A HISTORY OF
ECONOMIC THOUGHT
Tenth Edition

For BA/MA Students of Economics

V LOKANATHAN

Emeritus Professor of Economics
Sir Theagaraya College
Chennai - 600 021

S. CHAND
PUBLISHING

S Chand And Company Limited
(ISO 9001 Certified Company)

S Chand And Company Limited

(ISO 9001 Certified Company)

Head Office: Block B-1, House No. D-1, Ground Floor, Mohan Co-operative Industrial Estate, New Delhi – 110 044 | Phone: 011-66672000

Registered Office: A-27, 2nd Floor, Mohan Co-operative Industrial Estate, New Delhi – 110 044 Phone: 011-49731800

www.**schandpublishing**.com; e-mail: **info@schandpublishing.com**

Branches

Ahmedabad	: Ph: 27542369, 27541965; ahmedabad@schandpublishing.com
Bengaluru	: Ph: 22354008, 22268048; bangalore@schandpublishing.com
Bhopal	: Ph: 4274723, 4209587; bhopal@schandpublishing.com
Bhubaneshwar	: Ph: 2951580; bhubaneshwar@schandpublishing.com
Chennai	: Ph: 23632120; chennai@schandpublishing.com
Guwahati	: Ph: 2738811, 2735640; guwahati@schandpublishing.com
Hyderabad	: Ph: 40186018; hyderabad@schandpublishing.com
Jaipur	: Ph: 2291317, 2291318; jaipur@schandpublishing.com
Jalandhar	: Ph: 4645630; jalandhar@schandpublishing.com
Kochi	: Ph: 2576207, 2576208; cochin@schandpublishing.com
Kolkata	: Ph: 23357458, 23353914; kolkata@schandpublishing.com
Lucknow	: Ph: 4003633; lucknow@schandpublishing.com
Mumbai	: Ph: 25000297; mumbai@schandpublishing.com
Nagpur	: Ph: 2250230; nagpur@schandpublishing.com
Patna	: Ph: 2260011; patna@schandpublishing.com
Ranchi	: Ph: 2361178; ranchi@schandpublishing.com
Sahibabad	: Ph: 2771238; info@schandpublishing.com

First Edition 1973
Subsequent Editions and Reprints 1974, 75, 78, 79, 81, 83, 84, 87, 89, 92, 93, 95, 96, 97, 99, 2000, 2001, 2004, 2007, 2008, 2015, 2016
Tenth Edition 2018
Reprint 2019
Reprint 2020

ISBN : 978-93-525-3337-4   **Product Code:** H5HET41ECON10ENAJ18O

PRINTED IN INDIA

By Vikas Publishing House Private Limited, Plot 20/4, Site-IV, Industrial Area Sahibabad, Ghaziabad – 201 010 and Published by S Chand And Company Limited, A-27, 2nd Floor, Mohan Co-operative Industrial Estate, New Delhi – 110 044.

"The ideas of economists and political philosophers, both when they are right and when they are wrong, are more powerful than is commonly understood. Indeed the world is ruled by little else. Practical men, who believe themselves, to be quite exempt from intellectual influences, are usually the slaves of some defunct economist."

Lord Keynes

PREFACE TO THE TENTH EDITION

I am immensely pleased at the reception accorded to the earlier editions of *A History of Economic Thought,* which has prompted me to prepare a thoroughly revised and enlarged tenth edition of the book. The book covers the undergraduate syllabi of Economic Thought in majority of the Institutions in India.

In its 5th decennium, the book provides an expanded coverage on development of economic ideas and contributions of eminent nobel laureates. It covers the contributions of nobel laureates in economics up to 2016.

More in this Edition:

Shantiparva of Mahabaratha, Basaveshwara – M N Roy, Vakil and Brahmanand, Pandit Madan Mohan Malaviya, Vinoba Bhave, Jayprakash Narayan, Dr Ram Manohar Lohia, Deendayal Upadhyaya, B R Shenoy, Jyotirao Govindarao Phule, Rajarshi Shahu Maharaj, J C Kumarappa, Yashwantrao Balwantrao Chavan, J N Bhagwati, Maurice Dobb, New Keynesians and Joan Robinson.

I take this opportunity to thank the teachers and students for their generous and warm response. My special thanks are due to Prof. K Jothi Sivagnanam, Prof. R Srinivasan and Prof. P Anbalagan for their kind help in collecting some books and materials whenever I do the revision of the book.

My thanks are due to the publisher S Chand And Company Limited, for their excellent cooperation, quick and neat execution of the job. My special thanks are due to Surabhi Khare, Head Editorial – Higher Education for her encouragement and helpful suggestions and P Thanigaimalai, Sr Manager, Sales (Higher Education), Chennai Branch for his support.

I crave the indulgence of readers for constructive suggestions and errors if any that might have crept in inadvertently.

V LOKANATHAN

PREFACE

"A HISTORY OF ECONOMIC THOUGHT" is designed as a textbook for BA degree course of the Madras University and other Indian universities. It has been prepared in accordance with the revised syllabus prescribed for "Economic Thought" for BA degree students of Madras University. Students of postgraduate course may also find this book useful as a simple introduction to the subject. A list of questions has been given at the end of the book. In preparing this book, I have referred to many standard authors on the subject to whom I owe my gratitude.

My thanks are due to many of my colleagues at the college for their kind advice and helpful suggestions. My special thanks are due to my friend Shri L Subramanian, of Indian Oxygen Ltd., Madras, for typing out the manuscript neatly and carefully.

My thanks are due to the publisher, M/s S. Chand & Co. Ltd., for their excellent cooperation and for the quick and neat execution of the book.

I shall feel amply rewarded if the book is found useful by those for whom it is meant. I crave the indulgence of the readers for the errors that might have crept in inadvertently.

Suggestions for improvement are welcome.

Sir Theagaraya College,   **V LOKANATHAN**
Madras-21.
June, 1973

CONTENTS

1. Introduction 1-4

2. Ancient Economic Thought 5-18
   The Hebrew Economic Thought – The Greek Thought: Plato, Aristotle – The Roman Thought – The Islamic Thought

3. Economic Thought in Ancient India... 19-27
   Kautilya's Arthasastra – Economic Ideas of Thiruvalluvar – Santi Parva

4. Medieval Economic Thought 28-30

5. Mercantilism 31-40

6. The Physiocrats 41-48
   Quesnay – Turgot – Condillac

7. Adam Smith (1723-1790) 49-56

8. Jeremy Bentham (1748-1832) 57-59

9. Thomas Robert Malthus (1766-1834) 60-65

10. David Ricardo (1772-1823) 66-73

11. J. B. Say (1767-1832) 74-76

12. Bastiat (1801-1850) 77-78

13. Nassau William Senior (1790-1864) 79-80

14. John Stuart Mill (1806-1873) 81-85

15. The Historical School 86-89
    Wilhelm Roscher – Bruno Hildebrand – Karl Knies – Schmoller

16. The Nationalists 90-94
    Adam Muller – Friedrich List

17. Sismondi (1773-1842) 95-98

18. Utopian Socialism 99-109
    Forms of Socialism (State Socialism, Utopian Socialism, Christian Socialism, Anarchism, Marxian Socialism, Communism, Revisionism, Syndicalism and Guild Socialism) – Socialistic Pattern of Society, Utopian Socialists – Saint Simon, Saint Simonians, Fourier, Robert Owen, Louis Blanc, Proudhon

19. Karl Marx (1818-1883) 110-118

20. Fabian Socialism 119-120
    Sidney Webb – Bernard Shaw

21. The Marginal Revolution 121-130
    Gossen – William Stanley Jevons – Carl Menger – Leon Walras

22. The Austrian School 131-134

23. Alfred Marshall (1842-1924) 135-141

24. Indifference Curve Analysis – Iso-Product Curves 142-144

25. Neo-Classicism 145-150
    Knut Wicksell – J. B. Clark – Irving Fisher – Taussig

26. The Institutionalist School 151-154
    Veblen – J. R. Commons – W. C. Mitchell

27. The Keynesian Revolution 155-165

28. Joseph A. Schumpeter (1883-1950) 166-167

29. Neo-Keynesian – New Keynesian Economics 168-171

30. Joan Robinson (1903-1983) 172-176

31. Welfare Economics 177-180
    J. A. Hobson – A. C. Pigou – Pareto – J. R. Hicks

32. Maurice Dobb (1900-1976) 181-183

33. Comparative Economic Systems 184-189

34. Socio-religious and Socio-economic Reformers of India 190-196
    Basaveshwara – Jyotirao, Govindarao Phule –Rajarshi Shahu Maharaj

35. Recent Indian Economic Thought 197-277
    R. C. Dutt – Dadabhai Naoroji – Mahadev Govind Ranade – Gopal Krishna Gokhale – Mohan Das Karam Chand Gandhi – Jawaharlal Nehru – P. C. Mahalanobis – B. R. Ambedkar – C. Rajagopalachari – V. K. R. V. Rao – D. R. Gadgil – Indira Gandhi – Periyar E. V. Ramasami – Arignar C. N. Annadurai - C. N. Vakil – P. R. Brahmananda – J. N. Bhagwati – Brij Narain – J. K. Mehta – B. R. Shenoy – Pandit Madan Mohan Malaviya – Vinoba Bhave – Jayprakash Narayan – Ram Manohar Lohia – Deendayal Upadhyaya – M. N. Roy – J. C. Kumarappa – M. S. Swaminathan – Yashwantrao Balwantrao Chavan.

36. Recent Trends in Indian Economic Thought (Applied Economics) 278-280

37. Nobel Laureates in Economics 281-382
    1969 : Jan Tinbergen (Netherlands) and Ragnar Frisch (Norway)
    1970 : Paul A. Samuelson (United States)
    1971 : Simon Kuznets (United States)
    1972 : Kenneth J. Arrow (United States) and Sir John Hicks (Britain)
    1973 : Wassily Leontief (United States)
    1974 : Friedrich A. Von Hayek (Britain) and Gunnar Myrdal (Sweden)
    1975 : Tjalling Koopmans (United States) and Leonid V. Kantorovich (Soviet Union)
    1976 : Milton Friedman (United States)
    1977 : Bertil Ohlin (Sweden) and James E. Meade (Britain)
    1978 : Herbert A. Simon (United Staes)
    1979 : Arthur Lewis (Britain) and Theodore W. Schultz (United States),
    1980 : Lawrence R. Klein (United States)
    1981 : James Tobin (United States)
    1982 : George J. Stigler
    1983 : Gerard Debreu
    1984 : Sir Richard Stone
    1985 : Franco Modigliani
    1986 : James Buchanan
    1987 : Robert M. Solow
    1988 : Maurice Allais
    1989 : Trygve Haavelmo

1990 : Harry M. Markowitz, F. Sharpe and Merton Miller
1991 : Ronald Coase
1992 : Gary S. Becker
1993 : Robert W. Fogel and Douglass C. North
1994 : John C. Harsanyi, John F. Nash and Reinhard Selten
1995 : Robert E. Lucas JR.
1996 : James A. Mirrless and William Vickrey
1997 : Robert C. Merton and Myron S. Scholes
1998 : Amartya Sen
1999 : Robert A. Mundell
2000 : James J. Heckman and Daniel L. McFadden
2001 : George A. Akerlof, A. Michael Spence and Joseph E. Stiglitz
2002 : Daniel Kahneman and Vernon L. Smith
2003 : Robert F. Engle III and Clive W. J. Granger
2004 : Finn E. Kydland and Edward C. Prescott
2005 : Robert J. Aumann and Thomas C. Schelling
2006 : Edmund Phelps
2007 : Leonid Hurwicz, Eric S. Maskin and Roger B. Myerson
2008 : Paul Krugman
2009 : Elinor Ostrom and Oliver E. Williamson
2010 : Peter A. Diamond Dale T. Mortensen and Christopher A. Pissarides
2011 : Thomas Sargent and Christopher Sims
2012 : Lloyd Shapely and Alvin Roth
2013 : Eugene Fama, Robert Shiller and Lars Peter Hansen
2014 : Jean Tirole
2015 : Angus Deaton
2016 : Oliver Heart and Bengt Holmstrom

INTRODUCTION

Nature and Importance of Economic Thought

The History of Economic Thought deals with the origin and development of economic ideas and their interrelations.

History of Economic Thought is different from Economic History and History of Economics. While the history of economic thought deals with the development of economic ideas, economic history is a study of the material or industrial development of the people in the past. Though they are separate branches, we should remember that there is a close relationship between them. The economic ideas of people at any time are coloured and conditioned by their environment. For instance, the economic ideas of Plato and Aristotle were influenced by the institution of slavery, for slavery was a part of the Greek civilization of the past. And the Industrial Revolution in England and the development of the urban proletariat (working class) provided the basis for the socialist ideas of Karl Marx.

The history of economics deals with the science of economics. Economics as a science, that is, as a body of systematized knowledge, is only of recent origin. It is roughly two hundred years old. It is only after the publication of the "Wealth of Nations" by Adam Smith in 1776 that we have come to study economics as a science. That is why Adam Smith is regarded as the 'Father of Political Economy.' That is, the latter part of the 18th century may be taken as the starting point. But the History of economic thought is broader than the history of the science. Economic Ideas have been there ever since the birth of mankind. We find economic ideas even in the writings of the ancient Hebrews, Indians, Greeks, Romans and during the Middle Ages. Prof. Bell describes economic thought as "A study of heritage left by writers on economic subjects over a period of about 2,500 years; and it freely draws upon all phases of human knowledge."

Prof. Haney has defined the subject in the following words: "The subject, the History of Economic thought, may be defined as a critical account of the development of economic ideas, searching into their origins, interrelations and manifestations."

History of Economic Thought may be broadly divided into *two* parts. The first part deals with the origin and development of economic ideas before the development of economics as a separate science and the second part deals with the economic ideas since the birth of political economy (the science of Economics) as a separate science.

Theoretical Approaches: There are different theoretical approaches to the study of the history of economic thought. They are (*i*) chronological approach, (*ii*) conceptual approach, (*iii*) philosophical approach, (*iv*) classical deductive approach, (*v*) historical approach, (*vi*) neo-classical approach, (*vii*) welfare approach, (*viii*) institutional approach, and (*ix*) Keynesian approach.

(*i*) ***Chronological Approach:*** In the chronological approach, economic ideas are discussed in the order of time. One advantage of this kind of approach is that it ensures continuity and it enables the reader to fix the time at which the economic ideas have come into existence.

(*ii*) *Conceptual Approach:* In the conceptual approach, importance is given to the development of economic concepts or ideas. For instance, we study about things like marginal utility (Jevons), General Equilibrium (Walras), Quasi-rent, long and short run (Marshall) and Liquidity preference (Keynes). The advocates of this approach are not interested in the school of thought which has popularized a given idea.

(*iii*) *Philosophical Approach:* The philosophical approach was first adopted by Plato, the Greek Philosopher. In the past, economics was considered a handmaid of ethics. Naturally, philosophical approach was adopted by early writers to discuss economic ideas. Aristotle, Adam Smith, Quesnay and above all Marx, all held definite philosophical views. ('But Schumpeter is of the opinion that the above writers were, as a matter of fact, not influenced by their philosophical views when doing their work of economic analysis').

(*iv*) *Classical Deduction Approach:* The classical school (for example, Ricardo, Malthus and J. S. Mill) adopted deductive method which is an abstract one. The classical economists believed that the laws of economics are of universal application and that all economic laws could be formulated by a simple process of reasoning from one fundamental principle. The classical deductive approach, however, has come in for a lot of criticism at the hands of the historical school. The historical school maintained that only by patient and careful observation and by inductive method, one could build up a realistic economic theory.

(*v*) *Historical Approach:* The historical approach lays emphasis on the inductive method. The historians stress that we must have some knowledge of the previous stages of economic development if we are to understand the economic life of the present. We cannot study man's economic activity by neglecting his environment. They believed that the laws of economics are not universal in nature. They are relative conditioned by time, place, and historical circumstances. The historical school had its birth in Germany.

(*vi*) *The Neo-classical Approach:* The neo-classical approach aims at improving the classical theories by suitably modifying them by taking into account the modern developments in the theory of economics. The neo-classical approach is an attempt at the reconstruction of the classical theories. "Neo-classical economics" may be said to begin with the appearance of Marshall's *"Principles of Economics"* in 1890. Marshall's dual theory of value is a fine example of neo-classical approach. The neo-classical approach believes that "Induction and deduction are both necessary for the science, just as the right and left foot are needed for walking."

(*vii*) *Welfare Approach:* The welfare approach aims at providing a basis for adopting policies which are likely to maximize 'social welfare.' "Welfare economics is concerned with the conditions which determine the total economic welfare of a community." (Oskar Lange). While the classical approach emphasizes on cost, supply and production, the welfare approach emphasizes on utility, demand and consumption.

(*viii*) *Institutional Approach:* The institutional approach is a twentieth century phenomenon. "Institutional Economics" is essentially an American product. Veblen was the founder of this approach. The advocates of the institutional approach assert that the "price system" should not be the central theme of economics. They attach importance to group behaviour which is constantly changing. They consider economic laws as relative. They consider institution (habits, custom, legal forms) as the chief factor in governing human behaviour.

(*ix*) *Keynesian Approach:* A major development in modern economics is associated with the name of J. M. Keynes. His approach is so new and fundamentally different from that of the classical economists that the term 'Keynesian Revolution' has been applied to it. The essence of the Keynesian approach is that it deals with the problems of the economy as a whole, and not only with those of the individual consumer. One of the great contributions of Keynes was to tie economic analysis to the great public problems of the day. In short, while most of the early economists dealt with micro-economics, Keynes dealt with the problems of macro-economics—employment, interest, money, their interrelations and so on. Keynes' approach to economic problems centres on the goal of full employment.

Philosophy: The attitude of economists towards economics as a science depends upon their philosophical leanings to some extent. There are two main tendencies in philosophy. They are (*i*) *Idealism*, and (*ii*) *Materialism*. Idealism generally tends towards optimism. Plato (a Greek thinker), Kant and Hegel (German Philosophers) belonged to the school of Idealism. Materialism tends towards pessimism. The materialists believe that man is dominated by his natural environment. The materialists are generally individualistic and they believe in laissez-faire. Hobbes, Locke, Rousseau and Bentham belonged to the school of materialism. We must, however, remember that materialism and idealism are not independent of one another. They are just two sides of social life and they constantly react upon one another.

Method: The writers in Economics make use of two main methods to seek truth. They are called deductive and inductive methods. The deductive method is that which works from the general to the particular by mental process of analysis. It is an abstract method. Most of the classical economists (Adam Smith, Ricardo and J. S. Mill) made use of the deductive method. The inductive method works from the particular to the general and is based on facts. The inductive method may also be called the method of observation. The inductive method was adopted by the Historical school which had its origin in Germany. But the modern view is that, "Induction and deduction are both necessary for the science just as the right and left foot are needed for walking." Besides deduction and induction, there is another method which may be called the statistical method. This is nothing but a combination of the inductive and deductive method.

Importance of Economic Thought: There are two main views on the importance of the study of the history of economic thought. One group of economists asserts that there is no need to study the history of economic thought, especially the history of economic thought before the 18th century. They argue in the following manner. "It is true that ancient and medieval history are full of marvellous economic teachings, but as far as the history of the science is concerned, there is no need to go farther back than the physiocrats." They regard the 'history of economic thought' as 'the history of errors.' We must simply forget those errors. They believe that no useful purpose can be served by the study of the absurd opinions and doctrines that have long been exploded. This, however, is not a correct view. For even the study of error would enable us to avoid it in future.

Another set of economists believed that one cannot, moreover, be said to possess a knowledge of any doctrine, or to understand it until one knows something of its history" (Gide and Rist).

A study of the history of economic thought is important for the following reasons: First of all, through a study of the history of economic thought, we realize that there is a certain unity in economic thought and this unity connects us with ancient times. Of course, there are some writers on the subject who deny continuity in the evolution of economic thought. For instance, they regard the Middle Ages as a complete break because the thinkers of the Middle Ages emphasized on the negative aspects of life. This, however, is not totally true. For even during that period there was speculation on economic topics such as money, interest and the views of these thinkers were similar to those of Greek thinkers of the past.

Secondly, in spite of a tremendous improvement in the science of economics, even today the nature and scope of economics is under dispute. The study of economic thought will help us in understanding the origin of economics. So there is a great value in studying the history of economic thought. In the beginning, economics was not studied as a separate science. It was merely a handmaid of politics and ethics.

Thirdly, through a study of economic thought, we realize that most of the economic ideas are relative. They are conditioned by time, place and circumstances. Economic ideas are rooted in economic practice. Many economic ideas of the past had their roots in institutional arrangements. Aristotle justified slavery because slavery was an accepted social fact of the Greek civilization. Mercantilist theories of foreign trade and physiocratic notions about agriculture and Ricardian theory of rent are still with us.

Fourthly, a study of economic thought provides a broad basis for comparison of different ideas. It will enable a person to have a well-balanced and reasonable judgment. As he is familiar with most of the old theories with all their fallacies, he will not be confused easily by new ideas or fads. He will have the necessary background to form a correct judgment.

Fifthly, by a study of the history of economic thought, one may be able to take an objective point of view. The student will realize that economics is one thing and economists are another. There may be controversies among economists. But these controversies will not last long. They will die soon and there may be synthesis of different conflicting theories which will result in the evolution of economic laws.

Sixthly, by a study of the history of economic thought, a student will realize that "old doctrines never die; they only fade away, with a strange power of recuperation in an appropriate environment" (Alexander Gray). For instance, some of the ideas of Keynes, one of the greatest of modern economists, may be traced back to socialist writers such as Sismondi and Proudhon and to Malthus.

Lastly, a study of the history of economic thought will enable us to know the persons responsible for formulations of the principles that constitute the framework of economics as at present taught. It will also help us know at what period these principles were enunciated and what circumstances were accounted for their enunciation just at that period.

2 ANCIENT ECONOMIC THOUGHT

Nature and Significance

The study of ancient economic thought is essential for understanding the growth of economic theories and institutions in their proper light.

The economic life of the people in the early past exhibited some basic features. In those days, wants were a few and simple. Food, clothing and shelter were their essential wants. In the beginning, property was owned by the community and not by individuals. Barter was the rule. There was not much of economic activity. The society was custom-bound and tradition-oriented. But in the later stages, with the development of the tribal society, economic order became somewhat dynamic. The principle of division of labour came to be applied and there was the exchange of surplus products. But it should be noted that the early thinkers did not formulate any independent economic theories. Whatever economic ideas they had contained in the books of religion, philosophy, ethics and politics. For instance, usury (high rate of interest) was despised and legally prohibited. It was prohibited not on economic grounds but on ethical grounds. Taking interest was considered unethical.

Economic science had a tardy growth in the beginning because in those days economics was considered a handmaid of ethics and politics. In the words of Prof. Haney, "There was more speculation about morals than about economic life. Ancient philosophy in its social aspects was simple, the political, economic and ethical values being little differentiated and under the circumstances, the whole was pervaded by a moral tone." Their philosophy of life with emphasis on the negation of worldly (material) pleasures also explain to some extent the absence of comprehensive economic theories. Further, custom, tradition, and authority restricted freedom of choice, economic enterprise and growth of enterprise which are the characteristic features of a modern capitalist economy. Further, we also realize today that labour is an important factor of production. But most of the early thinkers underrated the role of labour in production and did not realize the dignity of labour. They considered labour as an ignoble function to be performed by slaves. But in modern times, "one of the most fruitful sources of economic speculation has been the earnest desire to better the conditions of the labouring class." Further, ancient economic communities lived as self-sufficient units. Production was carried on mainly for consumption. So the development of economics had to wait till the period of Reformation and Renaissance.

Significance of the study of Ancient Economic Thought: There are two main views regarding the significance of the study of ancient economic thought. Some writers such as Gide and Rist are of the opinion that the ancient economic thought is only of historical interest and it has no relevance to modern times. But Prof. Cannan felt that such a study was rewarding because it would enable the readers to know about the origin of the science, its development, and the environment under which the science developed. As Alexander Gray put it, "Political economy throughout has been in large measure an attempt to explain within the existing framework and assumptions of society, how and on what theory contemporary society is operating." In Economics, the heresies of today become the orthodoxies of tomorrow. No theory, however wrong it may appear at first sight, is completely discarded and demolished for ever. "Old doctrines never die, they only fade away with a strange power of recuperation in an appropriate environment" (Alexander Gray). So it is a profitable exercise to study the economic ideas of some of the early thinkers such as the Hebrews, the Greeks and the Romans.

THE HEBREW ECONOMIC THOUGHT

Introduction: The Hebrews had one of the ancient civilizations of the world. Their period dates back to 2500 B.C. It is believed by some scholars that Western civilization has its origin in the civilizations of the Hebrews of the biblical times and of the Greeks of the classical age. The main sources of information for the Hebrew period are the writings of the Hebrew prophets in which they had laid down the code of conduct and the old Testament.

Characteristics of the Economic Thought of the Hebrews: The economic philosophy of the Hebrews was simple. For the society in which they lived was not a complex one. Economic problems were never studied separately. Economic, political, ethical and philosophical ideas were intertwined. But religion and ethics predominated in their writings. The life of the common man was regulated by the code of conduct prescribed by a powerful priestly class. And the ethico-religious ideas of the priests were not conducive for economic progress. Their philosophy was characterised by lack of individualism and materialism. They looked down upon all industry other than agriculture. There was a relative indifference towards wealth. And there was a great degree of passivity and fatalism. All these things made any great industrial civilization impossible. The early thinkers had fixed ideas on many problems. "The general aim of social regulation was to maintain the social equilibrium, and, here as elsewhere among ancient peoples, static ideals dominated. This finds expression in the caste system and in the isolated national life." The Hebrews had some notions of social welfare but they could not think of any dynamic plan of action to implement them. In other words, there was no active 'social planning.'

Some Important Economic Ideas of the Hebrews: The Hebrews had definite ideas on subjects such as interest and usury, agriculture, property rights, taxation, weights and measures, adulteration, monopoly and the poor. Some of their important economic ideas are given below:

1. *Usury (Interest):* The economically weak were protected by a number of provisions. For instance, the Hebrew prophets condemned lending things upon 'Usury', that is, at interest. The Mosaic Law prohibited "Usury of money, Usury of Victuals, Usury of anything that is lent upon usury." It may be interesting to note that the law applied only to fellow Hebrews. Lending of money at interest to strangers, however, was allowed. The Hebrews were asked to show mercy in the case of loans to the poor. As money was borrowed by the poor in those days mainly for consumption purposes, the Hebrew prophets thought that it was unethical to charge high rates of interest on the loans borrowed by the poor. The Hebrew thought on interest, it may be noted, is similar to the ancient Indian thought on interest.

2. *Commerce and Just Price:* The Hebrew prophets formulated many laws against false weights and measures and adulteration of articles of consumption. They had legislation to curb monopolistic tendencies and speculation. Middlemen had no place in their business organisation. The export of essential food articles was forbidden. In times of scarcity and famine, hoarding of foodgrains was not permitted. And a ceiling was put on the profit margin of retailers. All these things aimed at safeguarding the interests the poor. Thus the Hebrews developed the concept of 'just price' in its primitive form.

3. *Labour:* The Hebrews, unlike the Greeks, realized the dignity of labour. But the pride of place was given to agricultural labour. Payments were made in kind. It is interesting to note that they had some laws to safeguard the interests of the workers.

4. *Agriculture and Industry:* The Hebrew civilization was essentially a rural and agrarian civilization. Agriculture was the main occupation of the Hebrews and they held it in high esteem. One of their maxims runs as follows: "Although trading gives greater profits, these may all be lost in a moment; therefore never hesitate to buy land." And one of their proverbs is, "He that tilleth the soil shall have plenty of bread." It has been said in the Jewish Encyclopaedia that agriculture was the basis of the national life, of the Israelites, State and Church both being founded upon it. Commerce and crafts were not held in esteem by the Jews.

5. *The Seventh Year:* A peculiar feature of the Hebrew Economic Thought was the observance of the seventh year or Sabbatical year. The Hebrews left their land fallow in the seventh year after tilling it for six years. It was done with the object of conserving the fertility of the soil. (It may be noted that later on when the manorial system was in vogue in England, the land was left fallow in the third year). Later on, they extended the institution of the seventh year to slaves and loans. The slaves of the Israelite race, after serving for six years, were freed in the seventh year with their wives. The biblical law required that such liberated slaves should be liberally furnished with food and other goods that would enable them to start out on a life of their own. Further, the seventh year required that all debts should be cancelled.

6. *The Jubilee Year:* The Jubilee year was another peculiar institution of the Hebrews. The Jubilee year was the 50th year. According to this provision, the land sold to someone was to revert to its owner in the 50th year. Thus, "a sale of land really amounted to no more than a lease." In those days, land was the main form of wealth. By the Jubilee year method, they tried to prevent concentration of wealth in the form of landed property in the hands of a few persons. This method might have prevented the acquisition of land of smallholders by owners of large estates. By the institution of seventh and Jubilee year, the lawgiver desired to prevent inequality in wealth, to preserve family and tribal property, and to keep his people attached to their country. Thus by the Jubilee year, the lawgiver tried to prohibit the permanent alienation of land from the original possessor.

7. *Money:* The Hebrews seemed to have understood the functions of money. There are references to different kinds of money in the Old Testament. This shows that money was used in the society described in the Old Testament. Money was used mainly in the form of bullion. They used bullion, ingots or rings in payment of goods. There was no question of stamped money. It is believed that stamping of coins began about 700 B.C.

8. *The Sabbath:* The Sabbath was the cornerstone of biblical social legislation. It was the weekly day of rest, relaxation and good living. It was enjoyed by the master of the house and his family as well as the slave and the maid servant. "The institution of the weekend was a social invention that has no parallel in the civilizations of Greece, Rome or other ancient cultures" (Spiegel).

The social philosophy of the Hebrews was simple. They were in the childhood of civilization. The organisation of society was tribal in its nature. Religion, ethics, law, economics and philosophy were all bound together. Morals were the central theme of their educational system. Religion dominated their lives. There was minute regulation of everyday life. Their philosophy was characterized by a lack of individualism and materialism and their ethico-religious ideas were not conducive to economic progress.

In the Bible, there are provisions for the poor protecting them from exploitation and permanent debt. There are attacks by the prophets on injustice and exploitation of the poor by the rich. It is true that Moses tried to prevent inequality of wealth. This led some writers to suggest that socialism had its first appearance in Israel. Far from it. All this does not make socialism and it is certainly very far from social democracy or democratic socialism. "Had the Mosaic law been carried out, the result would rather have been, perhaps, like a sort of periodically enforced communism."

Though in the economic thought of the Hebrews, statements about economic ideas were scattered and fragmentary, they had a disproportionately greater power of influencing men's minds when compared with the more recent refined scientific theories. We may conclude with the words of Eric Roll: "The views of the Hebrew Prophets, set in the ethical or metaphysical system of patriarchal society, may appear extremely primitive to a modern economist; but their power to influence men's minds is not necessarily inferior to that of many a refined and scientific theory; indeed it is often greater. The systems of philosophy, of which such isolated economic statements formed part, continue to live."

THE GREEK THOUGHT

Introduction

Greek thought, Roman Law and Christian religion form the basis of European culture. In 1875, Henry Maine said, "Except for the blind forces of nature, nothing moves in this world which is not Greek in its origin." Greece has a rich intellectual legacy. So it is not surprising that parallels have been found between Greek ideas and economic thoughts developed more than two thousand years later.

By about the 8th century B.C. in Greece, the institution of private property in land was established. There was a high degree of division of labour and trade. And the use of money was also established. The close bonds of tribe were broken and the society was divided into classes and ruled by landed aristocracy. The Greeks lived in city-states and they practised direct democracy. But at the time, in question, democracy lost much of its meaning and real power lay in the hands of the owners of the land and of an hereditary ruling class.

Slavery was an accepted fact of the Greek social life. Much of the productive work was done by slaves and resident foreigners. The slaves and resident foreigners formed the majority of the population. As the foreigners were not allowed to own land, most of them became traders and craftsmen.

The Greek city-state (polis) underwent many changes. We do not know much about the heroic period of Greece. It was only during the latter part that the Greek Philosophy made its main contribution to social thought. The main discussions of the Greek Philosophers centred around the city-state. They were interested in things such as *the good life, the just state and the happy man.* Thus we find that ethics and politics were intermingled and economics was considered a handmaid of ethics and politics. We should also remember that the word *economics* is of Greek origin and literally means "management of the household."

Plato (427-347 B.C.) and Aristotle (384-322 B.C.) were the two great thinkers of ancient Greece.

Plato (427-347 B.C.)

Plato belonged to the city-state of Athens and Athens was something special in Greece and the world. It produced many philosophers and artists and it was the centre of democracy and individualism. But Plato wrote in the days of the decline of Athens. Athenian democracy, in his days, lost much of its democratic content. In discussing the ideas of Plato, it is important to remember that Plato was essentially an Aristocrat. A new commercial class was coming up to power. There was too much of commercialism. And Plato's dislike of Athenian democracy of his days might be regarded as a spiritual revolt of a philosopher against the excess of commercialism.

On the analytical side, Plato's main achievement is the account of the division of labour and the origin of the city-state. Plato was the first person to offer a systematic explanation of the principles of society and of the origin of the city-state. He also gave a plan for the ideal social structure. The main ideas of Plato are found in "*The Republic*" and "*Laws.*"

Origin of the City-state and Division of Labour

According to Plato, "A state arises out of the needs of mankind, no one is self-sufficing, but all of us have many wants." After a consideration of the essential needs of mankind, Plato arrives at the conclusion, that the city arises because of division of labour. According to Plato, "Division of labour emerged from the natural inequalities among human beings." There are "diversities of natures among us which are adapted to different occupations." As a consequence of this that "all things are produced more plentifully and easily, and of a better quality, when one man does one thing which is natural to him and does it at the right time, and leaves other things." It may be interesting to note that Plato attributes the origin of the state to purely economic considerations.

Division of labour is one of the central concepts of Plato and it is of great importance in the history of economics. For, two thousand years later, Adam Smith used the same concept as the central theme of his analysis. It should, however, be noted that there are significant differences in the context and emphasis that Plato and Adam Smith place on division of labour. In Plato, division of labour is the basis of social organisation; the city-state is built upon division of labour. In Smith, division of labour is a device for the ultimate advantage of those who practise it. To Plato, inequalities in human beings result in specialisation. But Adam Smith wants to stress the point that specialisation results in the improvement in productivity. While Smith is concerned with the causes of wealth of nations, Plato uses the concept to explain the structure of the society. In the hands of Plato, division of labour is nothing but an idealization of the caste system.

The Ideal State

Plato's ideal state is a city-state. It is a small one with a constant number of citizens. There will be 5,040 citizens. Plato has chosen the figure because it is administratively convenient, as it is divisible by all numbers up to ten. Only then they will know each other. Just as population is stationary, wealth also will be more or less stationary. All economic and non-economic activity will be strictly regulated.

Plato's concept of a ruler is an ideal one. His ruler will be free from any motive of economic exploitation and he will accept rigorous standards of conduct.

In Plato's ideal state, there are two classes: The *rulers* and the *ruled*. The rulers are divided into *guardians and auxiliaries*. The latter (the ruled) are the artisans. As the artisans are engaged in the menial occupations of the production and exchange of wealth, none of them will have the ability necessary for running the government. The members of the ruling class will be set apart from early childhood. They will be carefully educated not only in philosophy but also in the arts of war, since they will have to protect their state against foreign attack. At the age of thirty, they will have to pass an examination. Those who pass the examination become the "philosopher kings." In other words, they become guardians in the fullest sense (real rulers). All those who cannot pass the examination remain auxiliaries (soldiers) and they are entrusted with general administrative duties.

Plato believed in rule by an *elite*. It was for this *elite* group Plato suggested a communistic way of life. The upper classes from whom leaders are trained must lead a spartan life. They must not have any property beyond what is necessary. They must not acquire homes or lands or moneys of their own. If they acquire them, they will become housekeepers and husbandmen instead of guardians. In other words, the upper classes will not have any private property and family. They will live together and share common meals, like soldiers in a camp. And the strange thing is they share women too. Thus there is communism in respect of goods as well as women. For, "friends have all things in common." The best political community is one made up of friends who share everything, women, children and all possessions. Members of the ruling class will not be allowed to possess gold or silver, "that mortal dross which has been the source of many unholy deeds." Plato does not want the rulers to own any property because the ruling classes will be corrupted if they acquire a taste of money and possessions.

There are two divergent views on the scope of Plato's communism. There is one set of writers who believe that if Plato had been alive today, he would have been the reddest of reds. For instance, Mr. Beer in his "social struggles in Antiquity" asserts it is quite clear that "Plato advocated communism for all Hellens (Greeks). Otherwise, there would be no point in the entire social criticism which he levels in both his works, against the economic, political and moral conditions of his country." But other writers such as Alexander Gray believe that Plato's communism is prescribed only for the limited class of the guardians, who are to live a semi-military life. "It is in fact the communism of the camp." Plato recommends communism solely for the upper sections. Schumpeter is also of the opinion that, "though Plato's influence is obvious in many communistic schemes of later ages, there is little in labelling him a communist or socialist or a forerunner of later communists or socialists." Plato's constitution does not exclude private property except on the highest level of the society.

Money, Interest and Trade

Though Plato did not seem to have any definite view on the nature of money, he seemed to have some notion regarding the medium of exchange function of money. He considered money as a 'symbol' devised for the purpose of facilitating exchange. He felt that citizens should not possess gold and silver but only token money. Thus they are not permitted to accumulate wealth in the form of full bodied money. We may consider Plato as the first sponsor of one of the fundamental theories of money which tells that the value of money is in principle independent of the stuff it is made of.

The citizens are not allowed to practise a craft or a trade. They are reserved only for the resident foreigners. Foreign trade is controlled. Only necessities may be imported, and only goods that are not needed exported. Retail trade is forbidden. And money should not be lent at interest. Inequalities of wealth will be reduced by imposing a ceiling on the amount of permissible wealth.

The economic ideas of Plato show that he was essentially a child of his time. In the city state of his time, slaves formed about one-third of the population and they performed most of the economic functions. He does not question the institution of slavery. His sympathies are with the aristocrats. His political ideas are authoritarian in nature. It is true he rejects private property and he hates commercial activities. But he was no fascist or communist. He hated war. For fascists, victorious war is the highest social ideal. But Plato was a man of peace. He advocated a rule of reason. Though he advocated communism for the ruling class, others were allowed to own property.

We have to note that the ideal state of Plato was far removed both from Athenian democracy and aristocratic Sparta. His ideal state was an Utopia. It is true that there are many difficulties in putting Plato's ideas into practice. But we must remember that the Utopians and the Romantics of the 19th century have drawn inspiration from Plato. Not only that, Plato was the first thinker who made an economic interpretation of history.

ARISTOTLE (384-322 B.C.)

Introduction

Aristotle was the first analytical economist. It was he who laid the foundations of the science of economics. Aristotle was the pupil of Plato and tutor to Alexander, the Great. But Aristotle differed from Plato on many important issues like the origin of the state, communal versus private property. Plato was of aristocratic origin but Aristotle was not. The main economic ideas of Aristotle are found in the "*Politics*" and the "*Ethics*". We shall now discuss the ideas of Aristotle on the state, slavery, property, value, money and interest.

The State

According to Aristotle, "The state, like the family and the village, originates in the bare needs of life." He explains the origin of the state in terms of the household. The household is "the association naturally formed for the supply of wants." The village grows out of the number of households and finally the state comes into existence. Man is by nature a political animal. Not only that, he is also a social animal. The state is possible because all men live together in a society. The aim of the state is promotion of good life. Thus Aristotle attributes the origin of the state to economic and political causes.

Aristotle's view of the ideal state differed from that of Plato. Plato advocated complete communism, which embraced not only property, but also wives and children. In his book "*Politics*", Aristotle has attacked the communistic elements of Plato's ideal Republic. He was against Plato's communism of wives and children. Aristotle was for the continuation of the institutions of family and private property. But like his master, he recognised and justified the institution of slavery.

In Aristotle's ideal state too, there would be the rulers and the ruled. These rulers are classified into the military class, the statesmen, the magistrates and the priests. We have to note that "these functions are not to be divided among different groups: according to age the members of the ruling class will perform these tasks of government; they will be soldiers when they are young and strong, statesmen in the prime of life, and priests in old age" (Eric Roll). Those who are ruled consist of the farmers, craftsmen and the labourers.

Private Property

While Plato advocated the community of property, Aristotle pleaded strongly in favour of the institution of private property. Aristotle's attack on the community of progeny is based mainly on the *incentive argument*: He argues that communal property will not be looked after as carefully as private property. According to Aristotle, private property is superior to communal property on *five* grounds: (*i*) Progress, (*ii*) Peace, (*iii*) Pleasure, (*iv*) Practice, and (*v*) Philanthropy.

(*i*) *Progress:* Private property is more productive than communal property and hence promotes progress. Goods that are owned by a large number of people receive little care. "The more numerous, the joint owners of anything, the less it is cared for." The principle 'what is everybody's business is nobody's business' will be applied here. Men will neglect their common property thinking that someone else is looking after it. As Aristotle put it, "Property should be in a certain sense common, but as a general rule, private; for when everyone has a distinct interest, men will not complain of one another, and they will make more progress because everyone will be attending to his own business."

(*ii*) *Peace:* Communal property is not conducive to social peace. Quarrels are bound to develop when the principle of "equal wages for equal work" is not followed. Under communal ownership, there is the possibility of some men doing more and better work getting small reward and others doing little work getting larger reward.

(*iii*) *Pleasure:* Private property will give pleasure to the owner. "So each man must possess some property which he can call his own." But this feeling will go if all persons "call the same thing mine."

(*iv*) *Practice:* The practical experience of ages proves that private property is a good thing. If communal property is such a good thing, people would have instituted it long ago. The institution of communal property is not workable. Things are not good just because they are new and untried.

(*v*) *Philanthropy:* Private property enables people to practise philanthropy. The institution of private property will promote moral goodness among the citizens. If a man has property, he can use a part of it for himself and he can share a part with his friends and even have a part of it for common enjoyment for "friends' goods are goods in common." Friends will have things in common.

Aristotle was against the imposition of ceiling on private property. He would rather plead for checking the growth of population. In his own words, "It is more necessary to limit population than property." If population is not checked, it will result in poverty and "poverty is the parent of revolution and crime."

While advocating the institution of private property, Aristotle appeals to the moral nature in man to put it to a good use. In other words, he suggests that private ownership should be combined with common use, at least among friends. And he cites a case, where in Lacedaemon, citizens made use of each others slaves and horses. Aristotle wants the owners of private property to accept public responsibility. Those with property must act as the Trustees of the Society. A similar idea has been echoed by Mahatma Gandhi in our own times.

Slavery: Aristotle's views on slavery are similar to those of Plato. Aristotle lived in a society to which slavery was essential. Slavery was a salient feature of the Greek civilization of his time. At the time of Aristotle, the institution of slavery was attacked by social critics. *Aristotle, justified slavery by saying that some people were slaves by nature.* Thus he regarded slavery as a natural phenomenon: "that some should rule and others be ruled is a thing not only necessary but expedient; from the hour of their birth, some are marked out for subjection, others for rule." But in his own days, some slaves were slaves not by nature but by law. And some of them were Greeks. So Aristotle suggested that Greeks should never enslave Greeks.

The analytical ideas of Aristotle from a purely economic point of view, may be studied under three headings: (*i*) The Scope of Economics, (*ii*) The Analysis of Exchange, and (*iii*) The Theory of Money.

(*i*) **The Scope of Economics:** The word *"Economics"* is of Greek origin and literally means "management of the household"; it is in this sense Aristotle uses the word in his book *"Politics."* According to Aristotle, economy is divided into *two* parts: (*a*) *Economy Proper,* and (*b*) *The Science of Supply.* The former deals with the management of the household while the latter is concerned with the art of acquisition. The household management (economy proper) deals with the development of the city-state from the village and the household. In discussing the second part that is the science of supply, Aristotle analyses the art of exchange through which the needs of the household are met.

(*ii*) **The Analysis of Exchange:** While discussing the science of supply and the art of acquisition, Aristotle speaks of two forms of exchange, one natural and the other unnatural. The natural form of exchange is merely an extension of the management of the household and meant for the satisfaction of men's natural wants. The unnatural form of exchange aims at monetary gain. While discussing this problem, Aristotle speaks of two kinds of uses. One is a proper use and the other improper or secondary use. The proper use of goods is the satisfaction of natural wants. A secondary or improper use occurs when goods are exchanged for monetary gain. Thus all exchanges for monetary gain are branded as unnatural. "For example, a shoe is used for wear, and is used for exchange, both are uses of the shoe." In these words, Aristotle laid the foundation of the distinction between value-in-use and value-in-exchange, which has remained a part of the economic thought even today.

Aristotle's theory of value is subjective and is based upon the usefulness of a commodity concerned. But Schumpeter believes that Aristotle was trying to give some kind of a labour-cost theory of price but he was not able to state it explicitly.

To support this argument, Schumpeter quotes a passage from Aristotle's "Ethics" (Book IV)— "As the farmer's labour compares with the shoemaker's labour, so the product of the farmer compares with the product of the shoemaker." Further, Aristotle looked at problem of value from an ethical angle. He was looking for a principle of justice in pricing and he found it in the "equivalence" of what a man gives and receives. Thus Aristotle evolved the concept of just price. "An Exchange is just when each gets exactly as much as he gives the other; yet this equality does not mean equal costs, but equal wants." (Haney).

Monopoly: Aristotle defined monopoly "as the position in a market of a single seller." He condemned it as unjust.

(*iii*) **The Theory of Money:** Aristotle's theory of money explains what money is and what money does. Aristotle explained the necessity of money while Plato explained about only one important function of money, namely, the medium of exchange function. Aristotle explained the other important functions of money (store of value and measure of value) as well.

Aristotle advocated a non-communist society. Naturally, in such a society, there would be exchange of goods and services. First there would be barter. Then the difficulties of barter like the absence of double coincidence of wants would result in the introduction of some commodity as a medium of exchange. Metals like iron and silver are good for the purpose. In the beginning, money was first defined simply by size and weight. Later on, stamped money came into existence. Stamping of coins was found to be necessary to relieve the people from the trouble of weighing the money metal. Aristotle was aware of the other two functions of money, namely, as a measure of value and as a store of value. He also believed that money might have come into existence through legislation by the State. This idea led some people to believe that Aristotle anticipated Knapp's State Theory of money which tells that money is a creature of the Law. Aristotle was also aware of the difference between *money* and *wealth*. He referred to the fable of King Midas whose touch turned everything into gold. A man who is rich may be without food.

Interest: Like most of the ancient thinkers, Aristotle, condemned interest. According to him, money was only a medium of exchange. It had no business to increase from hand to hand. "A piece of money cannot beget another piece, was the doctrine of Aristotle, and no economic idea of his had more lasting effect. The obvious conclusion was that interest is unjust" (Haney). Aristotle's views against interest have been summarized beautifully by Eric Roll in the following words: "The worst form of money-making is that which uses money itself as the source of accumulation: usury. Money is intended to be used in exchange, but not to increase at interest; it is by nature barren; through usury, it breeds, and this must be the most unnatural of all the ways of making money." A student of modern economics may not agree with Aristotle's theory of interest because it does not take note of the fact that money may be put to productive uses as capital. But we have to remember, that in the days of Aristotle, money was borrowed by the poorer classes mainly for consumption purposes, that too, for the satisfaction of the bare necessities of life. Hence, Aristotle thought that it was unjust and unethical to lend money at interest. The modern theory of interest is based upon loans for productive investment.

Conclusion

From the foregoing analysis, it is clear that Aristotle laid the foundations of the Science of Economics. He may be rightly called the *first analytical economist*. His explanation of the origin of the State is based on the study of a number of constitutions of the city-states of Greece. Thus he adopted the inductive method in explaining the origin and the growth of city-states. He explained in a clear way the principles of a society in transition from agricultural self-sufficiency to commerce and trade. The arguments he advances in defence of the institution of private property are classic and are valid even today. What the Fabian Socialists of the present century say with regard to property and wealth is not much different from what Aristotle said so many centuries back. Aristotle's view that property should be private but a part of it may be put to common use is a golden mean to solve the problem of inequalities of wealth. By his analysis he exposed the impracticable nature of the ideal communism of Plato. In the field of exchange, Aristotle laid the foundations of the distinction between value-in-use and value-in-change, which has remained a part of economic thought even today. But Aristotle's theory of interest should be judged keeping in mind the time and the society in which Aristotle lived. Most of the present textbooks, while dealing with the functions of money, say that money is a medium of exchange, a measure of value and a store of value. Aristotle understood and explained the above functions of money more than two thousand years ago. But Aristotle justified slavery. And the institution of slavery, which he justified, brought low his civilization.

THE ROMAN THOUGHT

Rome has not contributed much to the development of economic thought. What little it did was merely an echo of Greece. In other words, the Roman ideas on economics are merely second-hand ideas borrowed from Greece. While Greece produced thinkers and philosophers, Rome produced warriors and statesmen. The Romans were doers rather than thinkers. They were empire builders. Still an understanding of Roman ideas on certain economic and legal matters is essential to follow the continuity in the economic thought through centuries.

Initially, Rome was a city-state with agriculture as the base of its economy. Step by step, and by means of warfare, it became an empire. Agrarian struggles were quite common in the early stages of the development of the Roman empire. In the field of ideas, the Roman were greatly influenced by the Greeks. The wars and conquests resulted in serious economic dislocation and created many conflicts between the rich and the poor. Small farmers were hit hard by those struggles but the landowners, money-lenders and traders who were already rich became richer. Anyhow, it was only during the period of the decline of the Roman empire that at least a few of the Romans bestowed their attention on economic questions. We shall now discuss the salient features of Roman thought in the field of economics and law.

When we discuss the contribution of Romans to economic thought, we must remember that in Rome 'it was the most practical men who concerned themselves most with economic matters; and their most influential thought on economic questions, being in effect the economics of civil service and the law Courts, was never formally propounded.' Thus the economic topics in Rome were discussed by their philosophers who wrote on practical affairs, the agricultural writers and jurists.

The Romans regarded agriculture as the most profitable and the most respectful and the most delightful occupation. Of course, it is a common feature of all ancient thought. The Roman philosophers censured luxury and preached a life of simplicity. Cicero, one of the noted philosophers of the times, considered many occupations such as those of usurers (money-lenders), manual workers, retail traders, mechanics, fishmongers, butchers, cooks and the dancers as vulgar. Though he branded retail trade as vulgar, he approved wholesale trade on a large scale. Cicero maintained, "But of all occupations by which gain is secured, none is better than agriculture, none more profitable, none more delightful, none more becoming to a freeman." The Roman philosophers regarded money-lending as big a crime as murder.

Seneca, another Roman philosopher, considered money as the root of most evils. But he has pointed out how trade between nations takes place out of comparative advantage enjoyed by different countries and how they trade with each other for the mutual satisfaction of their needs.

Pliny, another philosopher of the times, condemned gold by saying that it had been "discovered only for the ruin of mankind."

The Roman writings on agriculture are more important for a student of the economic history of Rome than for a student of economic thought. For they deal largely with the practical principles of farm or estate management. The agricultural writers have discussed the problem of employment of slave labour on farm, the size of holdings and so on. With regard to the size of the farm, mostly they were in favour of a small farm. Their motto was *"To praise a large farm, but cultivate a small one."* The agricultural writers were writing at a time when the great estates (Latifundia) were the order of the day. The large estates were swallowing small estates. After some time, these were characterised by operational inefficiency. Some of the writers attributed the inefficiency of the large farms to the employment of slave labour on farm. In other words, they regarded slave labour as inefficient. In the words of Pliny, "it is the very worst plan of all to have land tilled by slaves let loose from the house of correction, as indeed in the case with all work entrusted to men who live without hope." In fact, Pliny asserted that *the large landed estates were the cause of the decline of Italy.*

While the Greek philosophers like Plato and Aristotle justified the institution of slavery, the Romans began to question the institution of slavery. Generally they regarded slave labour as inefficient, and uneconomical when applied to land. But slaves did not get kind treatment from their Roman masters. They were treated like oxen. When they became too old to work, they were sold.

Roman Law

Roman Law is the richest legacy of Rome to the world. The Roman Law plays an important role in the history of economic analysis. The laws of many countries have the Roman Law as their model. It may be noted here that the Roman judges were laymen and they had to be told what the law was. So the Roman judges were guided by some jurists. The jurists were men of position and leisure. They became interested in legal questions almost as a hobby.

The Romans had two sets of laws: (*i*) *Jus Civile* (The Civil Law), and (*ii*) *Jus Gentium*. The Civil Law applied only to the affairs of the citizens. But *the Jus Gentium*, on the other hand, referred to a body of laws that were applicable to commercial and other relations between non-citizens (foreigners) or between citizens and non-citizens. Later on *jus gentium* became the natural law (*jus naturale*) of the Greek type. Since the seventeenth century onwards, *jus gentium* has acquired the meaning of the Law of Nations.

The significance of Roman Law for the development of economic thought lies in the fact that the Roman Law deals with the institutions of *Private Property* and *contract*. The Roman law made the right to private property almost absolute and provided for the freedom of contract, including the right of the individual to dispose of his property. Of course, the Roman law led to certain abuses too. As Marshall put it, "To Roman ...... influence we may trace indirectly much of the good and evil of our present economic system." The Roman jurists upheld the rights of private property without limit and guaranteed freedom of contract to a great extent. This led to certain abuses under the cover of rights guaranteed by the Law.

"An important characteristic of Roman economic thought is the separation of the non-personal elements in law from the personal, and the emphasis placed upon the former .... In fact, one of the services of Roman thought was to divorce law from religion" (Haney). For example, the doctrine of the corporation is very important in modern economic life. Under this doctrine, the corporate assets are separated from the assets of the owners of the Corporation, and while the owners change, the corporation remains the same. This principle can be traced back to the Roman Law. Further, whenever the modern law contains references to reasonableness—reasonable price, reasonable value, etc.,—it can be traced to the Roman Law.

The Roman Law has also provided the definitions of concepts such as price, money, of purchase and sale, of the various kinds of loans and of the two types of deposits (regular and irregular). This has provided a starting point for later economic analysis. Eric Roll has summed up the contribution of the Roman law in the following words: "Thus while Aristotle becomes the philosopher of the Middle Ages and one of the sources of the canon law, it is Roman law which serves as an important basis for the legal doctrines and institutions of capitalism."

Conclusion

The great service of Romans to economic thought was the development of jurisprudence as a science. "Their historic mission was military and political and the national energies were mainly devoted to the public service at home and in the field..... As might be expected from the want of speculative originality among the Romans, there is little evidence of serious theoretic inquiry on economic subjects" (Ingram). We may conclude that, "though the Romans did not directly develop economic theory, a knowledge of their writings is essential to an understanding of the continuity of the history of economic thought" (Haney).

THE ISLAMIC THOUGHT

"The key to economic philosophy of Islam lies in man's relationship with God, His universe and his people, *i.e.*, other human beings, and the nature and purposes of man's life on earth" (Muhammad Nejatullah Siddique). Religion is the basis of Islamic economic thought.

Alfred Marshall, who defined Economics as a study of mankind in the ordinary business of life noted: "For man's character has been moulded by his everyday work, and the material resources which he thereby procures, more than by any other influence unless it be that of his religious ideals; and the great forming agencies of the world's history have been religion and the economy."

Man-God relationship is defined by Tawhid. The essence of Tawhid is total submission to God and man must lead his life according to his will. Though God is the owner of all natural resources on the earth, they can be exploited by man. All things that are available to man are in the nature of a trust. Man is accountable to Allah as life on the earth is a test.

While man shares his relationship with God, a definite relationship between man and man is also prescribed. This relationship is based on brotherhood and equality: "Tawhid is a coin with two faces: one implies that Allah is the creator and the other that men are equal partners or that each man is brother to another man."

According to the teachings of Islam, "God is the creator of the universe." People are the vicegerents of God on earth. They must live according to laws laid down by God, and revealed through Prophet Muhammad.

Islam rejects asceticism. Good life means a life of sufficiency and peace.

It is absolutely necessary that equal opportunity be given to all, so that they might earn the necessaries of life. As there are differences in abilities, talents and capabilities, there can be differences in material rewards. Inequality in ownership through things such as personal effort and inheritance are possible. As private ownership is temporary and real owner of everything is God, people must use the wealth and income earned by them by following the rules laid down by God. In other words, under Islam, wealth is a trust from God and its proper use is a test of faith. It is imperative that resources given by God are used to fulfil the essential needs of all human beings and provide them with decent living conditions. A good Muslim should not abuse the material resources given by God.

Consumption and Saving

A Muslim should not indulge in conspicuous consumption. There must be moderation in personal consumption. Savings for one's future personal needs and security are encouraged.

Wealth in the form of accumulated savings may be used to meet religious obligations, such as payment of zakat. Zakat is a religious levy resulting in a transfer of resources from the rich to the poor. The remaining wealth may be invested in personal business or partnership.

Zakat prevents concentration of wealth and income in a few hands. Not only that, it ensures the minimum necessary for subsistence to all persons.

Investment is encouraged to discourage hoarding and to promote economic growth.

Interest militates against the fundamental principles of Islam. In Islam, one should not earn interest. But economists would say that we have to pay interest for capital just as we pay rent for land and wages for labour. For, capital has a role to play in the modern economy. So the followers of Islam have adopted interest-free financial methods.

Interest-free Islamic banks have been established in Islamic nations. An Islami bank plays the role of a partner, investor and trader. The interest-free financial methods satisfy the criteria: God permits trading and forbids riba (interest).

As the giving and taking of interest is forbidden, the Islamic Banks conduct their operations on the basis of profit-loss sharing which is permitted in Islam. Islamic banks accept demand deposits and term deposits. Demand deposits are repayable on demand but without any interest. But time deposit holders get a share in the profits earned by the bank according to a profit-sharing ratio announced in advance.

The Islamic banks offer a wide range of services. Among them, Mudaraba is the most popular service. Under mudaraba, a party deposits its capital which the other party uses for trade or investment. And the profits are shared between the two parties according to a ratio agreed upon at the beginning of the project. There are some clients who receive funds from the banks and manage operations independently. The contract tells what the client has to do with money, the permissible expenses which can be deducted and the percentage of profits he will get. Loss is generally borne by the provider of capital. But there should not be any negligence or violation of the terms of contract by the client.

It may be noted that though interest is forbidden, rent is permitted. For instance, an Islamic bank may lease a building and get rent. The Islamic term for lease is *ijara*.

Interest-free financial institutions like Islamic commercial banks, Islamic investment companies, Islamic national and international holding companies, takaful (insurance) companies and Islamic development banks have emerged in the last two decades in many nations. And they are successfully competing with the traditional interest-bearing institutions in many countries.

A distinguishing feature of Islamic strategy of economic development is that economic growth and social justice go together. Individual profit motive is not the main driving force of the economic system as in a capitalistic economy.

Role of the State

The State plays a positive role in the economic life of people. It makes them follow the Islamic code of conduct either through education, persuasion and sometimes through coercion. It helps the market to function in a smooth manner. It modifies the allocation of resources and distribution of income effected by the market system. In the field of capital formation and production, it takes positive steps to accelerate growth with social justice.

Money and Banking

The State has the right to issue money and control its supply.

One of the salient features of Islamic banking is, it is banking without interest. While discussing modern banking, some writers attack the institution of credit and its creation by commercial banks.

Some modern writers like Siddique have made the following novel suggestion relating to the role of central banking:

"The central bank will offer refinance facilities against interest-free loans made by the commercial banks, in case these banks need additional cash to maintain their liquidity. The extent of accommodation provided by the central bank will be fixed as a ratio to loans made by commercial banks."

The Islamic Development Bank

The Islamic Development Bank has been established "to foster economic development and social progress of member countries and Muslim communities individually as well as jointly in accordance with the principles of Shariat." It will "participate in equity capital of productive projects and enterprises in member countries." It will "invest in economic and social infrastructure projects in member countries by way of participation or their financial arrangements." "It makes loans to the private and the public sectors for the financing of productive projects, enterprises and programmes. It has also established special funds and operates them for specific purposes including a Fund for assistance to Muslim communities in non-member countries." It also operates Trust Funds and accepts deposits. It provides technical assistance to member countries and assists in promotion of foreign trade, especially in capital goods and member countries.

The Islamic Development Bank, as it does not operate on the basis of interest, has devised unique methods not traditionally adopted by development banks, such as participation in development projects, supply of capital, management and sharing of profits and losses.

Labour and Industrial Relations

Islam emphasizes dignity of labour, honest work and wages to maintain a decent standard of living. There is emphasis on cooperation between labour and management.

Population Policy

Population control through family planning has been controversial subject in the literature of Islamic Economics. A majority of the authors oppose family planning on the ground that it has no place in Islamic culture. Their solution to population problem is: Augmentation and full utilization of the resources that the bountiful God has created and a perpetual effort at discovering hidden resources. Thus increasing production is suggested as a real solution to the problem.

Economic Development

Increase in production, distributive justice, environmental balance and improvement in the quality of life may be considered as the four dimensions of development in Islamic Economics.

Exchange, Price and Profit

Some of the Islamic economists (*e.g.*, Baquir) lay the blame on the use of money as a store of value, which makes exchange a means to the accumulation of wealth. This creates a distortion in the equilibrium between supply and demand. The remedy for this lies in zakat and the abolition of interest. By this way, money is confined to its basic role of mediating between production and consumption.

Monopoly, hoarding and speculation are all considered as un-islamic practices. If the market functions under conditions of free competition, prices will be normal. All prices—whether of factors of production or of products will then be 'just' or 'fair.'

There is disagreement among writers in Islamic Economics on the nature of profit. Some writers do not consider profits as reward for risk-taking or uncertainty-bearing. Profits are shared between the supplier of capital and the entrepreneur or the working partner in the mudarabah contract. In a way, it resembles interest. But we know that there are some differences between the nature of interest and profit in economic theory.

Conclusion

From the foregoing discussion, we find that Islamic economics is similar to political economy, its function being "the discovery of laws and analysis of real life in the context of an Islamic society in which the Islamic way of life is fully justified." (Baqir al Sadr).

Like the Historical school, they believe that economic laws are relative and are not capable of universal application. The only exception is the Laws of Returns.

We may also say that Islamic economics is normative rather than positive. In short, as Mannan puts it, "Islamic economics is a social science which studies the economic problems of a people imbued with the values of Islam."

ECONOMIC THOUGHT IN ANCIENT INDIA

The main sources of information regarding the economic thought in ancient India are *the Vedas, the Upanishads, the Epics (the Ramayana and the Mahabharata)* and some treatises, especially Kautilya's *Arthasastra*. Thiruvalluvar's 'Thirukkural' throws light on the economic thought in ancient South India. The Vedas depict the life and work in the early vedic period. The Ramayana and Mahabharata provide sociological account of the contemporary period. Kautilya's Arthasastra of the fourth century B.C. gives details of the political, social, economic and military organisation of the Mauryan Empire.

There are two divergent views on the philosophy of life in ancient India. There is one set of writers, mostly of Western stock, who believe that life, work and thought in ancient India was based on the negation of life. In other words, they believe that the people in ancient India did not have materialistic view of life and they were interested mainly in things of the soul. So they concluded, religion and philosophy dominated their lives. Here is a typical view: "The economic ideas of the ancient peoples of the East which may be gathered from their sacred books, have but a slight interest from the point of view of modern science. They can all be reduced to a few moral precepts. Commerce and arts were, as a rule, despised in comparison with agriculture." (*L. Cossa: Introduction to the Study of Political Economy*). This, however, is not a correct view.

The opposite view, which seems to be nearer the truth, has been shared mostly by Indian scholars. Pandit Jawaharlal Nehru, for instance, believed that the basic background of ancient Indian culture was not one of other-worldliness or world-worthlessness. In fact, he believed that the Vedic Aryans were so full of zest for life that they paid little attention to the soul. While commenting on the Vedas, he tells that, "There is no idolatry in them, no temples for the Gods. The vitality and affirmation of life pervading them are extraordinary." In fact, the Indus valley civilization which was pre-Aryan, non-Aryan and definitely superior to the Aryan civilization was in "some respects even superior to that of a contemporary Mesopotamia and Egypt." The scheme of life practised in ancient India is an example of comprehensive and coordinated planning.

The Caste System

A proper understanding of the caste system is essential for describing the economic life in ancient India. In the beginning, the basis of caste was profession and not birth. Cossa aptly described the caste system as "*division of labour gone to seed.*" It was only during the latter period that the caste system became rigid and led to many abuses. Originally, the society was divided into four classes: (*i*) The *Brahmins*, (*ii*) The *Kshatriyas*, (*iii*) The *Vaishyas*, and (*iv*) The *Shudras*. The Brahmins performed mainly the functions of priests. There were great thinkers among them who guided the policy of the nation. The Kshatriyas were the rulers and the warriors. The Vaishyas were the agriculturists, artisans and merchants. The Sudras were labourers and unskilled workers, other than the agriculturists. It must, however, be noted that the early caste system was a flexible one. For instance, even Brahmins could follow agricultural pursuits. Not only that, even inter-caste marriages were not unknown. Rigidity in the system came in much later. It was only then, the caste system was used as a tool to maintain the social equilibrium. We may not be wrong in saying that the caste system of the later period retarded economic growth to a certain extent. Even today, the caste system remains as one of the main institutional obstacles to economic growth in India.

The joint family system was another important institution in ancient India. Only now, it is disappearing slowly under the impact of industrialisation and urbanization. Unlike, as in Greece slavery was not there on a large scale in ancient India. There were only a relatively small number of domestic slaves and they were not treated badly. In ancient Rome, the master had the right to sell a slave and even put him to death.

As in all early civilizations, agriculture was held in high esteem in ancient India. In fact, the word *Arya* comes from a root word meaning 'to till', and the Aryans as a whole were agriculturists and agriculture was considered a noble occupation.

Monarchy was the most popular form of government in Ancient India. Kingship became hereditary and generally women were not allowed to become the rulers. The ruler was held responsible for all misfortunes. There was a certain amount of decentralization in their political set-up. Village assemblies enjoyed a measure of autonomy. The chief source of revenue was from land. It was predominantly an agricultural civilization and the basic unit was the self-governing village. The political and economic structure was built up from these village communities.

Hunting was a regular occupation chiefly for the food it provided. Silk, woollen and cotton textiles were the major manufacturing industries. There were powerful trade associations and craft guilds. The *Mahabharata* refers to the existence of trade and craft organisations: "The safeguard of corporations (guilds) is union." It is said that 'the merchant guilds were of such authority that the king was not allowed to establish any laws repugnant to these trade unions.' (*Cambridge History of India*).

Interest and Usury: Money-lending by higher castes was severely restricted in ancient India and interest rates were regulated. A significant point is that in ancient India they had a notion that there should be some maxim for interest payment. Further, they had careful regulations against false weights and measures. The social welfare concept was a salient feature of early economic thought. Trade flourished not only in the country itself but between India and foreign countries. Old Tamil poems tell us of the port of Kaveripattinam on the Cauvery river in the South which was a centre of international trade.

Buddhism and Jainism, in a way, are responsible for the popular but erroneous belief that renunciation and life-negation are the dominant features of the ancient Indian society.

We shall now describe some of the main ideas contained in Kautilya's *Arthasastra* of the fourth century B.C.

Kautilya's Arthashastra

Kautilya was the Prime Minister of Chandra Gupta Maurya. He is also known as Chanakya. He has been called the Indian Machiavelli. His book *Arthasastra* gives details of the political, social, economic and military organisations of the past, and especially of the Mauryan empire. We shall now describe some of the main economic ideas contained in the *Arthasastra* of the fourth century B.C.

1. *Wealth:* Generally, people in ancient India realized the importance of wealth for the welfare of mankind. In fact, acquisition of wealth was described as one of the four major goals of life, namely, Dharma (charity), *Artha* (wealth), *Kama* (love) and *Moksha* (salvation).

   Kautilya used wealth in a wide sense. He included things like money, property, precious metals and even forests. He has emphasized the importance of saving in acquiring wealth, "Wealth is to be acquired grain by grain, as learning is to be acquired every moment." A man's wealth might be used for the maintenance of his family or for giving away in charity.

2. *Varta:* Ancient thinkers used the word *Varta* to mean the science of national economy. Kautilya included agriculture, animal husbandry and trade in Varta. He substituted the word "*Arthasastra*" for "Varta" and widened its scope. 'Arthasastra' is a combination of Economics, Political Science, Ethics, Jurisprudence and Military Science.

3. *Agriculture:* Agriculture occupies a place of first-rate importance in Kautilya's *Arthasastra*. Kautilya suggested that even a Brahmin could follow agricultural pursuits provided the Brahmin did not himself hold the plough.

4. *Labour and Caste:* The caste system in ancient India was rooted in the division of labour. Kautilya did not recommend slave labour. But hired labour was there. Kautilya had laid down a code of labour discipline. For instance, he suggested that a wage worker who abandoned his work before the term had expired was to pay the whole amount of stipulated wages to his employer and a fine to the King. "On the other hand, if an employer dismissed a workman whom he had hired before the expiration of the term agreed upon, he must pay the full amount of wages stipulated and a fine to the King, unless the workman were to blame."

5. *Value and Trade:* The ancient thinkers of India seemed to have some notions on value which are relevant to modern times. The following statements make the above mentioned point clear. "Whatever is without another of the same kind, is as good as a gem, we should take the value of each commodity according to time and place but there can be no value (price) of that which is incapable of being exchanged." Again "whatever one pays for obtaining a thing must be taken to be the cost of value (mulya of that article). Value is determined by the easiness, or otherwise of obtaining, and also by the inherent utility or lack of it" (Shukracharya).

Kautilya devoted a good deal of attention to the problems of trade such as regulation and development of trade by the State and the different taxes to be levied on the commodities that entered into trade. He even advocated state trading in certain commodities through departmental agencies.

6. *Public Finance:* Land revenue was an important source of taxation in ancient India. The early writers have described the features of a good tax system. "The tax system should be such as not to prove a great burden on the public (*praja*), the king should act like the bee which collects honey without inconveniencing the plant" (Garola: *Kautilya's, Arthasastra*).

Kautilya's Arthasastra has an elaborate scheme of Public Finance. Kautilya advocated state participation in the economic sphere. In other words, he has emphasized the need for setting up state undertakings to step up the revenue of the State. He recommended a balanced budget.

Kautilya classified tax receipts into *three* types: (*i*) *Income earned through taxes on goods, produced within the country,* (*ii*) *income earned through taxes on goods produced in the capital,* and (*iii*) *income earned through taxes, on imports and exports.* Imports were usually taxed at the rate of 1/5th of the cost (value) of the commodity. It may be interesting to note here that Kautilya suggested imposition of heavy taxes on imports of luxuries and other articles which were not conducive to the welfare of the people.

Kautilya had given an elaborate scheme of land revenue system. He suggested different rates for different lands. The land revenue ranged between 1/12th and 1/3rd of the total produce of the land.

The following were the main items of Public Expenditure outlined by Kautilya. (*i*) National Defence, (*ii*) Public Administration, (*iii*) Salaries of Ministers and Expenditures on Government Departments, and (*iv*) Expenditure incurred on the maintenance of armies.

7. *Welfare State:* The ancient Indian writers had a clear idea of the welfare state. According to Shukra, "The State is a tree of which the King is the root and the counsellors are the main

branches, the commanders are the lesser branches; the armies are the blossoms and the flowers, the people are fruits and the land is the seed." The same idea has been echoed by Kautilya: "In the happiness of his (King's) subjects lies his happiness, in their welfare, his welfare."

Kautilya regarded wealth as the basis of strength and power of a country. So he suggested that industries producing gold, silver, diamonds and iron should be state-owned. Private enterprise was to be allowed in agriculture, weaving, arts and crafts and private property rights were recognised. However, production, distribution, exchange and consumption were regulated by the State with the object of promoting maximum efficiency and equitable distribution. Money-lending and interest were not despised in ancient India as in ancient Greece and Rome. Kautilya suggested that the just rate of interest should be 15 per cent as a general rule. But he allowed higher rates of interest on money lent to traders and sea merchants. Kautilya suggested a system of price controls in order to protect the interests of the consumers. The traders could add a maximum of only 8 per cent profit on domestic commodities and 10 per cent on imported goods. Traders who violated these rules were punished.

Thus Kautilya's 'Arthasastra' confirms the view that the ancient Indian society was not a simple one but a complex one with sophisticated ideas on economics, politics, ethics and public administration.

Economic Ideas of Thiruvalluvar

The economic ideas of Thiruvalluvar are contained in the "Thirukkural", a book of ethics. Thiruvalluvar belonged to the Sangam Age. Thirukkural is variously dated from the 3rd century A. D. Thiruvalluvar's work is marked by pragmatic idealism. We may note one point here before we discuss the economic ideas of Thiruvalluvar. The conventional divisions of life's aim are Dharma or aram (Ethics), Artha or Porul (polity), Kama or inbam (Love), and Moksha or Veedu (liberation). Thirukkural deliberately excludes the fourth objective, namely, Moksha or Veedu (liberation). This is another instance that shows that the belief of some western scholars that people in ancient India were always concerned about other-worldliness and things like Moksha (liberation) was a mistaken notion.

Valluvar's economic ideas are found mostly in the second part of "Thirukkural", the "Porutpal", or the part dealing with wealth. By 'Porutpal', Valluvar meant all that Kautilya meant by the word "Arthasastra."

Thiruvalluvar was a fundamental thinker. He has made the point that rains lend basic support to life. The basis of stable economic life is rain, because rain furnishes food. Agriculture which is the most fundamental economic activity depends on rain. "It is rain that both ruins and aids the ruined to rise."

On Poverty and Begging

Valluvar considered freedom from hunger as one of the fundamental freedoms that should be enjoyed by every citizen. Valluvar realised that the destruction of the poor was their poverty. And he considered it foolish to redress the ills of poverty by begging, He condemned poverty and begging as the greatest curses of a society. It is wrong to say that some were made to beg by fate. If people were to live by begging, he said, "May the Creator of the Universe who has decreed so, go abegging and perish."

Wealth

Valluvar tells about the importance of accumulation of wealth and he regarded wealth as only a means, and not an end. He said, "Acquire a great fortune by noble and honourable means," He condemned hoarding and described hoarded wealth as profitless riches. According to him, 'industry is real wealth' and 'labour is the greatest resource.'

Agriculture

According to Thiruvalluvar, "Agriculture is the most fundamental economic activity." Husbandmen are the axle-pin of the world; for on their prosperity revolves the prosperity of the other sectors of the economy. He regarded agriculture alone as the most independent vocation. "The ploughmen alone", he says, "live as the freemen of the soil; the rest are mere slaves that follow on their toil." Valluvar was for free enterprise in agriculture. He was for peasant proprietorship and he condemned absentee landlordism.

There are certain similarities between the views of Valluvar and Physiocrats of the 18th century France on agriculture. The physiocrats considered agriculture alone as the productive occupation. The merchants and manufacturers, according to the Physiocrats, "were an unproductive class." Valluvar too held the belief that agriculture was superior to all other occupations. "Husbandmen are the lynch-pin of society, for they support all those that take to other work, not having the strength to plough." He goes on to say, "Who ploughing eat their food, they truly live. The rest to others bend subservient, eating what they give."

For Valluvar, good ethics is also good economics. On charity and thrift, Valluvar says, "Give, always give, but let your giving be governed by your resources. Be thrifty, but not to verge, on miserliness." Valluvar has noted that, "generosity which is blind to its resources, perishes of its own accord." He was for a balance in all things.

Valluvar considered "the agriculturists", "the intellectuals" and "the capitalists" as the important ingredients of an economic society.

Public Finance

Valluvar deals with the problems of Public Finance such as Public Revenue, Financial Administration and Public Expenditure.

Though a tax is a compulsory payment made by a citizen to the State, Valluvar was against any undue compulsion in taxation. He compared a king who collected taxes by force to a highwayman. Valluvar refers to three main sources of revenue, (i) Wealth that comes by itself, (ii) customs, and (iii) tribute paid by defeated enemies (in modern times, we call this 'reparation').

It may be interesting to note that Valluvar did not refer to land revenue though the land revenue was a major source of revenue in those days. The traditional tax was about one-sixth of the produce. Valluvar took the land revenue for granted. For the payment of land revenue became a part of the normal duties of every citizen. In fact, it has been called a *Kadamai* or duty.

Public Expenditure

Valluvar was for balanced budget. "It is not a great misfortune for a State if its revenues are limited, provided the expenditure is kept within bounds." His guidelines for a budgetary policy seem to be these: "Budget for a surplus, if possible, balance the budget at other times, but never budget for a deficit." Of course, modern economists may not agree with this stand.

Valluvar recommended the following main items of expenditure, (i) Defence, (ii) Public Works, and (iii) Social Services. From an economic point of view, Valluvar recommended a welfare state.

Valluvar regarded education as an important factor that promoted economic progress. He considered drinking, gambling and prostitution as evils that did harm to the socio-economic life of a society.

External Assistance

Valluvar was against dependence on external assistance. "That alone is a country which has not to seek external resources. That is no country which has to depend on external resource." In other words, Valluvar was for a self-sufficient economy.

Valluvar and Kautilya

Sometimes, a comparison is made between the economic ideas of Valluvar and Kautilya. We have to note first that the basic economic ideas of Valluvar are different from those of Kautilya.

First, Valluvar accords the pride of place to agriculture and that is not the case in Kautilya's *Arthasastra*.

Second, Arthasastra is based on the caste system but Valluvar does not speak of the caste system.

Third, Thirukkural is based on ethical foundations. For Valluvar, good ethics is good economics. But a salient feature of *Arthasastra* is that Economics and Politics are divorced from ethics.

Fourth, taxation by consent is the main feature of Kural. But taxation by fear is the central teaching in that of Kautilya.

We may conclude by saying that the fundamental economic ideas of Thiruvalluvar are similar to those of Adam Smith rather than those of Kautilya. For both in Valluvar and Smith, economic ideas are based on a moral philosophy of life. Both of them advocated a democratic basis of society and valued individual freedom more than anything else.

Economic Thought in Medieval India

The medieval period of India is more or less a dark period in the development of economic thought in India. There has been no significant contribution to economic thought during this period. However, there is one work, that is of some importance from the point of view of economic thought. And that is Abul Fazl's *Aini-Akbari*. Abul Fazl was a mastermind during the period of Akbar. He has been called the Muslim Chanakya. Abul Fazl has described the revenue system of Todar Mal who was the revenue minister of Akbar. The book contains references to the various measures taken for providing relief to agriculturists such as *taccavi* loan and remission of land revenue. It also contains references to regulation of market and pricing.

SANTI PARVA

Introduction

Santi Parva, which is the twelfth-book of the great epic Mahabharata, is a collection of many passages on statecraft, ethics and human conduct. This was recited by Bhisma, the elder statesman as he lay dying on a pile of arrows after the great battle at Kurushetra.

Yudishthira was in great sorrow due to the loss of his brothers and relatives in the war of Kurushetra. Almost all the sages pacified the king who was in anguish.

The Santi Parva is divided into three sub-parvas namely, Rajdharmanusana Parva, Aapaddharma Parva and Mokshadharma Parva.

1. Rajdharmanusana Parva

Sages such as Vyasa, Narada, Devala and Kanva went to Yudhisthira to enquire about his anguish. Narada asked Yudhisthira about the reason for his sorrow. The latter then told Narada that he heard Karna who was born to Kunti secretly was his elder brother. Out of ignorance and as he was greedy towards the kingdom, he made his brother to kill another brother. He wanted to know why the wheels of Karna's chariot were caught up in the ground. Further, he wanted to know how Karna was cursed. Then, Narada told him all about Karna and the curses that had been pronounced on him on various occasions.

Karna realized that Arjuna was superior to him in archery. So he approached Drona and requested him to teach him how to wield the Brahmastra. Drona refused to teach him because he was not a brahmana of faultless conduct or a Kshatriya who had purified himself by much penance. Thereupon, Karna met Parasurama and deceived him by saying that he was a brahmana and became his disciple. He learnt from him many things in archery and the use of many astras.

One day, when Karna was practising with his bow in the forest, by accident, he killed a branmana's cow. The brahmana became angry and cursed Karna that in battle his chariot wheels would stick in the mud and he would be done to death, even like that innocent cow which he had killed.

Parasurama, who became fond of Karna, taught him all the archery he knew and instructed him how to use and also withdraw Brahmastra. But when Parasurama came to know through an incident that Karna was not a brahmana but Kshatriya, he cursed Karna that his knowledge of astras would fail him and what he had learnt from him through deception would not be of any use to him. The moral is that a person should not tell lies and deceive his teacher. Not only that, the anecdote brings to light the caste discrimination during the period.

Karna was very generous in making gifts. One day, Indra, who was Arjuna's father came in disguise as a brahmana and begged of Karna for a gift of the divine ear rings and the armour with which he had been born. Karna took them out and gave them away. From that time, Karna's strength was reduced.

Narada, then informed Yudishthira that Parasurama's curse, the anger and curse of the brahmana whose cow was killed by Karna and Vasudeva's strategy combined to bring about Karna's death. So he advised Yudhisthira not to think that he alone caused his death. But Yudhisthira was not consoled by these words.

Kunti also consoled him and told him not to blame himself. But Yudhisthira told Kunti that she deceived him by hiding the secret of Karna's birth from him. That made him commit the sin. Then he cursed "May women never be able to keep a secret henceforth".

2. On Principles of Administration

Santi Parva deals with some of the principles of administration. In accordance with the customs of the day, the King should first perform sacrifice called Ashwamedha and give donations as per scriptures and then discharge his duties. At the same time, he should follow the principles of household. Only when a person is selfless, he would attain eternal fame. For *mama* (my) is death and *na mama* (not mine) is eternal. A king should rule the earth looking after the people by following the path of Dharma.

Crime and Punishment

According to Santi Parva, in the matter of royal punishment, the following rules should be followed: "If a Brahmin commits mistake, punishment through speech is enough for him. Shouldering the responsibility is a suitable punishment given to the Kshatriya. Imposing fine is the punishment given to a Vysya. But it was said that a sudra is devoid of punishment". Thus, the King should protect the subjects.

It would not be fair for a king to abandon his kingdom that was won over through Dharma. Not only that, holding the authority is the utmost principle of a Kshatriya. According to Vyasa, a king should first experience the comforts of *Dharma, Artha* and *Kama* and then go to the forest. A king should not be lamenting like a fool. Grief has thousands of abodes. Happiness has more than thousands of opportunities.

It is not right to think that wealth is the source of happiness. If that were so, a poor man would not get any kind of happiness.

According to Vyasa, "a king can protect Dharma by slaying the trespassers of Dharma. There is no need for grief. There is no harm in killing a person of a family, because of which the sorrow of that family is removed. Similarly, if a nation obtains peace by destroying a family, then it is not a wicked deed by doing so.

A king should appoint persons only after ascertaining whether they are eligible for the posts. After Yudhisthara agreed to be the king, on the advice of Krishna, he learnt from Bhishma, the royal principles. Bhishma told him that without the four principles of human object, purpose of the king could not be accomplished only with destiny. So a king should always endeavour to obtain the four principles of human object. Bhishma described his principles as the butter of milk of the principles of polity.

On the etymology of the word "Rajan", the Santi Parva says that during Satya Yuga, there was neither a kingdom, nor a king, nor the punishment and nor its giver. By following Dharma, all the people were protecting each other. In the course of time, they did not follow the rules of Dharma and they became greedy. As a result, they came under the control of attachment. The science of morals are contained in a treatise called *Trivarga*. The fourth principle of human object is *Moksha*. Administration followed by Dharma is the main duty of a king. Thus, the science of morals and principal duties of a king are explained in Santi Parva.

II. Aapaddharma Parva

This sub-parva deals with the strategies to be followed during war and the principles of polity.

Suppose a king, who is in trouble by the decline of his army, wealth and prosperity is attacked by an enemy. In that case, if the enemies are endowed with Dharma and Artha or they follow the path of Adharma also, it would be better to make treaty with them.

A king should neither punish nor honour anyone relying upon the words of someone. It is the best principle to follow the footsteps of the best person. It is necessary for a king to collect the treasure. With the treasure only, Dharma and kingdom flourish. It may be interesting to note here that mercantilists also believed that a nation's power depended upon its wealth. A king should always try to obtain the strength. Strength is considered better than Dharma because the latter relied upon the former. If a king foresees troubles and plans for their remedy, we can call him a person with presence of mind. A king should always keep an eye on his enemies. Not only that, in times of difficulties, a person should suppress the wicked and protect the virtuous. If someone comes as a refugee, we must serve him.

If a strong person attacks a weak person, the latter should never have rivalry with the former. Intellect is the most powerful thing in a human being. A king should always forgive the opposition and wrong acts of a child, blind, deaf and strong persons.

Greed is the source of sin and all mistakes are caused by it. Control on senses is the only remedy to get rid of greed. And the symptoms of ignorance are attachment, envy, delusion, happiness, sorrow, naughtiness, lust, anger, pride, fatigue, lethargy, desire, being jealous of other's growth and commiting sins. If a person abandons sins, he will earn divine bliss.

Penance and truth are two important things in life. The thirteen flaws in human beings are anger, lust, grief, delusion, desire of doing bad, desire to kill others, pride, greed, malice, jealousy, blame, envy and pity. There are ways of getting rid of these flaws by righteous conduct.

III. Mokshadharmaparva

A person can get rid of the grief born out of the loss of wealth or death of wife, son or father by following the principles of Truth and Dharma and the causes of welfare. Good deeds such as charity, sacrifice and service to the teacher will bring solace to a person.

On the mode of behaviour to be followed by human beings. Santiparva tells that a person with good behaviour is the best. The principles and practices of good behaviour are: "One should not sleep at the time of sunrise. One should pray to the Sun god every day. After washing the hands, feet and face and by sitting towards the east, one should eat the food. One should remain silent while eating the food. Whether the food is tasty or not, one should eat the food in a pleasing way. One should never blame the food. It is laid down that human beings should eat only in the morning and the evening. There is no rule to eat in the middle. Whoever follows this will get the result of fasting. Dharma is the source of human beings. It is ambrosia for the gods in the heaven. The Moksha-dharmaparva says that a virtuous person experiences happiness, due to the strength of Dharma. Spiritual knowledge, meditation and worship are all the ways to attain the Supreme Brahman.

There is need for following the principles of non-violence and ending the greed for wealth. If a person followed Dharma as laid down by the scriptures, then he would obtain welfare in this and the other worlds. A life of detachment is also necessary to enjoy peace and tranquility.

Conclusion

The three sub-parvas of Shanti Parva deal with the statecraft – principles of administration, duties of a king and governance based on Dharma – strategies to be followed during war, the principles of polity and the need for avoiding greed and to lead a life of Truth and Dharma.

4 MEDIEVAL ECONOMIC THOUGHT

The period from the fall of the Roman empire in 476 A.D. to 1453 A.D., the year in which Constantinople fell into the hands of Turks, is generally regarded as the Middle Ages.

There are some who regard the Middle Ages as a complete break in the continuity of economic thought because the thinkers of the Middle Ages had emphasized on the negative aspects of life. This, however, is not a correct view. For even during that period, there was speculation on economic topics such as money, interest and price and the views of these thinkers were similar to those of the Greek thinkers of the past. As in Greek thought, economic speculation was only a by-product of ethical and political thought.

For an understanding of the Medieval economic thought, it is necessary to bear in mind the essential features of the society of the Middle Ages. The Society of the Middle Ages may be described as a *feudal system*. In that system, the society was held together by mutual obligations and services. People enjoyed status according to the ranks. "In all directions, medieval life was communal and cooperative in character." There were merchant guilds and craft guilds. The guilds were associations for mutual benefit and protection of the members. The regulation of trade was an important function of the merchant guilds. But we have to note that the people in Middle Ages lived to a large extent in a "natural economy." Though there is much talk of trade, merchant guilds and all that, the actual volume of trade must have been small for there was shortage of money and there were difficulties of transport. Men lived largely in small and self-sufficient units. On the religious side, the Church dominated the lives of men.

The Church, The Bible and Aristotle exercised a great influence on the life and thought of Middle Ages.

After the fall of the Roman Empire, the Church became a powerful institution. It tried to regulate the lives of men. It taught them that their earthly life was only a preparation for another. So people aimed at eternal salvation. Further, Middle Ages was marked by a non-national atmosphere.

Aristotle influenced the views of the thinkers of Middle Ages on many matters. Their views on the nature and functions of money, usury, the principles which should govern exchange and the nature of justice can be traced to Aristotle. Thus Aristotle became the philosopher of the Middle Ages and his doctrines became the foundations of *medieval* economic thought.

Christianity

Christianity had a profound influence on the life and thought of Middle Ages. The doctrines of Christianity appealed to the poor and the oppressed.

In the first place, Christianity taught the universal brotherhood of man. All men were the children of a common father. So they were brothers. This principle of brotherhood and universal love struck at

28

the very roots of class distinctions. So it became difficult to defend the institution of slavery which was a part and parcel of Greek and Roman civilizations and thought. Slavery was considered a sinful institution.

Secondly, Christianity taught that life in this world is only a preparation for another. So people must aim at salvation. As God, created all men equal, even a slave may enter the Kingdom of Heaven.

Thirdly, Christianity taught men about the dignity of labour. This is in contrast to the Greek view that labour was to be performed by slaves and menial workers. But the New Testament advised people to work with their own hands.

The concept of "just price" and the prohibition of usury are the two dominant economic ideas of the Middle Ages. In short, Medieval economic thought is based on the idea of "justice". As all men are brothers, they should behave as brothers, respecting each other's rights and position in life. Their relationship should be guided by justice. No one, under any circumstances, should take advantage of his neighbours. This is the essence of medieval economic thought. And the salient features of medieval economic teachings are seen in the writings of St. Thomas Aquinas.

St. Thomas Aquinas (1225-1274)

St. Thomas Aquinas has been regarded as the prince of Scholastics. The Scholastics or the schoolmen were medieval men of science. They are comparable to our university or college professors. The economic ideas of St. Thomas are found in his book, *Summa Theologica*. A complete and authoritative statement of medieval economic thought may be found in that book. The arguments of St. Thomas are based on the Bible, Aristotle and the Christian fathers. In fact, what he aimed at was a synthesis of Christianity and the doctrines of Aristotle. The economic doctrines of St. Thomas cover such matters as the institution of private property, the just price, and the prohibition of usury. On most of these things, St. Thomas more or less repeats the views of Aristotle. It must be remembered that he discusses economic matters incidentally in connection with religious and moral questions.

Private Property

St. Thomas believes that the institution of private property is in accord with the law of nature. It may be regulated by Government for common good and the owner is under duty to share the use of his possessions with others. To support his view that private property may be regulated, he refers to the regulation of property in the Old Testament by means of the Sabbatical year and the Jubilee year. In short, like Aristotle, he suggests that property should be private in possession, but common in use.

St. Thomas advocated charity. But charity need not go so far as to endanger the donor's or his family's status in society. It may be interesting to note that St. Thomas argues that *theft is permissible in the case in extreme necessity*.

Trade

The ideas of St. Thomas on trade were similar to those of the Canonists. The Canonists justified profits, if profits were used for self-support and for charity (*i.e.*, for the support of family). They justified trade, if it was done as a service by providing the public with goods. St. Thomas too justified moderate profits on the grounds of support, charity or public service.

The Just Price

St. Thomas discusses the problem of 'just price' in his *Summa Theologica*. According to him, "The worth or value of a good is its just price." Just price may also be described as "the current price prevailing at a given place and at the given time, to be determined by the estimate of a fair minded person. Thus, the just price was not an absolutely definite price. He said that, "To sell a thing for more than its worth, or to buy it for less than its worth, is in itself unjust and unlawful." Just as no one wishes to acquire a good at a price in excess of its worth, no one should try to sell it for more than its worth. St. Thomas refers to Aristotle's view that when an exchange takes place, it must be to the common advantage of buyer and seller. Only under exceptional circumstances, can a seller charge more than the just price. For instance, if a seller incurred a loss in parting with a good, he could charge a price slightly more than the just price. Aristotle emphasized that the value of a thing depended on its demand. St. Thomas too seemed to have believed that the value of a thing reflected its utility. In fact, in "City of Joy", one of his works, he has said that a "different value is set upon each thing proportionate to its use."

It must be remembered that during the Middle Ages, there was price regulation of many commodities by public authorities. The regulated price was based more or less on the just price.

Usury

The views of St. Thomas on usury were based on the Bible and Aristotle. Jesus said, "Lend freely, hoping nothing thereby." According to Aristotle, "Money is used mainly as a means of exchange." It is a consumptible good. The lender of money should not charge any interest. And in those days, money was borrowed mainly for purposes of consumption than of production. St. Thomas echoed the same view in the following words: "It is by its very nature unlawful to take payment for the use of money lent."

St. Thomas, however, said that under certain circumstances, interest could be charged on loans lent. Firstly, if a lender suffered any damage because of having parted with his funds, he could charge interest as compensation for losses. Secondly, if the lender lost an opportunity to make a gain by lending money, he could charge interest. Thirdly, if a borrower failed to repay the amount borrowed in time, interest could be charged as compensation for the delay. Lastly, if there was any risk involved, interest could be charged. After the close of the Middle Ages, the Scholastic doctrines gradually approved of interest on loans. Even leading economists like Keynes are convinced of the advantages of a low rate of interest. A low rate of interest will promote the inducement to invest. The schoolmen of Middle Ages advocated a policy that encouraged productive and profitable investment while at the same time keeping interest rates down.

St. Thomas Nicole Oresme (1320-1382 A.D.)

St. Thomas Oresme was one of the great thinkers of the later Middle Ages. He had made beautiful comments on the use and misuse of money. According to him, "There are three ways.... in which one may make profit from money, aside from its natural use. The first of these is the art of exchange, the custody of or trafficking in money, the second is usury, and the third is the altering of money. The first is base, the second is bad, and the third is even worse." He noted that the rulers of his Age resorted to debasement of coinage on a large scale. He attacked that practice by saying that, "... making a profit from the alteration of money is even worse than usury." He called the policy of debasing coinage as a tyrannical and fraudulent practice and described it as a "violent theft."

MERCANTILISM

Introduction

The economic ideas and policies which were followed by European statesmen from the 15th century until the second half of the eighteenth century have been generally described as mercantilism. The mercantilists thought that the wealth of a nation could be increased by trade. The meaning is there in the word "mercantilism" itself. Mercantilism is known by various names such as 'bullionism', 'Colbertism' and 'Kameralism.' The early mercantilists believed that the wealth of a nation consisted in the amount of bullion (gold and silver) possessed by it. So they suggested ways and means of increasing the stock of gold and silver in a country. Hence the terms *bullionism*. In Germany, Mercantilism was known as *Kameralism*. In the words of Haney, ".....Kameral affairs concerned the economy of the prince, and Kameralism was the art which maintained, increased, and administered the royal income." In France, mercantilism was known as *Colbertism*. For nearly three hundred years, mercantilism was a powerful force in England, France, Germany, Italy, Spain, and in almost every other European nation. It was followed in Russia too.

Factors that gave Rise to Mercantilism

The historical background should be taken into account in explaining the Mercantilist philosophy. Many political, social, economic and religious factors were responsible for the rise of Mercantilism.

Towards the close of the Middle Ages, nationalism became a strong force. Europe changed greatly as a result of the Renaissance, the Reformation, the invention of printing and the discovery of America. As a result of these changes, there was a fundamental political change. It resulted in the emergence of strong nation States like England, France, Germany and Spain. Feudalism came to an end and the king became powerful. Each nation wanted to preserve its independence and considered the other nation as its potential rival. In order to create a strong and powerful state, the mercantilists tried to regulate the political and economic activity of the people.

During the Middle Ages, life, both economic and political, was dominated by religion and ethics. But the political teachings of Machiavelli (1469-1527) and Jean Bodin (1520-1596) influenced the thought of the ruler.

There were other factors, economic in character, which gave rise to mercantilism. During the Middle Ages, money was scarce and emphasis was laid on self-sufficiency. The result was that there was little exchange. But from the sixteenth century onwards, *exchange economy* became the rule. Markets developed and money came to be increasingly used in exchange. The supply of money increased by the discovery of a large number of silver mines. Slowly, *competition* began to take its place as a factor in controlling industry. Machiavelli divorced Politics from ethics. He argued that what was ethically wrong could be politically right. As Alexander Gray put it, "Machiavelli thus became the unscrupulous despot's guide to power." Sometimes, mercantilism is viewed as the equivalent of Machiavelli and Bodin.

31

Further, war became expensive during the period of mercantilism. The King had to find more money to maintain huge standing armies and prices were rising. Some of the Mercantilists thought that the whole art of war was reduced to money and the easiest way to win a war was to find more money to feed, clothe and pay one's army. Thus they argued that money and not courage was the important factor in war.

The mercantilists were practical men. Naturally, they were interested in practical problems. Their main problem was the creation of a strong state. That is why it has been said that mercantilism is merely "state-making" on the economic side. Mercantilism was not an end in itself. It was only an economic means for a political end, the end being the creation of a strong state. According to Alexander Gray. "Mercantilism was the sum total of the means on the economic side, appropriate to the attainment of this end." The mercantilists regarded wealth as the source of a nation's power. They saw in wealth the secret of a nation's strength. Mercantilism arose out of those conditions.

General Outline of Mercantilism

One thing, we must remember at the outset is this. "The complete mercantilist, in fact, never existed." Among the mercantilist writers, there were differences of opinion on many theories which we generally describe as mercantilist theories. So, mercantilism, sometimes, is a misleading word. Mercantilism was rooted in practice. As a practical philosophy, it was the product of the minds of statesmen, civil servants, and business leaders of the day. The mercantilists came from different walks of life. Thus Thomas Mun (1571-1641) was an English Merchant, who served on the board of East India Company. J.B. Colbert (1619-1683) was the great French Finance Minister. Philipp Wilhelm Von Hornick (1638-1712) was a pamphleteer.

The fundamental aim of the mercantilist was to make his country strong. When he came to look for a test of strength, he found it in the wealth of his country—above all in that portion of wealth which consisted of precious metals like gold and silver. So the mercantilists attached a lot of importance to bullion because it was the most durable, the most useful and the most generally acceptable form of wealth. In other words, they regarded money and bullion as the sign of wealth.

If a country has mines, it can get gold and silver. And it can accumulate those precious metals by imposing restrictions on the export of gold. But if a country has no mines, it can get gold and silver only as a result of trade. Trade must be conducted and regulated in such a way that gold may come into the country. In order that a country may have more bullion, there must be a "favourable balance of trade." In other words, there should be an excess of exports over imports. "It was thus a primary principle of the typical mercantilist to maximize exports while minimizing imports." (Alexander Gray).

In the mercantilist scheme of things, trade was the most important occupation. Industry and manufacture were ranked second in importance. Agriculture was the least important of all. Though agriculture might feed the population it brought no money in the form of gold and silver into the country. So they thought it was not so important as trade and industry.

The State had an important role in the mercantilist order. Mercantilism was a policy of perpetual governmental activity. There was regulation of economic life by the Government.

The economic doctrines of the mercantilists were characterised by the following features. In their policies, (i) Mercantilists gave importance only for national advantage; (ii) They laid great emphasis on national policies for increasing the stock of precious metals; (iii) Their aim was maximum exports and minimum imports; (iv) They sought favourable balance of trade by direct promotion of exports and restriction of imports; and (v) The ultimate aim was the creation of a strong and powerful state.

We shall now discuss in detail the views of the mercantilists on the role of the State, money, rate of interest, population, and balance of trade.

Role of the State

The mercantilists believed that State intervention was necessary for the proper management of society's economic affairs. There was so much of state regulation of economic activity during the period of mercantilism in England that E. Lipson, a noted economic historian remarked that England during the heyday of the mercantilists experienced her first "*planned economy*".

With the object of maximising exports and minimising imports, the Government put heavy import duties to discourage imports of foreign goods and granted bounties and other tax concessions to encourage exports.

For instance, in England, the Government issued patents of monopoly whenever new processes were introduced by companies. It allowed direct importation of foreign workers in order to establish a new industry. It fixed prices and wages in order to encourage production. It passed navigation Acts to encourage shipping and Navy. It created privileged trading companies. And it helped in the establishment of colonies in order to secure raw materials as well as a market for the finished goods. As there was so much of economic activity and regulation by the State, mercantilism has been described as a policy of perpetual Governmental activity. Sometimes, economists find close relationship between mercantilism and state socialism of today.

The Role of Money

The mercantilists were of the view that money, usually in the form of precious metals or treasure, had an important role to play in determining the economic well-being of a nation. So they wished an indefinite accumulation of the precious metals. It was felt that an adequate supply of gold and silver, in the form of bullion, was essential to the safety of the nation. Treasure was needed for the waging of war, since with it all other things could be purchased. The mercantilists paid a lot of attention to the accumulation of precious metals and much of the criticism is against this aspect of the system. *It has been said that the mercantilists, grossly confused money and wealth.* But it is only fair to say that they regarded precious metals as a sign of wealth and they were aware of the distinction between money and wealth.

The mercantilists advocated storing of wealth in the form of precious metals because gold and silver were durable and they had high value per unit. Further, most of the mercantilists emphasized on the 'store of wealth' function of money. And in those days, precious metals were used as money. Of course, some mercantilists emphasised on the "circulation function" of money too. They believed that there was a close relationship between production—or employment—and the quantity of money in circulation.

The mercantilists were aware of the existence of unemployed labour and natural resources in the country. So they believed that the increase in the supply of money would help in increasing production and export of manufactures. Hence, their emphasis on the ways and means of increasing the stock of precious metals by maximising exports and minimising imports. They seemed to have realised that an increase in employment would result in increased aggregate consumption.

Rate of Interest

The mercantilists advocated a low rate of interest on economic grounds. They believed that economic development could proceed effectively only if the interest rate was low. And the rate of interest could be low only if the supply of money was adequate. So they argued that the accumulation of precious metals would tend to lower the rate of interest and increase the availability of credit. At the time when the mercantilists were writing, there were frequent complaints of "scarcity of money" in England and Holland. Naturally, the mercantilists thought in terms of increasing the supply of money. Further labour and other agents of production would be fully employed only if the money supply was adequate. We know now that deflation is bad because falling prices are unfavourable to economic development.

So they were opposed to any policy that caused falling prices. They considered rising prices lesser evil than falling prices.

The Balance of Trade

The "balance of trade" idea was the central doctrine in mercantilist thought. The mercantilists advocated foreign trade as a tool for increasing a nation's wealth and treasure. And they insisted on a favourable balance of trade (excess of exports over imports). Only then there would be an inflow of precious metals into the country. The mercantilists believed that State intervention was necessary to promote a "favourable balance of trade."

With the object of achieving a favourable balance of trade, the mercantilists followed a policy of discrimination, regulation and protection in trade matters. They followed a policy of discrimination between countries in the regulation of imports. This policy was followed either for trade gains or as an instrument of power politics.

With respect to eligibility of exports, the mercantilists gave priority for those commodities with a high labour content relative to value. Manufactures were favoured over agricultural products ready for consumption. Raw materials and minerals were regarded as wasteful. The sale of machines and emigration of skilled workers were regarded as injurious. The mercantilists gave priority for commodities with high labour content in their scheme of exports because there was an abundant supply of unskilled labour. The mercantilist *ideal* seemed to be zero imports and exports only in exchange for the precious metals. However, in practice, the mercantilist believed in importing only if it was essential; if the commodities could not be produced at home or if their production would require the transfer of resources from export industries.

Population

The mercantilists had a definite policy with regard to population. They believed that an *increased* population meant both an increase in the potential number of soldiers and sailors and an increase in the number of productive workers. They felt that "cheap and abundant labour was necessary to enable home products to compete successfully with those of foreign countries, hence the laws and regulations encouraging matrimony and parenthood." (Haney). So they followed measures to increase population. This encouragement to increase population formed an essential part of Mercantilism.

Representative Mercantilists

We shall consider the views of some of the leading mercantilist writers.

Thomas Mun (1571-1641)

Thomas Mun was an Englishman. He served on the Board of the East India Company. He has given a systematic statement of mercantilist principles in his book "England's Treasure by Foreign Trade" (1664). Thomas Mun was a prince among mercantilists. It has been rightly said by Alexander Gray that, "*Mun is perhaps the nearest approach to the perfect mercantilist.*"

Thomas Mun has stated the theory of balance of trade in the following words, "The ordinary means to increase our wealth and treasure is by foreign trade, wherein we must ever observe this rule: to sell more to strangers yearly than we consume of theirs in value."

Mun has suggested twelve methods by which a country could have a favourable balance of trade.

Firstly, Mun recommends the cultivation of waste lands. This step would help in reducing the imports of hemp, flax and tobacco.

Secondly, he suggests restraint on domestic consumption of foreign goods. This would also help reduce imports. Not only that, he advised people to refrain from unnecessary change of fashion.

Thirdly, Mun suggests that with regard to exports, "We must consider our neighbour's necessities." Not only that, the promotion of exports requires that proper attention must be given to commodity prices. If the goods are necessaries and the foreign buyer cannot buy it from any other source, then they may be sold at a high price. As for other goods, it is better to sell as cheap as possible rather than to lose the market.

Fourthly, the value of a country's exports could be increased by confining them to her own ships. In other words, Mun was aware of the importance of the service, or *invisible forms* in the balance of trade. So he emphasised the earnings from shipping services. It must be noted that when Mun wrote his book the Navigation Act of 1660, which restricted the use of foreign ships, had not been passed.

Fifthly, Mun advised a frugal use of natural wealth so that more might be left for export.

Sixthly, Mun suggested that the fishing in the adjacent seas should be developed by the English people. In those days, fishing was the main industry of the Dutch. It was the "golden mine" of the Dutch on which all their political and economic power was based. And the Dutch were rivals to British trading interests in East India. Mun hoped that "if this foundation (fishing) perish, the whole building of their wealth and strength both by sea and land must fall."

Seventhly, England should be made a distributing centre so that it would help her to increase shipping, trade and the King's customs.

Eighthly, Mun encourages trade with far off countries.

The *ninth* step Mun suggests is curious in a way. In this, he deviates from the normal mercantilist thinking. He suggests that in certain cases they could allow the export of money itself. His argument is this: *money begets trade and trade increases money*. He argues that merely keeping the money in the country will not make a quick and ample trade.

The *tenth* and *eleventh* points are more or less the same. He suggests that manufactures of foreign materials such as velvets and silks should be allowed to be exported free. This would provide employment and increase exports.

The *twelfth* and last point is a very vague one and of a general nature. He suggests that "we must endeavour to make the most we can of our own."

Like all mercantilists, Mun praised industry and condemned idleness and luxury. He praised the "industrious Dutch" and deplored the idleness of his countrymen who spent most of their time in idleness and pleasure, smoking, feasting and drinking. Mun was also aware of the fact that money was only a means to an end and that it would not serve its purpose if enough goods and services were not there to buy. His question was, "What shall we do with our money?". Thus he was aware of the fact that money by itself was barren.

Antonio Serra (1580-1650)

Antonio Serra was an Italian. His pamphlet, "*A Brief Treatise on the causes which can make Gold and Silver abound in Kingdoms where there are no Mines*" contains his mercantilist views. There are some countries blessed with gold and silver mines. But in other countries, according to Serra, the presence of gold and silver may be attributed to: (*i*) the quantity of industry, (*ii*) the quality of the population, (*iii*) extensive trading operations, and (*iv*) the regulations of the sovereign.

Serra has given the following reasons for the mercantilist's preference of industry to agriculture.

First, industry is safer than agriculture. The artisan is more certain of a profit than is the peasant. The peasant depends upon weather which is uncertain and the efforts of the peasant may result in loss. *Second*, industry is subject to the law of increasing returns, whereas agriculture is not. *Third*, industry has a sure market. *Lastly*, industry is more profitable than agriculture.

Further, like Mun, Serra said that in certain cases it would be beneficial to allow the export of money itself. But he emphasized that if money is exported it must be with an object. "If money is exported for any purpose whatever, it must return with a profit into the Kingdom from which it was sent."

Philipp Von Hornick (1638-1712)

Von Hornick was an Austrian pamphleteer. According to him, "the might and eminence of a country consists in its surplus of gold and silver." All other things necessary or convenient for its subsistence should be derived from its own resources without dependence on other countries.

Like Mun, Hornick has laid down certain rules for the accumulation of gold and silver. The following are the important points: (*i*) The country's soil should be used to the maximum extent. If possible, gold and silver mines are to be discovered. (*ii*) Commodities should be worked up in the country. (*iii*) Population should be encouraged to take up remunerative occupations. (*iv*) When once gold and silver are in the country, they must not be allowed to go out of the country for any purpose. It is significant to note that Hornick insists that gold and silver are not to be hoarded, but are to remain in circulation. (*v*) People must be content with their own domestic products and do without foreign products as far as possible. (*vi*) If it becomes absolutely essential to import certain goods payment should be made in kind by export of commodities. Payment should not be made in gold and silver. Further, finished goods should not be imported. They should be imported in the unfinished form and worked up in the country. (*vii*) Lastly, no imports should be allowed of a commodity, if there is sufficient supply of the same commodity in the country, even though the home-made good is of inferior quality and of higher price.

Mercantilism in Action

Mercantilist ideas ruled the thoughts and actions of statesmen for nearly three centuries in England and in Europe. Mercantilism was a *"policy of power."* It called for state action in many directions. In accordance with the mercantilist ideas, in England, the Government passed many Acts for the encouragement of tillage, corn laws and navigation laws and sumptuary laws. In England, Corn Laws were in force until 1846. The Corn Laws included regulations which encouraged corn imports above a given domestic price and allowed corn exports when domestic prices dropped beyond a certain level. It may be noted that the corn laws often resulted in the conflict of interest among landlords, corn merchants, consumers and the State. The Navigation Acts aimed at the development of the Navy for the importance of naval strength was not overlooked by the mercantilists. The sumptuary laws attempted to control consumption of various articles. In general, the principle restricted the use of imports. Foreign trade was also subject to State control.

Probably, it was in France under Colbert that the policy of State regulation was carried to the extremes. Mercantilism, in France, became an out and out restrictive policy. Mercantilism in France was known as Colbertism. Colbert, the Finance Minister of Louis XIV, was the greatest of seventeenth century French Mercantilists. He imposed detailed controls upon manufactures. He aimed at national uniformity of finished products. "The state exercised over manufacturing industry the most limited and arbitrary jurisdiction... it decided who should be allowed to work, what things they should be permitted to make, what materials should be employed, what processes followed.... An artisan could neither choose the place in which to establish himself nor work at all seasons, nor work for all customers."

In Germany, too mercantilist ideas were adopted to develop industry. In Germany, mercantilism was known as *Cameralism*. The entire situation in Germany during the eighteenth century was similar to that of France under Louis XIV.

An Appraisal of Mercantilism

From the foregoing analysis, it is clear that the following points form the essential features of mercantilism: (*i*) The mercantilists laid too much of emphasis on the advantage of gold and silver as compared with that of other commodities. (*ii*) They overestimated the importance of commerce and underestimated the relative importance of agriculture. (*iii*) They went wrong in supposing that a favourable balance of trade necessitated a benefit in the long run. (*iv*) They went wrong in assuming that what was gain for one nation was loss for another.

We should make an estimate of mercantilism by taking into account the circumstances and the time in which the policy was advocated. "When considered with reference to the problems of the time in which mercantilism flourished, it is difficult, if not impossible, to find fault with the system." Mercantilism, in essence, was an economic policy and an economic doctrine bound up with the political doctrine of nationalism. In short, 'mercantilism is state making' on the economic side. Further, we must remember that the mercantilists were practical men and not a school of economists. Until recently the mercantilists have suffered from the cloud cast over them.

Adam Smith is mainly responsible for the belief that the economic ideas of the mercantilists were "little better than nonsense." He has created the impression that the mercantilists confused money and wealth. We must admit that Adam Smith was unfair in his criticism of mercantilists in this regard. It may be right to say that the mercantilists regarded money and bullion as the sign of wealth. Adam Smith's "*Wealth of Nations*" is a challenge to mercantilism. According to Adam Smith, the wealth of a nation can be increased by adopting the principle of "division of labour". And division of labour is limited by the size of the market. The size of the market will depend upon the volume of international trade. But the mercantilist policy of protection and their efforts at maximising exports and minimising imports resulted in the shrinkage of international trade. Hence, it was detrimental to the progress of a nation. So, he advocated free trade policy so as to increase international trade. Further, it is said the mercantilists failed to realize that international trade would be of mutual advantage to the trading nations. The criticism against mercantilists has been carried too far. It is true that some of the mercantilist ideas contained errors. But as Haney has admirably summed up, "they are far from a mass of absurdities when considered, as they must be, with regard to time, place and above all, to the spirit of the people. It is nonsense to believe that exports can exceed imports in all countries. But the mercantilists never claimed this belief. They did not generalise. They were laying down the principles of a national political economy, not a cosmopolitan one. War was the normal thing, and a large degree of self-sufficiency a practical necessity."

England, France, Germany and Spain became strong nations by following a policy of mercantilism. Even Adam Smith admitted that the famous Navigation Acts were of advantage to England and approved of them from the point of view of defence. Thus the essence of Mercantilism proper was the application of the independent domestic-economy idea of self-sufficiency to nations' (Haney).

Some of the modern theories of money, interest and employment are based on the mercantilist ideas. Dr. Smith has rightly said, "It is the mercantilists, and not Smith, who are the spiritual predecessors of modem economics." Mercantilism implied a general view of society which is often overlooked. They developed a sort of macro-economic approach to the problems of the society. The mercantilists emphasized the need for maximising exports not only with the idea of accumulating gold and silver, but with the hope that a prosperous export sector would provide more employment. Even the emphasis of the mercantilists on more money can be justified on economic grounds. They were aware of the dynamic functions of money. "Trade", they said, "depended on plenty of money; where money was scarce, trade was sluggish; where it was abundant, trade boomed" (Eric Roll). An increase in the supply of money in a country would result in lowering the rates of interest. And a low rate of interest would serve as an inducement to invest. And the level of investment determines the level of output and employment. In fact, Knut Wicksell developed his theory of interest with the mercantilist ideas as the basis. Keynes was a great admirer of some of the mercantilist ideas. The mercantilists were aware of the fact that money is not merely a medium of exchange but a store of value. Keynes noted that the mercantilists were concerned with the economic system as a whole and they were interested in securing optimum employment of the system's entire resources. The mercantilists were the early pioneers of economic thinking and their practical wisdom was better than the unrealistic abstraction of Ricardo. Keynes has approved of two mercantilist ideas—more money for business expansion and more money for lowering the rate of interest. Thus Keynes praised the mercantilist contribution to statecraft.

The mercantilists, of course, were wrong in overemphasizing trade and under-estimating the importance of agriculture and other sectors in their strategy of development. In fact, physiocracy with its emphasis on agriculture may be described as a revolt against the mercantilist doctrines. Their theory of international trade with emphasis on a favourable balance of trade was faulty and not always beneficial to the economic development of a nation. But we have to note that mercantilism paved the way for many western nations for their transformation from 'commercial capitalism' to 'industrial capitalism.' According to Prof. Heckscher, mercantilism is to be regarded essentially as 'a phase in the history of economic policy' which contains a number of economic measures designed to secure political unification and national power. The mercantilist ideas are powerful even today. In the words of Eric Roll, "Down to the present day they all reappear from time to time in various guises as symptoms and weapons of economic conflict."

Decline of Mercantilism

Mercantilism declined in England and other parts of the world towards the end of the eighteenth century. The following were the main reasons for the decline of mercantilism:

1. Under the influence of the teachings of Adam Smith, the 'policy of plenty' began to replace the 'policy of power.'

2. The development of banking, both domestic and international, reduced the importance of bullion (gold and silver) and coins.

3. The expansion of market economy showed that real estates, factories and machinery were more important items of wealth than gold and silver.

4. The economic growth that took place during the Industrial Revolution made it possible for the society to rely on competitive forces and laissez faire rather than promoting and regulating monopolies.

5. The great progress made in science and technology taught people that a country could become richer not only by impoverishing its neighbours but also by mastering the forces of Nature in a more efficient way. It was also found that the wealth of all nations could be increased simultaneously.

6. During the period of mercantilism, economic life was highly regulated. There were many regulations protecting the quality of goods. But these regulations which were once necessary ultimately became a barrier to progress. So the regulations were withdrawn. But we should remember that the doctrines of mercantilism have not completely disappeared from the current scene. There are ideas and policies extant today that resemble the ideas of the mercantilists. A brief study of neo-mercantilism will explain this point.

Neo-Mercantilism

Towards the end of the eighteenth century, under the influence of the teachings of Adam Smith, mercantilism declined in England and other parts of the world. "*The policy of plenty*" began to replace the "*policy of power.*" Laissez-faire principles with their emphasis on individualism, unfettered competition and free trade ruled for more than a century and industrial revolution took place in Great Britain under a policy of laissez-faire. But towards the close of the 19th century, laissez-faire views declined slowly. And at the beginning of the twentieth century, the view prevailed that the government must assist and encourage industry and commerce. The new policy of State encouragement and assistance to industry is known as *neo-mercantilism*.

It must be noted that the policy of neo-mercantilism was not a movement for return to mercantilism. While mercantilism emphasized on the development of trade under state control, the neo-mercantilist policy envisaged a state activity of another kind—assistance, support, defence, rather than regulation and control.

After the First World War, America, France, Germany and England have followed typical mercantilist policies. They have placed emphasis on accumulation of gold. They have imposed high tariffs, fixed import quotas and formulated many exchange restrictions. The above policies were based on political considerations. Further, they aimed at salvaging the economy out of economic difficulties. The spirit of nationalism has become strong. During the twenties and thirties, conditions similar to those which existed during the period of mercantilism prevailed. For instance, there were great wars, rapid industrial and financial changes, currency and price instability, international competition for gold, and a tendency to concentrate power in the State.

We should, however, note that the neo-mercantilism of the post-war period differed in several respects from the older mercantilism. According to Haney, neo-mercantilism "depended more upon effective 'social planning' of economic life, either through complete centralization under a dictatorship or through mass action under a 'democratic' form of 'regimentation'. And it was backed by much greater and more precise statistical information."

Meaning of Mercantilism for Underdeveloped Countries

The mercantilists have dealt with many factors of economic growth such as consumption, investment, the role of Government, money and capital, foreign trade and population. Some of the economic ideas of the mercantilists have relevance to the underdeveloped countries of today.

The countries in which mercantilism flourished resemble present-day underdeveloped countries in some respects, and differ from them in others. For instance, England and Western Europe were better equipped with resources per head than are many present-day underdeveloped countries, especially the crowded ones like India. Population was growing much more slowly and the man-land ratio was more favourable. There was not much of international lending. But there was a great deal of unemployment and under-employment as we have today. International transfer relations are much better in many underdeveloped countries today than in the past.

The mercantilists, according to Heckscher had, "A belief in official intervention as a corrective to evils." Even today in underdeveloped countries, the State is assigned a key role in the process of economic growth. Economic development of England, France and Germany was made possible by the activities of millions of private entrepreneurs under the policy of non-intervention (laissez-faire) by those governments. But in the shortage of private entrepreneurial skill, the State has to play a dominant role in the developing countries. Not only that, it has to regulate production and distribution with the object of promoting growth with justice.

The mercantilists considered the non-agricultural sectors—foreign trade and manufacturing sectors—as strategic in the economic growth of a nation. They thought that a favourable development of foreign trade and manufacturing by State regulation and assistance, would give rise to a favourable development in agricultural and other less strategic sectors. But most of the underdeveloped countries like India are predominantly agricultural. In India, for instance, most of our traditional exports such as tea, jute, cotton and sugar depend either directly or indirectly on agriculture. So priority has to be given for schemes of agricultural development. For, if agriculture fails, our Plans will fail. Of course, agriculture alone cannot support the increasing population and generate the surpluses necessary for investment.

With regard to population, we must follow the teachings of Malthus rather than the mercantilists. There is a definite need for population control in our country. The mercantilists have assigned a most important role to money in economic development at all times. It is true that money is essential for economic development. But whenever certain bottlenecks developed in an economy, more money would mean only increase in prices. Further, the mercantilists failed to explain the conditions under which further increases in money would push up prices rather than increase employment. Thus while the mercantilists recognised the role of money in economic development, they exaggerated this role and underestimated the role of "real" factors. More money, especially, paper money may sometimes generate inflationary pressures. India is a case in point.

Capital deficiency is one of the main problems of underdeveloped countries. External assistance is uncertain and cannot be relied upon for ever. So self-help is the best help. We can promote capital formation in a country by promotion of exports. Even today gold plays an important role in international monetary transactions. Only by promotion of exports, underdeveloped countries can earn enough gold and foreign exchange. That there is shortage of foreign exchange in most of the underdeveloped countries, no one can deny. There is every need for seeking a favourable balance of trade by maximizing exports and minimizing imports. This part of mercantilist policy has relevance to most of the underdeveloped countries. The Governments of underdeveloped countries provide financial and non-financial assistance to the export sector, and imports of non-essential commodities should be restricted so as to conserve foreign exchange. Even the developed nations may be persuaded to have liberal trade terms towards their imports from underdeveloped countries. But unfortunately, some of the rich countries of today follow mercantilist policies in some form or other in their trade relations with poor countries. It is one of the causes for the chronic deficit in the balance of payments position of most of the poor countries.

THE PHYSIOCRATS

Introduction

The physiocrats were a group of writers who developed a body of economic theory in France in the eighteenth century. Their publications covered a period from 1756 to 1778. Though the physiocrats wrote only for a relatively short period, their ideas had a profound influence on the economic thought. That is why they are regarded as the founders of the science of political economy. In fact, Adam Smith was greatly influenced by the economic ideas of physiocrats. Francois Quesnay (1694-1774) and Turgot (1727-1781) might be considered as the chief representatives of the physiocrats. The term 'physiocracy' means *Rule of Nature.*'

The Factors which gave Rise to Physiocracy

France in 1750s provided a favourable climate of opinion for the emergence of physiocratic doctrines. There were many economic, political and social factors at work.

Firstly, physiocracy was essentially a revolt of the French against mercantilism. Under Colbert, the famous Finance Minister of France, mercantilism was carried to an extreme degree resulting in the neglect of agriculture and a lot of governmental regulation of industry. Agriculture was badly organised at that time. There was need for an economic theory to prove that the pursuit of mercantilist policies was detrimental to the progress and wealth of a nation. And the physiocrats provided the theoretical basis to attack mercantilism. The chief aim of the physiocrats was to reorganise the French economy by means of tax reform and by promoting a system of efficient, large-scale farming.

Secondly, the tax system of France at that time was corrupt, inefficient and unjust. The nobles and the clergy, who owned nearly about two-thirds of land, were exempted from direct taxation. On the other hand, the burden of taxation on the poor was heavy. The poor were affected by taxes such as the salt tax, the poll tax and by duties on goods passing from one province to another.

Thirdly, the finances of the French government were in a bad shape. The unnecessary wars and the luxurious life at court made the government bankrupt and the government started borrowing loans under unfavourable conditions.

Fourthly, the French peasants were exploited by the nobles and other wealthy classes by a number of methods. The landowners took a large share of the produce. The Government put heavy taxes. Even the markets for agricultural commodities were restricted because mercantilist policies were in favour of manufactured goods.

Fifthly, in general, economic performance and prospects in France appeared unfavourable as compared with that of Britain. Britain had already realized that it was a wrong policy to develop trade and manufacture at the expense of agriculture. Agricultural revolution was taking place in England with emphasis on large-scale farming and scientific techniques of production. So in France too, attention was diverted to the strengthening of agriculture.

41

Lastly, there were other forces at work for progress and change. The political and moral philosophers of those times underlined the importance of the *individual* in their discussions. They emphasized that *man* must be the centre of philosophy and politics. And the forces of *liberty* were at work.

Main Ideas of Physiocrats

We may discuss now some of the main ideas of the physiocrats.

Natural Order: The physiocrats developed the concept of 'natural order.' In fact, physiocracy has been described as *"the science of the natural order."*

According to the physiocrats, the natural order is an ideal order given by God. And it is different from the positive order made by man. In other words, the society which is governed by the laws of Nature is an ideal society and the society which is ruled by positive laws made by government is an imperfect society. Some of the physiocrats believed that the natural order existed at some time in the remote past. They identified it with the golden age of the ancients. The moral and religious philosophy of physiocrats is reflected in their concept of 'natural order'. They all believed in God and considered the natural order the work of God. According to Quesnay, "natural order is merely the physical constitution which God himself has given the universe." Only the natural order will increase the happiness of mankind "Divine in its origin, it was universal in its scope." In short, the natural order was the best and the most advantageous order for the physiocrats.

Property, security and liberty formed the very basis of their social order. It may be interesting to note here that the physiocrats were not interested in the concept of *equality*. The physiocrats believed in the interdependence of all classes and of their final dependence upon Nature.

The concept of natural order led to certain important practical results. The natural order implied that only under conditions of freedom, man can enjoy the maximum happiness and derive maximum advantage in economic matters. It followed that there should be minimum interference in economic affairs by Government. Government should have minimum functions. It must confine itself to such things as protecting life and property. In other words, they advocated *laissez-faire*.

The physiocrats believed that the individual interests were identical with the interests of the society and every man could be trusted to find out for himself the best way of attaining maximum advantage. Thus, physiocracy was based on a note of optimism.

Laissez-faire

The physiocrats were opposed to almost all forms of government restrictions. They advocated *"laissez-faire."* It means, "let things alone, let them take their own course." In effect, it means freedom of business enterprise at home and free trade abroad. According to this doctrine, the only function of government is to protect life, liberty and property. So there will not be much work for government. We must note, however, that laissez-faire does not mean that nothing will be done. There will be a lot of scope for individual effort. The only thing is the functions of the government will be reduced to the minimum.

Net Product

Land occupied a predominant position as an agent of production in the physiocratic system. They considered agriculture alone as the productive occupation. This was one of the characteristic features of the physiocratic system.

The physiocrats thought that industry, trade and professions were useful but *sterile*. They simply reproduced the value consumed in the form of raw materials and subsistence for workers. Only agriculture was productive for it produced a surplus, a *net product* above the costs of production. The physiocrats called this net product, *"The produit net."* In agriculture alone, the wealth produced was greater than wealth consumed. "Labour applied anywhere except to land is sterile, for man is not a creator." (Le Trosne).

We must remember that though the physiocrats described industry as sterile, they never said it was useless. Industry was unproductive in the sense that it produced no extra wealth. The idea of the physiocrats that land alone was productive was based on religion. They believed that the fruits of earth were given by God while the products of the arts were wrought by man who is powerless to create. In agriculture, Nature cooperated with man and helped in the creation of a surplus, the net product.

It follows from the above discussion that only labour engaged in agricultural operations is productive and labour engaged in all other occupations (trade, industry, professions) is unproductive.

The Circulation of Wealth

One of the major achievements of modern economics is the concept and the measurement of national income. The physiocrats anticipated national income analysis, though in a crude form. The economic ideas of the physiocrats regarding the flow of income through society is found in Quesnay's "*Tableau Economique*" (The Economic Table). The '*Tableau Economique*' is a graphic representation of the way in which the circulation of wealth takes place.

Quesnay has divided the society into three classes. In other words, the physiocratic system is based on the division of society into the following three classes:

1. *The Productive Class:* It consists of the farmers, who pay a rent to the landlords, who till the soil and pay the expenses of cultivation.

2. *The Proprietary Class (the class of proprietors):* The class of proprietors included the landlords and the King.

3. *The Sterile Class:* The class was composed of all those engaged in non-agricultural occupations. Merchants, artisans, domestic servants, members of liberal professions formed part of this class. It must be remembered that the physiocrats did not consider the sterile class as useless. It was sterile (unproductive) in the sense that it did not produce any 'net product.'

Of the above three classes, farmers alone are the productive class because soil is the only source of wealth. In the words of Quesnay, "May the sovereign and the nation never forget that the earth is the only source of riches, and that it is increased by agriculture."

After classifying the society into the above three classes, Quesnay traced the circulation of income among the three classes of the society in the following manner:

All wealth is produced by the productive class (the farmers). Let us suppose the value of the total produced in any year is equal to five million francs. Of this, the agricultural class (farmers) require two million francs for their maintenance. These two million francs do not circulate. The remaining produce worth three million francs is distributed in the following manner. Since the productive class requires manufactures, it buys them from the sterile class for one million francs. The remaining two million francs pass into the hands of landowners and the government in the form of rent and taxes. The proprietary class lives on these two million. It spends one million for food and the other for manufactures. According to the physiocrats, the sterile class produces nothing. But still it receives two million francs (one million from the productive class and another from the proprietary class). The sterile class uses the two million francs for buying the necessaries of life and the raw materials of industries from the productive class. Thus the two million which come into the hands of the sterile class return to their starting point, the agriculturists. Thus the original five million francs are replaced in the hands of the productive class. The cycle is complete. And the process goes on indefinitely.

At the time when it was published, the '*Tableau Economique*' was regarded as one of the greatest productions of the human mind. For instance, Mirabeau, one of the physiocrats, classified it among the three great inventions of mankind. The first is the invention of writing, the second the invention of money, the third the *Tableau Economique*. The circulation of wealth, represented by Quesnay, has been compared with the revolution which has been caused in biology by the discovery of the circulation of the blood. Cannan is of the view that, "in the fact that it attempts to give a comprehensive view of the total results of the industry of a year, it marks an enormous advance in economic theory." Quesnay's Economic Table is regarded as a pioneering attempt at 'National Income Analysis' and "mathematical economics." Quesnay was interested in statistical data and actually tried to estimate the values of annual output and other aggregates. Even in our own time, Leontief, who has developed the famous input-output analysis, has adopted the same principle of Quesnay's economic table. It may be interesting to note here that Karl Marx was the only first-rank economist of the 19th century who recognised the merit of Quesnay as an economist. In fact, in a general way, Quesnay's 'Net product' is similar to that of Marx's 'Surplus value.' Schumpeter has made this point clearly in the following words: "Exactly as Quesnay let land alone be productive of surplus value, so Marx let labour alone be productive of surplus value."[1]

If we want to understand the *Tableau Economique*, we must first of all keep in mind the fact that it represents the state of France in the eighteenth century and that Quesnay has before his eyes the *grande culture* based on cultivation by rich farmers paying a rent to the landlord. Quesnay's economic theory has an 'agrarian bias.' The Economic Table is based on the mistaken notion that agriculture alone is the productive occupation.

Value

The physiocrats did not treat the problem of value in a systematic way. Of course, in a vague manner, they were aware of the difference between value-in-use and value-in-exchange, the influence of cost of production and scarcity on value. For instance, Qnesnay, the founder of the physiocratic school, developed a cost-of-production theory so far as manufactured goods were concerned. He said that when manufactured goods were exchanged, only equivalents were exchanged. No profit (or surplus value) could arise.

Property

The physiocrats were great believers in the institution of private property. We may even say that they worshipped it as a divine institution. According to Quesnay, "The safety of private property is the real basis of the economic order of society." The physiocrats regarded property as "a tree of which social institutions are branches growing out of the trunk." But we must also note that the physiocrats imposed certain duties and responsibilities on the proprietary class. For instance, they must continue without fail to bring lands under cultivation. They must dispose of the wealth in such a way that it promoted the general interest of the society. They must not exploit the workers. They should protect the interests of the tenants and the agriculturists. And, above all, *the proprietary class must bear the whole burden of taxation*.

The Influence of Physiocrats on Applied Economics

The physiocrats exercised a lot of influence on applied economics. We shall study now their influence on trade, the functions of the state and the problems of taxation.

1. *Trade:* The physiocrats thought that all exchange was unproductive. For, according to them, exchange implied a transfer of equal values. The mercantilists thought that foreign trade provided the only possible means of increasing a country's wealth. But the physiocrats thought that foreign trade, like domestic trade, produced no real wealth. They argued that the only result was a possible gain, and one man's gain is another man's loss. But a country must get from other countries the goods which it cannot itself produce. Some of the physiocrats considered foreign trade a necessary evil. In arguing on the above lines, the physiocrats attacked Mercantilism which aimed at a favourable balance of trade. *But they favoured free trade*. Gide and Rist have a reasonable doubt: "But if they thought all trade was useless it is not easy to understand their enthusiasm for Free Trade." However, we can explain their enthusiasm for free trade in the following manner. At the time, the physiocrats were writing, domestic trade and industry in

---

[1.] Schumpeter: *History of Economic Analysis* p. 238 (1954 Edition).

France were subject to strict regulations under Colbertism, that is mercantilism of the French style. So they advocated freedom in domestic trade. They advocated free trade for international trade too. Further their advocacy of free trade was in consistence with their basic policy of *laissez-faire*. The 'natural order' implied that each would be free to buy or sell wherever he chose, within or without the country. The physiocrats believed that free competition with foreign merchants alone could secure the best possible price, and only the highest price would enable them to increase their stock of wealth and to maintain their population by agriculture. So the physiocrats must be regarded as the founders of the *Free Trade*.

2. ***The Functions of the State:*** In the 'natural order' of the physiocrats, the functions of the State would be reduced to the minimum. There would be very little legislation. The physiocrats believed that the most useful work any legislative body could do was to abolish useless laws. Their advice was "Remove all useless, unjust, contradictory, and absurd laws, and there will not be much Legislative machinery left after that" (Baudeau).

We have to remember that the physiocrats were no anarchists: "... it would be a great mistake to think of the physiocrats as anarchists. What they wanted to see was the minimum of legislation with a maximum of authority."[1] One of the duties of the State was to preserve the 'natural order' and to protect private property, the foundation of that order. Further, it must provide universal education and it can also undertake public works.

3. ***Taxation:*** The physiocratic theory of taxation is bound up with the theory of the net product. They believed that only the output of land provided a surplus. So they argued that taxes should be paid from the net product, for it was surplus. And they concluded that landed proprietors must bear the burden of taxation. In other words, they advocated a single tax system.

A third of the 'net product' was to be paid in taxes. "To the objection, that it was unjust to place the burden of taxation upon the shoulders of a single class of the nation, instead of distributing it equally among all classes, the physiocrats replied, that the statesman's ideal was not equal taxation, but the complete abolition of all taxation" (Gide and Rist). But we know now that a single tax on agriculture cannot meet all the needs of the State. But it may be interesting to note that most of the arguments in favour of direct taxation are to be found in the writings of physiocrats. Their theory of taxation is regarded as an excellent demonstration of the superiority of direct taxation over indirect taxation.

Main Representatives of Physiocratic School

Francois Quesnay (1694-1774) and Turgot (1727-1781) might be regarded as the chief representatives of the physiocrats.

Quesnay (1694-1774)

Quesnay was the founder and leader of the physiocratic school. He was the court physician of Louis XV. It may be interesting to note that he took interest in economics at the age of sixty-two. His main writings were: (*i*) An article on *"Farmers"* ("Fermiere", 1756), (*ii*) an article on *"Grains"* (1757), (*iii*) The *"Tableau Economique"* (1753-1758). Quesnay's ideas regarding the circulation of wealth are found in his *"Tableau Economique"*. Quesnay was in favour of strengthening and developing agriculture to increase the wealth of France. He attributed the ills of Kingdom to the poverty of the peasants. "Poor peasants, poor Kingdom, poor kingdom, poor king." He advocated freedom of trade and industry. The basic ideas of the physiocrats such as natural order, net product, circulation of wealth, a single tax system are all essentially the ideas of Quesnay.

Turgot (1727-1781)

It is customary to place Turgot among the main physiocrats. But we have to note that "he was never a

---

1. Gide and Rist: *A History of Economioc Doctrines* (p. 52).

thorough going physiocrat, and his ideas regarding value are much more scientific" (Gide and Rist). He realized the subjective character of value. Schumpeter describes him as a 'non-physiocrat with physiocrat sympathies.' The main ideas of Turgot are found in his "Reflexions" (1769). Turgot was a great success as an *intendant* (General Administrator) (1761-74). He was appointed Minister of the Navy in 1774 and a few months later he became Finance Minister to Louis XVI.

Turgot was an advocate of *laissez-faire*. He believed that an individual knows his own interest best. He believed in the productivity of agriculture. But he recognized the services of the non-productive class too. And he did not regard (landed) property as a divine institution. As Haney puts it, "He had a better understanding of the relation of saving to capital formation, he defended freedom to lend and borrow at interest, and he was opposed to the system of political autocracy which Quesnay favoured."

Condillac

Condillac's name must be mentioned here because his views on some of the economic problems were far more advanced than those of other physiocrats.

Condillac was the only physiocrat who regarded value as the foundation of the science of economics. He emphasized that value was based upon utility. "Value is not an attribute of matter, but represents our sense of its usefulness, and this utility is relative to our need. It grows or diminishes according to our need expands or contracts." Thus Condillac has laid the foundation of the psychological theory of value. He was also aware of the fact that value increases with scarcity and diminishes with plenty. Here we have the germ of the theories of the Marginal school.

Condillac has defined production in a non-physiocratic fashion. "Production means giving new form to matter." He also said that there was no difference between agricultural and industrial production, for they both transformed what already existed.

On the question of wages, too, the views of Condillac were far more advanced than the other physiocrats. The other physiocrats believed in the *Iron Law of Wages*. For instance, Turgot said that "the worker's wage is only equal to what is necessary for his subsistence." But according to Condillac, "Wages represent the share of the product which is due to the workers as co-partners." He did not refer to an Iron Law of Wages. On the other hand, he believed that wages were determined by the forces of supply and demand. And like Turgot, he justified the taking of interest.

Critical Estimate of Physiocrats

Physiocracy, in essence, was the revolt of the French against Mercantilism. It is from this angle, we have to judge the economic ideas of the physiocrats. While the Mercantilists were preoccupied with gold, the physiocrats laid emphasis upon 'real wealth' in the form of raw produce. The mercantilists aimed at maximizing exports and minimizing imports with the object of securing a favourable balance of trade. But the physiocrats, in general, regarded foreign trade as a necessary evil and attacked the favourable balance-of-trade idea of the mercantilists. While mercantilists believed in regulation of trade and industry, the physiocrats advocated freedom of trade and industry.

The physiocrats were wrong in considering agriculture alone as the productive occupation. Commerce and industry are equally important and equally productive as agriculture. There was a fundamental error in their economics. That is, they did not have a correct notion of production. Today, by 'production' we mean creation of utilities. But the physiocrats did not understand this simple truth. They had a materialistic conception of productivity. The physiocrats regarded manufacture as unproductive although it creates form utility, which is one form of production. The physiocrats are mainly responsible for the erroneous classification of labour into productive and unproductive labour basing on the fact whether the labour has resulted in the production of material or immaterial goods.

The greatest defect in the physiocratic doctrine is almost the total absence of any reference to value. As Gide and Rist put it, "They seldom mention value, and what little they do say, is often confused and commonplace. Herein lies the source of their mistakes concerning the unproductive character of exchange and industry......"

The physiocrats advocated complete freedom of trade and industry. But absolute freedom of trade and industry are not advisable. If we follow the *laissez-faire* doctrine, there will be little scope for social action.

The aim of the physiocrats was to develop agriculture. They regarded land as the only source of wealth. For land alone yielded a surplus (net product). It followed the landed proprietors alone should bear the burden of taxation. In effect, their conclusions went against the interests of the agricultural class. Further, their non-intervention policy helped industry more than agriculture. It must be noted that it was not their intention at all.

The weakest point in the physiocratic system is its theory of distribution. According to the physiocrats, rent is a free gift of nature. But Ricardo has pointed out that rent arises not because Nature is bountiful but because it is niggardly.

But we have to remember that the physiocrats have made important contributions to economic thought.

Firstly, they put economics on a scientific basis by applying scientific methods. They are rightly regarded as the founders of the political economy.

Secondly, economic development was a major concern of the physiocrats. They realized the importance of agriculture in securing a surplus for capital formation. So the physiocrats emphasized the need for transforming traditional agriculture into the large-scale agriculture based upon technologically advanced methods.

Thirdly, the physiocrats were the first school of economists who analysed capital and realized the importance of capital formation in economic development.

Fourthly, the physiocrats made important contributions to the theory of taxation. Often, much fun is made of their advocacy of single tax on agriculture. But we must remember that the physiocrats emphasized the need for agricultural surplus, as one of the main requisites of economic development.

Fifthly, the physiocrats have realized the inter-dependence of different classes in the economy. Quesnay's '*Tableau Economique*' where he describes the circulation of wealth among different classes has been a model for the modern input-output analysis of Leontief and general equilibrium analysis of Walras.

Sixthly, the physiocrats insisted that the government should confine itself to the minimum functions of maintaining life, liberty and property. The modern governments pretend to do so many things for their people. But the modern man will be happy if his government can succeed in protecting the basic rights of life, liberty and property.

Seventhly, in advocating *laissez-faire*, the physiocrats were opposing all obstacles to capitalistic economic development.

Eighthly, they advocated direct taxes rather than the indirect taxes which affected the poorer sections of the French society of their time badly.

Ninthly, they argued for capital formation through reduced consumption by the wealthy.

Lastly, the physiocrats must be given a high place among those who prepared the ground for the French Revolution.

Meaning of Physiocracy for Underdeveloped Countries

The salient features of physiocracy were: (*i*) their emphasis on agriculture to secure surplus for economic development; (*ii*) freedom of trade and industry both within the country and outside, (*iii*) agriculture alone should bear the burden of taxation, and (*iv*) minimum role for government. We shall see how far the ideas of the physiocrats are applicable to the underdeveloped nations where the main concern is economic development.

Most of the underdeveloped countries are predominantely agricultural societies. India is a case in point. In India, in the past agriculture accounted for nearly two-fifths of our national income. The success of our Five-Year Plans depends mainly upon the performance of our agriculture. The physiocrats emphasized that agriculture should provide the surplus for capital formation. Even in our country, there is need for transforming our traditional agriculture into modern agriculture by employing advanced technological methods. The agricultural sector in our country accounts for a sizable portion of our national consumption, saving and investment. Naturally, it affects our national output. Even today, there is terrible concentration of landed property in our country. So the wealthy sections of the agricultural sector should help promote capital formation by reducing their consumption of luxury goods. Agriculture often provided the surplus that helped in saving and investment, which in turn, helped the industrial development of France, United States, Germany and Japan. So there is lot of meaning in the physiocrats considering agriculture as the strategic sector in the economic development of a nation. They thought that the development of agriculture would help in the development of non-agricultural sectors too. They were right in considering agricultural surplus as a dynamic, growth-generating factor. But, with all that, we cannot depend entirely upon agriculture. Industrial development must take place side by side for we find that most of the developed nations of the world are highly industrialized and they enjoy high standards of living.

The physiocrats maintained that the agricultural sector should bear the burden of taxation (for capital formation) because they felt generation of surplus was possible only in the agricultural sector. Even today there is a well-informed opinion in our country that there is a lot of scope for mobilising more financial resources for our schemes of economic development from the agricultural sector. There has been a substantial development in the agricultural sector. But the tax proceeds from this sector have been more or less inelastic. Of course, direct taxation of agriculture alone would not meet the entire needs of the State. The underdeveloped countries should depend both on direct as well as indirect taxes for mobilization of resources.

The physiocrats believed in competition and opposed monopoly in all its forms. They hoped that under competitive condition there would be the best set of prices including suitable prices for agricultural products. In underdeveloped countries, the growth of monopolies is acting as a check on economic development.

The physiocrats did not attach much importance to external economic relations when a country was large and essentially self-contained. Our country is large but not self-sufficient even in such a bare necessity as food.

While the population policy of the mercantilists was in favour of increasing numbers, the physiocrats recommended the increase of agricultural output and net product, and not the increase of numbers.

The physiocrats were champions of *Free Trade*. But if the developing nations of the world are to adopt a policy of Free Trade, it would be very difficult for products from the newly set up industries of these countries to compete with the goods from the developed nations of the world. So they must grant protection to infant industries to a certain extent against dumping and by granting subsidies to industries in export Sector. Even the developed countries of the world today impose high tariffs to protect their domestic industries. So the present conditions in the world are not ideal for following a policy of free trade as advocated by the physiocrats.

Lastly, the physiocrats have assigned only minimum functions to the State. And they advocated *laissez-faire*. But the State has an important role to play in the economic development of the underdeveloped countries. The *laissez-faire* policy is not suitable both for developed as well as underdeveloped countries for different reasons. The main concern of the poor countries is to improve the standard of living of their people. That is possible only through schemes or plans of economic development. The government should be the main agent of economic development. Growth with social justice is our aim now. And this is possible only with social action and governmental intervention.

7

ADAM SMITH
(1723-1790)

The Classical School

Adam Smith is the founder of the classical school. He has been described as the "Father of Political Economy." His work "Wealth of Nations" (1776) is generally regarded as the starting point of classical school. According to Keynes, 'The classical economists' was a name invented by Marx to cover Ricardo and James Mill and their predecessors. But Keynes included in the classical school, "the followers of Ricardo, that is to say, who adopted and perfected the theory of the Ricardian economics." These economists include (for example) J. S. Mill, Marshall and Edgeworth. Thus Adam Smith, Jeremy Bentham, Thomas Robert Malthus, David Ricardo, J. B. Say and J. S. Mill are the leading economists of the classical school. Of them, Smith, Ricardo and J. S. Mill formed the classical trinity. The classical system rested on four main pillars—the Malthusian Population doctrine, the Wages-Fund Theory, the Ricardian Theory of Rent and the Labour Theory of Value.

The Essential Features of Classical School

The entire philosophy of the classical school was based on economic liberalism. The classical writers believed in personal liberty, private property and individual initiative and private enterprise. Classical ideas were liberal in contrast to mercantilist restrictions of trade and industry. We shall summarize now some of the basic features of the classical school.

1. The classical economists believed in *laissez-faire.* It implied a minimum role for government in economic matters. That government is best which governs least.

2. They believed in a market economy based on free and perfect competition. Production, exchange and distribution would be guided by market forces.

3. They assumed conditions of *full employment.* (It is this assumption that came in for a lot of criticism in the hands of J. M. Keynes). They thought that the economy was self-adjusting and would tend towards full employment without government intervention.

4. They believed that the individual by seeking his own interests would serve the best interests of society. In other words, they believed in the existence of a harmony of interests. (Ricardo, however, did not believe in the so-called harmony of interests).

5. The classical economists emphasized the importance of all economic activities, especially industry. The mercantilists believed that wealth was derived from commerce. The physiocrats had seen in agriculture the source of all wealth. The classical economists added industry to commerce and agriculture and regarded all of them as productive.

6. The classical school provided a method of analysing the economy and the economic laws that operate within it. They treated political economy as an abstract science in which fundamental principles of universal application might be laid down. In other words, they believed that economic laws were of universal application.

7. The classical economists were the first set of economists who paid a good deal of attention to the problems of economic growth and development.

8. The classical economists looked at the economy as a whole. This is what we call the macro-economic approach in modern times.

9. Lastly, the classical economists believed in J. B. Say's Law of Markets which said that *supply creates its own demand*. On that basis, they felt that general over-production and hence unemployment impossible. Malthus was an exception. He believed in the possibility of over-production under certain circumstances.

ADAM SMITH (1723-1790)

Introduction

Adam Smith was born in Kircaldy, Scotland in 1723. He was educated at the universities of Glasgow and Oxford. He became Professor first of Logic and then of Moral Philosophy at Glasgow. After teaching for more than a decade, he became a private tutor to the Duke of Buccleuch. He travelled for two years on the continent. While in France he came into contact with some of the leading Physiocrats of the day, including Quesnay and Turgot. The Physiocrats exercised a profound influence on Adam Smith. Adam Smith praised the physiocratic system "with all its imperfections" as "perhaps the nearest approximation to the truth that has yet been published upon the subject of political Economy." In 1778, Adam Smith was appointed as commissioner of customs in Edinburgh. He held that post for the remaining years of his life. He died in 1790.

Adam Smith published his *Theory of Moral Sentiments* in 1759. After that, he concentrated his attention less on ethical doctrines and more on jurisprudence and political economy. Adam Smith published his "*Wealth of Nations*" in 1776. (The full title of the book is *An Inquiry into the Nature and Causes of the Wealth of Nations*). Adam Smith's 'Wealth of Nations' was a challenge to mercantilism. Adam Smith was the first economist to deal with economic problems in a systematic manner. In other words, he was the first academic economist. He has been rightly called the "Father of the Political Economy". Alexander Gray has put it well when he said, "before Adam Smith there has been much economic discussions. With him we reach the stage of discussing economics."

We have already noted that Adam Smith's "Wealth of Nations" was a challenge to mercantilism. According to Adam Smith, the wealth of a nation can be increased by adopting the principle of 'division of labour.' And division of labour is limited by the size of the market. The size of market will depend upon the volume of international trade. But the mercantilist policy of protection and their efforts at maximizing exports and minimizing imports resulted in the shrinkage of international trade. Hence it was detrimental to the progress of the nation. So he advocated free trade policy so as to increase international trade.

According to Adam Smith, "Political Economy is an inquiry into the nature and causes of wealth of nations." In his book "*Wealth of Nations*", Adam Smith, first of all, emphasizes the importance of labour as the source of the wealth of a nation. Then he tells the wealth of a nation can be increased by the division of labour. Division of labour necessitates exchange. This leads on to the discussion of money as a means of exchange, and to value. After discussing the problem of value and price in his book, Adam Smith discusses the problem of wages, profits and rent. Then he criticizes mercantilism and physiocracy. The last section of his book deals with problems of public finance.

1. *Division of Labour.* According to Adam Smith, "Labour is the source of wealth of a nation." While the physiocrats regarded land alone as the productive factor and agriculture as the source of all wealth, Adam Smith gave importance to labour as the true source of wealth. The opening words in his book are, "The annual labour of every nation is the fund which originally supplies it with all the necessaries and conveniences of life."

After saying that labour is the source of wealth Adam Smith makes the point that division of labour will increase the productivity of labour and thereby the wealth of a nation Division of labour refers to the specialization of labour in different industries or different processes within the same industry. Adam Smith has illustrated the point in his famous example of the pin making industry. "One man draws out the wire; another straightens it; a third cuts it; a fourth points it; a fifth grinds it at the top for receiving the head; to make the head requires two or three distinct functions; to put it on is a peculiar business; ..... and the important business of making a pin is in this manner divided into about eighteen distinct operations. If one man performed all the above operations, that is, if there was no division of labour, he would produce just one pin or so in a day. He could not make more than twenty. But on the other hand, if division of labour was practised, the average production of each man was 4,800 pins.

According to Adam Smith, "*Division of labour is limited mainly by the size of the market.*" That is, only if there is a wide demand for a good, it will be produced on a large scale and there will be a lot of scope for the application of division of labour. In those industries which produce goods for international market, there will be great scope for division of labour. The scope for the application of division of labour also depends upon the nature of the good. For example, the scope for division of labour is not as great in agriculture as in the case of manufacturing industry.

Division of labour has the following advantages:

(i) *Increased output:* Division of labour will increase the output per worker. Adam Smith has given an excellent example for this in his "Wealth of Nations." He said that in his day, the pin-making industry involved as many as eighteen distinct operations. As a result, each workman produced as many as 4,800 pins. If he worked alone, that is, without division of labour, he would produce just one pin or so in a day. Certainly, he could not make more than twenty.

(ii) *Increase in the dexterity (skill) of workers:* By doing the same kind of work constantly, the worker gets a great skill in his particular line. Practice makes a man perfect.

(iii) *Saving in time:* A man can work continuously on a single operation. He need not spend time in changing tools or in passing from one process to another.

(iv) *Introduction of machinery:* It prepares the way for introduction of machinery. It will result in the invention of a great number of machines which facilitates labour. In other words, division of labour is the mother of invention.

Smith was not unaware of some of the disadvantages of division of labour. For instance, extreme division of labour would result in monotony of work. A worker by doing the same type of work again and again would find no pleasure in his work. He would be bored with his job. Not only that, if a worker confined himself to a few very simple operations all through his life, it would make him "as stupid and ignorant as it is possible for a human creature to become." Division of labour might also cause immobility of labour. And there was greater risk of unemployment in times of bad trade. In spite of the above disadvantages, Adam Smith argued that division of labour would increase the wealth of a nation.

2. *Value:* According to Smith, there are two kinds of value: (i) value in-use, and (ii) value-in-exchange. The first one expresses the utility of some particular object and the second one refers to the power of purchasing other goods. For example, nothing is more useful than water but it has little value-in-exchange. On the other hand, diamond has little value-in-use but it has great value-in-exchange.

The determination of value (value-in-exchange) has been one of the central problems in economics Adam Smith believed that labour was the real source of value. According to him, the value of a thing depended on the amount of labour expended upon its production. He said that it was "natural" that an article the making of which required two day's labour should have double the value of another that was the result of only one day's labour. In other words, the value of a thing depended upon the "toil and trouble of acquiring it." Adam Smith emphasized that, "*labour is the real measure of the exchange value of all commodities.*" This is the famous Labour Theory of Value. Thus "the theory that labour or effort is the cause of value (if value can be said to have cause) was first formulated by the father of political economy himself. It is curious to think that it was the same theory that was used with such good effect by Karl Marx in his attack upon capitalism." (Gide and Rist). We must also note that Smith made the distinction between natural price and market price. "When the price just covers the ordinary rate of rent, wages and profits expended in preparing and marketing the commodity, it sells at its 'natural price'." The market price may be below or above this, depending upon the supply actually on the market and the 'effectual demand'—the demand of those who were willing to pay the natural price. When the market price exceeds the natural price, there will be an increase in the supply of the product and price will be brought down to its natural level. Thus the natural price becomes "the central price, to which the prices of all commodities are continually gravitating."

Some Criticisms of the Labour Theory of Value

1. There is the difficulty of measuring labour or cost of production. Adam Smith used time as his measuring rod. But all workmen are not of equal efficiency and the less skilled may take longer than the skilled over a particular piece of work, and so put more labour into it.

2. Misdirected labour cannot have value. An article incapable of fulfilling the purpose for which it was intended can have no value, however much labour has gone into its manufacture. Even Karl Marx admits that "nothing can have value, without being an object of utility." He said, "misdirected labour does not count as labour."

3. It fails to explain the value of rare things, such as works of art or antiques. It is a great weakness of any theory of value if it does not explain the value of all things.

4. It ignores the influence of demand.

Wages

Adam Smith has not developed a clear-cut theory of wages. He noted that in modern times, wages were the result of a contract between worker and master and the contract was always to the advantage of the latter. Adam Smith's sympathies were always with labour.

According to Smith, "Masters could not reduce wages below a subsistence rate." Although, he suggested subsistence as the natural level of wages, he observed that the market level might be higher than the subsistence level whenever the society was progressing and the funds for employment were expanding more rapidly than population. Thus Adam Smith has taken into account both demand for labour and supply of labour in the determination of wages. We find in it the traces of the Wages-Fund Theory and the Malthusian theory of population. For instance, he tells that the demand for labour can increase only in proportion to the increase of "the funds which are destined for the payment of wages."

Adam Smith has also analysed the problem of wage differences. Smith has developed the *principle of equal advantage* to explain wage differences. According to this principle, under conditions of perfect mobility, the whole of advantages and disadvantages of different employment of labour will tend to equality. He has given the following factors for differences in money wages: (*i*) Agreeableness of the employment; (*ii*) The cost of learning the skill; (*iii*) The constancy of employment; (*iv*) The trust reposed in the workman; and (*v*) The probability of success.

Rent

Adam Smith has given a number of explanations for rent. At one place, he describes it as a "monopoly price." At another time, when he discusses commodity prices, he includes the rent of land as an element of cost and therefore a determinant of the product price. Further, in some other context, he tells that rent is determined by price. He considers that a high or low rent is the effect of a high or low product price.

Adam Smith was not disposed favourably to landlords as a class. He said that the landlords "loved to reap where they have not sown." But Adam Smith believed that the interests of the society coincided with the interests of the landlords. Rents did arise only when the society was progressing. The prosperity of the landlords symbolized the general good of the society.

Profit and Interest

Adam Smith was of the opinion that wages and profits moved in the opposite direction. "The increase of stock, which raises wages, tends to lower profit." As more and more capital becomes accumulated, the mutual competition among owners of capital for investment in the same trade will tend to lower its profits. However, Adam Smith made certain exception to the statement that wages and profits moved in the opposite directions. For instance, in new colonies both wages and profits may be high and in the "Stationary State" both wages and profits may be low.

According to Adam Smith, interest is the "compensation which the borrower pays to the lender, for the profits which he has an opportunity of making by the use of the money." He believed that interest would vary with profit.

Adam Smith has made use of his principle of equal net advantage to explain differences in profits and interest. We should remember that he made use of the same principle to explain differences in wages.

Capital

Adam Smith has realized the importance of the role of capital in the economic development of a nation. He was aware of the fact that capital accumulation is essential for the industrial development of a nation. In his own words, "*Capital limits industry.*"

In Adam Smith's "Wealth of Nations", capital appears in three forms: (*i*) as an instrument of production, (*ii*) as a fund maintaining the workmen, and (*iii*) as a source of revenue. Further, Adam Smith has classified capital into *three* portions.

  (*i*) The first portion is used for immediate consumption. It affords no revenue or profit (*e.g.*, stock of food, clothes, etc.).

 (*ii*) The second portion is the fixed capital which affords a revenue or profit without circulating or changing masters (*e.g.*, machines, buildings, improvements of land, as clearing, draining, enclosing, etc.).

(*iii*) The third portion is the circulating capital, which affords a revenue only by circulating or changing masters (*e.g.*, money, materials, completed works in the hands of the merchant or manufacturer which are not yet disposed of).

Adam Smith believed that the wealth of a nation could be increased by a proper division of labour. And division of labour was limited by the size of capital stock. He had also emphasized the role of saving in capital accumulation: "parsimony, and not industry, is the immediate cause of the increase of capital." Adam Smith was of the view that the portion of the income that was saved was "immediately employed as a capital." In other words, an act of saving at once becomes an act of investment. Saving is equal to investment. Smith did not pay much attention to the problem of hoarding. This became a leading doctrine for a period of more than 150 years. We should also add that Smith was in favour of labour-intensive investment during the development process. Smith believed that investment in agriculture was the most productive form of capital investment because in agriculture "nature labours along with man."

The Role of Money

The classical economists, in general, de-emphasized the importance of money. It was Adam Smith who had established this tradition. In fact, he attacked mercantilists mainly because they over-emphasized the role of money in an economy. According to Adam Smith, a nation's true wealth consists "not only in its gold and silver only, but in its lands, houses, and consumable goods of all different kinds." Money only serves as an instrument for the circulation of wealth and for the measurement of value.

Money does not add to the revenue of the society. But it is the 'great wheel of circulation.' It facilitates the circulation of goods and it is the production of the goods that makes up the revenue. Although the gold and silver coins that circulate in an economy form a valuable part of the capital of the country, they are dead stock and produce nothing.

Smith believed that paper money was preferable to gold and silver. For paper money required much less effort to produce. He likened gold and silver money to a highway that enabled goods to be brought to market without being itself productive. He thought that banking would save the labour of producing gold by providing paper money, just as a highway through the air would save land that might be used for other things. As long as paper money were convertible into gold, a small reserve of gold was enough. But we have to note that the mercantilists argued that consumable commodities are soon destroyed, whereas gold and silver are more durable. Not only that, gold being a universally acceptable medium of exchange, it can be spent in any direction.

Laissez-faire and the Harmony of Interests

Smith believed in the natural organisation of the economic order under the influence of personal interest. He was a great advocate of *laissez-faire*—non-intervention by government in business. According to him, governments are wasteful, corrupt and incompetent. So he advocated a minimum role for government. He said, "I have never known much good by those who affected to trade for public good." He believed that individuals, if left to themselves, would serve society even though it was not their intention. The individual was led by 'an invisible hand' to do good for the society. Man is "led by an invisible hand to promote an end which was no part of his intention." In other words, he believed that the interests of individuals coincided with the interests of the society. Smith applied the free-enterprise idea to both domestic and international affairs. He illustrated the idea of the harmony of interests with the following example: "It is not from the benevolence of the butcher, the brewer, or the baker, that we expect our dinner, but from their regard to their own interest."

Smith conceived the economic world as a great natural community created by division of labour. He also believed in the spontaneous origin of economic institutions and in their beneficent character. The above ideas have been referred to as '*naturalism and optimism* of Smith' by Gide and Rist.

Smith advocated free trade. He believed free foreign trade would promote greater division of labour. While the mercantilists believed that each nation enriched itself at the expense of its neighbour, Smith believed in an international harmony of interests: "The wealth of a neighbouring nation, however, though dangerous in wars and politics, is certainly advantageous in trade.... As a rich man is likely to be better customer to the industrious people in his neighbourhood, than a poor, so is likewise a rich nation." (*Wealth of Nations*: Book IV, Ch. 3).

Smith was always suspicious of businessmen who were ready to sacrifice the interests of the others to promote their own: "People of the same trade seldom meet together, even for merriment and diversion, but the conversation ends in conspiracy against the public or in some contrivance to raise prices." (Book I, Chapter 10). Smith believed that the actions of businessmen would promote general welfare only under conditions of competition. He always attacked government intervention on behalf of the narrow special interests of businessmen.

Role of Government

Smith advocated a minimum role for the state in economic affairs. He considered non-intervention by government in economic matters as a wise policy. In his view, governments are "always" and without any exception, the greatest spendthrifts in the society.

Adam Smith said that the State could perform only the following three major functions: (*i*) To protect society from foreign attack, (*ii*) To establish the administration of justice within the country, and (*iii*) To erect and maintain the public works and institutions that private entrepreneurs cannot undertake privately.

We shall, however, note that non-intervention for Adam Smith was a general principle and not an absolute rule. He justified legal control over interest rates, state administration of Post office, control over the issue of paper money by bankers, compulsory elementary education and so on. Further, though he was a champion of free trade, he favoured two kinds of protectionist tariff: (*i*) Those tariffs that protect a domestic industry essential to the defence of the country. ("Defence.... is of much more importance than opulence"), and (*ii*) Those that equalize the tax burden on a particular domestic industry by imposing a tariff on imports of that good. Smith also suggested that if free trade is to be introduced in a country after a long period of protectionism, it should be done gradually in order to avoid unemployment.

Canons of Taxation

Adam Smith recommended taxation to finance government activities. He has laid down some rules for a good tax system. Even today they are valid. They are known as the *canons of taxation*. They are the canons of equity, certainty, convenience and economy.

1. *Canon of Equity:* It is based on the principles of justice and ability to pay. It tells that people should pay taxes according to their respective abilities (Progressive taxation is based on this principle).

2. *Canon of Certainty:* There must be certainty about the tax which an individual has to pay. Things like the time of payment, the manner of payment and the quantity to be paid should be plain and clear to the tax-payers. A tax should not be arbitrary.

3. *Canon of Convenience:* A tax should be levied in such a manner or at such a time that it is convenient for the tax-payer to pay it. For example, the Indian farmer may be asked to pay the land revenue after the harvest is over.

4. *Canon of Economy:* Taxes should be collected at minimum cost to the government.

Even today the above canons of taxation are regarded as good working principles for planning a sound tax structure.

The Influence of Physiocrats on Adam Smith

There are a number of passages in "The Wealth of Nations" which indicate the influence of the Physiocrats on Adam Smith. But we should remember that though Adam Smith was profoundly influenced by the Physiocrats, he differed from them on certain important issues.

The naturalism, optimism and liberalism of Smith was derived largely from the Physiocrats. In Smith's idea of *laissez-faire* derived from self-interest and reaction against government interference, one can see the influence of physiocrats. Smith was so much influenced by the physiocrats that Dupont, an historian of economic thought, remarked that everything that is sound in "The Wealth of Nations" is derived from the Physiocrats whereas everything added by Smith is faulty. This, however, is not a correct estimate of Smith.

Smith never shared the views of the Physiocrats regarding the exclusive productivity of agriculture, and the single tax. The Physiocrats had only a partial view of production. To them, agriculture was the only source of wealth. But Adam Smith has tried to give a view of production as a whole. He believed that the services of all sections were essential for the production of wealth. He argued that the increase in national wealth could not be measured in terms of a single net product. A practical conclusion that followed from the above argument was that taxation should not fall upon one class as the physiocrats wished, but upon all classes: "The subjects of every state ought to contribute towards the support of the government as nearly as possible in proportion to their respective abilities, that is, in proportion to the revenue which they respectively enjoy under the protection of the State." This is the famous canon of equity.

However, the physiocratic influence on Smith can be seen in his classification of labour into productive and unproductive labour. He put all those who were engaged in the production of immaterial goods in the category of unproductive labour. For example, kings, soldiers, churchmen, lawyers, doctors, men of letters, actors, musicians and dancers all belonged to the category of unproductive labourers. Manufacturers and merchants, for instance, belonged to the category of productive workers. In other words, Smith had given a materialistic interpretation of wealth. According to Smith, "Material goods can be accumulated and are therefore a means of increasing wealth." But services are of the moment only. They vanish in the acts of production and consumption. From this point, Smith regarded them as unproductive, although in many cases they were useful. Further it is the physiocratic influence that made Smith talk about the special productivity of soil. The Physiocrats were champions of free trade. So was Smith.

Critical Estimate of Adam Smith's Contribution to Economic Thought and Policy

Adam Smith has been rightly described as the "Father of Political Economy." "The Wealth of Nations" has become the cornerstone of economic science. J. B. Say has rightly remarked, "when we read this work, we feel that previous to Smith there was no such thing as political economy." Adam Smith has influenced men of practical affairs. Pitt the younger, when he became minister, introduced many tax reforms and abolished certain trade barriers on the basis of the guidelines suggested in Smith's "Wealth of Nations."

Though Smith borrowed certain ideas from the physiocrats, "Smith was superior to Quesnay and perhaps to every writer since the time of Aristotle, in the extent and accuracy of his knowledge." However, Schumpeter said that "The Wealth of Nations" does not contain a single analytic idea, principle, or method that was entirely new in 1776." But in adopting the discoveries of others, he has made them his own. But Schumpeter, at some other place, has described, "The Wealth of Nations" as "the most successful not only of all books on economics but, with the possible exception of Darwin's *Origin of Species,* of all scientific books that have appeared to his day."

Adam Smith developed "the price system" or value economics.

Some of the main criticisms made against Adam Smith are as follows:

1. His approach is essentially materialistic. He does not regard wealth as a means to the higher ends of life.
2. There is undue emphasis on individualism. Further, his "individual" is an unreal one—too much of an "economic man" dominated by the "self-love" and "self-interest."
3. Smith's theory of distribution is sketchy and incomplete.

Notwithstanding the above criticism, we should note that Smith gave Political Economy a definition and made it a distinct science. And "he brought labour and capital into prominence, along with the land factor emphasized by the physiocrats."

Before Smith, the emphasis was always on the production of wealth. The producer was the starting point. But Smith shifted the emphasis from the producer to the consumer. "Consumption is the sole end purpose of all production, and the interest of the producer ought to be attended to, only so far as it may be necessary for promoting that of the consumer." Even today, the welfare of consumers is regarded as the test of economic policies.

Adam Smith was the first development economist who realized the importance of capital accumulation in economic development. Adam Smith's labour theory of value was the foundation for Marx's theory of surplus value, which the latter used as a weapon to attack capitalism. It has been rightly said that "the roots of ultimate contradiction made manifest to the world in the third volume of *Das Capital* lie imbedded in the first volume of the *Wealth of Nations* (Douglas)." We may conclude with the words of Gray that "It is again a tribute to the greatness of Smith that all schools of thought may trace to him their origin or inspiration."

JEREMY BENTHAM
(1748-1832)

Jeremy Bentham was not primarily an economist. But he has influenced the development of economic thought considerably. He was the son of an English lawyer. He studied Law but he never practised it. According to Haney, "Bentham's chief contributions to Economics lie in what he added to the philosophical, ethical, and psychological basis for the science. He was essentially a social philosopher, and was more interested in government and law than in economics."

Bentham was the leader of the utilitarian school. He was the author of the concept of utilitarianism. Just as Ricardo's name is associated with the theory of rent, Bentham's name is associated with the principle of utility. Bentham was the central figure of a group usually described as *Philosophical Radicals*.

Bentham's important publications, so far as political economy is concerned, was "Defence of Usury" (1787). It appeared a decade after Adam Smith's "Wealth of Nations" and preceded Ricardo. His other work "An Introduction to the principles of Morals and Legislation" (1789) has a wide influence on thought and legislative practice in England and on the continent.

Hedonistic Psychology

Bentham's thought is based on hedonistic psychology. Hedonism is the doctrine that pleasure is the chief good. Bentham thought that individual actions are motivated by a desire for pleasure and dislike of pain. Not only that, individual actions are governed by a calculated balancing of pleasures and pains. We have to note Bentham's hedonism is rational hedonism.

All men desire happiness. And happiness may be defined as the surplus of pleasure over pain. Pleasure and pain are therefore the main springs of human action. In Bentham's words, "Nature has placed man under the governance of two sovereign masters, pain and pleasure. It is for them alone to point out what we ought to do, as well as to determine what we shall do.... we owe to them all our ideas, we refer to them all our judgments, and all the determinations of our life."

Bentham believed that pleasures and pains are measurable. Of course, he was aware of the difficulties and limitations in the measurement of pleasure and pain. He said that pleasure or pain depended on a number of factors including its duration, intensity, certainty (or uncertainty) and nearness. He spoke of different degrees of pleasure. In Bentham's classification of pleasure, one can trace some of the phases or degrees of utility mentioned by Jevons and other members of the marginal utility school. *Bentham assumed that the feelings of different individuals are comparable, and pleasure can be measured through a "common measure" or denominator in the shape of money.*

Bentham also discussed the relationship between wealth and happiness. In his "Principles of The Civil Code", he argued that the happiness of an individual is not in proportion to his wealth. From this, we may say that Bentham seemed to have some vague notions about the diminishing marginal utility of money.

Bentham and his Principle of Utility

Based on hedonistic psychology, Bentham has formulated the utilitarian system of ethics and government: "The idea that men are governed by pleasures and pains, becomes the idea that they are governed by the 'principle of utility' and that the state should act or refuse to act accordingly" (Haney).

According to Bentham, "The aim of every individual is to maximize his pleasure and pleasure is 'good' for an individual." Bentham's utilitarianism is essentially hedonistic utilitarianism. Anything that promotes the greatest happiness of the individual is *good* for him. Bentham uses the words "benefit, advantage, pleasure, good or happiness" more or less with the same meaning. The test of greatest happiness decides what every individual ought to do, determining the difference between right and wrong.

"The Principle of Utility" is also known as *the principle of greatest happiness*. It considers as the highest good the greatest happiness of the greatest number.

From the principle of utility, Bentham derives a social ethics and a principle of government. First, the principle of utility shall govern actions of individuals. Secondly, the society also must be governed by the same principle because society is nothing but an aggregation of individuals. The community is a factious body. We can understand the common interest only by understanding the interest of the individual. The interest of the society is merely "the sum of the interests of the several members who compose it." The common interest can be formed by applying the apparatus of pleasure pain calculus. The only way to find out the common interest is to add individual A's pleasure-minus-pain to individual B's pleasure-minus-pain and so on. And that is the only way to measure the greatest good of the greatest number.

On the basis of the above reasoning, Bentham reaches two conclusions which are of great importance in the development of economic thought. The first one is that "natural rights" do not exist. The other is the doctrine of *laissez-faire*.

Bentham believes natural rights do not exist because rights depend upon laws and laws are made by government. And governments have come into existence by force and they are perpetuated by habit.

The above line of thought provides the basis for Bentham's individualism, and his advocacy of *laisser-faire* and free competition. His general rule for increasing the wealth or enjoyment of the nation is that "nothing ought to be done or attempted by government." His rule of government is, "Be quiet."

Bentham argued that there was no need for government action in economic matters for the following *two* reasons:

(i) (a) The wealth of society is nothing but the wealth of individuals who compose it; (b) each individual knows his interest better than anybody else. At another point, Bentham made the observation that "there is no true interest but individual interest."

(ii) Government action is not merely inexpedient, it is injurious. Government action involves restraint upon individuals. And where there is restraint, there is pain. Whenever the government gives subsidies and other financial assistance to some industries, they involve taxes and "taxes are the product of coercive laws applied to the most coercive purposes."

Bentham advocated unlimited freedom for competition. Though competition would cause distress to some individual competitors, it would be more than offset by the benefits of others and thus promote the greatest happiness of greatest numbers. In this connection, we should note that Bentham criticized Adam Smith's concession that government should fix maximum rates of interest.

Though Bentham gave "Be quiet" as his rule of government, he allowed certain activities of government. Though he considered legislation as a "necessary evil", he said that there must be some legislation in order to establish a system of punishments and rewards that would induce individuals to pursue actions leading to the greatest happiness of the greatest number. On the agenda of the government, he allowed the State to grant patents to inventors. He recommended escheats (a kind of tax) on estates which lack near relatives, taxes on bankers and stock brokers. Above all, he said that the proper aim of legislation should be to promote the greatest happiness of the greatest number. Thus he made place for 'general interest'. This of course, reveals an incosistency in his thought. For at one point he says that there is no true interest but individual interest. Now he talks in terms of 'general interest.'

Bentham and Adam Smith

First of all, Bentham accepted the economics of Adam Smith in general, rejecting the latter's proposal to regulate the interest rates. But still we must note that Benthamism was different from Smithianism.

Adam Smith believed in the harmony of interests. But Bentham did not believe in that. Adam Smith believed that in economic matters the individuals, following their own interest were led by an invisible hand to do good for the society at large. Bentham broke away from this optimistic 'nature philosophy.' He tried to make utilitarianism a rational principle which would serve to guide the law maker.

Secondly, Bentham's economic ideas are based on purely hedonistic philosophy.

Thirdly, Bentham mixes ethics and moral philosophy with economics, and turns the latter into sociology.

Criticism

Firstly, there is difficulty in calculating the greatest happiness of the greatest numbers. As men are not equal, and the same pleasure may be felt by different men unequally, it would be difficult to calculate the greatest happiness of the greatest number with any assurance of success.

Secondly, Bentham equated happiness with pleasure and reduced happiness largely to terms of quantities of pleasure. 'A sum of pleasures' may be an attractive phrase. But when it comes to estimates of human happiness or misery, arithmetic in economics is not much more helpful than economics in arithmetic. For there is no proof that by pursuing the happiness of the greatest number, we shall produce the greatest happiness.

Thirdly, Bentham thought the greater the equality in "masses" of wealth possessed by individuals, the greater the chances of equality in happiness. This line of thought has serious implications. It prepares the way for the sort of mechanical quantitative treatment of social problems. Not only that, it may put some ideas into the head of a ruler. For example, the ruler may think that he can maximize human happiness by exercising control over distribution of wealth. This may lead to regimentation of life. Of course, that was not the intention of Bentham because he advocated *laissez-faire* policy for the State.

Fourthly, the 'principle of utility' is a subjective concept. It will make economics an inexact science. Not only that, as it is an ethical concept, economics will become normative science. But the modern tendency is to make economics a positive science.

Summing up

In spite of all the criticism, the formula of the greatest happiness of the greatest number still remains valuable in economics and politics. It supplies a 'slogan' in the popular mind and supplies a standard with which one can judge state action.

Bentham was a social reformer. He believed that education of an individual would improve his calculation of pleasure and pain. He also suggested certain legal reforms. He was a great law reformer. He suggested laws to inflict pain on individuals who acted so as to cause more pain to others, than pleasure to themselves. But this line of thought may lead to more of social action or "socialism." In a way, such ideas were leading him away from *laissez-faire*.

Bentham's ideas had a profound influence on a group of liberal thinkers known as 'philosophical radicals'. J. S. Mill was one them.

Bentham finds an important place in the history of economic thought for the following reasons:

First, he dealt a severe blow to the natural philosophy of the physiocrats and Adam Smith.

Second, he developed rational utilitarianism as the basis for greater freedom in economic life.

Third, he was a great influence on J. S. Mill who was a champion of liberty and individualism.

Lastly, Bentham suggested the ideas of degrees of utility and their measurement to Jevons. So in a way he may be regarded as the forerunner of marginal utility school.

THOMAS ROBERT MALTHUS
(1766-1834)

Introduction

Thomas Robert Malthus was born in 1766. His father Daniel Malthus, a country gentleman, was a friend of most of the philosophers of his time. Malthus was the youngest son of the family. He received excellent education and for some time he worked as a curate. In 1807, he was appointed professor of History and Political Economy at a college founded by the East India Company in England. He remained there until his death in 1834. Keynes calls Malthus the first of the Cambridge economists. Malthus married when he was thirty-nine years of age and had three sons and a daughter. He was a good friend of David Ricardo. They enjoyed warm friendship in spite of the fact that they disagreed almost on all aspects of political economy except the Malthusian analysis of population problem. Malthus is famous for his theory of population. But another significant contribution of Malthus to economic analysis is *his theory of Market gluts* where he discusses the problems relating to *inadequacy of aggregate demand.*

Ricardo and Malthus are known as *pessimists* in the history of economic thought. Though Malthus was a classical economist, he differed from the other members of the classical school, on some of the important economic principles.

The main works of Malthus are: (*i*) *An Essay on the Principle of Population* (1798), and (*ii*) *Principles of Political Economy* (1820).

The Social Background of Malthusian Theory of Population

Malthus published his "Essay on Population" in 1798. By then, people noticed some of the evil effects of the Industrial Revolution. Unemployment, poverty and disease became serious problems and called for immediate attention. Taxes were put on the property owners to provide poor relief and the property owners considered those taxes burdensome. The landlords were attacked by other social classes on the ground that the "landlords loved to reap where they had not sown." In other words, landlords were described as an exploiting class. And the merchants and the manufacturers started challenging the political power enjoyed by landlords.

However, the immediate cause of the pessimism of Malthus was his father's optimism. Under the influence of Godwin, his father believed in the perfectibility of man and society. Young Malthus wanted to attack the optimistic philosophies of Godwin and Condorcet. Malthus was thirty-two, at the time he published his "*Essay on Population*." He was a bachelor at that time.

William Godwin (1758-1836) was a political philosopher. He believed in the philosophy of anarchism. He published 'An Enquiry concerning Political Justice and its influence on general Virtue and Happiness', in 1793. Godwin believed in individualism and opposed all coercive action by the state. He relied on the goodwill and sense of justice of individuals. He argued that men were ultimately guided by the rule of reason. Godwin believed in the perfectibility of human race. Since the character of men depends upon social environment, a perfect society will produce perfect people. According to

Godwin, "The main obstacles to progress are: (*i*) the institution of private property, (*ii*) economic and political inequalities, and (*iii*) the coercive state." Godwin's view of population was based on an optimistic note. He was hopeful that when the limit of population was reached, men would refuse to propagate themselves to the point of over-population. It was this optimism about the future of mankind that was attacked by Malthus.

The Marquis de Condorcet (1743-94) was a French intellectual and a social reformer. Though he came of an aristocratic family, he was a democrat in politics and a physiocrat in economics. He was a pacifist and an optimist. According to Condorcet, "Social progress depends on three fundamental principles: (*i*) equality among nations, (*ii*) equality of individuals within a nation, and (*iii*) the perfectibility of mankind."

Condorcet believed that the natural order tended towards economic equality, but the existing laws and institutions encouraged inequalities. Equality would remove all the social evils of the day and lead to man's perfection. On the question of population, Condorcet thought that as a result of beneficent reforms, population would increase but food supply would increase more rapidly. In case, food supply did not keep pace with the increase in population, Condorcet suggested birth control to limit the growth of population.

Malthus rebelled against the ideas of Godwin and Condorcet. He attributed poverty and misery not to evil human institutions but to the fecundity of human race. War acted as a check on population growth. Abolition of war would remove one of the remedies of over-population. Godwin's egalitarian, communistic society would mean more food for masses and would only increase population.

The Malthusian Theory of Population

The Malthusian theory of population is one of the well-known theories about the growth of population. Malthus published his "Essay on Population" in 1798. What he has said in that has come to be known as the Malthusian Law of population. *The Malthusian theory discusses the relationship between population and food supply*. It is based on the law of diminishing returns. In plain language, all that the theory tells is that population increases at a faster rate than food supply.

Malthusian theory of population is based on the following two fundamental assumptions: (*i*) Food is necessary for human existence; (*ii*) Passion between the sexes is natural and will remain nearly in its present state.

On the basis of the above two assumptions, Malthus states that "the power of population is indefinitely greater than the power in the earth to produce substance for men." According to Malthus, "Population increases in a *geometric ratio* (*i.e.*, at the rate of 2, 4 or 8, 16, etc.) while food supply increases only in an arithmetic ratio (*i.e.*, at the rate of 2, 4, 6, 8, 10 etc.)." Malthus believed that the population of a country, when unchecked, would double itself in every twenty-five years. But food supply will not increase as fast as population on account of the influence of the law of diminishing returns on land. So to begin with, though there will be enough food supply, after some years, there will not be enough food for all. For population outgrows food supply. So the growth of population has to be checked. This can be done by the application of some checks by Nature or by man himself or by both.

Malthus published the second edition of the *Essay* in 1803. It may be interesting to note that Malthus did not mention a tendency to diminishing returns in agriculture until the second edition of the *Essay*. His main point was that the pressure of population on food supply was ever present. In fact, in one of his letters to Nassau Senior, Malthus said, "except in new colonies, favourably circumstanced, population was always pressing against food, and was always ready to start off at a faster rate than that at which the food was actually increasing." It implies that a steady rise of living standards can never be associated in "old" countries with a growing population. This argument holds good to India; which is over-populated and poor.

Malthus has spoken of two kinds of checks to population growth: (*i*) *Preventive checks*, and (*ii*) *Positive checks*.

(*i*) *Preventive checks:* Preventive checks are in the form of moral restraint, postponement of marriage and so on. The preventive checks cause the birth rate to fall. Malthus suggested that those who could not afford children should either postpone marriage or never marry. It may be interesting to note that Malthus disapproved of vice as a preventive check. This included prostitution and birth control, both of which reduced the birth rate.

(*ii*) *Positive checks:* The positive checks are imposed by war, famine and disease. They increase the death-rate. If population is not checked by the above two methods, then, there would not be enough food supply for all. There would be famine, starvation and death. People would face starvation and live in misery. This, in short, is the Malthusian theory of population. Thus Malthus presents a dark and pessimistic picture about the future of mankind. Thomas Carlyle, a great social scientist, after reading Malthus called political economy the "dismal science."

We should further note that in the second edition of his *Essay*, Malthus added a new check to his argument, and that was moral restraint. By moral restraint, Malthus meant simply postponement of marriage. It may be interesting to note that Malthus condemned contraception under all circumstances as "improper arts to conceal the consequences of irregular gratification." It implied that Malthus did not approve of the birth-control methods preached by neo-Malthusians. But in India, birth-control techniques adopted in the family planning programmes are absolutely essential for checking the growth of population.

The crux of the population problem in under-developed countries today is this: They have on the one hand the high birth rates typical of agrarian economies, and on the other, the low death rates characteristic of industrialized economies. Economic development will cure this difficult situation in course of time. Until then, unless there is voluntary limitation of families, the Malthusian checks of famine and disease may operate. Mark Blaug is of the opinion that India "is over-populated because the death rate was lowered by the introduction of Western medicine, thus divorcing population growth from the current level of income. It follows that India would be better off if she could also 'Westernize' her birth rate."

The Malthusian theory was popular for nearly a century. It formed the basis of action for many governments. It influenced the thinking of many statesmen. Of course, the theory is not so popular today as it was a century ago.

According to Malthus, "The poor are responsible for their poverty and misery." Poverty and misery are the natural punishments for the poorer classes because they have failed to restrict their numbers. It follows from the above view that the government should not provide relief to the poor by means of "Poor Laws," etc. If aid is given for the poor, then more children would survive and aggravate the problem of hunger and misery. So Malthus suggested the gradual abolition of Poor Laws. The ideas of Malthus were incorporated in the Poor Law Amendment of 1834. The new poor law abolished all relief for able-bodied people outside workhouses.

Ricardo agreed broadly with the views of Malthus on population. But he was not so dogmatic as Malthus. He endorsed the view that "under favourable circumstances, population may be doubled in twenty-five years; but under the same favourable circumstances, the whole capital of a country might possibly be doubled in a shorter period." In that case, wages during the whole period would have a tendency to rise, because the demand for labour would increase still faster than the supply.

Criticism of Malthusian Theory of Population

The following are the main points of criticism against the Malthusian theory of population:

1. Population does not grow as Malthus has suggested. His ratios have been proved wrong by history. Malthus believed that once in every twenty-five years, population would double itself. There is no historical proof for this. In some countries (*e.g.*, France) some decades back population actually declined.

2. It is true that in many countries population has increased at a rapid rate. But food supply has also increased and people have not died of hunger in those countries. In fact, the standard of living today is much higher than it was a century ago.

3. The Malthusian theory is based on the Law of Diminishing Returns. Malthus has overlooked the possibility of scientific improvement in agriculture. For example, Agrarian Revolution took place in England along with the Industrial Revolution. That brought about a big increase in food supply and other agricultural products.

4. This is an age of international trade and commerce. If a country does not grow enough foodgrains for itself, it can import foodgrains from other countries. For example, India has been faced with the problem of food shortage since a long time. But we have been importing large quantities of foodgrains from countries like America and Canada.

5. Malthus has over-emphasized the relationship between population and food supply. "The problem of population as a whole is, then, not one of mere size, but of efficient production and equitable distribution. That is, it is a problem not of numbers alone but of wealth" (Seligman).

6. Lastly, Malthus thought that any addition to population is undesirable. But "every mouth brings with it a pair of hands." Since man is the source of labour, large numbers, sometimes, may mean greater wealth, strength and power.

Though the Malthusian theory of population does not apply to most of the Western nations which are highly industrialized, it applies to most of the underdeveloped countries like India and China which are dominated by agriculture. Malthusian theory has some force even today. In the poor countries of the world, over-population is a real danger. Not only that, if we look at the population problem in a broad way, that is, if we take the total population of the world and total food supply, it can be seen that after some years there will be shortage of food if the growth of population is not checked by some means or other. That is why many countries of the world today have adopted birth control measures and other family planning programmes. Further, we should not take the ratios of Malthus literally. We must remember that Malthus has used them as a convenient way of making his point of view. Like all other laws of economics, the Malthusian theory must be taken as a statement of tendency. As Briggs and Jordan put it, "Malthus is to be judged as a prophet rather than as a historian and as an economist rather than as a statistician."

The Optimum Theory of Population

The modern theory of population is known as the optimum theory of population. Malthus considered the problem merely as a question of numbers and food supply. But as Seligman put it, "the problem of population as a whole is, then, not one of size but of efficient production and equitable distribution. That is, it is a problem not of numbers alone but of wealth. Since man is the chief labour force, large numbers indeed, other things being equal, mean greater national strength and power."

The optimum theory does not look at the population problem as a question of numbers. It looks at it from the angle of production and efficiency. According to the optimum theory, every country will have an optimum or ideal population at which its output will be maximum. The optimum population is *"that population, which combined with the other available resources or means of production, will yield the maximum returns."* When a country has reached the optimum population, per capita output (output per head) will be the highest. According to Dalton, "Optimum population is that which gives the maximum income per head."

We should remember that the optimum population for any country is not a fixed one. For a country may have different optimum levels at different times.

Neo-Malthusianism

The Neo-Malthusian movement was started by Francis Place, an eccentric tailor who was connected with the beginnings of English trade union movement. The movement was started in 1820s. The propaganda of Francis Place was directly associated with the teachings of Malthus.

The Neo-Malthusians regarded themselves as the disciples of Malthus. They believe that Malthus has clearly demonstrated the need for checking the growth of population. But they do not approve of some of the checks suggested by Malthus to reduce the birth rate. Moral restraint is a case in point. They argue that enforced celibacy advocated by Malthus might involve more suffering even than want of food. And late marriages would only make people immoral by encouraging prostitution and by increasing the number of illegitimate births. The neo-Malthusians argue that there is nothing wrong in adopting birth-control measures. "There is reason to believe, however, that were Malthus now alive, he would not be a neo-Malthusian" (Gide and Rist).

The Malthusian Theory of Gluts

The Malthusian theory of gluts is one of the less known but more important contributions of Malthus to economic theory. Ever since 1930s, 'aggregate demand' has become a central problem in economics and Malthus is regarded as the forerunner of modern thought. In fact, Keynes found in Malthus, an early presentation of the theory of effective demand, of the need for unproductive consumption, and of government investment.

In his analysis of effective demand, Malthus differed from Ricardo and other classical writers. While Ricardo was interested in the theory of distribution of the product in the conditions of equilibrium, Malthus was interested in the volume of output day by day in the real world. And Malthus was of the opinion that the level of output at any time depended upon effective demand. He described effective demand as demand which is high enough to ensure a continual supply or a continuous process of production. In other words, production depended on the existence of effective demand, that is, demand which enabled the producer to cover cost plus profit.

Malthus argued in favour of unproductive consumption in order to maintain and increase effective demand. "It is absolutely necessary that a country with great powers of production should possess a body of unproductive consumers." Since the wages of workers are so low they cannot demand many goods. The capitalists, if they want they can consume the excess of products. But the capitalists are more interested in saving and accumulation of capital. Their actual habits and mode of living do not give them enough opportunities for unproductive spending on a sufficient scale.

While Adam Smith and Ricardo were in favour of saving and capital accumulation, without limit, Malthus argued against it because rapid accumulation of capital would result in the reduction of unproductive consumption and this in turn would check the progress of wealth. It must, however, be noted that Malthus was not against saving as such. But he suggested that a proper balance must be maintained between saving and consumption.

In the class of unproductive consumers, Malthus included landlords, menial servants, statesman, soldiers, judges and lawyers, physicians and surgeons and clergymen.

Malthus used the concept of effective demand to show that the economic system was not self-adjusting. Unless a large body of unproductive consumers was maintained, there would be periodic over-production, glut in the market and stagnation. Thus for the first time, in the history of English economic thought, Malthus has pointed out the possibility of crises in the form of trade cycles because of the inherent defects of the capitalist system. Many modern writers regard Malthus as the forerunner of many under-consumption theories. Thus Malthus had some insights into one of most important problems, of the modern economy: the maintenance of the level of aggregate demand.

Keynes, in his Essay on Malthus, has quoted one of the letters of Malthus to Ricardo to show how Malthus was concerned with the causes that determined the different levels of output at different times in a country: "....Besides I really think that the progress of society consists of irregular movements, and that to omit the consideration of causes which for eight or ten years will give a great stimulus to production and population, or a great check to them, is to omit the causes of the wealth and poverty of nations—the grand object of all enquiries in political economy.... We see in all countries around us, and in our own particularly, periods of greater and less prosperity and sometimes of adversity, but never the uniform progress which you seem alone to contemplate." ("Essays in Biography" by J. M.

Keynes). Keynes has expressed a feeling that "the almost total obliteration of Malthus's line of approach and the complete domination of Ricardo's for a period of a hundred years has been a disaster to the progress of economics."

Other Economic Views of Malthus

Rent: The views of Malthus on rent are found in "An inquiry into the Nature and progress of Rent" (1815). To a great extent, Malthus anticipated the Ricardian theory of rent. The early writers like Adam Smith and J. B. Say regarded rent as a monopoloy return. For instance, Adam Smith described landlords as monopolists who loved to reap where they had not sown. But Malthus regarded rent as a surplus that arose because of the bounty of Nature. It may be noted that he differed from Ricardo in this respect because the latter argued that rent arose not because of Nature's bounty but because of its niggardliness.

According to Malthus, rent arose because of the following factors:

1. There was shortage of fertile land.
2. This necessitated the cultivation of lands of inferior fertility.
3. The produce in each case is sold at "the natural or necessary price." The price of produce in each progressive country would be just equal to the cost of production on land of the poorest quality actually in use. Naturally, lands with superior fertility will get rent. Thus Malthus more or less anticipated the Ricardian theory of rent.

Value: The contribution of Malthus to the theory of value is negligible. He is somewhat confused about it. At one point, he criticises Adam Smith's theory of value and at another point he uses Smith's definition of value. That is, he describes value as the power to command other goods, including labour. Later, he tried to develop the cost of production theory of value. In other words, he tried to define value as the amount of (stored and current) labour plus profits.

The Contribution of Malthus to Economic Thought

1. Malthus was the first economist to devote an entire book to the study of the principle of population. Malthusian theory of population has become a starting point for all modern studies of the problem. He has been rightly described as the 'Founder of modern demography.'
2. The Malthusian theory is important from the fact that it enabled Darwin to formulate his theory of Natural selection. According to Haney, "Darwin himself has said that his theory of the struggle for existence was only the 'doctrine of Malthus applied with manifold force to the whole animal kingdom.'
3. Malthus collected a lot of historical and statistical data to illustrate his theory. So in a way he may be regarded as one of the founders of historical economics.
4. The Malthusian theory of population has introduced a dynamic factor into economics. Before Malthus, most of the economic analysis was based on the assumption of "other things being equal." But the Malthusian theory of population made it an unrealistic assumption for population was always changing.
5. Malthus is the forerunner of many under-consumption theories of trade cycle.
6. Malthus, though in a vague way, understood one of the most important problems of modern economy, namely, the maintenance of the level of aggregate demand. Keynes, who believed that level of employment depended on the level of aggregate effective demand, hailed Malthus as a pre-Keynesian. Malthus was the only classical economist who doubted the classical assumption of full employment equilibrium based on J. B. Say's 'Law of Markets.' In this respect, the plain common sense reasoning of Malthus was far superior to that of Ricardo's abstract logic. We may conclude with the words of Lord Keynes that, "If only Malthus, instead of Ricardo, had been the parent stem from which the nineteenth century economics proceeded, what a much wiser, and richer place the world would be today."[1]

---

1. Keynes: *Essays in Biography*, p. 144.

DAVID RICARDO
(1772-1823)

Introduction

Next to Adam Smith, Ricardo is the greatest name in the classical school of economics. Although Adam Smith was the founder of the classical school, David Ricardo became the leader of the school.

Life and Works

Ricardo was born in 1772 in a Jewish family in England. He was the third of seventeen children. Ricardo's father was a stock-broker. He entered his father's business at the age of fourteen. At twenty-one, he married a girl who belonged to a different faith. Ricardo himself changed his Jewish faith. This caused friction in the family and his father disowned him. So young Ricardo entered the stock market on his own with the aid of some friends who had advanced him some funds. Within a few years, he became rich. In fact, he became richer than his father. At forty-two, after amassing a huge fortune, he retired from business. When he died at the age of fifty-one, Ricardo left behind a legacy of £725,000.

Ricardo had no formal schooling beyond the age of fourteen. He turned to the systematic study of political economy rather late in life. When he was twenty-seven, he came across Adam Smith's "Wealth of Nations." That book kindled his interest in economics. Though Ricardo had an intellect as sharp as a razors's edge, he was a poor writer. In fact he wrote to his friend James Mill, "Oh that I were capable of writing a book." James Mill encouraged him to write on economic problems with the following assurance: "For as you are already the best thinker on political economy, I am resolved you shall also be the best writer."

Ricardo's chief work *"On the Principles of Political Economy"* was published in 1810. His other important work, a pamphlet, "The High Price of Bullion, a proof of the Depreciation of Bank Notes" was published in 1810.

Social Background of Ricardian Theories

Ricardo and Malthus are known as pessimists in the history of economic thought. But we must remember that the industrial environment of Adam Smith was different from that of Malthus and Ricardo. During the life of Ricardo, Industrial Revolution had already taken place with all its attendant evils. There was the factory system and the growth of population and the poverty of the working masses. There was rise in the price of grains, caused by depreciation of money and increased urban population. Lands of inferior fertility were brought into cultivation and land rents were increasing. The economy of the day in a way could be described as the capitalistic economy because of the large employment of capital.

The rising prices for food made "Corn Laws" a topic of great controversy. The landowners were interested in the continuance of "Corn Laws" because they could get high price for corn and consequently high rents. But the manufacturing classes asked for the repeal of corn laws hoping that such a step would result in a fall in the price of corn. Then with the fall in the price of corn, there would be fall in the wages and cheap labour would be available. Thus, there was a clash of interests between the landowners and the manufacturers. Naturally, under such circumstances, economic thinkers were forced to bestow their attention on problems such as rising prices, high rents, factors that determined wages, taxes and so on.

The Ricardian System

In order to understand Ricardian theories, it is essential to know some of the salient features of his method and assumptions.

1. First of all, Ricardo had an analytical genius. He was a deductive thinker. Though he was a man of business and had a lot of practical experience, he did not use the inductive method. He believed in abstract logic. He did not give historical or statistical facts to support his conclusions.

2. Ricardo was a firm believer in the doctrine of *laissez-faire*. And he was not interested in making large philosophical statements. 'Ricardo saw problems, not promises; and uncertainty, not progress.'

3. Ricardo considered money as a veil. He was interested in analysing fundamental economic problems as though they occurred in a money-less world. But Ricardo believed in the quantity theory of money which tells that the level of prices in the economy is proportional to the quantity of money in the economy.

4. Ricardo approached the problem of (exchange) value from the cost of production side. He accepted more or less the labour theory of value.

5. Ricardo incorporated the pessimistic views of Malthus with respect to population and food supply.

6. Lastly, Ricardian analysis of rent is based on the Law of Diminishing Returns.

On the Scope of Political Economy

While Adam Smith and Malthus regarded political Economy as an enquiry into the nature and causes of wealth, Ricardo considered Political Economy as "an inquiry into the laws which determine the division of the produce of the industry among the classes who concur in its formation." In his preface to his "Principles of Political Economy and Taxation," Ricardo stated that the produce of the earth was divided into rent, profit and wages and that "to determine the laws which regulate this distribution is the principal problem in political economy." *Ricardo has thus shifted the emphasis from production to distribution*. According to Eric Roll, "the main achievement of Ricardo is to be found in the theory of value and distribution."

Value

Ricardian theory of value is essentially a labour theory of value. We must remember Ricardo was concerned with relative values, not with absolute values. First of all, like Adam Smith, Ricardo has recognized two forms of value: (*i*) value-in-use, and (*ii*) value-in-exchange. Then he points out that for a commodity to have value-in-exchange, it must have utility. But he asserts that utility cannot be the measure of exchangeable value. According to Ricardo, the value of commodities depends upon two things, (*i*) Scarcity and (*ii*) the quantity of labour required to obtain them.

Ricardo agreed with Adam Smith that the value of most things depended on the amount of labour required to produce them. But there was another group of things, whose supply cannot be increased by labour. The exchange value of such non-reproducible commodities depended upon their scarcity. Rare statues, and pictures (works of art), scarce books and coins belong to this category. Ricardo thought that the supply of goods in the first category could be increased "almost without any assignable limit." For this category of goods, labour is the foundation of their value.

While Adam Smith applied labour theory of value to primitive societies, Ricardo applied it to capitalistic society as well. In fact, he believed that labour was the foundation of value in all stages of society. Because of certain modifications suggested in the labour theory as given by Adam Smith, Ricardian theory of value has been sometimes described as 93 per cent labour theory of value.

Ricardo has made a distinction between natural price and market price. Market price may deviate from the natural price (or value) because of temporary fluctuations of supply and demand. If market price rises above the normal price, profits will rise and more capital will be used to produce the commodity. On the other hand, if the market price falls, profits will fall and capital will flow out of the industry. In other words, short-run price depends on supply and demand and long-run price depends on the cost of production. And the relative costs of production of two commodities are proportional to the respective amounts of labour required to produce them.

The labour theory of value or the cost of production theory of value has been criticized on the following grounds:

1. There is difficulty in measuring labour or cost of production. Of course, Adam Smith used time as his measuring rod but all workmen are not of equal efficiency. The less skilled may take longer than the skilled over a particular piece of work and so put more labour into it.

2. Labour may be misdirected. An article which cannot fulfil the purpose for which it was intended cannot have any value, however much labour has gone to its manufacture. Even Karl Marx admitted that "nothing can have value without being an object of utility." Misdirected labour does not count as labour. So in order to get over this problem, Marx defined the amount of labour required as "socially necessary labour."

3. The main weakness of the labour theory of value is that it ignores the influences of demand.

We should remember that the labour theory of value became a powerful tool in the hands of Karl Marx to demonstrate that there was exploitation of labour in a capitalist economy. Marx found it very convenient for his argument to agree with Adam Smith and Ricardo that the value of a commodity depended on the amount of labour required for its production. On this basis, he asserted that the worker was entitled to the entire fruit of his labour. Marx emphasized that a thing can have value only if it is a product of human labour. We should, however, note that there is no hint of exploitation in Ricardo's analysis. It was Marx who made use of Ricardo's labour theory of value to speak about exploitation of labour by capitalists. Ricardo said that labour was the source of wealth. On this basis, Marx developed the socialist concept that the worker deserved that whole product. To this, he added the doctrine of class struggle.

RICARDIAN THEORY OF RENT

The Background for the Theory

At the time Ricardo formulated his theory of rent, rent was an important subject in England of that time because tenancy farming was widespread. The Parliamentary debate in 1815 on "Corn Laws" (which imposed tariffs on grain imports and thus provided protection to landowners) was the immediate issue that resulted in the development of the theory of rent. The Napoleonic wars came to an end and the farmers and landlords feared that there would be large-scale dumping of grain into England at low prices. In those days, the landowners dominated the Parliament and they asked for higher protection in the name of general welfare. But the businessmen and manufacturers spoke against higher tariffs on grain imports and asked for the repeal of the Corn Laws. The manufacturers made use of Ricardian theory of wages to support their argument. Ricardo said that wages would tend toward the minimum subsistence level. In that case, lower prices on grain and on bread would keep wages low. This would reduce the production costs of English manufacturers. Then British goods would compete more effectively in foreign markets. The businessmen further thought that if Britain imported more grains, they could export more manufactured goods. Thus there was a clash in the interests of landowners on the one hand and businessmen and manufacturers on the other. This conflict gave birth to the Ricardian theory of rent.

Although, Ricardo was not the first to originate the theory of rent, he developed it clearly and completely. Ricardo, by his theory of rent, tried to demonstrate that all classes, *except the landlords,* will be injured by the increase in the price of corn. He felt that improvements in agriculture and imports of cheap grain would prevent to some extent the tendency towards rising rents and falling profits. Therefore, Ricardo *opposed* the corn laws. He hoped that the abolition of tariffs on imports would promote the interests of the society at the expense of the landlords.

Rent Theory

According to Ricardo, *"rent is that portion of the produce of the earth which is paid to the landlord for the use of the original and indestructible powers of the soil."*

The Ricardian theory of rent is based on certain assumptions:

1. Rent is peculiar to land alone. Rent arises because of the peculiar characteristics of land, namely, that its supply is inelastic and it differs in fertility. Rent arises because of differences in the fertility of land. Rent is a *differential surplus*. All lands are not of equal fertility. Only those lands which are more fertile than others will get rent.

2. Land has some original and indestructible powers.

3. Land is subject to the law of diminishing returns.

4. There is perfect competition.

Ricardo explained his theory of rent with the aid of an example of colonization. Suppose some people go to a new country and settle down there. To being with, they will cultivate all the best lands available. There may be no need to pay any rent so long as such best lands are freely available. Suppose another batch of people go and settle down in the new country after some time. Naturally the demand for agricultural produce will increase. And in the course of time, the first grade lands alone cannot produce all the foodgrains that are needed on account of the operation of the Law of Diminishing returns. The law of diminishing returns is the basis of the Ricardian theory of rent. So second-grade lands will have to be cultivated in order to meet the needs of the growing population. If the second-grade lands are to be brought under cultivation, the price of grain prevailing in the market must be sufficient enough to meet the cost of production in the second grade lands. Otherwise, second grade lands will go out of cultivation. Since under conditions of competition, there will be only one price for a commodity, all the produce, whether it is from the first grade lands or from the second grade lands, will have the same price. When the second grade lands are cultivated, the first grade lands will yield a surplus over and above their expenses of cultivation. This surplus is called rent. In our present example, only first-grade land yields rent. The second-grade land covers only the expenses of cultivation. But suppose the demand for foodgrains further increases. The lands of inferior fertility (in our example, third-grade lands) will be brought under cultivation. Then even the second-grade lands will yield rent and the rent of the first-grade lands will increase further. The land that is just able to meet its expenses of production is known as a no-rent land or marginal land. Rent indicates the differential advantage of the superior land over the marginal land.

It has been stated that rent arises on account of differences in the fertility of land. Besides differences in fertility, rent may also arise on account of situational advantage. Some lands enjoy situational advantage. For example, they may be nearer to the market place. That may help producers to save on transport costs. Even if all lands are equally fertile, lands possessing situational advantage command some superiority over other lands. Thus rent arises on account of differences in fertility and in situation.

While discussing the relationship between rent and price, Ricardo has stated that rent does not enter price. According to him rent is determined by price. Rent is price-determined and not price-determinant. Rent is high because price (of corn) is high, price is high not because rent is high.

Ricardo has come to the conclusion that rent does not enter price because according to him, there are some no-rent lands. But still their produce has a price on the market and rent does not enter price here because the marginal lands do not get any rent at all.

1. Some of Ricardo's critics have raised objection against the order of cultivation described by him. According to Ricardo, the best lands are cultivated first. But there is no historical proof for this. Best lands are not always cultivated first.

2. Objection has been raised against the use of the phrase "original and indestructible powers of the soil." It has been argued that there are no such original powers of the soil and its powers are not indestructible. For the fertility of land may decrease in the course of time by continuous cultivation.

3. Ricardo's view that rent is determined by price and that it does not enter price has been attacked by many economists. From the point of view of a single firm, rent enters price.

4. Ricardian theory is based on the assumption of perfect competition. Only under conditions of perfect competition, all units of a good will be homogeneous and there will be only one price for a good at a time. But in the real world, imperfect competition is the rule.

5. Rent is not peculiar to land alone. Modern economists feel that the rent aspect can be seen in other factor incomes as well. According to the modern view, the term 'rent' is applied to "payments made for factors of production which are in imperfectly elastic supply." Thus the term 'rent' includes besides payments for the use of land, other payments for labour and capital as well. For instance, Marshall has introduced the concept of quasi-rent with reference to machines. According to him, "quasi-rent is the income derived from machines, and other appliances for production made by man." Marshall described rent as 'the leading species of large genus.'

Further, modern economists make use of the concept of *'transfer earnings'* to explain rent with reference to a particular industry. Transfer earnings refer to the amount that a factor could earn in its best paid alternative employment "Any payment in excess of this amount is a surplus above what is necessary to retain the factor in its best paid employment and so is rent."

6. Lastly, Ricardo overemphasized the role of diminishing returns. This law will hold good only if other factors, including the level of technology, are kept constant. But historically, improvements in agriculture have resulted in increasing returns per unit of labour in the most advanced countries.

Implications of the Ricardian Theory of Rent

The Physiocrats, Adam Smith and Ricardo considered rent as a surplus. But there is one big difference. While the physiocrats and Adam Smith regarded rent as a gift of Nature, Ricardo argued that rent arose not because of the bounty of Nature but because of its niggardliness. "The labour of Nature is paid, not because she does much but because she does little."

While Adam Smith saw harmony of interests between landlords and the rest of society, Ricardo saw a conflict of interest between the landlords and the rest of society. As population increases, the increased demand for food will raise its price. Lands of inferior quality will be brought into cultivation. Rent will therefore rise. Wages will also rise to give labour their minimum of subsistence. And profits will fall. Therefore, with the progress of population, Ricardo argued, "all classes *except the landlords* will be injured by the increase in the price of corn." Indirectly Ricardo's theory of rent suggested that landlords as a class were never interested in improvements in agriculture. He believed that improvements in agriculture and imports of cheap grain would prevent the tendency towards rising rents and falling profits. So, as a policy, Ricardo opposed the corn laws. The repeal of corn laws and other restrictions on the imported foodgrains would promote the interests of the society. Of course, the rents of the landlords would fall.

Ricardo said that rent did not enter into price. This had serious policy implications. It implied that even if high tax was imposed on rents, it would not raise the price of corn. In fact, on the basis of the Ricardian theory of rent, J. S. Mill suggested the socialization of rent by means of a tax on land. Sidney Webb, a socialist, considers the Ricardian theory of rent, "the very cornerstone of collectivist economy."

Wages

Wages are the price of labour. Like all other things, labour has its natural price and market price. The market price of labour depends on supply and demand. If there is an abundant supply of labour, market price of labour will be low and if there is scarcity of labour market price will rise. But, we must note that the market price will fluctuate around the natural price.

The natural price of labour depends on the price of necessities of life required by the labourer and his family. According to Ricardo, "the natural price of labour is that price which is necessary to enable the labourers, one with another, to subsist and to perpetuate their race, without either increase or diminution." If the prices of food and other necessaries rise, wages will rise and when the prices of food and other necessaries fall, wages will fall.

Ricardo believed that in the long run, both the natural price of labour and money wages would tend to rise because of the increase in the cost of producing food for increasing population. Improvements in agriculture and imports of foodgrains would lower the cost of living only temporarily. But ultimately, money wages will rise in order to meet the increasing costs of foodgrains.

Ricardo's idea that in the long run, the wages of workers will enable them to live only at a "subsistence level" is sometimes referred to as the "Iron Law of Wages." When the market price of labour rises above the natural price, there will be expansion in the families of workers. As population increases, wages will come down to their natural price. When the market price of labour is below the natural price, poverty and misery will reduce the working population and wage rates will rise. Thus, in the long run, workers will receive wages at minimum subsistence level.

The Iron Law of Wages is of little importance today. Nobody pays any serious attention to the theory except in the textbooks on the history of economic thought.

Profits

Ricardo has not given a clear-cut theory of profits. He has treated profits and interest as one and the same. But, Ricardo was emphatic about one thing. He firmly believed wages increased at the expense of profits. In other words, whenever there was an increase in wages, profits would fall. Thus according to Ricardo, wages and profits are diametrically opposed to each other. It implied that the interest of the employer and worker are eternally opposed. Ricardo believed that in the long-run, money wages would rise and the rate of profit would tend to fall.

It may be interesting to note here that though Ricardo believed that "the interest of the landlord is always opposed to that of the consumer and manufacturer" and the interests of worker and employer are always opposed, he never advocated state intervention to reduce the conflict of interest. He remained a non-interventionist and advocated *laissez-faire*.

Money

On the question of money, we should remember that Ricardo was interested in the urgent currency problems of his day.

Ricardo wrote on currency problems at a time when the market price of gold was increasing because of the introduction of irredeemable (inconvertible) paper standard by the Bank of England. Ricardo tried to explain why the market price of gold was rising and suggested ways of controlling it. He maintained that printing of bank notes was the main cause of rising prices of gold and other commodities. In other words, he believed in the quantity theory of money which tells that the level of prices in the economy is proportional to the quantity of money in the economy.

Ricardo advocated that Bank of England should restore gold standard. He believed the gold standard by acting as a check on the over-issue of currency would curb inflation. But he advocated economy in the use of gold and silver. To eliminate the cost of coinage and to economize gold, Ricardo suggested a sort of gold Bullion standard. He anticipated the gold bullion standard introduced in 1925, that is, during the inter-war period. Ricardo's currency reform was adopted by Parliament in 1819 and gold standard was introduced in 1821. And the gold standard remained the dominant monetary standard in Britain and many other countries for over a century, except during major wars and great financial crises.

The Theory of Comparative Cost

The theory of comparative cost is the major contribution of Ricardo to the theory of foreign trade. Adam Smith advocated free competition in foreign trade and his theory of trade was based on difference in absolute costs. According to Smith, every country would buy in the cheapest market. But Ricardo developed the theory of comparative costs. According to Ricardo, "Trade might take place of the advantages of both trading countries, even when one of them was more efficient in the production of *both* the commodities exchanged." The theory of comparative cost or comparative advantage may be stated as follows: "Under competitive conditions, a country tends to specialise in those commodities in the production of which it has the greatest comparative advantage" (Silverman). In recent times, Benham has stated the law as follows: "The principle of comparative costs or comparative advantage points out that two countries will gain by specialization and trade, provided that each has a comparative advantage of lower comparative costs in the commodities it exports."

Ricardo advocated that the more efficient country should export those commodities whose comparative cost is lowest, and it should import whose comparative cost is highest. The theory of comparative cost was the theoretical basis on which Ricardo advocated free trade policy. He believed that under a system of perfectly free commerce, the pursuit of individual advantage is admirably connected with the universal good of the whole.

We can illustrate the theory of comparative cost by the famous example given by Ricardo himself. Let us take two countries, England and Portugal and two commodities wine and cloth. Let us assume that Portugal is more efficient than England in both lines of production. Portugal can produce a certain quantity of wine by the labour of 80 men and a certain quantity of cloth by the labour of 90 men. But in England, the production of the same quantities of wine and cloth takes, respectively, the labour of 120 and 100 men. Under these circumstances, it would be of mutual advantage for both countries if Portugal specialized in wine and imported cloth, while England specialized in cloth and imported wine.

The theory of comparative cost is based on two fundamental assumptions:

First, Ricardo assumed that capital and labour did not flow between countries. (Otherwise both wine and cloth would be produced in Portugal itself).

Secondly, he assumed the law of constant costs rather than increasing costs as output expanded. (Otherwise, it would not be possible to carry on specialization to the fullest extent).

Criticism

The Ricardian theory of comparative cost has been criticized on the ground that it is based on the labour theory of value. Not only that, the theory is based on the assumption of full-employment.

Stationary State

Ricardo's view of the natural progress of society and the theory of stationary state may be described as follows:

To begin with, population is small. When the population is small, only the best lands are used for producing food. This, in turn, means rents are small and there will be a good deal of income to be shared between profits and wages. Everybody, except the landlord, is happy.

In the next stage of society since profits are high, capitalists will begin accumulating more capital. Then there will be more demand for labourers. The increased demand for labour will raise wages above the subsistence level. When wages are above the subsistence level, population will expand. When population expands, the society is forced to cultivate lands of inferior quality to produce the necessary increase in food supply. This, in turn, means diminishing returns and increased rents. The relative shares of wages and profits fall.

In the third stage, rents rise further and wages and profits fall. The process goes on until population is so large, the pressure on land is so great and rents are so high that wages are at the subsistence level and profits are so low that capitalists do not wish to accumulate more capital. *The society is said to have reached the stationary state at this point.* Since, wages are at the subsistence level, population will not grow. Since profits are very low, there will be no further capital accumulation and no further force to raise wages. The system has come to a halt. Only if there is some external change, such as improvement in agricultural methods, the movement will begin again.

The Ricardian theory of stationary state is a brilliant analysis because Ricardo brings together under one head the problems of production, growth and distribution of income which, in fact, remain the major economic problems even today. While Adam Smith looked at the stationary state as a dim and distant prospect, Ricardo considered it as a real possibility. The Ricardian system is a major milestone in the development of economic theory. In spite of all his abstract logic, to this day, Ricardo remains an economist's economist.

Conclusion

Opinions differ regarding the contribution of Ricardo to economic thought. According to Gide and Rist, "Next to Smith, Ricardo is the greatest name in economics. Ricardo is the supreme example of abstract reasoning. He will be remembered as the master of deduction in economics. According to Eric Roll, "the main achievement of Ricardo is to be found in the theory of value and distribution. In the opinion of Haney, "one of his (*Ricardo's*) great services lay in the fact that, more than any predecessor, he separated economics from other branches of knowledge, and from ethics and from government in particular. With Ricardo political Economy became Economics."

"He (Ricardo) succeeded even more than Smith in isolating the chief categories of the economic system. He left to his successors many unsolved problems, but he also indicated ways in which they might be solved."

Above all, Ricardo provided the foundation stones of socialism. The Ricardian theory of value is the starting point of modern socialism. Marx developed his theory of surplus value only on the basis of the labour theory of value. The Ricardian theory of rent has become a powerful tool for every Marxian in his general attack upon private property. The Ricardian theory of wages has become the battle-cry of socialism. For Ricardo has said that wages can increase at the expense of profits. It implied conflict between capitalists and workers suggesting them the idea of a class war. Thus, the so-called scientific socialists have approved of the arguments of Ricardo on value, rent, wages and profit. It has been rightly said by Alexander Gray, "If Marx and Lenin deserve busts, somewhere in the background there should be room for an effigy of Ricardo." However, Keynes has expressed the view that "the total obliteration of Malthus's line of approach and the complete domination of Ricardo's for a period of hundred years has been a disaster to the progress of economics" (J. M. Keynes: *Essays in Biography*). At some other place in the same essay, Keynes lamented that, "If only Malthus instead of Ricardo, had been the parent stem from which the nineteenth century economics proceeded, what a much wiser and richer place this world would be today." Jevons, one of the founders of the Marginal utility school, called Ricardo "that able wrong headed man" who "shunted the car of economic science on to a wrong line." Keynes criticized Ricardo for the latter's assumption of full employment based on J. B. Say's Law of Markets, which ruled out general over-production. (Keynes praised Malthus because he believed in the possibility of over-production). In spite of the above criticisms and varying estimates, we have to remember that Ricardo's teaching dominated political economy for nearly a century.

J. B. SAY
(1767-1832)

Jean Baptiste Say was a Frenchman who popularized the ideas of Adam Smith on the continent. His main work was *Traite d' Economic Politique* (A Treatise on Political Economy). It was published in 1803. Say had many ups and downs in life. At first he was in business. Later on he became a professor of Political Economy in a college in France.

Say came across Adam Smith's "Wealth of Nations" by chance and the book had a profound influence on him. He tells us that, "when we read this work, we feel that previous to Smith there was no such thing as political economy." Later on, Say interpreted the work of Adam Smith to the world. But it will be unjust to regard Say as a mere popularizer of Smith's ideas. He did not merely repeat the ideas of Smith but carefully reviewed them. He developed some of them and emphasized others. According to Say, "The work of Smith is only a confused assemblage of the soundest principles of Political Economy....; his book is a vast chaos of just ideas, jumbled with positive knowledge." So Say tried to popularize the ideas of Smith by presenting them in a lucid and orderly manner.

We shall now discuss the ideas of Say in detail.

Nature and Scope of Political Economy

Say had clear ideas about the nature and scope of political economy. According to him, political economy is a study of the laws which govern wealth. He divided the subject of economics into three main divisions: (*i*) Production, (*ii*) Distribution, and (*iii*) Consumption of wealth. In the field of distribution, Say said that national income would be distributed in the form of rent, wages, interest and profits. It may be interesting to note here that Say criticized the English economists for combining profits and interest. He maintained that the functions of an undertaker were different from those of a capitalist. He described the 'undertaker' as a *entrepreneur*. This term has found a permanent place in the science of economics.

While Ricardo throughout his analysis adopted the deductive method, Say was in favour of inductive method. He argued that methods similar to those used in natural sciences might be followed in Political Economy.

J. B. Say considered Political Economy as a purely theoretical and descriptive science. According to him, "The duty of an economist is to observe, to analyse and to describe but not to give advice." He must just explain the causes and stop with that. He must give no advice. Thus he regarded political economy as a positive science. Further, he believed that the laws of economics were of universal application.

Productive and Unproductive Labour

The physiocrats and Adam Smith had a materialistic conception of wealth. For instance, Smith considered all services as unproductive labour. He regarded the services of doctors, judges, lawyers and actors as unproductive labour. Say found fault with Smith for including only material things as wealth in economics. Say considered even services such as the advice of a doctor as "product." The doctor gives advice only after taking fees for consultation. "Its production consisted in saying it; its consumption in hearing it; it has been consumed simultaneously with its production." The idea that economic activity consists of the production of material as well as immaterial goods has been put humorously by Lionel Robbins in the following words: "We do not say the production of potatoes is economic activity and the production of philosophy is not."

The physiocrats considered agriculture alone as the productive occupation. Even Adam Smith, under the influence of physiocrats, attributed special productivity to agriculture. But Say refuted the idea. He believed that "Nature is forced to work along with man" not only in agriculture but everywhere. While Smith gives priority to agriculture, Say gives top priority to manufactures.

Say's Law of Markets

Say's 'Law of Markets' has found a permanent place for him among the galaxy of economists. The 'Law of Markets' is considered to be the greatest contribution of Say to economic thought.

During the days of J. B. Say, some businessmen and even economists thought that general over-production and unemployment were common occurrences. Say tried to disprove this belief by his law of markets.

Say's 'Law of Markets' tells that *supply creates its own demand*. In Say's own words, "It is production which creates market for goods." In other words, whatever is produced represents the demand for another product. Additional supply is additional demand.

It is true that goods and services are bought with money. But they are only superficially bought with money. We use money in exchange of goods because exchange based on money is more efficient than exchange based on barter. But goods and services, in fact, are bought with other goods and services. Let us assume that there is no money in an economy. Then, we can 'demand' one set of commodities only by offering other commodities for them. Whenever we produce an additional supply of commodities, we are adding to the demand for commodities at the same time. Thus products are always exchanged against other products. When a product is produced, it offers a market for other products, from the moment it is created. On the basis of the above reasoning, Say argued that there cannot be any general over-production. It implied that there will not be any mass unemployment and an economy will always be at a full employment equilibrium. In other words there will be no such thing as deficiency of 'aggregate demand.' Say, however, accepted that there can be over-production in a particular industry. That is, there may be partial over-production. For example, we may produce an additional 10 pairs of shoes and we may offer them in exchange for other commodities (*e.g.*, bread, biscuits, safety-pins). Through our increased supply, we are increasing 'demand' for these commodities. It is possible that the producers of these commodities (bread, safety-pins, etc.) may not want additional shoes at the existing prices. In that case, price of shoes in terms of other commodities will fall. In other words, the relative prices of other commodities have risen. Since every producer aims at profit maximization, next year we will not produce more shoes but more bread, biscuits and safety-pins. The above example tells us that partial over-production is the effect of producing what is not exactly wanted. The situation of partial over-production can be corrected when the entrepreneurs shift their resources from the production of things they cannot sell at a profit to the production of things they can sell at a profit. Thus, Say's Law of Markets denies the possibility of general over-production.

Implications of Say's Law of Markets

1. As 'supply creates its own demand,' there will be no general over-production. It implies that there can be no general unemployment. In fact, 'full employment' became one of the basic assumptions of the classical economics. Only on the basis of the assumption of 'full employment' the classical economists ruled out the possibility of 'trade cycles.'

2. According to this law, it will be profitable to have wide markets for they will increase the demand for goods and raise their prices.

3. Everyone should be interested in the prosperity of everyone else. 'It is foolish to divide the nation into producers and consumers; everyone is both.' Further, in a nation, all occupations (agriculture, manufacturing and trade) should flourish together.

4. The Law of Markets has been used in support of Free Trade doctrine. It implied that imports will not be detrimental to home production or industry. For what is bought from abroad is purchased with home products. When we buy some things from the foreigners, at the same time, we will be selling things to them and thus a market will be created for them.

5. Say was interested in the development of industry. By ruling out the possibility of the crisis of over-production, he wanted to avoid everything that might prove unfavourable to the extension of industry.

6. Say's Law became the basis for the *laissez-faire* policy of the government. As supply creates its own demand, it implies that there is automatic adjustment of the economy. The economy has built-in flexibility. So there is no need for State interference in economic matters. On this basis, in the field of Public Finance, Say asserted that "the very best of all plans of Finance is to spend little and the best of all taxes is that which is least in amount."

Criticism

Say's 'Law of Markets' was accepted as the true explanation of working of the economic system by most of the economists of the classical school. In fact, the economic writings of classical economists were based on the assumption of 'full employment' until Keynes published his "General Theory of Employment, Interest and Money' in 1936. Even Ricardo, the leader of the classical school, supported Say and approved that 'in reference to a nation, supply can never exceed demand.'

Malthus was the only classical economist who opposed Say's Law that "supply creates its own demand." He argued that demand might be deficient and cause unemployment. But he could not convince Ricardo, who took the same kind of view of Say because Malthus was unable to explain clearly how and why effective demand could be deficient and excessive. As keynes put it beautifully, "The great puzzle of Effective Demand with which Malthus had wrestled vanished from economic literature." However, Keynes regarded Malthus as a pre-Keynesian. And it was left to Keynes to prove that deficiency in aggregate demand could cause unemployment. Even Marx spoke of the possibility of technological unemployment in his Theory of Industrial Reserve Army.

Further we can show that Say's Law is unrealistic from the following argument. Say said that supply will create its own demand on the assumption that the incomes that are earned by people in the process of production are completely spent. But we know that when there is an increase in income, the entire income will not be spent. A portion of it will be saved. But the classical economists who supported Say believed that all that was saved was automatically invested. They thought that savings and investment could be influenced by the rate of interest. This is an incorrect view. For the main determinant of investment is the marginal efficiency of capital (expected rate of profit). So a fall in the rate of interest will not automatically increase investment. Thus there may be deficiency of demand and supply will not create its own demand.

Above all, the Great Depression of 1929-32 with all its evils of bad trade and mass unemployment struck a death blow to Say's Law of markets and the classical assumption of full employment.

Value

Say gave more importance to utility in his theory of value than his English contemporaries. He believed that we seek a thing because it possesses utility and it is utility that determines value. Thus Say tried to give a psychological theory of value based on utility. But we must note that he did not speak of '*marginal utility.*' While referring to reward for means (factors) of production, Say states that "the value of the means of production comes from the value of the product which may result, which is founded on the use which can be made of this product or the satisfaction which can be drawn from it."

Conclusion

J. B. Say plays an important role in the history of economic doctrines. We may sum up our opinion of Say with the words of Haney, "He was no Smith or Ricardo; but he was no mere popularizer ....The history of political economy would have been different without J. B. Say."

BASTIAT
(1801-1850)

Introduction

Frederic Bastiat was born in 1801 near Bayonne in France. He belonged to a family of wealthy merchants. He himself became in turn a merchant, a farmer, a justice of the peace, a councillor and finally a deputy in the Constituent Assembly of 1848. He died in Rome in 1850 at the age of forty-nine.

Bastiat's literary career was very brief. His first article appeared in 1844. The title of the article was: "Concerning the Influence of English and French Tariffs on the Future or Both Peoples." A series of articles he wrote appeared as a book, with the title, "Sophismes economiques" (Economic Sophisms). In 1845, Bastiat became secretary of the Free Trade Association in Paris and also took charge of a newspaper called 'Free Trade.' The most ambitious attempt of Bastiat was "Harmonies economiques" (Economic Harmonies). He completed only the first volume and it appeared in the year of the author's death in 1850. That work sums up the essence of Bastiat.

While Ricardo and Malthus are known as pessimists, Carey and Bastiat are known as optimists in the history of economic thought.

Free Trade versus Protection

Bastiat was essentially a journalist. Naturally, he paid more attention to the controversies of the day. He was a champion of Free Trade and he opposed socialism. He was for laissez-faire. He considered protection and socialism as devices of exploitation. The manufacturer who cannot make a profit seeks Protection, whereby the State will guarantee him a profit at other people's expense. And there will not be much of individual responsibility under socialism. Bastiat's articles had great appeal because of their pleasant wit and satire. While writing about the absurdity of giving indiscriminate protection to each and every industry, he referred to the petition of candle-makers and associated industries for protection against the unfair competition of the sun. The attack of Bastiat on protection and socialism is seen at its best in his 'The Economic Sophisms.'

Economic Harmony

The teachings of Ricardo and Malthus implied antagonism of interests. But as a laissez-faire economist, Bastiat believed that under the reign of liberty, there would be complete harmony of all legitimate interests.

Value

According to Bastiat, "Economics is the study of exchange." Wants, efforts and satisfactions form the circle of economics. Bastiat regarded various theories of value emphasizing on utility, scarcity, labour as one-sided. According to him, there are two kinds of utility: (*i*) "gratuitous" and (*ii*) "onerous." The former consists of materials and forces which are the free gifts of Nature. Onerous utilities lie in the service of man to man and they are bought by our own efforts. It follows that the free gifts of Nature have no value. The essence of value lies in human service. It means that where no service is rendered or received, there can be no value. Bastiat comes very near to the labour-cost theory when he holds that value lies in "effort." In his own words, "Value is the relation of two services exchanged." But, we should, however, note that it is not clear what the term 'service' includes.

Rent

Bastiat has criticized the Ricardian theory of rent. According to Ricardo rent is a payment made for "the original and indestructible powers of the soil." But Bastiat believed that rent of land is only a payment made for services such as the clearing away of forests, drainage, building of fences, fertilizing the soil etc.

Wages

Bastiat has presented an optimistic picture about the lot of wage-earners. He believed that as production increased, wages would also rise. The workers need not be afraid of the operation of the Iron Law of Wages. His two main conclusions in this regard were: (*i*) The labourer would tend to rise to the rank of a capitalist, and (*ii*) wages tend to rise.

Interest

According to Bastiat, "Interest is a payment made for postponement of consumption by capitalist." He also believed that there was harmony of interests between capital and labour. Though the share of labour in total produce increased with the progress of the society, and though capitalists received a smaller relative share of produce, they received a greater one absolutely, on account of the growth of capital. He believed in a falling rate of interest with the advancement of society.

Role of Government

According to Bastiat, the role of government is "essentially limited to maintenance of order, security and justice. All actions of government beyond this limit is a usurpation upon conscience, upon intelligence, upon industry, in a word upon human liberty."

Conclusion

According to Schumpeter, Bastiat's case "is simply the case of the bather who enjoys himself in the shallows and then goes beyond his depth and drowns." Of course, he was a brilliant economic journalist. But he was no theorist.

Bastiat stood on the shoulders of Say and Carey. There is a charge that Bastiat plagiarized Carey. But this is accounted for by the French sources that Bastiat and Carey had in common.

We should look at the writings of Bastiat as propaganda literature against protection and socialism. His belief that laissez-faire competition would ensure perfect and harmonious social order is basically unsound. His theory of rent is quite erroneous. On account of its shallowness and disregard of certain facts of social life, Bastiat's theory has not exercised much influence on the leaders of economic thought.

13

NASSAU WILLIAM SENIOR
(1790-1864)

Introduction

Nassau William Senior was born in 1790 in England. He was a highly educated Oxford man. He was called to the Bar. Later on, he became Professor of Political Economy at Oxford. It may be interesting to note that he became the first incumbent of Oxford economics chair when it was founded in 1825. He became a member of the Royal Commission on the Poor Laws in 1832. His writings belong mostly to the period 1827-52. His major work was "An Outline of Political Economy" (1836).

The Scope and Method of Political Economy

According to Senior, "The subject treated by the Political Economist .... is not Happiness, but Wealth." In other words, Political Economy is the science which deals with the nature, the production and the distribution of wealth. He regards economics as an abstract and deductive science. His view is that economics is a science and not an art. Practical questions "no more form part of the science of political economy..... than navigation forms part of the science of astronomy." Moreover, he does not want the economist to offer even a single piece of advice. The business of the economist is neither to recommend nor to dissuade, but solely to state general principles. According to him, "Reasoning is more important than observation."

According to Senior, "Political Economy is based on four propositions: (i) "Every man desires to obtain additional wealth with as little sacrifice as possible." (This is also known as *hedonistic principle*); (ii) The Malthusian principle of population; (iii) The Law of Increasing Returns in Industry; and (iv) The Law of Diminishing Returns in Agriculture.

Value

Senior defines value as "that quality in anything which fits it to be given and received in exchange." According to him, "the forces which determine value fall into two sets: the demand and supply of the one good, and the demand and supply of that for which it is exchanged."

Abstinence and Capital Formation

The concept of 'abstinence' as cost of production is the chief contribution of Senior to economic thought. In his own words, abstinence is "a term by which we express the conduct of a person who either abstains from the unproductive use of what he can command, or designedly prefers the production of remote to that of immediate results." In the formation of capital, he tells that, "some delay of enjoyment must in general have reserved it from unproductive use."

While discussing the agents of production, he avoided the use of the word "capital". According to him, the means of production are labour, natural agents and abstinence. In the place of land, he has used the expression "natural agents". By "abstinence", Senior refers to "that agent, distinct from labour and the agency of Nature, the concurrence of which is necessary to the existence of capital, and which stands in the same relation to profit as labour, does to wages." Abstinence is a sacrifice which must be rewarded because, "to abstain from the enjoyment which is in our power, or to seek distant rather than immediate results, are among the most painful exertions of the human will." By cost of production is meant "the sum of the labour and abstinence necessary to production." Thus Senior has introduced subjective factors into the cost of production. There are some writers who believe that Senior might have borrowed the concept of 'abstinence' from G. P. Scrope, who wrote before him that the profit of the owner of the capital is "a compensation to him for abstaining for a time from the consumption of that portion of his property on his personal gratification."

Utility and Demand

Senior believed that demand depended upon the "degree" in which a thing was desired. In a very vague way, he had in mind what is today known as the Law of Diminishing Utility: "Two articles of the same kind will seldom afford twice the pleasure of one, and still less will then give five times the pleasure of two." However, he considered limitation of supply as chief factor in the determination of value.

Theory of Wages

According to Senior, wages depend on "the extent of the fund for the maintenance of labourers, compared with the number of labourers to be maintained." This is more or less an echo of the Wages-Fund theory.

Law of Increasing Returns

The optimism of Senior shows itself in his doctrine concerning increasing returns from manufacturing. He believed that "every increase in the number of manufacturing labourers is accompanied, not merely by a corresponding, but by an increased productive power."

Conclusion

One of the interesting things about Senior is his emphasis on the subjective elements. In this, he differs from most of his predecessors. He attaches a lot of importance to 'utility' and 'abstinence' which are subjective in nature. He believed in a cost theory of value but his costs were physical and subjective. The critical powers of Senior were remarkable but he did not formulate any significant theories in economics though he was on the verge of stating the Law of Diminishing Utility and the Law of Increasing Returns. The postulates on which his analysis is based has been subject to a lot of criticism. The first one that "every man desires to obtain additional wealth with as little sacrifice as possible" is a mere truism. The Malthusian theory is not true at all times and in all places. And Senior has reduced the laws of returns to a crude generalisation: "additional labour when employed in manufactures is *more*, when employed in agriculture is less efficient in production."

Schumpeter is of the view that Senior has been treated with comparative neglect by many economists. He puts him in the same bracket as Malthus and Ricardo. According to him, "Senior was one of the three Englishmen whose works are the main stepping stones between A. Smith and J. S. Mill." Senior was indeed a great analytic economist.

JOHN STUART MILL
(1806-1873)

John Stuart Mill was the last great economist of the classical school. He systematized and popularized the whole body of the classical economic thought. In Mill's book, we find the classical doctrines in their final crystalline form. But it will be a mistake to dismiss Mill as merely a gifted popular writer and his book as a restatement of classical ideas. We must remember that Mill made some significant original contributions to political economy. The classical school was already in decline during Mill's last days. Even Mill himself departed from some of the main ideas developed by Smith and Ricardo. We may agree with Gide and Rist in their opinion that "with him classical economics may be said in some way to have attained its perfection and with him begin its decay."

Life and Works

J. S. Mill was born in 1806. He was the son of James Mill. James Mill was the economist who induced Ricardo to write on economics. J. S. Mill received extraordinary education under the direct supervision of his father. Mill began to learn Greek at three, Latin at eight. At eleven, he read the proofs of his father's book "History of India." He mastered algebra and geometry by the time he was twelve. Then he began to study logic. At thirteen, he began the study of economics. By the time he was eighteen, he had already edited the works of Bentham who is known for his principle of utility. At twenty, Mill had a nervous breakdown. Mill was appointed in the East India Company in 1823 and he was there for nearly thirty-five years. For a short time (1858-68) he was also a member of Parliament. He died in 1873.

Mill's main works on Economics were: (*i*) *Principles of Political Economy* (1848), (*ii*) *Essays on some unsettled questions of Political Economy* (1844). Mill was not merely an economist, he was a logician, reformer and a champion of liberty. His other important works were: (*i*) *System of Logic* (1843), (*ii*) *On Liberty* (1853), (*iii*) *Subjection of Women* (1869) and *Autobiography* (1873).

Mill as an Economist

The economic ideas of Mill are essentially the economics of Adam Smith and Ricardo. Mill believed in most of the fundamental ideas of classical economics. He believed in Bentham's principle of utility. He was a lover of individual freedom and a champion of liberty. Naturally, he advocated the *laissez-faire* ideas of physiocrats and Adam Smith. He believed in the Ricardian theory of rent and the Malthusian theory of population. The Law of Diminishing returns, he believed, was of universal importance. He has described it as the most important proposition in political economy. Like Bentham he was a social reformer. He advocated peasant proprietorship, co-operation, taxation of rent and restriction of inheritance rights. He believed in free competition. But, however, towards the end of his life he became attracted towards socialism. In fact he found it hard to bring a compromise between his individualistic ideas and socialistic ideas which involved state action, which in turn, might infringe upon individual freedom. In fact, this led to many logical inconsistencies in his economic thinking.

Mill was not a mere theorist. He was interested in the application of economic principles to the problems of the society. In fact, the actual title of his book was, *"Principles of Political Economy with some of their Applications to Social Philosophy."*

Mill, though, generally restated classical doctrines, he made a original contribution by saying that the laws of production were different from the laws of distribution. He made use of the distinction between the laws of production and laws of distribution to advocate his socialist reforms.

Mill defined Political Economy as a science dealing with "the nature of wealth, and the laws of its production and distribution." He divided his book into five parts. They deal with production, distribution, exchange, influence of the progress of society on production and distribution, and the influence of Government.

We shall now discuss, in detail, the economic principles as enunciated by Mill.

1. *The Law of Self-interest:* The Law of self-interest is also known as the hedonistic principle. It means that every individual desires well-being and each man knows what is good for himself. This has led to individualism. When we say that a person is seeking his own good, it does not mean that he desires the failure of others. It is true that Ricardo and Malthus spoke of the possibility of conflict between different classes (for example, conflict between landlords and other members of the society, and conflict between labour and capital). But Mill, like most other classical economists, believed in the general harmony of interests.

2. *The Law of Free competition:* Mill was a firm believer in free competition. When we admit that each individual is the best judge of his own interests, it implies that the best thing is to let each man choose his own path. In other words, *laissez-faire* is the best policy. On account of its emphasis on liberty, the classical school is also known as Liberal school. It has other names too—individualist school or orthodox school. Mill never regarded *laissez-faire* as a dogma or a scientific axiom. At best, it was a practical rule.

   The classical writers considered free competition as a supreme natural law. According to Mill, "every restriction of competition is an evil" and "every extension of it is always an ultimate good."

3. *The Law of Population:* Mill was a firm believer in the Malthusian theory of population. According to Gide and Rist, "In his dread of its dire consequences, he surpasses Malthus himself." Mill may be rightly regarded as a neo-Malthusian. He felt for the rights and liberty of women. Women are rarely consulted when maternity is forced upon them.

   One of the criticisms of Malthusian theory is that Malthus was unnecessarily worried about increase in numbers. The critics pointed out that every mouth brings with it a pair of hands. To that, Mill's answer is this: "It is in vain to say that all mouths which the increase of mankind calls into existence bring with them hands. The new mouths require as much food as the old ones and the hands do not produce as much." (*Principles,* Book I). A large family appeared to him as disgusting as drunkenness. According to O. H. Taylor, "He (Mill) became one of the early supporters of the birth-control movement which sought to spread the knowledge and use of contraceptives, and make planned parenthood universal."

4. *Value:* Mill considered value as more or less a settled problem. According to Mill, "Happily there is nothing in the laws of value which remains (1848) for the present or any future writer to clear up; the theory of the subject is complete."

   Mill thought his main task in the field of value was merely to restate Ricardian theory of value in simple terms. Like Ricardo, he distinguished between value-in-use and value-in-exchange and concentrated upon the latter. Like Ricardo, he stated that "The value of commodities.... depends principally on the quantity of labour required for their production." Later on he said that even wages enter into value. And finally, he ended up with a cost of production theory of value: "Profits.... as well as wages enter into the cost of production which determines the value of the produce."

   The criticism against Mill's Law of value is this. Wages and profits are monetary measures. The quantity of labour is physical amount. But Mill has lumped them together.

   In the case of those commodities whose supply is fixed for ever (Ricardo's non-reproducible commodities)—rare wines and old masters—Mill believed that their value depended on supply and demand and not on cost of production.

Mill has made an important contribution to the science of economics by modifying the law of demand and supply. The law tells that demand and supply cause a variation in price. Mill argued that it is equally true to say that the price causes a variation of demand and supply. Stated in this way, the law represents merely a vicious circle. Mill modified the law of supply and demand by saying that price is fixed at a *margin* where the quantity offered is equal to the quantity demanded. 'All price variations move about this point, just as the beam of balance oscillates about a point of equilibrium.' "The rise and fall continues until the demand and supply are again equal to one another." Mill thus gave the law of supply and demand a scientific precision.

The law of demand and supply explains only the variations of value. It does not explain the conception of value itself. For that, Mill looks into cost of production.

Mill believed that the law of supply and demand could be applied to money also. The temporary value of money depended on its supply (quantity in circulation) and demand (for exchange purposes). This is almost the quantity theory. But money has natural value too. The natural value of money, according to Mill, depends upon the cost of production of precious metals.

5. *The Law of Wages:* Mill's name is associated with wage-fund doctrine. Instead of saying that Mill originated the wage-fund doctrine, it may be right to say that he popularized the doctrine. Mill's statement of the wage-fund doctrine may be summarized as follows:

Wages depend mainly upon the demand and supply of labour. We may also say that wages, depend on the proportion between population and capital. According to Mill, "wages not only depend upon the relative amount of capital and population, but cannot under the rule of competition, be affected by anything else."

By population, Mill means here the number of the labouring class, or rather those who work for hire. By capital, he refers to that portion of the circulating capital which is set aside for the payment of wages, *i.e.*, the wage-fund.

Certain things follow from the wage-fund doctrine. The wage-fund doctrine was used to show that the attempts made by workers by means of trade union activity are useless. If workers in a section of industry manage to get an increase in wages by trade union activity, workers employed in other firms will be affected. The wage-fund, remaining the same, they will get lower wages. Further, wages can rise only at the expense of profits. When profits fall, savings will fall and this will affect the growth of capital. This, in turn, would affect the demand for labour. So the only way by which workers can improve their lot is by discouraging the growth of population. The influence of Malthusian theory can be seen here quite clearly.

The wage-fund doctrine was used as a basis for opposing trade unionism. But Mill believed that workers had every right to combine to raise their wages. So he abandoned the doctrine in later life.

The wage-fund concept is wrong because there is no predetermined proportion of capital that must go to labour.

6. *The Law of Rent:* Mill accepted Ricardo's law of rent. Like Ricardo, he believed that rent arose because of differences in fertility of land. In other words, he regarded rent as a differential surplus. Not only that, like Smith, he considered rent as the effect of monopoly because the landlord had 'exclusive power' over his land. And Mill emphasized the point that "the interest of the landlord is decidedly hostile to the sudden and general introduction of agricultural improvements."

7. *The Law of Profits:* Mill borrowed his law of profits from Nassau Senior. Senior considered profits as a reward for abstinence. We must note that in those days, economists made no distinction between profits and interest.

Profits are closely related to wages. Mill considered profits merely as a reward for abstinence; he believed it included wages of superintendence and reward for risk. He considered profits as a surplus after paying wages. Like Ricardo, he believed in the falling rate of profits. He also thought profits and wages varied inversely: "We thus arrive at the conclusion of Ricardo and others, that the rate of profits depends upon wages; rising as wages fall, and falling as wages rise."

8. *The Law of International Trade:* Mill developed Ricardian theory of international trade. Following Ricardo, he concluded that it was differences in comparative cost and not differences in absolute cost that gave rise to international trade. Mill went a step further and introduced the law of supply and demand into the field of international values. Mill believed that in the case of foreign commodities, the law that permanent value is determined by cost of production will not hold good. The value of foreign commodities depends rather upon the cost of producing the goods exchanged for them, that is, upon demand. In other words, according to Mill, international values obey a law of "equation of international demand." Again, in the words of Mill, "There is some proportion at which the demand of the two countries for each other's products will exactly correspond; so that the thing supplied.... will be completely paid for, and no more....". "Supply and demand are" in this case "but another expression for reciprocal demand."

Thus Mill concluded that trade equilibrium between two countries found each one exporting just enough to cover its imports. This was the "equation of international demand" or "The Law of International values."

Mill's law of international trade has provided the basis for new protectionist arguments. Mill himself suggested that the taxes on imports and exports might be so adjusted so that the former could bear the burden of taxes to a certain extent. But we have to remember that Mill was never an advocate of protection.

According to Jacob Viner, Mill's discussion of the relationship between reciprocal demand and the commodity terms of trade was in the main a pioneer achievement, and probably constitutes his chief claim to originality in the field of economics.

Stationary State

Mill, like other classical economists, described the stationary state. He thought that the increase of wealth must come to an end and society must enter upon a stationary condition. Improvements in technique, the law of diminishing returns, the accumulation of capital and the working of competition would combine to produce declining profits and rising rents. And if population growth is checked, there would be improvement in the conditions of working classes too.

Mill believed that the progressive state in which population and output rose was not conducive to improvement in the quality of life. On the other hand, the stationary state, characterized by stability of capital and population provided vast scope for human development and improvement in the quality of life. Mill believed that in a stationary state, there would be no competitive struggle and wealth would be evenly divided. In short, Mill looked upon the stationary state as a state of blissful equilibrium.

Mill's Individualist-Socialist Programme

Mill was not merely a political economist, he was a great social reformer. His sympathies were with labour and he was a supporter of working class movement. He often spoke of socialism with respect. He developed his economic ideas relating to socialism from leading socialist thinkers. For instance, he borrowed his ideas regarding the doctrines of heredity and unearned increment from Saint Simonians. From Sismondi, he learnt to develop his sympathy with peasant proprietorship. And he borrowed the idea of co-operative association from the socialists of 1848.

Mill strongly believed that the division of human race into two hereditary classes—employers and employed—cannot be permanently maintained. He believed that a day would come when labourers and capitalists would become partners in a co-operative enterprise or finally, there might be association of labourers among themselves. While discussing communism, Mill commented, "If the choice were to be made between communism with all its chances and the present (1852) state of society with all its sufferings and injustices, if the institution of private property necessarily carried with it as a consequence, the produce of labour should be apportioned as we now see it, almost in an inverse ratio to the labour.... if this or communism were the alternative, all the difficulties, great or small, of communism would be but as dust in the balance."

Though Mill was attracted towards socialism, we have to remember that he remained faithful to a liberal economy. His belief in individualism, free competition and *laissez-faire* made him adopt a peculiar socialist programme with emphasis on individual enterprise. That is why, his socialist programme has been described as 'individualist-socialist programme.'

To find a theoretical basis for advocating social reform, Mill has made a distinction between the laws of production and the laws of distribution. According to Mill, "The laws and conditions of the production of wealth, partake of character of physical truths. There is nothing optional or arbitrary in them.... It is not so with the distribution of wealth. That is a matter of human institution solely. The things once there, mankind, individually or collectively, can do with them as they like." (*Principles:* Book III).

It has been criticized that Mill did not see that production and distribution are interrelated and that interference with one involves interference with another. But we have to note that by making the distinction between the nature of the laws of production and distribution, Mill challenged the assumption of the classical economists that the laws of economics were of universal application and permanent in character. By saying that the laws of distribution were a matter of human institutions, Mill implied that redistribution of wealth could be carried out in an equitable manner by suitably changing the laws of distribution.

Mill aimed at reducing the inequalities of income and wealth, without at the same time affecting the individual liberty of action.

Mill's programme of social policy may be summarized as follows:

1. *Abolition of the wage system and the substitution of a cooperative association of producers:* Mill considered wage-system the enemy of progress for it deprived man of all interest in the product of his labour. Mill borrowed that ideal of co-operative community from the French socialists.

2. *The Socialization of rent by means of a tax on land:* This proposal was based mainly on the Ricardian theory of rent which considered rent as a differential surplus. Mill suggested a tax on land which would gradually absorb rent. The tax could be increased whenever there was increase in rents. This brilliant and revolutionary idea was used by the socialists to attack the landlords who were earning large incomes by way of rent. Mill advocated peasant proprietorship.

3. *Lessening of the inequalities of wealth by restrictions on the rights of inheritance:* Mill considered the right of inheritance, one of the basic obstacles to individual liberty and a source of danger to free competition, because it placed competitors in positions of unequal advantage. He believed that the 'accident of birth' should not determine the fortunes of persons on earth. As the right of inheritance is one of the basic causes of inequalities of wealth, Mill advocated restrictions on the right of inheritance. He argued that nobody should be allowed to inherit above a certain sum.

Mill believed that his above proposals of social reform would not conflict with the individualistic principle.

Conclusion

According to Cossa, Mill's "Principles" is "the best resume, the fullest, most complete and most exact exposition of the doctrines of the classical school that we have...." Mill was not only the last great economist of the classical school, he was the greatest of the orthodox economists during the two generations between Ricardo and Marshall. He did for Ricardo what J. B. Say had done for Adam Smith—*i.e.*, systematisation and popularization. Besides, he was an outstanding political scientist, social reformer, philosopher and a champion of liberty. Above all, he was "the first distinguished liberal economist with socialist leanings. He may be considered as a forerunner of Fabian socialism."

THE HISTORICAL SCHOOL

The historical school was dominant in Germany in the second half of the nineteenth century. The historical school was a revolt against the method and analysis of classical economics. Roscher, a Gottingen Professor, may be regarded as the founder of the school. The historical school, for the sake of convenience, has been divided into (*i*) the older Historical school, and (*ii*) the Newer (younger) Historical school. Roscher, Hildebrand and Knies "all belonged to the older school and Schmoller became the leader of the Newer Historical school. Even Friedrich List may be considered as a member of the Historical school. But on account of his emphasis on national problems, he has been dealt with in a separate chapter on nationalists. The term "Historical School" refers to "all those economists who emphasize the relativity of laws and institutions, the inductive method of reasoning from concrete historical data, and the interrelations among human motives and among the social sciences." (Haney).

The Social Background of Historical School

Germany became the home of the historical school because social, political and economic climate of the day was ideal for the birth of the historical school.

After the Napoleonic wars, there was a peace treaty. After the peace treatry, Germany was divided into thirty-nine states. Most of them were monarchical and undemocratic. Those German states, except Prussia, were weak and undivided. The struggle against Napoleon aroused feelings of patriotism and nationalism in Germany. Prussia, which was the largest, richest and most powerful state dominated Germany. The natives of Germany looked forward to Prussia to bring about the unification of Germany. So under the leadership of Prussia, nationalism became a strong force.

Further, some of the important economic institutions of nineteenth century Germany differed from those of Britain. So the same economic ideology could not be applied to both the countries. For instance, mercantilist policies were followed in Germany until 1871, even thought Britain gave it up a long time ago. Again, the economic analysis of classical economists was based on the assumptions of competition and freedom of enterprise. But economic life in Germany was subject to a number of regulations and the above analysis based on competition and freedom of enterprise appeared unrealistic in the context of the German situation. So the Germans felt that there was a wide gap between economic theory as taught in classical economics and concrete economic reality. As the history of Germany was different from the history of Britain, they thought the classical doctrines were irrelevant and inapplicable to Germany. So all these things made Germans attach more importance to nationality and history in economic analysis.

The Origin and Development of German Historical School
Wilhelm Roscher (1817-1894)

Roscher was the founder of the "Older historical school." This group wanted to supplement classical theory with historical facts. Roscher became Professor of political economy at Gottingen and later at Leipzig. He did not repudiate classical economic theory completely. What he tried to do was to find the historical basis for the abstract deductive economics of the classical school.

According to Roscher, "Political Economy is the science which deals with the laws of the development of the economy of a nation or with its economic national life." And one cannot understand the economic life of a nation unless one understands its language, religion, art, science, laws, the state and economy.... Thus, Roscher believed that Political Economy can be explained only in the closest relation to other sciences like history, jurisprudence, politics and civilization.

Roscher believed that by making historical comparisons, we can learn many lessons. Further the thorough application of the historical method will do away with a great number of controversies on important questions. Economic laws are not absolute truths. They are only relative. Each people and age has its own peculiar economy. The economist must be content to state the rules of government which are applicable to his particular economy, and are based on a study of various stages of industrial evolution.

Bruno Hildebrand (1812-1870)

Hildebrand was a German Professor. He was one of the early founders of the historical school. His book "The National Economy of Present and Future" appeared in 1848. In it, he challenged the teachings of classical economists and asserted that history could be used for the reconstruction of political economy.

Hildebrand found fault with Smith for believing (just like the Mercantilists and Physiocrats before him) that economic theories would apply to all times and places. The classical economists have forgotten the fact that a man, as a social being, is always a child of civilization and a product of history. Hildebrand believed that the "laws of development" should be the basis of political economy. Accordingly, he classified economic development into three phases—natural economy, money economy and credit economy. He considered the present money economy as a transitional stage. Credit economy will mark the complete stage of development.

Karl Knies (1821-1892)

Karl Knies was the most thorough expositor of the historical method of the older school. His book "Political Economy from the Historical Standpoint" appeared in 1853.

Knies denied the existence of natural laws. He believed that economic laws were only relative. They were not of universal application. They would not hold good at all times, in all places and circumstances. He criticized even Hildebrand's law of development. He is of the view that no complete parallelism between the past and the present exists. According to Knies, "Political Economy is simply a history of ideas concerning the economic development of a nation at different periods of its growth."

While the classical economists believed in the harmony of interests, Knies argued that self-interest was often in conflict with social welfare. Further Knies emphasized the importance of social institutions in studying the problem of distribution.

The early founders of historical school devoted a great deal of attention to the criticism of the classical method. They were for a theory of evolution and historical investigation. But they failed to agree on the aim and scope of political economy. They left it to the younger group of historical school to apply their principles.

The Newer Historical School

The Newer Historical school came into existence at the end of the 19th century in Germany. Gustav Schmoller was the leader of the new school.

The Newer Historical school abandoned the controversy concerning economic laws. They did not deny the existence of natural laws. But they agreed with their predecessors regarding their criticism of the classical assumptions and methods. They doubted even 'the laws of development' stressed by Hildebrand. As Schmoller put it, "We have no knowledge of the laws of history although we sometimes speak of economic and statistical laws." Further, the members of the "younger historical school" were not content merely with advocating the use of historical method. They wanted to put theory into practice.

Schmoller (1838-1917)

Gustav Schmoller was the leader of the "Newer Historical School." He was a professor at many German universities. Schmoller opposed the deductive method tooth and nail. In fact, he entered into a great debate with Carl Menger, the founder of the Austrian Marginalist School over the question of method. While Schmoller advocated inductive method, Menger supported deductive method. The debate was called the *Battle of Methods*. In a pamphlet called "Errors of Historicism", while defending theoretical analysis, Menger wrote: "The historians have stepped upon the territory of our science like foreign conquerors, in order to force upon us their language and their customs, their terminology and their methods, and to fight intolerantly every branch of enquiry which does not correspond with their special method." This controversy over method aroused many bitter feelings and ultimately it was resolved that both inductive and deductive methods are important and they supplement each other.

Schmoller emphasized on historical research in his book "Political Economy and Its method" published in 1894.

"The historical sciences provide empirical material and data which transform the scholar from a mere beggar into a rich man as far as knowledge of the reality is concerned. And it is this historical empirical material which, like all good observation and description, serve to illustrate and verify theoretical conclusions, to demonstrate the limitations of the validity of certain truths, and more than anything else, to obtain inductively new truths. This applies particularly to the more complicated fields of political economy, in which it is possible to advance only on the basis of historical investigations....."

Schmoller advocated social reform. And he believed that a more equitable distribution of income should be the guiding principle of social reform. He accused the older historical school of attempting to apply the lessons of history too quickly. He pleaded for much more historical study in order to establish an empirical basis for national economic theory.

The Essential Ideas of the Historical School

The essential ideas of the historical school have been divided into *critical ideas* and *positive ideas*.

Critical Ideas of the School

1. The classical economists believed that the laws of economics were of universal application. The Historical school argued that there was no justification for such a belief. According to them, economic laws were relative but not absolute. The historical school thus criticized the 'universalism' and 'absolutism' of the classical school. They thought that the laws of economics are always subject to change both in theory and practice. Economic laws are provisional and conditional. For instance, according to Knies, "The conditions of economic life determine the form and character of economic theory. Both the process of argument employed and the results arrived at are products of historical development.... The generalisations of economics are simply historical explanations and progressive manifestations of truth. Each step is a generalisation of the truth as it is known at that particular stage of development. No single formula and no collection of such formulae can ever claim to be final." Thus Knies has applied the doctrine of relativity to economics. The laws of economics are not as precise as the laws of physics and chemistry. Even Marshall defined an economic laws as a "statement of tendencies."

2. Another charge that is made against the classical school is that its laws are based on crude psychology. Adam Smith and other leading economists of the classical school believed that man was motivated by self-interest in his economic activity. The historical school argued that it was not always the case. There are other equally important motives such as desire for glory, the sense of duty, patriotism, love or simply custom. So it is not correct to say that man is always guided by selfish motives.

3. Lastly, historical school criticized the use of the deductive method by the classical school. They believed, in general, inductive method was better than deductive method. Of course, the controversy over the method no longer exists today. Discussion of method is considered today as a pure waste of time. According to Pareto, "The aim of the science is to discover economic uniformities, and it is always right to follow any path or to pursue any method that is likely to lead to that end." In fact, after a long debate over method Schmoller himself has said: "*Induction*

and deduction are both necessary for the science, just as the right and left foot are needed for walking."

The Positive Ideas of the School

The positive contributions made by the historical school are more important than its criticisms of the classical school.

1. We can study economic phenomena either from a mechanical approach or from an organic approach. The mechanical view does not explain the concrete reality. Its main weakness is that 'it isolates man's economic activity, but neglects his environment.' The historical school developed the organic approach. The production and distribution of wealth in a country depends upon so many factors—geographical situation, its natural resources, human endowments, the system of government and so on. As economic and other social phenomena are interdependent, we cannot study political economy separately except in combination with other social sciences. The historical school claimed that the historical method allowed it to study all aspects of an economic phenomenon.

   The Historical school believed in the words of Goethe: "A person who has no knowledge of the three thousand years of history which have gone by must remain content to dwell in obscurity, living a hand-to-mouth existence." We must know something about the previous stages of economic development if we are to understand the economic life of the present. In the words of Hildebrand, one of the founders of the historical school, "Man as a social being is the child of civilization and a product of history. His wants, his intellectual outlook, his relation to material objects and his connexion with other human beings have not always been the same. Geography influences them, history modifies them, while the progress of education may entirely transform them."

2. The historical school developed an evolutionary approach to the study of society. As the society is constantly changing, an economic doctrine or policy that is applicable for one country at a particular time may not be applicable for another country or another age. Thus by making use of the doctrine of relativity, the historical school tried to demonstrate that classical economic ideas which were suitable for England were not suitable for Germany.

3. The historical school promoted nationalism. The classical school was individualistic, whereas the historical school was nationalistic. That is why, while the classical economists advocated *laissez-faire*, the historical school advocated state intervention and even protection. We must also note one thing. At the same time, the historical school came into existence, Britain and Germany were in different stages of economic development. England already became an industrial power and the workshop of the world. But Germany was just then experiencing industrial revolution. So *laissez-faire* policy, which implied a free trade policy was advantageous for Britain to dump her goods in Germany. But Germany found it advantageous to have state intervention to protect her infant industries by means of protection.

Conclusion

According to Eric Roll, "Their one positive achievement was to stimulate research in economic history." The historical school had great influence on some leading theoretical economists like Alfred Marshall. However, one main criticism against the historical school is that there is over-emphasis on historical element in their studies. "History tells of sequences and coincidences; but reason alone can interpret and draw lessons from them." Through its nationalism, the historical school promoted German unification and economic growth. Today the historical inductive method has become complementary to the abstract deductive approach. Marx made great use of the historical method. In fact, his 'Das Kapital' may be considered a study in historical synthesis.

Though the ideas of historical school spread to England and France, they have never struck root there.

Lastly, the economists of the historical school are to be thanked for their valuable studies in economic history. These studies have provided us data for verifying and correcting the theory of the classical economists.

THE NATIONALISTS

The Nationalists were the politico-economic writers of the first half of the nineteenth century. They were found largely outside England, especially in Germany. The Nationalists were critics of the classical school. They attacked the individualism, cosmopolitanism and the free-trade doctrines of the classical economists. They advocated steps to increase the productive powers of the nations. While the classical economists looked at national wealth merely as the sum of wealth of individuals, the Nationalists considered individuals merely as dependent parts of the nation and thought that the wealth of the individuals depended upon the wealth and welfare of the nation. Thus the nationalists subordinated the interests of the individuals, to the interests of the nation.

The Social and Political Background of the School

At the beginning of the nineteenth century, the weakness of extreme individualism, and *Laissez-faire* in dealing with the practical problems of the day such as unemployment, poverty and war came to light. This gave rise to the emergence of liberal social reformers, socialists and Nationalists. The Nationalists aimed at increasing the aggregate productive powers of the nation.

Further, at the beginning of the nineteenth century, there was a lot of inequality among nations in their industrial development. The Nationalists suggested steps for promoting the industrial development of their nations. Those steps included protective tariffs. In fact, in some respects, Nationalism resembles Mercantilism. But we must remember that Nationalism was philosophically more sophisticated than Mercantilism.

Germany became the centre of Nationalism and it revolted against the teachings of Adam Smith and other classical writers which were more suitable for England than Germany. Germany at that time was industrially backward and it was a predominantly agricultural country. Not only that, Germany was divided into a number of weak states fighting against each other. The ultimate aim of the nationalists was unification of Germany so that it would become a mighty industrial power on par with Britain.

Among the nationalists, there were two groups: (*i*) *Philosophic* Nationalists. Muller was the most important of them. They stood for the ideals of stability and permanence. (*ii*) *The Protectionists:* List was the champion of the school. The protectionists emphasized the role of protective tariffs in the industrial development of the nation.

Adam Muller (1779-1829)

Adam Muller was the most important of the early nationalists who attacked classicism. Muller belonged to the school of philosophical nationalists or Romanticists as they were known in Germany.

Muller was born in 1779 in Berlin. He studied in Berlin and Gottingen. He entered government service after studying Law. He died in 1829.

Muller opposed the cosmopolitanism of Adam Smith. He was interested in the creation strong and wealthy state. In other words, he was interested in increasing the *wealth of his* not *wealth of nations.* He advocated protection towards this end.

In the philosophy of Muller, "the State comes first, and the individual has only signific relation to the State" (Alexander Gray). As the State is centre of all things, the problems of produ and distribution should be considered only in relation to the State.

Muller advocated the use of paper money instead of gold or silver because the latte cosmopolitan in character. Paper money on the other hand promotes the nationality. "World-m or metallic money, on the contrary, fosters the illusion that the holder's interests are dependent stream of world trade, and thus conceals the fact that he is much more directly dependent o internal trade of his own country and on his own sovereign. Gold and silver encourage the belie wherever the language of metallic gold is heard, there is a man's fatherland; paper money atta him to his own soil" (A. Gray, p. 327). "He even values war, because it brings into prominence ideas of the State and the nation as a whole" (Haney). In Muller's own words, "perpetual p cannot be an ideal of politics. Peace and War should supplement each other like rest and motion wonder ideas like these became powerful tools in the hands of Nazis for strengthening the machinery.

Muller was a great admirer of the Middle Ages. He wanted the world to go back to the Mid Ages. He considered money, Roman institutions and material luxuries as corruptors of man hated change. He was interested in the permanence of institutions. He was an admirer of u institutions, because according to him, the guilds and corporations of Middle Ages and the land. tenant relationships bounded men together. He was of the opinion that the poorer feudal set up were better off than in the money economy. One of the chief contributions economic thought is that he fought against the tendencies of modern economists to over goods and material enjoyment. One major criticism against Muller is that "he regarded the Ages as representing the normal condition of economic life for all times" (Haney).

Friedrich List (1789-1846)

List was the leader of the protectionist group among the nationalists. We may also consider him as the forerunner of the historical school.

By the middle of the 19th century, the doctrines of Adam Smith became popular in Europe Almost all accepted the classical doctrine of Free Trade. List in his book, "The National System of Political Economy" (1840) attacked the doctrine of Free Trade and advocated the policy of protection

List was born in Wurtemberg in 1789. He did not receive much of formal education either at school or college. He entered civil service at an early age and by his ability and hardwork attained a respectable position in government. In 1818, he became Professor of political science at the University of Tubingen. As university professor, List started attacking the bureaucratic methods and reactionary policies of the government in Wurtemberg. His anti-governmental views caused his dismissal in 1819. List then became active in promoting a strong political and commercial union of the German States. He worked for the abolition of internal customs tariffs which crippled the internal trade of Germany. List was elected to the State Legislature in 1820. As a member of the State Legislature, he advocated some administrative and fiscal reforms which were considered radical in those days. For instance, he advocated abolition of tolls on roads, state ownership of industries, taxes on feudal property, excise duties, a reduction in the number of civil service officers and a single direct income tax to meet the expenses of the government. These views were considered treasonable and he was put in prison. Later he was deported. List emigrated to America. He bought a farm and settled down in Pennsylvania. There he became an editor and a speculator in coal mines and railways. List lived in America from

1825 to 1832. The protectionist ideas of List gained more popularity in America than in Germany. List returned to Germany in 1832.

After his return to Germany, List advocated a railway network for Germany. He even gave a plan for railway development in 1833. He was happy to note that the Customs Union of the German States (*Zollvereiss*) was established in 1834. This he considered as the foundation of German unity. Towards the end of his life, List was unhappy because of the delay in German unification. Besides he suffered from ill health and financial difficulties and he committed suicide in 1846.

Economic Ideas of List

"The National System of Political Economy" (1840) is the great work of List. To understand the economic ideas of List, it is essential to understand the conditions of Germany in the nineteenth century. Germany was predominantly an agricultural country at that time and it was divided into a number of states. Those states, except Prussia, were not only weak but they were politically and economically divided.

List believed that political unity, that is, unification of Germany was absolutely essential for economic development of Germany. He considered the union of England and Scotland as one of the chief causes of the economic development of Great Britain. But Germany was divided into a number of states and separated by tariff walls: "Thirty-eight customs boundaries cripple inland trade, and produce much the same effect as ligatures which prevent the free circulation of the blood" (List). In a petition, List stated that, "In short, while other nations cultivate the sciences and arts whereby commerce and industry are extended, German merchants and manufacturers must devote a great part of their time to the study of domestic tariffs and taxes." Further, while there were so many internal tariffs, there was almost the complete absence of import duties. While the German states were closed to one another, owing to the absence of effective central control, they were open to other nations. For instance, after the French Revolution, the Restoration government of France imposed protective tariffs. So driven from France, Britain began to dump her goods on the German market at very low prices. The German merchants and manufacturers became alarmed and pleaded for economic unity and a uniform tariff and protection. It is in this context that we must study the ideas of List. List's book "National System" advocating protection appeared at the psychological moment. The backward condition of Germany made List the champion of economic nationalism.

List has developed his theories on two new basic ideas: (*i*) The idea of nationality as contrasted with that of cosmopolitanism, and (*ii*) The idea of productive power as contrasted with that of exchange values.

(*i*) *The Idea of Nationality versus Cosmopolitanism:* List rejected the liberal cosmopolitanism of Adam Smith on the ground that it ignored the nation. The individual's position depended on the strength of national power. But Adam Smith and his followers were interested in cosmopolitan or universal economy. Adam Smith was interested in the 'Wealth of Nations.' That is, he was interested in nations in general, or mankind. List felt that it was not a right approach. Nation must be the centre of the study. For it exists as a separate entity. Not only that, nations go to war with one another and do take advantage of one another when they can. National life is the basis of present life. Hence political economy must study the problems of national economy.

Classification of Nations according to Stages of Economic Development

List has divided nations into five categories according to the "degrees of culture" or "economic stages." According to List, Nations could be divided into five stages: (*i*) The savage stage, (*ii*) the pastoral stage, (*iii*) the agricultural stage, (*iv*) the agricultural and manufacturing stage, and (*v*) the agricultural-manufacturing-commercial stage.

List believed that a nation would become '*normal*' only when it attained the last stage. That was the ideal stage. Only when a nation attained that stage, it could support vast population, develop arts and sciences and retain its independence and power. In other words, it would attain nationality only then. List did not think that all nations could attain the highest stage of development. For instance, he thought that some of the tropical countries should be content to remain agricultural countries. But other countries such as Germany and America possessed the necessary material and human resources for development and they could reach the highest stage of development where there would be equilibrium between agriculture, manufacture, and commerce. List believed that a nation could not attain the highest stage of development in a spontaneous manner. The State should act so as to bring about it. So List rejected the *laissez-faire* doctrine of Adam Smith.

(ii) Exchange Values and Productive Power

List makes a distinction between exchange values and productive power. According to him, "The national power should not be estimated in terms of exchange value." What was important for a nation was not so much the actual amount of material wealth which it possessed but its productive power. The productive power depends upon the ability of a nation to replace what had been consumed. Each nation should take care to see that its future progress is assured. List believed that "the power of creating wealth is infinitely more important than the wealth itself." Sometimes a nation must sacrifice some present advantages so that it may derive more advantages in future.

List accused Adam Smith for emphasizing only on exchange values and not on productive powers. According to List, the productive powers of a nation depended upon many things such as moral and political institutions, liberty, control of government and parliamentary government. Above all, List gave top priority for manufactures in the category of productive power. "His theory of the importance of the productive power led him to postulate as ideal an equilibrium between the different branches of production." (Eric Roll). List believed that manufacturing alone would bring about the balanced development of all productive powers in a nation. Both manufacture and agriculture were essential for a nation. But without the development of manufacturing industry, other branches of production would not develop. Industry led to agricultural improvement and to a development of art and science. The true principle of division of labour must try to have a balance between agriculture and industry. List criticized Adam Smith's conception of division of labour as one-sided. After establishing the importance of manufacturing industry in developing the productive powers of a nation, List advocated the need for protection to develop industry.

It may be interesting to note here that List believed that in certain cases, military preparations, wars and war debts may increase the productive powers of a country. He gave England as an example. War increased the productive powers of England so much that the increased values it received annually far exceeded the interests on its increased war debts.

List's Ideas on Protectionism

List advocated a policy of protectionism in general. He believed that Germany could become a strong manufacturing country only by adopting a policy of protectionism. The essence of List's ideas on protectionism are given below:

1. The policy of protection should be adopted in a nation only if it had the natural basis for industry and its progress had been retarded by the competition of a powerful rival which had advanced in the industrial path. This is the famous infant industry argument. German industry was in an infant stage when compared with England which was a mature industrial nation. So, German industry should be protected against 'dumping' of goods by England.

2. Protection can be justified only when it aims at the industrial education of a nation. For instance, protection is not necessary for a country like England where industrial education is complete. Again, it is unnecessary for countries which do not have either the resources or aptitude for development. For example, List cites the countries in the tropical zone. They can at best be only agricultural countries.

3. Protection should be used to nurse only infant industries. When they grow strong enough to meet competition from rivals, protection should be writhdrawn. Of course, after that, protection

may be introduced only when it is necessary for protecting the inland manufacturing power in its very roots.

4. Lastly, it may be interesting to note that List was against protection for agriculture. He strongly believed that protection should not be granted to agriculture. He argued that agriculture benefited greatly from the existence of a powerful industry in the nation. And industry required cheap food and raw materials. And protection will raise the prices of food and raw materials. Further, differences in soil and climate gave agriculture a kind of natural protection. Not only that, protection was thought of as a temporary policy during a transitional stage. Since the ultimate aim was the highest development, there would be no need for protection for agriculture because when once a nation attained the highest stage of development, the policy of protectionism should be replaced by a system of universal free trade. So List opposed the idea of protection for agriculture.

Conclusion

The real originality of List consists in the fact that, "He was the first to make systematic use of historical comparison as a means of demonstration in political economy." (Gide and Rist). He has been rightly regarded as the forerunner of the historical school. By popularizing the idea of the stages of economic growth, List pointed out the need for State action and intervention to assist a nation to pass from a lower to a higher stage against the competition of more advanced nation. "Even as a scientific economist, List, however, had one of the elements of greatness namely the grand vision of national situation...." (Schumpeter).

SISMOND
(1773-1842)

Life and Works

Sismondi was a Swiss economist and historian. He was a leading critic of the classical school. Sometimes, he is also described as a socialist.

Sismondi was born in Geneva, Switzerland, in 1773. His father was a protestant clergyman. During the revolutionary Disturbance (1793-94) he and his family took refuge in England. On their return to Switzerland, they sold most of their property and left for Italy. In Italy, they bought a small farm. There Sismondi became something of a small fermer. Later he returned to Geneva. Sismondi was primarily an historian. His main historical works were: (*i*) History of the Italian Republic of the Middle Ages (16 volumes), and (*ii*) History of the French (29 volumes).

In his early years, Sismondi was a follower of Adam Smith and an ardent admirer of the class doctrines. It was only during his later years that he launched a direct attack on classical economics. Sismondi's reputation as an economist rests on his book "New Principles of Political Economy" which appeared in 1819. He lived until 1842.

Background

Sismondi was a contemporary of great economists like Malthus, Ricardo, J. B. Say and List.

Great events took place during the lifetime of Sismondi. He witnessed the French Revolution, the Napoleonic wars, the Industrial Revolution and the factory system. He noted the evils of wage-slavery and factory-system. Not only that, since 1815, economic crises (business fluctuations) became a common feature in English market. So poverty and economic crises became two important new facts. Critics started questioning the assumption of classical economists regarding the harmony interests. Even the doctrine of *laissez-faire* was found to be useless in dealing with new development. Sismondi tried to give an explanation of economic crises and suggested certain remedies too. shall now discuss the essential economic ideas of Sismondi in detail.

ECONOMIC IDEAS OF SISMONDI

The Aim and Method of Political Economy

According to Sismondi, political economy has a moral purpose. It is not concer such, but with wealth in relation to man. We must study about wealth in its rela charge against the classical economists is that they had taught only how to incr and they did not teach how to increase *national happiness*. Sismondi considere important than any other branch of economics. He believed that governmen progress of wealth in order to promote social justice.

According to Sismondi, "The wealth of a nation depended upon its enjoyment or happiness." Wealth is produced only to promote welfare or happiness. And happiness can be promoted by increase in consumption. So consumption plays an important role in Sismondi's economic analysis.

With regard to the method of economic analysis, Sismondi attacked Ricardo for being too abstract in his method. But he praised Adam Smith and Malthus. He said that "Smith attempted to study every fact in the light of its own social environment and his immortal work is, indeed, the outcome of a philosophic study of the history of mankind." He praised even Malthus who "possessed a singularly forceful and penetrative mind, had cultivated the habit of a conscientious study of facts."

Sismondi's Criticism of Classical School

The following are the main points of Sismondi's criticism of the economic ideas of classical school.

1. The teaching of classical economists encouraged unlimited production which resulted in over-production and economic crisis.

2. They advocated free competition which was another cause of over-production.

3. They preached the doctrine of harmony of interests which was not true. In an industrial society, he argued, class conflict was the rule.

4. The classical economists believed that the best form of government was no government at all. In other words, they advocated *laissez-faire*. Sismondi attacked the policy of *laissez-faire* and advocated State intervention.

The Idea of Class Conflict

Sismondi did not believe in harmony of social interests. On the other had, he was one of the early economists to speak of the existence of two social classes, the rich and the poor-the capitalists and the workers. He thought the interests of these two classes were opposed to each other and they were in constant conflict with one another. In fact, Marx and Engels, in their *Communist Manifesto,* acknowledged their indebtedness to Sismondi for formulating the idea of class conflict. Sismondi emphasized the point that small and independent workers on the farm and in the workshop were disappearing because of severe competition from capitalists who controlled large-scale industry. The concentration of capital in the hands of a few persons ruined the small-scale producers. And society has been divided into two classes—the owners and the proletariat. Property and labour are separated.

The Theory of Over-Production

This is the central idea of Sismondi. Sismondi feels that there is something fundamentally wrong in the conditions of capitalistic production. The inherent contractions in the system lead to over-production. The over-production which Sismondi speaks of is a general over-production of all commodities, and not merely over-production of certain commodities. By stating the idea of general over-production, Sismondi attacks Say's Law of Markets which rules out general over-production. Say's Law of Markets implies a full employment equilibrium. But Sismondi warns, "Let us beware of this dangerous theory of equilibrium which is supposed to be automatically established. A certain kind of equilibrium, if it is true, is re-established in the long run, but it is only after a frightful amount of "suffering."

According to Sismondi, over-production is the result of *three* causes: (*i*) *competition. It makes difficult for the producer to know the exact size of demand.* (*ii*) *Capital and not want that determines production* and (*iii*) *the separation of labour and ownership of capital.* According to Sismondi, "Production is based on the extent of capital at the disposal of the producer." Before determining the size of production, the producer must try to anticipate the size of demand for his commodity. But he does not bother himself to ask the question whether there will be enough demand for a commodity when it is produced. What he is interested to know is whether he is capable of producing more. So he goes on producing. There is also another problem. It is easier to expand production than to contract.

For a variety of reasons, it is almost impossible to restrict the size of firm or to close down. This accentuates the problem of over-production. So, he argues that over-production takes place because production is carried on not according to demand but according to the availability of capital.

Sismondi makes a distinction between annual production and annual revenue and tells that the annual production of any year is bought by the revenue of the preceding year. This, of course, is a wrong distinction and wrong belief. Sismondi tells that to avoid economic crisis, there must be an equilibrium between production and consumption. Nations may be ruined either by spending too much or too little. Sismondi's theory of over-production is essentially a doctrine of under-consumption. Sismondi is one of the early contributors to the business cycle theory.

The concentration of wealth in the hands of a few, narrows home market more and more, and so the industrialists are compelled to open up foreign markets. This results in nationalistic wars. Sismondi then developed the thesis that economic imperialism is inherent in capitalism.

Sismondi's theory of over-production is criticized on the ground that it is based on the distinction between annual production and annual revenue. But, we know that basically a nation's annual revenue is its annual production. Further, it is not the produce of two different years that is exchanged but the various products of the same year.

On Machinery

Almost all the classical writers considered machinery a great blessing to mankind. But Sismondi was of the opinion that at times machinery could cause unemployment and misery. The immediate effect of the introduction of machinery is to throw some workers out of employment. Then there will be more number of workers competing for fewer jobs. This would lower the wages of workers. This, in turn, would result in diminishing consumption and a slackening of demand. So machinery is not always beneficial. It will produce useful results only when its introduction is preceded by an increased revenue, and consequently by the possibility of giving new work to those displaced.

Sismondi and Malthusian Theory of Population

Sismondi attacked the Malthusian theory of population which is based on the assumption that population is limited by the means of subsistence. He argued that population would not increase at a faster rate than food supply. According to Sismondi, *"population depends on revenue."* In the industrial setup labour is separated from ownership. So the labourers are dependent on the capitalist for their revenue. They are at the mercy of the capitalist and in order to live they must accept any wages that are offered to them. The supply of labor is determined by the demand of the capitalist for wage labour. The worker has no control over his revenue. When the worker is independent, he has control over his revenue. He knows his present position and can estimate his future prospects. He can determine when to marry and produce children. Since labour and capital are separated, revenue is under the control of the capitalist. And it depends on the capitalists' demand for labour. So the capitalist who controls revenue can indirectly control the size of the population.

Role of Government

Sismondi opposed *laissez-faire* and advocated state intervention in the economic field. He believed that state intervention would guarantee the worker a living wage and social security. He thought that mere increase in aggregate production of wealth would not automatically increase the greatest happiness of the people. A smaller output with equitable distribution would promote greater happiness. He wanted the State to pass laws to regulate distribution. He believed that small-scale farming would promote good distribution of income. He was opposed to the idea of tenant farming. He advocated small-scale production in industry so as to avoid over-production. He favoured inheritance taxes. Since the new machinery often brought unemployment and caused over-production, he advised the government to curb new inventions by discontinuing patent rights. He insisted on the government to compel employers to provide security for their workers in old age, illness and unemployment. He even advocated that workers must get a share in profits.

idi and Socialism

smondi a socialist? There are two divergent views on this question. While some writers place mong socialists, others regard him merely as a leading critic of capitalistic doctrines and as a social reformer. Prof. Knies, one of the founders of Historical school, described Sismondi as a socialist. Haney is of the opinion that though Sismondi's influence was felt by the socialists, he was ocialist. In Haney's words, "Indeed, he has sometimes been wrongly classified as one."

It is true that Sismondi's sympathies were with labour. He spoke of the exploitation of labour. arguments often run like that of Marxism. He has expressed the view that labour is the source of weal' s explained how concentration of capital takes place. He has advocated government ll these ideas have, no doubt, influenced socialist thought. But he rejected Socialism.

ondi rejected communism. For he believed in the importance of private interest. He did vocate abolition of private property. He wanted to see a revival of the small and independent lucers and farmers.

nclusion

Gray is right in saying that "Sismondi as a writer of economics, is extremely difficult to hile having kinship with many schools, he is consequently at home with none" (A. Gray). best a social reformer, who stood for social security. To achieve this end, he advocated ntrol over economic life. He thought that the price system would not automatically produce test happiness of the people. He put consumption before production. And he attributed duction and economic crisis and the resulting disequilibrium to under-consumption. be regarded as a pioneer of the under-consumption theories. The remedy he suggested was to consumption relatively to production. Finally, he advocated redistribution of wealth without olutionary changes in the existing institutions. In short, he was a historian turned social reformer.

UTOPIAN SOCIALISM

Introduction

Socialistic ideas can be found even in the works of ancient writers. For instance, Plato, that eminent philosopher of Greece, had he been alive today, he would have been the reddest of the reds. He pleaded not only for abolition of private property but opposed even the institution of marriage in the case of the rulers. In fact, he advocated the idea of 'community of wives.' But socialism as a dominant social and economic philosophy is only of recent origin. It is essentially a nineteenth century product. Of course, socialist ideas were gaining ground towards the end of the eighteenth century.

The socialists, in general oppose *laissez-faire*. They advocate State intervention. They do not believe in the harmony of interests among different classes. They recognize the existence of class conflict. They advocate collective action and public ownership. And they believe in the perfectibility of man. There is a touch of idealism about their programmes.

Social Background of Socialism

The Industrial Revolution took place in England roughly during the period 1750 to 1850. Factory system came into existence and large-scale production became the rule. There is no doubt that the wealth of England increased. But there was terrible concentration of wealth in the hands of a few people. The rich became richer and the poor poorer. And there was exploitation of workers in the form of low wages, long hours of work, employment of child and women labour and so on. But the State did not do anything to reduce the suffering of the working masses owing to its *laissez-faire* policy. Disease, hunger and misery became the lot of workers. There were no political rights for women and they had no right of association in the form of trade unions. All these things gave birth to socialistic ideas.

Before we study about utopian socialism, in detail, it may be useful to know briefly about different forms of socialism.

Forms of Socialism

There are different forms of socialism: 1. State socialism, 2. Utopian socialism, 3. Christian socialism, 4. Anarchism, 5. Marxian Socialism, 6. Communism, 7. Revisionism, 8. Syndicalism, 9. Guild Socialism, and 10. Socialistic pattern of society

1. *State Socialism:* Under this system, the government in a capitalist society will own and operate certain sectors of the economy for overall social objectives rather than for profit. The Tennessee Valley Authority in the United States is a good example.

   State socialism is different from state capitalism. State capitalism refers to a system under which the government in a capitalistic society owns and operates industries with a profit motive. It will try to maximize profit or minimise loss. It will act just like a private entrepreneur. Under Bismarck, Germany took over the ownership and management of the railways in Germany. Bismarck was a state capitalist, not a socialist.

2. *Utopian Socialism:* It became a prominent social philosophy at the beginning of the 19th century. Saint-Simon, Charles Fourier and Robert Owen are regarded as the founders of Utopian socialism. Utopian socialism came into existence at a time when the workers were very weak and when they had no vote and when trade unionism was not yet developed. The Utopian socialists considered the competitive system of the capitalist society as unjust and irrational. They worked out schemes of perfect social arrangement and appealed to the workers to adopt them. They did not advocate class struggle. On the other hand, they appealed to the capitalists to co-operate with them and provide finances to implement their programmes. They set up some model co-operative communities. Utopian socialists such as Fourier and Owen sought reform in voluntary local communities. Since they have advocated associations with limited membership, they are sometimes known as "Associationists." The Utopian socialists were not always successful in their attempts.

3. *Christian Socialism:* It developed in England and Germany after 1848. Charles Kingsley was a leading advocate of Christian Socialism in England. The movement came into existence after the failure of the radical movements in England and France. The advocates of this system spoke of the Bible, religion and God's message to offer solace to the suffering masses. God's order was mutual love. They appealed to the rich to use their property as a trust for the benefit of everybody. The movement disapproved violence and class struggle. The Christian socialists advocated education for workers, factory reforms and co-operation. In short, the Christian socialists wanted to "socialize the Christian and Christianize the socialist." It may be interesting to note that Gandhi's ideas of trusteeship are similar to those of Christian socialists.

4. *Anarchism:* Proudhon was the leading advocate of anarchism. According to him, all governments are coercive and should be abolished. In the words of Bakunin, "The State is the root of the evil." We should, however, remember that the anarchists did not advocate a society without order. They believed in the essential goodness of human nature. It became corrupt only by the State and its institutions. They advocated that private property should be replaced by collective ownership. There would be mutual understanding, co-operation, and complete liberty in the ideal society of the anarchists.

5. *Marxian Socialism:* It is also referred to as "scientific socialism." It is based on the labour theory of value and on the materialistic interpretation of history. It presents capitalism as a decaying institution full of inherent contradictions. It regards history as a series of class struggles—the struggle between the master and the slave, the lord and the serf and the capitalist and the worker. It tells that the struggle between the capitalists and the workers will lead to revolution when the capitalist system will be overthrown and the dictatorship of the proletariat will be set up. Thus, socialism will come into existence.

Under socialism, there will be public ownership and management of the means of production. Private property will be allowed only in consumer goods. A socialist economy is a planned economy. Profit-motive will be eliminated. Price system will be there but it will play only a secondary role.

6. *Communism:* According to Marx, "Communism is the next higher stage of society." The working principle of socialism is "From each according to his ability, to each according to his *work*." The basic principle of communism is, "From each according to his ability, to each according to his *need*." This supposes superabundance of goods. But unfortunately scarcity is the inconvenient fact of life. In a truly communist society, money payments will be eliminated. The communists want to end money because they consider it as an invention by the capitalist class for the exploitation of workers. In the ultimate stage of society where there will be no class conflicts, the State will wither away. It should be noted that we do not have communism of the type we have discussed anywhere in the world today. The so-called communist countries (*e.g.*, Cuba, China) are only socialist societies.

7. *Revisionism:* Fabian socialism, which developed in England, is a good example of revisionism. They do not approve of class struggle, revolution and violence. They are for reduction of inequalities of income and wealth. But they believe in gradual change by means of education, persuasion and parliamentary reform. They are not for total abolition of capitalist institutions but for their modification. They advocate control over monopolies, state ownership of public utilities. Owing to the emphasis of the revisionists on ownership and management of public utilities by public authorities, revisionism, sometimes, has been called 'gas and water' socialism.

8. *Syndicalism:* Syndicalism, in its origins, is essentially a French movement. Later it spread to Italy. George Sorel (1847-1922) promoted and popularized syndicalism. The word 'syndicate' means so many things. But in French a 'syndicat' is the everyday word for a trade union. 'Syndicalism' then is merely 'trade unionism'. Strictly speaking, one should probably refer to the movement as 'revolutionary syndicalism....' The syndicalists did not believe in parliamentary reform. They advocated direct action on a large scale. Strikes should be resorted to promote revolutionary spirit among workers and they did not rule out sabotage as a weapon in the class struggle. They hoped that a general strike would overthrow capitalism, and industry would come under the direct control of workers. The syndicalists advocated abolition of private property.

9. *Guild Socialism:* G. D. H. Cole (1889-1959) was a great popularizer of guild socialism. He was a professor of economics at Oxford University. Guild socialism was essentially a British movement. It was an evolutionary movement which believed in gradual change and reform. The guild socialists felt the need for the existence of state to promote the general interests of citizens as consumers. But they were interested in the organisation of industry and in the control of industry by the workers. They did not want the government to run the industries. The government could develop only overall economic policy. They wanted every worker to be a partner in the firm in which he worked. This was the essential idea of 'industrial democracy' advocated by the guild socialists. There would not be two classes with conflicting interests— workers and capitalists. Instead, the society would be divided into producers and consumers. Guild will be the national association of workers and government, the national association of consumers. Thus consumers and producers would form partnership of equals.

Socialistic Pattern of Society

The present Indian economic system may be described as a mixed economy. We have a private sector and a public sector. It is essentially capitalistic, but includes elements of state capitalism and state socialism. Since 1956, the Indian Government had been trying to make the economy more and more socialistic in character.

In the 1950's, the Government of India adopted the establishment of 'socialistic pattern of society' as one of its major socio-economic objectives. Sometimes, our socialism is also described as 'democratic socialism.' The features of socialistic pattern of society may be described as follows: (*i*) India will continue to have mixed economy. (*ii*) In future, the state will play a larger role in economic matters. In other words, the role of the public sector will be expanded. (*iii*) The Commanding heights of the economy will be controlled by the state. The attempt at nationalization of banking and wholesale trade in foodgrains are cases in point. (*iv*) India will have a planned economy. But coercion will not be the basis. Democracy will be the basis of planning. (*v*) Reduction of inequalities of income and wealth is one of the major objectives of economic planning. Recently, attempts have been made to prevent concentration of economic power in the hands of a few persons. The appointment of Monopolies and Restrictive Trade Practices Commission to control monopoly power may be cited as an example.

But even after six decades of planning in our country, we find in spite of legislation on land reforms, progressive taxation policies, still there is concentration of wealth in the hands of a few persons. In the countryside, it has been noted that "Ten per cent of India's cultivators own more than 50 per cent of the land, while one per cent of them own nearly one-fifth" (Prof. Galbraith). According to some critics, we in India are not able to make any great progress towards establishing a socialistic pattern of society because we are trying to erect a socialistic superstructure on a capitalist base. Some of the key sectors are still controlled either directly or indirectly by powerful, vested interests.

Utopian Socialists

We have already noted that Saint-Simon, Charles Fourier and Robert Owen are the founders of Utopian socialism. We may also include Proudhon and Louis Blanc in the category of Utopian socialists.

Marx described all socialists who preceded him as Utopian socialists. He called his socialism 'scientific socialism.' In fact, Marx is a leading critic of Utopian socialism. His main criticism against them is that they had no knowledge of the proletariat as such. They made their appeal to the whole of society and they dreamed fantastic dreams of a new society. They appealed to morality. According to Marx, "from a scientific standpoint, this appeal to morality and justice does not help us an inch further." The Utopian socialists constructed the outlines of a new society out of their own heads and looked around for a capitalist to launch it. In other words, the Utopian socialists did not have a philosophy of history. Marx claimed that the function of scientific socialism was to reveal socialism as 'a necessary product of historical development.'

We shall now study the economic ideas of some of the leading Utopian socialists.

Saint-Simon (1760-1825)

Henri Comte de Saint-Simon came of a noble family. He had an adventurous life. At the age of sixteen, he took part in the American War of Independence. During the French Revolution he gave up his claim to nobility. Towards the end of the Revolution, by successful speculation in national property, he made a huge fortune. He was imprisoned for some time as a suspect and released afterwards. From the moment he was released, he began to regard himself as a prophet and philosopher. And he wasted his money in an extravagant manner by supporting young scientists, scholars and artists. Soon he became penniless and led a miserable life. He lived for several years at the home of a former servant. After the death of the servant, he lived upon the modest pension provided him by his family and the financial support of some businessmen. He died in 1825.

Saint-Simon is considered as the father of Utopian socialism. He developed his ideas before the birth of the working class movement in France. So naturally Saint-Simon made no appeal to the workers to struggle against their employers.

According to Saint-Simon, "The world in which we live is based on industry." So he advocated industrialisation. He considered idleness as sin. Work is worship for him. Saint-Simon has given a plan for *Industrial Parliament.* In the Industrial Parliament, there would be three chambers, each chamber looking after invention, review, and execution. The Invention chamber would consist of artists and engineers who would plan public works. The second chamber, that is, the Review chamber would be composed of scientists who would review the projects and control education. The Execution chamber would consist of leaders who would carry out the project and control the budgets. Saint-Simon's plan for Industrial Programme is a fine example of one of the early attempts to work out a centrally planned economy run by an educated elite.

Saint-Simon rejected the classical assumption of the harmony of interests. He recognized there was clash of interests. But he did not advocate class struggle. Instead he pleaded that workers should be dealt with in a humane way. Humanitarian considerations became the dominant theme of his writings.

Saint-Simon opposed the institution of private property and inheritance because it made the rich idle. He advocated collective ownership of property.

Saint-Simon was interested in creating the organisation which is most favourable to industry. He used the term in the widest sense. It includes every kind of useful activity, theoretical as well as practical, intellectual as well as manual. In the new industrial state, government will have a limited role to play. All that it has to do is to see that useful work is not affected. Since the government has to perform only a limited role, it will have only a small amount of money or power. The money required for industrial undertakings will be supplied by voluntary subscriptions, and the subscribers will themselves supervise the spending of their own money by the administration.

According to Saint-Simon, "The property of France can exist only through the effects of the progress of the sciences, fine arts and professions." The princes, the nobles, the Bishops, Marshals of France and the idle landowners contribute nothing to the progress of mankind. To a certain extent, they retard the progress. For they spend their wealth in such a way which is of no direct use to the sciences, fine arts and professions.

The above ideas of Saint-Simon can be found in what is known as *Saint-Simon's parable:*

"Suppose that France suddenly lost fifty of her best physicists, chemists, physiologists, mathematicians, poets, painters... engineers... bankers... businessmen... farmers... miners... metal workers... making in all the three thousand leading scientists, artists, and artisans of France."

"These men are the Frenchmen who are the most essential producers, those who make the most important products, those who direct the enterprises most useful to the nation, those who contribute to its achievements in the sciences, fine arts and professions. They are in the most real sense the flower of French Society; they are above all Frenchmen, the most useful to their country, contribute most to its glory, increasing its civilization and prosperity. The nation would become a lifeless corpse as it lost them..... It would require at least a generation for France to repair this misfortune...."

"Let us pass on to another assumption. Suppose that France preserves all the men of genius that she possesses in the science, fine arts and professions, but has the misfortune to lose in the same day Monsieur the King's brother and other members of the household.... Suppose that France loses at the same time all the great officers of the royal household, all the ministers (with or without portfolio), all the councillors of state, all the chief magistrates, marshals, cardinals, archbishops, bishops, vicars-general and canons, all the prefects and subprefects, all the civil servants and judges, and in addition, ten thousand of the richest proprietors who live in the style of nobles."

This mischance would certainly distress the French, because they are kindhearted, and could not see with indifference the sudden disappearance of such a large number of their compatriots. But this loss of thirty thousand individuals, considered to be the most important in the state, would not grieve them for purely sentimental reason and would result in no political evil for the state.

The princes, the great household officials, the Bishops, Marshals of France, prefects and the idle landowners are burden on national revenue. For every year large sums of money are spent on them in the form of salaries, pensions, gifts, compensations, for the upkeep of their activities which are useless to the nation. In the words of Saint-Simon himself, "....Society is a world which is upside down. The nation holds as a fundamental principle that the poor should be generous to the rich, and that therefore the poorer classes should daily deprive themselves of necessities, in order to increase the superfluous luxury of the rich."

Saint-Simon was arrested and tried for his above views which were considered as heresy in 1819, but he was acquitted.

Saint-Simon was a supporter of monarchy. He compared the nation to a pyramid. According to him, "Monarchy is the magnificent diamond which crowns the pyramid." It may be interesting to note that Saint-Simon did not advocate confiscation of private property.

Saint-Simonians

After the death of Saint-Simon, his disciples organised a school that became almost a religion. Auguste Comte, Rodrigues and Enfantin were all the leading disciples of Saint-Simon.

Saint-Simonians were great critics of the institution of private property. Their criticism of private property is directed from the point of view of distribution and production of wealth, and from the angle of justice and utility.

According to them, Saint-Simon had already emphasized that in the new order which he had envisaged workers and idlers could not exist side by side in the society. It was only the income from private property that tended to make the property owners idle. Not only that, since there was concentration of capital in the hands of a few persons, the few capitalists controlled distribution and this resulted in the exploitation of one man by another. Saint-Simon attributed exploitation to the existing social order based on private property.

The Saint-Simonians firmly believed that the institutions of private property and the right of inheritance should be abolished to increase production and to promote equitable distribution. They made use of historical arguments to show that private property was not a fixed or permanent institution. It must undergo change like other social institutions. They advocated collective system. According to Gide and Rist, "....The Saint-Simonian system is the prototype of all the collectivist schemes that were proposed in the course of the century." When the Saint-Simonians spoke of equality-they really meant equality of opportunity—an equal chance and the same starting-point for every one. "To each according to his capacity" was their slogan. They accepted the view that exceptional capacity should be able to enjoy exceptional reward.

Conclusion

The doctrine of Saint-Simonians is a mixture of realism and Utopianism. Saint-Simon's enthusiasm for large-scale industry provided the inspiration for big banks, railways, the Suez Canal and huge industrial undertakings. The Saint-Simonians realized the importance of the institutions of credit in an industrial society. The theory of profit-sharing, for the first time, in the history of economic thought, was developed by Saint-Simonians. And they anticipated most of the doctrines of subsequent socialists.

Fourier (1772-1837)

Charles Fourier was contemporary of Robert Owen, the famous British Utopian socialist. His appeals were usually addressed to the wealthy or to the king. He was not a revolutionary socialist. He came of a middle class merchant family. The family lost most of its possessions during the French revolution. Fourier worked as a clerk in many business houses. Because of difficult financial circumstances, Fourier acquired his education during leisure hours in reading rooms.

Fourier was a great critic of the existing industrial system. While Saint-Simon was in favour of large-scale industrial production, Fourier disliked large-scale production, mechanization and centralization in all forms. He felt that commerce was at the root of all corruption. He criticized the existing pattern of society that "accords its high protection to the agents of famine and pestilence."

Phalanxes or Phalansteries

Association is the leading idea in Fourier's system. Fourier believed that all the social problems could be solved by the organisation of society into co-operative communities which he called phalanxes or Phalansteries. He prepared a blue-print for those societies covering all details. Each association (Phalanx) would combine three hundred families. There would be 1,800 members. They would have nine square miles of land. They would carry on production in the interest of the group. Fourier gave priority for agriculture and handicrafts in the scheme of production. He believed that such a co-operative enterprise would increase production tenfold over that of private industry. As all people would live in honour and comfort, there would be no theft or law and order problem. He described the advantages of common kitchens and apartments. Fourier believed that *Phalanxes* would solve the problem of scarcity. He said that all "dirty work" in the Utopian colony would be done by children.

Fourier's views on labour and its reward are interesting for a student of economic thought. He believed that all labour might be pleasant. It was only overwork that made labour unpleasant. But overwork would be unnecessary in his *phalanxes*. He thought if a person worked between the ages of eight and twenty-eight, that is, if he worked for twenty years, he would earn to spend the remaining part of his life in leisure. He classified labour into three categories: necessary labour, useful labour and agreeable labour. The first two categories would receive the highest reward, and those who were engaged in agreeable or pleasant labour would get the lowest reward. All members would receive a certain minimum reward.

After all the members have been provided with minimum subsistence, the surplus produce would be distributed between labour, capital and talent and skill in the following manner. Labour would get five-twelfths of the share, capital four-twelfths, talent and skill would get three-twelfths of the share. It may be interesting to note that Fourier welcomed the idea of participation of private capital in his schemes. In fact, he appealed to the capitalists to finance his project by promising them a satisfactory return. The story goes that Fourier used to be at home every day at noon hoping that some capitalist would come to him with capital to finance his schemes. But all the waiting did not bear fruit.

Experiments were made in some countries with *Phalanxes*. But they all failed. The present '*communes*' in China, in a way, might be compared to *Phalanxes*. But there is one big difference. While Fourier opposed large-scale production and emphasized on voluntary co-operation, the present *communes* in China are marked by centralized control and planning and large-scale production.

Conclusion

There is a lot of truth in some of Fourier's critical remarks about the existing industrial system. He was one of the first social thinkers to underline the importance of co-operative production. Fourier believed that co-operative living would promote a new and noble social order. The *phalanxes* would promote social security from cradle to grave. An interesting thing about his scheme is that he assured a minimum subsistence for the members of his society in the early stages of development of his ideal society. His division of labour based on aptitudes and ability solves one of the problems of resource allocation in a non-price economy. According to Jacob Oser, "The Fourierist *Phalanxes*, though ultimately failures, influenced the labour movement at the time and inspired much thought on how to eliminate the wastes of private enterprise and promote a better economic system. The co-operative movement is in part a living monument to Fourier."

Robert Owen (1771-1858)

Robert Owen was the most famous of the Utopian socialists. He was born in 1711. He was the son of a Welsh iron-monger and saddler. He attended school only for a few years. Then he entered life. At an early age of twenty-eight, he became the owner of extensive cotton mills at New Lanark in Scotland. Soon Owen's spinning mills became the largest and the best equipped in Scotland. Later on Owen became a factory reformer, trade union leader, pioneer socialist, advocate of co-operatives, founder of Utopian communities and educational reformer.

The central thesis of Owen is this. Men are good or bad according to their environment. An improved environment, resting on improved education, provides the path to all progress. Since character is formed by circumstances, men are not responsible for their actions. So they should be moulded into goodness by a proper environment. It implies that there is no use of punishing people for being bad. Owen's theories and programmes are based on the belief that by providing better conditions, we could produce better people. While the classical economists believed that self-interest promoted the general interests of the society, Owen thought an individual would achieve greatest happiness only by serving the society.

Owen believed that men were naturally good but only the capitalist system made them bad. He considered *private property, religion* and the *institution of marriage* as barriers in the creation of an ideal communal order. He believed that these barriers would be removed in his ideal order, where the natural goodness of man would find free expression.

Owen believed that education alone would provide better environment for working people. So he set up the 'Institution for the Formation of Character' in 1816. By his educational reforms, Owen has found a place for himself in the history and theory of education.

Owen introduced his reforms at his own mills at New Lanark. Boys were not admitted into the factory until they were ten. Free education was available to the boys until the age of ten. He was the first person to found a nursery or infant school in Britain for children below the age of five. And for workers, he reduced the number of working hours, increased wages, abolished fines and punishments provided food and clothing at subsidized rates. And he extended even social insurance benefits. In short, he made New Lanark Mills, a model firm. It attracted a lot of visitors and became the Mecca of social reformers. We must remember that Owen preached social rather than moral reform. Owen's ideas influenced factory legislation in Britain to a great extent. The Factory Act of 1819 was passed only in response to his appeal to the government to enact factory legislation.

In the later part of his life, Owen's ideas became more communistic. He demanded the abolition of profits, speculation and even the institution of money.

Villages of Co-operation

Owen advocated the establishment of communistic settlements, which are known as "*parallelograms*" or '*villages of co-operation*.' He himself promoted such a model co-operative community to show the way. In 1825, he established the New Harmony colony on thirty thousand acres of Indiana. Owen thought that his new organisation would do away with the evils of capitalism and competitive system. It may be interesting to note that while Fourier allowed profit on the capital invested in his Utopian colonies, Owen favoured only a fixed rate of interest on capital. He thought that after some time, the owners of capital would voluntarily give it up. Within three years, the New Harmony colony experiment failed and Owen lost most of his fortune. Other villages of co-operation set up later in Britain also failed.

National Equitable Labour Exchange

Owen opposed the institution of money and profits for in his view they were two great evils. He wanted to eliminate these evils by bringing producers and directors into direct contact with one another. So in 1832, he founded the National Equitable Labour Exchange as a market where goods could be exchanged on the basis of notes representing labour time.

Owen thought money based on the value of precious metals confused the relation between the true values of goods in an exchange. So he advocated the use of labour notes based upon the labour time involved in producing the goods as a medium in its place.

Owen's experiment with exchange based on labour notes failed within five years.

Conclusion

Owen's ideas and experiments had a remarkable influence on socialism, co-operation and trade unionism. His criticisms of capitalism and his idea of collective action to organise co-operative communities had profound influence on socialists. Above all, he was a great social reformer.

Louis Blanc (1811-1882)

Louis Blanc is generally regarded as the founder of state socialism. He was a social reformer and a historian. He came of a royal family. But during the French Revolution, the family became poor. Blanc published his '*Organisation of Work*' in 1839. That brought him fame and he became a leader of the socialist movement.

While the other Utopian socialists believed their Utopian schemes could be implemented without State aid, Louis Blanc depended upon the State to help in the implementation of his ideal programmes.

Further early socialists were essentially *bourgeois*, that is capitalist or middle-class. But Louis Blanc may be regarded as an advocate of proletarian socialism.

Louis Blanc was a great critic of capitalism and competition. He thought they would ruin the working class as well as *bourgeois*. But he did not advocate class war. He considered even trade union activity as useless. He believed that State could be used as an instrument of progress.

He advocated *social or national workshop* where men in similar industries would co-operate. The social workshops would be initiated and financially supported by the State. We must note that these social workshops of Blanc were not the self-sufficient units of Owen or Fourier.

Louis Blanc advocated producers' associations. Even capitalists could join such associations and receive a fixed rate of interest as permitted by the State. The State might help in the setting up of producers' associations. As these associations would attract the best workers, they would drive capitalists out of business by their superior competitive efficiency.

Blanc firmly believed that the existing order could be changed into a better order only by the intervention of the government. In Blanc's ideal order, people would be rewarded not according to their productivity or service, but according to their needs or wants. And people will enjoy the right to work. The government should organize national workshops to give work to the unemployed.

Blanc's aim was to abolish individualism, competition and private property in his ideal social order. He thought competition was by and large unfair. It resulted in low wages and unemployment. So government should regulate competition and control production. As he was in favour of large-scale enterprise, he appealed to the government to provide the huge capital that was required for it. According to him, "the State is, or ought to be, the Banker of the Poor."

Conclusion

Louis Blanc is one of the first socialists who put the burden of reform on the shoulders of the State. He represents the transition from 'Utopian socialism' to 'Proletarian socialism.' Of course, he is also an 'associationist' like Fourier and Owen. Above all he is a moderate. Not only that, his ideas have some modern touch about them. His basic purpose is to prepare for the future without breaking violently with the past.

Proudhon (1809-65)

Pierre-Joseph Proudhon was a leading advocate of anarchism. We find in his ideas some salient features of proletarian socialism. In fact, some of the ideas of Marx may be traced back to Proudhon. Proudhon came of a poor family. In spite of extreme poverty, Proudhon received a certain amount of education. For sometime, he worked as a printer and was also unemployed for some period. He underwent imprisonment for some of his revolutionary writings. We shall now discuss some of the leading ideas of Proudhon on government, property, money and credit.

Anarchism

Proudhon was a champion of individual liberty and justice. He regarded anarchism as the ideal system. Anarchy, in his view, does not mean disorder, but only the absence of a master.

Attack on Government

In his "General Idea of the Revolution in the Nineteenth Century", Proudhon attacked government. According to him, in the beginning, government might have come into existence in the interests of the people. But he tells that experience shows that everywhere and always "the government.... has placed itself on the side of the richest and most educated class against the more numerous and poorer class; it has little by little become narrow and exclusive; and instead of maintaining liberty and equality among all, it works persistently to destroy them, by virtue of natural inclination towards privilege. We may conclude without fear that the revolutionary formula *cannot be Direct legislation, nor Direct government, nor simplified government, but it is No Government*. Neither monarchy, nor aristocracy, nor even democracy itself, in so far as it may imply any government at all, even though acting in the name of the people and calling itself the people. No authority, no government, not even popular, that is the revolution.... governing the people will always be swindling the people. It is always man giving orders to man, the fiction which makes an end of liberty.

Property

When Proudhon was thirty-one, he wrote a book, "*what is property?*" He answered "*Property is theft.*" So according to him, "Property is theft and property owners are thieves." But we have to note one thing here. By 'property' Proudhon meant large property that enabled its owner to earn income in the form of rent, interest and profit. Large property permitted people to live without working. He favoured small property ownership of houses, land and tools.

According to Proudhon, large industries should be owned by associations of workers and society must control those associations so that they may charge a just price, as near as possible to cost of production. But he was generally in favour of small scale production. And he advocated equality of incomes in spite of inequality in abilities and productivity.

Proudhon described the property-owners as robbers because they robbed the labour of their due share in production. He developed in a vague manner the concept of surplus value. He explains how a capitalist takes a profit from labourer's product. 'The capitalist pays each labourer of a group a mere day's wage. But in the combined labour of the group there is an advantage for which he does not pay. There is a union or harmony through which the product exceeds the sum of the individual products of the separate labourers.' (Haney). So he suggested that workers should receive an additional proportion of the product.

Proudhon developed a labour theory of value. According to him, "The absolute value of a thing is its cost in time and expense."

Bank of Exchange

To promote individual freedom and justice in exchange, Proudhon advocated abolition of gold standard. He realized the importance of credit. But he thought that 'bankocracy' monopolized it. So he advocated the establishment of Bank of Exchange. To begin with, the bank would be organized with a thousand subscribers. Paper money would be issued for goods according to the labour time required for their production. The amount of paper money which the bank would issue would be proportional to the gross output of the subscribers, and the paper would be negotiable among themselves. Proudhon thought inflation could never occur in such an economy because the amount of paper issued would be proportionate to the delivery of products. The banks would buy goods from members at between 50 and 100 per cent of the cost of production. As a matter of fact, the transaction would really be a loan on goods for a limited time, for the producer could sell the goods, repay the loan and keep the excess revenue. In other words, the Exchange Bank would provide free credit to workers on easy terms. It would charge only a small commission. Thus interest rate would be abolished. As loans are freely available to workers, they can buy capital goods and the existing class structure dividing the society into capitalists and labourers would disappear. Ultimately property and labour would be united. Proudhon opposed 'association of labour' because he considered it an encroachment upon the liberty of the labourers. According to Haney, a notable feature of Proudhon's thought is its emphasis on the collective or social character of modern production.

An Estimate of Utopian Socialists

Utopian socialism is 'unscientific socialism.' It is not based on scientific economic theory. It is largely ethical in character, bourgeois in its origin. But, "considered from the standpoint of their effect upon the stream of economic thought, these Socialists of the first-half of the nineteenth century, though their influence was largely indirect and rather gradual, are of considerable influence."

   The Utopian socialists raised the question of distributive justice. They began to question some of the social institutions which were considered to be permanent and fixed facts in the past. They pointed out that the institutions of private property and rights of inheritance were at the root of inequalities of income. As property was the main source of income in the existing social system, they argued that reduction of inequalities of income could be attained only through control of property or abolition of private property. Some of them advocated the need for state intervention to reduce inequalities by means of regulation of production and distribution. Some of them, like Robert Owen, were pioneers of the co-operative movement. But one main criticism against them is that they did not have a philosophy of history. They lacked a true historical sense of institutional development. It is said that because they lacked true historical sense, they failed to appreciate the social value of some of the basic institutions like private property, marriage and religion and they advocated their abolition.

KARL MARX
(1818-1883)

Karl Marx was the founder of scientific socialism. "Scientific Socialism" is different from "Utopian socialism." Marx considered the Utopian socialists as dreamers who had no knowledge of the proletariat as such. The aim of scientific socialism was to demonstrate socialism as a necessary product of historical development.

Karl Marx was born in Germany in a middle class Jewish family. During his childhood, the family converted to Protestantism. Marx studied Law, History and Philosophy in different German universities (Bonn, Berlin and Jena) and received the degree of doctor of philosophy at the age of twenty-three. He married the daughter of a baron who occupied a high government post. She proved to be the most devoted companion of Marx throughout his life.

Marx was a revolutionary even during his youth. He could not get teaching post in any German university because of his radicalism. So he turned to journalism. On account of his radical views, he was exiled from Germany. He took shelter in France. While in France, he studied French socialism and English political economy. He was exiled from France too at the request of the Prussian government. He stayed in Belgium for a while. Finally he settled down in London. He lived there until his death in 1883. While in London, he led the life of a recluse and spent most of his time in the British museum studying books on political economy and other things. Marx was a great scholar. His personal life in London was full of sufferings marked by illness and poverty and death of many of his children. Still he continued to study, write and organize. Marx organized the International Working Men's Association called the "First International."

Friedrich Engels (1820-95) was a close friend, collaborator and financial supporter of Marx. Engels was the son of a prosperous German cotton manufacturer. Engels looked after the family manufacturing interests in Manchester, England. At the same time, he was a scholar and he was engaged in revolutionary activities. He met Marx in 1844 in Paris. From that time onwards, they remained life-long friends and collaborators. But for the continuous financial assistance from Engels, Marx's family would have been starved to death. Not only that, Engels played a substantive role in the publication of Marxist literature.

Both Marx and Engels wrote the "Communist Manifesto" in 1848. In 1847, Marx wrote "The Poverty of Philosophy." It was intended as an attack on Proudhon's book, "The Philosophy of Poverty." The essential ideas of Marx on communism can be found in the Communist Manifesto. The Manifesto attacked capitalism as a system of "naked, shameless, direct, brutal exploitation", and its slogan was "workers of the world, unite." Marx published "The Critique of Political Economy" in 1859. But *Capital* (Das Kapital) is the major work and it is more or less a complete statement of Marxian system. Marx worked on this masterpiece for some decades. Only the first volume of '*Capital*' was published during the lifetime of Marx in 1867. Engels edited and published the second and third volumes of "Capital" in 1884 and 1894 respectively after the death of Marx. And the fourth volume was published after the death of Engels by a German socialist Karl Kautsky. He published it under the heading, "*Theories of Surplus Value*" (1910). "Capital" came to be called the Bible of "Scientific" socialists.

Philosophy

Marx made use of Hegelian philosophy with modification. He wanted to stand Hegelian philosophy "on its feet instead of on its head." He put Hegel's dialectic on a materialistic basis, and made social evolution a matter of material and economic forces. Marxian philosophy is called dialectical materialism.

Dialectical materialism explains how changes in society take place. According to it, "Change is nothing but development." And development takes place by stages. Each stage will be "higher" than the previous stage. An initial situation is called 'thesis', its successor is called 'antithesis' and the third stage is a 'synthesis'. But the process does not end here. It goes on, for change is continuous process. No idea, institution or situation is fixed. Each contains in itself the seeds of change. Thus capitalism succeeded feudalism and socialism will replace capitalism.

Dialectical process has been explained by certain rules. First, there is the *unity of opposites*. Second, there is the rule of *negation of negation* and the third rule refers to the *change of quantity into quality*. The first rule, unity of opposites explains how uneasy and hostile elements co-exist in a given situation. For instance, the capitalists and the workers temporarily co-exist in a capitalist society. Of course, they may be struggling against each other. The second rule, the negation of negation explains the mechanism of change. It simply tells that no system is permanent, however powerful it may appear at the moment. Thus feudalism gave place for capitalism. And capitalism will give place for socialism. The third rule refers to the change of quantity into quality. Engels illustrated this point in the following manner. If heat were applied to water in a kettle, at first, there would be only hotter water. But when the temperature of water increases to 212 degrees at sea level, a qualitative change would take place. Water will be changed into steam. Similarly, when the capitalists exploited the working masses, the early effect would be only misery. But there will be a qualitative change soon in human reaction. They will revolt against the existing order.

Hegel's dialectical powers are based on idealism. Human mind was very important for him. The outside world was only subsidiary to mental activity. But Marx gave materialistic interpretation of Hegelian philosophy. *To him change in the material would influence the mind and thoughts.*

So much for philosophy. Let us now study the Marxian system. Before we study Marx in detail, we should remember that "Marxism is at once philosophy, sociology, history and economics." (Robert Lekachman). So it may be profitable to study the Marxian system in broad outline before we go into details.

The Marxian System

The materialistic interpretation of history, especially the analysis of capitalist stage and the doctrine of class struggle form the basis of Marxian socialism which is international and revolutionary in character.

Materialistic Interpretation of History

Marx said in his preface to "Capital" that his aim was "to lay bare economic law of motion of modern society." Marx differed in his analysis from the classical economists in two fundamental respects. In the first place, the classical economists discussed problems such as rent, wages, and profits under capitalism and regarded the latter as a permanent fact. But Marx considered the capitalistic system itself as a variable. He treated capitalism as a transitory phase in the long run evolution of society. Again while the classical economists regarded economic laws as 'natural laws' that were of universal application, Marx considered economic laws as relative laws, valid only for a particular stage of historical development.

The central point in Marxism is the emphasis on the historical evolution of social, political and economic institutions. According to Marx, "*the mode of production in material life determines the general character of the social, political and spiritual, processes of life.*" Underlying all social changes, there is a fundamental and continuing development of the productive powers of society. The basic evolution of technology of production, in turn, determines the characteristic economic institutions, political arrangements and even intellectual and cultural values appropriate to the stage. Even capitalistic institutions should be regarded as a product of the productive powers of the society. So the capitalistic institutions are not permanent. They are only transitory. These institutions which are appropriate for a particular stage of development are subject to change. As the productive powers of society develop, the existing economic and political institutions should change for they are no longer appropriate. The existing institutions then become fetters on the expression of the new productive powers. They outlive their usefulness and they must be replaced by another set of institutions appropriate to the higher stage of economic development. This, in short, is the materialistic interpretation of history.

Class Struggle

Marx believed that the basic disparity between the evolving power of production and outdated institutions would express itself in "class struggle." This is the second fundamental way in which Marxian approach differed from that of the classical economists. While the classical economists believed in the harmony of interest, Marx made class conflict the dominant feature of social life. In Marx's view, *"all history is the history of class struggles."* In ancient times, there was the struggle between the master and the slave. Under feudalism, there was the struggle between the lord and the serf. And now under conditions of modern capitalism, the struggle is between the capitalists and the workers (the proletariat). The capitalists control the means of production and the workers depend on the capitalist for work. The main aim of the capitalist is to maximize profits. This he does by exploitation of labour. Low wages, long hours of work and employment of women and children so that they would provide cheap labour are some of the ways by which exploitation takes place. Exploitation is inherent in the capitalist system. As exploitation increases, there will be polarization of the society into two classes—the capitalists and the proletariat. Then conditions become ripe for the overthrow of capitalism by the united proletariat. In fact, capitalism itself creates conditions for its destruction. Thus, as the productive powers of the society increase, capitalism becomes inappropriate for that stage. This, in turn, results in antagonism between classes that puts an end to capitalism. And socialism will be the new order.

Marx the Economist

As an economist, Marx was a very learned man. In the words of Schumpeter, "criticizing and rejecting, or accepting and co-ordinating, he always went to the bottom of every matter. The outstanding proof of this is in his work, *Theories of Surplus Value*, which is a monument of theoretical ardour.... To his powerful intellect, the interest in the problem as problem was paramount, in spite of himself, and however much he may have bent the import of his final *results*, while at work he was primarily concerned with sharpening the tools of analysis proferred by the science of his day, with straightening out logical difficulties and with building on the foundation thus acquired a theory that in nature and intent was truly scientific whatever its shortcomings may have been."[1]

Marx was the first economist of top rank to see and to teach systematically how economic theory may be turned into historical analysis. Not only that, he knew how to rationalize history.

Marxism and Classicism

As an economist Marx was a pupil of Ricardo. It has been rightly said that, "Marxism is simply a branch grafted on the classical trunk" (Gide and Rist). So before we study about Marxian economic theory, it may be useful to study the relationship between Marxism and classicism. For, the economic theories of Marx are derived directly from the theories of the leading economists of the nineteenth century, especially from Ricardo.

   1. The Labour Theory of Value as developed by Ricardo is the economic basis of Marxism. In fact, Marx treated Ricardo as his master and substantially accepted the Ricardian theory of value.

---

[1]   J. A. Schumpeter: *Capitalism, Socialism and Democracy.*

2. Marx developed his theory of surplus value only from the Labour Theory of Value. So Marx developed his theory of surplus value from the Ricardian setup. We may also go a step further and say Marxian theory of surplus value is similar to the concept of 'net product' developed by Quesnay and other physiocrats. In the words of Schumpeter, "Exactly as Quesnay let land alone be productive of surplus value, so Marx let labour alone be productive of surplus value."

3. Marxian theory of unemployment, where he speaks of an 'Industrial Reserve Army', is based on the Ricardian theory of technological unemployment.

4. Marxian theory of falling profits had already been anticipated by the classical economists.

5. The conflict between wages and profits which Marx spoke of had been already discussed by Ricardo.

6. Marx's abstract, deductive method is essentially Ricardian in its nature. In other words, Marx made use of the same theoretical tools used by Ricardo.

Owing to close connection between Marxism and classicism, Labriola, a noted Italian Syndicalist commented that "*Das Kapital* instead of being the prologue to the communal critique, is simply the epilogue of bourgeois economics." Again, Sorel, a noted socialist writer, tells that "Marxism is much more akin to the Manchester doctrine than to the Utopian. We must never forget this." (The classical school is also known as Manchester school). Of course, Marx used classical theories to arrive at different conclusions. But we have to remind ourselves of the fact that Marx differed fundamentally from the classical economists on certain things. For instance, while the classical economists studied economic problems on the assumption that capitalism was fixed and permanent system, Marx regarded capitalism itself as a variable, subject to change. He considered it as a transitional stage. Again, while the dominant note of classical writings is based on class harmony, Marx regarded class conflict and class struggle as an historical fact.

We shall now study the Marxian economic theory. Marxian economic analysis may be presented in the form of a few propositions.

1. *Labour is the source of all value:* This is based on the Ricardian theory of value. Marx regarded this as a fundamental law.

2. Labour is paid in wages its own value. The value of labour is the amount of labour required to rear, train and maintain the labourer (Marx treats 'labour' as a commodity).

3. *Surplus value:* The capitalist employs workers for more hours than are necessary to maintain them and hence he is able to secure a surplus value which comes to him in the form of profit. For example, it may take on the average six hours a day for a labourer to produce commodities necessary to maintain himself. But the capitalist will employ the labourer not for six hours but for twelve hours a day. It means that the additional six hours produce a surplus above the wages paid to a worker. The capitalist takes away that surplus value. It is this that Marx calls exploitation.

4. The main aim of the capitalist is to increase the surplus value. The capitalist is not interested in producing large quantities of useful commodities for their own sake but he is interested in the expansion of surplus values.

5. The capitalist attempts to increase his surplus value by the accumulation of capital. Marx has classified capital into *two* basic forms: (*i*) Variable capital (labour) and (*ii*) Constant capital (machinery, etc.). Marx regarded machinery as the product of past labour.

6. The employment of constant capital (machinery, etc.) increases total production. But it causes technological unemployment and creates an industrial reserve army of the unemployed. This enables the capitalist to keep down the wages. Marx tells that constant capital does not create surplus value, for according to him labour (variable capital) alone is the source of value and is capable of creating surplus value.

Then, Marx speaks of certain inherent contradictions in the capitalistic system. He realized the importance of machinery in industrial production. But at the same time he mentioned that machinery would not be always beneficial to the labourer or capitalist. The introduction of machinery on a large scale would displace labour and create technological unemployment. Machinery will create a condition of relative over-population. It may be interesting to note that Marx did not agree with the view of Malthus that wages were at a subsistence level because of population pressure, in the biological sense. On the other hand, he thought, the capitalist, by introducing machinery, maintained an industrial reserve army of the unemployed. Naturally, with unemployment on a large scale, wages would tend to be at a very low or subsistence level.

By introducing machinery (constant capital) on a large scale, the capitalist also would not benefit much because it would not produce any surplus value. For according to Marx, "Labour and labour alone is the source of value." So the introduction of machinery keeps wages down and permits exploitation of labour. At the same time, it fails in the creation of surplus value.

On the basis of the above propositions, Marx arrives at certain conclusions regarding the falling rate of profit, concentration of capital, and business cycle crisis.

Falling Rate of Profit

Marx believed that under capitalism there was tendency for the rate of profit to fall in the long run. He explained it this way. He thought that there was a tendency for the employment of constant capital (machinery, etc.) to increase in relation to variable capital (labour) in the long run. In the Marxian terminology, there would be a continuous increase in the organic composition of capital. (If 'V' is the variable capital and 'C' is the constant capital and if 'O' is the organic composition of capital, then by definition $O = \dfrac{C}{C+V}$. Increase in the employment of constant capital takes place mainly because of the desire of the capitalist to accumulate more and more capital. Another reason is, the capitalist uses it as a method to keep wages low. If the capitalists employed more labour (variable capital), wages would tend to rise. To prevent this, they introduced more and more machinery. Thus they created a huge industrial reserve army and kept wages down. The introduction of machinery on a large scale cause unemployment and misery for the working classes. And for the capitalist, it results in a falling rate of profit. Marx arrived at this conclusion, namely, 'falling rate of profit' on the assumption that surplus value is created by variable capital only and that there is a tendency for the proportion of variable capital to total capital to decline in the long run.

Concentration of Capital

Marx believed that there was a tendency for capital to be concentrated in the large scale production. Not only that, it would be concentrated in the hands of a few persons. The large scale units definitely have superior competitive ability. The result is that small scale capitalists are driven out of business and they are forced to join the ranks of proletariat. Polarization becomes sharp and the society gets divided into two classes—the capitalists and the proletariat.

Economic Crisis

Marx believed that cyclical fluctuations in the form of prosperity and depression were inherent in the capitalist system. He had some insight into the problem of trade cycle. He thought that the average period of trade cycle was ten years. He described the different phases of a trade cycle as "moderate activity, prosperity, over-production, crisis and stagnation." Marxian theory of trade cycle is generally regarded as an under-consumption theory. Marx noticed that there was a fundamental conflict between the effect of capitalistic production and its aim. The effect of capitalistic production with its emphasis on the introduction of machinery was the increase in the productive powers of the society. But the aim of the capitalist was accumulation of capital and surplus value. This implied that there were large sections of the society (the labourers) without enough purchasing power to absorb the vast increase in production. That resulted in a crisis.

All the above mentioned things—mechanization, misery of the labourers, falling rate of profit, economic crisis concentration of capital—intensified the class struggle. The labourers would unite into a force capable of revolutionary action. The capitalists, on the other hand, forced by falling rate of profit and economic crises try to exploit labour as much as possible. "They stand now in naked opposition—capitalists and proletariat, defenders of the dying order and the creators of the new." (T. Gill). Then comes revolution. The expropriators are expropriated and a new society is born. We do not find full details about the new society in Marx.

Before we study the criticism of Marxian analysis, it may be useful for us to study Marxian theory of value and theory of surplus value in detail.

Marxian Theory of Value

Marxian theory of value is essentially the Labour theory of value. According to Marx, a thing can have value only if it is a product of human labour. Of course, Marx admits that "nothing can have value without being an object of utility." He said that "misdirected labour does not count as labour." So he qualified labour as "socially necessary labour."

Marx has made the usual distinction between use-value and exchange-value. But he has expressed the view that "use-value as such lies outside the sphere of investigation of political economy." Another point we have to remember is, by labour Marx referred to simple average labour. Skilled work is counted as multiple of unskilled average labour. According to him, the value of a product is measured in units of simple average labour.

Though Marxian theory of value is based on the Ricardian theory of value, we have to note that there is one main difference. While Ricardo believed that the relative values of different commodities were proportional to the amount of labour expended on them, Marx argued that labour time determined the absolute value of goods. By saying that value of a commodity depended on the amount of labour required for its production, Marx concluded that the worker was entitled to the entire fruit of his labour. So on the basis of the labour theory of value, Marx developed the theory of exploitation. In other words, to Marx the real purpose of labour theory of value was to serve as a basis for his theory of exploitation.

Marxian Theory of Surplus Value

Marxian theory of surplus value is based on the labour theory of value. According to Marx, "Commodities will tend to exchange in the ratio of the socially necessary labour time required to produce them."

In order to explain his theory of surplus value, Marx makes a distinction between simple commodity production and capitalist production. First of all, under capitalism, labour power itself becomes a commodity and is bought and sold on the market. Secondly, the main aim of the capitalist is to maximize profit. Marx has explained the distinction by means of two formulae: (*i*) C-M-C, (*ii*) M-C-M. Under conditions of simple commodity production, the producer sells his commodities for money. With that money, he buys the commodities of other producers for consumption purposes. So the cycle is commodity-money-commodity (C-M-C). But under conditions of capitalistic production, the formula is M-C-M'. The starting point is money. Money is used to buy other commodities, including labour power. The commodities are turned into other commodities, which are sold for a greater sum of money so that the capitalist makes a profit of M'-M. Marx called this profit, *surplus value*.

It is possible for the capitalist to make profit because labour power has the peculiar property of being able to create more value than is needed for its own subsistence. In other words, the worker can produce more in a day's labour than is needed for his own maintenance and that of his family. For instance, it may take on the average six hours a day for a labourer to produce commodities necessary to maintain himself. But the capitalist employs the worker not for six hours but for twelve hours a day. It means that the additional six hours produce a surplus above the wages paid to a worker. The capitalist takes away the surplus value because he has bought the worker's labour power. It is this that Marx calls exploitation. While paying the worker his wages, the capitalist still robs him of his due share. So, according to Marx, "Profits are 'legalized robbery'." The capitalists are able to buy labour power and take the surplus value because the workers do not own the means of production.

The working day of a labourer may be divided into two parts, during one of which the worker toils for himself and the other for the capitalist. Marx defined the ratio between the two as the *rate of exploitation.*

The rate of exploitation may be measured in the following manner. Marx classified capital into variable capital (wages) and constant capital (machinery, raw materials, etc.). We should also remember that Marx argued that variable capital alone increased value. The rate of exploitation was given by the formula S/v, where 'S' was surplus value and 'v' variable capital. We may also translate S/v as surplus labour time/necessary labour time. (We may describe the necessary labour time as the period required to produce the means of subsistence of the labourer and his family and surplus labour time as the extra portion of the day worked only for the benefit of the capitalist). Necessary labour time and surplus labour time form the working day.

The capitalists adopt various methods to increase the surplus value. First of all, they may prolong the working day, that is, they will increase the number of working hours. By that way, they can get more hours of surplus labour. Secondly, they may diminish the number of hours to produce the workers' sustenance. The capitalist may also employ women and children because they would require less for their upkeep than adults.

From the above discussion, it can be seen that the Marxian theory of surplus value is based on the Ricardian theory of value and the subsistence theory of wages.

We shall now look into the various points of criticism made against Marxism.

Criticism of Marxism

Marxian economics is essentially connected with Marxian socialism. It becomes rather difficult to criticize the economic ideas of Marx without taking into account his political philosophy.

1. Marx's materialistic interpretation of history is inadequate and one-sided. It is true that economic forces play an important role in shaping history. But there are other factors as well. So all that we can say is that history of man is moulded by many factors. Economic factors are only one of them, and not necessarily the most important.

2. Marx's generalization of all history as a history of class struggle is only partially true. The class struggle idea is made on the materialistic conception of history which again is only partial explanation of history. As Lekachman put it crisply, "classes refuse to polarize. False class consciousness is an international scandal. Monistic historical explanations are out of intellectual fashion."

3. There is nothing remarkable in the economic theories of Marx. In fact, even the most important of them will not stand critical scrutiny. For instance, the labour theory of value is the foundation of Marxian economics. But this fundamental theory of Marxism, namely, labour theory of value, was considered outmoded even at the time Marx wrote. We know now, utility plays an equally important role in the determination of value. In the famous example of Marshall, supply and demand are likened to two blades of a pair of scissors. Even if we take it for granted that value depends upon the cost of production, we know that all costs cannot be reduced to labour. Further, as labour is not homogeneous, there is difficulty of reducing different kinds of labour to a common unit. Because Marx was faced with all the above difficulties in explaining value, in his third volume of 'Capital' he wrote that, his theory explained only *total value* and proved only that the value of all goods combined must equal total labour time. He admitted that prices of particular goods rose or fell not as a result of labour time value changes, but from the effect of credit system, competition and so on. Further Marxian theory of value at first did not take note of time element in the determination of value. Of course, later on, Marx was forced to admit that the time element was after all an important factor in the determination of value. We

shall study later that Marshall made an excellent use of the time element to arrive at a compromise between the earlier theories of value (Labour theory or cost of production theory) and the marginal utility theory of value.

4. As Marxian theory of surplus value is derived from the labour theory of value, it follows that the moment the labour theory of value is overthrown, the theory of surplus value falls to the ground. If labour does not create value, or if value can be created without labour, then there is no proof that labour always creates surplus value.

5. There is no historical proof for Marxian theory of Industrial reserve army.

It has been rightly observed that "Marx's theory of value and surplus value have rather the significance of a political and social slogan than of an economic truth" (Beer). In fact, some of the leading economists of the next period (for instance, Alfred Marshall) not only rejected the tools of economic analysis used by Marx but completely ignored Marx as an economist. But some of the modern economists feel that Marxian economics is still relevant to modern time. For instance, let us see what Mrs. Joan Robinson speaks of Marxian analysis: "Until recently, Marx used to be treated in academic circles with contemptuous silence, broken only by an occasional mocking footnote. But modern developments in economic theory, forced by modern development in economic life—the analysis of monopoly and the analysis of unemployment—have shattered the structure of orthodox doctrine and destroy the complacency with which economists were wont to view the working of laissez-faire capitalism. Their attitude to Marx, as the leading critic of capitalism, is therefore much less cocksure than it used to be. In my belief, they have much to learn from him" (Mrs. Robinson in her foreword to "An Essay on Marxian Economics").

In spite of the above criticisms, we should remember that Marx's 'Capital' is a searching criticism of capitalism. His theory is an assault on the problems of industrialization. He conceived the problem on a grand scale and developed many insights into the problem of modern industrialization.

Marx was aware of the historical relativity of given social, economic and political institutions. He rightly emphasized the importance of economic element in the process of historic change. There is, of course, a view that the capitalist world of Marx was an abstract world of his own thought and his own creation. Groce in his "Historical Materialism" expressed the view that "The capitalist society studied by Marx, is not this or that society, historically existing, in France or in England, nor the modern society of the most civilized nations, that of Western Europe and America. It is an ideal and formal society, deduced from certain hypotheses which could indeed never have occurred as actual facts in the course of history."

We should also remember that Marx was aware of the importance of mechanized, large scale production as a typical form of advanced capitalistic system. Not only that, he was aware of the problem of expansion and contraction of industrial production (trade cycle) in a capitalist society and pointed out that such crisis was inherent in the growth process of capitalistic system. Of course, Marx was not the only one to mention the problem of trade cycle. But Marxian analysis led to many later developments in trade cycle theory.

During an interview in India, late Mrs. John Robinson has expressed the view that modern economists, especially the economists of leading capitalist countries, have diverted people's attention from the 'fundamental problems' raised by Marx. In her opinion, "Marxism has precisely what is lacking in other theories. It teaches about the structure of the society, about who gains and who loses, about those who are involved in production. To study and analyse these is clearly the task of economics."

Marx the Teacher

In the Marxian system, sociology and economics pervade each other. He has used economic and sociological terms almost as identical units. For instance, the economic category "labour" and the social class "proletariat" are made identical. Again, the functional distribution of national income into rent, wages, interest and profits, becomes in the hands of Marx the distribution between social classes and thus acquires a different meaning. Or as Schumpeter puts it beautifully, "Capital in the

Marxian system is capital only if in the hands of a distinct capitalist class. The same thing if in the hands of workmen, is not capital. Thus, Marx, by giving sociological connotation to economic theorems makes them a powerful tool to advocate his socialist ideology. We have seen how Marx tried to rationalize history. He gave economic theory in terms of historical analysis."

Marxism as an Ideology

In spite of many criticisms made against Marxian economics, we should note that Marxism as an ideology has still powerful appeal and is a dynamic force. In one sense, Marxism is a religion and Marx is prophet. No one has influenced the development of socialism so much as Marx.

Marxian synthesis has its merits and demerits. The chief merit of Marxian synthesis is that it brings historical, social, political and economic events into a single grand scheme. But at times, such a synthesis might be misleading and result in both bad economics and bad sociology.

Synthesis is a co-ordination of the methods and results of different lines of advance. It is difficult to achieve it. But Marx, the great teacher, succeeded in achieving a grand wedding of historical events, political facts and economic theorems. Marx's synthesis embraces all the historical events such as wars, revolution and legislative changes and all the social institutions, such as property, forms of government and so on. While most of the non-Marxian economists have treated the above institutions as the given data, Marx considers the above institutions as *variables* and subjected them to explanatory process of economic analysis. For instance, while the classical economists regarded capitalism as a permanent institution, Marx considered it as a variable subject to change.

For all the wars—the Napoleonic wars, the American civil war, the great French Revolution, etc.—Marx tries to give a theoretical explanation in terms of class warfare and of attempts at and revolt against exploitation. Marx, the economist is not content with giving technical answers to technical questions; instead, he teaches humanity the hidden meaning of its struggles. Marx had some prophetic vision too. He predicted the trend toward big business. Of course, he went wrong in predicting increasing misery for the working masses in capitalist countries. Again, Marxian theories of imperialism and class-struggle are not totally correct.

Marxism has been interpreted in a number of ways. Among the Marxists, we have "Orthodox" Marxists and "Revisionists". Lenin, the leader of the Russian Revolution, used Marxian theory as an explanation of "imperialism" and tried to overthrow the Czarist regime in a country which had not yet attained capitalistic phase. Again, his successor Stalin used communism in 1920s and 1930s to create a modern industrial society. In 1960s there was the ideological split between the Russian communists and the Chinese communists.

· Mao-Tse-tung (born 1883) revised most of the central doctrines of Marx. For instance, Marx thought that socialist revolutions would occur in the advanced industrial countries of Western Europe, led by the urban proletariat. But Mao believed that the possibilities for revolution were better in the poor agricultural countries. But on one important thing, both Marx and Mao had the same opinion. Both of them believed in force. According to Marx, "Force is the midwife of every old society pregnant with a new one." Mao believed that "political power grows out of the barrel of a gun." According to Mao, "The seizure of power by armed force, the settlement of issue by war, is the central task and the highest form of revolution. This Marxist-Leninist principle of revolution holds good universally, for China and for all other countries."

It is also interesting to note that Marxism as an ideology has the greatest appeal not in the most economically advanced countries such as the United States of America and England but in the underdeveloped countries which are trying to transform themselves into modern industrial societies.

FABIAN SOCIALISM

Fabian socialism, which developed in England, is a good example of evolutionary socialism. The British Fabian society was organised in 1884, a year after the death of Karl Marx. The society is named after Quintus Fabius Maximus, the famous Roman General who was a great "delayer". Fabius took all steps against his enemy, Hannibal, except to fight him on the battlefield. His motto was *"Hasten slowly"*. Similarly, the Fabian socialists told their followers that they must wait for the right moment, as Fabius did most patiently when warring against Hannibal, though many censured his delays. But when the time comes, they must strike hard, as Fabius did. Otherwise, their waiting would be in vain and fruitless. The Fabian society had a lot of influence in the British Labour party, in government circles, and among intellectuals.

Great intellectuals like George Bernard Shaw, Sidney Webb, Beatrice Webb, H. G. Wells, Bertrand Russel and Harold Laski were all the leading members of the Fabian society. Fabian socialism was dominated by the intellectuals who were drawn from the British middle class. Speaking of his middle-class origin, Shaw once remarked that he belonged to a family of 'downstarts'.

We should remember that fabian socialism is based not on Marxian economic theory but on Ricardo's law of the rent and Jevon's law of value. The Fabian socialists were greatly influenced by Henry George's book "Progress and Poverty" which advocated a single tax on land after abolishing all other taxes. They were also influenced by J. S. Mill who advocated socialization of rent.

The Fabian socialists do not approve of class struggle, revolution and violence. They are for reduction of inequalities of income and wealth. But they believe in gradual change by means of education, persuasion and parliamentary reform. They are not for total abolition of capitalist institutions but they are for their modification. They advocate control over monopolies, state ownership of utilities. Owing to the emphasis of the Fabian socialists, who are also sometimes described as revisionists, on ownership and management of public utilities by public authorities, the Fabian socialism sometimes has been called 'gas and water socialism.' The Fabian socialists advocate trade unionism, factory legislation, tax reform, nationalization of key industries. In short, the Fabian socialists advocate social justice through a gradual and peaceful socialization of means of production. Strangely, the Fabian socialists supported imperialism. The reasons are not far to seek. They belonged to the British empire and they did not want England to become a tiny pair of islands in the North Sea. They, especially Shaw, argued that a great power should govern the interests of civilizations as a whole.

Sidney Webb (1859-1947)

Sidney Webb was a leading Fabian socialist. He came of a middle-class family. He had a remarkable memory and he had a passion for social reform. Webb was a member of Parliament and also served as a Minister in Labour Government. His wife, Beatrice Webb (1859-1943), was the daughter of a very rich man. Her independent income enabled both of them to devote their attention to study the social problems in a systematic way. The Webbs founded the London School of Economics and Political

Science, which is now a part of the University of London. The Webbs published splendid literature on social problems.

The Webbs had no faith in producers' co-operatives such as the agricultural credit banks. They thought that such institutions were a part of the capitalist system for they were guided by profit motive. Not only that, the producers' co-operatives excluded their own employees from membership. The Webbs believed that consumers' co-operatives would ultimately replace capitalism with the "co-operative commonwealth". They regarded capitalism as a decaying civilization and they looked hopefully at Soviet communism, which they regarded as a new civilization.

Bernard Shaw (1856-1950)

Bernard Shaw heard one of the lectures of Henry George, the author of "Progress and Poverty", in 1882. Henry George, in his lecture, advocated a tax on the rent of land. Later, Shaw read the book "Progress and Poverty". That book made him a socialist. Since then he had advocated radical economic reforms. Shaw's economic ideas are found in his *"Fabian Essays"* and his *"Intelligent Woman's Guide to Socialism."*

Shaw rejected the Marxian theory of surplus value. Marx's theory was incomplete because it did not include the value of commodities which were not freely reproducible (such as old masters). Further, Marx denied productivity to resources other than labour.

Shaw's attack on private property is based on Ricardian theory of rent. He felt that private ownership of land resulted in a number of unjust privileges to landowners. So he said that "It is practically a demonstration that public property in land is the basic economic condition of socialism." Shaw attacked rent on land as well as urban rent. He regarded high rent as 'unearned increment.' And Shaw made no distinction between rent on land and interest on capital. Both rent and interest, he considered, as returns of exploitation. In fact, Webb and Shaw extended the rent theory even to include 'rent of ability' of superior workers. According to Stigler, "It is a most unusual feature of Fabian socialism that it attacked large labour incomes as well as property incomes. Much of the superior earnings of professional men and artists was attributed to the unequal distribution of income, which allowed a few men to prosper by catering to the whims of the rich." Shaw advocated widespread education and progressive income tax. He pleaded for reduction of inequalities of income. His argument against unequal distribution of income is that it will lead to unequal distribution of consumption. That is, productive resources will be diverted for the production of luxuries even before the vital necessities of subsistence are produced.

Conclusion

Like most of the popular social reformers, the Fabian socialists were not good economists. Naturally, they were not able to construct a coherent programme of economic reform. But we should note that they were very effective in their criticism of the existing order.

THE MARGINAL REVOLUTION

Introduction

The 'Marginal Revolution' took place in the latter half of the nineteenth century. The marginalist school developed in many countries at the same time. Different people worked independently of each other at first. Stanley Jevons in England, Carl Menger in Austria and Leon Walras at Lausanne, Switzerland are generally regarded as the founders of the Marginalist school. Hermann Heinrich Gossen of Germany is considered to be an anticipator of the marginalist school. The term "Marginal Revolution" is applied to the writings of the above economists because they made fundamental changes in the apparatus of economic analysis. And they started looking at some of the important economic problems from an altogether new angle different from that of the classical economists. Marginal economics has been used to analyse the single firm and its behaviour, consumer behaviour, the market for a single product and the formation of individual prices. Marginalism dominated Western economic thought for nearly a century until it was challenged by Keynesian attack in 1936. Keynesian economics, however, shifted the sphere of enquiry from micro-economics to macro-economics, where the problems of the economy as a whole are analysed.

The provocation for the emergence of marginalist school was provided by the interpretation of the classical doctrines, especially the Labour theory of value and the Ricardian theory of rent by socialists. Karl Marx made use of the Labour Theory of Value to develop his theory to attack the very foundations of capitalism. Again, Henry George made use of the Ricardian theory of rent to describe rent as an 'unearned increment' and advocated a tax on the rent of land. In other words, he advocated socialization of rent. Thus the socialists made use of the classical theories to say things which were not the intention of the creators of those theories. So the leading early marginalists felt the need for thoroughly revising the classical doctrines, especially the theory of value. They thought by rejecting the labour theory of value and by advocating the marginal utility theory of value, they could strike at the *theoretical basis* of socialism.

Meaning of Marginal Revolution and its Implications for the Theory of Value

The classical theory emphasized on supply, production and cost. But the marginalist school emphasizes on consumption, demand and utility.

Utility is key word of the marginalist school. And they have used the concept of marginal utility to shift the emphasis from supply to demand and from cost to utility as the basis of value. The marginal analysis is regarded as an innovation in the method of approach of the science. As has been already noted, the essential elements of modern technique, namely, the emphasis on demand, and utility and the recognition of marginal utility were developed in the 19th century. The utility approach is subjective approach.

Value is the central problem in exchange. The entire economic activity may be thought of as a network of exchange transactions in the market. We can consider the economic system as a number of interdependent markets. Then, the central problem of economic enquiry becomes the explanation of exchange process or explanation of the formation of price.

The classical economists explained value in terms of labour. It was an objective theory. The labour theory of value was significantly altered by some of the post-classical economists. But still they retained labour and cost as elements in the explanation of value. They developed a subjective real-cost theory. Even the subjective real cost theory was weak because it continued to regard labour as a determinant of value.

The marginal utility school takes consumption as the starting point. The school claims that its theory of value is independent of any social order. But, as we have already noted, the classical theory was not strong enough to withstand the attacks of the growing working-class movement. So the early marginalists abandoned the labour theory of value altogether. There is another point which we have to remember. Classical political economy was developed more or less entirely by English economists. Though Jevons was one of the founders of the marginalist school, continental writers, especially Carl Menger of Austria, made significant contributions to the development of the marginalist school. Menger was the founder of the Austrian school. That is why sometimes the marginal utility school is also referred to as the Austrian school. However, there was one basic difference between Jevons and Menger. While Jevons was still influenced by the utilitarian philosophy of Bentham, he gave the new theory of value, a non-utilitarian interpretation of value. The marginalists developed new and powerful tools of economic analysis. They made use of diagrams and mathematical methods. Economics became an exact science in their hands.

We shall now discuss the essential ideas of the Marginalist school.

Essential Ideas of the Marginalist School

1. The marginalist school, concentrated on the 'margin' to explain economic phenomena. According to this school, all economic decisions are made at the point of margin. The marginal utility school extended the marginal principle to all economic theories.

   We know that economists were troubled for a long time about the paradox of value. For instance, water had great value in use but very low value in exchange. On the other hand, diamonds which had very low value-in-use, had high exchange value. They offered explanations which sound funny to a student of modern economics. For instance, J. B. Say explained that air and water are so useful that their value is infinite and therefore we cannot buy them. The marginal utility theory helps us to explain this paradox. The confusion arose in the minds of the early writers because they did not distinguish between *total* and *marginal* utility. Though the total utility of water is great, its marginal utility is low. In the case of diamonds, as the supply is small, marginal utility tends to be high, though the total utility of diamonds is small. As value depends upon marginal utility, it commands a high value-in-exchange.

2. The approach of the marginalist school is micro-economic rather than macro-economic. The marginalist school does not deal with the aggregate economy. It deals with decision-making of individual buyers and sellers, price of a single commodity, the output of a single firm and so on. In other words, it is concerned mainly with the problems of partial equilibrium analysis.

3. The marginal school has adopted the abstract and deductive method of classical economists.

4. The marginal utility analysis is based on the assumptions of competition. There will be a large number of buyers and sellers and no one buyer or seller can influence the market decisions by his actions.

5. While the classical school considered cost of production, that is, supply, as the determinant of value, the marginalist school considered demand to be important element in the determination of value.

6. The analysis of the marginalist school is based on the subjective and the psychological approach.

7. The marginalist approach is based on the assumption of rational behaviour on the part of individuals. The marginalists assume that men act in a rational manner in balancing their pleasures and pains and in measuring marginal utilities of different goods.

8. The marginal school believes that economic forces generally tend towards equilibrium.

9. Lastly, the marginalists supported the *laissez-faire* policy of the classical economists. They thought, maximum social welfare could be attained by market forces such as competition and there should not be any governmental interference with natural economic laws.

We shall now discuss the ideas of some of the leading economists of the marginalist school.

Gossen (1810-1858)

Herman Heinrich Gossen is one of the most tragic figures in the history of economics. Gossen was an anticipator of the marginal utility theory. He published his book "Development of the Laws of Exchange Among Men" in 1854. He hoped that his book would revolutionize the science of economics. He claimed that he was doing to economics what Copernicus did for astronomy. But his ideas were never popular during his lifetime. One main reason for that was his treatment of the subject was highly mathematical. But Jevons and Menger praised the pioneering efforts made by Gossen in the development of marginal utility theory.

Gossen's analysis of the laws of human conduct exhibits *three* main features: (*i*) Utilitarianism, (*ii*) Consumption approach, and (*iii*) Mathematical method.

Gossen's analysis of economic system is based on hedonism. Bentham's utilitarianism can be seen there. According to him, "Man tries to maximize his pleasure, and minimize his pain. In other words, he believed that the aim of all human conduct is to maximize enjoyment." Gossen has given certain laws of human enjoyment. Of them, the first two laws are very important.

Gossen's First Law: It states that "The amount of one and the same enjoyment diminishes continuously as we proceed with that enjoyment without interruption, until satiety is reached." In modern times, this law is known as the *Law of Diminishing Marginal Utility*. In other words, the law tells that the marginal utility of a good for a person diminishes with every increase in the stock that he already has.

Gossen's Second Law: The second law tells that each man will spend his money on different commodities in such a way that the amounts of all enjoyment will result from a uniform level of satisfaction. In modern terms, Gossen's second law is known as the *Law of Equi-marginal Utility*.

Gossen's views on value are based on the above two laws. According to Gossen, the value of a thing depends upon the enjoyment which it can give. And individual units of the same good will have different values according to the quantity possessed. Beyond a certain quantity, a single unit will not have any value at all. Gossen emphasized that value must be considered only in relative terms. In his own words, "nothing in the external world possesses absolute value; value depends entirely on the relation between the object and the subject."

Gossen classified goods into different classes. First, there are the consumption goods. They satisfy our wants immediately. Second there are goods of the second class. They are jointly necessary for enjoyment. In modern times we call these goods complementary goods. (*e.g.,* tooth brush and tooth paste; car and petrol; carriage and horse). Goods of the third class are those which are used in the production of other goods. Gossen also noted that labour which creates means of enjoyment (utility) is also accompanied by pain (disutility). So he said that the utility of any product must be estimated after deducting the pains of labour required to produce it.

The foregoing analysis tells that Gossen's book contains the essential elements of the marginal utility school. Gossen was a great original thinker who believed that mathematical methods were absolutely essential to explain economic phenomena.

William Stanley Jevons (1835-1882)

Jevons was one of the founders of the marginal utility school. He was an English economist, who worked out the ideas of the marginalist school quite independently of Menger, the founder of the Austrian School.

William Stanley Jevons was born in Liverpool, England in 1835. He studied at University College, London. Jevons was appointed as an assayer of the mint in 1854 at Sydney in Australia and he worked there for five years. On his return to England, he entered teaching profession. He became professor of logic, political economy and philosophy, first in Manchester and later at University College, London. He was a many-sided genius. He published several books on logic and political economy. Jevons made many outstanding contributions to the development of index numbers. At the age of forty seven, in 1882, Jevons met with an untimely death by a drowning accident while swimming.

Jevons' main contribution to economic theory is to be found in his "Theory of Political Economy" (1871). His other important works are "The Investigations in Currency and Finance" which was posthumously published in 1884, "The Serious Fall in the Value of Gold" and "The Coal Question" (1865). Jevons was interested not merely in theory but also in the problems of applied economics. He also made an attempt to construct a theory of trade cycles. His theory is known as 'sun-spot theory.' The theory tried to establish a connection between the rhythm of harvests and trade. He thought harvests in any year were influenced by meteorological fluctuations (sun-spots and all that). Jevons failed in his attempt to provide a satisfactory explanation of the trade cycle. And the sun-spot theory today is only of historic interest.

Jevons' fame rests mainly on his contribution to the development of the marginal utility theory. He emphasized the mathematical character of economics. *"Our science must be mathematical simply because it deals with quantities.* Wherever the things treated are capable of being greater or less, there the laws and relations must be mathematical in nature. The ordinary laws of supply and demand treat entirely of quantities of commodity demanded or supplied, and express the manner in which the quantities vary in connexion with the price. In consequence of this fact the laws *are* mathematical. Economists cannot alter their nature by denying them the name; they might as well try to alter red light by calling it blue."

Jevons' economic analysis is based on hedonism, which, in turn, is the basis of Bentham's utilitarianism. He believed that the laws of economics could be derived from "the great springs of human action—the feeling of pleasure and pain."

According to Jevons, *"Value depends entirely upon utility."* He considered this a great innovation and revolutionary idea because the classical economists believed that the value depended upon the amount of labour expended in the production of a good. Jevons rejected the labour theory of value which dominated economic thought for a long time. He believed that labour once spent has no influence on the future value of any article. He argued that labour spent on the production of a commodity is gone and lost for ever. Many economic theories of classical economists were based on the Ricardian theory of value. Jevons described Ricardo as "an able but wrong-headed man who shunted the car of economic science on to a wrong line." He felt that Mill pushed the car further toward confusion. For Mill stated, "Happily there is nothing in the laws of value which remains for the present or any future writer to clear up; the theory of the subject is complete...." That, however, was not to be the case.

After saying that 'value depends entirely upon utility,' Jevons explains the term 'utility'. He describes utility as the quality possessed by an object of producing pleasure or preventing pain. Utility is relative. It is not an intrinsic quality. It merely expresses a relation between an object and a subject. Jevons then makes the distinction between total utility and *final degree of utility.* (In modern times, we call this 'final degree of utility' as 'marginal utility'. We should remember that none of the founders of the marginalist school used the term 'marginal utility' as such). It was Marshall who used the expression, 'marginal utility' as such. Like Gossen, Jevons concluded that successive increments of a commodity reduced the utility of every unit. According to Jevons, 'final degree of utility' denotes "the degree of utility of the last addition, or the next possible addition, of a very small, or infinitely small, quantity of the existing stock." In other words, "the final degree of utility varies with the quantity of commodity, and ultimately decreases as that quantity increases." If a commodity can be put to a number of uses, the theory of utility tells that the distribution between various uses should be so assigned that the final degree of utility in the various directions should be equal. The final degree of utility is the fundamental concept in Jevons' theory of exchange and distribution.

Jevons formulated his theory of value in the following manner:

Cost of production determines supply;

Supply determines final degree of utility; and

Final degree of utility determines value.

From the above theory, it can be seen that though Jevons dismissed the labour theory of value, he agreed that labour indirectly influenced value by varying the utility of the commodity through an increase or decrease of the supply. But he argued that labour would not directly influence value because labour itself varied in quality and efficiency. He further went on to say that 'the value of labour is determined by the value of the produce, not the value of the produce by that of the labour.' He described labour, which was a 'painful exertion' as a subjective, psychological cost. He felt that the main problem of economics was to satisfy our wants with the least possible sum of labour.

Jevons preferred the term "ratio of exchange" for value. And he defined that ratio of exchange as "the reciprocal of the ratio of the final degree of utility of the quantities of commodity available for consumption after the exchange is completed." In other words, when an act of exchange takes place between two persons, the marginal utility for each person will be proportionate to price. From the above argument, Jevons concluded that 'a person distributes his income in such a way as to equalize the utility of the final increments of all commodities consumed.' Lionel Robbins is of the opinion that Jevons was not very successful in elaborating a satisfactory theory of exchange: "His celebrated equations of exchange certainly showed one condition of equilibrium, namely, that equilibrium, for each party to exchange, what he called final degrees of utility must be proportionate to price. This is right enough so far as it goes on the simple assumptions Jevons was making. But it does not explain the formation of price under competitive condition."[1]

Jevons' other Theories

Jevons did not develop a general theory of distribution based on marginal productivity. He did not explain clearly, the law of diminishing marginal returns. It was J. B. Clark who gave the best formulation of the Law of Diminishing Returns and the marginal productivity theory of distribution. He accepted more or less the classical theory of rent. His theory of wages resembles the Residual claimant theory of Walker. Jevons concluded that 'the wages of a working man are ultimately coincident with what he produces after the deduction of rent, taxes and the interest of capital.' He defined wages as the residual share of the product. He was of the belief that wages 'are the effect, not the cause of the value of the produce.' However, Jevons' theory of capital and interest received much praise in the hands of Lionel Robbins for Jevons has emphasized the role of time element in the determination of interest. The essence of Jevons' theory of interest is that the rate of interest is among others a function of time for which factors of production are invested before yielding their final product.

Conclusion

Jevons was right in claiming that his theory of value based on utility would bring about a revolution in economic analysis. The term 'Jevonian revolution' may be rightly applied to his work. According to Schumpeter, Jevons "was without any doubt one of the most genuinely original economists who ever lived." It is true that his theory of marginal utility had been anticipated by economists like Gossen. But we should note that he heard of his forerunners only after he had written his book. Above

---

1. Lord Robbins: *The Evolution of Modern Economic Theory*, p. 177.

all, Jevons was as much a logician as he was an economist. In the opinion of Marshall, "There are few writers of modern times who have approached as near to the brilliant originality of Ricardo as Jevons has done."

Carl Menger (1840-1921)

Carl Menger was the founder of the Austrian school. He was in civil service for a brief period and later on became a professor of Political Economy at the University of Vienna. He published his book "Principles of Economics" in the same year (1871) in which Jevons published his book. Menger's book established his fame as the author of the 'Marginal Revolution' of the Austrian school.

According to Eric Roll, "Menger's contributions to economics fall into *three* main classes: method, money and pure theory."

Method

Menger advocated deductive method in economic analysis. In fact, he entered into a great debate with Schmoller, the leader of the 'Newer Historical School' over the question of method. While Schmoller advocated inductive method, Menger supported deductive method. The debate was called the "Battle of Methods." In a pamphlet called "Errors of Historicism" while defending theoretical analysis, Menger wrote, "The historians have stepped upon the territory of our science like foreign conquerors, in order to force upon us their language and their customs, their terminology and their methods, and to fight intolerantly every branch of enquiry which does not correspond with their method."

Menger emphasized that economic method must rest on an individualist foundation. He argued that without understanding the behaviour of individuals, we can never understand the total economic process. Like Jevons, he put the individual into the centre of the picture. His approach is an atomistic approach. But he differed from Jevons in one fundamental respect. While Jevons developed his theory on the basis of hedonism, Menger tried to develop a subjective theory of value free from hedonistic assumption. Again, what Jevons tried to say with mathematical tools, Menger managed to say it in plain language.

Money

After describing the inconveniences of barter, Menger explains how money acts as a universal medium of exchange. Money facilitates the quantification of subjective values. The values of goods can be expressed through money. In other words, money acts as a price index. Menger has given one of the best explanations of the function of money in the process of exchange and in the formation of price. Besides, in the field of applied theory of money, Menger made many important suggestions for implementing Austrian currency reform.

Pure Theory: Theory of Value

Menger's subjective theory of value is one of his lasting contributions to economic thought. Menger starts with wants and means. He defines utility in a relative sense.

Classification of Goods

Menger classified goods on technical grounds into goods of the first order, and of the second, third and higher orders. Goods of the first order are those which can be used for the immediate satisfaction of our wants (*e.g.*, bread). Goods of the second order (*e.g.*, flour) are used for the production of the goods of the first order which directly satisfy our wants. Goods of the third order (*e.g.*, wheat) are used for the production of goods of the second order. It goes on like that. Thus "beyond the bread is the flour; beyond the flour the grain; beyond the grain, the field and the plough; beyond the plough, the iron." (A. Gray). Menger makes use of this classification of goods to establish the relationship between the value of the goods of the first order and the value of the production goods of all kinds.

Menger further classified goods into: (*i*) economic goods, and (*ii*) non-economic goods. Economic goods are those goods whose supply is inadequate in relation to our wants. So we are compelled to economize them. In the case of non-economic goods, that is, those goods whose supply exceeds our need, there is no need to economize them. But Menger has made the point that the classification of goods into economic and non-economic goods is not a permanent one. It is only relative. Goods may move from the category of economic goods to that of non-economic goods, and vice-versa. It all depends on changes in wants, supply of goods, technique of production and so on. Goods of economic order are said to possess scarcity. It may be interesting to note that Auguste Walras, the father of Leon Walras, used the term 'rarete' in more or less the same sense used by Menger. Today, every person who has an elementary knowledge of economics knows that means are scarce in relation to wants. "But Menger was the first without using the word, to express precisely the quantitative relation between ends and means to which the word is now applied." (Eric Roll).

According to Menger, "Value arises from the limitation of goods in relation to wants." Only economic goods possess value. Free goods do not possess value. Menger's theory of value is subjective in character. "Value is a judgment of the mind; not a property of the thing or an independent entity." Like Jevons, Menger developed the idea that the value of a thing was proportionate to its marginal utility. Of course, Menger did not use the term as such. Menger considered even the measure of value as subjective. A commodity may have great value to one individual, little or no value to another. Its value depends on the requirements of different individuals and the amounts available to each of them. Menger emphasizes that value has nothing to do with cost of production or labour: "Whether a diamond was found accidentally or was obtained from a diamond pit with the employment of a thousand days of labour is completely irrelevant for its value.... goods on which much labour has been expended often have no value, while others, on which little or no labour was expended, have a very high value." Menger has also made the point that the value of any portion of goods when a supply exists, is represented by the least important use to which such a portion is applied.

Menger denied Adam Smith's dictum that exchange is due to a human propensity to truck. He argued that trading is undertaken to increase the satisfaction enjoyed by traders. For example, if a farmer has more grain than he needs and if a winegrower has more wine than he needs, it will be of mutual advantage for them to trade. When trade takes place, they will be in equilibrium when the ratio of the marginal utilities of two goods are the same for both of them. According to Menger, "The principle that leads men to exchange is the same principle that guides them in their economic activity as a whole; it is the endeavour to ensure the fullest possible satisfaction of their needs."

Imputation

Menger introduced the idea of *imputation* in pricing factors of production, that is, in the theory of distribution. He made use of the concept to analyse the problem of the value of goods of a higher order (including the factors of production). He tells that the value of goods of a higher order is "conditioned by the anticipated value of those goods of a lower order for the production of which they serve." Menger has made use of the concept of imputation to explain factor prices. He has extended the principle of marginal utility to the whole area of production and distribution. For example, the rent received by landowners is governed by the utility of the products grown on the land. In general, the present value of the means of production is equal to the prospective value (based on marginal utility) of the consumer goods they will produce. Of course a margin has to be subtracted for interest and profit.

Monopoly

Menger has pointed out the limitations on monopoly. "The monopolist is not completely unrestricted in influencing the course of events.... He cannot, therefore, sell large quantities of the monopolized good and at the same time cause the price to settle at as high a level as it would have reached if he had marketed smaller quantities." He has also mentioned about the policy of restrictionism that is generally

...y the monopolist. Menger has pointed out that the monopolist would fix the price of his ...he level that would give him maximum profit.

Conclusion

Menger was a careful and an original thinker. He was a great thinker because he could formulate his theories precisely in spite of the fact that he lacked the appropriate mathematical tools. His fundamental principle of marginal utility was his own. He was a pioneer in the field of 'Marginal Revolution' and his theoretical system was based on extreme individualism.

Leon Walras (1834-1910)

Leon Walras was one of the three founders of the marginal utility school. He was a Frenchman, who taught political economy at the Law Faculty of the University of Lausanne, Switzerland. He was the son of Auguste Walras, the noted economist who was the author of the term '*rarete*' which more or less means marginal utility. Before becoming the professor of economics at the university of Lausanne, Walras tried his hand at many things—engineering, journalism and novel-writing. He was not always successful in these attempts. The economic ideas of Leon Walras are found in his book 'Elements of Pure Economics' which was published in 1874.

Method

Walras used mathematical method. He used this method more thoroughly than Jevons. In fact, Walras is considered the founder of mathematical-utility school in economics. Walras felt that non-mathematical persons had no future in theoretical economics. They would only make bad economists. He hoped that one day "mathematical economics will rank with mathematical sciences of astronomy and mechanics." According to Walras, "Pure economics is, in essence, the theory of the determination of prices under a hypothetical regime of perfectly free competition." Walras developed a theory which combined a utility theory of value with a mathematically precise theory of market equilibrium. On account of his mathematical approach, Walras cannot be easily understood by all. That is why he has been described as an economist's economist.

Walras developed marginal utility theory independently of Jevons and Menger. Like Jevons and Menger, he bases exchange value on utility. He tells that value depends upon marginal utility. He uses the term '*rarete*' (a term used by his father) to mean marginal utility. He defines *rarete* as "the intensity of the last want satisfied." And he tells that the desire to equalize marginal utilities will lead to exchange. Walras believed that there was a direct relation between demand and price. And he thought that there was no such direct relationship between supply and price.

General Exchange Equilibrium

On the basis of his marginal utility theory, Walras has developed the concept of general exchange equilibrium. While Jevons dealt with the problem of exchange equations for only two commodities, Walras formulated equations to deal with the problem of exchange values of any number of commodities.

Under conditions of competition, equilibrium will be achieved when the price is such that supply and demand are equal. Walras develops in stages the concept of general equilibrium. He takes first exchange of two commodities, then exchange of several commodities. He also deals with the theory of production. Then he explains how equilibrium takes place through a series of equations.

The general equilibrium analysis of Walras is based on the following assumptions: (*i*) There is free competition, and (*ii*) consumers' tastes, technology and factors of production (land, labour, etc.) remain constant.

We may describe his general equilibrium analysis roughly in the following manner.

Walras divides the entire economy into *two* great markets: (*i*) *a product market,* and (*ii*) *a factor market.* In the case of the product market, the sellers consist of business firms who have produced the goods and the buyers are the households which consume the goods. In the factor market, the business firms become the buyers while the households who own the land, labour, and other factors of production become sellers.

According to Walras, "The buyers and the sellers go to their respective markets and each is guided by the desire to maximize his utility." Various prices and quantities are offered until general equilibrium is reached. When once general equilibrium is reached (i) no buyer or seller can increase his utility by any change in his own actions, and (ii) demand for products and factors of production will be exactly equal to supply.

An important thing about the general equilibrium analysis is that it considers the interrelationships among the many variables in the economy. For instance, when there is a change in the price of a good, say butter, it will not affect the demand for butter alone, it will affect the demand, price and supply of substitutes too. This, in turn will cause a shift in employment of factors of production as well. So the general equilibrium analysis gives us a picture of general system of the interdependence of prices, demand and supply. Its main purpose is to demonstrate mathematically all prices and quantities produced can be adjusted to the level of demand. In other words, in a state of equilibrium, the demand for any commodity will be equal to its supply.

Walras makes use of a device known as 'numeraire' to explain general exchange equilibrium. 'Numeraire' is the good which is used as a unit of account. It is a nominal thing representing goods. We have to note that it is not money in the ordinary sense of the word. Walras has made use of it to solve his equations.

In short, the general equilibrium theory of Walras tells that a change in one part of the economy can lead to changes throughout the economic system just as a stone thrown into a pond causes widening circles of ripples.

The general equilibrium analysis of Walras has been criticized on certain grounds. First, it is based on a static approach. It assumes many important factors such as tastes, form of competition, supply of factors to remain constant. It does not take note of changes that take place over time. Second, it does not help us to understand the problem of economic growth. Third, the analysis is essentially hypothetical and it does not provide a framework for actual price determination. Fourth, from his general equilibrium analysis, Walras seemed to argue that free competition resulted in maximization of utility. But some later economists like Wicksell argued that state intervention in competition by altering prices would bring about distribution in property and thereby promote the happiness of a majority of people.

Modern economists are not generally bothered about the origin of value. They are mainly interested in formulating a general theory of functional interdependence. Walras may be considered a pioneer in that trend.

Walras's theory of production is merely an extension of his general equilibrium analysis to the field of factor-pricing. It is only a special case of the theory of value. According to Eric Roll, "His solution was one of the earliest statements of the opportunity cost principle and of the modern marginal productivity theory."

Leon Walras was a born thinker. He may be considered as the founder of the "General Equilibrium Economics" besides being one of the founders of the marginal utility school. All those who deal with the problems of general equilibrium at the present time start with Walras and acknowledge his influence.

An Estimate of Marginal Utility School

It is generally agreed that the marginal utility school really made a revolutionary advance in economic analysis. Of course, the school has its own critics. One of the major points of criticism against the marginalist school is that it rationalizes human behaviour too much. Critics say that it is rather difficult to find their economic man—"the rational maximizer of utility." Second, their theories of market prices are based on the assumption of perfect competition, which we do not have in the real world.

They have not dealt with the problems of monopoly price in any detailed manner. Third, they have not taken note of the influence of trade unions on wages. In other words, their theories do not deal with the problems of 'big business, big labour, big government'. Fourth, they have not dealt with the problems affecting the process of economic growth. Fifth, they have not developed any theories of trade cycle. They have said little or nothing on some of the central problems of modern economics, namely, the problems of unemployment and depression. Lastly, they believed that marginal utility was quantitatively measurable. This assumption came in for a lot of criticism. That is why modern economists make use of the 'indifference curve approach' to study consumer's equilibrium where they deal with the problems of *different levels* of satisfaction and not with different amounts of satisfaction. Modern economists like Pareto and J. R. Hicks have shown that general equilibrium theory can be constructed without assuming a quantitatively measurable utility. Modern economics makes use of a theory of consumers' preference in which the consumer is asked if he prefers one set of goods to another, not by how much he prefers them.

The economists of marginalist school also realized the interdependence of economic life. Instead of having a theory of value, and another theory of production and yet another theory of distribution, the economists of the marginal school demonstrated how all these aspects of economic activity are related to each other. In the opinion of Prof. T. Gill, "Probably the most important technical contribution lay in the development of the tools of what we can call *marginal analysis*. The particular concept of marginal utility may have gone by the board, but in its place there are marginal rates of substitution, marginal products, marginal costs, marginal revenues, marginal rates of transformation and a host of other such terms which are at the very core of economic theory today."[1]

---

1. Richard T. Gill, *Evolution of Modern Economics*, p. 61.

THE AUSTRIAN SCHOOL

Carl Menger was the founder of the Austrian school. Austrian Economics is derived mainly from Menger's *Principles of Economics* (1871) and *Problems of Economics and Sociology* (1883). The Austrian school of Economics differs in essential respects from the Classical school, the Historical school, and from the Marxian, Institutional and Mathematical economics.

Bohm-Bawerk and Friedrich Von Wieser, who belonged to the second generation of the Austrian school are often regarded as the co-founders of the school. In fact, Carl Menger, Wieser and Bohn-Bawerk are considered as the three pillars of the Austrian school. It may be noted that Austrian Economics is not a completely uniform system accepted in every detail by all the members of the group. Even the leaders of the school disagreed with one another on several issues. However, in the 1890s, marginalism, diminishing marginal utility, costs as foregone utility and imputation of value to complementary factors were considered as the characteristic tenets of the school. In later years, major emphasis was placed by the followers of the school on methodological individualism and subjectivism. The Austrian school is generally regarded as non-mathematical. The writings of Bohm-Bawerk and Wieser helped to spread Austrian Economics throughout the world. The later generation Austrians such as Ludwig Von Mises and Friedrich A. Von Hayek had great influence among economists.

Main Principles of the Austrian School

Most of the members of the Austrian school believed in the following tenets:

1. *Methodological individualism*: They believed that in the explanation of economic phenomena, we have to go back to the actions of the individuals. Groups cannot act except through the actions of individual members.
2. *Methodological subjectivism*: To explain economic phenomena, we have to depend upon the judgements and choices made by individuals on the basis of their knowledge and expectations regarding external developments and consequences of their own intended actions.
3. *Marginalism*: It refers to the principle that in all economic decisions, relating to value, cost, revenue, productivity and so on are determined by the significance of the marginal (last) unit, or lot, added to or subtracted from the total.
4. *Tastes and preferences*: Subjective valuation (utility) of commodities and services determines the demand for them. In other words, market prices are influenced by consumers. The allocation of a consumer's income among various uses is influenced by the diminishing marginal utility of each good.
5. *Opportunity cost*: The cost of production reflects the most important of the alternative foregone if productive services are employed for one purpose rather than for the (sacrificed) alternatives. The opportunity cost was first called Wieser's law of costs.

Time Structure of Consumption and Production

The decisions to save reflect "time preference" regarding consumption in the immediate, distant or indefinite future. Similarly, investments are made to obtain larger outputs from given inputs by means of processes taking more time.

Carl Menger (1840-1921)

The main contributions of Carl Menger, the founder of the Austrian School, to economics fall into three classes: "method, money and pure theory." (A detailed account of Menger's contribution is given in the previous chapter dealing with the Marginal Revolution).

Friedrich Von Wieser

The publication of *Source and Principal Laws of Economic Value* in 1884 by Wieser is the next important step in the development of the Austrian theory. He applied Menger's theory to the phenomena of costs and distribution.

Wieser explained value in terms of marginal utility. This is what Jevon's called earlier "final utility."

In his book *Natural Value, Wieser* explained the value of the factor of production in terms of the "productive contribution" of the factor—a theory of *Positive imputation*.

In his last work, *Theory of Social Economics* (1914), Wieser draws a distinction between "cost instruments of production" which are reproducible and applicable to more than one use, and "specific instruments of production" which, like land are naturally scarce and limited to a single use. Cost instruments, as they are subject to many uses, can have their productivity imputed by comparing numerous equations. But specific instruments are treated as residual claimants. They are assigned such portions of the marginal utility of the joint product as are not imputed to the cost instruments with which they are used (labour and capital). We may note that this is only a broadened version of rent concept.

It may be noted that though Wieser denies that cost of factors of production determines the value of the product, he admits that costs have an indirect effect. His idea is that only men's interests, based on utility, induce them to estimate value at cost. According to Haney, "This development of the conception of cost as subjected to utility is one of his (Wieser's) contribution to the theories of the Austrian school." In Wieser's own words, "the cost value does not determine the use value; the use value exists of itself, and sanctions the cost value." (*Natural Value* p. 177).

Bohm-Bawerk (1851-1914)

The main contributions of Bohm-Bawerk are found in *Capital and Interest* (1884), *Outlines of the Theory of Commodity Value* (1886), and the *Positive Theory of Capital* (1888).

Bohm-Bawerk has elaborated the division of value into subjective value and objective value. He has replaced the old division of value into use value and exchange value by these terms. One of his chief merits lies in his treatment of objective value or purchasing power. He made an excellent attempt to develop and complete theory of objective exchange value and price.

Exchange value, in the objective sense, is nothing but the capacity of a good to command other goods in exchange.

Bohm-Bawerk attempts to show that exchange value depends upon individual valuations. First, he takes an isolated pair. Then he introduces competition among a group of buyers. Then he speaks of competition among several sellers. Finally, he considers two sided competition.

According to Bohm-Bawerk, objective exchange value is determined somewhere between (*i*) an upper limit set by the valuations of the last, or least desirous, buyer included in the exchange and the most capable seller excluded on the one hand, and (*ii*) a lower limit established by the valuations of the least capable seller—the last seller—and the most desirous seller excluded.

In Bohm-Bawerk's own words, "if, finally, we substitute the short and significant name of "Marginal Pairs" for the detailed description of the four parties whose competition determine the price, we get this simple formula: The market price is limited and determined by the subjective valuations of the two "Marginal pairs.""

Like Wieser, Bohm-Bawerk admits that cost plays a part in determining value, but only a subordinate and indirect one.

Bohm-Bawerk's Theory of Capital and Interest

The two basic principles in Bohn-Bawerk's theory of capital are: (*i*) Perspective undervaluation of the future' (Irving Fisher calls it "impatience") and (*ii*) roundaboutness of production. The perspective undervaluation of the future induces consumers to discount the expected utility of future consumption (or the importance of future needs). Hence saving (non-consumption of income) and the supply of capital become scarce. "Roundaboutness of production" refers to the use of productive services (labour, land) over longer periods of production (investment). It makes these services more productive and that explains the demand for capital. We shall elaborate the arguments a little further.

Bohm-Bawerk's theory of interest is known as the Agio theory of interest because it is built on the concept of 'Agio'. It means a premium which the present always carries as compared with the future. Generally, a man prefers present satisfaction to future satisfaction. It is considered that the present goods are more valuable that future goods, just as a bird in hand is worth two in the bush. So when people save they have to postpone their enjoyment of goods. Since people generally do not like postponement of satisfaction, if you want them to postpone their present satisfaction, you have to pay them some compensation and that compensation is interest.

People prefer present consumption to future consumption for the following psychological and technical reasons. The psychological reasons are they over-estimate future resources and under-estimate future needs. Hope is the cause of the former and lack of imagination and weakness of will are the cause of the latter. These two causes operate to increase the marginal utility of goods in the present compared with their marginal utility in the future. They create an '*agio*' (Premium); and to call forth a supply of present in return for future goods, that '*agio*' has to be paid.

The third factor is of a technical nature. According to Bohm–Bawerk, the whole progress of civilization on its technical side consists in the adoption of more 'roundabout' methods of production. From the making of simple tools and instruments, to the production of most elaborate modern machines, progress has meant more and more intermediate stages between the original factors and the finished consumption goods. And people consider present goods more valuable than future goods. And "interest measures the difference between the value of present and of future goods of like kind and like amount." In other words, people believe that present goods are technically superior to future goods. Since the theory is based on the psychology of people, it is sometimes called the psychological theory of interest.

The Time Preference theory of Irving Fisher is basically the same as the 'Agio' theory of Bohm-Bawerk. But Fisher did not agree with the third factor given by Bohm-Bawerk, namely technical superiority of the present goods over future goods as one of the reasons for 'agio'. That means, indirectly, we bring in productivity as a factor. But it may be wrong to say that Bohm-Bawerk has completely ignored marginal productivity as a factor for the determination of interest. In fact, as Briggs and Jordan put it, "he was on sound ground in stressing the connection between time and interest, for the productivity of capital or more accurately, of capitalistic methods of production, cannot be separated from the element of time."

We may also note that Bohm-Bawerk's theory of capital and interest was rejected by Menger and Wieser, but its main ideas were accepted by many other economists.

Joseph Schumpeter, Mises, Friedrich A. Von Hayek, Haberler, Fritz Machlup, Oskar Morgenstern and Paul N. Rosenstern Rodan are the notable economists who belonged to the later generations of the Austrian school.

If we do not go by national or residential criteria, we may recognize many non-Austrian Austrian economists. In fact, Gide and Rist wrote as early as 1909 that "lately the Austrian school has become more American that Austrian." On the European continent too there were many Austrian economists. Knut Wicksell of Sweden was the most important among them. In England, Philip Wicksteed was the most eminent of the early Austrian economists. One can see the similarity of thought or the "Austrian connection" in the works of the American economists like J. B. Clark and Irving Fisher.

Criticism

1. According to Haney, "the general shortcoming of the Austrian theories both of value of cost-goods in general and of interest in particular, lies in the assumption of an independent value existing in the products secured, which value they seek to reflect back upon the instruments of production."

2. Another shortcoming of Bohm-Bawerk's thought is that he ignores the problem of the determination of wages. He does not answer the question, "how is the product divided between labour and capital"?

3. Marshall criticized the economists of the Austrian school for their over-emphasis on demand aspects.

4. The Austrian theory is too individualistic. It is too rationalistic in that it overlooks, important institutional factors and important motives.

In spite of the above criticism, a great merit of the Austrians is their attempt to extend their theory of value in a logical way to the factors of production and to the distribution of income among them.

ALFRED MARSHALL
(1842-1924)

Introduction

Alfred Marshall was the leader of the second generation of the marginal utility school. One great difference between the economists of the earlier marginal utility school and Marshall is this: While the early economists of marginalist school, for instance, Jevons, rejected classical theory of value based on cost of production completely, Marshall made an attempt to bring about a synthesis of the classical theory and the new theory based on marginal utility. On account of this, Marshall is sometimes also described as a leading neo-classical economist.

Marshall was born in a middle class family in London in 1842. He was the son of a cashier in the Bank of England. His father was something of a domestic tyrant. Of course he gave good education to his son. Marshall specialized in mathematics at Cambridge and later on studied economics. He was professor of economics at Cambridge from 1885 to 1908.

Marshall's masterpiece, "*The Principles of Economics*", appeared in 1890. His other important works included "Economics of Industry" (1879), "Industry and Trade" (1919), "Money, Credit and Commerce" (1924).

Marshall did not try to demolish the economics of Smith, Ricardo and Mill. But he tried to supplement it. As has been already noted, he sought a synthesis of the utility theory of the Austrian economists and the cost of production theory of the classical economists. With great understanding and insight, he saw truth in the theories of both schools of thought and put those theories together as a connected whole. In the words of Haney, "Marshall's synthesis, as we may call it, is not perfect, but it is a masterpiece, and *as a whole* has probably never been surpassed as an explanation of economic life." Marshall described his "Principles of Economics" as "an attempt to present a modern version of old doctrines with the aid of the new work and with reference to the new problems of our own age."

We shall now study the essential features of Marshall's economics.

Nature and Scope of Economics

According to Marshall, "Political economy or Economics is a study of mankind in the ordinary business of life; it examines that part of individual and social action which is most closely connected with the attainment and with the use of the material requisites of well-being. Marshall's definition of economics is known as the materialist welfare definition of economics. Marshall agreed with the view of Adam Smith that economics studies about wealth. But it was only a part of the study. In his own words, "Thus it is on the one side a study of wealth; and on the other and more important side, a part of the study of man." Prof. Robbins is a great critic of the materialistic welfare definition of Marshall. It misrepresents the science as we know it. Robbins tells that "whatever economics is concerned with, it is not concerned with the causes of material welfare as such."

It may be interesting to note that Marshall's treatise was the first to establish the use of the term 'Economics' from 1890 on in England and the United States. In the nineteenth century, the term commonly in use was "Political Economy". According to Marshall, economics is not a body of concrete truth. In the opinion of Keynes, "this engine, as we employ it today is largely Marshall's creation.... The building of the engine was the essential achievement of Marshall's peculiar genius."

Economic Laws

Marshall regarded economic laws as statements of tendencies. He was aware of the fact that they were not as exact as the laws of physics or chemistry. According to him, "The Laws of economics are to be compared with the laws of tides, rather than with the simple and exact law of gravitation."

Diagrammatic Approach

Though Marshall was an expert in mathematics, he had his own doubts about the value of mathematics in economics. But he was in favour of using diagrams to illustrate the theories. In fact, he translated many of the theorems of Mill and Ricardo into diagrammatic language. Keynes describes him as the "*founder of modern diagrammatic economics.*" We should also note that Marshall was not interested in pure theory as such. He wanted to preserve the contact between economic theory and economic policy.

Marginal Utility and Demand

According to Marshall, demand is based on the law of diminishing marginal utility. The law tells that the marginal utility of a thing diminishes with every increase in the amount of it a person already has. We should remember that the law of diminishing utility is based on the following assumptions: (*i*) It refers to a given moment in time; (*ii*) There are no changes in habits and tastes; and (*iii*) All units of the good are homogeneous.

Marshall stated the general law of demand as follows: "The greater the amount to be sold, the small must be the price at which it is offered in order that it may find purchasers, or in other words, *the amount demanded increases with a fall in price, and diminishes with a rise in price.*"

On the basis of diminishing utility, Marshall has developed the law of substitution, known as the Law of equi-marginal utility in consumption. The law tells that demand is based not only on the law of diminishing marginal utility but on the balancing of marginal utilities. A consumer will spend his money on different goods in such a way that their marginal utilities are proportionate to their prices. Marshall believed that the marginal utility of a good could be measured in terms of money. Because money provided the measuring rod of utility, he thought, economics was the most exact of social sciences.

Consumer's Surplus

Marshall has added the term consumer's surplus (consumer's rent) to economic literature. Consumer's surplus measures the difference between the potential price which a consumer is prepared to pay and the actual price he pays. The concept of consumer's surplus has been derived from the Law of Diminishing Marginal Utility.

Marshall has defined the concept as follows: "*The excess of a price which a person would be willing to pay for a thing rather than go without the thing over that which he actually does pay is the economic measure of this surplus satisfaction. It may be called consumer's surplus.*"

The concept of consumer's surplus has been attacked on the ground that it is impossible to measure consumer's surplus though it is generally true that one may get a feeling of surplus satisfaction in the case of certain goods. But we must remember that Marshall introduced the concept to show that just as we can speak of producer's surplus we can also speak of consumer's surplus. He has made use of the concept to demonstrate the effects of taxes on commodities with elastic and inelastic demand. With the help of the concept, he tried to show which kind of government intervention was desirable. In spite of strong criticism of the concept of consumer's surplus, it has become the basis of welfare economics. In the opinion of Eric Roll, "The whole field of welfare economics of which Marshall's disciple and successor, Professor Pigou, is its founder, really rests on considerations of which the consumer's surplus doctrine is the intellectual ancestor."

Elasticity of Demand

Marshall has introduced the concept of elasticity of demand to explain the rate of change of demand. The rate at which demand may change when price changes is known as *elasticity of demand*. The law of demand simply tells us that when price falls, demand increases. But it does not tell to what extent demand will change for a given change in price. The concept of elasticity of demand relates the percentage fall in price to the percentage increase in quantity demanded.

The elasticity of demand at any price can be measured by the percentage change in the amount demanded divided by the percentage change in the price. It can be explained in a simple formula:

$$\text{Elasticity of demand} = \frac{\text{Percentage change in the amount demanded}}{\text{Percentage change in the price}}$$

According to the definition of Marshall, "If we write 'P' for price and 'x' for quantity demanded, the elasticity of demand in respect of any specified price or quantity is, $\frac{dx}{x} \div \frac{dP}{P}$."

The concept of elasticity of demand is very useful in economic theory and practice. It is useful in studying the problem of value under monopoly. The monopolist generally fixes a higher price for commodities with inelastic demand rather than those with elastic demand. Again, the monopolist can practise price discrimination only when the elasticity of demand is different in different markets. The concept is also useful in studying the problems of taxation. Generally, the government taxes commodities with inelastic demand at a higher rate than those with elastic demand. Again, the concept is useful in studying the influence of trade unions on wages. In his "Essays in Biography" Keynes wrote, "In the provision of terminology and apparatus to aid thought I do not think that Marshall did economists any greater service than by the explicit introduction of the idea of elasticity."

Supply and Cost of Production

According to Marshall, supply is governed by cost of production. And cost of production is measured in terms of money. But behind the monetary costs, there are the real costs. Thus Marshall has distinguished between real cost of production and expenses of production. Supply increases when price rises. In other words, the supply curve slopes upward to the right.

Marshallian Theory of Value and Time Element

For a long time, there was a controversy regarding what determined the value of a commodity. The classical economists said that the cost of production (supply) determined value. But the economists of the early marginalist school said that demand, based on marginal utility, determined the value of a commodity. But Marshall said that both supply and demand determined value. Marshallian theory of value combines marginal utility with subjective real cost. According to Marshall, the forces behind both supply and demand determine value. Behind demand is marginal utility. It is reflected in the demand prices of buyers, *i.e.*, the prices at which given quantities will be demanded. Behind supply is real cost, that is marginal effort and sacrifice. It is reflected in the supply prices of sellers, that is, the prices at which given quantities will be supplied. According to Eric Roll, "The novelty of this view, compared with the Austrian version, is that cost of production comes into its own once more as a determinant of value."

Marshall likened supply and demand to two blades of a pair of scissors. It is useless to ask which does the cutting. In his own words, "We might as reasonably dispute whether it is the upper or under blade of a pair of scissors that cuts a piece of paper, as whether value is governed by utility or cost of production. It is true that when one blade is held still, and the cutting is effected by moving the other, we may say with careless brevity that the cutting is done by the second; but the statement is not strictly accurate, and is to be excused only so long as it claims to be merely a popular and not a strictly scientific account of what happens."

Marshallian theory of value, owing to its emphasis both on supply and demand as forces governing value, is also known as the *Dual Theory of Value*. It is important to note that the theory emphasizes the role of *margin*. Value is determined by the forces of supply and demand at the margin. It is *marginal utility* and *marginal cost of production* that govern value.

On the basis of time element, Marshall classified value into four kinds: (*i*) Market value, (*ii*) Short-period value, (*iii*) Long-period value (Short period value and Long period value are jointly called 'normal value'), and (*iv*) Secular value.

The market price of a commodity may be defined as the price ruling at a particular period. In the case of market price, the supply is fixed (the market supply curve is a vertical straight line) and price depends mainly upon demand. In other words, demand is the most important determinant of market price. For example, let us take the case of perishable good, say fish. A certain amount of fish will be supplied in the market on a particular day. Its price will be determined largely by demand.

In the case of short-period price, we think of supply as the amount which can be produced at the given price, with existing equipment and labour. In other words, "the short-run is defined as that period during which the variable inputs can be increased or decreased, but the fixed plant cannot be changed. So in the case of short-period price, demand and supply are both important in determining price and the supply curve is based on variable costs."

In the case of long period, supply means 'what can be produced by plant which itself can be remuneratively produced and applied within the given time.' In the long run, cost of production is the most important determinant of price.

When there is an increase in demand, generally it will raise the short-period supply price. Because, as more workers are employed, marginal productivity of labour will diminish owing to the influence of the law of diminishing returns. Not only that, sometimes, less efficient workers may have to be employed. But the long-run is a period long enough for making changes in conditions of supply. More factories can be built, more machinery can be employed and more workers can be trained. Supply can be increased without an increase in price. Marshall defined long-run normal price as one which in the long-run would exactly balance supply and demand and which would be equal to long-run total cost of production. The normal price will change whenever there is a change in the efficiency of production. Marshall has also made the point that market price will tend to fluctuate around normal price.

Marshall has also conceived of gradual or secular changes in normal value. Secular changes in normal values are caused by changes in economic data: population, tastes, capital, organisation and so on.

Marshall's introduction of time-element in economic analysis is one of his many significant contributions to economic thinking. In conceiving of market broadly into short and long-period, his object was to trace "a continuous thread running through and connecting the applications of the general theory of equilibrium of demand and supply to different periods of time." By means of distinction between the long and the short-period, the meaning of 'normal' value was made clear.

Prime Costs and Supplementary Costs

Marshall divided costs into prime costs and supplementary costs to analyse the problem of value in the short period. Now-a-days, we call prime costs as variable costs and supplementary costs as constant or fixed costs. Prime costs (variable costs) include things such as wages and raw materials. They change in the short-run with changes in the scale of production. Supplementary (constant) costs are fixed costs. They include things such as depreciation of the plant, interest on loans, rent and salaries of top-executives. Supplementary costs cannot be changed in the short-run.

The distinction between prime and supplementary costs is made to show that in the short-period, a firm will generally continue in production if it covers only its prime costs. But in the long-run, a firm must cover all its costs, supplementary as well as prime. So the distinction between fixed and variable costs is largely a short-period distinction. The so-called variable costs are merely those that are variable in the short period, and even the supplementary (fixed) costs become variable in the long period.

External Economies and Internal Economies

Marshall classified economies of scale of production into internal economies and external economies. Economies that are possible to a single firm are called internal economies. Economies that are possible to an industry as a whole are called *external economies*. External economies arise from the localisation of industry, that is, when most of the firms comprising an industry are concentrated in one area.

Internal Economies: According to Marshall, "The chief advantages of production on a large scale are economy of skill, economy of machinery and economy of materials." A large firm also enjoys marketing economies. It can generally buy more cheaply than a small one. It often sells in large quantities and at the same time it gets a good price. In the opinion of Marshall, "The economies of highly organised buying and selling are among the chief causes of the present tendency towards the fusion of many businesses in the same industry or trade into single huge aggregates; and also of trading federations of various kinds, including German cartels and centralized co-operative associations."[1]

Marshall was also aware of the economies of small scale production: ".... the small employer has advantages of his own. The master's eye is everywhere; there is no shirking by his foremen or workmen, no divided responsibility, no sending half-understood messages backwards and forwards from one department to another. He saves much of the book-keeping and nearly all of the cumbrous system of checks that are necessary in the business of a large firm."[2]

External Economies: External Economies are dependent on the general development of the industry. External economies arise out of the localization of industry, that is, by the concentration of many firms of a similar character in particular localities.

Localization of industry will help in the development of hereditary skill. Subsidiary industries will develop in the neighbourhood. It will help in the use of highly specialized machinery. Further localized industry will offer a local market for special skill.

Representative Firm

Marshall introduced the concept of representative firm to explain the causes which govern the supply price of a commodity. Supply price of a commodity, he thought, would depend upon the cost of representative firm.

The representative firm is *not* a new producer just struggling into business, who works under many disadvantages and who is content for a time with little or no profits. It is also *not* a huge and leading firm with great ability and good fortune and has vast business and huge well-ordered workshops that give it a superiority over almost all its rivals. But Marshall's representative firm must be one which has had a fairly long life, and fair success, which is managed with normal ability, and which has normal access to the economies, external and internal, which belong to that aggregate volume of production.

Thus, in the words of Marshall, "a representative firm is in a sense an average firm.... And a Representative firm is that particular sort of average firm, at which we need to look in order to see how far the economies, *internal and external,* of production on a large scale have extended generally in the industry and country in question."

Marshall's concept of 'representative firm' has been described as a fictitious concept which is not of much use in applying to real situations. In the opinion of Haney, "His (Marshall's) idea

---

1. Marshall: *Principles of Economics*, p. 235.
2. *Ibid*, p. 237.

of 'representative firm' appears as a device to bridge the gap between long and short periods, and savours of the question begging use of averages which is all too characteristic of classical economics."

Law of Returns

Marshall has stated the Law of diminishing returns as follows:

"An increase in the capital and labour applied in the cultivation of land causes in general a less than proportionate increase in the amount of produce raised, unless it happens to coincide with an improvement in the arts of agriculture." In plain language, the law tells that we cannot double the output simply by doubling labour and capital applied in the cultivation of land.

Marshall believed that *generally* agriculture was subject to the law of diminishing returns in the long run, while the manufacturing industry was subject to the law of increasing returns. In his own words: ".... We say broadly that while the part which nature plays in production shows a tendency to diminishing return, the part which man plays shows a tendency to increasing return."

Marshall has stated the law of increasing returns as follows: "An increase of labour and capital leads generally to improved organisation, which increases the efficiency of the work of labour and capital."

Therefore, in those industries which are not engaged in raising raw produce, an increase of labour and capital generally gives a return increased more than in proportion.

Marshall has stated the Law of constant returns as follows:

"If the actions of the laws of increasing and diminishing returns are balanced, we have the law of constant return, and an increased produce is obtained by labour and sacrifice increased just in proportion."

Marshall made use of the laws of returns to arrive at certain policy conclusions. For instance, he concluded that an industry of increasing returns especially in a new country will produce more cheaply if it expands under tariff protection. It is the infant industry argument. But he felt that the difficulty with such a policy was that it would become a tool of power politics and it might not be put to proper use.

Distribution

In the field of distribution too, Marshall made use of the element of time to describe how factor-incomes are determined.

Rent: While Ricardo considered rent as an income that is peculiar to land alone, Marshall felt that the rent aspect can be seen in other factor prices as well. In fact, he has introduced the concept of quasi-rent to make this point. Even the rent of land is not seen as a thing by itself. He argued that, "the rent of land is only the chief species of a large genus of economic phenomena." But like Ricardo, Marshall thought, rent was always price-determined.

Quasi-Rent

Marshall has introduced the concept of quasi-rent in economic literature. In the short run the incomes of many factors are in the nature of rent. Marshall called them *quasi-rent*. According to him, "Quasi-rent is the income derived from machines and other appliances for production made by man."

In economics, the term rent is generally used to denote the income from a factor whose supply is permanently inelastic. Land is the main example of such a factor. Its supply is fixed both in the short run as well as in the long run. But in the short run, the supply of machines and other man-made goods too is inelastic. Suppose there is an increase in demand for machines, their supply cannot be increased in the short run to meet the change in demand. So they will earn an income similar to rent. But the difference between land and man-made appliances is that the supply of land is permanently fixed while that of the latter is fixed only in the short run. In the long run, the supply of machines and other man-made goods can be adjusted to meet changes in demand. Quasi-rent will disappear in the long run.

Wages: According to Marshall, "Wages like any other factor of production, depend on both demand and supply." The demand for labour is a derived demand, which depends upon the demand by consumers for final products. If the supply of labour increases, the marginal productivity of labour will fall, and wages will fall. Marshall said that wages are not determined by marginal productivity of labour alone. Of course, the doctrine of marginal productivity throws into clear light one of the causes that govern wages. Thus, Marshall did not discard the marginal productivity theory of wages and interest. But he argued that this should be regarded as a part only of a complete theory of distribution.

Interest: Marshallian theory of interest is essentially the Abstinence theory of interest of Nassau Senior. But he preferred the word '*Waiting*' instead of abstinence. He said, "The sacrifice of present pleasure for the sake of future, has been called *abstinence* by economists. But this term has been misunderstood for the greatest accumulators of wealth are very rich persons, some of whom live in luxury, and certainly do not practise abstinence... since, however, the term is liable to be misunderstood, we may with advantage avoid its use, and say that accumulation of wealth is generally the result of postponement of enjoyment, or of a waiting for it.

Marshall regarded profits as the reward for organisation or entrepreneurship, which we call as the fourth factor of production. According to Marshall, "Normal profits include interest, earnings of management and reward for organisation." Marshall's treatment of profits is considered to be rather vague.

Marshall's Contribution to Monetary Economics

Marshall made some original contributions to monetary economics.

1. Marshall analysed the quantity theory of money as a part of the general theory of value. He always expressed the view that value of money is a function of its supply on the one hand and demand for it, on the other as measured by "the average stock of command over commodities which each person cares to keep in a ready form."

2. He made the distinction between the real rate of interest and the money rate of interest.

3. He enunciated the "purchasing power parity" theory to explain the rate of exchange between countries with mutually inconvertible currencies. Of course, it was Prof. Cassel who restated the theory in a form applicable to modern conditions. But it was anticipated by Marshall in The Memorandum appended to his third volume before the Gold ad Silver Commission.

4. Marshall suggested the "chain" method of compiling index numbers.

5. Marshall based the proposal of paper currency for the circulation based on gold-and-silver symmetallism as the standard. Marshall was not in favour of bimetallism. Symmetallism refers to the method by which a bar of silver of, say, 2,000 grammes is wedded to a bar of gold, say, 100 grammes. Under symmetallism, the government must always be ready to buy or sell a wedded pair of bars for a fixed amount of currency. Marshall thought that this plan could be started by any nation without waiting for the concurrence of others.

6. Lastly, Marshall explained how an increase in the supply of money reflected itself in an increase in prices.

Conclusion

When Marshall died in 1924, Keynes described him as the "greatest economist in the world for a hundred years." Marshall was the first economist who devoted his life to building up the subject as a separate science, standing on its own foundations, with high standards of scientific accuracy as the physical or biological sciences.

Marshall's main contributions to economics are: (*i*) the clear distinction between the long and the short period, (*ii*) the doctrine of consumer's surplus, (*iii*) the doctrine of quasi-rent, (*iv*) the expansion and refinement of the rent concept. Marshall has demonstrated that the old doctrines of demand and supply, normal value, cost of production and so on can be applied with modification to explain modern economic problems. We may conclude with the words of Prof. Haney that "Alfred Marshall will stand in the history of economic thought as one who made more progress toward a united and consistent theory of value and distribution than any predecessor."

INDIFFERENCE CURVE ANALYSIS – ISO-PRODUCT CURVES

The indifference curve analysis has been developed by the English economist Edgeworth (1845-1926) and the Italian economist, Pareto (1848-1923) to analyse consumer demand. It has been developed as an alternative to the Marshallian utility analysis of demand. In recent times, J. R. Hicks has further developed the indifference curve analysis.

The main objection against utility analysis is that it assumes that marginal utility can be measured quantiatively. Further, it is based on the assumption that only one commodity is consumed at a time. It cannot be applied to situations where an individual consumes two or more goods at a time. But indifference curve analysis may be used to analyse consumer demand when an individual consumes two or more goods at a time.

The utility analysis is based on cardinal approach, whereas the indifference curve analysis is based on ordinal approach. The indifference curve analysis avoids quantitative measurement of marginal utility. An indifference curve represents a level of satisfaction. It is almost impossible to *measure* levels of satisfaction. For we do not have units of measurement. We can say whether one indifference curve represents a higher or lower level of satisfaction than another, but we cannot say by how much satisfaction is higher or lower.

Each consumer will have a scale of preferences. An indifference curve shows all those combinations of goods which occupy the same position in the consumer's scale of preference, which will give him the same level of satisfaction. We call it an indifference curve because the consumer will be indifferent between different combinations so long as be remains on the indifference curve.

An indifference map may consist of a set of indifference curves. Generally we make the following assumptions about the shape of indifference curve.

1. An indifference curve always slopes downwards from left to right.

2. All indifference curves are convex to the origin. It is because of the diminishing marginal rate of substitution. It implies that the marginal significance of a commodity in terms of the other will always diminish progressively as one acquires more of the former good.

3. No two indifference curves can ever cut each other.

Consumer's Equilibrium

By making use of the indifference curve analysis, we can study the problem of consumer's equilibrium. When we make use of the indifference curve apparatus we assume that: (*i*) The scale of preferences of the consumer remain the same throughout the analysis; (*ii*) He will spend the entire amount on one good or another; (*iii*) He is one of many buyers; (*iv*) All goods are homogeneous; and (*v*) The consumer acts in a rational manner and maximizes his satisfaction.

The indifference curve simply tells us about the scale of preferences of the consumer, that is, consumer's personal tastes. But the consumer's actual purchases will be influenced by his income and the price of the goods in question. The *price-opportunity line* or the *price-line* tells us about the opportunities that are open to the consumer in the market for acquiring the commodity at its current price, whereas the indifference curves show his tastes independently of market conditions. We must remember that the indifference map and the price line are quite independent of one another.

By superimposing the price-line on the indifference map, we can show how the consumer reaches an equilibrium position. The consumer will be in an equilibrium position, that is, he will be maximizing his satisfaction at that point where the price line is tangent to an indifference curve. For at any such point of tangency, the price line and indifference curve have the same slope. It implies that the marginal significance of the good in terms of money will equal price. The consumer will have the combination of the goods appropriate to this point on his indifference curves.

We can make use of indifference curve analysis to study many kinds of economic problem and the goods in question can be consumption goods, capital goods, work, leisure or money. We can study consumer's indifference maps between all possible commodities. For the consumer to be in equilibrium with respect to all goods, the marginal significance of all goods in terms of money must equal their money prices.

Income Effect, Substitution Effect and Price Effect

We can make use of indifference curve analysis to study consumer's equilibrium even when there is a change of money income, or the prices of goods or both.

Income Effect: In the case of income effect, income changes but prices remain constant. So the consumer may become better or worse off. If he gets more income he will have more to spend and he will be better off. If he gets less income, he will have a smaller amount to spend and he will be worse off.

Substitution Effect: In the case of substitution effect, price may change but the consumer's money income may also change in such a way that he is neither better nor worse off. Of course, he will buy more of those goods whose relative price has fallen. He will substitute the relatively cheaper commodities for the relatively dearer commodities.

Price Effect: In the case of the price effect, price changes but money income remains constant. When there is a change of price, money income remaining the same, there will be a change of *real* income. Substitution will also take place. The consumer will buy more of the food whose price has fallen. So price effect is a combination of the income effect on the one hand and substitution effect on the other.

Criticism

The indifference curve analysis has been criticized on the following grounds:

1. It is based on unrealistic assumptions. For instance, it is based on the assumption of perfect competition. But imperfect competition is the rule in modern world.

2. Prof. Hicks in his indifference curve analysis has assumed that institutional price controls are absent in the economy. But countries at war and planned economies make it increasingly apparent that such institutional controls are more important than supply and demand.

3. It rationalizes human behaviour too much.

4. There are some who regard that the indifference curve analysis is merely old wine in a new bottle. Though the name marginal utility has been changed to 'marginal rate of substitution', still, the basic idea has been retained. According to Eric Roll, "Above all the very concept of subjective utility still forms the ultimate sanction for the indifference curve no less than Marshall's utility curve." But Hicks asserts that "the replacement of the principle of diminishing marginal utility by the principle of diminishing marginal rate of substitution is not a mere translation. It

is a positive change in the theorem of consumer demand." A great merit of indifference curve analysis is that it tries to get away from the cardinal measurement of utility.

A Note on Iso-Product Curves

Modern economists make use of Iso-Product curves or Isoquants or Equal Product curves to discuss the laws of returns. The term 'iso-quant' was introduced by R. Frisch. It was, however, Professors Allen and Hicks who have brought the term into general use.

The Iso-Product curve is similar to an indifference curve. It is based on the following assumptions: (*i*) Technical production conditions are given and constant; and (*ii*) Factors are combined in the most efficient manner under the given production conditions.

The Iso-Product curve shows all those combinations of factors which will give a certain product, just as an indifference curve shows all those combinations of goods which provide a certain level of satisfaction. We may describe an iso-product curve as that curve which represents various combinations of two factors of production that yield the same results.

Difference between Iso-product Curves and Indifference Curves

There are important differences between iso-product curves and indifference curves:

1. While it is impossible to find any unit in which to label indifference curves, we can label iso-product curves in terms of amounts of products made.

2. While we cannot measure satisfaction in physical units, we can measure the output of a homogeneous product in physical terms without any difficulty. We can find out by how much output is higher at one point than at another. But we cannot find out by how much satisfaction is higher on one curve than on the other.

The shape of the iso-product curve will be the same as the shape of the indifference curve. That is: (*i*) It slopes downwards from left to right; (*ii*) All iso-products are convex to the origin; and (*iii*) No two iso-product curves can ever cut each other.

We can make use of iso-product curves to discover how returns to factors of production will change as amounts of factors used are altered in certain ways. In other words, by making use of the iso-product curves, we can study the general relationship between input of factors and output of product.

NEO-CLASSICISM

After the marginal revolution, many new schools developed in England, Austria, Sweden and America. The leader of the new school attempted a synthesis of the new ideas of marginal utility school with the ideas of the old classical school. Neo-classical synthesis has been described as "a marriage of micro and macro economics." Classical economics refers to the early nineteenth century theories developed mainly by Ricardo and later on formulated in the best manner by J. S. Mill in his *Principles*. Marshall might be regarded as the leader of the neo-classical school in England. As Haney put it, "By breaking down partitions, cutting windows, and adding rooms he remodelled the classical system so effectively that since the appearance of the "*Principles of Economics*" in 1890, his "Neo-classicism" has been recognized in the English speaking world as the most secure, convenient, and harmonious stepping place now available for economic science." Knut Wicksell became the leader of the Swedish school or the Scandinavian school. In America, J. B. Clark, Taussig and Irving Fisher were the notable neo-classical economists. According to Taylor, "F. W. Taussig remained as a theorist closer than others to the old classical, Ricardo-Mill tradition, and only half-absorbed or accepted the new ideas of his generation; but he had great wisdom, produced much good work, and taught and formed a great many younger American economists of outstanding merit. Irving Fisher stood out as the one great American *mathematical* economist—on his own, not Walrasian lines."

The neo-classical economists have made significant contribution to the theory of money, interest and profit. We shall now study the ideas of some of the leading neo-classical economists.

Knut Wicksell (1851-1926)

Knut Wicksell was the founder of the Swedish school. He was born in 1851. At first he studied philosophy and mathematics. He took interest in economics only when he was thirty-five. After ten years' further study in France, Germany, Austria and England he took his doctorate in economics. From 1900, he taught at the University at Lund, Sweden. He died in 1926.

Wicksell developed new theories concerning the rate of interest, and the price level. His theory concerning the relationship between the money rate of interest and the general price level has been his important contribution to economic theory. In the words of Haney, "He is a pioneer in co-ordinating theories of price and of interest with a theory of the value of money." The greatness of his theories came to light only after the writings of Professor Hayek and Mr. J. M. Keynes. Wicksell published his classic work, "*Interest and Prices*" in 1898. His other important work is "*Lectures on Political Economy.*" (It was originally published in German in 1910 but translated into English in 1934 and 1935). Wicksell was influenced by the writings of Bohm-Bawerk, the famous Austrian economist and Walras, one of the founders of the Marginal Utility school. He was also influenced by some English economists such as Wicksteed and Edgeworth and by Italian economist Pareto. He was also aware of the writings of Marshall. Thus there was a good deal of classical and neo-classical thought in the writings of Wicksell. But he makes marginal utility the basis of his approach and like Walras, he makes use of mathematical equations.

Main Theories of Wicksell

The following are the important contributions of Wicksell to economics. *Firstly*, he analysed the relationship between the rate of interest and the general level of prices. He analysed the role of interest in generating inflationary or deflationary price movements. *Secondly*, he discussed the role of government and the central bank in promoting price stability. *Lastly*, he developed the saving-investment approach (modern aggregate supply-demand) approach to monetary phenomena. Wicksell's savings and investment approach was one of the sources of Keynesian Economics. Keynes himself praised Wicksell as one of his forerunners. The main aim of Wicksell was to synthesize monetary theory, trade cycle theory, public Finance, and price theory into one system.

Wicksell's Theory of Capital and Interest

Wicksell became interested in the problem of fluctuations in prices or, what we call nowadays as business cycle. Why do prices rise or fall? That was the one great question that bothered Wicksell. While attempting an answer to the question, Wicksell turned to the analysis of the rate of interest.

Wicksell defined capital as a *"coherent mass of stored-up labour and saved-up land."* He described interest as the "marginal productivity of waiting." Time element is an important factor in his theory of interest. In a precise form, Wicksell defined interest as the difference between: (*i*) the marginal productivity of saved-up labour and land; and (*ii*) the marginal productivity of currently used labour and land.

Natural Rate of Interest and Monetary Rate of Interest

Wicksell distinguished between the natural or normal rate of interest and the money rate (or market rate) of interest. According to him, natural rate of interest was determined by basic technological factors. In other words, the natural rate of interest was equal to the marginal productivity of capital. The money rate of interest was the rate actually charged in the money market at a particular moment of time. Wicksell made use of the distinction between the natural rate of interest and money rate of interest to explain the fluctuations in saving and investment. When the natural rate of interest was above the money rate, businessmen would make more profit by increasing their capital investment. So this would lead to an expansionary phase in the economy as a whole. On the other hand, when the natural rate was below the monetary rate, the demand for a new capital would fall to a very low level and there would be bad trade. Only when the two rates (natural rate and money rate) of interest were equal, prices would be stable. The significance of Wicksell's analysis lies in the fact that he made an effort to link together the real and monetary sides of the economic system. He noted that fluctuations in the economy (expansion or contraction) took place whenever the real factors, operating on the natural rate of interest diverged from the monetary rate of interest. Wicksell emphasized the role of government and the central bank in promoting stability of the economy. He suggested that wholesale prices could be stabilized by controlling interest rates. Further Wicksell emphasized on the economy as a whole. Not only that, he applied the idea of supply and demand, which was usually used for determining the prices of particular commodities, to the general price level. In other words, Wicksell paid attention to the problems of aggregate supply and aggregate demand.

Wicksell made some important observations about investment and savings and their effects on the economy as a whole. He observed that during a boom period, when investment is high, savings will not keep pace with investment. He was also aware of the fact that savings and investment decisions were not the same decisions. Savings were made by people for one set of motives and investments were made by another set of persons for altogether different motives. The discrepancy between savings and investment will have important effects on the economy as a whole. Keynes regarded Wicksell as his forerunner because the latter anticipated some of Keynes's important ideas.

Monetary Reform: Wicksell advocated suspension of free coinage of gold and suggested that world must have an international paper standard. Such a standard, he thought, would solve the problem of shortage of gold. He feared that the growing production and stock of gold would result in inflation of currency and rising prices. Wicksell believed that when once the international paper standard was introduced, the gold standard "would sound like a fairy tale, with its rather senseless and purposeless sending hither and thither of crater of gold, with its digging up of stores of treasure and burying them again in the recesses of the earth." Under the new system, each country would have its own system of notes and small change. These notes would have to be redeemable at par by every Central Bank, but would be allowed to circulate only inside the country.

Views on Competition: Wicksell realized the limitations of perfect competition in the retail market. He anticipated the theory of monopolistic or imperfect competition. He regarded every retailer as a partial monopolist. As every retailer has his own circle of customers, prices would be stable. The retailer would not change his price often. Wicksell also made the point that increase in the number of sellers would not always be to the advantage of buyers. In fact, he was aware of the anomaly that "competition may sometimes raise prices instead of always lowering them as one would expect."

Population: Wicksell advocated limitation of population not by Malthusian 'moral restraint' but by recourse to deliberate contraceptive method. He was a neo-Malthusian in this respect.

Taxation: He opposed the regressive tax system of his day, favoured mild progression in income tax. He supported the taxation of inheritance.

Welfare: He recommended welfare services, particularly education.

Conclusion: Wicksell's greatest contribution to economic theory lay in the field of money and prices. A great merit of Wicksell is that as a monetary theorist, he anticipated many keynesian doctrines.

J. B. Clark (1847-1938)

J. B. Clark was the master of 'American Marginalism.' Clark has extended the marginal utility principle to the field of production and distribution. The marginal productivity theory of distribution is one of his significant contributions to economic thought. His important works are: (*i*) *Philosophy of Wealth* (1885), and (*ii*) *Distribution of Wealth* (1899).

According to Clark, in a "static" condition, the factors of production receive shares corresponding to the productivity of their final or marginal increments.

Dynamic Theory of Profits

Clark made a significant contribution to the theory of profits. To explain the emergence of profits of the entrepreneurs, Clark distinguished between a stationary economy and a dynamic economy. A stationary economy is one in which the fundamental data of the economy do not change. Conversely, dynamic economy is defined as one in which some of the five possible types of changes are found : population, tastes, capital, technique and the forms of industrial organisation.

Clark argued that profits could not exist in a stationary state. According to him, "Profits would appear only in a dynamic economy." In his own words, "Profits are then the result exclusively of dynamic change." When economic data change, the entrepreneur is faced with new problems in co-ordinating capital and labour. Profits are an indication of the measure of his success in readapting the process of production to the changed situation.

Prof. F. H. Knight was a great critic of Clark's theory of profits. While admitting that without change there would be no profits, Knight argued that all changes would not give rise to profits. He has argued that it is not change as such 'but the divergence of actual conditions from those which have been expected and on the basis of which business arrangements have been made' that cause profits. According to Prof. Knight, 'the most fundamental function of organisation is the meeting of uncertainty.' And there was a good deal of uncertainty and risk with regard to unforeseen changes. For example technical risks, competition risks, trade cycle risks, risks that arise out of change of governmental policy cannot be foreseen in advance and are non-insurable. So profits, he concludes, are the reward for uncertainty. "Dynamic changes give rise to a peculiar form of income only in so far as the changes and their consequences are unpredictable in character." (F. H. Knight).

But in spite of the above criticism, we have to note that Clark made a significant contribution to economic analysis by introducing the distinction between dynamic doctrine and economic statics.

Irving Fisher (1867-1947)

Irving Fisher has been hailed as America's 'greatest scientific economist' by J. A. Schumpeter. Fisher was a mathematician turned economist. Besides his contribution to monetary economics, Fisher made considerable contribution to the theory of statistics (Index Numbers). He was a pioneer in the field of econometrics, which made statistical methods a part of econometric theory. His main works are: (*i*) *Mathematical Investigations in the Theory of Value and Prices,* (1892), (*ii*) *Nature of Capital and Income* (1906) and (*iii*) *The Rate Interest* (1907).

Fisher's theory of interest is based on time-preference. His explanation of interest is similar to that of Bohm-Bawerk. He regards interest as the result of time preference—a preference for present psychic income (satisfaction) over future income.

Fisher's significant contribution to monetary theory, however, was his formulation of the quantity theory of money based on the equation of money.

The quantity theory of money explains the relationship between money and the level of prices. (We know that the value of money depends upon its purchasing power, which in turn, depends upon the price level).

The quantity theory of money tells that 'one of the normal effects of an increase in the quantity of money is an exactly proportional increase in the general level of prices.' Fisher believed that there was a close and direct connection between money and prices.

Fisher has stated his theory in the form of an equation known as the "Equation of Exchange":

$$MV + M'V' = PT,$$

where 'M' is the quantity of money, 'V' is the velocity of circulation of money, M' is the quantity of bank money (demand deposits), V' is its velocity of circulation of M'. 'P' is the average level of prices, and 'T' is the volume of goods and services sold.

Fisher argued that 'P' depended mainly upon 'M'. He arrived at some policy conclusions on the basis of his theory. As the price level depends upon the quantity of money, the way to stabilize the overall price level and thereby the economy is to control the quantity of currency in circulation.

Criticism

Fisher's quantity theory of money has been criticized on the following grounds:

1. It over-emphasizes the role of money in the determination of prices.

2. It is based on the unrealistic assumption of full employment.

3. The theory cannot explain why prices do not rise even when the quantity of money is increased during a period of depression. The fact is that both the quantity of money and the level of prices depend upon the level of incomes. So to find out causes of changes in prices, we must find out the factors which bring about changes in the level of incomes. Modern economists have tried to explain the phenomenon in terms of 'effective aggregate demand.'

4. The quantity theory only attempts to explain changes in the value of money and does not show how the value of money itself is determined.

5. Lastly, it is inadequate as a theory of money because it takes no account of the influence of the rate of interest.

In spite of the above points of criticism, we have to note that the quantity theory contains at least one fundamental truth, namely, that, there is a connection between the quantity of money and its value. The theory is true over long periods. It emphasizes the necessity of regulating the supply of money in a country. It points out the dangers in the over-issue of currency at any time. Modern governments often find deficit financing an easier way of financing schemes. But the theory warns that if at any time, there is over-issue of currency in a country, it will result in inflation with all its evils.

Trade cycles

Fisher did not think that business cycles were inherent in the economy. According to him, the trade cycle was entirely a monetary phenomenon. The cure for it, consisted in stabilizing the price level.

Fisher considered things like over-production, under-consumption, mal-adjustment between agricultural and industrial prices, over-confidence, over-investment, over-saving, over-spending as inadequate explanations of business cycles. They play only subordinate role in the really great booms and depressions. In the opinion of Fisher, the two dominant factors which cause business cycles are: (*i*) over-indebtedness (especially in the form of bank loans); and (*ii*) deflation (or appreciation of dollar). Thus Fisher had a strong conviction that the two economic maladies which he called "debt disease" and "dollar disease" were more important causes of booms and depressions that all others put together.

Taussig (1859-1940)

Frank William Taussig was an American economist who attempted a synthesis of classical economic theory with the modern theory. According to Taylor, "F. W. Taussig remained, as a theorist, closer than others to the old, classical, Ricardo-Mill tradition, and only half absorbed or accepted the 'new' ideas of his generation." He was a teacher of economics at Harvard. He was America's great authority on international trade and especially the tariff. His important works are: (*i*) *Tariff History of the United States* (1888); (*ii*) *International Trade* (1927); (*iii*) *Wages and Capital* (1896); and (*iv*) *Principles of Economics* (1911).

Taussig made important contributions to the theory of wages and profits and the theory of international trade.

Wages: Taussig has given a modified version of marginal productivity theory of wages. According to him, "*Wages stand for the marginal discounted product of labour.*"

The marginal productivity theory of wages tells that under perfect competition, wages will equal the value of the marginal product of labour. But Taussig argues that some goods take a considerable time to produce; an entrepreneur pays his factors for months or even years before his products are made and produced. In Taussig's words, "The operations of the capitalists consist in a succession of advances to labourers." So the entrepreneur cannot afford to pay the labourers the full value of their marginal product, but only its *discounted* value, that is, the present value of what he will receive when he sells the product. In the opinion of Taussig, "The capitalist class secures its gain through the process of handing over to the labourers less in the way of consumer goods than the labourers eventually produce. The product of labour is *discounted* by the capitalist employers."

All the criticisms that are made against the marginal productivity theory may be made against Taussig's discounted marginal productivity theory. Here is an assessment of the theory by Prof. Earl Rolph: "There would be no logical objection to saying that all agencies receive the discounted value of the future yield of the immediate product, but there are very strong objections to saying that some factors receive a discounted return and that other factors do not. This is the fundamental fallacy of the discounting approach and the issue is not a purely verbal one."

Profits

Taussig looks at profits as a form of wages. He adopts Marshall's approach to the question of profits. Profits are the earnings of a representative firm or entrepreneur. Of course, Taussig was aware of the fact that it was difficult to draw a satisfactory line of demarcation between wages and profits.

The wages theory of profits has been rejected by most of the economists because it is unrealistic and unscientific to include a theory of profit in a general explanation of wages.

International Trade

On the basis of the quantity theory of money, Taussig developed the idea that gold movements lead to equilibrium in the international trade by influencing prices and money wages. But he was not fully satisfied with the explanation. It was left to Mrs. Joan Robinson and others to develop a new balance of payments theory in terms of incomes. Keynes's "General Theory of Employment, Interest and Money" provided the stimulus for the new theory. We may illustrate the theory by taking two countries A and B. If the country A increases its imports from country B its income and employment will fall while income and employment in B will rise. When a country's income rises it will import more, and when its income falls, it will import less. So, falling incomes in A will decrease imports from B, and rising incomes in B will increase imports, from A. So the imbalance in trade will be corrected either partly or wholly even *without gold movements*.

THE INSTITUTIONALIST SCHOOL

Introduction

Institutional Economics is essentially an American product. It is a twentieth century phenomenon. The leader of the Institutionalist school was Thorstein Veblen (1857-1929). Other important members of the school were John R. Commons (1862-1945) and Wesley Clair Mitchell (1874-1948). The Institutionalist school had a lot of influence on government policies in the United States, especially, during the "New Deal" period.

Social Background of the School

In the nineteenth century, American capitalism achieved many things—a powerful industrial system, a large increase in national income and so on. But, the conditions of the working classes were rather bad. Their level of living did not increase much as the national income increased. On the other hand, working conditions were characterised by long hours of work. There was housing shortage and there was no job security. Towards the 19th century, monopolies became a powerful institution and economic and political power was concentrated in the hands of big business. *Laissez-faire* policy was used to the convenience of the influential sections of the society. And whenever it was advantageous to the business community, the government did not hesitate to pass legislation granting tariff protection. And political corruption was not uncommon. Thus American society was characterized by big business and absentee ownership. There was the growth of an American leisure class, built upon a foundation of capitalist industry. So some of the economists were not satisfied with the existing economic doctrines of the classical and marginal school. Some thought in terms of socialism whereas others thought in terms of reforming the society, by having social control over institutions. The institutionalists belonged to the latter category. They were attracted towards some of the ideas of German historical school.

The Essential Ideas of the Institutionalist School

1. The Institutionalist school emphasized the role of institutions in economic life. We have to note that an institution is not merely an organisation or establishment like a school or bank. The term 'institution' includes customs, social habits, laws, ways of living and modes of thinking. Thus slavery is an institution. Belief in slavery is also an institution. Celebration of certain days as festival days is also an institution. We may say, that communism was an institution in Russia and anti-communism is an institution in America. According to the institutional school, *economic life is regulated by economic institutions and not by economic laws*. Naturally the institutionalists are interested in analysing and reforming the institutions of credit, monopoly, absentee ownership, distribution of national income and so on.

2. They believed that group social behaviour is more important to the analysis of economic problems than the individual behaviour emphasized by the marginalist economists.

3. They believe that the economy must be studied as a whole. It is in contrast to the 'atomistic' approach of the marginalist school.

4. They advocate the evolutionary approach in economic analysis. Darwin, and not Ricardo, is their model. The study of the evolution and functioning of economic institutions should be the central theme in economics. One must have a knowledge of history, political science, sociology, philosophy and psychology to understand economic problems.

5. They reject the idea of 'normal equilibrium.' According to them, mal-adjustments in economic life are not departures from normal equilibrium but are themselves normal. They reject "price system" economics.

6. Economic laws are not of universal application. They are relative to time and place. In other words, they believe in the doctrine of relativity.

7. They reject the classical assumption of harmony of interests. They recognize clash of interests and class conflict.

8. They believe that market economy cannot ensure social welfare. They advocate liberal democratic reforms to reduce inequalities of income and wealth.

9. They advocate inductive method rather than deductive approach. They reject the abstract reasoning of the marginalists as unrealistic.

10. They repudiated the pleasure-pain psychology of the marginalists.

The Institutional School and the Historical School

There are in general certain similarities between the institutionalist school and the historical school. First of all, both emphasize the importance of institutions. Secondly, both schools stress the doctrine of relativity. Thirdly, they believe in change and evolution. Fourthly, they attack the 'value economics' of the classical school based on abstract reasoning and motive of self-interest. Lastly, both schools aim at a realistic description of human behaviour. "The Austrian school attacked the Historical school. The Institutionalists attack the Austrian!" (Haney). But there is one difference. The Historical School concentrated largely on the question of logical method. They did not have much of an idea of evolution in the Darwinian sense.

Veblen (1857-1927)

Thorstein Veblen is regarded as the founder of "Institutional Economics." Many regard Veblen's work as an outstanding American contribution to political economy. He was the son of Norwegian immigrants and he was born on a farm in Wisconsin. He received a doctorate in philosophy from the Yale University. Veblen did not get a suitable academic position in any of the American Universities in spite of his doctorate degree and profound originality. He was never at one place. All through his life, he had to move from college to college. His marriage was a failure and he was more or less a lonely man. Veblen was a product of his time.

Veblen's first and mot popular book "*The Theory of the Leisure Class*" was published in 1899. His other important works were: (*i*) *The Theory of Business Enterprise* (1904), (*ii*) *The Instinct of Workmanship and the State of the Industrial Arts* (1919), and (*iii*) *The Engineers and the Price System* (1921).

Veblen used peculiar terminology in his books. He was the author of terms such as "leisure class" and 'conspicuous consumption'. Veblen was not satisfied with the methods and doctrines of the classical economists and marginalists as explanations of contemporary economic institutions and phenomena.

Veblen has adopted the evolutionary approach. He pointed out the limitations of the marginal utility principle. He attacked classical economic theory based on hedonism, and rejected the concept of economic man, as always balancing pleasure and pain.

The main idea of Veblen is that the institutions condition and determine man's survival and development. Institutions are of many types. They may be customs or habits, property and so on.

According to Veblen, "The main economic institutions are property and technological methods." In the beginning, technological information was open to all classes. But as industrial arts develop, there is increase in the scale of production. Production exceeds our necessities and there is a surplus. Certain groups by making use of their property rights manage to take away this surplus and live in leisure. Thus 'the leisure class' comes into existence. The leisure class becomes interested in money-making. Then self-interest begins to clash with common good. In due course, machinery comes under the control of the moneyed class. They run industrial establishments as absentee owners. They make profits in a number of ways—by restricting production, by fixing high prices, and by financial manipulations in which credit plays an important role. The moneyed interests overcapitalize with the hope of making speculative earning. Such activities result in business crises. Veblen notes that there is a fundamental conflict in the capitalist society between all those who work in a socially productive way and the members of the 'leisure class' who make money as 'absentee owners' by directing the technique of production.

Veblen regards life as an endless change and in this he was greatly influenced by Darwinian idea of evolution. He has attributed progress to the survival of the fittest habits of thought and the adaptation of individuals to a changing environment. He tells that institutions must change with changing circumstances.

Veblen attacked marginalists because he thought that their theory supported the present scheme of the distribution of wealth and income. He considered the standard economic theory as business economics which had been developed to defend the business community. He argued that theory was not applicable to the society as a whole. He was interested in social economics instead of the business economics of price, profit, and ownership.

We find that there are certain similarities between the ideas of Veblen and Marx. Both attack the foundations of the classical economics. Like Veblen, Marx has rejected the concept of economic man whom he described as 'the image of the bourgeois.' Again like Marx, Veblen emphasizes change and movement and like Marx he builds his system on the basis of conflict between two opposing forces. But Veblen's explanation of historical change is not as clear and as comprehensive as that of Marx.

Conclusion

One of the chief contributions of Amercian economists are those in the statistical and descriptive branches of the subject. The economists who developed all these branches were influenced by Veblen. But Veblen has been criticized on the ground that he over-emphasized the role of 'institutions' in economic life. As Haney summed up, "The laws of economics work through institutions, but they are more fundamental than institutions. The central core of economic theory is about as "non-institutional" as it was in Veblen's day. In the opinion of Prof. Gordon, "Despite some of the new developments in the theory of the firm and of market behaviour, micro theory is still concerned primarily with the kind of "equilibrium economics" which Veblen so severely criticized." Veblen is more admired by sociologists than economists.

J. R. Commons (1862-1945)

John Rogers Commons was a leading member of the institutionalist school. While Veblen concentrated on the sociological aspects of the society, Commons contributed to the study of the legal aspects of institutions. He concerned himself about legal concepts such as 'property', 'the corporation', 'the reasonable value' and 'going concern.'

John R. Commons was born in Indiana in 1862 in an impoverished family. He graduated at the age of twenty-six. He never took his doctorate degree. He was not always successful as lecturer. He changed many jobs. Finally, he settled in the teaching profession when he got a job at the University of Wisconsin in 1904.

Commons was a great social reformer. Like Webbs, he helped in the drafting of many programmes of reform and social legislation. He wrote a Civil Service Law, helped the passing of small loan legislation and drafted Wisconsin's Unemployment Reserve Act. He did not believe in the harmony of class interests. He noticed clash of interests in the society. He advocated an increasing role for government in resolving the conflicting interests among many different groups.

In his book "Institutional Economics", he defined institution as a *"collective action in control of individual action."* It may be noted that this definition is different from the one given by Veblen. Veblen defined an institution as a widely prevalent habit of thought. Commons emphasized the mutual dependence of men and the need for co-operation. He emphasized the need for collective action to reconcile the clash of interests which the institution of private property created.

In his "Legal Foundations of Capitalism", Commons emphasized the role of courts in the social arrangements. He classified transactions into *three* types: (*i*) bargaining transaction, (*ii*) rationing transaction, and (*iii*) managerial transaction. He criticized the economists for paying too much of attention to the first type and for neglecting the other two. A bargaining transaction is a market transaction between individuals of equal status. A rationing transaction transfers ownership and modifies property rights. It is based on an authoritative relationship. Examples for rationing transactions are the tax burden fixed by government and wages fixed for individuals by trade unions. A managerial transaction is also of an authoritative type. Example for this is a company manager commanding the services of a worker. Commons thought that a study of all the transactions was essential for a proper analysis of economic problems.

Commons was a great supporter of trade union movement. He thought it was necessary to the collective bargaining power of workers. But he was not for overthrowing the capitalist system. He believed in gradualist approach to trade unionism. Today most of Commons's ideas on social reform are generally accepted. In short, Commons made his institutional economics a tool for social reform.

W. C. Mitchell (1874-1948)

Wesley Clair Mitchell was one of the three great figures of the institutionalist school. He was a student and admirer of Veblen. He gave an empirical basis for Institutional economics. An analysis of business fluctuations was his great contribution to economic thought. He did pioneering work in the statistical field and he thought that his statistical studies would provide a firm foundation for institutionalist ideas of his teacher, Veblen.

Mitchell was born in Illinois. Though he came of a poor family, he managed to receive university education. He took his doctorate from Chicago University. He occupied many important positions. In 1915 he wrote a monograph called, "The making and use of Index Numbers", which is a classic on the subject. However, Mitchell's classic, "Business cycles and their causes" was published in 1913. After the First World War, Mitchell organized the National Bureau of Economic Research which has done pioneering investigations of national income measurement, business cycles, productivity changes, price analysis and many other subjects. Mitchell firmly believed that deductive reasoning was useless unless its results were checked and corrected by inductive investigation.

Mitchell's greatest contribution was in the study of business fluctuations. He attributed business cycles to the imbalance between production and distribution. When imbalances occur, it results in glut on the market with unsold goods. And men and machines are unemployed. Business cycles recur because there is no proper business planning. Business fluctuations are aggravated by factors such as widening of markets, the growth of monopolies, the migration of people from the countryside to cities and dependence of the farmers on markets instead of being self-sufficient as in the past.

He arrived at the following conclusions regarding business cycles after thorough statistical investigations. Firstly, business cycles are a feature of a monetary economy. Secondly, business fluctuations are widely diffused throughout the economy. Thirdly, intensity of the cycle depends on the prospects of profits. Lastly, business cycles are generated by the economy itself. They are not accidental disruptions of equilibrium. They are a disease of the capitalism.

Mitchell believed that careful social or national planning would mitigate the evils of business fluctuations while at the same time preserving economic liberty.

Mitchell's theory of trade cycles is a superb contribution to economic analysis. Veblen depicted economics as a science of change. But it became a science of measurement in the hands of Mitchell.

THE KEYNESIAN REVOLUTION

JOHN MAYNARD KEYNES (1883-1946)

Introduction

John Maynard Keynes was one of the greatest and the most controversial economists of the twentieth century. Many major developments in modern economics are associated with his name. His book, "The General Theory of Employment, Interest and Money" marks a turning point in the history of economic thought. The book has brought about many fundamental changes in economic theory and policy. Hence the term "Keynesian Revolution" is often applied to describe the economic ideas of Keynes. Sometimes, Keynesian economics is also described as "New Economics". Of course, there are some critics who say that there is nothing new in "New Economics". But they form only a small minority. 'New political economy concerns itself with the problems of the economy as a whole, rather than with those of the individual consumer.'

Life and Works

John Maynard Keynes was born in 1883 in a family of intellectual eminence. He was the son of John Neville Keynes, a noted economist. His mother was a Mayor of Cambridge as lately as 1932. He was brought up in the most intellectual society of Cambridge. He studied economics at Cambridge under Marshall and Pigou. In 1906, he entered civil service. It may be interesting to note that the architect of "New Economics" got his worst marks in Economics. His comment was "The examiners presumably knew less then I did" He worked in India Office for some time. Then he went to Cambridge University to teach economics. He lectured on money. He was a member of the Royal Commission of Indian Currency and Finance (1913-1914). He served in the Treasury from 1915-1919. He was principal representative of the Treasury at Paris peace conference after World War I. As Keynes was opposed to the way in which the peace settlement was forced upon Germany, he resigned his official position in 1919. It was after that he wrote "The Economic Consequences of Peace." After his resignation, he returned to teaching and became bursar at King's College. In 1940, he rejoined the Treasury and guided his country in war finance. After the war, he played an important role in organizing International Monetary Fund and the International Bank for Reconstruction and Development. In 1942 he became Lord Keynes.

Keynes was a great lover of arts and books. In 1925, Keynes married Lydia Lopokova, a great star of the Russian Imperial Ballet. According to Mrs. Alfred Marshall, marrying Lydia was 'the best thing Maynard ever did.' She proved to be a delightful companion and a tireless nurse in the years after he had a serious heart attack in 1937.

Keynes was a many-sided genius. He made many important contributions to the fundamentals of economic science. He was equally successful in the practical application of economics on critical occasions. Naturally, Keynes had a lot of influence among academic economists as well as men of practical affairs. To find an economist of comparable influence, one would have to go back to Adam Smith.

Keynes, the great economist, died in 1946 from a heart attack.

The important works of Keynes included: (*i*) *Indian Currency and Finance* (1913); (*ii*) *The Economic Consequences of the Peace* (1919); (*iii*) *A Treatise on Probability* (1921); (*iv*) *A Tract on Monetary Reform*; (*v*) *The Economic Consequences of Mr. Churchill* (1925); (*vi*) *The End of Laissez-Faire* (1926); (*vii*) *A Treatise on Money* (Two Volumes) (1930); (*viii*) *Essays in Persuasion* (1931); (*ix*) *Essays in Biography* (1933); (*x*) *The General Theory of Employment, Interest and Money* (1936); and (*xi*) *How to pay for the War* (1940).

Background of Keynesian Economics

The development of the economic ideas of Keynes had a great deal to do with the great depression of the 1930s. In fact, his ideas developed when Keynes was trying to analyse the problem of trade cycles, one of the greatest maladies of the capitalist economies. Unemployment became a severe problem during the period. In the past, economists, segregated the study of business cycles from general economic theory. But Keynes tried to unite the monetary theory with the general economic theory. While Keynes was trying to find out an explanation of the factors that caused sudden changes in the level of economic activity, his theories took shape. As he was thinking and writing during a period of depression, naturally, he became more concerned with the problems of depression rather than with those of inflation. On account of the pre-occupation of Keynes with the problems of depression, Keynesian economics has been dubbed as 'depression economics.' This, however, is not a correct description of Keynesian economics. Instead of describing Keynes as a "depression" economist, it may be appropriate to describe him as an 'anti-deflation' and 'anti-inflation' economist.

Further the economic thinking of the period was concerned with the problems of secular stagnation of the capitalist society. The mature free-enterprise, capitalist economies of the Western world seemed to be less vigorous after World War I than before. In fact, Karl Marx, predicted the doom of capitalism and fears about the gradual decline and fall of capitalism were increased after 1929, the year of great depression. So Keynes tried to demonstrate that there was nothing fundamentally wrong with the basic structure of capitalism as such. But he pointed out the need for putting an end to the policy of *Laissez-Faire* in order to make capitalism strong. He has emphasized in his book "*The End of Laissez-Faire*": "The important thing for government is not to do things which individuals are doing already, and to do them a little better or a little worse, but to do those things which at present are not done at all." Keynes argued that government should intervene actively in economic matters to promote full employment. Most of the economists in the capitalist economies regard Marx as 'the prophet of doom' and Keynes as 'the prophet of boom.'

We shall study the relationship between Keynesian approach and the classical approach before we study Keynesian economics in detail.

Keynes and Classical Economists

Usually by classical economists, we mean Adam Smith, James Mill and their predecessors. But Keynes included the neo-classical economists including Marshall, Pigou and Edgeworth in the category of classical economists, in his "General Theory of Employment, Interest and Money." And his attacks, in general, are directed against the neo-classical economists like Prof. Pigou. We shall now study the points where he differed from the classical economists.

1. According to Keynes, "The classical economists were concerned with the distribution of the social product rather than its amount." For instance, Ricardo believed that political economy is not an enquiry into the nature and causes of wealth but it is "an enquiry into the laws which determine the division of the produce of the industry among the classes who concur in its formation." In other words, classical economists tried to explain the determinants of the relative shares in the national income of the different factors of production rather than the forces which determined, the level of that income. The level of income may also be called the level of employment. But Keynes was interested in analysing the factors that determined the level of output or income or employment at any time.

2. The classical approach (especially those of the neo-classical economists like Marshall) is micro-economic approach which is interested in the problem of partial equilibrium analysis. It is difficult to provide an adequate explanation of the forces determining the general level of employment in a country on the basis of partial equilibrium analysis. It can only explain how unemployment may occur in particular industries. But Keynesian approach is macro-economic approach and deals with general equilibrium analysis. 'Macro-economics deals with aggregates such as total output, total expenditure on consumer's goods and on investment, the average level of prices, wages and interest rates, and how these aggregates affect on one another and act on the economic system as a whole.' The general equilibrium analysis of Keynes helps us to show whether employment in all industries will be high or low at any particular time.

3. The classical economics is based on the assumption of full-employment equilibrium. This assumption was derived from J. B. Say's Law of Markets. The law stated that "supply creates its own demand." That is, there can be no such thing as 'deficiency of aggregate demand.' On the basis of Say's Law, the classical economists, with the exception of Malthus, argued that there was the possibility of over-production of particular commodities but not over-production in general. In other words, they ruled out general unemployment and over-production. They thought the economy was self-adjusting. Keynesian economics is a rejection of Say's Law of Markets.

The classical economists, in general, ignored the problem of crises. They failed to realize the possibility of different levels of economic activity with the same amount of resources. So Keynes describes their analysis based on full employment equilibrium as a special case which is not applicable in general. For instance, classical economic theories contain no analysis of the economics of less than full employment and as such they have not provided any satisfactory explanation of business cycles. But Keynesian theory is a general theory which is applicable to different levels of employment.

4. While the classical economists studied economics from the point of view of long-run equilibrium, Keynes emphasized on short-run considerations. He was not interested in the long-run equilibrium. "For in the long-run we are all dead" as he put it humorously.

5. The classical economists praised savings and thrift. But Keynes advocated spending and thriftlessness during a period of depression. Keynes attacked savings, especially during the period of depression because too much of savings curtailed effective aggregate demand and hence affected investment and employment.

6. Classical economists like Pigou suggested a policy of general cut in wages to solve the problem of unemployment. Pigou attributed the fall in demand to rising prices. He thought prices rose because of increase in the cost of production, which in turn, was the result of increase in wages. He argued that if a policy of general wage cut was followed during a period of depression, cost of production would fall, which in turn would reduce prices and demand would increase. This would increase employment. Keynes opposed the policy of general cut in wages for he considered it a remedy worse than the disease itself. When there is a general unemployment, a general cut in wages will only cause a reduction in demand by reducing incomes and would not solve unemployment. It would aggravate the problem.

7. The classical economists considered the general theory as something separate from monetary theory. This compartmentalisation has resulted in a lot of confusion. As Keynes put it, "we have all of us become used to finding ourselves on the one side of the moon and sometimes on the other without knowing what route or journey connects them....". One of the greatest achievements of Keynes has been to link the general theory with the monetary theory. This idea is explicit in the title of his great book, *"The General Theory of Employment, Interest and Money."*

8. While the classical economists analysed economic problems in static terms, Keynes introduced

certain dynamic elements in the form of expectations into his theory. They play an important role in determining the marginal efficiency of capital. "The *General Theory* has helped to make us think of Economics in dynamic rather than in static terms."

9. The classical economists regarded interest as a reward for waiting or abstinence or time element. They also thought the equilibrium between savings and investment was brought about by the rate of interest. But Keynes introduced the element of liquidity preference in his theory and thought that the rate of interest was determined by liquidity preference on the one hand and supply of money on the other.

10. While the classical economists advocated 'balanced budget' as a rule, Keynes advocated deficit budget during a period of depression. He thought that deficit financing could be used as a tool for achieving economic recovery, that is to raise the level of output and employment.

11. The classical economists believed that whenever there was an increase in the quantity of money, it would result in a rise in the general level of prices. The famous quantity theory of money as formulated by Fisher, was based on the assumption of full employment. But Keynes argued that as long as full employment level was not reached, an increase in money supply would only increase output and not prices. An increase in the supply of money would cause inflation only after full employment level had been reached. Of course, Keynes was aware of the possibility of inflation occurring even before full employment level was reached when certain bottlenecks developed in the economy.

12. While the classical economists advocated laissez-faire, and a 'thorough-going competition', Keynes pleaded for the end of *Laissez-Faire* and pointed out the need for government intervention. Keynesianism was purposive in the area of public policy. It is rooted in practice. One of the chief contributions of Keynes to economics is this. He succeeded in relating academic economics to the economics of government. For instance, he advocated cheap money policy and public works programmes to revive an economy during the period of depression.

The foregoing analysis clearly shows that it is not right to regard Keynesian economics as simply classical economics, further developed or embroidered. It represents a genuine break from classical economics. In fact, in one of his letters to Shaw, Keynes wrote that he believed his work *General Theory* would revolutionise economics in the course of the next ten years. He was right in the assessment of his own work.

We should not, of course, forget the fact that, in spite of the great deviations from the traditional theory, there are certain similarities between Keynesian economics and classical economics. For instance, Keynes has accepted the traditional assumption of purely competitive society. We do not come across any major discussions on monopolistic and oligopolistic competition in the 'General Theory.' Of course, he makes a few side comments here and there. As Prof. Gill summed it up, "producers, in the Keynesian world, engage in simple profit maximization just as they did in the world of Walras or Ricardo. Marginal analysis is used extensively throughout. Furthermore, Keynes presented his theory in the essentially static form characteristic of the late 19th century analysis. There is no growth in the Keynesian system, nor any formal analysis of process of change. Fundamental conditions—technology, population, stock of capital—are taken as given."[1]

We shall now study the essentials of Keynesian economics.

Keynesian Theory of Employment

The starting point of Keynesian Theory of Employment is the principle of effective demand. Total employment depends on total demand (aggregate effective demand) and unemployment results from a deficiency of total demand. Keynes found in Malthus an early presentation of the theory of effective demand, of the need for unproductive consumption, and the government investment.

We should remember that Keynesian Theory of employment relates to the short run. In the short run employment is determined by aggregate demand, which in turn depends on the *propensity to*

---

[1]. Richard T. Gill: *Evolution of Modern Economics*, p. 91.

consume and the *amount of investment* at a given time. The term 'aggregate demand' refers to the total volume of purchases which consumers, investors and government are willing to undertake. So the various components of aggregate demand are consumption demand, investment demand and government demand.

Aggregate Demand, Aggregate Income and Aggregate Output

Employment depends on demand and aggregate demand is equal to aggregate income. Hence, we may say that the general theory of employment is also a theory of aggregate demand or aggregate income. Since the value of the total output is equal to total income, Keynesian Theory of employment may also be called a theory of aggregate output. Employment results in the production of output on the one hand and on the creation of income on the other.

The Propensity to consume: The level of consumption at any time depends upon the level of income. Keynes has introduced a "fundamental psychological law" in relation to income and consumption. According to this law, when there is an increase in a person's income, he will generally divide it between added consumption and added saving. For the society as a whole, an increase in national income (national product), will result in increase in total consumption and total saving. The term, 'propensity to consume' explains the functional relationship between consumption and income. It tells us how consumption varies when income varies. Keynes tells us that a high propensity to consume is favourable to employment.

The Inducement to Invest: Business investment demand is a complex phenomenon and depends upon many factors. But the two most important factors which determine investment are the rate of interest and the marginal efficiency of capital. Marginal efficiency of capital refers to the expected rate of profit from new investment. The rate of interest, one of the factors, which determine the volume of investment, depends upon: (*i*) the state of liquidity preference and; (*ii*) the quantity of money. The term 'liquidity preference' refers to the desire of people to hold some of their assets in the form of money. The quantity of money refers to the amount of funds in the form of coins, paper currency, and bank deposits outstanding in the hands of the public.

Liquidity preference depends upon three important motives: (*i*) Transaction Motive; (*ii*) Precautionary Motive; and (*iii*) Speculative Motive. Of the three motives, speculative motive is very important in relation to the rate of interest. Keynes defines the speculative motive as "the object of securing profit from knowing better than the market what the future will bring forth."

We have noted that the consumption demand, investment demand and government demand are the various components of aggregate demand. But if we ignore the government for a while, the immediate determinants of income and employment are consumption and investment spending. The money that is spent on final goods and services, whether for consumption or investment, generates income.

If consumption, investment and income are designated as C, I and Y respectively, then

$$Y = C + I$$

Saving is the difference between income and consumption. If we designate saving by S, then,

$$S = Y - C$$

By solving the two equations, we get

$$S = I.$$

It means that aggregate savings and investment are equal. But they may not be always in equilibrium. The classical economists believed that savings were automatically invested. They thought that the decisions to save and the decisions to invest were essentially the same decisions. But Keynes, like Wicksell, argued that savings decisions were not the same as investment decisions. Savings and investment were made by different people for different reasons and were influenced by different factors. Thus, sometimes savings might exceed investment. When this happened, it would result in the deficiency of aggregate demand, which in turn, would cause a fall in income and general unemployment.

Keynes thought that the gap between savings and investment could be filled by government intervention, either directly by taxes and government expenditure or indirectly by actions influencing the supply of money.

We may now summarize the Keynesian theory of employment:

1. Total Income depends on the volume of total employment.

2. Employment depends on effective demand.

3. Effective demand is determined by the propensity to consume and the volume of investment.

4. As the propensity to consume is more or less stable, employment depends on the volume of investment.

5. Investment depends on the rate of interest and the marginal efficiency of capital.

6. The rate of interest depends on liquidity preference and the quantity of money.

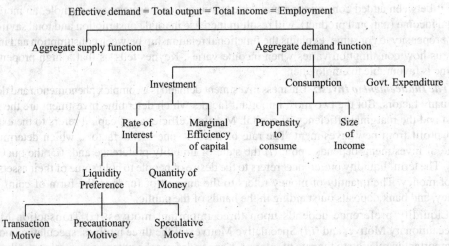

Keynesian theory of Employment

Propensity to Consume or the Consumption Function

In the estimate of Hansen, consumption function (propensity to consume) is the greatest contribution of Keynes to economic analysis.

The ultimate aim of Keynesian theory is to explain what determines the volume of employment. The starting point of the theory is the principle of effective demand. It tells that employment depends on consumption expenditure and investment expenditure. Consumption depends on the size of income and propensity to consume. (Investment depends on the marginal efficiency of capital and the rate of interest). A high propensity to consume is favourable to employment. One of the remedies for solving unemployment is to increase propensity to consume.

The propensity to consume is also called '*consumption function*' because it shows the functional relationship between income and consumption. We have to note that the propensity to consume does not mean mere desire to consume. It refers to the actual consumption, that takes place, or is expected to take place, out of varying amounts of income.

We must note the distinction between the average propensity to consume and the marginal propensity to consume. If 'C' designates consumption and 'Y' income, average propensity to consume is $\dfrac{C}{Y}$. If Rs. 800 are spent out of an income of Rs. 1,000, the average propensity to consume is 800/1,000 or 8/10. It means 80 per cent of the income will be spent for consumption.

The marginal propensity to consume is the ratio of a small change in consumption to a small change in income. It may be designated by $\dfrac{\Delta C}{\Delta Y}$, where symbol Δ (delta) stands for a small increment.

The propensity to consume is relatively stable.

Marginal Propensity to Consume and The Investment Multiplier

Keynes borrowed the concept of multiplier from R. F. Kahn, his colleague at Cambridge University. The propensity to consume tells us that there is a definite relationship between consumption and income at all levels of employment.

We may establish a definite relationship between investment and income. 'From the marginal propensity to consume, we can tell *how much* income and employment will increase as a result of a given increase in investment.' If the propensity to consume is given, we can say that a definite ratio exists between any increase in income (ΔY) and any given increase in investment (ΔI). This ratio between the increase in income and increase in investment is called *investment multiplier.*

We may illustrate the relation between the marginal propensity to consume ($\Delta C/\Delta Y$) and the investment multiplier ($\Delta Y/\Delta I$) by a simple example.

Let us suppose, there is Rs. 100 increase in income Rs. 90 of the increased income are spent on consumption and Rs. 10 on investment. Then the marginal propensity to consume is 90/100 $\dfrac{\Delta C}{\Delta Y}$.

The multiplier is $\dfrac{100}{10}\ \dfrac{\Delta Y}{\Delta I}$ = 10. In a general form we may say that the multiplier is equal to the reciprocal of one minus the marginal propensity to consume. In the above example, the marginal propensity to consume is 9/10, one minus 9/10 is 1/10, and the multiplier is the reciprocal of 1/10 and that is 10.

We may also describe the multiplier as the reciprocal of the marginal propensity to save which is always equal to one minus the marginal propensity to consume. Thus, if the marginal propensity to consume is 9/10, the marginal propensity to save is 1/10, and the multiplier is 10.

According to Keynes, "The size of the multiplier varies directly with the size of the marginal propensity to consume." Whenever the marginal propensity to consume is high, the multiplier is high and vice versa.

Marginal Efficiency of Capital

Marginal efficiency of capital plays an important role in the Keynesian system. It is one of the co-determinants of investment. Marginal efficiency of capital refers to the rate of prospective earnings on capital. In plain language, it is the expected rate of profit of a new investment.

As more capital goods are produced, the marginal efficiency of capital declines. Investments will continue to the point at which the marginal efficiency of capital is equal to the rate of interest.

The marginal efficiency of capital is highly variable. It fluctuates with every change in businessman's expectations of future profits from present investment. Keynes said that marginal efficiency of capital will have a tendency to decline for the following two reasons: First of all, the expected rate of profit will decline as more and more investments compete with each other; secondly, as demand for capital goods increases, the supply price of capital goods will increase. Keynes thought that it was difficult to maintain full employment in a capitalist economy unless the rate of interest was low enough. But if the marginal efficiency of capital was falling more rapidly than the rate of interest because of pessimistic tendencies among businessmen, a decline in the rate of interest will not increase investment. Keynes, in his later writings, stressed more on the declining marginal efficiency of capital rather than high rates of interest as the parent of depression.

It may be interesting to note that Keynes, like Ricardo and Marx, thought that there was a long run tendency for the rate of profit to fall.

The Rate of Interest

The Rate of Interest is a cornerstone in the Keynesian system. It is one of the major determinants of the level of investment.

Keynes rejected the classical notion of rate of interest as the reward for saving or waiting as such. The classical economists believed that saving was influenced by the rate of interest. But Keynes thought savings depended much more on the level of income.

According to Keynes, interest is the reward for parting with liquidity. In other words, it is the reward for not hoarding.

Liquidity preference refers to the desire of the people to hold their assets in the form of money. Keynes has given three important motives of liquidity preference: (*i*) The transaction motive; (*ii*) The precautionary motive; and (*iii*) The speculative motive. Of the three motives, speculative motive is more important in relation to the rate of interest. Keynes defines the speculative motive as "The object of securing profit from knowing better than the market what the future will bring forth." Although the rate of interest is closely related to the speculative motive, the other two motives cannot be ignored because money held for one purpose is a perfect substitute for money held for other purposes.

After introducing the concept of liquidity preference, Keynes said that the rate of interest was determined by the state of liquidity preference on the one hand and quantity of money on the other. The stronger the liquidity preference, the higher would be the rate of interest and the greater the quantity of money, the lower would be the rate of interest. A decrease in the liquidity preference will tend to lower the rate of interest and a decrease in the quantity of money will tend to raise the rate of interest.

The quantity of money depends on central bank policy. The central bank can increase or decrease the supply of money through its monetary policy.

The classical economists thought a lower rate of interest would reduce saving. But Keynes thought that normally a lower rate of interest would stimulate investment, thereby increasing income and saving. Pigou said in 1950: "Nobody before him (Keynes)... had brought all the relevant factors, real and monetary at once, together in a formal scheme, through which their interplay could be coherently investigated."

Role of Government

Keynes pleaded for the end of *laissez-faire* and believed that government could play an important role in promoting full employment. For instance, he said that the government should stimulate private investment during a period of depression by lowering the rate of interest. This could be done through a suitable monetary policy of the central bank. But Keynes was aware of the limitations of lower interest rates in promoting investment. So he thought that an effective way to overcome depression was to undertake enough deficit spending (deficit financing) to achieve full employment. In other words, he suggested, '*socialization of investment*'. The State could determine the aggregate level of investment. Of course, ownership of capital would be still in the private hands.

Keynes also believed by redistribution of income, through a progressive taxation policy, the government could increase the propensity to consume.

Keynes advocated public works programme to stimulate investment. He believed that pyramid building, earthquakes, even wars may serve to increase wealth. He thought that "Ancient Egypt was doubly fortunate, and doubtless owed to this its fabled wealth, in that it possessed *two* activities, namely, pyramid building as well as the search for the precious metals.... the Middle Ages built cathedrals and sang dirges. Two pyramids, two masses for the dead, are twice as good as one; but not so two railways from London to York."[1]

---

[1] *The General Theory of Employment, Interest and Money*, p. 131.

Keynes accepted even wasteful government deficit spending on useless projects in the absence of useful projects:

"If the Treasury were to fill old bottles with banknotes, bury them at suitable depths in disused coal-mines which are then filled up to the surface with town rubbish and leave it to private enterprise on well tried principles of *laissez-faire* to dig the notes up again, there need be no more unemployment and with the help of the repercussion, the real income of the community, and its capital wealth also, would probably become a good deal greater than it actually is. It would indeed be more sensible to build houses and the like; but if there are political and practical difficulties in the way of this, the above would be better than nothing."

Keynesian Revolution and its Impact

"The General Theory of Employment, Interest and Money" is probably the most influential book of the 20th century in economics. It has influenced economic theory as well as public policy. The work has shown the way to solve unemployment problem. One of the chief contributions of Keynes was to tie economic analysis to the great public problems of the day.

So far as the impact of the "General Theory" on economic analysis is concerned, we should note that it has had an immediate and dynamic effect. Keynes has added a number of tools to economic analysis—'Marginal propensity to consume, liquidity preference, marginal efficiency of capital' are all but a few examples. Economists have experienced a considerable enrichment of their "mental furniture" by reason of the Keynesian contribution. In the estimate of Prof. Alvin H. Hansen, "The consumption function is by far the most powerful instrument which has been added to the economist's kit of tools in our generation." Keynesian ideas have given a stimulus to the further development of macroeconomics.

Another important contribution made by Keynes was in the use of expectations. Keynes's integration of expectation with his theory of money and marginal efficiency was a notable advance in economic analysis.

While the classical economists assumed full employment. Keynes emphasized on under-employment equilibrium (that is, equilibrium at less than full employment). The 'under-employment equilibrium concept is regarded as one of Keynes's most significant gifts to economics. In fact, it is the theme of the 'General Theory.' The present interest in full employment economics and short-run economics owes much to Keynes.

Keynes was not without his critics. For instance, Knight commented on the general theory as follows: "We must simply 'forget' the revolution in economic theory and read the book as a contribution to the theory of business oscillations."

In the opinion of Hansen, Keynes's break with the classicists was complete on the rate of interest and the relation of savings and investment.

Sometimes, Keynesian economics is dubbed as 'depression economics.' But we may be right in describing Keynes as 'anti-deflation' and 'anti-inflation' economist. For he felt, 'inflation is unjust and deflation is inexpedient.' While the classical economists thought they could control inflation by a high rate of interest, Keynes felt the other way. In his own words, "The remedy for the boom is not a higher rate of interest but a lower rate of interest. For that may enable the so-called boom to last. The right remedy for the trade cycle is not to be found in abolishing booms and thus keeping us permanently in a semi-slump; but in abolishing slumps and thus keeping us permanently in a quasi-boom."

Keynes opposed gold standard because he thought that under gold standard the freedom of the monetary authorities to manufacture money and hence deal with unemployment is restricted.

Keynesian economics had a profound influence on social philosophy and public policy. Keynes taught that the *laissez-faire* capitalist system based on market economy would not generate sufficient aggregate demand to maintain full employment. He argued for State intervention to prevent general unemployment. The State could promote full employment either by lowering the rate of interest or by undertaking public works programmes. Keynes argued that interest payments no longer served any useful purpose. Many governments have followed 'cheap' money policy during a period of depression. Keynes thought the State could prevent depression in a more significant and direct manner by influencing consumption expenditure and investment expenditure. By suitable changes in tax policy, it can influence consumption expenditure. For example, during a period of depression, the government may reduce taxes so that more money will be left with people for consumption purposes. The government can also participate directly in investment activities. It will supplement private investment. He said that the government must take up the responsibility to see that there is no general deficiency of aggregate demand. In other words, he advocated 'socialization of investment'. In short, he believed that more and more recourse should be had to fiscal policy (taxation, spending and borrowing policies) than to monetary policy. As Gerhard Colm puts it, "It is almost impossible to think of fiscal policy in the modern world, without thinking of John Maynard Keynes, and particularly the *General Theory*. In fact, he gave the concept of fiscal policy a new meaning, and the operations of government finance a new perspective, it is perhaps not going too far to say that Keynes thought of survival of liberal capitalism in terms of fiscal policy correctly understood and boldly carried out."

The 'New Deal' policies in America were greatly influenced by the economic ideas of Keynes. Further Keynes played a significant role in establishing the International Monetary Fund and the International Bank for Reconstruction and Development.

Marx and Keynes: We notice that Marx and Keynes had certain similar ideas. Both of them were interested in macroeconomics. Both of them regarded inadequate demand as the cause of trade cycles. Both emphasized the falling rate of profit. Both believed that the rewards for capitalist groups were excessive. But, while Keynes thought the capitalist system could be preserved through the modifications of the capitalist institutions and changes in policy, Marx predicted the inevitable decline and fall of capitalism. While Marx became the 'prophet of doom', Keynes became the 'prophet of boom'. Keynes was anything but a socialist. He was the very opposite of Marx and Keynesian philosophy should be regarded as a major alternative to Marxism. Of course, Keynes conceded that Marx had some idea of the unemployment problem in a capitalist society.

Post-Keynesian Economics

The ideas of Keynes have helped a great deal for the development of macro economics. There has been a lot of discussion on the concept of 'consumption function', one of the cornerstones of the Keynesian system.

Again Prof. Duesenberry made use of the concept *demonstration effect* to point out the interdependence of consumption decisions among different consumers. He argued that a person's desire to buy goods would be influenced by the purchases of other consumers. So consumption, as a percentage of income, would depend not on a person's absolute level of income but on his relative position in the over-all income distribution. Duesenberry also pointed that consumption level in one period might be affected by the previous consumption level achieved by higher income. When once the consumers reached a certain level of income, they would be reluctant to go down to a lower level of consumption even when income was falling.

In recent times, Milton Friedman has given another theory of consumption function. He has divided a consumer's income into "permanent income" and "transitory income." He has argued that consumption is mainly a function of "permanent income." Changes in "transitory income" such as windfall gains or loss will lead only to changes in accumulated balances or holding of durable goods. Changes in "transitory income" will not generally affect ordinary consumption.

The Critique of Keynesianism

Schumpeter felt that Keynesianism was not applicable at all times and in all places. In his own words, "Practical Keynesianism is a seedling which cannot be transplanted into foreign soil; it dies there and becomes poisonous before it dies. But in addition, they would also understand that, left in the English soil, this seedling is a healthy thing and promises both fruit and shade. Let me say once and for all: all this applies to every bit of advice that Keynes ever offered." The above criticism is valid in a way. For, the doctrines of over-saving and inadequate consumption spending are not applicable to the underdeveloped countries of the world. In those countries, inadequate saving is one of the factors that is limiting the growth of investment and income. In the underdeveloped countries of the world which are predominantly agricultural, the major problem is not involuntary mass unemployment, a characteristic feature of the developed industrial societies of the West but *disguised unemployment.*

On the basis of the critique of Keynesianism, one school-the monetarist school-began its analysis in the late 1940s with Milton Friedman as its leader. The school did not reject macro-measurements and macro-models of the economy. Instead, it embraced the techniques of treating the entire economy of having supply and demand equilibrium. But they regarded inflation as solely to the variations in money supply, rather than as being a consequence of demand. They argued that the focus should be on monetary policy which was largely ignored by early Keynesians. They felt that monetarism had an ideological as well as practical appeal. At least, on the surface, monetary policy does not imply as much government intervention in the economy as other measures. The monetarist critique made keynesians take a more balanced view of monetary policy, and inspired a number of revisions to Keynesian theory.

Lucas critique of keynesian economics has resulted in the emergence of another influential school. This is based largely on the developments in macroeconomic theory, and in particular the rational expectations hypothesis. Lucas and others argued that Keynesian economics required remark- ably foolish and short-sighted behaviour from people. This is in total contradiction of the economic understanding of their behaviour at a micro level. Neo-classical economists introduced a set of macroeconomic theories based on optimising microeconomic behaviour (*e.g.,* real business cycles).

Prof. Hayek, a free market economist, is a great critic of Keynesianism. In his famous book, "The Road to Serfdom" (1944), Hayek criticized keynesian economic policies for what he called their fundamentally collective approach. He argued that such theories required centralized planning, which leads to totalitarian abuses. He felt expanding government programmes would stifle the private sector and the civil society.

James Buchanan noted that since keynes had roots in the classically liberal or free market tradition, he was more concerned with what was good policy, not on how it would be executed. In the book, "Democracy in Deficit" he notes that keynes never thought out how, for example, deficit spending would give a blank cheque for politicians to run deficits even when orthodox keynesianism did not find it proper. Macroeconomics has responded to the critique of keynesianism by incorporating more detailed microfoundations into basically keynesian models.

One of the great weaknesses of the "General Theory" was in the area of economic growth. Keynes was interested only in the short-run analysis and short-run policy measures. Recently, attempts have been made to modify Keynesian theory in long-run dynamic terms. R. F. Harrod's "Towards a Dynamic Economics" (1949) is a notable contribution in the field. Harrod and Domar have recently developed a growth model making use of the basic ideas of Keynes. Harrod pointed out that Keynes' treatment of investment was one-sided. While Keynes emphasized the role of investment in creating aggregate demand and hence more employment, ignored the fact that employment represented an addition to capital stock and that the latter had an effect on the productive capacity of the economy in the long run. So Harrod-Domar in their model attempted to show what happened when the stock of capital, population and technology were all expanding over time. That way, they have tried to bring growth back into Keynesian economics. Thus the *General Theory* has stimulated theoretical and empirical research so much that we may apply the term "new economics" to Keynesian economics without exaggeration.

JOSEPH A. SCHUMPETER
(1883-1950)

Joseph A. Schumpeter was born in the Austrian province of Moravia (now Czechoslovakia) in 1883. He was educated in Law and Economics at the University of Vienna. He was a lover of peace and hated war in any form. Naturally, during World War I, he expressed his anti-German sentiments. For a while, he served as Finance Minister of Austrian Republic in 1919. Later on he became professor at the University of Bonn in Germany. And in 1932 he joined the Harvard University in America and taught there till his death. Schumpeter was the first foreign-born economist who became the president of the American Economic Association.

Schumpeter was a great scholar. His works included, (*i*) "The Theory of Economic Development" (1934), (*ii*) "Business Cycles" (1938), (*iii*) "Capitalism, Socialism and Democracy" (1947) and (*iv*) "The History of Economic Analysis." The last work was edited after his death by his wife.

Leon Walras and Karl Marx exercised a profound influence on Schumpeter. Schumpeter was much impressed by the emphasis of Walras on the interdependence of economic quantities. And he had a great admiration of Marx's understanding of the process of economic change. One thing he liked most about Marx was that while "criticizing and rejecting, or accepting and co-ordinating, he always went to the bottom of every matter." But Schumpeter was no Marxist. He was devoted to the institutions of capitalism. But he thought that the very forces that accounted for the success of capitalism would destroy it. He agreed with Marx that capitalism was doomed. But the reasons that Schumpeter gave were different from those that were given by Marx.

Schumpeter considered economic life as essentially a process of change and development. He was mainly interested in explaining the theory of capitalist economic development and the business cycles. His theory of trade cycles rests upon the hypothesis that the mechanics of evolution itself works to produce wave-like movements. According to him, the essential process in economic change is the introduction of innovations and the innovations are introduced by the entrepreneur who is the central figure in the scheme of economic development. Innovation refers to the changes in the methods of supplying commodities. Innovation may consist of the introduction of new goods or new methods of production, opening new markets, conquering new sources of supply and things like that. We should remember innovation is something more than invention. An invention becomes an innovation only when it is applied to industrial processes.

The entrepreneur carries out new combinations and introduces innovations. He is different from a salaried manager or an industrialist, who runs a business without trying new ideas. The entrepreneur is a pioneer in introducing new products, new processes and new forms of business organization or in exploiting new markets.

Without the activities of the entrepreneurs and their innovations, economic life would reach static equilibrium. Profits and interest would disappear and there would not be any accumulation of wealth. The entrepreneur, who is guided by the profit motive, seeks profit through innovation and he transforms the static situation into the dynamic process of economic development. He diverts labour and land to investment. As current savings are not enough, the entrepreneur depends upon credit to provide the means for his enterprise.

According to Schumpeter, economic development arises from within the economic system itself. It is not imposed from outside. Another point that Schumpeter makes is that innovations do not occur continuously but they appear in clusters. The activities of the enterprising entrepreneurs create a favourable climate for investment. Others follow suit. Credit expands, prices and incomes rise and there is all-round prosperity. But this prosperity does not last forever.

The boom has in it the seeds of depression. The boom creates conditions which are unfavourable to continued progress. Rising prices act as a check on investment and the competition of new products with old ones cause business losses. When businessmen repay their debts, it aggravates the deflationary process and depression sets in. So the trade cycles represent the process of adaptation of the economy to innovations. The economic system tends towards equilibrium but innovations disrupt that tendency. The main point is that the process that generates economic growth also generates economic fluctuations. So long as there are innovations and economic growth, there will be business fluctuations and depression represents a struggle of the economy toward a new equilibrium. In short, Schumpeter considered the action of entrepreneurs as a dynamic factor which disturbed economic equilibrium.

Schumpeter was of the definite opinion that capitalism would not survive. But he differed with many leading economists like Ricardo, Malthus, Marx and Keynes regarding the precise nature and causes of the decay of capitalism. Schumpeter rejected the Ricardian law of diminishing returns and the Malthusian theory of population which were given as obstacles to economic growth. He rejected Marx's argument that economic conditions of capitalism would produce successively more severe crisis. And he disapproved of the stagnation thesis of Keynes on the main ground that opportunities for great innovations have not been exhausted. Further, although the process of opening up new countries has been completed. Schumpeter believed that new opportunities would appear.

Schumpeter thought that capitalism would decline for the following reasons: (*i*) The entrepreneurial function was becoming obsolete, (*ii*) the protective political strata of capitalism was being slowly destroyed, and (*iii*) there was the slow but steady destruction of the institutional framework of capitalist society.

Schumpeter observed that the function of the entrepreneur was becoming obsolete and innovation was being reduced to routine. The entrepreneur was becoming just another office worker. In the process of capitalist evolution, the industrial bourgeois class would lose not only its income but its function as well. Schumpeter believed that the true pacemakers of socialism were not the intellectuals or agitators who preached it but great innovating entrepreneurs like Rockefellers. He has humorously said that "this result may not in every respect be to the taste of Marxian socialists."

Schumpeter agreed with Marx that big business destroyed small and medium-sized firms. This in turn would make the political position of the industrial bourgeoisie in democratic politics politically weak. The destruction of the political strata which provide the strongest defence of the capitalism also mean self-destruction of the system. Schumpeter was worried that farmers who were great defenders of capitalism were declining as a percentage of the population. With the destruction of the institutional framework of capitalism and with a lot of governmental control in economic matters, capitalism lost much of its substance. In Schumpeter's words, "... It is capitalism in the oxygen tent—kept alive by artificial devices and paralysed in all those functions that produced the successes of the past. The question why it should be kept alive at all is, therefore, bound to be put before long."

Schumpeter thought that with the increasing role of the Government in the economic sphere, capitalism would become 'guided capitalism' and with the nationalisation of industries, "guided capitalism" would become "state capitalism". Under state capitalism, there will be government ownership and management of selected industrial sectors, complete government control in labour and capital market and government initiative in domestic and foreign enterprise. Some may even describe the system as socialism. It is a matter of taste. But under state capitalism, there will be friction and inefficiency. The disadvantages of such a system can be eliminated only under pure capitalism or full socialism. Schumpeter, however, believed that some of the essential human values would be preserved under state capitalism. It is interesting to note that even Veblen, the founder of the "Institutionalist school", reached pessimistic conclusions about the long-term viability of capitalism as we know it.

NEO-KEYNESIAN – NEW-KEYNESIAN ECONOMICS

Neo-Keynesian Economics

The term 'Neo-Keynesian Economics' refers to the doctrines of a small but influential group of post-Keynesian Cambridge (England) economists. They accept the basic ideas of John Maynard Keynes found in his '*General Theory of Employment, Interest and Money*' (1936). The well known neo-Keynesian economists are Joan Robinson, Nicholas Kaldor, Luigi Pasinetti and Piero Sraffa. They are all associated with Cambridge University. The work of the Polish economist, Michel Kalecki, who independently worked out a general theory of employment similar to that of Keynes is also important in neo-Keynesian economics. The neo-Keynesians have much in common with David Ricardo and Karl Marx. Sometimes, their work is called neo-Ricardian and/or neo-Marxian.

The neo-Keynesian writings are found mostly in *The Cambridge Journal of Economics*. Similar ideas are found in the Journal of *Post-Keynesian Economics* published in the United States.

There is difference in the interpretation of Keynes by the neo-Keynesians and the orthodox Keynesians (Hicks, Samuelson, Tobin). Neo-Keynesians claim that they have an answer to the problems of "Stagflation". Stagflation refers to the simultaneous occurrence of rising unemployment and inflation. The orthodox Keynesians consider stagflation a paradox and they have no answer to it. So policy–makers started discrediting Keynesianism.

There was decline in the influence of orthodox Keynesians, during the 1970s. At that time, neo-Keynesian theory had an appeal to those who disagreed with the ideas of monetarism as well as mainstream neo-classical economists. One can see leftist overtones in the writings of neo-Keynesians. But they are not considered as socialists as such. The neo-Keynesians generally favour, in addition to fiscal policy, an incomes policy to control price inflation.

Investment and Growth

Investment or capital formation plays a central role in Keynesian theory of employment. But Keynes has confined his analysis to the short period. In the short period, investment is considered as a strategic factor for disbursing purchasing power into the economy as a means of expanding effective demand and thereby increasing employment. The neo-Keynesian theory of growth takes account of the long term consequences of investment in adding to productive capacity in future periods. Based on earlier work by Roy Harrod, Joan Robinson and Nicholas Kaldor analysed the conditions necessary for sustained growth. Some level of current investment will be enough to sustain full employment and keep the economy growing at a steady rate. But Robinson's theory of growth suggests that conditions essential for steady growth are highly improbable under decentralized market capitalism.

Keynes laid great emphasis on uncertainty about future in explaining the difficulty in maintaining sufficient private investment to achieve sustained high-level employment. When expectations go wrong, businessmen adapt either by altering the level of their output or by changing price or some combination of the two. In Keynesian analysis, adjustments are made mainly in output. But Robinson and Kaldor give importance to price adjustments as well as to output adjustments. Keynes has assumed competition, whereas neo-Keynesians take account of strong monopoly elements in the product markets. Kalecki's concept of degree of monopoly can be used as a measure of market power to fix prices. This has been integrated into the neo-Keynesian theory of growth.

The neo-Keynesians agree that fiscal policy may be used to promote steady growth. But they do not consider money as a strategic factor in policy.

The neo-classical synthesis integrates Keynesian short-run theory with neo-classical long-run theory. But neo-Keynesianism stands as an alternative to neo-classical synthesis.

Distribution Theory

Keynes recognized "arbitrary and inequitable distribution of wealth and income" and "massive unemployment" as the two major weaknesses of capitalism. But he was not concerned much about the theory of distribution.

The neo-Keynesian theory of income distribution is perhaps the most revolutionary part of their entire theory. They have divided Keynes consumption function into two parts: the propensity to consume out of wages and the propensity to consume out of profits. In the simple neo-Keynesian models, they make the assumption that workers spend all their wages on current consumption. The decisions of the capitalists to invest and to consume will determine their profits. Capitalists can increase their share of national income by investing more or by consuming more. Kalecki (1968) has made this point in a telling way when he said; "Workers spend what they earn and capitalists earn what they spend." Thus in neo-Keynesian economics, investment plays a strategic role in determining the distribution of income between wages and profits as well as determining the level of national income to be distributed.

In the neo-Keynesian theory of distribution, Kalecki's concept of the degree of monopoly has replaced the unrealistic assumption of perfect competition in the neo-classical theory. And the degree of monopoly directly affects the income distribution. An increase in the degree of monopoly will increase the relative share of profits in the national income at the expense of wages.

There is a lot of difference between the neo-Keynesian macroeconomic theory of income distribution and the neo-classical microeconomic theory of distribution. The latter is based on the application of general theory of pricing to the factors of production (labour and capital) according to marginal productivity principles. During the 1950s, Joan Robinson challenged the meaningfulness of the neo-classical production function.

Reswitching

For some time, there was controversy between the orthodox Keynesians and the neo-Keynesians on the reswitching problem. Contrary to the neo-classical theory of capital and interest, Samuelson agreed that a technique of production that may be optimal (cost the least) at a low rate of interest, may not be optimal at an intermediate interest rate, but may again become optimal at a high rate of interest. Pasinetti, a neo-Keynesian economist, demonstrated the logical possibility of reswitching of production techniques. The neo-Keynesians made use of the reswitching possibility to show that the marginal productivity theory of distribution was not meaningful except as an apology for the receipt of large incomes by owners of capital. Neo-Keynesians believed in the conflict between capital and labour in sharing the national income. This resembles the popular view of Ricardo and Marx that when wages rise, profits fall and vice-versa.

A Second Revolution

The neo-Keynesian claim that they have brought about a second revolution in economic theory (the first revolution was the Keynesian revolution).

It may be noted that Keynes accepted that the neo-classical theory was true under conditions of full employment. But the neo-Keynesians did not agree with this view. The marginal productivity theory is one of the pillars of the neo-classical economics. It deals with the efficient allocation of resources through rational pricing based on marginal productivity and treats income shares just as a special case of marginal productivity theory. But the neo-Keynesians vehemently attacked the marginal productivity theory.

The neo-classical economists gave importance to the concept of equilibrium. But the neo-Keynesian economists gave importance to 'history'. This brings economics closer to Marx. Thus the neo-Keynesians challenged the very foundations of the neo-classical economics.

New Keynesian Economics

New Keynesian economics is a school of modern macro-economics that strives to provide microeconomic foundations for Keynesian Economics. It developed partly as a response to criticism of Keynesian macroeconomics by the economists who propagated New Classical macroeconomics.

In the 1990s, there was the "uncoupling" of money supply and inflation. The "big bang" marketization in the former Soviet Block witnessed repeated failures. This encouraged the revival of Keynesian ideas by giving microeconomic foundations to Keynesian macroeconomic analysis. These theories have been called New Keynesian economics.

During the 1980s, Keynesian macroeconomics went out of fashion as a policy tool, and as a field of study. Some economists felt that combining economics with behavioural science, game theory and monetary theory were more important areas of study. At the policy level in the West, Margaret Thatcher, Prime Minister of U.K. and Ronald Reagan, President of USA advocated slashing the size of the government sector. However, towards the end of 1980s, economists shifted back to the study of macroeconomics and policy makers began to look for ways and means of managing the global financial network.

New Keynesian approach to macroeconomics is based on two assumptions. Like the New-classical approach, New Keynesian economic analysis assumes that households and firms have *rational expectations*. But there is a difference between the two schools. The New Keynesian analysis generally assumes a variety of *market failures*. Especially, the New Keynesians assume that there is *imperfect competition* in price and wage setting to explain why prices and wages can become sticky. That means, wages and prices do not adjust instantaneously to changes in economic conditions.

Wage and price stickiness and other market failures present in New Keynesian economic models imply that the economy may fail to attain full employment. Therefore, the New Keynesians believe that fiscal and monetary policies followed for macro-economic stabilization can lead to a more efficient macroeconomic outcome than a laissez-faire policy would.

The first wave of New Keynesian economics developed in the late 1970s. Stanley Fischer developed the first model of *Sticky information* in his 1977 article, *Long-Term Contracts, Rational Expectations and the Optimal Money Supply Rule*. Fischer adopted a "staggered" or "overlapping" contract model. Let us suppose that there are two unions in the economy and they take turns to choose wages. When it is a union's turn, it chooses the wages it will set for the next two periods. This is in contrast with John B. Taylor's model where the nominal wage is constant over the contract life. We may note that both Taylor and Fischer contracts share the feature that only the unions setting the wage in the current period are using the latest information: Wages in half of the economy still reflect old information. The Taylor model had sticky nominal wages in addition to sticky information. The early New Keynesian theories were based on the basic idea that, given fixed nominal wages, a monetary authority (a central bank) can control the employment rate.

During 1980s, the New Kernesian economists developed the concept of menu cost (lumpsum cost) in a framework of imperfect competition to explain price stickiness. The concept of menu cost was originally introduced by Sheshinski and Weiss (1977) in their paper looking at the effect of inflation on the frequency of price changes. The idea of applying it as a general theory of Nominal Price Rigidity was put forward by many economists such as George Akerloff and Janet Allen in 1985-86.

The New Keynesians developed an important concept called *Coordination Failure* to explain recessions and unemployment. During recession, a factory can go idle even, though there are people willing to work in it, and people willing to buy its production if they had jobs. In such a situation, economic downturns appear to be the result of coordination failure. The 'invisible hand' of Adam Smith fails to coordinate the optional flow of production and consumption. Russel Cooper and Andrew John in their 1968 paper *Coordinating Coordination Failures in Keynesian Models* gave a general form of coordination as models with multiple equilibria where agents could coordinate to improve each of their respective situations.

Labour Market Failures: Efficiency Wages

New Keynesian economics have offered many explanations for the labour market to clear. In a Walrasian market, when there is unemployment, unemployed workers bid down wages until the demand for the workers meets the supply. The New Keynesians developed theories explaining why markets might leave willing workers unemployed. One of the important theories they developed was the efficiency wage theory that was used to explain long-term effects of previous unemployment. They maintained that short-term increases in unemployment become permanent and lead to higher levels of unemployment in the future.

In a model developed by Shapiro and Stiglitz, workers are paid at a level where they do not shirk, preventing wages from falling to full-employment levels. This and other shirking models became very influential. In efficiency models, wages are paid to workers at levels that maximize productivity instead of clearing the market. For example, in developing countries, firms might pay more than the market rate to ensure that their workers can take nutritious food to increase their productivity. Sometimes, higher wages are paid to workers to increase their loyalty and morale. This, in turn, might lead to better productivity.

Taylor Rule

In 1993, John Taylor formulated, what has come to be known as *Taylor Rule*. This is a monetary policy rule that stipulates how much the central bank should change the nominal interest rate in response to changes in inflation output or other economic conditions. The rule, in particular, stipulates that for each one-percent increase in inflation, the central bank should raise the *nominal interest rate* by more than one percentage point. This aspect of the rule is often called *Taylor Principle*.

The New Keynesian Phillip's Curve

The New Keynesian Phillips curve was originally derived by Roberts in 1995. The curve is used in most of the Dynamic Stochastic General Equilibrium (DSGE) models to analyze monetary policy. The New Keynesian Phillips curve tells that this period's inflation depends on current output and the expectations of next period's inflation.

Policy Implications

New Keynesian economists agree with Neo Classical economists that in the long run, the classical dichotomy holds. That is, changes in money supply are neutral. But, as prices are sticky in the New Keynesian model, an increase in the money supply or a decrease in the interest rate does increase output and lower unemployment in the short run. Some New Keynesian models confirm the non-neutrality of money under many conditions. It may, however, be noted that the New Keynesian economists, do not recommend expansionary monetary policy for short run gains in output and employment as it may raise inflationary expectations. They advocate using monetary policy for stabilization.

Conclusion

The foregoing analysis shows that the New Keynesian economists have contributed many new concepts and theories to economics to gain insights into current economic problems and they have made a number of policy prescriptions in many areas. And the theories they have given have helped revive interest in Keynesian ideas.

JOAN ROBINSON
(1903-1983)

Introduction

Joan Robinson was one of the most famous British economists of the 20th century who belonged to the Cambridge school. In the beginning, she was a Marshallian. Afterwards, she became an ardent Keynesian and finally she emerged as one of the leaders of the Neo-Ricardian and Post-Keynesian Schools. The neo-keynesians are also called as neo-Marxians. The neo-Keynesian writings are found mostly in the *Cambridge Journal of Economics*. Similar ideas are found in the *Journal of Post-Keynesian Economics* published in the United States of America. Mrs. Robinson made many fundamental contributions to different areas of Economics.

Joan Robinson was born at Camberley, Surrey, England on October 31, 1903. She studied economics at Girton college, Cambridge and after graduation, in 1925 she married a young economist Austin Robinson. Both of them came to India in 1926 and they got involved in a research committee on Anglo-Indian economic relations. The couple returned to England in 1929. Joan Robinson taught in Cambridge from 1931 to 1971. She became a full-time professor in 1965. As she made a number of original contributions to Economics, most of the economists thought that she richly deserved the Nobel Prize in Economics but she did not get it probably because of her Marxist leanings. Two of her students, Amartya Sen and Joseph stiglitz won the Nobel prize in Economics.

Joan Robinson was a frequent visitor to the Centre for Development Studies (CDS) at Thiruvananthapuram in Kerala until 1982. During mid 1970s, she was a visiting Fellow at the Centre and she instituted an Endowment Fund to support public lectures at the CDS.

Her Major Works

Joan Robinson's major works include: *The Economics of Imperfect Competition (1933). An Essay on Marxian Economics (1942), The Production Function and Theory of Capital (1953), Accumulation of Capital (1956), Essays in the Theory of Economic Growth (1962), Economic Philosophy: An Essay on the Progress of Economic Thought (1962), Economic Heresies: Some Old Fashioned Questions in Economic Theory (1971) and Contributions to Modern Economics (1978).*

The other works for the lay readers include *Introduction to the Theory of Employment (1973), The Cultural Revolution in China (1969), An Introduction to Modern Economics* (1973) with Joan Eatwell.

The Economics of Imperfect Competition

The Economics of Imperfect Competition is one of her lasting contributions to economic theory.

We do not have perfect competition or pure monopoly in the real world. The market structure we see around us contains the elements of both competition and monopoly. Two main conditions of perfect competition are: (1) there will be many sellers and (2) there will be a homogeneous good. If anyone of the conditions is missing, we may say the market is not perfect. The real world situation has been described as *imperfect competition by Joan Robinson* and *monopolistic competition by E.H. Chamberlin.*

The term 'monopolistic competition' has been coined by Chamberlin in his book *The Theory of Monopolistic Competition* (1933) to cover all market situations lying between pure competition and monopoly. To describe the same situation, Joan Robinson has used the expression 'imperfect competition' in her book, *The Economics of Imperfect Competition* (1933). Chamberlin classified the markets into 'Large Group' and 'Small Group: However, it has become customary to study the real world market situation (i.e. imperfect competition) by classifying it into monopolistic competition and oligopoly. Under monopolistic competition, there will be a large number of sellers but there will be *product differentiation.* Under oligopoly, there will be a few sellers. There may or may not be product differentiation under oligopoly.

'Product differentiation' and 'selling costs' are important features of monopolistic competition.

Product Differentiation

Product differentiation is a characteristic feature of monopolistic competition. As under perfect competition, there will be a large number of sellers even under monopolistic competition. But they will not sell a homogeneous good. Each unit of the product which is being produced by many firms is a close but not a perfect substitute for each other unit. Not only that, there is some legal obstacle (such as the laws relating to patents and trademarks) that prevents any firm from producing and selling a product that is in all respects identical with that being currently offered by any other firm.

Product differentiation is merely a technical term for a familiar fact. What is substantially the same article in a physical sense is supplied by different firms in different ways. Matches, Cigarettes, tinned goods of various kinds are typical examples. Each brand is characterized by a special name or trade mark which in effect is sold as a special product. So its producer becomes a partial monopolist because he has the monopoly of the supply of this particular brand. He is only a partial monopolist because his particular brand has to meet the competition of possible substitutes and this possibility of substitution limits monopolistic powers.

There is a great deal of monopolistic competition in manufacturing, retail trade and the supply of various services.

Selling costs

Chamberlin has introduced the concept of selling costs in the theory of the firm. Under monopolistic competition, another set of costs, apart from production costs, is required for the marketing of the product. Such costs are called selling costs. Selling costs are different from production costs. Selling costs, in a strict sense, are incurred for changing the demand curve of a product for the purpose of shifting the demand from one commodity or brand of commodity to another. Costs of raw materials and transport, for example, are production costs. Examples of selling costs are advertising of all varieties.

When competition is imperfect and when there is product differentiation, the market can no longer be taken as given, it has to be created. Advertising does this in several ways. Salespersons, salaries, expenses of sales departments (the cost of providing special facilities and comforts to customers etc.), the cost of shop window displays are all examples of selling costs.

Under monopolistic or imperfect competition, there will be a good deal of excess (unused) capacity. As a result, the average cost is higher under monopolistic competition than under pure competition.

Joan Robinson coined the term "monopsony" in her book, *The Economics of Imperfect Competition.* It is used to describe the buyer converse of a seller monopoly. Monopsony is generally applied to a buyer of labour, where the employer has wage setting power that allows him to exercise exploitation and pay workers less than their marginal productivity. Joan Robinson used monopsony to describe wage gap between women and men workers of equal productivity.

Joan Robinson famously called economic theory "a box of tools". Keynes called it "…. an apparatus of the mind, a technique of thinking, which helps its possessor to draw correct conclusions".

Schumpeter is of the view that Theory of Monopolistic Competition or Imperfect Competition is of direct applicability to practical questions.

While writing about it, he says: "Everyone knows that this new arm of the economists' analytic engine was added, in different forms, by English and American authors who worked independently of one another – a striking proof of the intellectual, still more than practical, need for this type of theory and a not less striking illustration of how the logic of the scientific situation may drive different minds along similar lines of advance" (Joseph A. Schumpeter, *History of Economic Analysis, 1954*).

Robinson's *An Essay on Marxian Economics* (1942) was fresh, insightful and critical. It was one of the first studies that took Karl Marx seriously as an economist. After that, Marxian economics attracted the attention of many serious thinkers in the field of economics.

Accumulation of Capital

Joan Robinson published *The Accumulation of Capital* in 1956, which is one of her great works. The book tried to extend Keyne's theory to account for long-run issues of growth and capital accumulation. She published another book. *Essays in the Theory of Economic Growth in 1962.* This book is a lucid exposition of growth theory. In it, she developed the concept of *golden age*.

Her work on capital accumulation started when she was investigating the problems arising out of capital aggregation. Based on the writings of Piero Sraffa and Robinson, the Neo-Ricardian Classical revival began. In the "Cambridge Capital Controversy", Joan Robinson led the Cambridge assault on the American Neo-Keynesians.

The Cambridge capital controversy is about the nature of capital goods. Joan Robinson in her 1954 article. "The Production Function and the Theory of Capital" attacked the traditional neo-classical view that capital could be measured and aggregated. The views of Kaldor and Robinson became the Cambridge position. On the other hand, the American economists including Paul Samuelson and Robert Solow claimed that capital could be aggregated. In other words, Robinson repudiates aggregate production functions of capital.

Robinson and *Kaldor* are doubtful whether marginal productivities calculated from such production function can be used to explain wage and profit rates and the relative shares of labour and property in GNP. They further doubt whether economists, can work with a detailed breakdown of numerous heterogeneous capital goods – different types of machines – to get quantitative results at all like the neoclassical case – in an actual realistic mixed economy marked by uncertainty and uneven growth.

Though Robinson and Kaldor have not agreed upon an alternative to aggregative analysis, in the macroeconomic analysis of income distribution they are more or less of the view that it is the fast growth that produces high profits, rather than vice-versa.

We shall now briefly outline Joan Robinson's Model of Capital Accumulation. It is a simple model based on the 'Capitalist rules of the game'. But "it is not so much concerned with an automatic convergence to a moving equilibrium in a capitalist economy, as with studying the properties of equilibrium growth".

Assumptions of Mrs. Robinson's Model

1. There is a laissez-faire closed economy;

2. Capital and labour are the only productive factors in such an economy;

3. Capital and labour are employed in fixed proportions in order to produce a given output;

4. There is neutral technical progress;

5. There is no shortage of labour and entrepreneurs can employ as much labor as they wish;
6. There are only two classes – the workers and the entrepreneurs – between whom the national income is distributed;
7. Workers save nothing and spend their wage income on consumption;
8. Entrepreneurs consume nothing but save and invest their entire income (from profits) for capital formation. "If they have no profits, the entrepreneurs cannot accumulate and if they do not accumulate, they have no profits"; and
9. There are no changes in the price level.

In Robinson's model, net national income is the sum of the total wage bill plus total profits which may be shown as

$$Y = wN + pK$$

where Y is the national income, w, the real wage rate, N, the number of workers employed, p the profit rate and K the amount of capital. Y is a function of N and K and profit rate is crucial in the theory of capital accumulation.

Profit rate is the ratio of labour productivity minus the real wage rate to the amount of capital utilized per unit of labour. That is,

$$P = \frac{l - w}{\theta}$$

where the profit rate (p) depends upon income (Y), labour productivity (l), the real wage (w) and the capital–labour ratio (θ)

On the expenditure side, net national income (Y) equals consumption expenditure (C) plus investment expenditure (I)

$$Y = C+I$$

As Joan Robinson makes the assumption that workers save nothing and spend their entire wage income on consumption and entrepreneurs consume nothing (out of profits) but save and invest their entire income for capital formation, we have

$$S = I$$

As the growth rate of capital ($\Delta K/K$) is equal to p, (the profit rate), it depends on the ratio of net return on capital relative to the given stock of capital. If income remains constant and the wage rate decreases or income increases and the wage remains constant the profit rate would tend to increase. In this way, the entrepreneurs maximize their profits.

The Golden Age

In addition to the growth rate of capital ($\Delta K/K$), another ΔN factor which determines the growth rate of an economy is the growth rate of population ($\Delta N/N$). When the growth rate of population equals the growth rate of capital, i.e. $\Delta N/N = \Delta K/K$, the economy is said to be in full employment equilibrium. Joan Robinson calls it "golden age" to describe the steady growth with full employment. In her own words: "When technical progress is neutral and proceeding steadily without any change in the time pattern of production, the competitive mechanism working freely, population growing (if at all) at a steady rate and accumulation going on fast enough to supply productive capacity for all available labour, the rate of profit tends to be constant and the level of real wages to rise with output per man. Then there are no internal contradictions in the system. Total annual output and the stock of capital then grow together at a constant proportionate rate compounded at the rate of increase of the output per man. We may describe these conditions as a golden age" (Robinson, The Accumulation of Capital, P. 99). Robinson also Indicates that golden age represents a mythical state of affairs not likely to obtain in any actual economy.

Joan Robinson says that an economy is in a golden age when the *potential growth ratio* is being realized. The potential growth ratio represents the highest rate of capital accumulation that can be permanently maintained at a constant rate of profit.

Joan Robinson's model is sometimes considered as an elaboration of Harrod's growth model. But we must note that Joan Robinson's theory of capital accumulation depends on profit-wage relation and on labour productivity whereas Harrod's theory depends on saving – income ratio and on capital productivity.

Robinson stresses the importance of labour in capital accumulation whereas Domar underlines the importance of capital.

Professor Kenneth Kurihara, while commenting on Joan Robinson's model says: "J. Robinson's chief contribution to post – Keynesian growth economics seems to be that she has integrated classical value and distribution theory and modern Keynesian saving – investment theory into one coherent system".

Towards the end of her life, Robinson concentrated on methodological problems in economics. She was thoroughly dissatisfied with "equilibrium" theories and she tried to revive the original message of Keynes' *General theory*.

Joan Robinson was also interested in the problems of underdeveloped and developing countries and made substantial contribution in that direction.

Conclusion

There is no doubt that Joan Robinson was one of the most brilliant economists of the 20th century. The theory of Imperfect competition and the theory of Capital Accumulation are her lasting contributions to economics.

WELFARE ECONOMICS

Introduction

'Welfare Economics' has now become a distinct branch of economic science. Prof. Pigou is regarded as the father of welfare economics. It is rather difficult to define the boundaries of welfare economics. Anyhow, according to Reder, "Welfare economics is the branch of economic science that attempts to establish and apply criteria of propriety to economic policies." Oscar Lange, an eminent economist of the socialist camp, in his *Essays on the Foundations of Welfare Economics* has given the simplest and the most useful definition of welfare economics: "Welfare economics is concerned with the conditions which determine the total economic welfare of a community."

Is the economy functioning well? Is the society's system of distribution good? What can be done about improving total well-being? To what extent the government must intervene to promote economic welfare? These are all some of the leading questions about which the welfare economics is concerned about. The liberal economists argue that in a Welfare State, the policies of the State must aim at maximizing welfare. They contend that value judgments must enter into policy-making decisions.

The idea of welfare in economics has been there ever since the time of Adam Smith. Adam Smith considered a larger per capita output as a result of larger production as an index of welfare. Bentham and the Utilitarians too made a significant contribution to the concept of welfare. Bentham spoke of the promotion of the greatest happiness of the greatest number as the goal of happiness. This idea of 'greatest happiness of greatest number' he borrowed from Francis Hutcheson.

J. S. Mill also gave some ideas of promoting welfare in his peculiar individualist-socialist programme. In recent times, Marshall considered economics as the science dealing with the causes of material welfare. In a way, Marshall was a welfare economist. Marshall introduced the concept of consumer's surplus and thus presented welfare economics with an analytical tool. But his Principles of Economics was only an engine of economic analysis and not a programme of social reform. It was left to Pigou, the brilliant pupil and successor of Prof. Marshall, to give a complete statement of welfare economics. Before we study about Pigou and his contribution to welfare economics, it may be useful to sketch briefly the economic ideas of Hobson, a pioneer in welfare economics.

J. A. Hobson (1858-1940)

The ideas of Hobson on welfare economics are found in his book "*Work and Wealth*". Hobson made use of economic theory to advocate moderately radical social reforms to promote human welfare. He rejected the classical economists assumption of perfect competition as a typical market situation. He did not believe in the harmony of interests, another basic assumption of the classical economists. While the classical economists considered *laissez-faire* as the best policy, Hobson advocated government intervention to carry out a programme of social reform to promote welfare.

Hobson developed the under-consumption theory of trade cycle. He believed that under-consumption and over-saving led to over-investment which resulted in over-production and glut on the market. Keynes praised Hobson for his under-consumption approach to trade cycle. Hobson gave an excellent description of imperialism. He believed that the inability of the capitalist economy to keep the economy fully employed led to imperialism. Lenin praised Hobson for giving a beautiful account of imperialism. Above all, Hobson advocated greater equality of income for ethical and economic reasons. He thought measures aimed at reducing inequalities of income would promote economic welfare and increase consumption spending and thereby solve the problem of unemployment.

Hobson believed that over-saving would lead to under-consumption and business depression. He considered over-saving as a vice. He attributed over-saving and under-consumption to the faulty distribution of income in the society. And over-saving and under-consumption create business cycles.

On the basis of the analysis of over-saving and under-consumption, Hobson developed his theory of imperialism. Imperialism and expansionist policies are followed by the capitalist societies because they find in the new colonies a market for the goods that cannot be sold in the home market. He thought that if there was a proper distribution of incomes in the society, the home market would be capable of indefinite expansion and there would be no fear of over-production and no need for exploiting colonies by following a policy of imperialism.

Hobson believed that an equitable distribution of income would put an end to over-saving, underconsumption, depression and imperialism. Over-saving was the result of concentration of income in the hands of a few wealthy persons. "The proportion of saving is generally in direct ratio to the size of income, the richest saving the largest percentage of their income, the poorest the smallest."

Hobson believed that income could be redistributed through trade union action to raise wages, pension. This would raise the standard of living of labourers and hence increase the level of their consumption. He suggested a more effective programme for an equitable and socially advantageous re-distribution of income through State intervention. The programme included regulation and operation of industry by government and taxation to raise revenue for public consumption. Hobson advocated taxes especially on monopoly gains, high rent and interest. The revenue from taxation should be used for providing social services such as health and education. In times of bad trade, the state can undertake public works programmes.

Hobson criticized the classical economists for their valuation of cost and utility in terms of money. He argued that valuation of industry should be done in terms of human effort and satisfaction. For example, he said that the human cost of saving arises only in the case of poor people with small incomes. There was no sacrifice involved in saving by the rich. He suggested that society should distribute the cost of production according to the ability of individuals to bear the costs and it should distribute the goods among consumers according to their capacity to derive utility from them.

As a pioneer in Welfare economics, Hobson finds a permanent place in the history of economic thought.

A. C. Pigou (1877-1959)

Arthur Cecil Pigou succeeded Prof. Marshall as the Professor of Economics at the University of Cambridge. After Marshall, he became the leading neo-classical economist. He is the founder of "Welfare Economics." His leading ideas on welfare economics are found in his *The Economics of Welfare* (1920). Prof. Pigou in his book has attempted to provide a theoretical basis for social reform to promote welfare.

Prof. Pigou defined economic welfare as "that part of social welfare that can be brought directly or indirectly into relation with the measuring rod of utility."

The law of diminishing marginal utility is the basis of Pigou's welfare economics. Like Marshall, Pigou has extended the law of diminishing utility to money. He has assumed that the marginal utility of money diminishes as more and more money is acquired. On that basis, he argued that under certain conditions, greater equality of incomes could increase economic welfare. In his own words, "The old law of diminishing utility thus leads securely to the proposition: Any cause which increases the absolute share of real income in the hands of the poor, provided that it does not lead to a contraction in the size of the national dividend from any point of view, will in general, increase economic welfare."[1]

Pigou rejected the classical economists' assumption of harmony of interests. The orthodox economists thought what was good for the individual was good for the society. They thought that total welfare was nothing but the sum of the welfare of individuals. Pigou rejected that idea and distinguished between social and marginal private costs and benefits.

Social and Marginal Private Costs and Benefits

The private marginal cost of a commodity is the cost of producing an additional unit. The social marginal cost is the expense or damage to society as a consequence of producing that commodity. Private marginal benefit can be measured by the selling price of the commodity. And social marginal benefit refers to the total benefit that society gets from the production of the additional unit.

Pigou has made the distinction between private and social costs to show that sometimes social costs may be greater than private costs. For example, the sparks from railway engines may damage the trees by the side of the railway line and the owner may not be compensated for the damage. When a factory is built by an entrepreneur in a residential district, he destroys much of the value of the property of other people. Again, the increased sale of alcoholic drinks may be profitable to the producer and the seller (and to the government) but increased social costs are incurred when policemen and prisons become necessary to maintain law and order.

There are of course cases in which the social marginal net product will increase private marginal net product. In other words, private actions will increase society's benefit to a great extent. For example, scientific research is generally of greater value to society than to the person who has done research and to the inventor.

Pigou observed that under conditions of monopolistic competition, there was a lot of competitive advertising which was a social waste.

According to Pigou "many of the problems of the society arise out of people's attitude to future". They prefer present satisfaction to future satisfaction because their telescopic faculty is defective. As a result of this irrational time preference for present, resources are directed for increasing present consumption at the expense of future needs. So Pigou concluded that government should not encourage the tendency of people to devote too much of their resources to present use for it diminishes economic welfare. This argument of Pigou has led to certain policy conclusions. The government should avoid any tax on saving. It must either abolish or reduce property tax, death duties and progressive income tax in order to maximize economic welfare. It follows that taxes on consumption are preferable because they encourage saving. Pigou, of course, was aware of the fact that heavy taxes on consumption goods would affect the poorer sections of the society.

It is interesting to note that while Hobson attacked over-saving, Pigou wanted to increase saving in order to promote economic growth. Pigou's analysis is based on the assumption of full employment. And he thought that what was saved was automatically invested.

As industrialists are generally interested in maximizing profit, government intervention sometimes may be necessary to promote welfare. The measures included among other things: (*i*) Taxes on alcoholic drinks and competitive advertising, (*ii*) subsidies to encourage research, and (*iii*) laws against false weights and measures and the adulteration of food products.

Pigou assumed that interpersonal comparisons of utilities (satisfactions) was possible. This is a weak point of Pigou's approach. Modern economists assert that it is impossible to measure comparisons of satisfactions among different people.

THE NEW WELFARE ECONOMICS

Pareto (1848-1923)

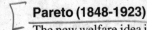

The new welfare idea is based on the assumption that individual marginal utilities are not measurable. Economists like Lionel Robbins believe that 'there is no way of comparing the satisfaction of different people.' The ideas of new welfare economics may be traced back to Pareto who rejected the cardinal notion of utility. In other words, he believed that utility was not measurable. He also thought that it was impossible to make interpersonal comparison of utility. He made use of the indifference curve analysis to avoid measuring utility quantitatively.

Pareto made use of the concept of *social optimum*. (This is often referred to as Paretian optimum) to explain the idea of maximum social welfare. Social optimum (or maximum welfare) situation is reached when we cannot make some one better off without making some one else worse off. A main weakness of Pareto's concept of welfare is that it can be applied only to unambiguous cases. It cannot be applied to ambiguous cases. For example, a certain policy of the government may benefit some and harm others. For such cases, we cannot apply Pareto's concept of social optimum. In the recent years, economists such as Hicks, Paul Samuelson and Little have tried to remedy the defect in Pareto's concept. Yet another charge against Pareto is that if we were to adopt his optimum, indirectly it was a plea for status-quoism and for non-intervention by government. Further it is rather difficult to put Pareto's concept of social optimum into practice.

J. R. Hicks

J. R. Hicks has pointed out three main weaknesses in Pigou's approach to welfare economics. First of all, Pigou had correlated economic and general welfare. Second, he had made interpersonal comparison of utility. Third, he had identified the sum of consumer surpluses with the real value of the national dividend. To remedy the defects in the analysis of Pigou and Pareto, Hicks, Kaldor and Scitovysky and some modern economists have introduced the concept of compensation principle and reorganisation principle. The compensation principle is generally known as new welfare economics. 'Reorganisation' refers to alterations in economic circumstances. For instance, there may be change of tax structure, tariff policy and so on. A change in tax structure which helped some one without affecting some one else improved welfare. Theoretically, it was an ideal reorganisation. But it was difficult to come across such actual situations. So Hicks has introduced the compensation principle. According to the compensation principle, a society's economic welfare would increase if it were possible for those who gained from a reorganisation to compensate those who lost and still retain some net advantage. Hicks has given the compensation principle as follows: "If A is made so much better off by change that he could compensate B for his loss and still have something left for, then the reorganisation is unequivocal improvement." Of course, there are a number of practical difficulties in identifying those who have gained and those who have lost.

In recent times Prof. Samuelson has made use of the concept of *social welfare function* to explain ideas of welfare economics. He believes that economics should be essentially a normative science. The social welfare function is a method by which the social scale of preferences can be derived from individual scale of preferences. This can be done either voluntarily or by some dictator in a centrally planned economy.

Conclusion

The main difference between 'positive' economics and 'welfare' economics is this: The aim of positive economics is to explain and welfare economics is to prescribe. One of the major achievements of new welfare economics is that it has identified more or less precisely the conditions of maximum welfare. For example, Reder has said that ".... If welfare is to be a maximum, it must be impossible to increase it by varying the output of any product consumed by a consumer including variations from zero." As a rough guide to what ought to be done, welfare theory is of great use.

MAURICE DOBB
(1900-1976)

Introduction

Maurice Dobb was a British economist at Cambridge University. He was one of the pre-eminent Marxian economists of the 20th century.

Maurice Dobb was born on July 24, 1900 in London. He received his early education at charterhouse school in Surrey. Dobb joined Pembroke college, Cambridge to study economics. He was a brilliant student at college and gained firsts in both parts of the economics tripos in 1921 and 1922. After that, he joined London School of Economics for graduate studies. He earned his Ph.D. degree in 1924. Then he returned to Cambridge to become a university lecturer. His association with J.M.Keynes helped him get the job at the university. He had strong belief in communism and he was open about that to his students. Dobb was a remarkable expounder of Marxian theory. In 1920, Dobb joined the communist party and he played a key role in strengthening the communist movement at the university. In other words, he was politically active. At the same time, he did not neglect economics. Dobb focused on the vulnerability of the capitalist system to economic crisis (e.g. business cycles with alternating periods of depression and prosperity. Depression is a period marked by unemployment and bad trade). He gave the example of the United State of America when referring to capitalist money assisting military agendas instead of public works.

Dobb was elected as a Fellow of Trinity college at Cambridge in 1948. During that time, jointly with Piero Sraffa, he assembled the selected works and letters of David Ricardo and published them in eleven volumes.

His Works

Dobb was a prolific writer. He published twelve academic books, more than twenty four pamphlets and a large number of articles meant for the general public. He often wrote on political economy describing the connection between the social context and problems in society and how that influences market exchange. In his Marxian economics class, he used to say that economic relations of men determine social associations of men. Dobb was of the firm belief that the capitalist system created classes and with class comes class warfare.

Amartya Sen and Eric Hobsbawn are the two distinguished students of Maurice Dobb. Sen won the Noble Prize in Economics in 1998 and Bharat Ratna in 1999.

Dobb's important works include: *Capitalist Enterprise and Social Progress (1925) Russian Economic Development since the Revolution (assisted by H.C. Stevens) (1928), Wages (1932), Russia Today and Tomorrow (1930), On Marxism Today (1932), "Economic Theory and the Problems of a Socialist Economy" (1933), EJ, Political Economy and Capitalism: Some essays in economic tradition* (1937), *Marx as an Economist: An Essay (1943), Studies in the Development of Capitalism (1946), Soviet Economic Development since 1917 (1948), on Economic Theory and socialism. (1955),*

Economic growth and underdeveloped countries (1963), *Welfare Economics and the Economics of Socialism* (1969), *the Sraffa system and critique of the Neoclassical Theory of Distribution* (1970), *Theory of Distribution* (1970), *Theories of value and Distribution since Adam Smith. Ideology and economic theory* (1973), *and the development of socialist economic thought. Selected Essays* (2008).

Economic Thought

Dobb's economic writings had a decisive influence on post - Keynesian economics. His main objective was to develop a modern Marxian political economy. Naturally, he became the most important Marxian political economist of the twentieth century. All the intellectual pursuits of Dobb reflect his commitment to emancipation of economics from the tyranny of capitalistic crisis, and chronic underdevelopment of the majority of the nations during the post-imperialistic and post-colonial era of capitalist development. Dobb was of the view that capitalistic development and growth succeeded only in a limited way but failed to develop underdeveloped regions and nations. He firmly believed that socialistic planning was a viable and far more realistic alternative for the majority of the underdeveloped nations.

Dobb as an economist was primarily interested in the interpretation of the neoclassical economic theory from a Marxist point of view. He gave an excellent critique of capitalist, centrally planned socialist and market socialist models that were based on the neo-classical framework of static equilibrium. He criticized the market socialist model of Oskar Lange and the contributions of neo-classical socialists of an illegitimate "narrowing of the focus of study to problems of exchange – relations". (Economists and the Economics of Socialism, 1939).

According to Dobb, the main economic challenges for socialism are related to production and investment in their dynamic aspects. The three major advantages of planned economies, as identified by him are: *antecedent co-ordination, external effects and variables in planning.*

Antecedent Co-ordination

Planned economies employ antecedent co-ordination of the economy, whereas in a market economy, decisions are made on the basis of expectations, which again are based on uncertainty. This lack of information often leads to disequilibrium that can only be corrected in a market *expost* (after the event) and thus resources are wasted. An advantage of antecedent planning is removal of significant degrees of uncertainty on the basis of co-ordinated information and decision-making prior to the commitment of resources.

External Effects

Dobb recognized the relevance of external effects to market exchanges. Generally, an economic agent in an exchange does not take note of the externalities of production and consumption. But significant externalities are present in modern market economies. Planning can take into account a wide range of social effects. And this has important applications for efficient industrial planning, including decisions about the external effects of uneven development between sectors and regions, external efforts of public works and development of infant industries. This is in addition to negative externalities.

Variables in Planning

Things that appear as "data" in static framework can be used as variables in a planning process and they can be adjusted in the plan according to the circumstances. They include rate of investment, distribution of investment between capital and consumption, choice of production techniques, geographical distribution of investment, relative rates of growth of transport, fuel and power and of agriculture in relation to industry.

According to Dobb, Marshall's marginal economics was a special case of stable development (of a market economy) and Marxian political economy was the more general theory of instability, or boom and bust development.

Dobb has constructed the Marxian theory of crisis that does not look at the crisis as a simple case of falling rate of profit or under-consumption. To him, capitalistic crises are complex and historically contingent phenomena depending on the specific institutional psychology of society.

Dobb in his book, *Political Economy and capitalism: Some essays in economic tradition*, tells that capitalism is characterized not by competition between small businesses but top monopoly – like economic power. Then, he speaks of monopoly capital. He has developed a coherent theory of crises based on the institutional psychology of monopoly capital, whereby the rate of profit is rising and instability high. Dobb was also of the view that Keynesian aggregate demand management was insufficient in its ability to deal with the severity of capitalistic instability. In his last book, *Theories of Value since Adam Smith* (1973), Dobb summarises Marx's idea of crisis and gives a modern Marxian theory of unstable development.

Dobb, in his studies of Soviet Russia's economic development wanted to demonstrate to the world that planned development, especially industrialization, had been a remarkable economic success in Soviet Russia. For a number of years, he taught western economists about Soviet development. This is one of his significant contributions.

Dobb in his analysis of Marxian interpretation of economic history has dealt with Marxian interpretation of both feudalism and capitalism and the rise of the bourgeois and working classes and the transition from feudalism to capitalism.

Dobb in his *Theories of Value and Distribution since Adam Smith* (1973) offers a defence of classical economy in general and Marxian political economy in particular. His basic argument is that classical political economy maintained that distribution of income and wealth is not merely the function of supply and demand but of historical modes of primitive accumulation and institutionalized systems of power. For example, Adam Smith maintained that rent was not determined by market forces but by the monopoly privilege of the land owning class. For Dobb, Karl Marx was a quintessential political economist. Of course, Marx maintained that wages and profits were a function of class struggle, not merely supply and demand.

Conclusion

We find from the above analysis that Dobb has made major contributions to Marxian economics, especially in Marxian economic history, theories of monopoly capital, theories of capitalistic economic crises, economic development and growth and he has also made a significant contribution to economic analysis of Soviet economic development.

COMPARATIVE ECONOMIC SYSTEMS

Introduction

We have many types of economic systems such as capitalism, socialism, nazism and fascism. Of all the systems, capitalism and socialism are the two most important economic systems. The U.S.A. is a good example of capitalistic system and former Soviet Russia is an excellent example of socialistic system. A study of comparative economic systems has now become a subject of practical importance. In the past, many text-books in economics paid very little attention to the subject of differences between economic systems. But to-day it is recognized that while some economic laws or principles are valid in all types of economic systems, others are valid only in particular systems. For instance, while the Law of Diminishing Returns is applicable to all types of economics systems, the Marginal Productivity Theory of Distribution may not be applicable under socialism. A purely communistic society aims at 'from each according to his ability and to each according to his needs.' Under such conditions, the theory of income distribution which emphasizes marginal productivity would have no significance.

We shall outline the salient features of capitalism and socialism, and study some of their merits and weaknesses.

CAPITALISM

Features of Capitalism

Right to private property, freedom of enterprise, economic motivation, profit motive, price system and competition are some of the important economic institutions of capitalism.

1. *Private Property:* It is one of the basic institutions under capitalism. Private property, in fact, refers to a group or bundle of rights extended to an individual by society as a whole. The right to property includes also the right of inheritance. The individual can decide how his property shall be disposed of after his death. But we have to note that the right to private property is not an absolute right. It can be modified and limited by social action. In practice, even under capitalism, property rights are often restricted severely by the government.

2. *Freedom of Enterprise:* This is another basic institution of capitalism. Freedom of enterprise refers to the general right, which each individual has, to engage in any line of activity which appears desirable to him. It includes the choice of occupation or business. However, individuals are forbidden from indulging in anti-social activities such as stealing, burglary and organization of murder for profit. Similarly, people are not allowed to function as doctors or lawyers unless they have completed extensive courses of training to prepare them for the work and have passed rigorous examinations.

3. *Economic Motivation and the Profit Motive:* Economic motivation is another important institution of capitalism. It means that individuals under capitalism are motivated by the desire

for economic gain in their economic activities. It is believed that this desire for economic gain makes people work harder and longer than any other motive.

Economic motivation is often confused with what is called the profit motive. They are closely related. The profit motive is a part of economic motivation. But the two terms are not the same thing. For instance, private profit plays only a minimum role under socialism where Government owned and operated most of the industries. But economic motivation could continue to function there. In other words, economic motivation as a whole is much broader than profit motive.

4. *The Price System:* Most of the basic economic decisions relating to production, distribution, exchange and consumption of goods under capitalism are made on the basis of prices, price relationships and price changes. The price system is a very important institution of capitalism. Attempts made under socialism to modify its operations or eliminate it entirely have posed many difficult problems. In recent times, even socialist economists have adopted a system of "shadow prices" (accounting prices) in their plan models.

5. *Competition:* Competition is another basic institution of a capitalistic economy. There will be a large number of buyers and sellers in the market. No one buyer or seller can alter the price by his own actions. There will be free mobility of factors of production and so on. Competition is said to be regulator of economic activity. Competition brings about correlation between producers and consumers. The desires of the consumers are expressed on the market through prices. Of course, in practice, markets are not organized on the basis of competition in the strict sense in which we have described it. Government imposes a number of restrictions and modifications on the market. Not only that, many industries under capitalism are owned by a few large firms. In other words, oligopoly is the dominant type of market.

During a period of war, economic institutions of capitalism will be subject to serious modifications at least on a temporary basis. For example, during World War II, in the U.S.A., the Government controlled production to a great extent.

Evaluation of Capitalism

It is rather difficult and complicated to evaluate any economic system as a whole. However, we shall list some of the so called merits and weaknesses of capitalism.

Merits of Capitalism

1. It is claimed that production under capitalism is generally at a higher level than under any other system. Once decisions have been reached as to what commodities and services should be produced, the advocates of capitalism claim that the capitalistic economy proceeds to produce these goods with great efficiency.

2. The great increases in production in the capitalistic system have brought about improved standards of living to citizens living in capitalistic societies.

3. The economic development of countries such as the U.S.A. and England has taken place only under capitalistic system.

4. The distribution of income is highly unequal under capitalism. But it is argued that inequality is the result of the automatic operation of the price system. And it is even claimed that great inequality in the distribution of income, as it exists under capitalism is desirable because it promotes capital formation.

5. Lastly, it is claimed that individuals enjoy a great degree of political and economic freedom under capitalism. There is freedom of choice by consumers. This is referred to as consumer's sovereignty.

Weaknesses of Capitalism

1. Production is not adapted to human needs and desires. It is argued that in a (capitalistic) system

marked by gross inequality in the distribution of income, prices in the market do not measure accurately either the needs and desires of persons or the real costs of production. Luxuries for the rich are turned out even before necessities for the poor are produced. It is simply wrong. But it is not the fault of the entrepreneurs who produce for profit; it is the fault of the pattern of income distribution.

2. It is true that great increases in the total volume of production have occurred in some of the leading capitalistic economies like that of the United States over the years. But the critics of capitalism argue that the system is not nearly so productive as it should be. There are some who suggest that the national income could be doubled with the existing quantities of productive agents at the disposal of the economy.

3. There is the problem of monopoly with all the attendant evils of restriction of production and abuse of profit motive.

4. The capitalistic productive system is less efficient than it should be because of a variety of competitive wastes. Unused capacity and duplication of facility or idle capacity is sometimes wrongly referred to as over capacity or excess capacity.

5. Another type of competitive waste is found in excessive varieties of goods. In other words, there is undue proliferation of styles, shapes, sizes and colours of goods. Though variety is a good thing, undue proliferation is definitely wasteful.

6. There is a good deal of wasteful advertising in the capitalistic system. The competitive or combative advertising result in misutilization of scarce resources.

7. The capitalistic productive system is criticized for its wasteful competitive exploitation of natural resources.

8. Economic instability is a weak point of capitalism. Often, capitalistic economies are caught in the grip of business cycles with alternating phases of prosperity and depression. The great depression of 1929-32 is a case in point.

9. Lastly, a major weakness of capitalism is that the system is marked by great inequality in the distribution of income. Inequality results in waste and inefficiency. Not only that, wrong kinds of goods will be produced. As has been already noted, production will not be adapted to basic human needs and desires. Great inequality in income distribution is considered bad because it arises largely from the receipt of unearned income by various persons. It is claimed that under capitalism the individual enjoys a great amount of economic and political freedom. But the great inequality in the distribution of income reduces this freedom to almost nothing. The poor man is never free. Choice of occupation, consumer's sovereignty are only legal rights which the poor can never exercise effectively in practice.

SOCIALISM

Features of Socialism

We shall describe some of the economic institutions under Socialism.

1. *Private Property:* Under ideal socialism, the right to private property would be limited to consumption goods since most of the means of production would be owned by the society as a whole. For example, in the socialistic economy of former Soviet Russia, the material means of production were owned almost completely by society as a whole. The land of the country was nationalized as of February 1918, and is completely owned by society as a whole. According to M. T. Florinsky, even by the end of the second Five-Year Plan (1937), some 98.7 per cent of the land and capital of the system had been brought into socialized or collective ownership. Only very small amounts of capital were in the hands of individual peasant farmers and handicraft producers.

2. *Freedom of Enterprise:* As most of the material means of production are owned by the society as a whole, freedom of enterprise to make private profit is limited. Of course, individual workers enjoy considerable freedom of occupational choice, under socialism.

3. *Economic Motivation and Profit-Motive:* Economic motivation is there under socialism to some extent. Private profit motive is much less significant under socialism than under capitalism. In an ideal socialistic economy, private profit motive would be virtually eliminated, since private individuals in general would not be allowed to own and operate enterprises for private gain. But other forms of economic motivation are there. For example, moderate differentials in wages are permitted between different industries and occupations. The desire of the people to work for the good of the society as a whole, public honours for unusual accomplishments in production are some of the other types of motivation emphasized under socialism. The socialist economy also relies to some extent on other motives such as enthusiasm for socialism and economic planning, and socialist competition.

4. *The Price System:* The price system and the institution of money are there under socialism. But the price system plays only a secondary role for the basic economic decisions relating to production and distribution are taken by the institutions of economic planning. In recent times, the socialistic economies have made use of "shadow prices" to achieve efficiency in production and to bring the market demands and supplies of economic goods into balance.

5. *Competition:* Competition is there but it is different from competition under capitalism. Workers compete for better and more pleasant jobs and consumers compete for the available limited supplies of various consumers' goods. That is all. In other fields competition would be replaced by the dictates of economic planning.

6. *Planning:* Socialism and planning more or less go together. Communism is an extreme form of socialism.

Merits of Socialism

We may list some of the accomplishments of modern socialism.

1. *Adapting Production to Human Needs and Desires:* Under socialism, production is adapted to meet the socially desirable human needs and services. In planning for production, the socialistic system would not produce the "wrong kinds of goods." Super-luxuries like palatial homes would not be produced for any one until all consumers were assured of adequate food, clothing, shelter and other economic goods. Not only that, a socialistic economy is in a better position to provide some of the non-market wants such as the desire for full employment, complete social security, a high level of public health, and other things.

2. *Technical Efficiency:* It is believed that technical efficiency will be high under socialism. Another advantage of socialism is that production would be for use rather than for profit.

3. *Elimination of Competitive Wastes of Capitalism:* The planned production in a socialistic society would not be dependent upon the activities of a large number of private persons. So it was thought that most of the "competitive" wastes of capitalism could be eliminated under socialism. For example, there would not be undue proliferation of styles, shapes, sizes and colours of goods. And there would not be wasteful advertising.

4. *Absence of Business Cycles:* It is generally claimed that a socialistic economy is free from business cycles. It is generally agreed now that business cycles are caused by imbalances in the relationship between saving and investment. Under socialism, as both saving and investment are controlled by economic planners, it should be possible always to keep saving and investment in balance.

5. *Distribution of Income:* We do not find gross inequalities in the distribution of income among persons and families under socialism. Because of the relatively equal distribution of income

under socialism, the production of the "wrong kinds of goods" would be eliminated by planned production.

6. *The Issue of Freedom:* The severe restrictions on the right to private property and on freedom of enterprise restrict individual freedom to a certain degree. But the socialists argue that for all practical purposes, these rights mean very little to most individuals under capitalism. The individual in a socialist economy enjoys some basic economic rights. For example, the right to work is more or less assured. Unemployment is not a major problem in a socialist economy because it is a planned economy. Further, the individual would have a free choice of occupation.

Weaknesses of Socialism

1. *Problems of Planned Production:* Though planned production under socialism has some advantages in comparison with capitalistic production, it is agreed that planned production need not necessarily be suited to the basic needs and desires of the people. Planned production has its own difficulties. Further, it is said that under socialism, many important economic decisions are made "arbitrarily" rather than "rationally". The decisions of the planners might be "rational" in a broad sense of the term, but they are considered "arbitrary" because those decisions are not always based on the basis of prices and costs.

2. *Socialism and Dictatorship:* Generally, there will be some sort of dictatorship under socialism. As Benham puts it, "A dictator is not necessarily a good economist, nor is there any guarantee that he will receive good advice and follow it. He is in a position to do great harm as well as great good. His personal prejudice and ambitions may lead to famine, or may plunge the country into war."

3. *Efficiency in Production:* Since the State enjoys a considerable degree of monopoly, critics of socialism argue that in the absence of competition, it is rather difficult to test the productive efficiency of state-owned units.

4. *Avoidance of Business Cycles and Mass Unemployment:* Though it is accepted that a socialistic economy enjoys a greater economic stability than a capitalistic economy, critics point out that in actual practice a socialistic economy would operate to conceal business depressions rather than to eliminate them. There is some truth in it.

5. *Too Many Things at a Time:* As the economic planners under socialism want to do so many things at a time, their position is similar to that of a cat watching twenty or thirty rat-holes at the same time.

Conclusion

Both capitalism and socialism have advantages and disadvantages. We may say that a system which worked out exactly in accordance with the socialistic model is better than an actual capitalistic system. On the other hand, an ideal theoretical capitalistic system is regarded by some to be better than any socialistic system in practice.

MIXED ECONOMY

Introduction

The two major systems of the world are capitalism and socialism. But there is no economy on the earth which is purely capitalistic or socialistic in nature. In other words, the purity of the two classic systems of capitalism and socialism has almost disappeared. We have only a mixture of two. The so-called socialist economy of Russia retained some of the essential elements of capitalism and in the capitalistic economy of the U.S.A., one can see a number of socialistic institutions. *Laissez-Faire* capitalism has become outmoded. In fact, Samuelson, the Nobel Laureate, describes even the U.S.A., as a mixed economy. Most of the developing economies may be described as mixed economies.

India as a Mixed Economy

In India, we have a mixed economy, where there is a public sector and a private sector. In general terms, we may say that a mixed economy is a deliberate attempt to have the best of both worlds (of capitalism and socialism). In it, public and private enterprise would be combined to maximize social welfare. Private enterprise would continue to play a large part in it. For example, our Five-Year Plans consist of two sectors: (*i*) Public Sector and (*ii*) Private Sector. With the acceptance of socialistic pattern of society as a broad socio-economic objective by the government in the 1950s, the role of public sector had increased over time till 1991.

The government took note of the concept of mixed economy while formulating the Industrial Policy after independence. Thus defence and strategic industries like manufacture of arms and ammunitions and railways are monopoly of the State. Some key industries like iron and steel, coal, air-craft manufacturing and shipbuilding were controlled by the State. Other industries like sugar, cotton textiles, cement and paper are in the private sector. But they were controlled and regulated by the State.

For a long time, the public sector enterprises were incurring huge losses. But now, at least some of them are in a good shape and they contribute sizeable sums to capital formation in the country. Of course, some services rendered by public enterprises have to be sold at a price lower than cost. Not only that, industries in which profit motive is not strong enough but which cater to national needs are operated by the State.

Recently, the government has accepted the idea of *joint sector*, where the private enterprise will have the opportunity to develop with State participation. In the joint sector enterprises, the government will play an effective role in guiding policies, management and operations. We may look at the joint sector as a tool for social control over industry without resort to outright nationalization. The government made it abundantly clear in the industrial policy of 1973 that joint sector will not be used to allow large houses, dominant undertakings and foreign companies to enter fields from which they are otherwise precluded. Since 1991, with the advent of liberalization, privatization and globalization, there has been downsizing of the government and the role of the public sector has decreased.

Thus in a mixed economy like India, the private sector and the public sector are expected to play a complementary role to each other.

SOCIO-RELIGIOUS AND SOCIO-ECONOMIC REFORMERS OF INDIA

BASAVESHWARA

Introduction

Basaveswara was a 12th century Indian philosopher, social reformer, Kannada poet and statesman. The *Basavarajadevara ragale* by the Kannada poet Harihara (c.1180) is the earliest available account on the life of the social reformer. Harihara was a near contemporary of the social reformer. However, *Basava Purana*, a sacred 13th century Telugu text of the South Indian Hindu Lingayat community by Palkuraki Somanatha gives more or less a full account of the life and ideas of Basava. Bhima Kavi wrote an updated Kannada version of the text in 1369. Both are considered sacred texts by Lingayats. Basava was also known as *Bhakthibanduri* (the treasurer of devotion), *Basavanna* (elder brother Basava) and Basaveswara (Lord Basava).

Life and Work

Basava was born in a Saivite Brahmin family in North Karnataka. He studied in a Hindu temple in a town called Kudalasangama. Basava's wife was the daughter of the Prime Minister of Bijiala, the Kalachuri King. He started his career as an accountant in the court of the king. When his maternal uncle (the Prime Minister) died, the king invited him to be the chief minister. It may be noted that the king also married Basava's sister Padmavati.

As Chief Minister of the Kingdom, Basaveswara initiated social reforms and religious movement focussed on Saivism. He recognized and empowered ascetics known as *Jangamas*. He spread social awareness through his literary works known as *Vachanas* in Kannada language. He rejected discrimination based on caste and gender, superstitions and rituals such as the wearing of sacred thread. But, he introduced *ishtalinga* necklace with an image of the Shiva Linga to every person regardless of his or her birth so that it would be a constant reminder of one's bhakti (devotion) to Shiva.

As the Chief Minister of the Kingdom, he introduced an innovative public institution, *Anubhava Mantapa* (The Hall of Spiritual Experience). It was a public assembly and gathering that welcomed men and women from all socioeconomic backgrounds to discuss spiritual, economic and social issues of life in open.

According to traditional legends, Basaveshwara was founder of the Lingayats. But modern scholars, based on historical evidence, are of the view that Basava was the poet-philosopher who revived and refined an already existing tradition. His verses such as Kayakave Kailasa (work is the path to Kailash (bliss or heaven or what we call work is worship) became popular.

Some of the important works in *Vachana Sahitya* attributed to Basaveshwara are *Shat-Sthalavachana* (a discourse on six stages of Salvation). *Kala-jnana-vachana* (Forecast of the future) and *Mantra-gopya, Ghatachakra vachana* and *Raja-Yoga-Vachana*.

Basava Philosophy

Basaveshwara developed and inspired a new devotional movement known as *Virashaivam.* He gave importance to devotional worship and rejected temple worship and rituals led by Brahmins. He was for personalized direct worship of Shiva through practices such as individually worn icons and symbols like a small *linga.* He believed that this brought Shiva's presence to everyone and at all times without gender, class or caste discrimination.

Basaveshwara, again and again, made use of two concepts, namely *Sthavara* (that is, what is static, standing) and *Jangama* (what is moving easily). Temples and ancient texts represented the former, whereas work and discussion represented the latter. Basavanna 820 translated by Ramanujan gives a beautiful illustration of these concepts.

The rich

Will make temples for Shiva

What shall I,

A poor man do?

My legs are pillars

The body the shrine

The head a cupola of gold

Listen, O Lord of the meeting rivers,

Things standing shall fall,

But the moving ever shall stay.

Basavanna championed the cause of vernacular language, Kannada, in all spiritual discussions so that everyone could understand the spiritual ideas. To him, one's own body and soul are the temple. Basava Philosophy is based on the trinity *guru* (teacher), *Linga* (personal symbol of Shiva) and *jangama* (constantly moving and learning). To him true god is "self-born, one with himself". Though Basaveshwara rejected rituals, he encouraged wearing *ishtalinga,* Rudraksha seeds or beads on parts of one's body and applying *Vibhuti* (sacred ash on forehead) as a constant reminder of one's devotion and principles. As further aid to faith, he encouraged people to use the mantra *Shivaya Namah* or Om Namah Shivaya. Basava favoured the path of direct, personal devotion (bhakti) for liberated, righteous life. Some scholars (e.g. Tripati) find similarities in the teachings of Basaveswara and the 11th century *Vishistadvaita* philosopher Ramanuja. The community that Basava helped form is also known as *Sharanas* and the community is largely concentrated in Karnataka. According to one estimate, towards the end of the 20th century, there were about 10 million Lingayat Hindus in Karnataka.

Social Reformer

Basaveshwara was a great social reformer. He advocated that every human being was equal irrespective of caste, and that all forms of manual labour were important. In other words, he believed in the dignity of human labour. According to Basava, it was not birth but one's conduct or behaviour that determined a true saint and Shaiva bhakti. The sharanas embraced all persons, irrespective of caste and gender into their fold and the large family of Shiva devotees could adopt any occupation of their choice. In the Virasaiva sect, birth did not determine one's occupation. Basava's approach is different from that of Adisankara. While Basava emphasized the path of devotion, Adi Shankara emphasized the path of knowledge.

Ethical Foundations of Virasaivam

Basava's teachings are based on ethical foundations. In one of his *vachanas,* he wrote:

Do not steal, do not kill. Do not utter lies;

Do not lose your temper. Do not detest others.

Do not glorify yourself. Do not blame others

> *This alone is purity within This alone is purity without*
> *And this alone is the way to please our Lord*
>   *Kudalasangama*

Those precepts sound simple and they contain the quintessence of all religions and ethical codes. Only by leading a pure life based on the above ethical code, a person can win the grace of God. Kudalasangama was the personal deity of Basaveshwara.

Contribution to Kannada Language

During Basava's time, most of the religious and ethical texts were in Sanskrit and in poetry. But Basava wrote in Kannada and in prose. This helped the common man to understand his teachings easily. Not only that, this helped the development of Kannada language and Basava's teachings became popular among the masses.

Kayaka

Basava wanted his followers not to neglect their normal duties. To him, *Kayaka* (work) is worship. But they should also lead a spiritual life. As everybody was required to take up some *Kayaka*, the economy of the country improved.

Basava was a very modest person. He used to say, 'There is none smaller than I'.

Basava lived at a time when temple entry was prohibited for the oppressed classes. By rejecting temple worship and by introducing *ishtalinga* necklace, with an image of the Shiva Linga to every person regardless of caste, at one stroke, he aimed at abolishing religious discrimination based on caste.

Similarly, by introducing an innovative public institution known as *Anubhava Mantapa* to enable men and women from all socioeconomic backgrounds to discuss socioeconomic and spiritual issues based on their experience, he tried to abolish gender discrimination.

By emphasizing that work is worship and by teaching the dignity of labour, he wanted every person to engage in some occupation or other, leading a pure and spiritual life. He discouraged laziness and helped especially the poor, to earn income. For poverty is lack of income. His emphasis on labour helped the economy grow.

Lastly, by avoiding Sanskrit and by writing in Kannada that too in prose, and by encouraging all discourses in the mother tongue, he helped in the development of Kannada language and literature and the education of the masses.

Conclusion

Thus Basaveshwara brought about great reformation in religion, ethics, economics, social conduct and in language and literature.

JYOTIRAO GOVINDARAO PHULE

Introduction: Early life

Jyotirao Govindarao Phule was born on April 11, 1827 in a poor and virtually illiterate family that belonged to Mali caste of gardeners and vegetable farmers in a village in Satara district (now in Maharashtra State). The family settled in Pune and prospered by selling flowers, garlands and flower arrangements for religious and social events like weddings. The family enjoyed the patronage of the last of the Peshwas and Phule's father and uncles served as florists under him. Hence the family came to be known as Phule (flower-man).

Govindarao was Phule's father. He carried on the family business along with his brothers. Phule's mother died when he was only a nine month old child. The Mali community did not give much importance to education at that time. So, after completing his education at primary level. Phule was asked to join the other members of the family at work in business and on the farm. But a good

Samaritan, a Christian convert from the same Mali caste as Phule, recognizing the intelligence of Phule advised his father to admit the boy in a school run by a Scottish Mission. His father did so. That was a turning point in the life of Phule. He completed his English schooling in 1847. He married a girl from his own community at a young age of thirteen as per the prevailing custom.

An incident in his life made him feel deeply about the caste discrimination. In 1948, he attended the wedding of his friend, who was a Brahmin. He took part in the marriage procession. For that, he was chided and insulted by the boys' parents. They told him, as he came from a lower caste, he should have had the sense to keep away from the wedding procession. At that time, he felt the injustice of the caste system. In the same year, Phule visited the first girls' school in Ahmadnagar that was run by Christian Missionaries. In 1948, Jyotirao read Thomas Paine's book *Rights of Man* (1791) which helped him develop a keen sense of social justice. At a relatively young age, he realized that people from so called lower castes and women were at a disadvantage. In other words, he became aware of social discrimination based on caste and gender. He further realized that education for the disadvantaged groups was of vital importance for their emancipation and empowerment.

His Contribution

Mahatma Jyotirao Govindarao Phule is sometimes regarded as the Father of the Non-Brahmin Movement. He also contributed greatly to the emergence of labour, peasant, dalit and women empowerment movements. He worked against the practice of untouchability, casteism and caste and gender based discrimination. Some of his important works are *Gulamgiri, Rayots whipcord, Jati Bhed Vivek Saar, Brahmanache Kasab, Sastar* (Parts 1 & 2).

Social Activism

Phule aimed at the reformation of an exploitative social system. He aimed at a broad socioeconomic transformation. He wanted to make people free from superstitious beliefs and abolish the economic frame-work of exploitation. He propagated importance of education, especially among the disadvantaged groups including women.

On the importance of education, he wrote the following famous poem:

"Lack of education leads to lack of wisdom, which leads to lack of morals / which leads to lack of progress / which leads to lack of money / which leads to the oppression of the lower classes / see what state of the society one lack of education can cause.

Jyotirao was not a man of words alone. He was a man of action. To give education to girls, Jyotirao and his wife Savitribai Phule started the first school for girls (by an Indian) in India in 1848. For this, he was forced to leave his parental home. He also opened schools for Shudra and Ati-shudra non-Brahmin communities in Pune and elsewhere. Phule aimed at the elimination of the stigma of social untouchability surrounding the lower castes by opening his house and the use of his well to draw drinking water to the members of the lower castes.

Jyotirao championed the cause of widow remarriage and established a home for upper caste widows in 1854. Not only that, he started a home for newborn infants to prevent female infanticide.

Phule's *akhandas* are based on the *abhangs* of Indian saint Tukaram, who was a Shudra. As already noted, Phule did not like discrimination based on caste. His critique of the caste system began with his attack on the Vedas, the most fundamental texts of the upper caste Hindus. He considered them to be a form of false consciousness. It is believed that Phule introduced the Marathi word *dalit* (broken, crushed) as a description for those persons who were outside the varna system. The term was later popularized in the 1970s by the *Dalit Panthers*.

Satyashodhak Samaj

Accordingly on September 24, 1873, Phule formed Satyashodhak, Samaj (Society of the Seekers of Truth) to focus on the rights of depressed classes and women. Phule was its first president and treasurer. He opposed *idol worship* and denounced the caste system. Sathyashodhak Samaj promoted rational thinking and rejected the need for priests. Phule's wife Savitribai Phule became the head of the women's wing.

After the death of Phule in 1890, his followers spread the message of the Samaj in the remote parts of Maharashtra and North Karnataka. After Mahatma Phule, Chatrapati Shahu Maharaj not only lent moral support to the Samaj, he also implemented the programmes of the Samaj in Kolhapur state. In 1920, Satyashodhak Samaj was transformed into a political movement known as *Non-Brahmin Movement*.

Occupation

It may be of interest to note that besides being a thinker, social reformer and author of many constructive programmes, Phule was a businessman too. For sometime, he worked as a contractor for the government and supplied building materials for the construction of the first masonry dam in India at Khadakwasla near Pune in 1870. In 1863, he entered into a business that supplied metal casting equipment.

In 1876, Phule was appointed Commissioner (Municipal Commission Member) to Pune Municipality and he served in that capacity, which was an unelected position until 1883. In fact, in an 1882 memorial, Phule styled himself as a "Merchant, cultivator and Municipal contractor".

Phule was bestowed with the title of *Mahatma* (Great Soul) on May 11, 1888 by another social reformer from Bombay, Vithalrao Krishnaji Vandekar.

Jyotirao wanted to organize his followers and workers so that they might assimilate his rational ideas and bring them into effect. So Jyotirao decided to set up an organization to preach his ideology.

The main objects of the Sathyashodhak Samaj are:

1. To redeem the Shudras and Ati-Shudras from the influence of Brahmanical scriptures under which the Brahmin priests fleeced them; to make them conscious of their human rights and to liberate them from mental and religious slavery;

2. All men are the children of one God, who is thus their parent; and

3. There is no requirement of intermediary such as priest or a preceptor to approach the mother or the father to offer his prayer to God;

Membership of Satyashodhak Samaj was open to all the castes and creeds including Mahars, Mangs, Jews and Muslims.

The subjects discussed at the meetings of Satya Shodhak Samaj included:

1. The necessity of the temperance and compulsory education;

2. Encouragement of Swadeshi goods;

3. Dislodging the Brahmin priest from the position he held in the religious field;

4. Making arrangements for performing marriage at minimum expenses;

5. Freeing men from the beliefs in astrology, ghosts and demons;

6. The main attack was upon the caste system and idol worship, and

7. Emphasis was also on the principle of the Fatherhood of God and brotherhood of Man.

Work of Satya Shodhak Samaj

Satya Shodhak Samaj aimed mainly at liberating the Shudras and Ati-Shudras and preventing them from exploitation by the upper castes, especially the Brahmins. Jyotirao Phule refused to regard the Vedas as sacrosanct. He opposed idolatry and denounced the Chaturvarna system. The Satya Shodak Samaj spread rational thinking among the common masses and opposed the need for a Brahmin princely class as educational and religious leaders. Mahatma Phule opposed worthless ritual and intermediary between God and man. The Samaj believed neither in the caste system nor in the basic fourfold division of society. The language of the Samaj was the language of the masses and not Sanskrit.

Conclusion

From the foregoing discussion, we find that Mahatma Phule was a great social reformer, who by his writings, actions and constructive programmes, fought against caste and gender discrimination, encouraged education for all, long before the emergence of human capital theory and its significance for human development. Besides education for women, he encouraged widow remarriage. His legacy through Sathyashodhak Samaj has been carried on by Chatrapati Shahu Maharaj in Kolahapur State. In Tamil Nadu, which is in the southernmost part of India, Periyar E.V. Ramasami who was another great social revolutionary, lived and fought against social and economic discrimination based on caste and gender and superstitious beliefs in the name of religion.

RAJARSHI SHAHU MAHARAJ

Introduction

Chatrapati Shahu Maharaj (also known as Rajarshi Shahu Maharaj) was born on June 26, 1874. He was the first Maharaja of the Indian princely state of Kolhapur between 1884 and 1922. He was a social revolutionary and became the pillar of social democracy. He was the first king in India who implemented reservation policy. He provided 50 percent reservation in Kolhapur state on July 26, 1902. His ideal was caste-free India and he worked towards the abolition of untouchability. He was a pioneer of Student Hostel movement for Bahujan Samaj. He derecognized Brahminical supremacy and religious bureaucracy of Brahmins. He wanted to put an end to the monopoly of Brahmins in employment as priests in temples. And he introduced many revolutionary and progressive legal reforms. After the death of Mahatma Phule, Chatrapati Shahu Maharaj carried on with the Satyashodhuk movement.

Accession

Shahu was born of Appasaheb Ghatge and Radhabai, a daughter of the Raja of Mudhol in Karnataka. He was their eldest son. When he was born, he was given the name Yeshwantrao Ghatge. His father was Chief of Kagal (Senior). Shahu was not a direct (male-line) descendant of the Bhonsle dynasty. He was adopted by Anandibai, widow of Raja Shivaji IV, in March 1884. Shahu's family was intimately connected with the ruling dynasty of Kolhapur through a series of intermarriages during many generations. This connection made him a suitable candidate for adoption by Anandibai. As Shahu was only a ten year old boy at the time of adoption, the British Government of India appointed a council of Regency to oversee the affairs of the State during Shahu's minority. At the age of twenty in 1894, he was invested with ruling powers.

Social Reforms

Shahu introduced many reforms to improve the lot of the people, especially those who belonged to the lower castes. He did much to make education and employment available to all. He subsidized education fully so that free education could be provided to all. He opened several hostels in Kolhapur state for students hailing from different non-Brahmin communities, including the dalits. It facilitated the education of the rural children and the poor low caste children. He provided 50 percent reservation for Shudra and Ati-Shudra persons in employment in the State. The newspaper *Nagpur Today* reported on July 26, 1902 "Chatrapati Shahuji Maharaj gave reservation to Bahujan Samaj to the tune of 50% on July 26, 1902 for the first time in the history of India".

This is one of the earliest reservation programmes in the country. All these measures were implemented in 1902. Shahu Maharaj built a college named Rajaram College.

Vedokta Controversy

When the Brahmin priests of the royal family refused to perform the rites of the non-Brahmins in accordance with the Vedic hymns, Shahu Maharaj took the daring step of removing the priests and appointed a young Marutha as the religious teacher of the non-Brahmins with the title of *"Kshatra*

Jagadguru (the world teacher of the kshatriyas). This was known as the "Vedokta" controversy. There was a lot of resentment and opposition from Brahmins and some eminent persons like the great patriot Bal Gangadhar Tilak. But he was not the man to retrace his steps in the face of opposition. He soon became the leader of non-Brahmin movement and united the Marathas under his banner.

Uplift of Women

The position of women in India at the end of the 19th century was in a pitiable condition. Children and widows were the main victims of the social customs of the day. So, Sahu Maharaj introduced many measures to prevent child marriage in the state. Not only that, he encouraged widow remarriage and inter-caste marriages. And he encouraged the education of girls by providing free education.

Good Governance

Chatrapati Shahu Maharaj's concern for good administration can be seen from his statement, "Although I am on the throne of Kolhapur, I feel proud to call myself as soldier, farmer and labourer". While addressing a meeting in Madras (Chennai) he said, "I am here not as king but friend to those whose pitiable condition shall melt, even a stone hearted person". The importance he gives to the dignity of labour in the economy and the society and his concern for the poor are brought out well in these statements.

Lover of Games and Sports

Shahu Mahraj was a great lover of games, sports and music. He was very fond of wrestling and encouraged it in his kingdom.

Sahu Maharaj and Sathyashodhak Movement

After Mahatma Jyotirao Phule, the non-Brahmin movement was led by Shahu Maharaj of Kolhapur. He started a number of branches of Sathya Shodhak Samaj (Seekers of Truth) in many parts of Kolhapur state. We have already noted that he provided 50 percent reservation for non-Brahmin Shudhras and Ati-Shudhras in employment. He abolished Devadasi system, prohibited child marriage, untouchability and encouraged widow-remarriage. By these measures, Sahu Maharaj brought about social transformation among the depressed classes and backward classes. He encouraged and financially helped Dr. Ambedkar to launch the Dalit movement and to start the paper *Mook Nayak*. Shahu Maharaj presided over the Managaon Parishat of Mahars in 1921. Though Kolhapur state was small in size, Shahu Maharaj's name and fame spread to entire Maharashtra, north Karnataka and parts of South India. In 1920, Satya Shodhak Samaj was transformed into a political movement known as 'Non-Brahmin Movement'.

In 1903, Shahu Maharaj attended the coronation of King Edward VII and Queen Alexandra, and in May that year, he received the honorary degree LLD from the University of Cambridge.

Chatrapati Shahu Maharaj died on May 6, 1922.

Conclusion

Shahu Maharaj was described by his biographer A.B. Lathe as "The greatest Maharaj that ever sat on the throne of Kolhapur and one of the powerful men that the nation ever produced in its long and brilliant history". When the postal department issued a stamp dedicated to the memory of Shahu Maharaj, on the first issue citation, the Government of India hailed him as "a social revolutionary, a true democrat, a visionary, a patron of the theatre, music and sports".

RECENT INDIAN ECONOMIC THOUGHT

Indian Economic Thought in the recent past has been influenced by many factors such as the mass poverty, Indian nationalism, anti-British sentiments and contact with the West.

India during the British Raj provides a classic example of arrested economic growth. The colonial and imperial policy of Britain resulted in the exploitation of the Indian economy. In order to encourage their industries, and to promote the market for their machine-made goods, the British policies resulted in the decline and downfall of Indian handicrafts. It resulted in poverty and underemployment. The policy of Free Trade followed by Britain was all to the advantage of her manufacturing industry. Even the policy of discriminating protection granted to some of the Indian industries did not go a long way in developing the Indian industry. During the British Raj, India became the market for the manufactured goods of Britain. At the same time they got many raw materials from India at cheap rates. In short, the British were in India not for our good, but for our goods.

During the period of the Nationalist movement, the Indian leaders attributed the mass poverty in India to the British rule. Naturally, they thought in terms of freedom from colonial rule as the remedy. Economic theory in India during the nationalist movement was concerned with one main aim. That was to provide a momentum to the nationalist movement. Some of leaders formulated certain economic theories to show that the British Government was exploiting the Indian masses in a number of ways. Another thing we notice about the recent Indian economic thought is that it has concentrated much attention on applied economics rather than on pure theory. In other words, our economists were concerned mainly with Indian economic problems. Heroic attempts have been made to estimate India's national income, population, and many agricultural problems. Not only that, those who wrote on economic problems in the recent past were not always professional economists as such. However, since the advent of planning in India, our economists have contributed a sizable literature to the study of problems of economic planning in the social context of a planned economy under a democratic setup.

We shall now study the main economic ideas of some of our leaders in the recent past such as R.C. Dutt, Dada Bhai Naoroji, Ranade, Gopal Krishna Gokhale and Mahatma Gandhi.

R.C. Dutt (1848-1909)

Romesh Chandra Dutt was born in a Bengali family in 1848. He joined the Indian Civil Service in 1869 and served in many capacities. He retired early from government service. Later on, he lectured on Indian History at the University of London. The economic ideas of Dutt are found in his two important books: (*i*) *Economic History of India* (2 volumes); and (*ii*) *Famines in India* (2 volumes). Gadgil described Dutt's 'Economic History of India' as 'almost the first history of a colonial empire.' Thus while the first book deals with the economics of colonialism, the second one deals with the conditions of agricultural population in India and the causes and remedies of famines in India.

Dutt was a nationalist. In 1899, he was elected President of the Indian National Congress.

Economic Ideas of Dutt

Dutt was concerned mainly with the problem of poverty in India. According to him, the chief cause of India's poverty was British Rule. Low productivity of Indian agriculture and fall of handicrafts, he attributed to the British Rule. Even famines, he thought, were caused by the policies of the British rule. Though the immediate cause of famine was the failure of rains, he traced the ultimate cause of famines to the chronic poverty and resourceless condition of the Indian peasants. The Indian peasants were made poor by the uncertain land taxes and the decline and fall of cottage industries. Indian agriculture was characterized by low productivity and absence of irrigation facilities on a large scale. Indian handicrafts, unable to face the competition of machine-made goods of England, declined. Dutt was of the opinion that "all our village industries have been killed by a free competition with the steam and machinery of England. Our cultivators and even our village industrial classes therefore virtually depend on the soil as the one remaining source of their subsistence." Further the village self-government also became a victim of the British rule in India. In his 'Economic History of India,' Dutt remarked, "One of the saddest results of British Rule in India is that effacement of that system of village self-government which was developed earliest and preserved longest in India among all the countries of the earth."

The poverty of India was aggravated by the extravagant, selfish and unsound financial administrative policies followed by Britain. He felt that nearly one-half of revenues received in India were remitted out of the country. He thought that a nation could be wealthy and prosperous only if the proceeds of taxation were spent among the people of that country and for them.

Remedies

Dutt suggested the following remedies to remove the poverty in India.

(*i*) Indian cottage industries should be revived for this would solve the problem of under-employment and unemployment, (*ii*) Land tax should be reduced. He suggested that all taxes on land, except land revenue, should be abolished. He noted that, in general, the Indian tax payer was taxed 40 per cent more than the tax payer of Great Britain and Ireland, (*iii*) Indian revenues should be largely spent in India itself, (*iv*) Irrigation facilities should be extended so as to reduce the dependence of our agriculture on the vagaries of monsoon, (*v*) He emphasized that the government should try to effect economies in expenditure, (*vi*) He suggested that the rate of interest on public debt should be lowered and sinking fund must be created to liquidate public debt, (*vii*) He pleaded for' Indianisation' of government services. In other words he suggested that Indians should get larger employment opportunities in Indian Civil Service, (*viii*) He suggested that the excise duties on goods produced by Indian mills should be abolished in order to promote industrialization of India.

Conclusion

R.C. Dutt may be regarded as one of the builders of modern India. He has combined history, politics and economics to demonstrate the impact of British Rule in India, and the causes of India's poverty. He did not stop with analysing causes. He suggested remedies, too.

Dadabhai Naoroji (1825-1917)

Dadabhai Naoroji, the *Grand Old Man of India*, was born on September 4, 1825 in a Parsi family of Bombay. In life, Naoroji had the distinction of being first in many things. He was the first Indian to be made a Professor at Elphinston College, Bombay, the first Indian to become a Member of House of Commons (British Parliament), the first Indian to become a Member of the Royal Commission and the first Indian to make the National Income Estimate. After teaching for a while at Elphinston College, he went to England in 1855 to look after business. There he took lively interest in politics and did many things to educate the British public opinion about the duties of England to India. Naoroji was an ardent nationalist. He was elected President of the Indian National Congress in 1886 and 1906. While at college, one of Naoroji's teachers called him '*the promise of India*'. The teacher was right. Naoroji became the *Father of Indian Nationalism*.

Economic Ideas of Naoroji

The economic ideas of Naoroji are found in his monumental work "*Poverty and Un-British Rule in India.*" The poverty of India was the theme of his book. He considered it the main economic problem of India. He made a survey of the per capita income in Bombay presidency for the years 1867-70. He noted that it was as low as Rs. 20 indicating the grinding poverty of the masses. He thought that the per capita income should be at least Rs. 34 to meet the bare necessities of life. He attributed the poverty of India to the policy of continuous exploitation followed by the British Government.

The Drain Theory

Dadabhai Naoroji is famous as an economist for his '*Drain Theory*'. He attributed the poverty of India to the British rule. He felt that under the British rule, India had the 'lordliest and costliest administration in the world.' The consequence of foreign domination was the drain of the wealth of India into England. He thought the extravagant cost of British administration had a disastrous effect on the Indian economy. Naoroji estimated that the drain which was to the tune of £3 million at the beginning of the 19th century increased to £30 million towards the end of the last century. According to Naoroji, this heavy drain of wealth from India into England was one of the main causes of the poverty of India.

The drain of wealth took place in a number of ways. First, large remittances were made by European officials of their savings in India. Second, large remittances were made in the form of salaries and pensions. Third, India often had to pay for government expenditure in England and of course in India too. Fourth, non-official Europeans made remittances from their business profits in India. The money which has gone out of India to England has once again come back as British capital and foreigners have monopolised trade and industry. It has once again resulted in the drain of wealth. Thus the drain has become continuous and it has affected capital formation in India.

Dadabhai Naoroji has collected a lot of statistical data to prove his drain theory. He examined the figures of imports and exports between the years 1835 and 1872 and pointed out that the value of the exports exceeded that of imports by £500 million. The drain would have been greater, if interest had been calculated on the amount. No country could bear such a drain upon its resources without sustaining very serious injury.

Naoroji pointed out that every war which the British fought after 1858 beyond the frontiers of India was clearly and mainly for safeguarding the imperial interests of Britain. He, therefore, argued that Britain should pay her proper share of the maintenance of the British Army in India.

Further, when the Railways were built in India, India had to spend large sums on salaries and allowances to European staff for all the top posts were manned by the Britishers. Indians were employed largely on low paid jobs. Large sums of money also went out of India in the form of profits on railways to England. Thus the benefits of railways were enjoyed largely by the foreigners and the burden of foreign debt was borne by India. In the case of other countries, the English men merely sent their capital. But in the case of India, the English capitalists did not merely lend, but with their capital they themselves invaded the country.

Dadabhai Naoroji felt that former rulers who plundered India's wealth by their invasions now and then were now better than the British rulers. He said, "The former rulers were like butchers hacking here and there, but the English with their scientific scalpel cut to the very heart.... There is no wound to be seen, and soon the plaster of the high talk of civilisation, progress and what not covers up the wound." He felt that it was wrong to consider India as Nature's tragedy and the Indian agriculture, a gamble in the hands of the monsoon. He said that, "If India did not progress under the Englishmen, there was no justification for their existence here."

Naoroji suggested the following measures to remove India's poverty and to reduce the drain.

1. India and England should pay all salaries to their people within their boundaries. With regard to the Englishmen employed in India and the Indians employed in England, there should be a fair and reasonable apportionment between the two countries.

2. As the Englishmen were paid reasonable salaries while they served in India, there was no need to pay pension to them.

3. As there was no danger of invasion of India by sea, and as all advantages from the Indian Navy went to England, India should not be charged any portion of the expenditure incurred on the maintenance of the Indian navy.

Conclusion

Though Naoroji's treatment of national income, as Dr. V.K.R.V. Rao pointed out, was based on "the Physiocratic concept of materiality of income" (Naoroji did not include 'services' in his calculation of per capita income), we should not forget the fact that Dadabhai Naoroji was the first Indian to calculate national income on per capita basis. His drain theory indicated broadly how there was perpetual exploitation of Indian wealth by the British administration. Above all, he explained the problem of poverty in India in a scientific manner based on statistical data.

Mahadev Govind Ranade (1842-1901)

Ranade was born on January 18, 1842 at Nasik. He took his M.A. degree from the University of Bombay. He studied Law too. He taught economics at the University of Bombay for some time. Later on, he practised Law. Then he entered the judicial service and became judge of the Bombay High Court. He was in the post till his death in 1901.

Ranade was a great nationalist. He helped in founding the 'Deccan Education Society'. The aim of the society was to spread modern Western education to the rising generation without exposing it to the anti-national bias of English educators.

The economic ideas of Ranade are found in his "*Essays on Indian Political Economy*" (1898). "*The Rise of Maratha Power*" (1900) is an important historical work of Ranade.

ECONOMIC IDEAS OF RANADE

On the Method and Scope of Political Economy

Ranade attacked the deductive method of the classical economists. He was in favour of the inductive and historical method. Again, while the classical economists believed that economic laws were of universal application, he thought they were only relative. In other words, he believed in the doctrine of relativity. He said that the traditional assumptions of economic theory were true only for England. In the above ideas, Ranade was influenced by Friedrich List, the leader of nationalist school in economics, who maintained that economic laws were relevant only with reference to a particular nation. List believed that what was important was to improve the 'productive powers' of the nation.

Ranade emphasized the importance of economic education in promoting the wealth of a nation. He said, 'the nation's economic education is of far more importance than the present gain of its individual members, as represented by the quantity of wealth measured by its value in exchange. In a sound and normal condition all the three departments of national activity must be fully developed.

Commerce and manufactures are, if possible, more vital in their bearing on education, on the intelligence and skill and enterprise of the nation than agriculture." Ranade was of the view that in any science, theory and practice should go together. "Theory is only enlarged practice and practice is theory studied in its relation to proximate causes."

India's Poverty

While Dutt and Naoroji believed that poverty of India was the result of the British rule, Ranade believed that mass poverty had been there in India even before the advent of the British rule. Of course, he agreed that poverty was intensified by the impact of the West on India. He gave the following reasons for the poverty of India. Firstly, there was too much of dependence on agriculture. This situation, of course, has been brought about by the economic policy of the government which encouraged export of raw materials. Secondly, industries in India were in a backward state owing to their inability to face stiff foreign competition. Thirdly, the credit system was highly disorganised and banking facilities were inadequate. Lastly, the land policy of the government was also defective because the assessment of revenue was highly arbitrary. Thus Ranade attributed the poverty of India to the existence of a preponderantly agricultural economy, low rate of industrialization, inadequate credit facilities and a defective land policy.

Suggested Remedies

Ranade opposed the *laissez-faire* policy of the State and believed that the State must play an important role in removing the poverty and in promoting the wealth of the nation. He said that "the State should come forward with such measures as may prove helpful in the development of the economy of the country, to the maximum advantage of the people." Further he said, "The State is now more and more recognized as the national organ for taking care of national needs in all matters in which individual and cooperative efforts are most likely to be not so effective and economical as national effort.... To relegate them to the simple duty of maintaining peace and order is really to deprive the community of many of the advantages of the social union." In fact, Ranade thought in terms of a planned economy for India with the object of establishing a welfare state. But he did not work out the details.

Ranade opposed the policy of the Free Trade because it was detrimental to the interests of the nascent industries of India. So he advocated a policy of protection to the Indian industries. Not only that, he wanted the government to follow a positive policy for promotion of industrial development of India. Further, he advocated State action to promote large scale farming. In other words, Ranade believed that a balanced and planned development of agriculture, industry and commerce was essential for promoting the economic development of India.

To solve the problem of population pressure in certain regions, Ranade advocated a balanced redistribution of population by sending people from thickly populated areas to sparsely populated areas. He thought the State could play a role in the resettlement of the people.

Ranade advocated changes in land policy to serve the interests of the cultivators of the soil. He said that the farmers might be allowed to pay their tax in kind, if it was convenient for them. He pleaded for a permanent ryotwari land settlement for a minimum period extending from 20 to 30 years. Further he advocated re-organization of credit system and formation of committees of capitalists to finance agriculture.

Conclusion

Ranade occupies a significant place in recent Indian economic thought. According to Prof. Karve, he was the first economist who suggested planning. Further, in order to make economic studies more realistic and meaningful Ranade suggested the study of economic problems in the national context. He was really a national economist. His suggestion for reorganization of credit system to provide agricultural finance resulted in the establishment of land mortgage banks. Besides being an eminent economist and able historian, he was a leader of thought and great patriot. Karve has described him as the 'prophet of liberal India'.

Gopal Krishna Gokhale (1866-1915)

Gopal Krishna Gokhale was born on May 9, 1866. He taught History and Economics at the Ferguson College, Poona from 1896 to 1902. In 1899, he was elected to the Bombay Legislative Council. He was the founder of the *Servants of India Society*. In 1905, he was elected the President of the Indian National Congress. Besides the above things, he served in many capacities. He visited England many times.

Economic Ideas of Gokhale

In economic matters he was the disciple of Ranade. Gokhale was an expert in fiscal economics. He was mainly interested in the problems of financial control and fiscal administration in India. He suggested a number of reforms in taxation and budgetary policies.

His view on the Indian budget was that it should be passed item by item. He thought that such a thing would help those who are conversant with Indian conditions to comment on the budget. Gokhale was not in favour of surplus budgets. He thought a succession of surplus budgets would make the government indulge in extravagant expenditure. He thought it would be "specially true of countries like India where public revenues are administered under no sense of responsibility, such as exists in the West, to the governed." Gokhale objected to the practice of using budget surpluses for repaying the debt incurred for the construction of Railways. As the railways were a commercial undertaking, he thought it should meet its debt commitments from its own income and not from the proceeds of taxation.

Gokhale suggested an equitable distribution of tax proceeds between the Centre and the provincial governments and local bodies. He suggested that land revenue, excise and forests might be put in the provincial list; opium, salt, customs, posts and telegraphs might be given to the Imperial government. The quinquennial revenue settlement might be given to the local bodies.

Gokhale advocated decentralisation of power, from the Centre down to villages.

In 1896, the government decided to increase the duty on salt in order to meet a deficit of £1.5 million which arose as a result of the annexation of Burma. Gokhale opposed the increase in salt tax for he thought that it would place a heavy burden on the poorer sections of the community. Again in 1879, the Government removed the 5 per cent import duty on Lancashire manufactures (textiles) and in 1896 imposed $3\frac{1}{2}$ per cent excise duty on all cotton goods produced by Indian Mills. Gokhale who understood the real motive of the above tax measures attacked the change of tax policy with regard to textiles as follows in the Imperial Legislative Assembly: "In deference to the representation of Lancashire Mill owners.. . . India was compelled to impose an excise duty upon her own cotton manufactures. That is to say she was forced to tax an internal industry at a peculiarly inopportune time for the benefit of Lancashire. She was practically sacrificed to the political exigencies of the movement."

Gokhale suggested certain reforms in the land revenue system. He suggested that in the Ryotwari areas, the revenue should not be more than 20 per cent of the gross produce where the cultivators paid revenue directly to the government.

Gokhale was highly critical of the large increase in public expenditure. When the Royal Commission was appointed in 1895 "to enquire into the administration and the management of the military and civil expenditure, and the apportionment of charges between the government of the United Kingdom and of India for the purposes in which both are interested", Gokhale gave evidence before the Commission as one of the non-official witnesses. He divided his evidence into three portions—the first one dealing with the *machinery of control*, the second with the *progress of expenditure* and the last portion dealing with the *apportionment of charges between England and India*.

Gokhale made the point that the machinery of control was defective. In England and other countries, public expenditure was controlled by the tax payers, it was a different case in India. In India, there was no popular control over the public expenditure. The Indian tax payers had no say in the matter.

On Public expenditure, Gokhale expressed the view that ever since the transfer of power from the East India company to the Crown, there was a tremendous growth of public expenditure. The average expenditure for the five years before the mutiny, which stood at Rs. 3 crores, increased to Rs. 73 crores. Gokhale pointed out that the huge expenditure incurred in the maintenance of large European army, the Europeans in the native army and in the civil service imposed a heavy burden on India. He accused the government of misutilization of Indian money for furthering its imperial designs for extending North and North-Eastern Frontiers, for fighting Afghan and Burmese wars. He said that in order to maintain the balance of power in Asia, the British Government was incurring huge military expenditure. He estimated the ratio of ordinary military expenditure to total expenditure at 35 per cent.

With regard to the apportionment of charges between the United Kingdom and India, Gokhale suggested that the India office charges should be shared on 50 : 50 basis, the army charges due to the Imperial Reserve should be paid by England, the public debt of India should be charged to the Crown, and the Crown should pay a reasonable share of the cost of maintaining the British army stationed in India.

Gokhale suggested the following measures: (*i*) economy in public expenditure. He said in normal times, public expenditure should not exceed public revenue. (*ii*) Military expenditure should be cut down to the minimum. (*iii*) Indianisation of civil service, and (*iv*) Audit should be made independent.

Conclusion

Gokhale made a remarkable contribution to the study of fiscal administration in India. His ideas regarding budgets, fiscal policy, provincial autonomy and military expenditure are superb. He was a master of all the subjects he had dealt with. Gokhale realized the importance of well informed public opinion of governmental policies. Above all, he was the political guru of Mahatma Gandhi. Gandhi took him as his model.

GANDHIAN ECONOMICS

Mohan Das Karam Chand Gandhi (1869-1948)

Mahatma Gandhi, the 'Father of the Nation', was born in Porbander on October 2, 1869. In a way, the history of India's struggle for Independence is the story of Mahatma Gandhi's life.

Gandhi studied Law in England. After his return to India, he was called to the Bar. After two years, he went to South Africa as a lawyer. It was there that Gandhi learnt his first lessons in political education. It was there that he evolved the concept of satyagraha or non-violent agitation.

After his return from South Africa, Gandhi became the leader of the Indian Nationalist Movement. He started the non-violent, non-cooperative movement to attain the goal of Independence. In 1930, he led the Salt Satyagraha and in 1940 launched the Civil Disobedience Movement. In 1942, he started the 'Quit India' movement. He was jailed many times for his political activities. On January 30, 1948, Gandhi was shot dead by a fanatic.

Before studying the economic ideas of Gandhi, it may be worth-while to take note of certain formative influences. Gandhi was influenced greatly by Tolstoy and Ruskin. Tolstoy's book, "*The Kingdom of God is within you*" and Ruskin's "*Unto this Last*" had a profound influence on Gandhi.

From the Philosophy of Tolstoy, he derived the concepts of *egalitarianism, simplicity* and *asceticism* which later on became the foundation of his economic ideas. Further, the idea of *'bread labour'* popularized by Tolstoy influenced Gandhi and strengthened his conviction that machine technology should be avoided. The concept of 'bread labour' made Gandhi believe that a man who did not do body labour had no right to eat. From Ruskin, he developed a distaste for material progress. Anarchists like Prince Kropotkin developed in Gandhiji, a hatred against centralization of economic and political power.

There is a vast literature on Gandhian economic thought. Dr. J.C. Kumarappa's "Gandhian Economic Thought" gives a complete idea of Gandhi's economic ideas. Besides, a number of pamphlets and articles such as *Cent per cent Swadeshi, Constructive programme—Its meaning and place, Economics of Khadi, Hind Swaraj* written by Gandhi himself give us some idea about his economic philosophy. Shriman Narayan's "Relevance of Gandhian Economics" also tells us a good deal about Gandhian Economics.

Gandhian Economics

Gandhian Economics is based on ethical foundations. In 1921, Gandhi wrote, "Economics that hurts the moral well-being of an individual or a nation is immoral, and, therefore, sinful." Again in 1924, he repeated the same belief: "that economics is untrue which ignores or disregards moral values."

According to Prof. C.N. Vakil, "One has to interpret Gandhiji's economic ideas and build up what may be described as Gandhian Economic thought from what he did and said in this connection. Gandhian Economic thought is based on four fundamental principles: *Truth, Non-violence, Dignity of Labour* and *Simplicity*. One principle that played significant role in Gandhi's life was: simple living, and high thinking. Gandhiji was a practical idealist. The economics of Gandhi might also be described as the economics of non-violence. Gandhi opposed modern capitalism because it is based on the exploitation of human labour. To Gandhi, moral progress is more important than material progress."

We shall discuss now some of the salient features of Gandhian economic thought.

1. *Village Republics:* To Gandhi, the village was India. He was interested in developing the villages as self-sufficient units. He opposed extensive use of machinery, urbanisation and industrialization on the ground that it led to *pauperisation* of villages and large scale unemployment in the countryside. He thought that industrialisation on a large scale would "necessarily lead to passive or active exploitation of the villages as the problems of marketing and competition come in." Later on, he added, "under my scheme, nothing will be allowed to be produced by the cities which can equally well be produced by villages. The proper function of cities is to serve as clearing houses for village products." He thought the development of rural civilization on the basis of self-sufficient villages would result in the decentralisation of political and economic power. He opposed modern industrial civilization because he wanted to protect the rural civilization.

2. *On Machinery:* Gandhi described machinery as 'great sin'. He said that "Books could be written to demonstrate its evils.... It is necessary to realize that machinery is bad. If instead of welcoming machinery as a boon, we should look upon it as an evil, it would ultimately cease." Because of his antipathy to the machine, Gandhi's critics called him a mediaeval mystic, who was vainly trying to put back the clock of human progress by his opposition to machinery and large scale production. This criticism, however, is based on a misunderstanding of his real attitude to machine. The idea that Gandhi was opposed to machinery or large scale production as such is one of the many superstitions about Gandhi. Gandhi was not against machinery in general. As he put it, "The spinning wheel itself is a machine, a little toothpick is a machine, what I object to is the craze for labour-saving machinery. Men go on saving labour, till thousands are without work and thrown on the open streets to die of starvation.... Today machinery merely helps a few to ride on the backs of millions." But he was against all destructive machinery.

He welcomed such instruments and machinery that saved individual labour and lightened the burden of millions of cottagers. For example, he was not against the use of Singer sewing machine.

Gandhi emphasized that he was against large scale production only of those things that villagers can produce without difficulty. He believed that the machinery method was harmful, when the same thing could be done easily by millions of hands not otherwise occupied. He wrote in 1934, "Mechanization is good when the hands are too few for the work intended to be accomplished. It is an evil when there are more hands than required for the work, as is the case in India." In 1938, in "Harijan" he wrote, "If I could produce all my country's wants by means of 30,000 people instead of 30 million, I should not mind it, provided that the thirty million are not rendered idle and unemployed." In short, Gandhi was aware of the menace of technological unemployment. He emphasized the need for labour-intensive methods of production in a country with surplus labour.

Gandhiji's ideas on machinery are still relevant. In spite of more than six decades of planned and machine using and power driven economic development, unemployment is still there and is growing.

3. *Industrialism:* Gandhi considered industrialism as a curse on mankind. He thought industrialism depended entirely on a country's capacity to exploit. Not only that, an industrialized nation in order to find new markets for her goods produced under large scale production would tend to follow a policy of colonialism. It will lead to wars and all that. Man will become a slave to machine and lose his dignity. Gandhi categorically said, "I do not believe that industrialisation is necessary for India." He described industrialism, a manifestation of capitalism, as the control of majority by a small minority. He believed that industrialism, would not remove the poverty of India. As he put it, "We know that each nation has its own characteristics and individuality. India has her own; and if we are to find out a true solution for her many ills we shall have to take all the idiosyncrasies of her constitution into account and then prescribe a remedy. I claim that to industrialize India in the same sense as Europe is to attempt the impossible" (*Young India*: August 6, 1925). That is why Gandhi suggested the development of village industries. The Charkha movement was inspired by great practical wisdom. "From the strictly economic point of view, the most urgent problem of India is the universal under-employment of the peasant." (J.M. Murray: *Mahatma Gandhi*).

Gandhi opposed large scale industrialism also on grounds of social justice. Machinery would enrich the few at the expense of the many. He thought it would result in the concentration of economic power in a few hands. Gandhi hated privilege and monopoly.

Gandhi said that machinery should not be used as a means of exploitation of others. There was a progressive change in his attitude to machinery and large scale production. In 1940, he visualized "electricity, ship building, iron works, machine-making and the like existing side by side, with village handicrafts." Hitherto industrialisation has been so planned as to destroy the village and village crafts. In the state of future, it will subserve the villages and their crafts. Gandhi advocated state ownership of public utilities. In short, Gandhi imposed the following conditions for using machinery: (*i*) They must not deprive people of employment. (*ii*) They must not exploit the villages or compete with village crafts. (*iii*) They must help the village artisan to improve his efficiency. (*iv*) They must not lead to monopoly and concentration of wealth in a few hands. (*v*) They must not lead to exploitation at the national or international level. (*vi*) Lastly, when involving large capital or large number of employees, they must be owned by the state and administered wholly for the public good.

4. *Decentralization:* Non-violence was the basic principle of Gandhi's life. Since the foundations of large-scale production were laid on violence, Gandhi advocated decentralisation. He advocated

a decentralized economy, i.e., production at a large number of places on a small scale or production in the people's homes. Gandhiji said, "If you multiply individual production to millions of times, would it not give you mass production on a tremendous scale? But I quite understand that your mass production is a technical term for production by the fewest possible number through the aid of highly complicated machinery. I have said to myself that this is wrong. My machinery must be of the most elementary type which I can put in the homes of millions." In other words what Gandhi wanted was *not mass production, but production by the masses*. He wanted the revival and development of cottage industries. Mass production really does not help the masses. As Dr. Schumacher put it, "It is claimed that mass production, if it does find a market, is the most effective instrument for the rapid accumulation of the surplus wealth and that this surplus will then percolate to the unemployed masses. Yet it is a fact of universal experience that no such 'percolation' takes place; a dual economy emerges in which the rich gets richer while the poor stagnates or gets poorer." Gandhi believed that "an ideal constitution for India must be based on the organization of well-knit and co-ordinated village communities with their positive and direct democracy, non-violent cottage economy and human contacts." Gandhi wanted to revive the cottage industries because he thought only there "production was simultaneous with consumption and distribution and the vicious circle of money economy was absent. Production was for immediate use and not for distant markets. The whole structure of society was founded on non-violence."

5. *Village Sarvodaya:* According to Gandhi, "Real India was to be found in villages and not in towns and cities." So he suggested the development of self-sufficient, self-dependent villages. He wanted every village to develop into a little republic, independent of its neighbours in so far as its vital wants were concerned. *Village Swaraj* was his ideal. And he laid the conditions of an ideal village. Gandhi said: "Indian independence must begin at the bottom. Thus every village will be a republic or *panchayat* having powers. It follows therefore that every village has to be self-sustained and capable of managing its own affairs even to the extent of defending itself against the whole world."

In his scheme for the revival of village economy, Gandhi has given top priority for the Khadi programme. Gandhi said: "Khadi is the sun of village solar system. The planets are the various industries which can support Khadi in return for the heat and the substance they derive from it."

6. *Bread Labour:* Gandhi realized the dignity of human labour. He believed that God created man to eat his bread by the sweat of his brow. *Bread Labour* or body labour was the expression that Gandhi used to mean manual labour. He did not regard all manual labour as the "curse of Adam." He said: "It is only when a man or woman has done bodily labour for the sake of service that he or she gets any right to live." He asserted that "man cannot develop his mind by simply writing or reading or making speeches all day long. Gandhi made use of the concept of 'bread labour' to tell people to utilize their idle hours which in villages are equal to the working days of six months in the year. Gandhi preached and practised the gospel of manual work. On account of his emphasis on manual labour and opposition to machinery, some critics have dubbed Gandhi as a mediaeval mystic who was trying to put back the clock of human progress.

7. *The Doctrine of Trusteeship:* Gandhi has developed the doctrine of trusteeship to provide an alternative to Marxian socialism. He thought it was surely wrong to presume that Western socialism or communism is the last word on the question of mass poverty. In Gandhi's ideal social order, 'the individual will be at the Centre and the State has to promote his welfare.' But under Marxism, individual will be subordinate to the State. Again while Marx considered force and violence as inevitable in the birth of a new order, Gandhian socialism is based on non-violence. In this respect Gandhi was the very opposite of Marx.

Gandhi made a distinction between "*possession*" and "*possessiveness*". In his view, the evil lay not in possession as such but in the attitude of possessiveness. Gandhi desired the capitalists to become trustees of the nation by running their business with integrity and efficiency and for the welfare of the people.

Sometimes, it is alleged that by means of his trusteeship doctrine, Gandhi was trying to give a new lease of life to the capitalist system. It is often alleged that Gandhiji, by advancing his trusteeship theory, had retarded the forces of revolution in the economic sphere because the capitalists could not be expected to function as real trustees of their own free will without legislative compulsion. But the doctrine of trusteeship "does not exclude legislative regulation of the ownership and the use of wealth." Gandhi only wished to give one more chance to the owning class to reform itself in the faith that human nature is never beyond redemption.

The following are the salient features of the trusteeship formula of Gandhi's ideal social order:

(*i*) Trusteeship provides a means of transforming the present capitalist order of society into an equalitarian one. It gives no quarter to capitalism, but gives the present owning class, the chance of reforming itself. It is based on the faith that human nature is never beyond redemption.

(*ii*) It does not recognize any right of private ownership of property except in as much as it may be permitted by society for its welfare.

(*iii*) It does not exclude legislative regulation of the ownership and the use of wealth.

(*iv*) Thus, under state-regulated trusteeship, an individual will not be free to hold or use his wealth for selfish satisfaction or in disregard of the interest of society.

(*v*) Just as it is proposed to fix a decent minimum living wage, even so, a limit should be fixed for the maximum income that could be allowed to any person, in society. The difference between such minimum and maximum incomes should be reasonable and equitable and variable from time to time so much so that the tendency would be towards obliteration of the difference.

(*vi*) "Under the Gandhian economic order, the character of production will be determined by social necessity and not by personal whim or greed".

8. *On the Food Problem:* Gandhi was against any sort of food controls. He thought such controls only created artificial scarcity.

9. *On Population:* Gandhi opposed the *method* of population control through contraceptives. He was, however, in favour of birth control through Brahmacharya or self-control. He considered self-control as a sovereign remedy to the problem of over-population. Gandhi did not agree with the view that food shortage was caused by excessive growth of population. He believed that "by a proper land system, better agriculture and a supplementary industry, the country is capable of supporting twice as many people as there are today."

10. *On Prohibition:* Gandhi advocated cent per cent prohibition. He regarded the use of liquor as a disease rather than a vice. He felt that it was better for India to be poor than to have thousands of drunkards. Once Gandhi wrote that "if he were appointed dictator of India, only for an hour, he would, in the first instance, close all the liquor shops without compensation, and compel the mill-owners to start refreshment rooms to provide harmless drinks to the workmen." Of course, Gandhi was aware of the fact that the evil of drinking cannot be stopped by mere legislative action. Gandhi did not agree with those who held the view that the introduction of prohibition would cause a steep fall in the revenue of the State and that enough funds would not be available for social service expenditure on items such as education.

The Relevance of Gandhian Economic Thought to Modern India

Many economists tend to dismiss Gandhian economics as Utopian in nature. They regard Gandhi as a medieval mystic who tried to put back the clock of human progress. But much of the criticism is based on gross misunderstanding of Gandhi's views. It requires sympathy, understanding and vision to appreciate Gandhi's economic philosophy. Gandhian economics is based on ethical values and the dignity of man and it is regarded as the only enduring alternative to prevalent Western notions of scientific socialism and communism.

Gandhi was a practical idealist. His economic thought is basically sound and is relevant to our times. His economic ideas are not medieval and out of date.

Gandhian thought has significant relevance for modern India and many things which have happened since he passed away have not diminished but heightened its relevance. In 1963, after more than a decade of planning, Mr. Nehru, the first Prime Minister of India noted that still there was a goodly number of people in India who had not profited by planning and whose poverty was most painful. He said, "I do think that some method should be found to remedy the situation." In that context, he observed: "I begin to think more and more of Gandhi's approach." Again Dr. Ropke in his *Humane Economy* observed, "It is regrettable that India seems to follow materialist socialism rather than Gandhi's humane wisdom."

It is often thought that Mahatma Gandhi was essentially a religious ascetic who was averse to the fruits of modern science and technology. It is an unfortunate misconception. He was not against machinery as such. All that he meant was that in a country like India where capital was scarce and labour abundant, it would be profitable to use labour-intensive industries. He was afraid that use of machinery on a large scale would result in technological unemployment. Gandhi said, "If the Government could provide full employment to our people without the help of Khadi and village industries, I shall be prepared to wind up my constructive programme in this sphere."

In his *Asian Drama*, Gunnar Myrdal has broadly supported Gandhi's emphasis on village and cottage industries because "South Asian countries now run the risk of creating petty islands of highly organized Western-type industries that will remain surrounded by a sea of stagnation." He has further observed that "The development of industries in direct competition with existing cottage industries could take work and bread away from millions with no immediate alternative source of employment or income. This would not be rational from a planning point of view. As for the workers in the South-Asian cottage industry, there is no prospect of any large scale adjustment for decades to come, particularly as the labour force will increase rapidly until the end of the century." In underdeveloped countries, full employment of human resources will depend not on mass production but on production by masses. It is gratifying to note that during the Second Five-Year Plan period, in the basic strategy of the Plan, the small-scale and cottage industries were given priority for solving the problem of unemployment and rural underemployment. In an economic system based on large-scale production, generally the rich get richer while the poor stagnate or become poorer. Even during the Third Five-Year Plan the planners had to accept they had to rely more and more on village and cottage industries to solve the problem of unemployment.

Gandhi's emphasis on non-violence, decentralisation, village swaraj are all relevant today. Gandhi firmly believed that communist methods of violence and class-war are unsuitable to Indian conditions.

The mad race in industrialisation and urbanization has resulted in the pollution of air and water. Environmental pollution is slowly becoming NUMBER ONE problem of the industrialized nations of the world. In the ideal social order based on village economy, environmental pollution will not be a problem.

It would have been a better thing if the state governments had continued the policy of prohibition without looking at it as a profit and loss account. Gandhi was right in opposing controls. For the licence-permit-quota policies of the government have resulted in monopolies and concentration of economic power in a few hands.

Gandhi belongs to the future, and not the past, His message is eternal. He once wrote, "... So long as my faith burns bright, as I hope it will even if I stand alone, I shall be alive in the grave and what is more, speaking from it." We may conclude with the words of Louis Fisher, a great admirer of Gandhi: "If man is to survive, if civilization is to survive and flower in freedom, truth and decency, the remainder of the twentieth century and what lies beyond must belong not to Lenin or Trotsky, not to Marx or Mao or Ho or Che but to Mahatma Gandhi."

JAWAHARLAL NEHRU (1889-1964)

Introduction

Jawaharlal Nehru, one of the chief builders of Modern India, was the first Prime Minister of Independent India and he was there in that post till his death in 1964. He was a great patriot, thinker and statesman. Above all, he was a citizen of the world. He had a passion for science and modernity. Democracy, secularism, planning and socialism are the main contributions of Jawaharlal Nehru to India. His views on economic and social problems are found in the innumerable speeches he made and in the books he wrote. Nehru was a man of letters. His entanglement in politics was a great loss to literature. His important works include *Autobiography, The Discovery of India and Glimpses of World History*.

There are two divergent views on the philosophy of life in ancient India. There is one set of writers, mostly of Western stock, who believe that life, work and thought in ancient India was based on the negation of life. In other words, they believed that people in India did not have materialistic view of life and they were interested mainly in the things of the soul. So they concluded, religion and philosophy dominated their lives. This, however, is not a correct view. The opposite view, which seems to be nearer the truth, has been shared mostly by Indian scholars. Nehru, for instance, believed that the basic background of ancient Indian culture was not one of other worldliness or world-worthlessness. In fact, he believed that the Vedic Aryans were so full of zest for life that they paid little attention to the soul. While commenting on the Vedas, he tells that, "There is no idolatry in them, no temples for the gods. The vitality and affirmation of life pervading them are extraordinary."

Democracy and Secularism

Jawaharlal Nehru was a firm believer in democracy. He believed in free speech, civil liberty, adult franchise and the Rule of Law. He has made Parliamentary democracy, a working proposition in the country. Democracy collapsed in most of the neighbouring States that became independent along with India, whereas democracy has survived in this great nation.

Secularism, is another signal contribution of Nehru to India. In our country, there are many religions— Hinduism, Islam, Christianity, Buddhism, Jainism, Zoroastrianism, Sikhism and so on. But there is no domination by religious majority. Secularism means equal respect for all religions. Therefore, secularism also means divorce of religious institutions from the State. It also means that religious establishments should be kept separate from political establishments. In addition to democracy and secularism, Nehru was interested in science and technology and modernization of our traditional society.

Planning

Jawaharlal Nehru was responsible for the introduction of planning in our country. The 'prehistory' of Indian Planning tells us in a clear fashion the decisive role played by one man: Jawaharlal Nehru. It was he who converted Congress to the idea of planning, and he who continued to insist on its importance at times when other, superficially more immediate, questions were tending to push it in the background. This inspiration and leadership continued throughout the 1950s and into the 1960s, upto the very end of Nehru's life. Of course, he became responsible for a number of serious mistakes in Indian Planning. But he made planning acceptable to the masses and the educated and politically-vocal Indians. We may be right in saying that upto 1964, India's plans were Nehru's plans.

Nehru believed in democratic planning. In his own words, "If left to normal forces under the capitalist system, there is no doubt at all the poor will get poorer and a handful of the rich richer." Planning is essentially a process whereby we stop those cumulative forces at work which make the poor poorer, and start a new series of cumulative forces which enable the poor to get over the barrier of poverty. In Russia, this was done, but at a terrific cost in human suffering. The problem which we have to face is how to cross the barrier of poverty without paying that terrible cost and without infringing individual freedom."

To Nehru, the Plan was essentially an integrated approach to development. Initiating the debate on the Second Plan in the Lok Sabha in May 1956, Nehru spoke on the theme of planning. He said, "The essence of planning is to find the best way to utilize all resources—of manpower, of money and so on...... We want to arrive at a state when we can assess accurately what the next stage is going to be, visualise our problems in advance and take appropriate action before events force our hands. That is, after all, the object of planning..... There is no other way but planning for an underdeveloped country like ours."

Planning for Nehru was essentially linked up with industrialization and eventual self-reliance for the country's economic growth on a self-accelerating growth. It may be interesting to note here that Mahatma Gandhi and Jawaharlal Nehru, saw eye to eye on very few social and economic questions. They differed on fundamental matters such as socialism versus capitalism, factory industry versus cottage industry, and centralization versus decentralization.

Gandhi considered industrialism as a curse on mankind. He categorically said, "I do not believe that industrialisation is necessary for India." He believed that industrialism would not remove the poverty of India and he suggested the development of village industries. Gandhi opposed large-scale industrialism also on grounds of social justice. He thought it would enrich a few at the expense of many and it would result in the concentration of economic power in a few hands. But Jawaharlal Nehru was for industrialization. Addressing the conference of the All India Manufacturers' Organization in April 1956, Nehru said: "If we really wish to industrialize, we must start from the heavy, basic, mother industries. There is no other way. We must start with the production of iron and steel on a large scale. We must start with the production of the machine which makes the machine. So long as you have not got these basic things, you are dependent on others and can never really grow rapidly enough. Once you have got these basic things, you grow as rapidly as you like. It depends upon your own energy, you are not bound down by an external factor; you start a process of self-growth. " In his emphasis on industrialisation. Nehru was greatly influenced by the strategy of planning followed by former Soviet Russia.

Nehru carried through this basic strategy of planned development. While Nehru felt that large-scale industries were essential to India's economic development, the Gandhians put their faith in small-scale decentralized enterprise. The 1934 resolution of the Working Committee on Swadeshi reaffirmed in 'unequivocal terms' the impermissibility of competition...... on Congress Platforms and in Congress exhibitions between mill-made cloth and hand-spun and hand-wooven Khadi and stated that for articles other than cloth, Congress activity should be restricted to useful articles manufactured in India through cottage and other small industries which are in need of popular education for their support.

Nehru circumvented this sizeable road-block in the following way:

"It is clear that the Congress considered it unnecessary to push large-scale industries through its organization and left this to the state as well as to their own resources. It did not decide in any way against such large-scale industry. Now that the Congress is, to some extent, identifying itself with the State, it cannot ignore the question of establishing and encouraging large-scale industries..... It is clear therefore that not only is it open to this committee and to the Planning Commission to consider the whole question of large-scale industries in India, in all its aspects, but that the committee will be failing in its duty if it did not do so. There can be no planning if such Planning does not include big industries. But in making our plans we have to remember the basic Congress Policy of encouraging cottage industries." (Note of Congress Policy, 21 December 1938 in Shah, Rep. NPC, p. 35). The National Planning Committee in 1948 suggested that support and protection of cottage industries was necessary only until the country reached 'the ideal of self-sufficiency.' There are some critics who point out that issues of fundamental importance have been raised in Congress only to be left in confusion. Nehru's 'step by step' policy was producing some muddy compromises.

The concepts of perspective planning, medium-term planning and Annual Plans were introduced into the technology of Indian Planning during Nehru's time. Nehru had no doubt in his mind about the fifteen-year objectives. The most important of course was the removal of poverty. It was not enough to increase the national income or the per capita income; it was also important to ensure minimum levels of living for the vast masses who groaned under sub-standard levels of living.

Time and again, Nehru emphasized that the strategy governing planning in India was to industrialize and that meant the basic industries being given the first place. At the same time, Nehru did not believe in rigidity and doctrinaire approach. He proclaimed his belief in "our capacity in India to win over people rather than fight them." He firmly believed that "we can bring about social changes and development by the pressure of democracy and also by a friendly, co-operative approach rather than the approach of struggle and elimination." Thus he believed in the humane approach.

Nehru, the Socialist

Socialism is another contribution of Nehru to India. He put the country on the road towards a socialistic pattern of society. But Nehru's socialism is democratic socialism. Right from 1920s, Nehru always strove to see that the relevant Congress resolutions indicated 'an approval of socialistic theories.' Nehru always held that Congress *de facto* went socialist in 1929. In one of the Lok Sabha debates in 1961, he said, "Ever since 1929, the Congress has had two objectives in view, democracy and socialism. Socialism was not put in its objective and creed and all that but in its resolutions it appeared. Gradually, the idea has developed, but the basic concept has been there in the Congress since 1929."

During the period of the formulation of the Second Five Year Plan. Nehru and his economic adviser Mahalanobis developed a distinct Indian Planning ideology, to which the Avadi meeting of the National Congress gave expression in its resolution on the 'socialistic pattern of society.'

Whether others with him really believed in socialism, we do not know. But Nehru's public approval of socialism virtually became an act of policy. At a meeting of the National Development Council (NDC) in November 1954, in a speech about his Planning Philosophy he said:

"The picture I have in mind is definitely and absolutely a socialistic picture of society. I am not using the word in a dogmatic sense at all, but in the sense of meaning largely that the means of production should be socially-owned and controlled for the benefit of society as a whole. There is plenty of room for private enterprise there, provided the main aim is kept clear." Accordingly, the Second Plan involved a great deal of public enterprise. Nehru himself underlined this in the emphasis which he placed on heavy industry, particularly machine-building industry. On the other hand, in the same speech. Nehru emphasized the need for the development of 'small and cottage and village industry' as a means of satisfying the demand for consumer goods, providing employment, and diversifying the rural economy. As one of the means of achieving his objectives, he envisaged changes in the Government's industrial policy. He said that it was necessary that "the whole industrial policy should be revised. The Government wanted to encourage private enterprise; but they wanted to encourage the State enterprise even more." These objectives were incorporated in the 1956 Industrial Policy Resolution. Nehru also realized the need for external assistance in the early phases of planning for development.

Conclusion

We may note that Nehru was not really a socialist in the Marxist sense with its doctrine of class war, violent revolution and dictatorship of the proletariat. Nehru believed that there was no need for contradiction between socialism and individualism. In one of his letters to Subhash Chandra Bose he wrote in 1934 "...... I suppose, I am temperamentally and by training an individualist and intellectually a socialist..... I hope that socialism does not kill or suppress individuality; indeed I am attracted to it because it will release innumerable individuals from economic and cultural bondage." Thus, there can be no doubt that Nehru was not a doctrinaire socialist. The private sector had an assured place in his system. And his socialist society was not of a totalitarian character nor did it subordinate the individual to the State.

Nehru's basic policies were right for India. There can be no real controversy about the emphasis he laid on human dignity, world peace, democracy, secularism, planning and development, socialism, national integration, science and technology. But one of the fundamental attacks on the policies of Nehru has been in respect of the strategy of planning. It has been alleged that the priorities, assigned by him in India's planned development have been based on a mistaken imitation of Soviet Planning and that higher priority should have been given to agriculture and consumer goods industries instead of capital goods industries. But we may note that the emphasis placed on capital goods industries was result of his desire to furnish the country with domestic supplies of the crucial inputs of economic growth so that the rate of growth could be much faster than if the country had to rely essentially on foreign aid for its requirements of capital and intermediate goods. And it is not correct to suggest that Planning under Nehru did not give sufficient priority to agriculture.

There is also criticism about the 'softness' of the Indian Government during the Nehru era and the adverse effects it had on the pace of social and economic development of the nation. Nehru was soft in his policies because he thought it was necessary in a pluralistic and traditional society wedded to democratic principles. That is why, he did not want to bring about the changes by the mere use of Governmental power and brutal force.

P.C. MAHALANOBIS

Introduction

Any discussion on plan models with reference to India usually starts with a discussion of the aggregative models associated with the name of Professor P. C. Mahalanobis, who is regarded as the Father of Statistics in India. Mahalanobis was a member of the Planning Commission and he was a close adviser to Nehru on economic affairs, especially on matters relating to planning.

Mahalanobis has developed a one-sector model, a two-sector model and a four-sector model. The one-sector model is similar to Harrod-Domar model in many respects. The two-sector model bears remarkable resemblance to a much earlier model developed by the Soviet economist, Feldman in 1928. The four-sector model is an exercise in numerical calculation of investment allocation in the short run.

Mahalanobis' one-sector Model

As we have already noted, Mahalanobis' one-sector model resembles very-closely Harrod-Domar growth model.

During the course of a lecture delivered in 1952 Mahalanobis used a simple model to draw the following quantitative conclusions: "If it is desired to double the per capita income in India say, in 35 years (with population continuing at the present rate), then the per capita net national income must increase at the rate of 2 per cent a year, and the total net national income must increase at the rate of at least a three-and-a quarter per cent (3-1/4%) per year. To attain this rate of growth, it would be necessary to make new investments at the rate of something like 10 or 11 per cent of the net income per year, that is the rate of investment must be roughly of the order of Rs. 900 or Rs. 1,000 crores per year. This means that there must be additional investments to the extent of something like Rs. 400 or Rs. 500 crores per year over and above what is being invested at present. The figures given above are of course, extremely rough and are only dimensional in nature."

In Mahalanobis model, growth was defined as the rate of increase of income (per person). Professor Mahalanobis has included population growth in the model. Otherwise, in its mathematical form, it would have been difficult to distinguish it from Harrod-Domar model. While the Harrod-Domar model is a descriptive model in describing certain movements in a market (capitalist) economy associated with its process of growth, the Mahalanobis model is an operational model. It provides a simple computational formula for working out the consequences of varying the rate of investment in terms of varying long-term growth paths.

We may note here that Mahalanobis did not say anything about the manner in which the rate of investment was to be raised to the level of 10-11% of the national income to achieve a reasonably high rate of growth. Further, he had no occasion to draw a distinction (as the Planning Commission did in the First Plan model) between average and marginal rate of saving. He treated the average rate of saving as constant, whereas in the Planning Commission's model it was the marginal rate of saving that was assumed to be so.

Mahalanobis' Two Sector Model*

The two-sector model is the most famous of Mahalanobis models. He presented the model in 1953.[1] This model is very similar to a model that was published as early as 1928 by the Russian economist Feldman.

In the two-sector model, Mahalanobis identified the rate of growth of investment in the economy with the rate of growth of output in the capital goods (sector) industries within the economy. One of the important assumptions of the model is this: The economy is divided into two parts according to the final use of products, consumer goods and capital goods. There is no sector defined as producing intermediate goods.

The approach in the two sector model has the following developmental philosophy: If you want a high rate of growth of consumption in the long run, then the best policy is to give priority to the development of investment goods industries over consumer goods industries, even though the latter might have higher capital-output ratios and even though you cannot eat machines. It may be noted that this development philosophy was at the bottom of Soviet Planning experience in the 1930s.

The above approach was carried over later into a more elaborate formulation (four-sector model) by Prof. Mahalanobis for preparing the Draft Plan formulation of the Second Five Year Plan. The new features introduced into the model were meant primarily to take into account the employment aspects of development and in particular, the problem of absorbing the additions to labour force during the period of the Second Plan.

The Plan Frame (P. C. Mahalanobis: Draft Recommendations for the Formulation of the Second Five Year Plan, 1956-61) which appeared on 17th March 1955 was based on a four-sector model of the Indian economy. Into the Plan Frame were built certain assumptions that were already accepted policy, such as a 5 per cent annual rate of growth and the production of 6 million tons of iron and steel in the last plan year.

In the Plan Frame, Mahalanobis gave top priority to the promotion of rapid growth 'by increasing the scope and importance of the public sector, and the development of heavy industries to strengthen the foundations of economic independence.' Production of the required supplies of consumers' goods would be mainly 'through household and hand industries,' which were to be protected against competition from the factory made articles. Agricultural productivity came fifth in the list, followed by housing, health and education, the liquidation of unemployment (ten years) and an increase in the national income of 25 per cent.

The argument in favour of this developmental pattern runs as follows:

Heavy industry was to increase the country's capacity for capital formation and thus the general rate of industrialization and to make India independent of foreign imports of producer goods. The labour-intensive household industries would offset inflationary tendencies by meeting the increased demand for consumer goods and create relatively more employment.... among the poorer sections of

---

*   This is sometimes, referred to as Mahalanobis-Feldman Two-sector Model.
[1]   P.C. Mahalanobis, "Some Observations on the Process of Growth of National Income." Sankhya, Vol. 12, Part 4, Sept. 1953.

the people so that a greater portion of the increase in income would go to them.' Factory produced consumer goods had to be limited in quantity, in order to conserve resources and maximize welfare, until such time as unemployment had been liquidated, their expansion could be justified only when domestic supplies of certain items (*e.g.*, antibiotics) could be increased in no other way, or when the factory product was an important earner of foreign exchange. As for agriculture, it was assumed that, the necessary increases in production could be obtained by the more intensive application of the specifics already adopted: Land Reforms, National Extension and Community Development, Public Credit and Co-operatives.

On the subject of 'balanced development and controls,' the Plan Frame stressed the need for 'adequate increases' in basic services such as electricity, irrigation, transport and communications; for financial operations (*e.g.*, public sector investments, expenditure on social services) to avoid both inflation and deflation; for the maintenance of adequate foodgrain and raw material services, and for the use of physical controls, if need be, to deal with short-run shortages. Surprisingly, the Plan Frame suggested that deflation rather than inflation was likely to be the main problem.

There is no need for specific justification for the emphasis on the public sector, as this was already government policy. The public sector was to expand relatively faster than the private sector and its contribution to capital formation was to be increased by government's entry into the fields of banking, insurance, foreign trade and internal trade. The private sector was to be made to 'conform in a general way' with the overall production programme. It was to be offered various inducements to take up forms of investment given priority in the plan.

To provide resources, the rate of investment would have to rise from 7 to 11 per cent of national income over the plan period. Resources for the public sector would be obtained by increased taxation, the profits of public enterprises, and deficit financing (to a limit of Rs. 1000-1,200 crores). Payment for increased imports of capital goods was to be met by foreign assistance, the withdrawal of sterling balances, the curtailment of non-essential imports, and the promotion of exports.

The experience of the Second and Third Five Year Plans emphasized the lack of realism in the assumptions upon which these proposals were based. The problem of inflation was grossly underestimated and the financial difficulties were brushed aside. The balance of payments situation was given little consideration, the prospects for agriculture were exaggerated and the capital-output ratio was put far too low.

When the Plan Frame was presented for comment to the Planning Commission's Panel of Economists, the body in its report stressed the complementarity of agriculture and industry and the 'importance of maintaining and expanding agricultural production in the Second Plan period.' The report criticized Mahalanobis's excessive reliance on deficit financing. For it might disrupt the price structure and create instability.

Only one economist, Professor Shenoy, disagreed in *toto* with Mahalanobis's idea about planning. But as he was committed to *Laissez-faire* methods in a doctrinaire fashion, no one, except a few businessmen, took much notice of his criticism. But before the publication of the Plan Frame, Professor B.K. Madan made some criticisms of Mahalanobis's approach in the papers he presented to the Planning Commission. He expressed three disagreements on matters of principle. The first one related to Mahalanobis's 'short-term' approach to the unemployment problem. Professor Madan was of the view that the emphasis on the protection of village industry was misplaced. 'Decentralized industry' he wrote, 'has considerable advantages from the socio-economic point of view and can be successful in the economic race, if it is technically assisted with power and machine. But decentralisation with technical stagnation is a retrograde policy which will lead to economic reaction, not development.' Second, there was the question of balance. According to Madan, "The prevention of inflation required a larger expansion of consumer goods production than the Plan Frame provided for." He further argued that there was no point in aiming at 'practical self-sufficiency' in the production of capital goods, and that the strengthening of the infrastructure of the economy (i.e., irrigation, transport and communications, power, education, public health and housing) should continue to be given major emphasis. Thirdly, he was of the view that the Frame's estimates of the increment in productivity obtainable from a given quantum of extra investment were unrealistic, But Madan and other critics did not succeed in producing a viable alternative framework in quantitative terms. So, the Plan Frame soon became 'the book of the plan.' It was something unfortunate. Although Mahalanobis had performed a valuable service in raising the planners' sights, he had also done them disservice by presenting them with a document which was based on unrealistic assumptions, and which made no serious attempt to discuss priorities in terms of costs and benefits. There are some critics who say that Mahalanobis, must bear much of the blame for the subsequent planning muddles. For he created a planning 'orthodoxy' founded upon nothing much more solid than an enthusiasm for heavy industry and a preference for Soviet-type methods. In conclusion, we may note that in spite of many limitations, Mahalanobis's model is historically important and the Plan Frame became the corner-stone of the Second Five Year Plan of India.

DR. B.R. AMBEDKAR

Dr. B.R. Ambedkar[1] (1891-1956) was a versatile personality. He was the architect of the Indian Constitution, a custodian of social justice and a champion of socialism and state planning.

Almost all the social and political questions which Dr. Ambedkar discussed had an economic dimension. Some of the economic problems he studied included the agrarian reforms of the Indian economy in the context of small holdings and their remedies, the problems of the Indian currency, the evolution of provincial finance in India and the problem of planning and state socialism.

Ambedkar's economic writings included "*Ancient Indian Commerce*" (a thesis submitted to the Columbia University for the award of the Master of Arts degree in 1915), "*National Dividend of India: A Historical and Analytical Study* (a thesis for which he was awarded Phd. degree in economics) by the Columbia University in 1916. A revised version of his Phd. Thesis was published as "The Evolution of Provincial Finance in British India: A study of the Provincial Decentralization of Imperial Finance". Ambedkar's thesis on "*Provincial Decentralization of Imperial Finance in British India*" was accepted for the M.Sc. degree in 1921. And his thesis "*The Problem of the Rupee*" was accepted for the award of the D.Sc., degree by the London School of Economics in 1923.

The main economic ideas of Dr. B.R. Ambedkar may be studied under four broad headings: (*i*) Financial Economics, (*ii*) Agricultural Economics, (*iii*) Economics of Caste, and (*iv*) Economics of Socialism.

I. Financial Economics

Much of the work done by Ambedkar during his stay abroad mostly during the period 1913-1923, was in the field of Financial Economics. He made a pioneering study of the evolution of provincial finance in British India. It studied mainly the provincial decentralization of Imperial Finance.

According to Dr. Ambedkar, "The inadequacy of imperial finance was mainly due to an unsound fiscal policy. The Government depended heavily on a few taxes such as land tax, customs and salt tax which affected the agriculture, trade and industry and the poor respectively." Under the injurious revenue system of the Imperial Government, the taxing capacity of people decayed so that notwithstanding the numerous resources from which it derived the revenue, the Imperial Government was unable to make both ends meet". In addition to this, there were internal charges on war debts. In short, as Dr. Ambedkar put it, "the bulk of the money raised by injurious taxes were spent in unproductive ways". And education formed no part of the expenditure incurred, and useful public works were lamentably few.

---

[1]   Bhimrao Ramji Ambedkar.

To remedy the serious defects of the Imperial finance, a full federal system was advocated by some officials. Richard Strachey was notable among them. But the idea was opposed by some. Instead, a new arrangement was made under which the revenues and charges remained imperial in their status, but their management was provincialized. Ambedkar refers to the system as "Imperial finance without imperial management." This, in brief, was the origin of the scheme of provincial budgets.

Dr. Ambedkar divided the evolution of provisional finance into three stages: (i) Budget by Assignments (1871-72 to 1876-77); (ii) Budget by Assigned Revenues (1877-78 to 1881-82); and (iii) Budget by Shared Revenues (1882-83 to 1920-1921).

Budget by Assignments (1871-72 to 1876-77)

Under the system of budget by assignments, assignment of funds from the imperial treasury was adopted as a method of supply to balance the provincial budgets. So Dr. Ambedkar called it "Budget by assignments". While commenting on the system Dr. Ambedkar said, "The assignments made to the provincial governments for the year 1871-72 had been declared to be fixed and recurring". Recurring they were, fixed they were not; for, every year since the start, the Government of India kept on adding to and withdrawing from provincial budget, items of charges already incorporated in them. In accordance to these modifications in the incorporated charges, the imperial assignments had to be either reduced or augmented as necessity dictated".

Dr. Ambedkar considered the scheme of provincial budget as economical and beneficial. According to his assessment, "under the system, revenue increased, receipts from services expanded and evasion decreased". But the most radical defect in the system of budget by assignment consisted in its rigidity.

Budget by Assigned Revenues (1877-78 to 1881-82)

Under the system, in place of fixed assignment, the provinces were given certain sources by revenue. The yield depended upon good management. The scheme provided elastic source of revenue. It provided provision to meet the growing needs of the provincial services. This was another stage in the evolution of provincial finance. Because of its distinct mode of supply adopted, Ambedkar called this stage as "budget by assigned revenue". According to him, under the new provision, "the deterrent effect of a deficit to bear and the stimulating effect of a gain to reap made the mechanism of provincial finance as perfect as it could be made from the standpoint of economy in expenditure and productiveness in resource.

Budget by Shared Revenue (1882-83 to 1920-21)

Under the earlier system, the budget was grouped under two distinct categories: wholly imperial and wholly provincial. The new provision carved out a third category of account to be made of jointly imperial and provincial. Ambedkar described the system as "budget by shared revenue". The principle of shared revenue was applied to all the provinces with effect from 1882-83. The earlier system was marked by constant revision at short durations. A great merit of the new system was that in the year 1881-82 settlement, it was made a definite rule that they shall be quinquennial in duration; that is, they shall not be subject to revision before the end of the fifth year from their commencement. The settlement was made quasi-permanent in 1904, and permanent in 1912 and it was there till 1921. And from April 1, 1924, provincial finance in British India entered a new phase.

According to Edwin Seligman, "the value of Dr. Ambedkar's contribution of this discussion lies in the objective recitation of the fact and the impartial analysis of the interesting development that has taken place in his native country. Lessons are applicable to other countries as well, nowhere, to my knowledge, has such a detailed study of the underlying principles been made."

The Problem of the Rupee

In his work, *"The Problem of the Rupee: Its origin and its solution,"* Ambedkar expressed the view that at the close of the Moghul Empire, India, judged by the standards of the time, was economically an advanced country. He found that India had a large trade, well developed banking institutions. Credit played an important role in business transactions. India enjoyed large balance of payments surplus. Later on, the management of Indian currency and foreign exchange at the hands of the British authorities became highly irresponsible and the performance was disappointing.

The Fowler Committee recommended gold exchange standard for India in the place of gold standard. Dr. Ambedkar was totally opposed to the recommendation. As he put it, "While some people regard that report as classical for its wisdom, I regard it as classical for its nonsense." But John Maynard Keynes supported gold exchange standard. Dr. Ambedkar entered into a major debate with him. In his own words, "Our differences extend to almost every proposition he has advanced in favour of the exchange standard. This difference proceeds from the fundamental fact which seems to be quite overlooked by Professor Keynes that nothing will stabilize the rupee unless we stabilize its general purchasing power. That exchange standard does not do. That standard concerns itself only with symptoms and does not go to the disease, indeed, on my showing if any thing, it aggravates the disease."

Prof. Edwin Cannan, while writing a foreword, when the thesis appeared in the form of a book wrote: "I do not share Mr. Ambedkar's hostility to the system, nor accept most of his arguments against it and its advocates. But he hits some nails very squarely on the head, and even when I have thought him quite wrong, I have found a stimulating freshness in his views and reasons. In practical conclusion, I am inclined to think he is right".

Ambedkar had expressed concern at the decline in the external value of the Rupee from 21.63 pence in 1875-76 to 16.73 pence in 1891-92.

II. Agricultural Economics

In 1918, Ambedkar published a paper *"Small Holdings in India and their Remedies"*. Citing Adam Smith's "Wealth of Nations", he made a fine distinction between "consolidation of holdings" and "enlargement of holdings". To him, "consolidation of holdings" was a practical problem whereas "enlargement of holdings" was a theoretical problem. The latter demanded a discussion of the principles which governed the size of a farm.

In any discussion on the size of land holdings, the concept of "economic holding" becomes important. He was very critical of the then existing notion of economic holding which equated a large holding with an economic holding. As he put it, "it is believed that a large holding is somehow an economic holding. It may be said that even Prof. Jevons has fallen a victim to this notion". He criticized the Baroda Committee report also. The committee was appointed to make proposals for the consolidation of small and scattered holdings in the Baroda state in 1917. In his sharp criticism of the Report, he said that, "the case with the Baroda Committee is much worse. Prof. Jevons at least sticks to one definition of an ideal economic holding, but the report of the Baroda Committee suffers from a plurality of definitions."

The definitions of an ideal economic holding, including the one given by Prof. Jevons, view it from the standpoint of consumption rather than production. According to Ambedkar, 'In this lies their error; for consumption is not the correct standard by which to judge the economic character of a holding. It would be perverse accounting to condemn a farm as not paying because its total output does not support the family of the farmer though as a *pro-rata* return for each of its investments, it is the highest.'

Ambedkar's significant contribution to agricultural economics lies in his suggestion that input-output relationship should be true economic test. He had, in his mind, factor proportions and their ideal combination. He believed that industrialization would have a beneficial effect upon agricultural development. He was worried about the rise in the proportion of India's rural population from 64.4% in 1891 to 67.5% in 1901 and 71.5% in 1911.

To Ambedkar, the evil of small holdings in India was not fundamental, but was derived from the parent evil of the maladjustment in her social economy. He observed that population pressure was the chief cause of subdivision and fragmentation of landholdings. The absence of alternative source of income is another cause of subdivision of holdings These things put a premium on small pieces of land. His remedy to the problem is to transfer the idle labour in agricultural sector to non-agricultural channels of production. In his own words, "...this will in one stroke lessen the pressure and destroy the premium that at present weighs heavily on land in India". One can see in this traces of some of the popular remedies suggested to solve the problem of what came to be known as "disguised unemployment" in 1950s. Ambedkar also believed that "...industrialization must precede consolidation. It should never be forgotten that unless we have constructed an effective barrier against the future sub-division and fragmentation of a consolidated holding, it is idle to lay out plans for consolidation. Such a barrier can only be found in industrialization, for it alone can reduce the extreme pressure which causes sub-division of land."

III. Economics of Caste

According to Dr. Ambedkar, the concept of "Chaturvarna" (division of Hindu society into four categories: Brahmin, Kshatriya, Vaisya and Shudra) will fail because the original four castes had multiplied into more than 4,000 castes. It makes the whole concept of division of labour ridiculous. While he agreed that civilized society needed some kind of division of labour, he asserted that in no civilized society should it degenerate into a division of labourers on the basis of hierarchy and watertight compartments. He believed that the caste system based on birth, and on the social status of parents, would not improve individual or social efficiency. And it would not also help the individual to develop his capacities to an optimum level.

The scheduled caste people were the worst sufferers of the evils of caste system. They were considered as "untouchable classes" in the past. And they were socially, educationally, and economically backward. They were known by different names: "Harijans" (a term coined by Narasimha Mehta and popularized by Mahatma Gandhi), "exterior castes", "depressed classes." "Chandalas" and "Panchamas" (the fifth class). The persons who belonged to these castes suffered from many social and economic disabilities.

When the term "depressed classes" was introduced, at the time it was considered superior to the term "untouchables". But Dr. Ambedkar considered the term degrading and contemptuous. In response to representation made by Dr. Ambedkar, the name was changed to scheduled castes by the British Government. But Mahatma Gandhi has preferred to call them "Harijans" meaning, "the children of God".

Dr. Ambedkar believed that caste was an obstacle to social mobility. It resulted in social stratification. He was of the firm view that individuals must be free to change their occupations. Moreover, the caste system caused social tensions.

In an undelivered speech, which he wrote in 1936, he said, "..... unless you change your social order, you can achieve little by way of progress. You cannot mobilize the community either for defence or for offence. You cannot build anything on the foundation of caste. You cannot build up a nation, you cannot build up morality. Anything that you build up on the foundation of caste, will crack and will never be whole."

Dr. Ambedkar felt that money alone did not go to determine the social status of a person in our society. Caste and heredity played a dominant role in determining the social status. Those who do menial jobs (*e.g.*, scavenging) might still be looked down, notwithstanding increase in their money wages. It may be noted that scavengers occupied the lowest status even among the so called "untouchables" in the past. Dr. Ambedkar pointed out that many poor brahmins enjoy better social status than relatively rich shudras.

We may note that Pandit Jawaharlal Nehru had similar views on the caste system. "The ultimate weakness and failing of the caste system and the Indian social structure were that they degraded a mass of human beings and gave them no opportunities to get out of that condition educationally, culturally and economically."

The caste system has resulted in the absence of social democracy in India as distinct from political democracy. Dr. Ambedkar, in his final address to the Constituent Assembly said: "On the social plane, we have in India a society based on the principles of graded inequality which means elevation of some and degradation of others. On the economic plane, we have a society in which there are some who have immense wealth, as against many who live in abject poverty. On the 26th January, 1950, we are going to enter into a life of contradictions. In politics, we will have equality and in social and economic life, we have inequality. In politics we will be recognizing the principle of one man one vote and one vote one value. In our social and economic life, we shall by reason of our social and economic structure, continue to deny the principle of one man one value .... If we continue to deny it for long, we will do so only by putting our political democracy to peril."

IV. Economics of Socialism

Dr. Ambedkar was a socialist. He was a champion of state socialism. He advocated the nationalization of all key industries and suggested state ownership of land and collective farming. He was for state monopoly of insurance business. Not only that, he advocated compulsory insurance for every citizen.

Ambedkar's idea of state socialism is based on a unique political philosophy which is a blend of Marxism and Buddhism. He admits that "a comparison between Karl Marx and Buddha may be regarded as a joke". The Marxists may laugh at the idea of treating Marx and Buddha together because to them Marx is so modern and Buddha is so ancient.

According to Ambedkar, "Karl Marx is no doubt the father of modern socialism and communism but he was not interested mainly in propounding the theory of socialism, that had been done long before him by others. Marx was more interested in proving that his socialism was scientific. His crusade was much against the capitalists as it was against those whom he called the Utopian socialists. He disliked them both. It is necessary to note this point because Marx attached greatest importance to the scientific character of his socialism. All the doctrines which Marx propounded had no other purpose than to establish his contention that his brand of socialism was scientific and not Utopian.

By scientific socialism, what Karl Marx meant was that his brand of socialism was inevitable and inescapable and society was moving towards it and that nothing could prevent its march. It is to prove this contention of his that Marx principally laboured."

Ambedkar was not a blind follower of Marx. In fact, he questioned the very (economic) basis of class conflict and thought it was irrelevant to the Indian situation. And he did not consider the economic interpretation of history as the only interpretation. Further more, he did not accept that the proletariat had been progressively pauperized. And he did not believe in the Marxian claim that socialism was inevitable.

According to Ambedkar, what remains of Karl Marx is a "residue of fire", small but still important." He gave the residue in the following *four* propositions:

1. The function of philosophy is to reconstruct the world and not to waste its time in explaining the origin of the world.
2. There is conflict of interest between classes and classes.
3. Private ownership of property brings power to one class and sorrow to another through exploitation.
4. It is necessary for the good of the society that the sorrow be removed by the abolition of private property.

Taking the above points from the Marxian creed, Ambedkar made a comparison between Buddha and Karl Marx and brought the similarities and differences between Buddha and Marx. He concluded by saying that "the differences are about the means. The end is common to both." The means adopted by Buddha were to convert a man by changing his moral disposition to follow the path voluntarily. The means adopted by the communists are equally clear, short and swift. They are: (*i*) violence and (*ii*) dictatorship of the proletariat.

Dr. Ambedkar advocated the establishment of state socialism with parliamentary democracy and without dictatorship. He wanted "to retain parliamentary democracy and to prescribe state socialism by the Law of the Constitution so that it will be beyond the reach of a parliamentary majority to suspend, amend or abrogate it. It is only by this that one can achieve the triple object, namely to establish socialism, retain Parliamentary Democracy and avoid Dictatorship.

Conclusion

There is no doubt that Dr. Ambedkar was a great economist. But his academic work as an economist was eclipsed by his greater contributions in the field of law and politics. Above all, he was a great social reformer.

C. RAJAGOPALACHARI

Sri C. Rajagopalachari was no economist in the ordinary sense of the term. He was a great statesman and an able administrator with an intellect as sharp as a razor's edge.

Till late 1950s, the economic philosophy of Rajaji was more or less same as that of the Indian National Congress Party which was the ruling party. But in due course, he was disillusioned with the policies and programmes of the Congress Party, especially Planning and the Industrial policy with its emphasis on a big role for Government, and emphasis on a system of licences, controls, permits and quotas. He described the Congress Government as 'Licence-Permit Quota Raj'.

The fundamental economic philosophy and principles advocated by Rajaji since the late 1950s are the same as the philosophy and the principles of the Swatantra Party (Party of Freedom) which he founded in 1959.

In the words of Rajaji, "The Swatantra Party stands for the protection of the individual citizen against the increasing trespasses of the State. It is an answer to the challenge of so-called socialism of the Indian Congress Party. It is founded on the conviction that social justice and welfare can be attained through the fostering of individual interest and individual enterprise in all fields better than through state ownership and Government control."

We shall discuss now some of the basic economic ideas of Rajaji.

1. *Individual Freedom:* Rajaji believed that the progress, welfare and happiness of the people depended on individual incentive, enterprise and energy. He stood for the principle of maximum freedom for the individual and minimum interference by the state. Of course, he approves of the obligations of the State to prevent and punish the anti-social activities, to protect the weaker elements of society, and to create the conditions in which weaker elements can thrive and be fruitful.

   In other words, he is opposed to the increasing state interference.

2. *Faith in people and in Gandhiji's principle of Trusteeship:* He believed in the inherent goodness and altruistic nature of human beings and therefore wanted the State to have faith in people. He supported the doctrine of Trusteeship advocated by Gandhiji.

   Rajaji felt that, the policies of the government should be founded on people and not on state compulsion and the encouragement of hatred and conflict between class and class expropriation, and more and more powers to government officials at the expense of the freedom of the citizens.

3. *Respect for Fundamental Rights guaranteed by the Constitution:* Rajaji was of the view that the policies of Government in power and the plan forecasts gave room for a lot of uncertainty, Therefore, he felt that a sense of stability and incentive for individual effort could be restored only by, strict adherence to the fundamental rights and guarantees specified in the Constitution

as originally adopted in respect of freedom of property, trade and occupation, and just compensation for any property compulsorily acquired by the State for public purposes.

4. *Fulfilment of Basic Needs:* Rajaji was of the view that in the policies adopted for national development, priority must be assigned to the basic needs of the people, namely food, water, housing and clothing.

5. *Right to educate children according to one's choice:* Rajaji believed that every citizen has a fundamental right to educate his children according to his choice and in a free atmosphere untrammelled by official directives and that State should afford facilities for such education without discrimination.

It may be noted that Rajaji suggested a scheme of basic education where a student after studying a few hours in school would spend some more hours in getting training in vocational education, generally in the occupation followed by his/her parents. But the scheme was opposed by some on the ground that it would perpetuate occupation based caste and result in social stratification.

6. *Increasing Food Production:* Rajaji gave top priority for increasing food production and he believed that the best way to attain that was through the self-employed peasant proprietors who are interested in obtaining the highest yield from the land.

Rajaji wanted to bring about agricultural improvement by providing material and psychological inducements. But he was not for disturbing the harmony of rural life. He was of the view that there should be no disturbance of ownership, management and cultivation of land. And he wanted more effective programme in respect of irrigation and the supply of material, implements, credit and marketing facilities. While Rajaji believed in the need for giving every kind of help to agriculture, he was totally opposed to the idea of collective farming and bureaucratic management of the rural economy. He suggested that steps might be taken for maintaining a reasonable and steady price for agricultural produce, which was in parity with other prices.

7. *Industry:* In industry, Rajaji believed in incentives for higher production and expansion inherent in competitive enterprise. At the same time, he wanted adequate safeguards for the protection of labour, and against unreasonable profits, prices and dividends where there is no competition.

Rajaji stood for restriction of State enterprise to heavy industry such as are necessary to supplement private enterprise in that field, national services such as Railways, and starting of new enterprises which are difficult for private initiative.

Rajaji was opposed to State entering the field of trade and disturbing free distribution. He was against controls and official management with all its wastefulness and inefficiency.

Rajaji believed that in the field of production, the free choice of the producer and the consumer must be given an important place.

8. *Preservation of the freedom of small artisans, craftsmen and traders:* Rajaji wanted to preserve the freedom of small self-employed artisans, craftsmen and traders who were in the danger of losing their occupation and income by reason of the policy of Statism. He pointed out that the disappearance of these persons would add to our unemployment problem.

9. *Greater thrift in public expenditure:* Rajaji advocated greater thrift in public expenditure. With regard to taxation, his view was that it should be kept at such low level that it should not interfere with the standard of living of the people, both urban and rural. Tax revenue should be just necessary and sufficient for carrying on administration and such social and economic services as are taken by the State. Taxation should not be too high to prevent capital formation and private investment.

10. *Opposed to deficit financing and foreign loans:* Rajaji was opposed to a programme of planned development based on crippling taxation, abnormal deficit financing and foreign loans which are beyond the capacity of the country to repay.

11. *Opposition to policies that created inflation:* Rajaji was opposed to all policies that led to excessive inflation and high prices. For these things reduced the value of savings and fixed incomes and created undue hardship for the present generation in the hope of a gain in the distant future which was uncertain.

12. *Reduction in the cost of public administration:* Rajaji believed in the reduction of the cost of public administration. He did not want the Government to do things which the private individuals and agencies were already doing because he felt that it would result in unproductive waste of national resources.

13. *Decentralized distribution in industry:* Rajaji felt that the State would serve the nation best by providing facilities for a decentralized distribution of industry. According to him, the State should limit its own regulatory function to the prevention and punishment of anti-social activities.

14. *Full employment and balanced development of industries:* Rajaji pleaded for the creation of opportunities for full and lasting employment in all sectors of life. He believed in a balanced development of capital goods industries, organized consumer goods industries and rural industries that provide supplementary employment in the small scale processing of the products of agriculture.

15. *Fair deal for labour:* Rajaji was for fair deal for labour and for linking wages to increased productivity. He believed in the workers' right to organise for the purpose of collective bargaining. He was for harmonising the interests of capital and labour when they got into conflict.

16. *Belief in the rule of Law and Independent Judiciary:* Rajaji was against putting any form of political pressure on officials that would prevent them from discharging their duties in a fair and just manner without discrimination. Rajaji was a firm believer in the Rule of Law and an independent Judiciary.

17. *Faith in Gandhian teaching and people:* Rajaji was a firm believer in the teachings of Gandhiji. Like Gandhiji, he believed in maintaining faith in the people, and in the efficiency of truth and non-violence.

Conclusion

One can see in the economic ideas of Rajaji the basic principles of *Laissez-Faire* philosophy advocated by the physiocrats. Rajaji's ideas of maximum individual freedom, minimum role for Government, lower taxes, minimum expenditure by government and balanced budget are all part and parcel of *Laissez-Faire* philosophy.

After nearly 60 years of our planning experience in India, the recent major changes in our economic policy with its accent on deregulation, decontrols, privatization, in a way, show that Rajaji was right in some of his basic economic thoughts.

V. K. R. V. RAO

According to professor P.R. Brahmananda, "the great trinity of pre-independent and post-independent Indian economists consisted of Gadgil, Vakil and Rao. These scholars were imbibed with a missionary zeal and analysed the Indian economic problems with a view to designing and propagating economic policies/programmes and plans to India's national advantage."

Dr. V.K.R.V: Rao was a prolific writer. Some of his important books and articles are *"What is wrong with Indian Economic Life?"* (1938), *"National Income of British India"* (1940), *"Investment, Income and the Multiplier in an Underdeveloped Economy"* (1952), *"Deficit Financing, Capital Formation and Price Behaviour"* (1953), *"Essays in Economic Development"* (1964), *"Education and Human Resource Development"* (1970), *"Gandhian Alternative to Western Socialism"* (1970), *"Indian Road to Democratic Socialism"* (1977), *"Inflation and India's Economic Crisis"* (1973), *"Food, Nutrition and Poverty"* (1982) and *"India's National Income,"* 1950-1980 (1987).

V. K. R. V. Rao was deeply interested in three large themes. They were: (*i*) National Income, (*ii*) Food, nutrition and the distribution of food (and income) (This theme gave him an angle on poverty) (*iii*) Employment and occupational distribution.

National Income Methodology

As an applied economist, Rao's name is remembered for his pioneering work on the national income of India. Rao was a pupil of J.M. Keynes and he worked with Colin Clark. H.W. Singer considered V.K.R.V. Rao "the best equipped of all Keynes' pupils to develop the national income concepts suited to India and developing countries generally; to analyse the concepts of investment, saving and the multiplier in an underdeveloped economy; and to study the compatibility of the national incomes of industrialized and underdeveloped countries."

Before Rao, economists who made estimates of the national income of India did so from the angle of measuring poverty of India and attributed India's poverty largely to the British Rule in India. But Dr. Rao "perceived the problem of estimation as a purely scientific exercise. This was his unique achievement at that time and gave credibility to his work." (P.R. Brahmananda).

Over the years, Rao became more and more conscious of the analytical limitations of inter-country comparisons of national and per capita income. His mind was bothered by three main issues: First, a great deal of marketed and exchange value derived output in developed countries gets unrecorded and under-estimated in developing countries. Second, a significant portion of national income in developed countries represents compensating or counter-vailing costs of final goods. This is so both in material production and tertiary sectors. Third, there is no scientific basis for estimating values of government expenditures because all of the expenditure may not have a marketable/commercial significance.

In his 1983 book on national income, Rao focused on the links between income and consumption, the behaviour of capital-output ratios, national and regional poverty changes and differences, rural-urban differences in income and differences in relative outputs and relative occupational patterns.

Dr. Rao may be rightly described as the unquestioned leader in the area of national income (of India).

Rao's paper on "Full Employment and Economic Development" was one of the earliest contributions in the field of development oriented towards employment. In the words of Singer, the theme, "subsequently occupied the minds of many people and proved particularly seminal in the development of the ILO World Employment programme.

In the later stages, when questions of poverty and basic needs came to the forefront in debates on economic development, we find that Rao gave early attention to "the human factor in economic growth." In fact, it was the title of one of his well-known papers.

International Development Authority

During the years 1947-1950, Rao was the chairman of the United Nations Sub-Commission for Economic Development. At that time, he was the guiding spirit of the Sub-Commission which shaped early thinking on development problems in the U.N. He was the author of the proposal for an International Development Authority. At that time, the proposal was strongly criticised. But today, the idea is embodied both in the International Development Agency (IDA), the soft money agency of the World Bank, and the UN Development Programme (UNDP).

International Food Aid

Rao was influential in creating ideas and shaping policy in the international aspects of the attack on world poverty, not only through his contributions to questions of international aid and improved flows of external resources, but also through his activities in the field of food aid. His paper on "International Aid of Surplus Food for Economic Development" is evidence of his contribution.

Support for Socialism

During the early phases of planning in India, Rao supported the case of a socialist India, where the State would control the commanding heights of the economy and the public sector would play a dominant role in economic development. He was soft till early 70s on inflation but his attitude to inflation changed slowly thereafter. He came round to the view that the permanent cure for inflation would require a control on the annual growth rate of money supply.

During the 1950s, and 1960s Rao was a strong advocate of priority for heavy industry. But from 1970s, he emphasized the need for giving priority for agriculture and rural development. He became concerned about growing, inequalities in urban and rural incomes. Towards the fag end of his life, Rao started emphasizing the Gandhian ideals of simplicity, sacrifice and hardwork.

Rao's Views on Industrialization

In his pamphlet "What is wrong with Indian Economic Life?" (1938), Rao gave the following reasons for low per capita income and low levels of per capita nutrition in India.

(*i*) Uneconomic holdings with sub-division and fragmentation;

(*ii*) Low levels of water availability for crops;

(*iii*) Excess population pressure on agriculture due to the absence of a large industrial sector;

(*iv*) Absence of capital and of advance protection keeping down growth of home industry; and

(*v*) Absence of autonomy in currency policy, and in general in monetary matters encouraging holding of gold. The significance of the pamphlet lies in the fact that it looked at the Indian economic problem as a whole and in a relatively integrated manner.

In his presidential address to the Indian Economic Association in 1949, Rao focused on the need for high level of capital formation for achieving rapid economic development of India.

In an article in the "Indian Economic Review" in 1952, he attributed the low levels of productivity of land and labour to low level of capital formation. In the same year, Ragnar Nurkse published his book, "*Capital Formation in Underdeveloped Countries*" wherein, he said that low capital formation is the major cause of low level of development of poor countries.

Rao, in his paper on "Deficit Financing" argued for supplementing voluntary savings by a measure of planned forced savings. It may be noted that the Taxation Enquiry Committee Report also recommended forced savings through excise duties on commodities of mass consumption.

We may note that Rao supported Nehru's approach to economic development which was based on Mahalanobis model. In the early stages, Rao strongly believed that industrialization would provide a solution to the population pressure in agriculture. He honestly felt that industrialisation would solve the problems of unemployment and poverty. But he became disappointed after watching the performance of planning in India for a few decades. Towards the close of his life, Rao suggested that priority must be given to rural development in India's Five Year Plans.

Village Clusters

In his scheme of rural industrialization, Rao felt that rural communities had to be given a viable base. Therefore he suggested that a cluster of villages should form a unit for rural development, so that both social and economic interactions between villages could develop, and they could effectively generate and fashion their own development with a more meaningful participation by people. Rao thought that the prospects of absorbing the huge rural workforce into rural areas was rather limited and therefore he emphasized that the economic base of rural areas had to be made more viable through the diversification of rural economy and improving its infrastructure.

From 1971 census, Rao found that villages with less than 1,000 population constituted as many as 78 per cent of all villages, which were inhabited by 38 per cent of the total rural people. On the other hand, only 23 per cent of the rural people lived in villages with 5,000 and above population. And the situation did not improve very much by 1981. According to 1981 census, villages with less than 1,000 population were 73% accounting for 38 per cent of rural population. On the other hand, villages with 5,000 or more population accounted for 15.5 per cent of rural population. That is why Rao suggested that "the base has to be cluster of villages.... having a total of population of around 5,000 persons. The unit area for rural development has to be large enough to be viable, diversified enough to enable integration and at the same time, small enough to establish sense of community identity and a feeling of belonging". According to Rao, "neither a small village nor a taluk (or Block) met the purpose of being a unit area for development." It may be noted that Rao did not, in general favour a wholesale resettlement of rural households for this purpose. He did not have "collective farms" or "communes" in mind when he suggested the concept of "cluster of villages". Far from it, Rao was happy that later a Panchayat Raj system in Karnataka took his advice and adopted a cluster of villages as the basic unit of the organization. Of course, the upper limit set for the village cluster was 10,000 instead of 5,000 as suggested by Rao.

Investment, Income and Multiplier

Rao's examination of the interrelation between investment, income and multiplier in an underdeveloped economy (1952) was his major contribution to macroeconomic theory. He followed the above with a paper on full employment and economic theory (1953) and another paper on deficit financing for capital formation and price behaviour in an underdeveloped country (1953). In the words of professor Brahmananda, "these three papers, along with that on Nature and Purpose of Economic Activity, would probably represent his best theoretical contribution."

Conclusion

As a thinker, teacher, economic adviser and direct policy-maker, Dr. V.K.R.V. Rao followed the footsteps of his great teacher, John Maynard Keynes.

D.R. GADGIL

Professor Gadgil was an eminent and practical Indian economist. He has written a number of books and articles. His important publications included *The Industrial Evolution of India in Recent Times* (1924), *Imperial Preference for India* (1932), *Regulation of Wages and other Problems of Industrial Labour in India* (1943), *War and Indian Economic Policy* (1943) *Federating India* (1945), *The Federal Problem in India* (1947) and *Economic Policy and Development* (1955).

Industrial Evolution of India

The 19th century writers like Ranade and R.C. Dutt studied the process of de-industrialisation brought about by East India Company and later by the policies of the British Government. But along with the decline of the small industries, a new stage of industrialisation started beginning with cotton textiles and jute industries. These industries were stared largely with foreign capital. In cotton textiles alone, Indian capital predominated. For a long time, practically there was no study of the growth of the new industries. Of course, the Industrial Commission Report of 1918 and the Fiscal Commission Report of 1921-22 covered most of the problems in their Reports. But, still there was no systematic study of these new industries. So there was a great need for a comprehensive study of the growth of industries by an economist. This gap was filled by B.R. Gadgil's book *"The Industrial Evolution of India"* (1924).

The first edition of the book covered the period 1860-1914. In subsequent editions, Prof. Gadgil covered the period upto 1939. Though Gadgil modestly considered his work mainly as a 'sketch of economic history' we may note that at the time he wrote, it was the best study of the contemporary problems of Indian industry.

Gadgil started with the sudden and complete collapse of the old handicrafts in the 19th century and then traced the development of the means of transport, the commercialisation of agriculture and the increase in population pressure on land. He found that there was a close connection between agricultural and industrial prosperity.

Gadgil has divided the entire period 1880-1939 into four sub-periods (1880-1895, 1895-1914, 1914-1928, and 1929 to 1939). According to Gadgil, they were alternating periods of prosperity and adversity.

According to Gadgil, "the most notable feature of the economic transition of the period 1860-80 was the decline of handicrafts." This was caused by the railway policy, free trade policy of the then Government and lack of technical education.

During the period 1880-95, commercial crops like cotton and jute assumed importance in Indian agriculture. Irrigation benefited mostly the commercial crops and agriculture in general, was prosperous. During the period, the established industries such as cotton textiles, jute industry, plantations progressed steadily but practically there were no new industries. It may be noted that the first Factory Act came in 1881 against the use of low cost labour in India. Gadgil gave good description of the conditions of industrial labour at the end of the 19th century.

The period 1895-1914 started with the severe famines of 1896-97. There was a severe setback in agriculture and in industry. Gadgil, of course, did not mention the beneficial effects of the Swadeshi movement on the growth of industries and financial institutions in India in general and Eastern India in particular. The movement created a demand for Indian goods. As he put it. "The greatest beneficiaries of the boycott of Lancashire cloth in Bengal were the Bombay cotton mills."

There was a valuable discussion on the 'Transition in Agriculture' during the period. In it, he focused on the problems of rural indebtedness, the danger of the land passing into the hands of non-agricultural classes (moneylenders) from agriculturists.

While discussing the period from 1914-1928, Gadgil advocated cooperative credit for the rural areas. He discussed the question of exchange rate and foreign trade in the 1920s and made the currency policy partly responsible for the slow growth of the Indian industry. During the period, Gadgil observed that there was a favourable change in the attitude of the Government towards industry and he said that "the attitude of the State throughout the earlier period was one of absolute *Laissez-faire* and that 'tariff policy was largely shaped by the wishes of the English manufacturers and early labour legislation was prompted by them.'

According to Gadgil, two important events of the period 1929-39 were the worldwide trade depression and the emergence of provincial autonomy. The depression brought down the agricultural prices heavily and the Government did nothing to help agriculturists. Though popular ministries were formed in 1937-38 under the scheme of provincial autonomy, they could not do much to mitigate the sufferings of cultivators. Although, there was increase in factory production under protection, there was a fall in the purchasing power of agriculturists. After 1935, India had shown signs of general industrial prosperity. But, as Gadgil put it, "While in all countries of the world, old prejudices were rapidly thrown over, and an enormous amount of experimentation in the direction and control of economic life was undertaken, India alone marked time".

Gadgil divided the period before 1914 into three stages: the stage of acquisition, the stage of consolidation and the stage of exploitation. It may be noted that the term "exploitation" was used in the sense of utilisation. The British attempted, with the help of their new technology to exploit the natural resources of the country.

Gadgil described the period from 1917 to 1939 as one of transition. This period witnessed positive policies such as protection and provincial autonomy.

Some of the modern writers are critical of Gadgil's description of the different sub-periods from 1860-1914 as parts of a cycle of prosperity and adversity. We may, however, note that a person doing research on economic history of India in the early 1920s was handicapped by lack of data. As Bhabatosh Datta put it, "The national output data were incomplete, the sectoral output data were not comparable over time and there was only a very crude index of price movements. Still, Gadgil's work remains even today the best single account of the growth of industry, railways, towns, as well as of agriculture and irrigation in the half century before the First World War."

Industrial Labour

Gadgil's publication *"Regulation of Wages and other Problems of Industrial Labour in India"* (1943) deals with topics such as wages, wages and employment, standard of living of workers, industrial relations and effects of rationalisation of industries.

According to Gadgil, the two great evils of the then existing wage systems were:

(*i*) Low level of payment made to industrial workers and (*ii*) disparity between the wages paid for similar work. This has created discontent among industrial workers and conflict between labour and capital. In order to remove disparity in payment of wages and to improve the lot of workers, Gadgil suggested that wages should be regulated at a higher level. It would improve the efficiency of workers.

In addition to higher wages for workers, Gadgil suggested that the state should introduce welfare programmes such as industrial housing, employment insurance, paid holidays and health insurance to improve the working and living conditions of workers, While analyzing the effects of rationalisation, Gadgil felt that though rationalisation would increase the national income and employment in other industries in the long run, he was afraid that it would create the problem of unemployment in the short run.

War and Economic Policy

According to Bhabatosh Datta, "Probably the best work on the subject of war economy in India was D.R. Gadgil and N.V. Sovani's *War and Indian Economic Policy* (1943). The book is divided into two parts—one on currency and prices and the other on financial and economic policy.

In the first part of the book, the authors noted that there was a close correlation between the growth in the note circulation and the rise in the wholesale prices. In other words, they attributed the inflation during the period to increase in money supply.

For the first time, Gadgil and Sovani made distinction between internal government borrowing from private savings and borrowing from banks. They recognized the inflationary potential of the latter. They also identified the nature of deficit financing and its inflationary impact in India.

In the second part of the book, Gadgil and Sovani exposed the fallacy of the official argument that there was no inflation in India. To check inflation and to provide relief to the masses, they suggested a sound economic and financial policy which included an increase in direct taxes, public borrowing, full utilisation of productive resources, economy in administrative expenditure, control over investment and profits, price control and rationing, transport regulation with priority to the movement of essential commodities, and co-ordination of all these activities. They concluded by saying "unless the control of prices, of the distribution of necessaries, of wages and profits, of transport and supplies, of acreage under crops, of the working of artisan industry, and of machine industry are all co-ordinated, and made to sub-serve one single centrally devised plan, the success of war economic policy is highly doubtful.

Conclusion

D.R. Gadgil has made a pioneering contribution in the analysis of the industrial evolution of India. And he studied in depth the problems of industrial labour. His study of war economy of India is considered to be the best work on the subject.

INDIRA GANDHI

The economic philosophy of Indira Gandhi is found in her writings and speeches and policy statements with particular reference to India's economic development through the public sector and the Five Year Plans. She is the author of *"Eternal India"* which is her version of *"Discovery of India"*. In working on this book, she collaborated with a French photographer. Her life and achievements are best chronicled in the four volumes of *"The Spirit of India"*. While following the basic economic policies and programmes of her father Pandit Jawaharlal Nehru, the first Prime Minister of India, Indira Gandhi radicalised them with bold innovations in order to complete India's unfinished revolution.

Indira Gandhi described herself as "*Desh Sevika*" (Servant of the Nation). She remained so through the challenging times and she died a martyr.

Socialism

Like her father Nehru, Indira Gandhi believed in democracy, socialism, planning and secularism. But she has often observed that Indian socialism must be evolved in accordance with the nation's innate culture and traditions and should not become a "carbon copy" of the socialist patterns obtaining in other countries.

Indira Gandhi's broadcast over All India Radio on January 26, 1969 after becoming the Prime Minister gives her political and economic philosophy and her adherence to the foreign policy of non-alignment advocated by her father.

Indira Gandhi firmly believed in securing a better life for the Indian masses by planned economic development. She had abundant faith in the people of India.

At the time, when she became Prime Minister, India was faced with a number of problems which needed immediate attention. There was the failure of monsoon and as a result fall in agricultural production. Economic aid from abroad did not come in the right time and in right amount. Export earnings did not increase to the expected level. Ensuring food to people in the year of scarcity became the first duty of the government. So Indira Gandhi wanted to give urgent attention to the management and equitable distribution of foodgrains. She proposed to import large enough quantities of foodgrains to make up the deficit in production. Her Government had prepared a well-thought out plan so that water and chemical fertilizers, and new yielding varieties' of seed as well as technical advice and credit reached farmers. She laid stress on self-reliance in agriculture.

Role of Public Sector

Indira Gandhi has continued to assign a prominent role to public sector in the rapid expansion of basic industries, power and transport. She felt that in our circumstances it was not only desirable but necessary. At the same time, she felt that public enterprises must be managed efficiently and they should produce sufficient profits for further investments.

Mixed Economy

Indira Gandhi reaffirmed her faith in mixed economy. She was of the view that within the framework of our plans, there was no conflict between the public and private sectors. In our mixed economy, private enterprise has flourished and has received help and support from the government.

Indira Gandhi always endeavoured to work for peace and international co-operation. In her own words "Peace we want because there is another war to fight–the war against poverty, disease and ignorance. We have promises to keep with our people–of work, food, clothing and shelter, health and education. The weaker and under-privileged sections of our people–all these who require special measures of social security have always been and will remain uppermost in my mind."

The 10-Point Programme

The 10-point programme passed by the AICC in June 1967 was based on Prime Minister Indira Gandhi's draft. Through the 10-point programme, in a way she served notice that banks and general insurance would be nationalized, there would be State trading in exports and imports as well as in foodgrains, the expansion of co-operatives and regulation of monopolies, the abolition of privy purses and princely privileges and the improvement of rural economy.

We shall discuss the 10-point programme in a little more detail. Indira Gandhi felt that the following 10-points call for consideration to attain a socialist democratic society in India.

1. *Social Control of the Banking Institutions:* The Congress election manifesto mentioned that "it is necessary to bring most of the banking institutions under social control in order to serve the cause of economic growth and fulfil our social purposes more effectively and to make credit available to the producer in all fields where it is needed."

2. *Nationalisation of general insurance.*

3. *Commodity-wise progress in state trading in imports and exports:* Indira Gandhi was of the view that export and import trade should be progressively undertaken through state agencies.

4. *State Trading in Foodgrains:* A national policy of distribution of foodgrains, particularly to the vulnerable sections of the community should be worked out and for this purpose, the Food Corporation of India and co-operative agencies should be utilised to the maximum extent.

5. *Expansion of Cooperatives:* Consumer co-operatives should be organized to cover urban and rural areas for the supply of the more essential commodities to the community at fair prices.

6. *Regulated removal of Monopolies:* The Government wanted to implement the recommendations of the Monopolies Commission Report to curb monopolies and concentration of economic power.

7. *Provision of minimum needs to the entire community.*

8. *Unearned increments in urban land values:* The Government wanted to impose limitation on urban income and poverty. It wanted to take concrete steps for placing restrictions on individual holdings of urban land for preventing racketeering in land in urban areas.

9. *Rural works programmes, Land reforms etc.:* The rural works programmes would give opportunities for employment especially to the landless and at the same time help create some overheads in agriculture such as agro-industries, feeder roads, minor irrigation and cattle development.

10. *Privileges of ex-rulers:* The privileges and privy purses enjoyed by the ex-rulers are inconsistent with the concept and practice of democracy. So she was of the view that the government should examine and take steps to remove them.

Indira Gandhi has always championed the cause of the weaker sections, minorities and the underprivileged.

Bank Nationalisation

Indira Gandhi took a bold step in nationalising 14 of the biggest commercial banks incorporated in India in July 1969.

As early as December, 1954, Parliament took the decision to frame our plans and policies within a socialist pattern of society. Indira Gandhi explained that "control over the commanding heights of the economy is necessary, particularly in a poor country where it is extremely difficult to mobilise adequate resources for development and to reduce the inequalities between different groups and regions."

"Banks play a vital role in the functioning of any economy... To the millions of small farmers, artisans and other self-employed persons, a bank can be a source of credit, which is the very basis for any effort to improve their meagre economic lot."

Indira Gandhi further went on to say that "an institution, such as the banking system, which touches—and should touch—the lives of millions, has necessarily to be inspired by a larger social purpose and has to subserve national priorities and objectives. That is why there has been widespread demand that major banks should be not only socially controlled but publicly owned..... That is also why we nationalised, more than a decade ago, the life insurance business and the State Bank, or the Imperial Bank as it was then called. That is also why we have set up, directly under the aegis of the state a number of financial institutions to provide medium or long-term credit to agriculture and industry.

Indira Gandhi firmly believed that "public ownership of the major banks will help to eliminate the use of bank credit for speculative and unproductive purposes."

The Government had already adopted social control over banks. By nationalisation, the government wanted to achieve its objects speedily. Especially, it wanted to expand credit to priority areas which have hither to been somewhat neglected. The measure aimed mainly at the removal of control by a few and provision of adequate credit for agriculture, small industry and exports.

Indira Gandhi emphasized one point strongly. That is that "sound business does not mean that credit should be provided only to those who can furnish security in the form of property and that it should be denied to others even if the projects proposed by them are otherwise credit-worthy. She said that the whole emphasis should shift from credit-worthiness of persons to credit-worthiness of purpose. She earnestly hoped that nationalisation would lead to a more equitable distribution of credit throughout the country.

20-Point Programme

On July 1, 1975, Indira Gandhi, as the Prime Minister of India, announced a dynamic new economic policy based on the 20-point programme.

The following are the 20-points:

1. Continuance of steps to bring down prices of essential commodities. Streamlined production, procurement and distribution of essential commodities. Strict economy in government expenditure.
2. Implementation of agricultural land ceilings and speedier distribution of surplus land and compilation of land records.
3. Stepping up of provision of house sites for landless and weaker sections.
4. Bonded labour, wherever it exists will be declared illegal.
5. Plan for liquidation of rural indebtedness. Legislation for moratorium on recovery of debt from landless labourers, small farmers and artisans.
6. Review of laws on minimum agricultural wages.
7. Five million more hectares to be brought under irrigation. National programme for use of underground water.
8. An accelerated power programme. Super-thermal stations under state control.
9. New development plan for development of handloom sector.
10. Improvement in quality and supply of people's cloth.
11. Socialisation of urban and urbanisable land. Ceiling on ownership and possession of vacant land on plinth area of new dwelling units.
12. Special squads for valuation of conspicuous construction and prevention of tax evasion. Summary trials and deterrent punishment for economic offenders.
13. Special legislation for the confiscation of smugglers' properties.
14. Liberalisation of investment procedures. Action against misuse of import licences.
15. New schemes for workers' association in Industry.
16. National permit scheme for road transport.
17. Income-tax relief to middle class exemption limit placed at Rs 8,000.
18. Essential commodities at controlled prices to students in hostels.
19. Books and stationery at controlled prices.
20. New apprenticeship scheme to enlarge employment and training, especially of weaker sections.

In addition to the general programme of development, the 20-point programme was undertaken as a special activity to lighten the hardships of various target groups. Many of its objectives were fulfilled.

Legislation for the abolition of bonded labour was adopted in 1976.

Steps were taken to confiscate smugglers' properties. Lakhs of people of lower and middle income groups have been exempted from income tax. The national permit scheme for road transport was enforced. The target of providing irrigation to 5 million hectares had been fulfilled. A national scheme for the use of ground water has been taken up. Super thermal power stations were established. Substantial progress was made even in the other items of the 20-Point programme.

Encouraged by the welcome changes that have subsequently taken place in the economic and social life of the people and the new challenges that had arisen. Indira Gandhi, again, as the Prime Minister (after staying out of power for a brief spell) announced the new 20-Point programme on January 14, 1982.

The New 20-Point Programme

Under the new 20-Point programme, Indira Gandhi proposed to:

1. Increase irrigation potential, develop and disseminate technologies and inputs for dry land agriculture.
2. To take special efforts to increase production of pulses and vegetable oilseeds.
3. Strengthen and expand coverage of Integrated Rural Development and National Rural Employment Programmes.
4. Implement agricultural land ceilings, distribute surplus land and complete compilation of land records by removing all administrative and legal obstacles.
5. Review and effectively enforce minimum wages for agricultural labour.
6. Rehabilitate bonded labour.
7. Accelerate programmes for the development of scheduled castes and scheduled tribes.
8. Supply drinking water to all problem villages.
9. Allot houses/sites to rural families who are without them and expand programmes for construction assistance to them.
10. Improve the environment of slums, implement programmes of house building for economically weaker sections, and take measures to arrest unwarranted increase in land prices.
11. Maximise power generation, improve the functioning of electricity authorities and electrify all villages.
12. Pursue vigorously programmes of afforestation, social and farm forestry and the development of bio-gas and other alternative energy sources.
13. Promote family planning on a voluntary basis as a people's movement.
14. Substantially augment universal primary health care facilities, and control of leprosy, T.B. and blindness.
15. Accelerate programmes of welfare for women and children and nutrition programmes for pregnant women, nursing mothers and children, specially in tribal, hill and backward areas.
16. Spread universal elementary education for the age group 6–14 with special emphasis on girls, and simultaneously involve students and voluntary agencies in programmes for the removal of adult illiteracy.
17. Expand the public distribution through more fair price shops, including mobile shops in far-flung areas and shops to cater to industrial workers, students' hostels, and make available to students textbooks and exercise books on a priority basis and to promote a strong consumer protection movement.
18. Liberalise investment procedures and streamline industrial policies to ensure timely completion of projects. Give handicrafts, handlooms, small and village industries all facilities to grow and to update their technologies.

19. Continue strict action against smugglers, hoarders and tax evaders and check black money.

20. Improve the working of the public enterprises by increasing efficiency, capacity utilisation and the generation of internal resources.

It may be noted that new 20-Point programme had in it some of the points listed in the 20-Point programme announced in 1975. The new 20-Point programme has been detailed into overall plan of development. In the words of Indira Gandhi, "It pinpoints areas of special thrust which will show immediate tangible results for various sections of our population. It is imperative to ensure that Harijans and Tribals and minorities in general have the fullest protection."

When the 20-Point programme was first announced in 1975, Indira Gandhi cautioned people not to expect miracles. As she put it, "Then as now there is only one magic which can remove poverty and that is hard work, helped by a clear sense of purpose and discipline."

Self-reliance and Removal of Poverty

The Five Year Plans which were drawn up when Indira Gandhi was the Prime Minister laid stress on "growth with stability", "progressive achievement of self-reliance" and "removal of poverty" (*Garibi Hatao*) and "growth with social justice".

Conclusion

Planning, democratic socialism, nationalisation of banks, 20-point programmes (with emphasis on fulfilment of minimum needs), self-reliance, social justice, dominant role for the public sector are all some of the important ideas, policies and programmes which formed part and parcel of the social and economic philosophy of Indira Gandhi.

PERIYAR E. V. RAMASAMI

Periyar E.V. Ramasami, the great humanist and social revolutionary of Tamil Nadu was born in the year 1879. 'Periyar' in Tamil means 'a great person' or 'an eminent person' or a 'sage'. He was born 10 years after Gandhi was born and 10 years before Nehru was born. His political and social life began in 1919 and continued until his death in 1973. One cannot understand Periyar's economic thought without understanding his social and political philosophy and his views on religion and caste. His socio-economic ideas have great relevance even today.

The economic and political ideas of the social reformers of South India can be understood in a proper way only by keeping in mind the political and social conditions in South India during the first quarter of the 20th century.

Social life in South India at the beginning of the 20th century was marked by social conflict between the Brahmin and the non-Brahmin communities. The Brahmins were a few in number and the non-Brahmins formed the majority. But owing to the impact of the British colonial rule, the Brahmins who formed a very small proportion of the total population occupied a dominant position in the political, administrative and economic spheres due to their unusually high literacy rates.

It was against the dominant influence of the Brahmins in the above areas, and to advance, safeguard and protect the interests of the non-Brahmin community, the Dravidian movement came into existence. And Periyar played a leading role in it.

Periyar was a basic thinker. Like Karl Marx, criticizing and rejecting, or accepting and co-ordinating, he always went to the bottom of every matter. To his powerful intellect, the interest in the problem as a problem was paramount.

Atheism, rationalism, self-respect movement and socialism may be considered as the pillars of Periyar's socio-economic philosophy.

Periyar opposed religion. He did not believe in God. He wanted to eradicate caste from the society. He was against God, religion and varnashramadharma which created caste distinctions because he believed that these institutions were abused for the exploitation of man by man. As he aimed at a casteless and classless society without discrimination based on caste or gender and as he perceived the above institutions to be root causes of all kinds of discrimination, he wanted to strike at the root by opposing caste and religion and by not believing in God. If we look at his atheism, rationalism and self-respect movement from this angle, we will get a correct perspective of the teachings of Periyar.

Atheism

The term 'atheism' is derived from the Greek 'a' (not) plus 'theos' (God) and denotes the doctrine of disbelief in a Supreme Being. In this sense, Socrates, Marx and Freud are all atheists. Marx called religion the opium of man.

Periyar had no faith in God or religion because he believed that these institutions encouraged superstition. As he was determined to get rid of the ancient meaningless practices in the society, he became a non-believer.

Periyar earnestly believed that religion and God as practised and worshipped in India had proved to be a dangerous disease and must be eradicated for the sake of the progress of the society and development of intelligence and capabilities of the people.

We may, however, note that Periyar never asked his followers to follow his teachings blindly. Almost always he concluded his lectures on religion and god with an observation that he was stating his views and the listeners could accept or reject them according to their rational thinking.

Rationalism

Rationalism is the philosophy that regards reason as the only basis for beliefs or actions.

Periyar considered himself a humanist (*manida dharmavadi*). The good society which he dreamed of was a 'human society'. According to him, a human society should be rational and should have the capacity to think but the existing society was an animal society, meaning that it was irrational. As man also has the sixth sense, it enables him to think, to change according to the context, and to progress. He emphasizes that only those who 'think' of any act with their 'intellect' are men and all others who do not think are 'mere animals'. In order to lift a man from his animal existence to a rational being, he advocated the destruction of things like religion, caste, vedas and gods. The essence of Periyar's rationalism was that man should look at everything with his own intelligence. He should think whether it is consistent with practice, reality and experience. And he should accept that which is right and reject the others. He firmly believed that all the social ills like poverty, ignorance and hatred among men were caused by irrationalism or lack of proper use of rationalism and not by 'bad time', God or the ruler. As people spent most of their leisure time and money on activities based on superstition, he lamented that "man's leisure time has been used only for destroying his rationality, and leading him to slavery, and not to make use of progress by rationality."

Self-Respect Movement

The Self-Respect Movement started by Periyar in 1925 has brought about a silent revolution in the thinking of the people of Tamil Nadu. In Tamil, the movement is known as *Cuya Mariyadai Iyakkam* or *Tan Mana Iyakkam*.

The Self-Respect philosophy is based on the firm belief that human actions should be based on rational thinking. It asserts that freedom of every man to think and act in a manner best conducive to the common weal, even as it reserves for everyone the right of challenging, and if need by revolting against authority, if such authority has been constituted for the exclusive advantage of a self-seeking class. And in its immediate implication, it would mean the marshalling up of all available forces to carry on an organized campaign against social oppression, and determination on a progressive programme of modernizing life.

The main principles of Self-Respect Movement are:

1. There shall be no kind of inequality among people living in a society;

2. In the economic life of a society, there shall be no difference such as rich and poor, and land and all resources being held in common;

3. In the human society, men and women shall be treated as equal in every respect without any kind of difference;

4. Attachment to caste, religion, varna, country and the God shall have to be eradicated from the society and there shall prevail friendship and unity in the human society all over the world;

5. There shall be no division as owner and worker and all shall equally work for all needs of all men and derive the benefits in equal measure; and

6. Every human being shall be free to act according to his reason, understanding, desire and perspective and shall not be subject to slavery of any kind in any manner.

The achievement of social and economic equality is the central theme of Self-Respect philosophy. Periyar wanted to fight the inequities arising out of the caste system and religious practices. He made use of the movement to purge the society of all the exploitative social practices in the name of religion.

Socialism

Periyar's belief in socialism got strengthened after his visit to Soviet Russia. He used the words *samadharman* and *podu udaimai* whenever he talked of socialism. He used the word *samadharman* to denote an egalitarian society—a society which recognizes no social or economic superiority or inferiority.

Periyar firmly believed that the first step towards socialism was eradication of distinction based on birth, which in turn, determined the caste of a person. Periyar emphasized more on social equality than on economic equality in his *samadharman* philosophy. For, he believed that social in equalities arising out of birth would remain active under any economic system and prevent any change in society and would revive even the economic inequalities which were abolished. Periyar also felt that there was no point in borrowing any socialist philosophy from abroad since the first duty facing a socialist in India was to abolish the *varna-jati* system. He was of the firm view that no amount of communism (meaning common ownership) could bring about any reform in a caste-ridden society that denied equal rights of enjoyment. He made a specific point that it was under the *jati* system that several people became rich and acquired superior status. He considered the communist system as a panacea for all social problems.

To Periyar, *samadharman* or socialism meant removal of degradation of the Dravidian race, abolition of caste, equal property, and provision of food, education and housing for all.

Poverty in India

Periyar attributed the mass poverty in India to wasteful expenditure by people. They spent a lot of their money on rituals, temple worship, extravagant marriages and so on. He observed that standard of living was rising in India because of the contact with the Western countries, but it was not accompanied by increase in income. He noted that the present economic system encouraged concentration of income and wealth in a few sectors.

Periyar, like Dadabhai Naoroji, blamed the British rule and its exploitative policy for the poverty of the Indian masses.

Periyar believed that the economic backwardness of a large majority of the non-Brahmin population was due to their belief in *varnashramadharma* and the superstitious beliefs about karma and rebirth which compelled people to spend their income on unproductive religious activities. To develop the economy and to improve the lot of the people, Periyar believed that *varnashramadharma*, religious thoughts and preoccupation with temples, festivals and rituals should be eradicated.

As the majority of the poor depended upon agriculture for their livelihood, and as agriculture was marked by low productivity, Periyar advocated modern methods of cultivation and formation of co-operative finance corporations to provide credit to farmers at low rates of interest.

On Industrialization and Mechanization

Periyar believed that mass poverty in India can be removed only by industrialization and mechanization. Gandhi believed that the development of village and cottage industries were necessary for improving the economic lot of the villagers. But Periyar hated the intense manual labour involved in cottage industries, that too, for producing small output. Not only that, the *varna* system reserved all manual labour to the *shudras*. Periyar considered Gandhi's basic education scheme as irrelevant in the age of technological and scientific progress. He thought the basic education scheme would make the shudras as the servile and menial class forever. For the same reason, he opposed Rajaji's elementary education scheme wherein the students were asked to have training in hereditary (parental) occupation during a part of the day. He considered that as a scheme by Rajaji to reintroduce the *varnashramadharma* through the back door.

Periyar considered mechanization as necessary, convenient and suitable for the progress of mankind and civilization. He did not agree with the view that mechanization would result in unemployment. He asked a basic question: Why should some be owners (capitalists) and the others be treated as workers? He thought that the classification of people into workers, owners, farmers, zamindars, mirasdars and so on representing different levels of hierarchy was the by-product of *varnashramadharma*. He was of the firm belief that to attain genuine equality, that is *samadharma*, we must do away with the inequalities arising out of birth as well as occupation. And upward social mobility implies vertical occupational mobility. He described the Dravidian movement as the workers' movement as the majority of the persons in the movement were employed as workers and were non-Brahmins.

We may note that Periyar's views on industrialization and mechanization are in contrast to Gandhi's views on industrialization. In this respect, Periyar was closer to Nehru than to Gandhi. But in India, the problems of poverty and unemployment are intertwined. How far the capital-intensive technology adopted in the process of industrialization of the West is suitable for India with unlimited supply of labour and disguised unemployment in the countryside is a question to be examined objectively.

One of the basic ideas of Periyar was that a labourer's son should not be a labourer. He saw in it an effective way of destroying caste. He wanted communal reservation in jobs because he thought that it would dismantle the occupational structure of castes.

On Khadi, Handloom and Match Industries

Periyar considered khadi as an uneconomic proposition and a very backward industry that would keep the villagers in poverty. He described handloom industry as an industry of barbarian age. He felt that handloom industry 'must die' or 'must be killed' as it involved loss of time and enormous labour and it gave meagre income. He considered handloom weaving, a kind of slavery. While a weaver could never become rich, many others could become rich by exploiting the weaver. In his own blunt way, he said that handloom industry contained half the 'foolishness and barbarity' of the khadi industry and should not be revived. He considered only the match industry as a useful and flourishing cottage industry and recommended the reduction of excise duty.

On Trade Unions

Periyar advised workers to keep away from politics and to prevent external leadership. He said that workers of a union should elect a leader from among themselves and they should not have a politician as their union leader. In a crude way, he expressed the view that fools were better than dishonest people. He felt that workers should trust their 'masters' until they could form their union and elect a leader among themselves rather than entrusting their unions to politicians.

Periyar further stated that workers' problem was people's problem as 90 per cent of the people could be labelled as 'labourers'. But it was not treated that way by the government and the society. Periyar went to the extent of suggesting that workers should fight the government rather than the owners for attaining their rights as the government was giving support to owners and ownership.

Village Uplift

Periyar felt sad about the exploitation of villages by towns and spoke against the very concept of village industries as distinct from urban industries. He called upon the villagers to give up superstitions, become rational, realize their plight and leave villages. Periyar advocated that the plan for village reform should start with the destruction of village as an institution. We may note here, Dr. Ambedkar too, after realizing that so long as the institution of village was there, caste system could not be eradicated, advocated destruction of the village as a social institution. But to Gandhi, the village was India and he firmly believed that India's battle for economic development had to be won or lost in the villages.

Periyar suggested a plan of action for the integration of towns and villages so that the vast differences between them in occupational pattern, availability of basic goods, educational conditions and lifestyle would disappear.

The salient features of Periyar's action programme for modernization of villages are given below:

1. mechanization of agriculture, that is, agricultural operations like ploughing, sowing, digging wells and harvesting are to be done by machines;

2. reformulation of agricultural land to facilitate mechanization and separation of land unsuitable for this for growing other crops;

3. marketing of agricultural products, through farmers' cooperatives so that the proceeds would go to the agriculturists;

4. combining several villages as a small town for provision of a school, hospital, park, cinema, drama, reading room, library, radio station, roads, bus transport, police station, a well-educated judge and shops;

5. organizing mobile exhibitions;

6. establishing appeal courts and providing for field camps of officers for redressal of grievances; and

7. establishing small industries.

One can see in the above action programme, Periyar's emphasis on mechanization of agriculture, farmers' cooperatives, 'cluster approach' to villages (a scheme suggested by V.K.R.V. Rao at a later date) and encouragement of small industries. Periyar was also of the view that agricultural work should be shared equally by all without distinctions of caste and without any notion of superiority or inferiority. He not only wanted to raise the standard of living of the villagers but he wanted to remove the rural-urban disparities.

On Women's Rights

'Empowerment of women' has become a fashionable term nowadays. But long before the term became vogue, and feminine movement came into existence, Periyar worked for the improvement of the status of women and for the their rights.

It may be noted that the title "Periyar" meaning "the Great Man" was conferred on E. V. Ramasami (known until then by the initials of his name of EVR) by women at one of their conferences in 1936 and from that day, people started addressing him as "Periyar".

Periyar felt that in the male dominated Hindu society, women were treated as slaves, play things and ornamental pieces. He spent a lot of time and energy in liberating women from their bondage or slavery. He gave equal priority for raising the status of women, abolition of untouchability and discrimination based on caste. He thought that the liberation of women was as important as the removal of untouchability to become fit for self-government. He regretted that nearly 50 per cent of the manpower of the country was wasted because of the slavery of women (*pen adimai*).

Periyar advocated Self-Respect marriage system not only to boycott Brahmin priests and Brahministic rituals, but also to give a new idea of freedom and equality' to wedding couples. According to the concept of Self-Respect marriage, marriage is a contract between a man and a woman and it relates to the two persons concerned and it has no divine bondage or anything of that sort. It approves 'love-marriage' as against 'arranged marriage'. It allows divorce at the instance of either partners and does not consider marriage as a sacred agreement. Under the system, women have property rights equal to men.

Periyar had some radical views on the rights of women and marriage. He felt that for women to enjoy real freedom, the institution of marriage should be abolished. He went to the extent of advising women to stop bearing children. He was a great advocate of birth control and he said that the propaganda on birth control was much more important than the propaganda on prohibition or eradication of epidemics. He also supported the right to abortion as a necessary ingredient of women's freedom.

Periyar made some suggestions to bring about equality between men and women. He felt that by reserving 50 per cent of jobs to women, the desire for havmg male child would be checked and this would also help in family planning (which in turn would control population growth). And women's employment itself would directly lead to birth control and this could become an excellent method of family planning.

Periyar encouraged widow remarriage. He thought that prohibition of widow remarriage was foolish, unnatural and inconsistent with natural human instinct and unheard of in any other part of the world. He firmly believed that the right to divorce for women was the most essential safeguard for them.

Thus Periyar suggested many things for the empowerment of women.

On Education

Today we all know that education plays an important role in the economic development of a nation. Investment in human capital is as important as investment in physical capital.

One of the basic changes advocated by Periyar in the field of education was that all lessons in the school curriculum relating to devotion to God, religion and the king should be removed because they stood as obstacles to knowledge and inculcated a slavish mentality.

Periyar gave many concrete suggestions for reforming educational system. He thought that the educational system which existed then was long and expensive and it was suitable only for the rich people. So he advocated compulsory education for all upto a level and then there must be diversification for vocational education. He was against public expenditure on higher education. Probably, Periyar with his keen intellect, found out that the rich benefited more from subsidized higher education than the poor.

Conclusion

Periyar, the great humanist and social revolutionary of Tamil Nadu campaigned for nearly fifty years for the uplift of the subordinate and disadvantaged social groups of Tamil Nadu and as a result of his rationalist teachings, there has been a great awakening among the masses. In 1970, the UNESCO award was given to him and the citation read: "Periyar, the prophet of the New Age, the Socrates of South-East Asia, Father of the social reform movement, and arch enemy of ignorance, superstitions, meaningless customs and baseless manners." In a non-violent manner, and without political power, by his teachings over a period of fifty years, Periyar has brought about a silent revolution by changing the social slavery that was in existence for over a period of 2000 years.

In India, in the last two thousand years, a great social revolution has taken place only in Tamil Nadu. It was Periyar, the leader of the Dravidian movement, who brought about that revolution.

ARIGNAR C. N. ANNADURAI (1909–1969)

Conjeevaram Natarajan Annadurai, popularly known as 'Anna' was born in a middle class family on the 15th September, 1909 at Kanchipuram in South India, a town famous for its silks and temples. The word 'Anna' means in Tamil 'elder brother'. For the first time, in the field of Politics in India, Anna brought to bear the relationship of a closely knit family in running his political party. In all his letters in the party organ, he addressed his followers as *Thambis* (younger brothers). The word 'Arignar' in Tamil means a savant.

Anna had his schooling in his home town and higher education at Pachaiyappa's college in Madras (Chennai). At college, he distinguished himself as a great orator both in Tamil and English. He passed his B.A. (Honours) degree examination in Economics, Politics and History in the year 1935 and stood first in the University.

During the anti-Hindi agitation in 1938, when Anna and Periyar were put in the same prison, Anna came under the direct influence of Periyar, and a master-disciple relationship developed among them. Anna was to Periyar, what Nehru was to Gandhi. And he was attracted to the socio-economic and political philosophy of Periyar. Thereafter, Anna became an ardent follower of the Self-Respect Movement and a leading advocate of the demand for Dravidanad, and a great champion of social and economic justice in the society.

The Justice Party whose leadership was dominated by the privileged classes was converted into a mass movement by Anna under the leadership of Periyar and it was renamed Dravida Kazhagam (Dravidian Federation) at the Salem Conference in 1944. The name was changed by a resolution brought forward by Anna and came to be known as 'Annadurai Resolution'. In the words of Anna, this resolution brought the party "from palace to platform".

Differences arose between Periyar and Anna in due course and Anna left Dravida Kazhagam and started the Dravida Munnetra Kazhagam (D.M.K.), meaning Dravidian Progressive Federation on September 17, 1949. With the launching of the D.M K., a social movement took on the character of a political party. The party aimed at 'establishing a new social order based on the cardinal principles of democracy, rationalism and socialism. We may note that Periyar's socio-economic philosophy is also based on these basic tenets. In order to achieve the goals of the party, it thought it necessary to resist the Northern domination and work for a separate, independent, Sovereign Federation of Dravidian Socialist Republics, comprising the present four southern states of India–Tamil Nadu, Andhra Pradesh, Kerala and Karnataka.

During the formative period, the D.M.K. did not contest General Elections. But in the Tiruchirapalli conference (1956), it took the historic decision to contest the elections. In the words of Anna, "we realised that we must either be politically capacitated or be ruined by democracy". And the D.M.K. captured political power in the state in the year 1967 and became the ruling party. Anna became the Chief Minister. The decision to contest elections was a shrewd move by Anna because he felt that without political power, it would rather be difficult to translate the policies of his party into action.

China attacked India in 1962 across the Himalayan borders. At that time, as a true patriot, Anna gave up the demand for an independent Dravida Nadu. Anna considered that it was the sacred duty of his party to rush to the help of the Indian government in its efforts to protect and safeguard the sovereignty of the Indian soil. Not only that, the Government of India wanted to bring forward a Constitutional Amendment Bill which debarred any secessionist party from contesting the General

Elections. As a pragmatist, and under altered circumstances, Anna did not want to commit political suicide by clinging on to the demand for Dravida Nadu. Anna realised that he could achieve his goals within the framework of the Indian Union by getting more powers for the states. The D.M.K. party constitution was accordingly amended. From then on, Anna emphasized on more autonomy for States and pleaded for reduction of regional disparities.

Anna's tenure as Chief Minister was rather short. But during that short period, he implemented many policies which were dear to his heart. After a serious illness, Anna died on 3rd February, 1969. The funeral of Anna was attended by the largest number of people in the world. The event has entered the Guinness Book. That was his *charisma* and he received so much love and affection from the people of Tamil Nadu.

We shall now describe briefly some of his views on social, economic and political affairs.

Democracy

Anna was a born democrat. He firmly believed that "democracy is not a form of government alone, it is an invitation to a new life, an experiment in the art of sharing responsibilities and benefits, an attempt to generate and coordinate the inherent energy in each individual for the common task." He abhorred tyranny and dictatorship.

Rationalism

Anna was a great rationalist. He hated the superstition and exploitation of man by man in the name of religion, which, in turn, had obscured the purity of religion. He was against idol worship, institutionalization of religion. He hated people attributing *karma* and all that as an explanation of their poverty. He believed in "one God and one caste". He considered service to humanity as the service to God. When asked to comment on the action programme of Periyar, his political guru, of breaking idols of Lord Vinayaka (Sri Ganesh), Anna replied that he would not break the idols of Vinayaka and he would also not break coconuts for Him.

Socialism

Anna believed in scientific socialism. He was a Marxian in thought but a Gandhian in approach. He was not a doctrinnaire communist or socialist. He firmly believed in non-violence. And he saw God in the smile of a poor man. According to him, "Concentration of wealth in the hands of a few is like a deluge. That would destroy not only the weaker sections of society but even those possessing it."

In his maiden speech in Parliament, while referring to socialism, Anna said, "Socialism is not mere welfare, because socialism is something other than guaranteeing welfare .... I am aware, according to Laski, that equality is not identity of treatment, but affording equal opportunities for all."

Anna lamented that in our country, equal opportunities were not provided to all, especially to the disadvantaged groups like the SCs/STs and the backward classes.

Professor Galbraith described Indian socialism as 'post-office socialism'. He said so because most of our public sector enterprises were working on "no-profit, no-loss" basis. As we had invested crores of rupees in the public sector undertakings, Anna wanted them to give returns by way of profits so that we could plough them back. He made it clear that he was not against planning or public sector undertakings. He was all for them. All that he wanted was to improve the efficiency of these undertakings by avoiding wastage and corruption.

Anna was critical of socialism as practised by the ruling Congress party. In the name of pragmatism, the then ruling Congress party has diluted the ideology of socialism. Socialism is something where the profit motive would be curbed to the minimum and the service motive would be on the top. In his own words, "If the profit motive is curbed down and the service motive is lifted up, even then you don't attain socialism to the fullest extent, but you are on the path to socialism". But in India, what we have "is not a mixed economy, but an adulterated economy. You are taking up the bad from socialism and you have got a curious mixture." Anna felt bad that even after twenty years of freedom, in spite of all the talk about planning, socialism and all that, the Government has not provided basic goods like drinking water, food, housing, employment and justice. Although the goal of socialism was accepted, the government has not succeeded in reducing the disparities between the rich and the poor. Anna agreed with the view that in India, production was getting more and more oriented to luxury items instead of necessaries for the common man.

Self-Determination

Anna looked at India as a sub-continent. To him, India was a geographical expression turned into a political entity by historical circumstances.

He demanded separate sovereign Dravidanadu because he wanted self-determination for the state. He was against language imperialism and imposition of Hindi on the people of his State. He hoped that "if it is separated, it will become a small nation, compact, homogeneous, and united, wherein sections of the people in the whole area can have a community of sentiment. Then we make economic regeneration more effective and social regeneration more fruitful."

As we have already noted, Anna gave up the demand for separate Dravida Nadu during the Chinese invasion of India in 1962.

On Inflation

Anna agreed with the view that one of the main causes of inflation was concentration of wealth in the hands of a few. These few moneyed people, not only spend extravagantly but also develop a tendency to hoard. This has resulted in the prices going up because money that was to be put to productive use, was utilized for destructive purposes.

On Food Imports

Anna laid stress on self-sufficiency in foodgrains. He felt sad that in a predominantly agricultural country like India, even after the implementation of three Five Year Plans, we had to import foodgrains from other countries like America. At that time we were importing huge quantities of foodgrains from America under P.L. 480 programme. It is true that but for these imports of foodgrains, there would have been starvation deaths on a large scale. But his point was that such a situation arose because of implementation lags. Not only that, there was no change in the mindset of those in charge of implementation of the plans. He thought that the government could be impeached on the counts of food, education and defence, even if the charge of ignoring the poor was ignored.

On Calling Madras State as Tamil Nadu

Anna fought for renaming Madras State as Tamil Nadu for historical, cultural and commonsense reasons.

In the past, Madras state was known as Tamil Nadu. In *Silappathikaram*, a great Tamil classic, there is reference to *Then Thamiz Nannadu* meaning sweet and good Tamil Nadu. And Tamil culture, which is Dravidian culture, is distinctly different from the Aryan culture. The commonsense reason, in Anna's own words, is "Madras after all is the capital city of Tamil Nadu, just as Ahmedabad happens to be the capital city of Gujarat, as Chandigarh happens to be the capital city of Punjab. If this logic of naming the state after the name of the capital city is to be followed, Kerala should be renamed Trivandrum, Andhra is to be renamed Hyderabad, Punjab is to be renamed Chandigarh (Note: At that time, Chandigarh was the capital of Punjab but now Chandigarh is the capital of Haryana) and Gujarat should be renamed Ahmedabad."

Anna also pointed out that nobody would lose anything by renaming Madras state as Tamil Nadu. On the other hand, the Tamilians as a whole, would get a sentimental satisfaction because Madras state has been given the ancient name of Tamil Nadu.

On Foreign Aid

Anna was concerned about the mounting external debt and India's heavy dependence of foreign aid in the form of loans. He was not against foreign aid as such. In his own words, "in a world which is becoming smaller and smaller, no country can live without interdependence. Our purpose in questioning it is only to find out whether the amount is being put to the best use, whether we are developing our repayment capacity, whether the creditor countries have got implicit confidence in us whenever we demand more and more aid."

On Taxation in India

Anna knew pretty well that no government could live without taxes. Nobody thinks that a Welfare State or even a Police State can be run without taxes. But he was concerned about the regressive nature of taxation in India with its heavy reliance on indirect taxes for its revenue. The burden of indirect taxes fell on the common man who was already reeling under poverty. He was of the view that the government should mobilize more resources from public sector undertakings.

On the expenditure side, Anna noted that though the government realized the investment in human resources was as important as investment in physical resources like machinery and buildings, when it came to the allocation of financial outlays, only meagre sums were allocated to education and healthcare. And there was poor husbanding of available resources. He cited a report of the World Bank team to support his viewpoint: "....Priorities are lopsided; *e.g.*, big irrigation projects are preferred to the much needed fertilizer plants. Even the minimum land reforms have not been implemented. Legislation is passed but no real effect is taken for implementation."

Anna further cited an appraisal made by a Soviet team about the investment pattern in India: "The policy of becoming self-sufficient in too many lines at the same time, has backfired. The number of big projects undertaken to become independent of imports, is very large. If it had concentrated on a few schemes and completed them with maintenance requirements, the results would have been far more rewarding. They would have maximized production; there would have been adequate returns and the public sector would have gained prestige".

On Handlooms

Anna paid special attention to the popularization of handloom cloth consumption by masses so as to help the handloom weavers and to mitigate their sufferings. In fact, Anna himself sold handloom cloth in public places, along with other frontline leaders.

On Rupee a Measure Scheme

In order to help the poor people, Anna introduced a scheme for supplying rice at a subsidized price. After he came to power, he followed a policy under which rice was sold at one Rupee a measure in large cities like Madras and Coimbatore to help the vulnerable sections there.

Achievements of Anna

Anna considered the following as his main achievements during his short tenure as the Chief Minister of Tamil Nadu.

1. Renaming of Madras State as Tamil Nadu;
2. Legalization of Self-Respect marriages; and
3. Prevention of imposition of Hindi in Tamil Nadu and introduction of two-language formula (Tamil and English) by passing an unanimous resolution in the Assembly.

Conclusion

As a true disciple of Periyar, Anna was wedded to the basic principles of rationalism, socialism and Self-Respect. Not only that, he was a great orator, man of letters, great Parliamentarian and he had a modern mind. He translated many of Periyar's views on social reform into action. Anna worked till the end of his life for the uplift of the common man. And he knew the 'limit of dissent' in Politics. His giving up of the demand for a separate and independent Dravida Nadu is a case in point.

C.N. VAKIL

Introduction

C.N. Vakil was one of the eminent economists of India. He was interested in economic theory as well as practice. He passed his M.A. degree examination of Bombay University and stood first in the university. Then he went to London and worked under Edwin Cannan for his M.Sc. Degree. From 1927, he served in the Department of Economics in varied capacities. He was Assistant Professor from 1921 to 1927, Professor from 1927 to 1930 and Director, School of Economics and Sociology from 1930 to 1956. From 1957 to 1960, he was Director, UNESCO Research Centre at Calcutta. He was Economic Adviser to the Government of India (Department of Planning and Development) in 1945-46. He was a member of the Experts Committee of the I.L.O. in 1956. He was a member of the U.N. Panel of Experts on Industrial Management in 1957. He was visiting professor at the university of Indiana in 1965. And he participated in the First World Congress of Economists held at Rome in 1956. He was appointed as the Vice-Chancellor of South Gujarat University, Surat in 1968.

Vakils' important publications include *Our Fiscal Policy* (1922) *Currency and Prices in India* (1927) *with* Dr. S.K. Muranjan, *Economic Outlook in Federal India* (1933), *Industrial Policy of India* (1934) with M.C. Munshi, *The Falling Rupee* (1942), *The Financial Burden of the War on India* (1943), *Economic Consequences of the Partition* (1948), *Economic Consequences of Divided India (1950) with* Cirvante, Desai and Brahmanand, *Planning for an Expanding Economy* (1956) with P.R. Brahmanand and Poverty and Planning (1963).

Fiscal Policy of India

Prof. Vakil studied the fiscal policy of India from 1861 to 1920 in order to submit a memorandum to the Fiscal Commission in 1921. His main argument was that during the above period, the interests of India were not taken into account by the British rulers. He pointed out no country would sacrifice its national interests for the sake of imperial unity. In his own words: "Every member is ready to do her part for such a unity, without doing injury to her national interests. The reasons for India to adopt such a policy are stronger than in the case of the other and smaller members of the Empire". (C.N. Vakil, Our Fiscal Policy, 1922, P.iv).

Financial Developments in India

Prof. Vakil was of the view that public expenditure in India during the British period did not promote the economic development of the country. Because of mass poverty, the taxable capacity of the people was very low. So he suggested that agriculture and industry should be developed; there should be educational development and better sanitation facilities and above all military expenditure should be drastically cut. Only then, there would be improvement in the incomes of the people and increase in taxable capacity.

He wanted more financial powers for the provinces so that they could spend more on nation building activities. The increased revenue of the provinces could be used as earmarked expenditure for the development of education, sanitation, agriculture and industry. If necessary, the provinces could raise more revenue by levying succession duty, marriage duty and by tapping other sources.

Deficit Financing

Prof. Vakil strongly opposed deficit financing as a means of financing Five Year Plans in the Post-Independence period. He considered the Keynesian concept as a short term remedy to fight depression in the developed countries. He felt that deficit financing has resulted in inflation and poverty.

He suggested the appointment of Public Expenditure Commission to monitor and reduce public expenditure. The British Government set up a Public Expenditure Commission in 1921.

Economic consequences of Divided India

While dealing with the economic consequences of partition and division of the country into India and Pakistan, he dealt with important issues relating to the distribution of area between the two countries, the refugee problem and the financial implications and effects of partition on agriculture, industry, currency and banking, transport, foreign trade, public finance and insurance.

He concluded that partition had a severe strain in both the countries. India, somehow, got over the short term effects of partition within three years. But the common man suffered because of continuous inflationary pressures and shortage of many essential commodities.

Devaluation of Indian Rupee

The Rupee was devalued in June 1966. Vakil believed that the devaluation would provide an incentive for foreign investment. He described it as anti-inflationary, employment oriented and a check on smuggling.

To restore confidence among the people and to put the economy on the right track, Vakil suggested a revised and balanced budget, freezing of all incomes (e.g. wages, profits) at least for some time, avoidance of unnecessary consumption, promotion of exports, increase in production and keeping prices under control.

International Trade

With regard to protection to safeguard indigenous industries from stiff competition from foreign countries, Vakil was of the view that protection should only be for a temporary period and once an industry has been properly established, it should be able to face competition on its own. That is the only way to safeguard the interests of the consumer which the policy makers usually ignored in such matters.

He was in favour of starting joint ventures abroad and trade with OECD countries in primary products. He further proposed setting up of an Import – Export Bank for international trade, commerce and financial matters.

Poverty in India

Professor Vakil was of the view that poverty in a country could be attributed to defects in its production or its distribution. He classified the causes of poverty into internal causes and external causes.

The internal causes are seasonal employment in agriculture, a few earning members in each family with many dependents, the presence of a large number of able bodied beggars miscalled sadhus, climatic conditions that discourage continuous and sustained work, fatalism (belief in Karma and all that) and faulty education system.

The external causes cited by him are international trade and commerce which is not to our advantage, commercial and industrial relations with other countries, especially England which resulted in the draining of our resources.

The remedies suggested by Vakil include increase in production and equitable distribution of income and wealth, consolidation of agricultural holdings, use of better inputs in terms of seeds, implements and manure, sinking of large number of wells, creation of irrigation facilities, strengthening of cooperative movement and education and training in modern methods of cultivation.

To overcome the problem of rural indebtedness, Vakil suggested the establishment of Land Mortgage Banks, and provision of credit to farmers through cooperative banks. He advocated the development of cottage industries to provide more employment opportunities, especially for those who did not want to migrate during agricultural lean season.

Prof. Vakil was for land tax in line with income tax, where a certain exemption limit could be fixed based on the income from land.

He was against industrial exploitation by foreigners. And he was for certain social changes. They include prevention of early marriage, lowering of mortality rates and incidence of diseases, provision of proper sanitation, and removal of purdah system. Vakil believed that free and compulsory education was a desirable objective.

Vakil lamented on the huge expenditure incurred on the bureaucracy: "A large percentage of plan expenditure for rural development, about 60 percent, was spent for administration. It was not known whether or not remaining 40 percent reached the farmer. Therefore, the machinery for implementing the same, had to be created as the existing bureaucratic machinery has failed to function effectively so far".

Planning and Development

Prof. Vakil and P.R. Brahmananda gave an alternative approach to Mahalanobis model for planning and development during the formulation of the Second Five Year Plan for India.

The model is based on the assumption that there is unlimited supply of unskilled labour in rural areas of developing countries. They form a massive reserve army of labour. In other words, there is disguised unemployment in agriculture on a large scale. But this disguised unemployment has vast savings potential. To tap that, those who suffer from disguised unemployment can be transferred from agriculture, without decreasing agricultural production and their labour can be utilized for producing real capital goods. So, for the development of the Indian economy, what we need is not basic and heavy goods as argued by Mahalanobis, but wage goods.

In contrast to Mahalanobis model which emphasized on fixed capital, Vakil and Brahmanand model laid emphasis on wage goods or what they called 'liquid capital' in determining the growth of income and employment. Again, while the Mahalanobis model laid stress on heavy and fixed capital, the Vakil and Brahmananda model laid stress on variable capital in the tradition similar to that of economists such as Marx, Ragnar Nurkse and Arthur Lewis.

When surplus workers are transferred from agriculture to industry, there would be need to provide higher levels of consumption to workers engaged in non-agricultural activities than those in the farm sector. That means there is need for enough wage goods, especially food. If there is wage goods gap, we cannot increase employment in developing economies with abundant supply of labour. The rate of transfer of unemployed workers from agricultural sector to non-farm sector (capital goods sector) depends upon the supply of wage-goods. Thus the provision of wage goods constitutes the most important element in Vakil and Brahmananda model.

In Vakil and Brahmananda model, there is complementarity between consumption and investment, whereas in the Mahalanobis model, there is conflict between consumption and investment. The latter model is based on the assumption that more consumption at present means less investment and that means low rate of growth of income and employment. (For more details on wage goods model, see section on P.R. Brahmananda)

Conclusion

The foregoing discussion outlines briefly the many contributions of Prof. C.N. Vakil to economic theory and policy. His analysis of fiscal policy, monetary policy and the economic consequences of partition are all based on empirical evidence. He was strongly opposed to deficit financing. The remedies he suggests are pragmatic and based on practical wisdom. The planning model which he developed with P.R. Brahmananda is one of his lasting contributions to planning and economic development.

P.R. BRAHMANANDA

Introduction

P.R. Brahmananda was born of P.R. Ramaiya, a well-known Kannada journalist and freedom fighter of princely Mysore state and P.R. Jayalakshmamma, who was a Deputy Mayor of Mysore.

Brahmananda obtained his Honours degree from Maharaja's college in Mysore in 1946. Later, he joined Bombay University and studied under great economists such as C.N. Vakil and D.T. Lakdawala, who was Chairman of the Planning Commission during the Janata rule at the Centre. He did his Ph.D. under the guidance of Prof. Lakdawala, Like his father, he was also a Gandhian.

Prof. Brahmananda belonged to the Bombay School of Economics. When he passed away on January 23, 2003, V.R. Panchamukhi described him as one of the brightest stars of economic profession. He was the soul and body of the Indian Economic Association (IEA) and Indian Economic Journal. D.S. Awasthi, a former Secretary of IEA once remarked" it is easier to say on which area of economics P.R. Brahmananda has not written" (The Indian Economic Journal, October – December 2002-03, Vol. 50 No.2, P.100).

His Works

Prof. Brahmananda was a versatile spirit. His writings ranged over virtually all areas of economics. But monetary economics and development economics claimed most of his attention. His writings in these areas are considered as his major contribution. But he also wrote frequently on topics in agriculture, public finance, industry, labour and trade.

Some of his important writings are: *Planning for an Expanding Economy,* which he wrote jointly with C.N. Vakil in 1956 is rated as his lasting contribution to Indian Economics. It presents an alternate approach to planning in a labour surplus agricultural economy, based on wage-goods model for increasing employment and income as opposed to Mahalanobis model which was the basis of the Second Five Year Plan of India (1956-61).

The New Classical versus the Neo-Classical Economics (1967) is an implicit critique of Economic Theory contained in Sraffa's book "Production of Commodities by Means of Commodities" (1961), *Gold Money Rift* (1969) developed the classical approach to international liquidity and outlined a neutral approach based on an international quantity theory of money; *Determinants of Real National Income and Price Level* (1977) gives Indian monetarist approach to economic policy with empirical testing of various ideas in the Indian context; *Productivity in the Indian Economy – Rising Inputs for Falling Outputs* (1982) applies the theory of productivity growth empirically to Indian conditions and outlines the approach in terms of surpluses and their productivities; *Planning for a Wage-goods Economy* (1995) gives an elaborate account of the Wage-goods model and explains why the economics of developing countries like India have to be different from the economics of industrially developed countries with high incomes; *Nobel Economics – A historical Commentary from the Classical Angle* (1999). It gives the history of modern economic analysis seen through the contributions of Nobel Laureates in Economics; *Money, Income, Prices in 19th Century India – A Historical, Quantitative and Theoretical Study* (2001) analyses the monetary history of India with empirical data for a long period through the lense of modern classical economics and is considered as his great work.

Brahmananda's other contributions include *The Economics of Welfare Maximisation* (based on his Ph.D. dissertation supervised by D.T. Lakdawala); *The Falling Economy and How to Revive It (1977).* It is his Indian Economic Association's Presidential Address); *Planning for a Futureless Economy: a critique of the 6th Plan (1978); The I.M.F. Loan and India's Economic Future (1982);* *Economic Theory and Labour Economics* (1966). This is his Presidential Address at the Labour Conference.

It may be noted that Prof. Brahmananda was a prolific writer. His writings over a period of more than five decades reached a figure of 801 contributions, out of which 36 are books.

Wage-Goods Model

Vakil and Brahmananda, in their book *Planning for an Expanding Economy (1956)* modified the classical theory of growth of income and employment in the context of developing countries suffering from disguised unemployment in agriculture. While Mahalanobis laid stress on the role of fixed capital in determining the growth of employment and income, Vakil and Brahmananda emphasized on wage-goods or what they called *liquid capital*. In their approach to planning, they gave the highest priority to wage-goods industries, especially, agriculture in allocation of resources for investment.

Poverty and unemployment are the two most important problems of the developing countries. In their book published in 1956, they defined wage-goods gap with reference to the magnitude of disguised unemployment. But subsequently, they defined wage-goods gap with reference to the magnitude of poverty. According to them, to remove poverty and increase employment and income, it is essential to increase the aggregate supply of wage-goods and bridge the wage-goods gap. In short, they explain poverty in terms of basic wage goods gap.

Wage goods include (1) food grains, cereals, pulses, (2) milk and milk products, (3) edible oils, (4) fish, eggs and meat, (5) sugar and sugar products (6) fruits and vegetables, (7) spices (8) tea (9) coffee, (10) cloth, (11) matches, (12) soap, (13) salt and kerosene.

Besides the above goods, which are in the nature of private consumption goods, there are other goods which are provided at the collective level. They are "drugs for common use, medical and hospital facilities, minimum educational and library facilities, minimum utility services like water, electricity, roads etc., recreational services and facilities". In addition to these goods, across the regions, there may be other wage-goods depending upon conventional and physiological-cum-nutritional requirement of labourers.

There is wage-goods gap in an economy because the capital stock or productive capacity designed and directed to produce wage-goods is deficient. To remove poverty, this deficiency in the capital stock has to be removed.

We may note that the overall stock of capital in a country may be adequate, but the capital stock to produce basic consumer goods may be deficient. That is because all types of capital stock cannot be used for the production of wage-goods. For example, steel plants and machine making factories cannot produce wage-goods such as food grains, kerosene, cloth, and sugar.

Sometimes, economists make a distinction between capital in "putty" form and capital in "clay" form. Putty capital is a generalized form of capital. It can be used for producing all types of goods such as capital goods, luxury goods and basic goods. But capital in clay form can be used only for specific goods for which it is designed.

Brahmananda is of the view that 'so long as capital is in a putty, all-purpose suited form, it can be directed towards creation of any sort of specific capacity but when once putty capital become capital goods in the form of factories, projects like mills, machinery, plants, mining and power stations and transport networks, it partakes "the nature of clay, fit for particular purpose".

The stock of wage-goods and the raw materials and the accessories used in the production of these wage – goods represent the putty capital because "if stocks of wage-goods exist, labour power can be purchased and deployed for whatever specific capacities are needed in the country".

The availability of wage goods helps in the employment of labour for producing capital. And if that capital is designed for the production of wage-goods, there will be sustainable growth of employment and income. Thus, Vakil and Brahmananda emphasize the importance of wage goods (liquid or variable capital) than fixed capital for the growth of the economy and for removal of poverty and unemployment. In their own words, 'the way out of poverty is, therefore to pay immediate attention to making good the capital gap in respect of wage-goods capacity. This, in its turn, would imply drastic alteration in the pattern of investment in the economy'.

The expansion of basic wage goods will help in the removal of poverty as well as disguised unemployment. To Vakil and Brahmananda, poverty and unemployment are not two different problems. They are two aspects of the same problem (inadequate supply of wage-goods) and they can be dealt with by increasing the supply of wage goods.

In the wage-goods model, "the rate of growth of real income is determined by the proportion of savings to income and the portion of such savings devoted to the expansion of the wage-goods sector".

The wage-goods model focuses only on labour in the production process. But we all know that in modern times, production involves the coordination of land, labour and capital by the entrepreneur. By taking note of this criticism, in later years, Brahmananda developed a strategy known as "Extended Wage-goods Strategy". He included in his priority sector 'integrated wage-goods complex'. It consists of not only the wage goods but also those capital goods which are required for the production of wage goods. That makes his model more consistent and realistic.

In the earlier model of Vakil and Brahmananda, consumption multiplier was defined with particular reference to the removal of labour suffering from disguised unemployment from agriculture. But in later years, in the modified model, they developed a multiplier which related the increase in the supply of wage goods to increase in real income. It has been called *consumption – real income multiplier.*

It is true that by withdrawing some workers (disguised unemployed) from agriculture, a certain amount of wage-goods can be released for providing productive employment in the creation of capital assets. But Vakil and Brahmananda thought that the wage-goods so released alone would not provide employment to all the potentially available labour force. Therefore, they laid emphasis on the increase in the production of wage-goods, especially food grains, to fill the wage-goods gap to achieve full employment conditions.

The wage-goods model in its original form tells that the growth in employment depends solely upon the supply of wage goods and that the capital goods (that is, heavy industry products) do not play any important role in expanding employment opportunities. This has been criticized. Prof. Dantwala has rightly pointed out "it is a mistake to consider capital goods and wage goods as exclusive and unrelated categories. Anyone who studies the composition of inputs needed for transformation of traditional agriculture should be able to appreciate the inter-connection between the two". Another weakness of the model is that it ignores the need for bringing about appropriate technological and institutional changes to generate more employment opportunities in the agricultural sector itself.

In spite of the above criticism, a great merit of Vakil and Brahmananda's book is that" it addressed itself to the task of building an indigenous theory of Indian economic development and is thus very close in spirit to the works of the founding fathers of Indian Political economy, Dadabhai Naoroji and Mahadev Govind Ranade" (Dilip M. Nachne, E.P.W., March, 2003, P.871)

Brahmananda's Contribution to Various Issues of Topical Significance

Some of the important contributions are his critique of 1966 rupee devaluation. He gave a famous agenda for anti-inflation and he called it SEMIBOMBLA. It was a 'Memorandum on a Policy to contain Inflation' with C.N. Vakil and others, submitted to the Prime Minister in April, 1975. He submitted another Memorandum called FULLMANGAL. It was a 'Memorandum on a Policy for Inflation Reversal and Guaranteed Price Stability with FULLMANGAL, submitted to the Prime Minister in April, 1975. He also wrote a critique of the IMF loan *(The IMF Loan and India's Economic Future)*. In one of his final writings on public policy, Liberalisation in the Indian Economy; Ecstasy so Far and the Agony Ahead, he expressed his concerns about the future course of liberalization.

Conclusion

We find from the foregoing discussion that Monetary Economics and Development Economics claimed most of Brahmananda's attention. His book *Planning for an Expanding Economy* (1956) which he wrote jointly with C.N. Vakil is considered as his lasting contribution to Indian Economics. And he never hesitated to comment fearlessly on public policy.

J.N. BHAGWATI (1934)

Introduction

Jagdish Natwarlal Bhagwati is famous for his research in international economics and for his advocacy of free trade. He is a champion of globalization. He is a professor of Economics and Law at Columbia university.

Bhagwati was born in a Gujarati family in Bombay Presidency on July 26, 1934. He did his B.A. degree course at Sydenham College, Bombay. Then he went to England for his further studies. There he studied at St. John's College (Cambridge University) and received his Second B.A. degree in Economics. From there, he went to U.S.A. and joined M.I.T. where he got his Ph.D. in Economics. His Ph.D. supervisor was Charles P. Kindleberger and the title of his thesis was "Essays in International Economics". Bhagwati is married to Padma Desai, also an economist. Their joint 1970 study "India: Planning for Industrialization" was a notable contribution at the time.

Career

Bhagwati returned to India in 1961 after completing his Ph.D. degree in U.S.A. First, he taught for a short period at Indian Statistical Institute, Calcutta. Then, he moved to Delhi to teach at Delhi School of Economics from 1962 to 1968. From 1968 to 1980, Bhagwati served as economic professor at the Massachusetts Institute of Technology (MIT).

Bhagwati is currently Professor of Economics, Law and International Affairs at Columbia University, and Senior Fellow for International Economics at the Council on Foreign Relations. In the past, he has held many important positions at the international level. He was special advisor to the U.N. on globalization; he was economic policy adviser, to the Director-General of General Agreement on Tariffs and Trade from 1981 to 1993 and external adviser to World Trade Organization in 2001. He was a member of the group appointed by the Director-General of W.T.O. on the future of the WTO. He was special policy adviser to the United Nations in 2000. He was on the Advisory Committee to the Secretary-General of UNO on the New Partnership for Africa and he was also a member of the Eminent Persons Group under the leadership of Brazilian President on the future of United Nations Conference on Trade and Development (UNCTAD).

Bhagwati currently serves on the Academic Advisory Board of Human Rights Watch (Asia) and the Board of Scholars of the Centre for Civil Society.

In 2000, Bhagwati was a signatory to an *amicus* briefing coordinator by the American Enterprise Institute with the Supreme Court of the United States. The amicus contended that the Environmental Protection Agency should contrary to a prior ruling be allowed to take into account the costs of regulations when setting environmental standards.

His Works

Bhagwati is a champion of free trade and is described as 'the most creative' international trade theorist of his generation. He has a number of books including *Why Growth Matters: How Economic Growth in India Reduced Poverty and the Lessons for Other Developing Countries" "Termites in the Trading System: How Preferential Agreements undermine Free Trade", "Defence of Globalization" (2004).* "Why Growth Matters…" describes the beneficial effects of economic growth and how they can be imitated in the other developing countries. "The Termites in the Trading System" discusses the harmful effects of preferential trade agreements. In his book "Defence of Globalization", he argues "….this process (of globalization) has a human face, but we need to make that face more agreeable".

Besides books, he has written a number of articles including "The Contemporary Crisis and its Determinative Factors within Globalization Framework (2013), "An Overview of the New Architecture of International Monetary System" (2007), "The Globalization Phenomenon and the Financial Institutions" (2008), "Financial Markets and Real Economy" (working Paper, 2012), "Financial Institutions Policies within Globalization. Framework (2010), "Networks and "Financial Systems"

(2004), "Global Imbalances and Capital Flows to Emerging Market Countries" (Emerging Markets Forum Background Paper 2004). In this Background Paper, he underlines that a dominant factor in the international and financial system over the last seven to eight years has been the almost continuous rise in the current account deficit in the balance of payments of the United States from an average of about US $ 90 billion a year throughout.

Taxing the Brain Drain: Bhagwati is of the view that there is a way to compensate for the brain drain from the less developed countries (LDCs) to the developed countries (DCs). A supplementary income tax can be imposed on immigrants' earnings in the developed countries; the funds raised in this manner can then be routed through the United Nations to the less developed countries for development spending. Bhagwati first mooted the idea in 1972. Since then, the proposal has attracted attention in both the less developed countries and the developed countries, as well as in the discussions of international agencies.

Two important discussions were held in 1976 at Nairobi Conference on Trade and Development (UNCTAD) and the International Labour Organization (ILO) Conference on World Employment. The International Conference in February, funded by Rockefeller Foundation, dealt with the feasibility and optimal format of such a tax, from the point of view of constitutionality, compatibility with human rights and revenue possibilities in developed countries receiving the most immigrants. The proceedings, plus legal and economic conclusions are published in the form of a book in Bhagwati and Partington (eds.) *Taxing the Brain Drain: A Proposal (1976). The* Second Volume in this series is *The Brain Drain and Taxation: Theory and Empirical Analysis:*

There are some economists who feel that Jagdish Bhagwati should have been awarded the Nobel Prize in Economics long back because he was the most important international trade economist of his generation – that generation falling between Bertil Ohlin and James Meade, who shared the Nobel Prize in 1977. His student Paul Krugman won the Nobel Prize in 2008.

Domestic Distortions

Bhagwati could have been awarded the prize for a single scientific paper. "Domestic Distortions, Tariffs and the Theory of Optimum Subsidy", which he wrote jointly with V.K. Ramaswami. It was published in the *Journal of Political Economy* in 1963 and is considered as a landmark in the Postwar theory of commercial policy. In the paper, they have specified the condition under which free trade is, and is not, optimal, in the presence of distortions (market failures).

Before their paper, economists believed that free trade was always the best policy for a small country without market failure and for a large country without market failure, the best policy was optimum tariff.

Domestic distortions may arise because of the presence of externalities in production or consumption or labour market rigidities such as wages. It was vaguely realized that a tariff might not be optimal. There might be a better way to correct the domestic distortion without tampering with free trade. But there was some confusion.

Bhagwati and Ramaswami removed the confusion by their *targeting principle*: the optimum policy intervention is that which targets the market failure directly, rather than indirectly. If the market is an externality in production, the best policy response will be a production subsidy that would increase the production of a good that would confer positive externality or reduces the production of a good which confers a negative externality.

Awards and Honours

Bhagwati has received a number of awards and degrees. They include Mahalanobis Memorial Award of the Indian Econometric Society (1974), Fellow of the American Academy of Arts and Sciences (1982), Seidman Distinguished Award in International Political Economy (1996), Padma Vibhushan Award (2000), Lifetime Achievement Award of the Indian Chamber of Commerce (2004), and Order of the Rising Sun, Gold and Silver Star (2006).

Conclusion

We may conclude with the words of Paul Samuelson, a Nobel Laureate, during Bhagwati's 70th Birthday festschrift in January 2005: "I measure a scholar's prolificness not by the mere number of his publishings Just as the area of a rectangle equals its width times its depth, the quality of a lifetime accomplishment must weight each article by its novelties and wisdoms…. Jagdish Bagwati is more like Haydn: a composer of more than hundred symphonies and no one of them other than top notch… In the struggle to improve the lot of mankind, whether located in advanced economies or in societies climbing the ladder out of poverty, Jagdish Bhagwati has been a tireless partisan of that globalization which elevates global total factor – productivities both of richest America and poorest regions of Asia and Africa".

BRIJ NARAIN (1888-1947)

Introduction

Brij Narain was an eminent economist and prolific writer of Pre-Independent India. His writings are marked by original thinking and analytical clarity. He was Professor of Economics at the Sanatan Dharma College, Lahore and Honorary Professor of Economics at the Punjab University. He met with a tragic end at a relatively young age. He was killed on August 14, 1947 during partition (in the communal riots).

Some of his important writings include *Essays on Indian Economic Problems* (1919), *Indian Economic Life* (1929), *India in Crisis* (1934), *Tendencies in Indian Economic Thought* (1935) *Indian Socialism* (1937) *Marxism is Dead* (1939), *Charkha, Marxism and Indian Socialism* (1941), *Principles of Economics* (1941) *Indian Economic Problems* (1944), *Money and Banking* (1946), and *Economic Structure of Free India* (1946).

Principles of Economics

Prof. Brij Narain was of the view that the laws of economics have universal application. They can be applied to developed countries as well as underdeveloped countries. In this, he differed from Ranade, who, like the members of the Historical School, believed that the laws of economics were relative in nature.

Indian Economics

Prof. Brij Narain was of the view that the term *Indian Economics* was vague. As he put it, "the demand (for Indian Economics) as we have seen is partly based upon a misconception of the true character of present day Economics. There is a sense in which principles of economics are of universal application". He maintained that the value of Indian economics was limited to the collection of facts relating to Indian economic life. To believe that these facts would form the basis of new science would be a sheer folly. In his own words, "Indian Economics thus means a mass of statistical and other material which would be of invaluable help in the solution of the Indian economic problems. It does not mean a science with peculiar laws or principles or any proposed solutions of Indian economic problems or any new method or methods of dealing with them". In short, Indian economics was "a study of Indian economic life in the light of our knowledge of general principles of Economics".

Industrialism

Prof. Brij Narain believed that only industrialism of the western type would make India a rich country. He felt that the arguments against industrialization of India were not based on facts. As he put it; "It does not correspond to facts. The motives to economic activity in India are essentially the same as those which operate in western countries". He argued that "those who oppose industrialism should remember two things – than an agricultural country means a poor country, and the growth of civilization with all that it implies depends upon the growth of town life, which in turn, depends upon the growth of industrialism. Revive the village community, if that is possible, restore the village by all means, but that is not how the problem of Indian poverty can be solved". He cited the examples of U.K., U.S.A. and Japan to illustrate how industrialism helped them become developed countries. He attributed the industrial backwardness of India to the laissez-faire policy followed by the British government. He criticized the policy of discriminating protection because it did not help the industrialism of the country.

Rural Development

Prof. Brij Narain felt that the scope for improving the working and living conditions of rural population by the establishment of rural industries was rather limited. To bring about improvements in agriculture, he suggested the diversion of surplus agricultural labour to manufacturing industries. It may be noted that similar suggestions were made by Arthur Lewis, Ragnar Nurkse and Vakil and Brahmananda in recent times. He suggested active participation of the State in agriculture. For instance, he suggested nationalization of agriculture to prevent sub-division and fragmentation. And he wanted land revenue to be abolished and a graduated tax to be introduced on agricultural incomes.

Prof. Brij Narain advocated for the establishment of a central bank in India.

Democratic Planning

During the great depression of 1930s, he advocated socialist planning of Soviet type for India to tide over the problems created by the crisis. The impact of the business depression was very severe on India and the efforts made by the government was not 'planning' in its real sense. Economic planning in India was capitalistic planning, that is, planning consistent with freedom of enterprise. In regard to industries, planning in India meant very little more than protective tariff. What was happening then was not planning but "protection".

In his own words, "Our industrial development is proceeding without any plan or system. No attempt is made to create basic or key industries. No attempt is made towards machine-making industries. It is futile to hope that such industrial development as has taken place now will provide the means, within any reasonable period of time, of lessening the pressure of population on the soil". (India in the Crisis, P. 277). He strongly felt that "the problem of planning in a country of small peasants, each working on his own account is insoluble except through nationalization of production" (Ibid., p. 277). He wanted economic planning on a comprehensive scale as in Soviet Russia. For, "in a socialist economy, the place of competition is taken by deliberate selection.... Socialist planned economy is of a unitary character. In the domain of industry, attention is concentrated on machine-making and development of the sources of power. In agriculture, collective farming with power-driven appliances is the distinguishing feature. Production is on a large scale or economic planning in the socialist state is on the basis of machine, whether in agriculture or in industries" (ibid, pp. 278, 288).

Prof. Brij Narain felt that in agriculture there was an urgent need to reduce the pressure of population on land to solve the problem of disguised unemployment. The surplus labour can be taken off land and they may be provided non-farm jobs in the villages. Village industries may be organized on a new basis. Agriculture can be modernized and there was need for increasing the purchasing power of masses. The problems in the rural areas cannot be solved by inflation. They can be solved only by more production and equitable distribution of wealth. But he was not for fascist planning. He wanted cultural planning. Under cultural planning, the educational system would be adapted to the economic needs of the nation. He was against religious fanaticism because that would result in communal strife. However, it may be noted that in the later part of his life, his admiration for planning waned and he moved away from it and advocated democratic planning.

Charkha, Marxism and Indian Socialism

Prof. Brij Narain was not in agreement with the Gandhian idea of non-violent economy because he felt that it was more concerned with individual salvation than with social reconstruction. As he put it, "in politics, we are not concerned with individual souls as in religion and our main objective is the safety and material prosperity of a group of human beings". Therefore, charkha economics cannot be the basis of economic development of India. He was opposed to Marx's idea of international communism. He pointed out: "if the international struggle for existence is a fact, it follows that socialism can never develop into communism in any one country. The "withering away" of the State in any country might mean loss of independence for that country or its dismemberment". For him, international communism was dead, though there was socialism in individual countries. According to him, "the main content or aim of Indian socialism is the ending of exploitation of man by man and a planned production and distribution of wealth". (*Charkha, Marxism and Indian Socialism*, p. 136). In short, he was against charkha economics of Gandhi and Marxism based on violence. And he was opposed to laissez-faire policy. He was in favour of democratic planning. There would be a planned economy with controlled private enterprise. As he put it: "If the control of private enterprise by the State can give us an economic structure for planning, we do not care for the social revolution. India is not ready for social revolution which might bring a workers' state into existence" (*Economic Structure of Free India*, p. 59). In Brij Narain's vision for the economic structure of Free India, we find the features that resemble the mixed economy which India adopted after Independence for its planning.

Commenting on the economic thought in India, he said that the Indian economists did not contribute to the development of economic theory. They studied Indian economic problems, their work being historical in nature. They attached more importance to economic institutions, of concrete problems and of the impact of world forces on the Indian economy (*Tendencies in Recent Economic Thought, 1935, p. 5*)

Prof. Brij Narain was interested in the use of statistical methods and mathematics in the interpretation of economic facts. He considered economics as a statistical science.

Conclusion

Prof. Brij Narain was one of the eminent original thinkers of Pre-Independent India. He advocated western industrialism and democratic planning. He rejected Gandhiji's charka economy as well as Marxian international communism. By advocating the use of statistical and mathematical methods in economics, he wanted to make economic analysis precise and scientific. He occupies a unique position among the economists who lived before Independence.

J.K. MEHTA (1901-1980)

Introduction

Prof. J.K. Mehta was a philosopher – economist. He was Head of the Department of Economics at Allahabad University. After his retirement in 1965-65, he became the Honorary Professor in the department until his death on August 10, 1980. He was a original thinker and prolific writer. He made significant contribution to the philosophical interpretation of economics.

His main contributions are found in *Studies in Advanced Economic Theory* (1946) *Lectures on Modern Economic Theory* (1959), *Foundations of Economics* (1966) and Macro Economics (1969). Public Finance: Theory and Practice (1949) jointly with Dr. S.N. Agarwal.

Definition and Scope of Economics

Mehta defined economics as follows: "Economics is the science that studies human behaviour as the effort to minimize pain in the long run or in other words, as an endeavour to gain freedom from wants and reach the state of happiness" (Economics: Pure Versus Applied, 1962:31).

Prof. Mehta dealt with the nature and scope of economics from a philosophical and psychological bent of mind. He considered maximization of utility as nothing but minimization of pain. As wants are many and means are a few, only some wants can be satisfied at a time. He tells that "since utility is obtained by removing wants and since the degree of utility in each case is equal to the degree of pain caused by the consciousness of the want, utility consists merely in the removal of pain".

All wants cannot be satisfied permanently because they are recurring in nature. Therefore, pain cannot be minimized to zero. So he concludes that we can get real relief from pain by not only removing our wants but by seeing that no new wants arise in future.

Let us take two categories of persons – the short-sighted and those with foresight. For the first category, economics is the study of human behaviour regarded as an effort directed at the attainment of the end of maximizing utility, for the latter it is the science that studies human behaviour as the effort to minimize pain in the long run, or in other words, "an endeavour to gain freedom from wants" (J.K. Mehta, Advanced Economic Theory, 1964, p.8) To him "Economics is a science which studies human behaviour as a means to the end of wantlessness (Ibid. p. 9).

State of Wantlessness

Prof. Mehta is of the view that "the real end of our activities consists in reaching the state of wantlessness, for in no other way can permanent freedom from wants or complete absence of pain be secured. This makes economics a science that studies human behaviour as an attempt to reach the state of wantlessness" (Advanced Economic Theory, p.9)

Freedom from wants requires control over the mind and the body. We all know that it is the mind that moves the body. It may be noted that wantlessness does not mean actionlessness. It is conscience that determines human behaviour. When a person yields to environment, her desire for worldly possessions would disappear. Mehta says: "wantlessness, then, consists neither in not eating and drinking, nor in not earning income. All that is required is to do all such things with a selfless motive to earn not for our own use but for the use of all those whom our conscience would like to be served. Such a wantless attitude to life would secure, therefore, not only our own happiness but would enable us to contribute to social welfare".

One can find in Mehta's concept of the state of wantlessness, an echo of Lord Buddha's teaching that desire is the cause of misery of humankind.

Static Economics and Dynamic Economics

The branch of economic analysis which confines its attention to equilibrium positions is called "statics". "Comparative Statics" is severally considered as the most useful variety of statics. It compares equilibrium positions corresponding to two or more sets of external circumstances. Supply-demand exercise belongs to this category.

Static analysis concentrates only on equilibrium positions. It does not concern itself with the time it takes for an equilibrium position to be achieved, nor with the path by which variables approach their equilibrium states. This is one major concern of dynamic analysis. In simple terms, dynamics is the study of the movement of economic variables from one equilibrium position to another.

To Mehta, "dynamics is not a positive concept; it is the negation of statics. Statics can be changed into dynamics by introducing the time element as a variable. He is of the view that statistical analysis of economic phenomena (a timeless analysis) and dynamical analysis (in which time figures as a variable) are tending to merge into one. As he puts it beautifully, "Break up dynamics into bits and it reduces itself to statics. Assemble them together and you get dynamics again (1962:13).

According to Professor Mehta, dynamic analysis is not concerned with the end – results: its concern is to show the path an economy takes to arrive at the final result. He feels that his approach to developmental economics corresponds to Tinbergen's; economic dynamics involving endogenous processes.

Consumer's Surplus

Prof. Mehta calls consumers surplus *buyer's rent* or *buyer's surplus*. It is the difference between the utility that he expects to derive from the consumption of the commodity and the cost of buying"

(Ibid, 4th edition, 1964, p. 73). He also tells that the greater our want for commodities now as compared to future wants, the greater the consumer's surplus.

Theory of Interest

After discussing the earlier theories of interest such as abstinence or waiting theory of interest, productivity theory (of interest) of capital, and time-preference theory, Mehta defined interest as the "earning of capital" which is determined by its marginal productivity.

The classical theory of interest says that the rate of interest is determined by the demand for and supply of saving. According to Keynes, interest is the price paid for parting with liquidity. Professor Mehta is of the view that the classical theory of interest and Keynes liquidity preference theory, as a matter of fact, are one and the same.

Welfare Economics

Mehta expressed the view that a person's welfare at a given time was measured by the amount of satisfaction that he enjoyed at that time. He looked at welfare as an ethical concept. According to him, "social welfare is a kind of welfare which is located or felt in the mind of a particular man". He accepts that measurement of social welfare is a tough task. Only a superman is competent to measure the sorrows and joys of others. But even he would make mistakes. He felt that every study of economics had been a welfare study in some sense. Prof. Mehta was in agreement with Hicks and Kaldor who modified Pareto Optimality by introducing compensatory criterion wherein, after a change, the gainers would still gain after compensating the losers. That would maximize social welfare.

He further states: Social welfare is not to be computed by adding up the welfare of all the individuals. It is just an idea of the welfare of one composite unit – the society (Economic Essays, p.11). Prof. Mehta in his essay, concludes by saying: "Social welfare has no objective tests. But how does that matter? Even in the study of pure economics, we dwell in a region that has little relevance to the so-called practical life" (Ibid, p.11)

Prof. Mehta attempted philosophical interpretation of economics for the pursuit of economic truths. He thought there was a close relationship between philosophy and economics even when traditional methods were applied. "Not only that, towards the end of his journey in search for 'truth in economics.

Prof. Mehta realized that the knowledge sought in the external world – the knowledge of economics, physics, chemistry, zoology, aeronautics, and like disciplines – is unreal'. (1967:209). He says: "For our happiness, for the solution of all our problems, the knowledge that we need is to be found in the Bible, the Geeta, the Quran, the Zand Avastha, and in short, the holy books of all the faiths. Putting that knowledge to effective use, we can assure the peoples of the world a joyful existence freed from the knotty problems of life which the existing sciences have attempted to solve but succeeded in making them Knottier still'. (where one and the many meet' 1967: 209)

Economics of Fasting

Generally, by fasting we mean not eating and not drinking except the drinking of water. But Prof. Mehta says that if a man has to fast, his body and mind both must fast. A complete mental fast means that the person concerned should stop thinking. Non-eating helps in removing the poisonous matter from the body. Similarly, if a person stops thinking, it will help in attracting fine matter. It will improve the quality of action and ultimately the quality of life. And at the same time, it will remove undesirable thoughts. He tells that a person should undertake fast when he is in pain.

Prof. Mehta extends his ideas on fasting to a firm. Just as a person undertakes fast when he is in pain, a firm that is sick, that is, which cannot produce and sell according to demand and has lot of unsold stock should go on fasting. He speaks of two kinds of fast: The first one relates to bodily fast. That is, the firm should not add to its plant and machinery, and stock of goods. The second kind of fast is mental fast. That is, the organizer of the firm should entertain pious thoughts. He should not try to increase market share at the cost of his rivals in the market and he should not contemplate introducing capital-intensive and labour-saving policies based on technological advancement and create unemployment for workers. Non-violence should be the basis of his approach to business: As Metha puts it, "Owing to violence and selfishness, some businesses are diseased. They should be persuaded to undertake a fast." (J.K. Mehta, Philosophy and Economics of Fasting, P. 23)

Economic Growth

When there is no growth in an economy, it is said to be in static equilibrium. But when it is still growing, it is either in a state of disequilibrium or dynamic equilibrium. Growth implies the growth of population and the growth of income. Prof. Mehta feels that growth in per capita income is an appropriate measure of economic growth. He is of the view that growth and progress are not one and the same thing. Similarly, development may lead to material progress, but it need not lead to moral progress.

Economic growth can be accelerated by improvement in human efficiency and by increasing the quality of human stock. In other words, he stresses on the role of both human capital and physical capital in economic growth. And he laid great emphasis on the quality of organization. He appreciated the importance given to savings for capital formation (investment) by classical economists.

The important role accorded by Schumpeter to entrepreneurs and innovations has also come in for praise by Prof. Mehta.

As far as the backward economies are concerned, he pointed out the need for change of social, cultural and infrastructure for economic growth to take place because these societies are custom-bound and tradition-oriented.

As far as the developed nations are concerned, like Malthus, he anticipated the Keynesian diagnosis of deficiency of aggregate demand as the main cause of the problem of unemployment. In his own words, the main problem in a developed economy is "not insufficient income but insufficient consumption (J.K. Mehta, Macroeconomics, 1969, P. 229).

Conclusion

Prof. Mehta richly deserves to be called a philosopher – economist. Rooted in Indian culture, in his economic thought, he brought together philosophy, mathematics and economics. His reflections on economics are based on ethical and religious foundations.

B.R. SHENOY (1905 – 1978)

Introduction

Prof. Shenoy was an eminent classical liberal economist of India. He was born in the village of Bellikoth, near Mangalore in Karnataka on June 3, 1905. Shenoy was a brilliant student. He got first class in Master's Degree in economics from Benares Hindu University in 1929. Then he enrolled for M.Sc. and Ph.D. in economics at the London School of Economics, Prof. Hayek was his Ph.D. guide. Hayek was a great champion of free trade and vehement critic of centralized planning. He considered planning as the road to serfdom. Shenoy was greatly influenced by the liberal economic philosophy of Hayek. His Ph.D. thesis at London School of Economics was "Some Aspects of a Central Bank for India". While at London School of Economics, he published two articles namely "An Equation for the Price Level of New Investment Goods" and "Interdependence of Price Levels" in the Quarterly Journal of Economics. These two articles established Shenoy as a young economist with competence in monetary and fiscal economics.

After his return to India, Shenoy taught at Wadia College (Pune). Then he taught at the University of Ceylon, Gujarat University and the London School of Economics. He was also associated with a number of policy–making institutions and bodies. He worked at the Ceylon Commission on Currency, the Ceylon Department of Currency, the Reserve Bank of India, the International Monetary Fund

(IMF) and the World Bank. In 1968, Shenoy resigned from Gujarat University and founded the Economic Research Centre in New Delhi. The Centre advocated the ideas of economic liberalism.

His Works

Shenoy was a prolific writer. His writings include *Post-War Depression and Way-out* (1944). In it, he pointed out the dangers involved in financing the Bombay Plan through newly created money and bank credit. Other important works are: *Problems of Indian Economic Development* (1958), *Indian Planning and Economic Development* (1963), *Fifteen years of Indian Planning* (1966), *Indian Economic Policy* (1968), *Indian Economic crisis: A Program for Reform* (1968), *PL480 Aid and India's Food Problem* (1974), *Food Crisis in India: Causes and cure* (1974), *Economic growth and social Justice* (1977) *Ceylon currency and Banking* (1941), *and the Sterling Assets of the Reserve Bank of India* (1953).

In the *Sterling Assets of the Reserve Bank of India,* Shenoy made an effort to accurately calculate the World War II expenses and the actual value of foreign exchange reserves with the Reserve Bank of India. Shenoy suggested devaluation of Rupee to attain proper parity with the pound sterling.

Economic Planning

Soon after Independence, there was a debate about the system and the path to be followed for our economic development. At that time – there were three broad proposals: one was the Gandhian model based on village economy and Trusteeship; the second one was the Bombay Plan which was based on the assumption that government intervention and regulation was absolutely necessary, especially in capital goods production. The third proposal was Nehruvian model based on socialistic pattern of society with a subsidiary role for private enterprise. Ultimately, Nehruvian model was followed for more than four decades. During this period, India became a mixed economy where the private enterprises were subjected to a lot of control and regulation. There was what Rajaji called Licence – Permit – Control Raj. There was not much choice and competition. Licences, permits, import substitution, export restrictions, quantitative restriction of bulk exports, reservation for small-scale exports were the order of the day.

Shenoy advocated that private enterprises should be allowed to compete both at home and abroad in most of the sectors other than defence, roads and railways.

When the economic crisis took place in India in 1991, we had to go for a huge loan from International Monetary Fund and it imposed a number of conditions for structural reorganization and liberalization. The conditions levied by IMF were similar to the suggestions made by Shenoy during the 1950s and 1960s. Liberalization, privatization and globalization became the essential features of new economic policy.

Note of Dissent

The liberal economic philosophy of Shenoy is reflected well in the "Note of Dissent" which he submitted when he was a member of the Panel of Economists appointed to appraise India's Second Five Year Plan (1956-61) which aimed at heavy industrialization.

In his Note of Dissent, Shenoy did not subscribe wholly to the views of his colleagues on (1) the size of the Plan, (2) Deficit Financing as a means of raising real resources for the plan, and (3) certain policy and institutional implications of the Plan.

1. Size of the Plan

The Second Plan was built on the basis of a 25 to 27 percent increase in the national income in five years. As the increase in investment required for the Plan Frame was fairly ambitious, Shenoy thought that unless foreign assistance became available in a very large measure, there would be the risk of inflation. In his own words, "To force a pace of development in excess of the capacity of the available real resources must necessarily involve uncontrolled inflation. In a democratic community, where the masses of the people live close to the margin of subsistence, uncontrolled inflation may prove to be explosive and might undermine the existing order of society. In such a situation, one cannot subsidize communism better than through inflationary deficit financing". (Note of Dissent, p2). If, methods of a communist economy with centralized planning were adopted, he thought individual liberty and democratic institutions would be wiped out by administrative or legislative action. In short, he considered the Second Plan an over-ambitious plan.

The over-ambitious character of the Plan Frame is also reflected in the rate of increase it aims at in the national income. Allowance being made for favourable monsoons, the increase in the national income during the Fist Plan is estimated at 12 to 13 percent, or an annual increase of 2.4 to 2.6 percent. The corresponding increase in the Plan Frame is 5 percent per annum or 25 to 27 percent (Ibid, p4) He is of the view that "the available real resources (savings) for development cannot for sometime be expected to be of an order that would permit anything like a doubling of the rate of growth in national income (Ibid p.4)

He further says: "As no plan can be bigger or bolder than the available resources, the size of the investment programme should be reviewed periodically to ensure that it keeps within the limits of savings. If such a review should reveal a shortage of resources, it would be shortsighted to fill the gap by credit creation or deficit financing as this will be self-defeating" (p.5)

Economic development is not merely a matter of credit creation or deficit financing. If there is scarcity of savings, it will result in scarcity of needs of production, and in administrative and organizational difficulties, which limit the pace of development and which credit creation cannot correct.

Indian poverty and the massive rural under-employment are the result of a continued shortfall of savings and investments below the demographic rate.

2. Deficit Financing

Deficit financing is generally used as an instrument for initiating a process of higher investment and higher incomes by fuller utilization of unemployed and underutilized resources.

Deficit financing does not create real resources. Together with the issue of loans, collection of small savings etc., it is one of the devices for appropriating, for the public sector, the real resources which exist in the economy.

It may be noted that Shenoy is not totally against deficit financing. As he put it; "Deficit financing is essential in an underdeveloped economy to permit full use of resources. By the same token, deficit financing should stop severely short of the point at which inflation begins. Inflation does not, on balance, add to the aggregate real resources".

'Inflation tends to be self-perpetuating. With rise in price and wages, the original estimates of the cost of the projects taken in hand will be out of date. More deficit financing would be necessary for their completion. And, as they cannot be left half-finished, there would be a pressure for further deficit financing. The best protection against inflation is to prevent it by keeping the investment programmes within the available resources (Pp 10-11).

3. Policy and Institutional Implications

Besides dealing with the size of the plan, deficit financing and inflation, in the Note of Dissent, Shenoy has dealt with other issues such as legal and administrative measures, extension of nationalization, continuance of controls, price support of agricultural produce.

Shenoy was of the view that heavy reliance on legislation and administrative measures to increase the rate of savings to permit a bigger and bolder plan would gradually undermine our democratic social order and individual liberty. Hence he suggested exploring the scope for foreign aid and foreign loans without strings and foreign private capital to supplement domestic saving for accelerated economic development.

Taxes on Lower Income Groups

As the standard of living of the lower income groups in India is very low, there is not much scope for imposing taxes on them. Finance for the Plan must be raised from the middle and the upper income groups. Taxes and other devices that would tend to reduce further the income of the lower income groups should be avoided. He was not for amendment of Article 286(3) of the Constitution in order to enable the government to tax articles "essential to the life of the community".

Extension of Nationalisation

Shenoy opposed general extension of nationalization on principle. According to him, "Nationalisation should be ordinarily limited to public utility concerns and to concerns, involving national security. Otherwise, State intervention should be concerned with the prevention of monopolies or quasi-monopolies. (P. 13) Moreover, civil servants are not trained in efficient management of business and industrial concerns in a competitive market economy, which is a highly specialized function.

Continuance of Controls

Shenoy was of the view that controls and physical allocations were not a necessary adjunct to planning. So he said: "Steps should be taken to remove controls as early as may be possible. Controls and allocations are an essential characteristic of communist planning. They do not very well, fit in, under planning in a free enterprise market economy.

Price-Support of Agricultural Produce

Shenoy recognized the importance of constructing licensed warehouses, and for provision of credit and marketing facilities to farmers. But he was not for price-support of agricultural produce. He considered that a risky venture in India. He felt that such a policy would force the economy down the inclined plane of inflation. He said that even in the United States, price support of agricultural produce only survived. It had not succeeded. It had undue stockpiling of agricultural commodities and in the past had involved a great deal of wastage of stocks through deterioration. He further felt that selective price support policy was a poor answer to this difficulty. Price support policy would cause a distortion in agricultural production and economic instability. The price situation in India was too complex to be resolved by price support of agricultural commodities or other inflationary measures such as deficit financing. He strongly felt that price support and deficit financing were no remedies to individual over-production, and to export difficulties.

Conclusion

Prof. Shenoy was a great defender of free-market economies and integration with the world economy. He was a man of moral courage. Nobel economist Milton Friedman paid rich tribute to Prof. Shenoy in the following words: "Prof. B.R. Shenoy was a great man who had the economic understanding to recognize the defects of current planning in India, and was even rarer, the courage to state his views openly and without equivocation. Rarely such a man blesses our society". Further, he went on to say: If one reads Shenoy's report now, it sounds like a retrospective description of what happened rather than a forecast. But needless to say, though most economists display a deep respect for Shenoy's courage and personal qualities, he remains a prophet without honour in his own country".

PANDIT MADAN MOHAN MALAVIYA

Introduction

Pandit Madan Mohan Malaviya was popularly known as Mahamana Malaviya. He was a many-sided personality. He was a teacher, brilliant lawyer, patriot, propagator of Hindu Dharma, ideals and religion, a dynamic political organizer, great educationist, social worker, journalist, editor of leading newspapers and journals. Above all, a great human being. He was the finest flower of the Indian culture.

Early Life

Pt. Madan Mohan Malaviya was born on 25th December, 1861, at Prayag, in a family of six brothers and two sisters. His father and grandfather were Sanskrit scholars. His father Pt. Baijnath was an excellent Kathavacak (narrator of stories from Bhagavat). After initial training in Sanskrit, Malaviya learnt English in a school and passed his B.A. from Muir Central College in 1884.

His early desire was to become a famous Kathavacak like his father. But his dream was not fulfilled. Because of poverty at home, on the persuasion of his mother, he took up a job as teacher at a government school for a salary of Rs.40 per month in 1884.

Legal Practice

After working in the school as a teacher for a few years, he joined LLB course in 1889 and passed it in 1891. Malaviya first practised in the District Court in 1891 and then moved on to practise in the High Court from 1893. Soon, he became a brilliant civil lawyer. Sir Mirza Ismail once remarked, "I have heard a great Lawyer say that if Mr. Malaviya had so willed it, he would have been an ornament to the legal profession. Though Pt. Madan Mohan Malaviya was having a roaring practice, during his 50th birthday in 1913, he gave up his legal practice to serve the country. Referring to this decision, Gopalakrishna Gokhale said, "Malaviyaji's sacrifice is a real one. Born in a poor family, he started earning thousands monthly. He tasted luxury and wealth but giving heed to the call of the nation, renouncing all he again embraced poverty".

Journalism

Pt. Malaviyaji was a great public speaker, writer, editor and publisher. He edited a number of newspapers and magazines both in Hindi and English. When the English Government tried to bring in the Press Act and Newspaper Act in 1908, Malaviya opposed the move and campaigned against it. At that time, he realized the need for an English newspaper to make the campaign effective throughout the country. So, he started an English daily *Leader* with the help of Pt. Motilal Nehru. He was its editor from 1909 to 1911. In 1910, *Maryada*, an Hindi paper was started by him. He was actively involved in *Hindustan Times* from Delhi. He started in 1933 *Sanatana Dharma*, a magazine dedicated to religious and dharmic interests.

Hindu Ideals and Religion

The basic training he received at home in the principles of Hindu Dharma helped him to have strong belief in right thinking, right expression, right conduct and right attitude in every field of activity. He was a firm believer in Sanatana Dharma. He played an active role in organizing 'Madhya Bharat Hindu Samaj Conference at Allahabad in 1805. The conference discussed about the social good and welfare of the nation.

India's Independence Struggle and Congress Movement

Malaviyaji served the Congress for almost 50 years and worked with 50 Congress Presidents. He was the President of Congress four times: 1909 (Lahore), 1918 (Delhi) 1930 (Delhi) and 1932 (Calcutta). He was closely associated with Allahabad Municipal Board till 1916. He had rich legislative experience. Not only that, he was a member of Industrial Commission during 1916-1918 and he attended the Second Round Table Conference in 1931.

Malaviyaji bid farewell to active politics in 1937. In Politics, he occupied a position that was midway between the moderates (the followers of Gopalakrishna Gokhale) and the extremists (the followers of Bala Gangadhar Tilak).

Educationist

Pt. Maulaviya recognized the value of education in the life of an individual and a nation early in life. He also realized the difficulties faced by poor students in getting education. By collecting a donation of ₹ 1.3 lakhs, he started a hostel by name Macdonald Hindu Boarding House to accommodate

230 students. And he dreamed of bigger things in education. The Banaras Hindu University which he established in 1916 is a standing testimony to his grand vision.

Pt. Malaviya would analyse a problem keenly. He had an innate ability to come out with a workable solution to any problem however difficult it is. He was a team worker and a good motivator. He was a very good fund raiser. He could collect huge donations for a public cause and convert his vision into a reality.

Social work

As Pt. Malaviya was entangled in politics, he encouraged his son Ramakant to start Yatri Sevadal in 1912. It became, 'Deen Rakshat Samiti' in 1914. Again, in 1915, it became 'Prayag Seva Samiti' with Pt. Malaviya as its Chairman. By 1918, it became 'Akil Bharatiya Seva Samiti' with a broad objective of service to the needy during Kumbh Mela, floods, earthquakes and other natural calamities. It had centres at many places. In 1918, a sub-unit on the model of 'Boy Scouts' was started under the aegis of Akhil Bharatya Seva Samithi. It may be of interest to know that a patriotic leader was the Chief Scout and 'Vande Mataram' was sung instead of British national anthem.

During a period of plague, Pt. Malaviya worked hard to hospitalize the sick and rehabilitate others into safe places. He arranged for mass feeding and shelter for the poor and the needy. This shows that he was full of human kindness.

Pt. Malaviya was deeply concerned about the plight of the Harijans. In Calcutta, he gave *mantra diksha* to the untouchables in 1928, even before the Harijan movement started by Gandhiji on 1st August 1933. He also carried out the 'Shuddi Movement' by initiating Harijans with diksha-mantra on 12th March 1936 on the banks of Godavari. Later he conducted Shuddikaran and Mantra-diksha in a number of places. And he was the President of the Conference in Bombay (1932) for the removal of untouchability.

Pt. Malaviya opposed the construction of a dam across the Ganga in Haridwar as that would have reduced the flow of water in the canal. And he was President of the Special Session of Hindu Mahasabha in Gaya in 1922, in Kashi in 1923 and he was its leader till 1927. He started the Cow Protection Society in 1941.

Conclusion

Mahatma Gandhi called Malaviyaji *Prata Smarniyal*, which means, a pious person whose name when remembered in the morning would lift one out of the mire of one's sordid self. Gandhiji compared Tilak to the lofty Himalayas, Gokhale to the deep seas and Malaviyaji to the crystal clear sacred water in which he decided to have ablution. With a sweet and graceful nature, and with abundant love for humanity, he led a blameless life. Edgar Snow, a famous journalist, wrote that Pt. Malaviya's personality radiated "the sweetness and simplicity of a child, yet his words carried the conviction of a man with a settled philosophy of life".

The great philosopher Dr. S. Radhakrishna called him *Karmayogin*. Pt. Malaviya was not merely a representative of Hinduism but the soul of Hinduism. In him, we find the combination of idealism and practical wisdom. According to Dr. S. Radhakrishnan. Pt. Malaviyas "….. while preserving the imperishable treasures of our past, he is keen on moving forward with the times". The philosopher adds the following triad to the sacred triads of Kashi: the trinity of Kashi, Banaras Hindu University and Pt. Madan Mohan Malaviya.

VINOBA BHAVE

Introduction

Vinoba Bhave was one of the great disciples of Mahatma Gandhi. He was born in a Brahmin family on September 11, 1895 in a village called Gagode in Kolaba in Raigad district of Maharashtra. His father Narahari Shambu Rao was a trained weaver with a modern and rationalist outlook. He was greatly influenced by his mother Rukmini Devi, a religious woman from Karnataka. At a very young age, after reading Bhagavad Gita, he was greatly influenced by it. After reading an article written by Gandhi in a newspaper, he put his formal educational certificates into fire, abandoned his studies and became Gandhiji's disciple after meeting him on June 7, 1916. Vinoba joined in Gandhiji's work for the regeneration and freedom of India. As Vinoba himself put it, "I experienced with Gandhi the peace of the Himalayas, the revolutionary spirit. Peaceful revolution, revolutionary peace, the two streams united in Gandhi in a way that was altogether new".

Vinoba was a great scholar, linguist and spiritual leader. His writings covered diverse areas of religion, philosophy and education. At Gandhiji's Ashram, Vinoba evinced keen interest in teaching, studying, spinning and improving the life of the community. He was also involved in Gandhiji's constructive programme related to Khadi, village industries, new education, sanitation and hygiene.

In 1925, Gandhi sent Vinoba to Vaikom in Kerala to witness the entry of Harijans to the temple. The Vaikam struggle was launched by Periyar E.V. Ramasami, a great leader of the non-Brahmin movement in the South. Vinoba underwent imprisonment many times for his involvement in freedom struggle. In 1940, Gandhiji chose Vinoba to be the first individual Satyagrahi to offer non-violent resistance to the British rule. Vinoba Bhave also participated in Quit India Movement in 1942. Throughout his life, Vinoba was committed to the practice of non-violence, spirituality and he believed in the universal power of love.

Bhoodan-Gramdan Movement

In 1951, Vinobha Bhave attended the Third Annual Sarvodaya conference at a village near Hyderabad in South India. The venue was 300 miles away from his ashram at Pavnar, near Nagpur. He walked all the way to Hyderabad. At that time in Telengana, land problem was a burning issue and violent protests were there by the landless with the support of the community. Vinoba believed that the future of India was a contest between the Gandhian philosophy based on peace and non-violence and Marxian ideology of violence. While in Hyderabad, Vinobha and other Gandhians were facing a challenge to their faith in non-violence.

On the historic day of April 18, 1951, Vinoba entered Nalgonda district in Telengana where the communists were very active. At that time, Telengana peasant movement on the land use reached the peak. It was a violent struggle launched by the poor peasants against the local landlords. Bhave felt that the rural rich must participate in the voluntary distribution of land. The organizers arranged for Vinoba's stay at a village namely Pochampalli which had 700 families. Nearly, two-thirds of the villagers were landless. Vinoba received warm welcome at the village. He visited the Harijan colony. Among other things, the Harijans asked for eighty acres of land – forty acres of wet land and forty acres of dry land for forty families. In other words, each family wanted just two acres of land. Then, Vinoba asked "if it is not possible to get land from the government, is there not something villagers themselves could do? At that time, to everyone's surprise, Sri Ramachandra Reddy, the local landlord stood up and said that he would give 100 acres for those people. At the evening prayer meeting conducted by Vinoba Bhave, the landlord reiterated his promise to donate 100 acres of land to the Harijans of the village. This is the genesis of the Bhoodan movement.

Vinoba then thought that the Bhoodan movement had the potentiality to solve India's land problem. After sometime, the movement developed into Gramdan (Village Gift) movement. This was designed as a part of the comprehensive movement for the establishment of Sarvodaya Society (The Rise of All Socio-economic – political order). In October 1951, Vinoba took a decision to get as gift fifty million acres of land for the landless from the whole of India by 1957. Then the Bhoodan movement became a mass movement. It is one of the finest examples of constructive work movement. The movement gained momentum till 1957 and afterwards it began to wane. Vinoba walked through the country nearly 20 years and received four million acres of land.

Before that, the Bhoodan movement was transformed from land-gift movement to village-gift or Gramdan movement. In the Gramdan movement, the whole or a major part of the land was to be donated by not less than 75% of villagers who were required to relinquish their right of ownership over their lands in favour of the entire village, with a power to equitably redistribute the total land among the families of the village with a proviso for revision after some intervals. The individual land-gift scheme was still there but much attention was not paid to it.

The Gramdan idea did not become popular in non-tribal areas and this was one of the reasons for the decline of the movement at the end of 1950s. Somehow with its ups and downs, the movement continued till 1974. There were other allied programmes such as Sampattidan (Wealth-gift), Shramdan (Labour gift) Jeevandan (Lifelong commitment to the movement by co-workers), Shanti-Sena (peace-army) and Sadhandan (gift of implements for agricultural operations)

In launching the Bhoodan movement, Vinobha Bhave adopted Gandhian philosophy of peace and non-violence to solve the basic economic problem of land collection and equitable redistribution of land among the landless. This movement, in a way, kept the Gandhi's programme of socioeconomic reconstruction alive. Jayaprakash Narayan, a renowned Marxist at one time was attracted by the movement and became closely associated with it because he thought that the Bhoodan movement was a great endeavour to bring about revolution in human relations based on the Gandhian philosophy of non-violence. The impact of the movement on Jayaprakash Narayan was so great that he devoted his entire life to the construction of Sarvodaya society.

The Bhoodan movement is not without its critics who are of the view that the movement in a way decelerated the land reforms in the country. Not only that, a major problem of the agrarian sector is subdivision and fragmentation of holdings. The redistribution of the Bhoodan land would only aggravate the problem. Something like collective farming (without compulsion on a voluntary basis) or cooperative farming would have improved the productivity of land.

However, the Bhoodan and the Gramdan movements attracted the attention of many great thinkers. Louis Fischer, a celebrated journalist said: "Gramdan is the most creative thought coming from the East in recent years. Hallam Tennyson, the grandson of Poet Alfred Tennyson, wrote a book on Vinoba Bhave with the title, "The Saint on the March". Chester Bowles, the American Ambassador in his book "The Dimensions of Peace" observed, "We experienced in 1955, the Bhoodan movement is giving the message of Renaissance in India. It offers a revolutionary alternative to communism, as it is founded on human dignity". The British industrialist Earnest Burder was so much impressed by the Bhoodan movement, he implemented Gandhian concept of Trusteeship by allotting 90% of shares of his company to his industrial workers. David Graham, an English journalist described him as a "creative rebel". Arthur Koestler, in 1959 observed that the Bhoodan movement presented an Indian alternative to the Nehruvian model of western development.

Conclusion

While speaking of Vinoba, S. Radhakrishnan said: "Indeed, his life represents harmonious blend of learning, spiritual perception and compassion for the lowly and the lost". In 1958, Vinoba Bhave received Raman Magsaysay Award for Community Leadership. And in 1983, he was awarded the Bharat Ratna posthumously.

We may conclude by saying that whatever might be the limitations of the Bhoodan movement, it was a great attempt for a peaceful and non-violent solution of India's land problem and for the reconstruction of Sarvodaya society.

JAYPRAKASH NARAYAN

Introduction

Jayprakash Narayan was born in a Kayestha family on October 11, 1902 at a village named Sitabdiara in Chhapra district in Bihar. In later years, he was popularly known as J.P. and Lok Nayak.

He was born of Harsu Dayal Srivatsava and Phul Rani devi. His father was a state government official. Jayprakash Narayan was a brilliant student at school and college.

In October 1920, Jayprakash Narayan was married to Prabhavati Devi, who was a freedom fighter in her own right. Narayan was working at Patna at that time. As his wife could not stay with him, Gandhiji invited her to stay at his Sabarmati Ashram. While at College, Jayprakash was attracted by the non-cooperation movement launched by Gandhiji against the Rowlett Act of 1919.

After completing all the courses at Vidyapeeth, Jayprakash Narayan decided to continue studies in the United States. At the age of 20, he sailed aboard a cargo ship and reached California on October 8, 1922. First, he was admitted to Berkely in January 1923. But he had to move from one university to another for financial reasons. To pay for his tuition and other college expenses, Jayprakash Narayan did all kinds of sundry jobs. This helped him gain an insight into sufferings of poor workers. While in the U.S.A. he pursued his favourite subject sociology.

While at Wisconsin, Jay Prakash came across Karl Marx's *Das Capital* and studied it. The success of the Russian Revolution of 1917 made him believe that Marxism was the way to alleviate the sufferings of the masses. Then he read a lot of writings of M.N. Roy; a great intellectual and communist theoretician. Jayprakash Narayan's paper 'Social Variation' was declared the best paper of the year.

Politics

Jayprakash returned to India in 1929 as a Marxist and Nehru invited him to join the Congress in the same year. Mahatma Gandhi was his mentor in the Congress. During the freedom struggle, he was jailed many times. When the Congress Socialist Party was formed within the Congress, Jayprakash Narayan became its Secretary with Narendra Dev as its President. Jayprakash became famous during the Quit India Movement in 1942.

Bihar Movement and Total Revolution

Jayprakash focused his attention on state politics since the late 1960s. 1974 was a year of high inflation, unemployment and there was shortage of essential goods of mass consumption. At the request of the organizers of the Nav Nirman Andolan movement, at the age of 72, he led a silent procession in Patna. At a public meeting in Patna on June 5, 1974, he declared: "This is a revolution, friends! We are not here merely to see the Vidhan Sabha dissolved. That is only one milestone on our journey. But we have a long way to go.. After 27 years of freedom, people of this country are wrecked by hunger, rising prices, corruption of oppressed by every kind of injustice.. it is a Total Revolution we want, nothing less". He mobilized the youth power by leading the students' movement in Bihar. It slowly developed into people's movement known as the *Bihar movement*. It was during this movement Jayprakash Narayan gave a call for peaceful Total Revolution. In collaboration with V.M. Tarkunde, he found the NGOs *the Citizens for Democracy* in 1974 and *People's Union for Civil Liberties* in 1976. Thus 1974 and the following years proved to be very eventful in the life of Jayprakash Narayan.

Total Revolution

Jayaprakash Narayan once stated that Total Revolution is a combination of seven revolutions, namely political, social, economic, cultural and ideological or intellectual, educational and spiritual. He wanted to bring about a change in the society in conformity with the ideals of Sarvodaya. It may be noted that from Marxism, he moved to socialism and ultimately to Sarvodaya.

After his release from detention owing to serious illness, he returned to Patna. Then he wrote to his followers explaining the circumstances of Bihar movement and his commitment to Total Revolution. That letter gives the salient features of the Total revolution. They are given below:

From the beginning, Jayaprakash Narayan had been saying that the objectives of their movement was total revolution. It aimed at bringing about a revolutionary change in all aspects of both society and individual. That is why, he called it total revolution or comprehensive revolution. It could not be achieved in a day or in a year or two. To achieve total revolution, along with the struggle that had to be carried on for a long time, constructive and creative activities must be carried on. The double process of struggle and construction is necessary in order to achieve total revolution.

The situation at that time was people were in fear and thousands were in prison, so people who are interested in the country and the society should concentrate on some constructive activities like education. Education, in the country, from the primary to the secondary stage was in a bad stage. But very little was done to improve the situation. There was discontent among the students. Something must be done to improve the quality of education.

There are other similar problems. For example, the economic and social problems of the Harijans and the tribals. Economically, they are poor and backward. Socially, their position is even worse. There is discrimination against the Harijans. They are treated as untouchables by the so-called upper castes. The situation is rather explosive. The soldiers of total revolution have to find a constructive solution to this explosive situation. They must find a way to enter into their hearts and bring them into the mainstream of Indian society. Without this constructive service, total revolution would remain incomplete.

In the existing situation, he outlined four aspects of the work for total revolution: struggle, construction, propaganda and organization. Under the circumstances, they should concentrate on the construction aspect. For example, the main plank of the programme should be that people's minds should be turned against the evils such as dowry system, caste distinctions, untouchability and communalism and they must work unitedly for social and cultural integration. Total revolution is permanent evolution. It will always go on and keep on changing the lives of people and the society. This revolution will not have a complete halt. Of course, according to the needs of the situation, its form will change, its programme will change, its processes will change (Jayaprakash letter to the People of Bihar, 1975).

On Society

Jayaprakash Narayan felt that even after nearly three decades of independence, there had been no real change in the social, economic and political structure of the society. Zamindari is abolished, land reform bills have been passed, untouchability has been legally prohibited, and so on. The small and marginal landowners, the landless, the backward classes and the Harijans – these form the majority in most states, perhaps the nine-tenths of India. Yet their position continues to be miserable. The Adivasis are still the most backward section, barring the Harijans. And the money lenders mercilessly cheat and exploit the Adivasis.

On Socialism

"Some industries, banks, life insurance have been nationalized. Railways were nationalized long ago. Now large public sector industries have been established. But all this adds upto state capitalism and inefficiency, waste and corruption. State capitalism means more powers to the State, mainly the State bureaucracy, or what Galbraith aptly calls 'the public bureaucracy'. There is no element or trait of socialism in all this. The working class and the public or, let us say, the people have no place in all this except as workers or consumers. There is no economic democracy, which is so much talked about, nor even industrial democracy". This does not mean that Jayprakash Narayan was opposed to socialism. He was deeply concerned about socialism. That is why he was pointing out all this. It is a pity that our socialists very largely equate socialism with nationalization.

Jayprakash Narayan was concerned about the steady decline in political, public and business morality. He lamented at the poverty of Bihar. Newspapers said that Bihar was the richest state in minerals. It has good land and minerals. Why then was Bihar the poorest state in India?

To bring about a systemic change in society, Jayprakash Narayan called for a total revolution. But the revolution should be brought about in a peaceful manner without impairing the democratic structure of society and affecting the democratic way of life of the people. "All this could never be accomplished if the functioning of democracy were restricted to elections, legislation, planning and administrative execution. There must also be people's direct action. This action would almost certainly comprise among other forms, civil disobedience, peaceful resistance, non-cooperation in short, Satyagraha in its widest sense," For such a Satyagraha, there is need for self-change. Those wanting to change must also change themselves before launching any kind of action (Notes on Bihar movement, 1975; (Source: Transforming the Polity – Centenary Readings from Jayprakash Narayan)

National Emergency

The Allahabad High Court found Indira Gandhi guilty of violating electoral laws. Jayaprakash Narayan called for Indira to resign and he wanted the military and the police not to obey unconstitutional and illegitimate orders. He advocated *Sampoorna Kranti* (total revolution), which was a programme of social transformation. Immediately, after that, Indira Gandhi preclaimed National Emergency on the midnight of June 25, 1975. Jayaprakash Narayan was arrested along with many opposition leaders and the dissenting members of her own party (the 'Young Turks'). He was released on November 12, 1975 when his health deteriorated. He had kidney failure and he was on dialysis for the rest of his life.

Indira Gandhi revoked the emergency on January 18, 1977 and announced elections. The *Janata Party,* consisting of all those who were opposed to Indira Gandhi was formed under the guidance of Jayprakash Narayan. The Janata party won the elections and became the first non-congress party to form government at the Centre.

Jayaprakash Narayan passed away on October 8, 1979 in Patna, Bihar. He was awarded Ramon Magsaysay Award in 1965 for public service. And in 1999, he was awarded *Bharat Ratna* – posthumously for Public Affairs.

RAM MANOHAR LOHIA

Introduction

Ram Manohar Lohia was born in a Vaishya family on March 23, 1910 at Akbarpur in Uttar Pradesh. He was a thinker, politician and activist who was a prominent figure in socialist politics and freedom movement for Indian independence. His mother died in 1912, when he was just two years old and he was later brought up by his father, who never remarried. His father's commitment to Indian nationalism influenced him during his childhood. After completing his school education, he attended Banaras Hindu University to complete his intermediate course. He then joined Vidyasagar College under the university of Calcutta and earned is B.A. degree in 1929. Then, he left for Germany to join Frederick William University (today's Humboldt's University of Berlin, Germany). He chose national economy as a major subject as a doctoral student from 1929-1933. His Ph.D. thesis paper was on *Salt Taxation in India.* It focused on Gandhi's socioeconomic theory. While in Germany, Lohia helped organize the Association of European Indians and became its secretary. The main focus of the organization was to preserve and expand Indian nationalism abroad.

He devoted his life for fighting against injustice through the development of an Indian version of socialism.

Lohia's major writings in English include, *The Caste System (1964), Foreign Policy (1963?) Fragments of a World Mind (1949), Guilty Men of India's Partition (1970) India, China and Northern Frontiers (1963), Marx, Gandhi and Socialism (1963) and Collected Works of Dr. Lohia (ed. Dr. Mastram Kapoor).*

Lohia in Indian National Congress

As soon as he returned to India in 1933, Lohia joined the Indian National Congress. As he was attracted to socialism, he helped lay the foundation of Congress Socialist Party in 1934. He became actively involved in it. It was founded as a left-wing group within the Indian National Congress. He was on the Executive Committee of Congress Socialist Party and edited its weekly journal. Not only that, Lohia formed a new branch in the Indian National Congress called the All India Congress Committee (a foreign affairs section). Nehru appointed Lohia as its first secretary. He served as secretary for two years. During those two years, he helped in the evolution of India's foreign policy in future.

When World War II broke out, Lohia vehemently opposed Indian participation on the side of Great Britain in the war. He was arrested on May 24, 1939 for ant-British remarks but released the next day out of fear that there would be youth uprising. After a few months, Lohia wrote an article called "Satyagraha Now" in Gandhiji's Newspaper "Harijan" on June 1, 1940. Within a few days, he was arrested and sentenced to two years imprisonment. While pronouncing the sentence, the magistrate remarked, "He (Lohia) is a top class scholar, civilized gentleman, has liberal ideology and high moral character". It may be noted that Lohia never propagated violence. After coming out of the prison in December 1941, he wrote articles to spread the message of toppling British imperialist governments from the countries of Asia and Africa. He was a visionary too. He visualized a situation where new Indian cities would self-administer themselves and there would be no need for police or army.

When Gandhiji launched the Quit India Movement in 1942 to urge the withdrawal of British authorities from India, many prominent leaders, including Gandhiji were jailed. At that time, Lohia and other Congress socialist party leaders such as Jayprakash Narayan mobilized support from the underground. For such resistance activities, Lohia was jailed again during 1944-46.

When the time came for India's freedom, Hindu-Muslim riots were there. Lohia strongly opposed partition of India. He appealed to both Hindus and Muslims to follow the non-violent path of Gandhiji and stay united.

Dr. Ram Manohar Lohia was the first person to introduce the unification of some 650 Indian princely states to form larger states. This idea was later adopted by Sardar Patel, the first Home Minister of India.

Dr. Ram Manohar Lohia favoured Hindi as the national language of India. His argument was: "The use of English is a hindrance to original thinking; progenitor of inferiority feelings and a gap between the educated and the uneducated public…." He wanted people to unite to restore Hindi to its original glory.

Lohia encouraged public involvement and active participation of people in post-freedom reconstruction. He exhorted people to construct canals, wells and roads voluntarily in their neighbourhood. He volunteered himself to build a dam on Paniyari and it is standing till this day and it is called *Lohia Sagar Dam*. Lohia famously said "Satyagraha without constructive work is like a sentence without a verb". He felt that community involvement in public works would bring about unity and sense of awareness among the people. And he played an important role in getting reservation for the minorities, lower castes and women in the Legislature.

Lohia was against privatization of education. He wanted to abolish private schools and establish upgraded government schools that would provide equal opportunity to study for all boys and girls irrespective of caste. And he was for decentralization of power so that the general public would have more power in governance. Lohia was a socialist and he wanted to unite all the socialists of the world so that they could have a powerful platform. He established World Development Council and his ideal was international government to maintain peace in the world.

During and after Independence in 1947, Lohia played an active role in politics. When there was difference of opinion on many fundamental issues with Jawaharlal Nehru who became the first Prime Minister of India, Lohia and other Congress Socialist Party members left the Congress in 1948. He became a member of Praja Socialist Party when it was formed in 1952 and he was its general secretary for a short period until he resigned in 1955. Then he started a new socialist party and edited its journal *Mankind.* As leader of the new party, he advocated many sociopolitical reforms such as abolition of the caste system, the adoption of Hindi as India's national language and stronger protection of civil liberties. In 1963, he was elected to the Lok Sabha.

Conclusion

Lohia died in October 1967 in New Delhi. He left behind no property or bank balance. His only concern was how to free people from foreign domination, social oppression and economic exploitation.

DEENDAYAL UPADHYAYA

Introduction

Deendayal Upadhyaya was born in 1916 at a village Chandrabhan (now Deendayal Dham) in Mathura district. His parents died when he was very young and he was brought up by his maternal uncle. At school and college, he excelled in studies. He did his B.A. at Sanatan Dharma College, Kanpur and M.A. in English literature at St. John's College, Agra and won a gold medal. Deendayal appeared for provincial services examination. He got selected but he declined to join duty because he was interested in working with the common man. He did B.Ed. and M.Ed. at Prayag and entered public service.

Rashtriya Swayam Sevak Sangh (R.S.S.) and Jana Sangh

Deendayal came into contact with R.S.S. when he was doing his B.A. at Sanatan Dharma College in Kanpur. There, he met K.B. Hedgewar, the founder of R.S.S. and the meeting and subsequent intellectual discussions with the founder of R.S.S. had a deep impact on him. In 1942, he became a full-time worker of the R.S.S. After undergoing training in Sangh education, Upadhyaya became a lifelong *Pracharak* of the RSS. From 1955, he became the Joint *Prant Pacharak* (Regional Organizer) of Uttar Pradesh. Deendayal was a man of great idealism and he had tremendous organizational ability. He was a social thinker, educationist, economist, politician, writer, editor, journalist, excellent public speaker and above all a great organizer. He was considered an ideal Swayamsevak by the RSS leaders. He started *Rashtra Dharma* in 1940 for spreading the ideology of nationalism. Later he started *Panchjanya* a weekly and *Swadesh,* a daily.

When Syama Prasad Mookerjee founded Bharatiya Jana Sangh in 1951, Deendayal was appointed General Secretary of the Uttar Pradesh branch. Later, he became All-India General Secretary of Bharatiya Jan Sangh. Syama Prasad Mookerjee was so much impressed by the work of Deendayal, he made the famous remark: "If I had two Deendayals, I could transform the political face of India".

When Mookerjee died in 1953, the burden of building up the party fell on the shoulders of Deendayal. As General Secretary of the party, he built it up brick by brick. And he became the ideologue of the party.

Integral Humanism

Deendayal conceived Integral Humanism as the political philosophy of Bharatiya Jana Party. Integral Humanism advocates the simultaneous and integrated program of the body, mind and intellect and soul of each human being. It is a synthesis of the material and the spiritual, the individual and the collective. He visualized for India a decentralized polity and self-reliant economy with village as the base.

Deendayal outlined his philosophy of governance to party workers in 1964 and presented an expanded version in 1965 at the plenary session of BJP. He delivered the final version in the form of four lectures under the title *"Integral Humanism"* in Bombay. The title was chosen to contrast it with "Radical Humanism", put forward by M.N. Roy, the former communist leader (L.K. Advani).

Deendayal Upadhyaya was of the firm view that India after independence should not rely upon Western concepts such as individualism, democracy, socialism, communism or capitalism. He believed that Indian polity after independence was raised upon the superficial western foundation and not, rooted in the traditions of India's ancient culture. He felt that the Indian mind was suffocated by

Western theories and that created a "roadblock" to the growth and expansion of original Bharatiya (Indian) thought. So there was need for "fresh breeze". The answer was Integral Humanism.

Deendayal welcomed modern technology but it must be adapted to suit Indian conditions. He believed in constructive approach. He believed in *Swaraj* (self-governance). He wanted his followers to cooperate with the government when it was right and oppose it when it went wrong.

Deendayal Upadhyaya claimed the Bharatiya Jan Sangh was pledged to the service not of any particular community or section but of the entire nation.

Upadhyaya was capable of taking bold and principled decisions. When seven of the nine Jan Sangh MLAs in Rajasthan opposed the Zamindari Abolition Act, he expelled them without fear or favour. He had moral authority over his party workers.

Subramanian Swamy, a BJP leader in his book. *Hindus under Siege* describes Integral Humanism as follows: "IHT (Integral Humanism Theory) recognized that in a democratic market economy, an individual has technical freedom of choice but the system without safeguards fails to accommodate the varying capabilities and endowments of a human being. Since the concept of survival of the "fittest prevails in a system, therefore some individuals achieve great personal advancement while others get trampled on or disabled in the ensuing rat race. We need to build a safety net into our policy for the underprivileged or disabled while simultaneously rewarding the meritorious or gifted. Otherwise, the politically empowered poor in a democracy who are in a majority will clash with the economically empowered rich who are the majority, thereby causing instability and upheaval in a market system".

In another *book India and China: A Comparative Perspective,* Subramanian Swamy considers Integral Humanism Theory as the only alternative to Marxism and capitalism presented after 1947 but it did not gain currency for political reasons. While capitalism suffers from the "one dimensional concept of the human pursuit of material progress" Integral Humanism Theory envisages a system that permits competitiveness while seeking adjusting complementaries, harmonizing material progress with spiritual advancement.

L.K. Advani, one of the senior leaders of the BJP, who considers Deendayal Upadhyaya as his political guru in his book, *My country*, *My Life* explains Integral Humanism policy as follows:

"Deen-Dayalji felt that both capitalism and communism were flawed philosophies....one considers man a mere selfish being hankering after money, having only one law, the law of fierce competition ... whereas the other views him as a feeble lifeless cog in the whole scheme of things. The centralization of power, economic and political is implied in both. They pit one section of the society against the other, the individual against the collective, man against Nature". He adds: "Integral Humanism did not receive the attention the western political theories did". He feels that it is worthy of being placed alongside the works of Mahatma Gandhi and Ram Manohar Lohia, with both of whom Deendayalji had so much in common".

Socioeconomic Ideas

Some of Deendayalji's political opponents called him right-wing and pro-capitalist. But he stood for some of the basic policies of a socialist economy. For example, he wanted the maximum income by way of salary to be not more than 20 times the minimum salary. And he was for nationalization of all infrastructure industries Deendayal criticized Nehru for being a socialist while laying taxes but a capitalist in dealing with the amassing of profits by the capitalists. Deendayal favoured economic freedom and opportunities for entrepreneurs. He was against state monopolies. He was for decentralization of the economy to empower the masses at the grassroots level so that they could make economic and developmental choices.

Deendayal was against big business. Gandhiji did not favour mass production. He favoured production by the masses. Similarly, Deendayal favoured large production by small units that is, "manufacture by the masses for the masses".

Deendayal spoke of a "national sector" It is a kind of public-private partnership. He was for economic freedom along with the right to work. He favoured private ownership of land in agriculture and he was strongly opposed to collective farming of Soviet Style. Upadhyaya was keen that "we should finish the unaccomplished task of land reforms and agricultural marketing" (AP. Mahesh Chandra Sharma: Economic Philosophy of Deen Dayal Upadyaya). Deendayal wanted the country to attain self-sufficiency in foodgrains but he was against building up of excessive buffer stocks resulting in the distortion of the market and leakages and wastages. And he thought that the policy of administered prices by the government would not be effective in controlling inflation.

Upadhyaya was a great critic of all the Five Year Plans because they did not help much in solving the problems of unemployment and inequality. They did not focus on infrastructure; agricultural production, education and public health. He was in favour of appropriate or intermediate technology instead of mechanization.

Deendayal was interested in protecting the interests of labour. Trade unions Bharatiya Kisan Sangh and Bharatiya Mazdoor Sangh were largely inspired by him. He declined Padma Bhushan from the Government when Vajapayee was the Prime Minister because he did not approve of the policies of the Government of the day.

Conclusion

Upadhyaya's death occurred under mysterious circumstances on February 11, 1968 near Mughalsarai railway station in Uttar Pradesh. He had boarded an express train from Lucknow bound for Patna. His body was found in the Mughalsarai station yard .Till date, his death remains a mystery. Was it an accident? a simple case of murder for gain? or was it assassination? To many, it remains, more or less, an unsolved puzzle.

M.N. ROY

Introduction

Manabendra Nath Roy (M.N. Roy) was born on March 21, 1887 in a Brahmin family at Arbelia, located in the 24 Parganas, near Calcutta (now Kolkata) in West Bengal and was given the name Narendranath Bhattacharya.

Narendranath Bhattacharya's early schooling took place in Arbelia. In 1898, when the family moved to Kodalia, Bhattacharya continued his studies at Harinavi Ango-Sanskrit School until 1915 where his father was employed as a teacher. Later he joined the National College under Sri Aurobindo, before moving to the Bengal Technical Institute, where he studied Engineering and Technology. However, he gained his vast knowledge only through self-study.

Nationalist Revolutionary

During the end of 19th century, revolutionary nationalism spread among the middle classes of Bengal under the influence of Bankimchandra Chatterjee and Swami Vivekananda. Bankim impressed upon Roy that true religion required one not to be cloistered from the world, but to work actively for the public good. Similarly, Swami Vivekananda stressed on social service and emphasized that Hinduism and Indian culture were superior to western religion and culture.

In July 1905, the partition of Bengal was announced. Roy organized a meeting and march against partition. For that, he was expelled from school. Then he left for Kolkata.

The Indo-German Conspiracy

Many revolutionary Indian nationalists, including M.N. Roy believed that only through an armed struggle against the British Raj, they could free India from the British empire. So they looked to a rival imperial power, Germany as a source of funds and armaments. When World War I broke out, the Indian Revolutionary Committee organized by the expatriate Indian nationalists in *Britain* approached the German Government for aid for armed struggle against the British in India. Germany agreed to provide money and materials to launch Indian War of Independence against the British rule. In 1915, M.N. Roy left India to receive arnaments. The mission failed and Roy did not see his motherland again for 16 years.

International Revolutionary

Roy developed interest in Marxism, when he was in New York. As the British spies were on the lookout for him, he fled to Mexico in July 1917 with his wife Evelyn. He received monetary help from the German authorities for the trip and other activities. In Mexico, he founded the Socialist Party in December 1917. In 1919, he converted it into Communist Party of Mexico and became the Founder of the first communist party outside Russia. In 1920, Roy attended the Second World Congress of the Communist International in Moscow. He was warmly received by Lenin in Moscow. At Lenin's request, Roy wrote a Supplement to Lenin's *Preliminary Draft Thesis on the National and the Colonial Questions* incorporating his own ideas on the subject. Roy served as a member of the Cominterm's Presidium for eight years. Meanwhile, Lenin asked Roy to prepare the East, especially India for Revolution. Roy published his major reflections *India in Transition* from Moscow. In 1922, he published the *Vanguard*, organ of the *émigré* communist Party of India. Then, in 1926 he published *The Future of Indian Politics,* followed by *Revolution and Counter-revolution in China* (1930). Roy led a comintern delegation appointed by Stalin to develop agrarian revolution in China and he reached Canton in February 1927. Though he handled the mission with great skill, it turned out to be a fiasco because of the differences among the members of the delegation. On his return to Soviet Russia, Stalin refused to meet Roy. To spare himself from Stalin's anger, Roy escaped from Russia to Berlin citing medical reasons.

Return to India and Imprisonment

M.N. Roy returned to India after a long gap of many years in December 1930. On his return, Roy met Jawaharlal Nehru and Subash Chandra Bose. Nehru, later recalled that in spite of significant political differences, he was attracted to him by his remarkable intellectual capacity.

Roy's political activity in India proved to be brief. On July 21, 1931, he was arrested in Bombay on the basis of an arrest warrant issued in 1924 on the charge of "conspiring to deprive the King Emperor of his sovereignty in India". After a summary trial, on January 9, 1932, he was sentenced to 12 years of rigorous imprisonment.

Roy was not apologetic about his advocacy of the use of armed struggle against British Colonialism. He declared: "The oppressed people and exploited classes are not obliged to respect the moral philosophy of the ruling power ... *A despotic power is always overthrown by force.* The force employed in this process is not criminal. On the contrary, precisely the guns carried by the army of the British Government in India are instruments of crime. They become instruments of virtue when they are turned against the imperialist state".

Roy filed an appeal in his case to Allahabad High Court and the sentence was reduced from 12 years to 6 years by the Court. His health was badly affected during the prison life and he was released in November 1936 in broken health. Nehru invited him for recovery and rest in Allahabad. It was then that Roy urged Indian communists to join the Indian National Congress to radicalize it. At the congress Session in 1936, Roy recommended the capture of power by *Constituent Assembly.* In 1937, Roy published his weekly *Independent India.* When it appeared, it was welcomed by progressive leaders like Nehru and Bose. Of course, some staunch communists accused him of deviation.

Radical Humanism

During the last years of his life, M.N. Roy was disillusioned with both bourgeois democracy and communism. He formulated an alternative philosophy which he called *Radical Humanism.* He gave a detailed exposition of it in *Reason, Romanticism and Revolution.*

He called his new philosophy *Integral Scientific Humanism* or *New Humanism*. He claimed that his views were based on reason and morality and not on any dogma.

Roy's New Humanism was cosmopolitan in outlook. It could not think in terms of a nation or a class but only in terms of man. As a radical humanist, Roy's approach was individualistic. He rejected the nationalism of the congressmen and the theory of class struggle of the communists. Radical Humanism conceives freedom as freedom of the individual.

In the beginning of his political career, Roy was greatly impressed by the philosophy of Marx and accepted Marxism because he believed that Marx was a humanist and that he was deeply concerned about man.

Roy realized in his later years that the dictatorship of the proletariat with planned economy did not result in the greatest good of the greatest number. In his own words, "The abolition of private property, state ownership of the means of production and planned economy do not by themselves end exploitation of labour nor lead to an equal distribution of wealth (Roy, Radical Humanism, 1952, P. 31).

Roy believed that revolution should be brought about not through class struggle or armed violence but through education. He did not mean education in the conventional sense of reading and writing. He meant it in the cultural sense of a high degree of human development. He knew that his revolution could not be achieved suddenly. It could be achieved only through the slow process of education.

Roy was very critical of many Marxian concepts such as class struggle, materialistic interpretation of history and surplus value.

Roy did not consider surplus value as something peculiar to capitalism alone. He argued that there would not be any progress without capital formation (investment) and investment was not possible without saving. There must be surplus of production over consumption and surplus value in the form of profit. And he considered capitalism better than feudalism because the former provided greater scope for saving and investment.

Roy was against the state ownership of the means of production. His radical democracy was against the exploitation of man by man. It aimed at economic liberation of the masses and creation of conditions for their advancement towards goals of freedom. In the place of the extremes of capitalism and socialism, he favoured cooperative economy.

The basis of Radical Humanism is freedom for all men and women. And the policies and programmes of the party will be rational and ethical. Roy believes that "the basic idea of a new revolutionary social philosophy must be that the individual is prior to society, and individual freedom must have priority over social organization. (Roy, 1952, op.cit., P. 284)

Conclusion

Roy's social and political philosophy evolved from militant nationalism to communism and to Radical Humanism. In the later stages of his life, he gave more, importance to individualism and liberalism. And he put man at the centre of the stage. In his humanist philosophy, democracy is the base, rationalism is the centre and sovereignty of man its apex. In short, Roy's Radical Humanism is his most important and lasting contribution to the modern political and social philosophy.

J.C. KUMARAPPA (1892-1960)

Introduction

J.C. Kumarappa, an Indian patriot and economist was a close associate of Mahatma Gandhi. He developed a school of thought based on Gandhiji's teachings. He called it "Gandhian economics".

J.C. Kumarappa was born in a devout christian family in Thanjavur on January 4, 1892. He was the sixth child of Solomon Doraisamy, a Public Works Department Officer and Mrs. Esther Rajanayagam.

After studying in Madras (now, Chennai), he left for London in 1912 to study Chartered Accountancy Course. After completing the course and after working for a few London Banks and Auditor's firms, he returned to India in 1919. For a few years, he continued as an auditor and set up his own firm of auditors in Bombay. He was Vice-Principal and part-time Professor of Davar's College of Commerce at that time.

In 1928, he went to the United States of America and did his B.Sc. in Business Administration at Syracuse and M.A. in Economics at Columbia University under Dr. Seligman. His Ph.D. Thesis was *"Public Finance and Our (Indian) Poverty"*. That changed him from a British Loyalist to a Staunch Indian nationalist. He returned to India in 1929 to continue his auditing work. But a meeting with Gandhiji on May 9, 1929 totally changed his life. Gandhi was much impressed with Kumarappa's Ph.D. thesis and agreed to publish it as a serial in "Young India". Not only that, as he found that Kumarappa's approach to economics was similar to that of his, he requested him to undertake a village survey in Gujarat. The Survey, "A Survey of Matar Taluka in Kheda District" won the admiration of all and became a classic. Kumarappa strongly supported village industries and promoted village industries Associations. When the All India Village Industries Association (AIVIA) was formed by the Congress in 1935, with Gandhiji as President, Kumarappa became the secretary and organizer. He edited, "Gram Udyog Patrika" and wrote a book, "Why the Village Movement" for AIVIA. Besides, Kumarappa undertook economic survey of the states of 'C.P. and BERAR' and 'Northwest Frontier Province' and they won the appreciation of many economists.

When Subash Chandra Bose formed the National Planning Committee with Jawaharlal Nehru as Chairman, he became a member of the Committee. But as he did not see eye to eye with the other members of the committee with regard to their approach to India's economic and social development and as he believed in decentralized participatory planning, he resigned from the committee after three months.

Kumarappa actively participated in the freedom movement and he underwent prison terms for his participation in programmes such as Quit India Movement and also for his writings in 'Young India'. He was also the editor of *Young India* for some years.

Some of Kumarappa's important writings include: *1) Economy of Permanence* (1984), *Why the Village Movement* (1958); *Cow in Our Economy* (1963); *Gandhian Economic Thought* (1962); *An Economic Survey of Matar Taluka* (1952); *Public Finance and Our Poverty* (1930) *and Village Industries* (1947).

Kumarappa formulated his economic theories based on Christian values and Gandhian concept of "Trusteeship", non-violence and emphasis on human dignity and development in the place of materialism. He rejected Marxism's emphasis on class war and force in implementation. Similarly, he rejected material development, unfettered competition and efficiency in free-market economies. Kumarappa in line with Gandhiji visualized an economy wherein the basic human needs would be satisfied while rooting out socio-economic conflict, unemployment and poverty. In short, he embraced the philosophy of non-violence.

And he rejected the idea that British rule in India was ordained by Providence.

Kumarappa wrote two books *Economy of Permanence* and the *Precepts of Jesus* (1945) while he was in jail during 1943-45. As Gandhiji found that these two books were of universal value and application, in his capacity as Chancellor of National University, Gandhiji conferred on Kumarappa Doctor of Village Industries (DVI) and Doctor of Divinity (DD).

The sub-title of Kumarappa's book *Economy of Permanence is A Quest for Social Order Based on Non-Violence*. In the book, he outlines his ideas on economic development. In Nature, all creatures co-exist in such a way that each fulfilled its role. As he put it, "… In this way, nature enlists the co-operation of all its units, each working for itself and in the process helping other units to get along their own too. When this works out harmoniously and violence does not break the chain, we have an economy of permanence". He further adds: "In an economy of permanence, everybody helped each other out. In contrast, there was the economy of transience, in which everyone tried to do well only for himself/herself. An economy of transience was violent; it chewed up nature". Kumarappa's favourite example for this was the way pesticides and chemical fertilisers were used to produce crops in ever increasing amounts. Sure, the crops got produced, but after a while the soil got spoilt; no more lush green fields. An economy of permanence, on the otherhand, did not destroy nature.

We find that the essential features of his *Economy of Permanence* are co-existence, co-operation, harmony and non-violence. Today, "sustainable development" has become a fashionable term. This is precisely what Kumarappa envisaged in his book.

Environmentalism

Like many of Gandhiji's followers, Kumarappa was interested in environmentalism. Along with Mirabehn, he argued against construction of large dams and other irrigation projects. He felt that small projects were effective. Similarly, organic manure was better and less hazardous than chemical fertilizers and pesticides. And forests should be managed with the goal of water conservation rather than revenue maximization. The British Government paid little attention to these aspects. Ramachandra Guha, an eminent historian, calls Kumarappa "The green Gandhian" describing him as the founder of modern environmentalism.

After India's Independence in 1947, Kumarappa worked for the Planning Commission of India and the Indian National Conference to develop national policies for agriculture and rural development. He went to China, Eastern Europe and Japan on diplomatic assignments and to study their systems and programmes for rural development.

Kumarappa was a member of the delegation sent by the Government of India in July 1947 to a meeting of shippers in London. The mission of the delegation was to protect the economic interest of India in maritime transport. In his later years, he became a critic of the policies of the government that went against the interest of the rural economy. At the end of 1947, Kumarappa was appointed as Chairman of the Agrarian Reforms Committee constituted by the All India Congress Committee and he travelled all over the country for two years. The Committee gave its final report in July 1949. It suggested a number of important recommendations on management of land and agriculture.

It may be noted that Kumarappa was never interested in power politics. He passed away on January 30, 1960.

Conclusion

Kumarappa was a true follower of Mahatma Gandhi. Like Gandhiji, he was a great believer in non-violence. He had an abiding interest in rural development. He was interested in sustainable development of village industries. Because of his interest in environmental protection, he has been rightly hailed as "The Green Gandhian".

M.S. SWAMINATHAN

Introduction

M.S. Swaminathan is an Indian geneticist. He is known for his leading role in India's Green Revolution, a program under which high yielding varieties of wheat and rice seedlings were planted in the fields of India. Swaminathan is known as *Indian Father of Green Revolution*. He is the founder and Chairman of M.S. Swaminathan Research Foundation. His vision is to rid the world of hunger and poverty. His aim is to take India to the stage of sustainable development, by means of environmentally sustainable agriculture, sustainable food security and the preservation of biodiversity. He calls it *Evergreen Revolution*.

M.S. Swaminathan was Director General of the Indian Council of Agricultural Research from 1972 to 1979. He was Principal Secretary. Ministry of Agriculture from 1979 to 1980. And he was

Director General of the International Rice Research Institute during 1982 to 1988. And he became the President of the International Union for the Conservation of Nature and Natural Resources in 1988. In 1999, *Time* magazine placed him in the list of the "20 most influential Asian people of the 20th century". He was one of the three persons from India in the list, the other two being Mahatma Gandhi and Rabindranath Tagore.

Early Life

M.S. Swaminathan was born of Dr. M.K. Sambasivan and Parvathi Thangammal Sambasivan in Kumbakonam on August 7, 1925. His father taught him that the word "impossible" exists mainly in our minds and that given the requisite will and effort, great tasks can be accomplished. His father was a follower of Mahatma Gandhi in the freedom movement. In support of Swadeshi movement, which emphasized the use of Indian handloom cloth rather than imported mill cloth, as a symbolic act, his father took the lead in Kumbakonam in "burning his foreign clothes". The aim of the Swadeshi movement was to free India from dependence on foreign imports and to protect village industry. His father played a leading role in temple entry to Dalits. It was a part of the Indian independence movement in Tamil Nadu. He imbibed the spirit of service to humanity at a very early age.

Education

When his father died, Swaminathan was a young boy of eleven years and his uncle became his guardian. He passed his matriculation examination from Catholic Little Flower High School in Kumbakonam. And he did his undergraduate course at Maharajas College in Trivandrum in Kerala during 1940-44 and earned a Bachelor of Science Degree in Zoology. Then he studied at Madras Agricultural College (now known as Tamil Nadu Agricultural University) where he got another Bachelor of Science degree in Agricultural Science. He joined the Madras Agricultural College because he wanted to pursue a career in agricultural sciences. In his own words: "My personal motivation started with the great Bengal famine of 1943 when I was a student at the university of Kerala. There was an acute rice shortage, and in Bengal about 3 million people died from starvation. All of our young people, myself included, were involved in the freedom struggle, which Gandhi had intensified, and I decided I should take to agricultural research in order to help farmers produce more".

In 1947, he joined the Indian Agricultural Research Institute as a Post-graduate student in genetics and plant breeding. He obtained post-graduate degree in Cytogenetic and plant breeding in 1949.

He wrote Union Public Service Examination and qualified for Indian Police Service. But he chose the UNESCO Fellowship to continue his Indian Agricultural Research Institute research on potato genetics in Netherlands. In 1950, he went to study at the Plant Breeding Institute of the University of Cambridge School of Agriculture. There, he earned Ph.D. degree in 1952; Swaminathan accepted a post-doctoral research associate ship at the University of Wisconsin Department of Genetics. Though he had job satisfaction with his research work, he returned to India in 1954, after declining the offer of a full-time faculty position. As he put it, "I asked myself, why did I study genetics? It was to produce enough food in India. So I came back". In other words, he wanted to serve the nation and free it from the import of foodgrains.

His Writings

M.S. Swaminathan is a prolific writer and tireless researcher. He has published a number of scientific papers in the fields of crop improvement, cytogenetics and genetics and phylogenetics in reputed national and international journals.

In addition, he wrote books on the general theme of his work, biodiversity and sustainable agriculture for the alleviation of hunger. Some of his books are: (1) *An Evergreen Revolution* (2006); (2) *I Predict: A Century of Hope Towards an Era of Harmony with Nature and Freedom from Hunger* (1999); (3) *Gender Dimensions in Biodiversity Management (ed.)* 1988; (4) *Implementing the Benefit*

Sharing Provisions of the Convention on Biological Diversity: Challenges and Opportunities (1997); Agrobiodiversity and Farmers' Rights (1996); Farmers' Rights and Plant Genetic Resources: A dialogue (ed.) (1995); and Wheat Revolution: a Dialogue (1993).

Awards and Prizes

M.S. Swaminathan's professional achievements are spectacular. He received many awards and prizes.

Swaminathan received the First World Food Prize. At that time, the Secretary General of the United Nations wrote: "Dr. Swaminathan is a living legend. His contributions to Agricultural Sciences have made an indelible mark on food production in India and elsewhere in the developing world. By any standards, he will go into the annals of history as a world scientist of rare distinction". The United Nations Environment Programme described him as "the Father of Economic Ecology".

During a lecture at the 2006 Norman E. Borlaugh International Symposium on October 19, 2006, Swaminathan spoke on "The Green Revolution Redux: Can we replicate the single-greatest period of food production in all human history?" In it, he discussed the cultural and social foundations of the Green Revolution in India and the role of historic leaders in India, such as Mahatma Gandhi in inspiring the Green Revolution thereby calling for the alleviation of widespread hunger.

Swaminathan is a member of many prestigious scientific bodies. He is a fellow of the Royal Society of London, the U.S. National Academy of Sciences, the Russian Academy of Sciences, the Chinese Academy of Sciences and the Italian Academy of Sciences.

Swaminathan was awarded Padma Sri in 1967, Padma Bhushan in 1971 and Padma Vibhushan in 1989. He was selected for Ramon Magsaysay Award for Community Leadership in 1971. In 2000, he was awarded Indira Gandhi Prize for Peace, Disarmament and Development "for his outstanding performance in the domain of plant genetics and ensuring food security to hundreds of millions of citizens in the developing world. Swaminathan won recognition for his creative efforts toward promotoing international peace, development and a new international economic order; ensuring that scientific discoveries are used for the larger good of humanity, and enlarging the scope of freedom.

In 1999, he was honoured with UNESCO Mahatma Gandhi Gold Medal for his outstanding work in extending the benefits of biotechnology to marginalized and poverty-stricken populations in developing countries and in securing a sound basis for sustainable agricultural, environmental and rural development.

In 1997, he won the highest award for International Cooperation on Environment and Development, given by the Government of China for outstanding contributions to the lofty cause of environmental protection and development and for his signal accomplishments in the field of international cooperation.

In 1985, he received international award from Association for Women's Rights in Development (AWID) for his significant contributions to promoting the knowledge, skill, and technological empowerment of women in agriculture and for his pioneering role in mainstreaming gender considerations in agriculture and rural development.

The honours, awards and the international recognition that he received speak volumes about his contribution to Green Revolution.

When Swaminathan returned to India after earning his Ph.D. degree, India at that time was importing huge amounts of food grains. He thought that importing food was like importing unemployment because 70 percent of our population was involved in agriculture and importing meant supporting farmers in other countries. When he took over as Director of Indian Agricultural Research Institute in New Delhi, he found agriculture in a bad shape and he wanted to improve agricultural productivity. With help from Rockefeller foundation, Swaminathan found a crossbred wheat seed, part Japanese and part Mexican that was fruitful. He later bred this plant to produce the grain favoured by the Indians. In 1966, he set up 2000 model farms in villages outside New Delhi to demonstrate to the farmers what the new seed could do. Swaminathan needed 18,000 tonnes of Mexican seed. In spite of financial crunch, the then Prime Minister Shri Lal Bahadur Shastri provided the necessary financial support. Otherwise, there would have been a famine in the country. The first harvest with new seeds was three times more than the previous year's harvest. That was the beginning of the Green Revolution. Mrs. Indira Gandhi, who succeeded Lal bahadur Sastri, was at first skeptical about Swaminathan's optimism to stop import of foodgrains. However, she gave him a free hand to organize a new agricultural programme. He turned India from a food deficit economy to food surplus economy. As a result of Green Revolution, India's food grains output in 2012-13 was 255 million tonnes as compared to 89 million tonnes in 1964-65.

Conclusion

By his research in genetics and plant breeding, M.S. Swaminathan has made great contribution to national as well as international agricultural development. It is heartening to note that at present his focus is on Evergreen Revolution. He wants to provide freedom from hunger to the masses in harmony with Nature. No wonder, he has been recognized as the "Father of Economic Ecology".

YASHWANTRAO BALWANTRAO CHAVAN (1913-1984)

Introduction

Yashwantrao Balwantrao Chavan (Y.B. Chavan) was the first Chief Minister of Maharashtra after the division of Bombay state and he was the Fifth Deputy Prime Minister of India. He was a patriot, a tall congress leader from Maharashtra, co-operative leader, great administrator and a patron of Arts and Literature.

Chavan was born in a Maratha Patil family on March 12, 1913 at a village in Satara district (now in Sangli district) of Maharashtra. Chavan lost his father when he was very young and he was brought up by his mother and uncle. His mother taught him the virtues of patriotism and self-dependency. From a young age, he was attracted by the freedom struggle. He took active part in the struggle for Independence from the age of 17. Chavan was fined in 1930 for his participation in the Non-Cooperation Movement led by Gandhiji and in 1932 he was sentenced to 18 months for hoisting the national flag.

Chavan earned his B.A. degree in history and political science in 1938 from Bombay University. Even as a student, he became a social activist and was associated with the Congress party and its leaders such as Pandit Jawaharlal Nehru and Sardar Vallabhai Patel. He became Satara District Congress President in 1940. He took his LLB in 1942.

Chavan was one of the delegates at the Bombay Session of the All India Congress Committee (ICC) in 1942. It was there that Gandhiji gave the call for Quit India Movement. Chavan was arrested for his participation in the movement and he was released only in 1944.

Role in Government

Y.B. Chavan was first elected MLA of the Bombay State from the South Satara constituency in 1946 and he became Parliamentary Secretary to the Home Minister of the State. And he was appointed Minister of Civil Supplies, Social Welfare and Forests in the next government with Morarji Desai as the Chief Minister. Chavan was a signatory to the Nagpur Pact (1953) that assured equitable development of all regions of the present Maharashtra State. In 1957, he was elected as Leader of Congress Legislature Party and became the Chief Minister of the bilingual Bombay State. From 1957 to 1960, he was a member of the All India Congress Working Committee. He played a leading role in the formation of the Marathi speaking Maharashtra State. Y.B. Chavan became the first Chief Minister of Maharashtra on May 1, 1960.

Chavan's vision for the economic development of Maharashtra was based on balanced development of both industry and agriculture across all regions of the state. He wanted to realize this vision through cooperative movement. Legislation regarding democratic decentralized bodies and

Agricultural Land Ceiling Act were two major pieces of legislation passed during his tenure as Chief Minister of the State.

When Krishna Menon resigned as Defence Minister in 1962 in the wake of India–China border conflict, Y.B. Chavan became the Defence Minister. He deftly handled the delicate post-war situation, took many decisions to empower the armed forces. Not only that, along with Nehru, he negotiated with China to end the hostilities. It may be noted that Chavan was the Defence Minister in Lal Bahadur Sastri's government during Indo-Pakistan War of 1965.

Chavan was appointed Home Minister of India by Prime Minister Indira Gandhi on November 14, 1966. Next, he was appointed as Finance Minister of India on June 26, 1970 by Indira Gandhi. Again on October 11, 1974, he was appointed as Foreign Minister by her. When Internal State of Emergency was declared by Indira Gandhi in June 1975, Chavan continued in her government. When general elections were declared in 1977, Congress was routed and even Indira Gandhi lost her parliamentary seat. In the new Parliament, Chavan was elected Parliamentary leader of the Congress party and as Congress was the biggest opposition, he became the Leader of Opposition.

There was a split in the Congress party at its annual session in Bangalore (now Bengaluru). There, Chavan parted ways with Gandhi and joined the rival party. That created a major setback for him in his political career. However, he was appointed as Home Minister and Deputy Prime Minister in Prime Minister Charan Singh's cabinet in 1979.

Chavan returned to Congress (I) after Indira Gandhi came to power after winning the general elections in 1980. He was appointed the Chairman of the 8th Finance Commission in 1982.

Chavan passed away after a heart attack in Delhi on November 25, 1984.

Patron of Marathi Literature

Chavan took a keen interest in the development of Marathi language and literature. He established *Marathi Sahitya Mandal* and supported Marathi Sahitya Sammelan (conference). He initiated compilation of *Marathi Vishwakosh* (Marathi language encyclopedia).

Conclusion

The foregoing account reveals that Y.B. Chavan was a great Marathi leader. He was the only Marathi leader who held four important portfolios of the Union Government. They are Defence, Home, Finance and External Affairs. He discharged his duties and functions in an able manner. In Maharashtra, he was called Prati-Shivaji, which means New Shivaji or New Avatar (incarnation) of Shivaji.

Yashwantrao Chavan Pratishtan (Foundation) was established in 1985 in Bombay (now, Mumbai) to "perpetuate his memory by acknowledging his rich, outstanding and valuable contribution to society and democratic institutions and development process in India's socio-political life and to undertake activities and programmes particularly for the elevation of common man and promote his cherished ideas nurtured in freedom struggle and thereby strengthening socio-economic fibre of India".

RECENT TRENDS IN INDIAN ECONOMIC THOUGHT (APPLIED ECONOMICS)

There has been a remarkable progress in the study of economics in India since Independence. In the words of professor Bhabatosh Datta, "The economists in India are no longer confined to certain special fields only nor to the pursuance of certain special lines of approach. They have firmly established their position among the economists all over the world. The output of good work has been enormous".

Before Independence, some foriegn scholars, most of whom were civil servants, did excellent work on Indian economic problems. The subjects covered by them ranged from economic history to day-to-day problems such as land revenue and rural credit. But after Independence, economic development through planning became a topic of absorbing interest among Indian as well as foreign scholars. The formulation of Five Year Plans in India has led to a steady evolution of economic thinking on questions relating to planning theory and techniques.

Planning

The First Five Year Plan, though was essentially, a collection of several projects, contained at the same time the essential features of Harrod-Domar model.

Any discussion on plan models with reference to India usually starts with a discussion of models developed by Mahalanobis. He has developed a one-sector model, a two-sector model and a four-sector model. The two-sector model bears close resemblance to a much earlier model developed by the Soviet economist, Feldman in 1928. The four-sector model is an exercise in numerical calculation of investment allocation in the short run.

Mahalanobis approach in the two-sector model had the following development philosophy. "If you want a high rate of growth of consumption in the long run, then the best policy is to give top priority to the development of investment goods industries over consumer goods industries". We may note that this development philosophy was at the bottom of Soviet planning experience in the thirties.

The Mahalanobis model was criticized on the ground that it ignored foreign trade and that it also ignored the structural rigidities in the Indian political and economic system.

By the time, the Third Plan (1961-66) came to be designed, new exercises were undertaken both by Indian and foreign scholars. And the assumption of a closed economy was replaced by more realistic assumptions.

And there was a special emphasis on consistency conditions. Rostow's concept of "self-sustained growth" was expanded to include "self-reliant growth". In the subsequent plans, the dynamic multi-sector consistency models marked a great advance.

Along with the progress made in the formulation of plan models, there was considerable improvement in the analysis of particular problems. Issues such as investment criteria for a planned system, choice of techniques (capital-intensive versus labour-intensive technology) were discussed in detail. From the Second Five Year Plan onwards, the question of the relationship between physical planning and financial planning was disussed at length. It may be noted that Mahalanobis model emphasized on physical planning rather than on financial planning.

According to Jagdish N.Bhagwati and Sukhamoy Chakravarty, the Indian discussion of the choice of technique was concerned primarily with the selection of an appropriate social rate of return on a unit of invested capital. For example, K.N. Raj dealt with some aspects of the Bhakra Nangal Project in the Punjab and N.V. Sovani and N. Rath examined the economics of the Hirakud Dam.

We may note that the whole discussion on Indian Planning models was linked with deep theoretical analysis of theory of investment and the broader theory of economic growth.

Agriculture

The economic analysis of agricultural policy has focused on questions relating to agricultural price and distribution policy and also the economic efficiency of alternative forms of land tenure and agrarian organization.

The social aspects of alternative policies with respect to agrarian organization have claimed attention of the Indian economists. As Dantwala, the eminent Agricultural economist puts it, "It may be pertinent to enquire as to what has provided the main inspiration for the proposal to impose a ceiling on individual ownership of land: the urge for distributive justice or the necessity of a more rational use of the land surface? The impromptu answer would perhaps be: both. But it would be honest to admit that the prime motivation is distributive justice. In the context of the acute land hunger and millions of dwarf farms, ownership of large areas of cultivated land by a few is con sidered highly inequitable, justifying the imposition of an upper limit to individual ownership."

Some of the important Indian studies have been the analysis of: (*i*) the economic "rationality" of farmers, (*ii*) the response of marketed surplus and production to price changes, (*iii*) the relationship of the land tenure system and agrarian organization to the efficiency of factor use and to the elasticity of marketed surplus, production and investment, to price change and (*iv*) the question of the existence and measurement of disguised unemployment.

Some of the notable works in the field of agricultural economics are those of M.L. Dantwala, K.N. Raj, Sovani and Rath, V.M. Dandekar, Raj Krishna, Mathur, A.M. Khusro, B.S. Minhas, T.N. Srinivasan, Hanumantha Rao, Vaidyanathan, D.R. Gadgil, P.K. Bardhan, Krishna Bharadwaj, Bhaba. tosh Datta and A. Bhaduri.

Industry

There has been considerable interest in the problems of industry since Independence. The Industrial policy statement of 1956 for a long time became the basis of Government programmes in relation to public and private sectors.

R.K. Hazari's Report (1987) exposed some aspects of concentration of economic power and the abuse of the industrial licensing system. This led to a number of studies on the relative roles of the public sector and the private sector, on monopolistic elements, on the concentration of economic power and on industrial growth problems in general.

A major change that took place in the industrial sector was the increasing dependence of the industries in the private sector for long term loans on specialized public sector financing institutions.

Some of the important works in industrial economics are those of J. Bhagwati, T.N. Srinivasan, A.K. Bagchi, B.N. Aktar, R.K. Hazari, D. Lal and S.L.N. Simha.

Foreign Trade

The Indian policy literature on foreign trade has been concerned mainly with issues raised by foreign aid, private foreign investment, and trade and exchange rate policies.

With respect to foreign aid, the use of "aid to end aid" by a specified time horizon has been the framework within which some important planning exercises have been done. Ultimate "self-reliance" is the aim.

There was considerable controversy on the tying of aid by commodity, especially P.L. 480 imports.

Most of the literature on private foreign investment revolved round two questions: (*i*) Is private equity investment superior to official loan, transfers? (*ii*) What restrictions must be placed on the inflow of private capital, from the view point of social welfare?

The literature on India's trade and exchange rate policies has focused on the drawbacks of a regime based on quantitative restrictions. (*e.g.*, import controls).

Some of the outstanding contributions in the field of international trade are those of J. Bhagwati, Padma Desai, A.K. Biswas, P.K. Bardhan. A.K. Bhaduri, S. Chakravarthy, G. Mathur, B.S. Minhas and A.K. Sen.

Definition and Measurement of Poverty

Rath and Dandekar have done some important work on the measurement of poverty in India. A common element in most of the definitions of poverty based on the subsistence level is the lack or inadequacy of income. "Want of adequate income, howsoever defined is poverty" (Dandekar 1981).

The poverty line in terms of a specific income level varies, depending on assumptions relating to what constitutes "daily needs of life" and the cost of those items. Dandekar has mentioned four such criteria for the definition of the current poverty line: (*i*) the proportion of expenditure taken up by specified essential items such as food; (*ii*) the calorie value of food; (*iii*) the cost of a balanced diet; and finally (*iv*) the cost of essentials for a tolerable human existence." Amartya Sen focused on the inequality among the poor and argued that for many purposes, such as the evaluation of the effects of policy on poverty, it is necessary to look carefully at the distribution of income below the line.

Basic Needs

It may be of interest to note that India, with its "minimum needs programme" adopted basic needs strategy before the term became popular. Ashok Rudra has dealt with in detail the basic needs concept and its implementation in Indian development planning.

Human Capital

Since 1960s, economists have emphasized that investment in human capital is a major contributor to economic growth. Some of the important works in the field are those of A.M. Nalla Gounder (a pioneering study on investment in education in India), V.N. Kothari, P.R. Panchamukhi, J.P. Naik, Malcolm S. Adiseshiah, Atmanand Misra, D. Nanjudappa and J.B.G. Tilak. Some foreign scholars like Mark Blaug and Maureen Woodhall have also made significant contribution to the study of the issues relating to human capital in India.

Conclusion

The foregoing analysis shows that Indian economists have made significant contributions to economic analysis of planning, agriculture, industry, foreign trade, poverty measurement, basic needs approach and investment in human capital.

NOBEL LAUREATES IN ECONOMICS

Introduction

Nobel prizes are a series of annual awards provided for by a fund in the will of Alfred Nobel and by a gift from the Central Bank of Sweden. There are six classifications, to reward persons who have made outstanding contributions for the benefit of mankind in: (*i*) Physiology or Medicine; (*ii*) Physics; (*iii*) Literature; (*iv*) Chemistry; (*v*) Peace; and (*vi*) Economics.

It may be interesting to note that Alfred Nobel did not include economics in his will. From 1901 to 1968 there was no Nobel Prize in economics, just as there still is no such prize in mathematics. The Nobel Prize in Economics established (funded) by the Central Bank of Sweden was first awarded in 1969. The winner is selected by the Royal Swedish Academy of Sciences.

The awards usually are presented in Stockholm, with the King of Sweden officiating, annually on December 10, the anniversary of Alfred Nobel's death. Each prize includes a gold medal, a diploma and a gift of money which varies from year to year.

Nobel Laureates in Economics

The following is a list of Nobel Memorial Prize winners in Economics up to 2016:

1969 : Jan Tinbergen (Netherlands) and Ragnar Frisch (Norway)

1970 : Paul A. Samuelson (United States)

1971 : Simon Kuznets (United States)

1972 : Kenneth J. Arrow (United States) and Sir John Hicks (Britain)

1973 : Wassily Leontief (United States)

1974 : Friedrich A. Von Hayek (Britain) and Gunnar Myrdal (Sweden)

1975 : Tjalling Koopmans (United States) and Leonid V. Kantorovich (Soviet Union)

1976 : Milton Friedman (United States)

1977 : Bertil Ohlin (Sweden) and James E. Meade (Britain)

1978 : Herbert A. Simon (United Staes)

1979 : Arthur Lewis (Britain) and Theodore W. Schultz (United States)

1980 : Lawrence R. Klein (United States)

1981 : James Tobin (United States)

1982 : George J. Stigler

1983 : Gerard Debreu

1984 : Sir Richard Stone

1985 : Franco Modigliani

1986 : James Buchanan

1987 : Robert M. Solow

1988 : Maurice Allais

1989 : Trygve Haavelmo

1990 : Harry M. Markowitz, F. Sharpe and Merton Miller

1991 : Ronald Coase

1992 : Gary S. Becker

1993 : Robert W. Fogel and Douglass C. North

1994 : John C. Harsanyi, John F. Nash and Reinhard Selten

1995 : Robert E. Lucas JR.

1996 : James A. Mirrless and William Vickrey

1997 : Robert C. Merton and Myron S. Scholes

1998 : Amartya Sen

1999 : Robert A. Mundell

2000 : James J. Heckman and Daniel L. McFadden

2001 : George A. Akerlof, A. Michael Spence and Joseph E. Stiglitz

2002 : Daniel Kahneman and Vernon L. Smith

2003 : Robert F. Engle III and Clive W. J. Granger

2004 : Finn E. Kydland and Edward C. Prescott

2005 : Robert J. Aumann and Thomas C. Schelling

2006 : Edmund Phelps

2007 : Leonid Hurwicz, Eric S. Maskin and Roger B. Myerson

2008 : Paul Krugman

2009 : Elinor Ostrom and Oliver E. Williamson

2010 : Peter A. Diamond Dale T. Mortensen and Christopher A. Pissarides

2011 : Thomas Sargent and Christopher Sims

2012 : Lloyd Shapely and Alvin Roth

2013 : Eugene Fama, Robert Shiller and Lars Peter Hansen

2014 : Jean Tirole

2015 : Angus Deaton

2016 : Oliver Heart and Bengt Holmstrom

We shall briefly describe the contribution of these Nobel Laureates in Economics in the ensuing sections.

JAN TINBERGEN

Jan Tinbergen was selected to share the first Nobel Prize in Economics with Ragnar Frisch in 1969. They were awarded the prize for their developments in the science of econometrics, an approach to economics that uses mathematical models to describe economic environments. In selecting these two eminent economists for the award, the Royal Swedish Academy of Sciences considered not only the extension of knowledge for knowledge's own sake, but also its applied aspects, its potential benefits to mankind.

Tinbergen has done pathbreaking work in international trade, economic development and planning, econometrics and economic theory.

It is convenient to divide Tinbergen's life and work into three periods. The first period includes the years from the end of the twenties to World War II. During this period, Tinbergen together with some other economists and statisticians created econometrics as a science. During the war years, Tinbergen was by and large isolated from international contacts. During the second period, the decade 1945—55, he was the Director of the Central Planning Bureau of Netherlands. It was then that he laid the foundation for modern short-term economic policies. During the third period, beginning in the middle fifties and continuing many years ahead, Tinbergen has devoted almost exclusively to the methods and practice of planning for long-term development, in particular of under-developed countries, and international co-operation.

Ragnar Frisch, Jan Tinbergen and Irving Fisher established the Econometric Society in 1930. It is "an international society for the advancement of Economic Theory in its relation to statistics and mathematics." Tinbergen made some of the most fundamental early contributions to econometrics. Notable among them are the so called cobweb theorem and the related contributions to dynamic theory, and the attempts of statistical testing of business cycle theories. The Cobweb theorem became a starting point for modern dynamic theory with the use of difference equations as a characteristic feature. Tinbergen himself applied the mathematical technique to the business cycle problem as early as 1931 in an article on ship-building cycle. By the end of the thirties, it had become a standard method of dynamic analysis in economics.

Tinbergen's second great contribution to econometrics was his pioneering work on statistical testing of business cycle theories. His work, *A Method and its Application to Investment Activity and Business Cycle in United States of America*, 1919-1932 was published in two volumes in 1939 by the League of Nations, Geneva. These two volumes opened up a completely new branch of economics: empirical macro-economics. Keynes at that time attacked Tinbergen's work as "alchemy". But that criticism fell flat to the ground.

Jan Tinbergen presented a model for the Dutch economy in 1936. The aim of the model was partly to discover the dynamic properties of the Dutch economy and partly to construct a basis for economic policy decisions.

Tinbergen published *The Theory of Economic Policy* in 1952 and *Centralisation and Decentralisation in Economic Policy* in 1954. These works created a basis for rational thinking and quantitative calculation in economic policy. It may be interesting to compare Tinbergen's theory of economic policy with the so-called modern welfare economics. The latter was mainly concerned with Pareto-optimal situations under conditions of perfect competition. The welfare economists have developed elegant and technically refined models. But these models proved rather sterile and difficult to apply to practical policy problems. But Tinbergen's theory of economic policy is quite simple. It is concerned with actual macropolicy targets of governments in actually existing economies and has proved powerful and applicable to current policy problems. This is a characteristic feature of all the scientific work of Tinbergen. He has never been very much interested in theory for theory's own sake. When once he evolves a method that works "empirically", he does not waste time on further theoretical refinements.

By the middle of the fifties, Tinbergen has started devoting more and more of his attention to the problems of economic co-operation and development. His interest in co-operation was closely related to the creation of European common market. In the field of development, poor countries attracted his attention. In this area, he was guided by idealistic views on mankind and his deep devotion to humanitarian activities.

In the field of long-term economic planning for growth, Tinbergen has been looking for simple, crude methods that "work" under the primitive conditions of policy-making in underdeveloped countries. His long-term Planning models have been designed on the basic assumptions that only a minimum statistical information is available, and that the skill of planners, administrators and politicians is limited. Broadly, his planning models may be divided into three types. The first model can be characterized as "planning by stages". First, a simple macro model of the Keynes and Harrod-Domar type is used to determine the total investment and savings required for the planning period considered. Then follows a sectoral stage where the total volume of investment is distributed by sectors by the application of a small input-model and sectoral capital-output coefficients. Sometimes, it may be followed by a regional stage. The final stage consists of the choice of concrete investment projects within each sector according to investment criteria which depend upon the policy targets of the country. This is considered the most widely used model for planning in underdeveloped countries. It has been pointed out by critics that this model does not ensure efficiency in the economic systems. It is considered a major drawback of the model. Another deficiency in the model is that it does not plan for implementation in terms of instruments to be used.

In the second model, the first and the second stage in the first model are lumped together and policy instruments are incorporated more explicitly in the solution. This is similar to the models developed by Ragnar Frisch and is a combination of Harrod-Domar, Keynes and Leontief input-output models. Computer facilities are essential for working out this model.

The third type of model is known as the semi-input-output method. It differs radically from the other approaches in that it starts out from individual projects and simply lets the macro-plan emerge as the sum of micro-plans. In this model, project appraisal is made on the basis of shadow prices. An interesting thing about the model is that even international commodity prices are taken into account. This brings the problem of competitiveness at international prices into planning process right from the beginning. The main problem with this model is that observable shadow prices do not exist. In the absence of shadow prices, planning for efficiency in resource allocation becomes a difficult job in underdeveloped countries.

Other Contributions

Besides the outstanding innovations in theory and policy mentioned above, Tinbergen has worked on issues such as national accounting, imperfect competition, stability in economic systems, international factor-price equalisation, the theory of interest, international commodity agreements, problems of education and growth, balance of payment and choice of techniques.

Conclusion

We may now sum up his main contributions to economics:

1. He was a pioneer in modern economic dynamics;
2. He helped to establish econometrics;
3. He is the founder of empirical macro-economics;
4. He contributed to a great extent towards the creation of the modern techniques of economic forecasting and prediction;
5. He is the founder of the modern theory of economic policy; and
6. He has contributed significantly to modern development planning in backward countries.

RAGNAR FRISCH

Ragnar Frisch was selected to share the first Nobel Prize in economics with Jan Tinbergen in 1969. They were awarded the prize for their developments in the science of econometrics, an approach to economics that uses mathematical models to describe economic environments.

Ragnar Frisch, Jan Tinbergen and Irving Fisher established the econometric society in 1930. It is "an international society for the advancement of economic theory in its relation to statistics and mathematics". It aims at the unification of the theoretical-quantitative and empirical-quantitative approach. In fact, the term "econometrics" was coined by Ragnar Frisch in late 1920s. The word has been coined with the idea of bringing out the connection of a science with measurement. Incidentally it may be mentioned that it was Frisch who coined the words, "micro-economics" and , "macro-economics".

The contributions of Ragnar Frisch to economics are many and varied. We may broadly classify his contributions under three heads: (*i*) His attempts to make economics an exact and quantitative science (*ii*) His efforts in making economics as an aid in the formulation of a rational economic policy; and (*iii*) His contributions to the development of economic dynamics.

Frisch has made significant contribution in the field of utility analysis. From the utility function, he has derived the conditions of demand elasticities. He has analysed the problem in his article "A complete scheme for computing all direct and cross-demand elasticities in a model with many sectors". This method was used for building large models for preparing national budgets for Norway.

Frisch has made notable contribution in the field of production theory. The definition of factor-quantity and product-quantity is fundamental in the theory of production. In the dynamic theory of production, the time shape of input and output elements is of basic importance. These ideas are found in his book, *Theory of Production*.

Frisch's article "Propagation problems and Impulse problems in Dynamic Economics" is an exercise in dynamic analysis. The above article appeared in *Economic Essays in Honour of Gustav Cassel* (1933). In it, the idea of erratic shocks was first brought forward by Frisch. The idea of erratic shocks caused by things such as technological advances, innovations, wars and natural disasters has been used to explain disturbances which occur quite frequently and at random intervals in an economy. Thus, the concept has been made use of in the explanation of business cycles.

Since the depression of thirties, Frisch had started taking interest in the problems of economic recovery and development planning. His book, *Circulation Planning* deals with the problems of restarting production and circulation processes in an economy caught in the grips of depression caused by deficiency in demand.

After World War II, Frisch developed economic policy models. The decision models he developed were based on input-output analysis. He was a pioneer in the field of comprehensive programming models. His book, *Planning for India, Selected Explorations in Methodology* throws light on the model constructed for Indian Planning.

Frisch has developed a number of concepts and tools in dynamic economics by his articles such as *statics and dynamics in economic theory* and *on the notion of equilibrium and disequilibrium*.

Frisch's theory of business cycle is found in his article, *The relation between primary investment and reinvestment*. He has explained business cycle in terms of the acceleration principle and reinvestment effects. He has given importance to time element in investment decisions. He has introduced the dynamic element in consumption also. The introduction of dynamic element into consumption is very important at a time when pure economic theory has undergone a revolution of thought from statistical to dynamical models. According to Kenneth J. Arrow, Frisch's work on polypoly theory and his analysis of the phenomena of "economic pressure" might be considered as his important contribution to economic dynamics.

Frisch is also popular for his theory of cost of living indices. He has presented many original ideas in his article, *Annual Survey of General Economic Theory: The Problem of Index Numbers* (1936).

Conclusion

In selecting Ragnar Frisch along with Jan Tinbergen for the award of the first Nobel Prize in Economics, the Royal Swedish Academy of Sciences considered not only the extension of knowledge for knowledge's own sake, but also its applied aspects, its potential benefits to mankind.

PAUL A. SAMUELSON

Paul A. Samuelson of United States was awarded the Nobel Prize in Economics in 1970 for his influential and widely read works, which have raised the level of scientific analysis in economic theory. He has done more than any other living economist to raise the level of scientific analysis in the field of economic theory and he has developed many new economic theories.

Samuelson was the first economist from the United States to receive the Nobel Prize in Economics. He made some of his best contributions to economics even while as a graduate student. He wrote three articles on the theory of consumer choice as a graduate student. It was as a graduate student that he developed the accelerator-multiplier interaction principle. His dissertation at Harvard was published in 1947 as *Foundations of Economic Analysis*.

Samuelson is one of the world's best known economists. His association with the Massachusetts Institute of Technology, where be teaches, began in 1940. His book *Economics* has sold more than three million copies in 24 languages. When the 1970 award was announced, Samuelson joked, "they don't give Nobel Prizes for writing textbooks". According to Milton Friedman, Samuelson "as a mathematical economist has helped to reshape and improve the theoretical foundations of our subject (Economics). This is the work for which this remarkable versatile man won the Nobel Prize".

Samuelson always emphasized that economics to be a realistic science, should make use of more and more of mathematics. He is both an economist and a mathematician. He is of the view that "economics has been getting more technical. Often that means more mathematical. From the standpoint of ultimate research at the frontier, that is probably inevitable and perhaps a good thing". He also feels that mathematics should be taught after the students gain some understanding of the fundamentals in economics.

Samuelson rejected the theory of demand based on cardinal (marginal utility) approach. He has developed the *revealed preference theory* which can justify the downward slope of the demand curves even though the individual consumer cannot describe his scales of preference by drawing indifference maps. Since this analysis asks the consumer to reveal the nature of his preferences by showing which goods he prefers in a set of circumstances, it is known as the revealed preference theory.

The fact that the revealed preference theory can explain the demand curves without the assumptions that the consumers can define or describe their indifference maps is one of its advantages. According to Sir John Hicks, one major advantage of revealed preference theory is that it is explicitly designed to allow econometricians to make use of it. Further, while indifference curve analysis can be used to analyse situations where there is weak ordering, revealed preference theory can be used to deal with situations where the consumer is choosing between strongly ordered combination of goods.

Samuelson has developed a principle to show that an economy may be in a vicious circle where the acceleration principle and multipler interact to produce a cumulative deflationary (or inflationary) spiral.

The analysis can also explain how a downturn can result from the previous expansion itself. The accelerator-multiplier interaction principle has been put to excellent use in some of the modern theories of the business cycle (*e.g.*, Hicks's theory of business cycle).

Samuelson has made notable contribution to *New Welfare Economics*. He has made use of the concept of social welfare function to explain the ideas of welfare economics. He believes that economics should essentially be a normative science. The social welfare function is a method by which the special scale of preferences can be derived from individual state of preferences. This can be done either voluntarily or by some dictator in a centrally planned economy.

In recent times, Samuelson has developed a new concept called "Net Economic Welfare" (NEW). In the past, economic welfare was measured mostly in terms of total output of goods and services or Gross National Product (GNP). If we decide to work fewer hours per week, take more vacations per year, the GNP goes down. But our leisure has gone up. Now that people enjoy more leisure, we may say that welfare has gone up. What we want is welfare, not mere growth. So the GNP is corrected for changes in leisure. Even the work done by women at home is included. For, it is productive, even though not paid employment. Similarly, correction is made for pollution which affects the quality of our life. Samuelson advocates NEW growth for developed countries like the United States and countries in Western Europe. Economic growth (in terms of GNP), of course, is of crucial importance for developing countries like India. These countries do not mind a little pollution during the process of industrialisation of their predominantly agricultural economies.

The fundamental theme of the first edition (1948) of Samuelson's famous text book *Economics* was the problem of the deep depression of the 1930s especially the problem of unemployment. A major focus was on the great contributions of John Maynard Keynes, especially his *General Theory of Employment, Interest and Money*. In recent times, he has contributed a lot to the understanding of the new problems such as cost-push inflation and stagflation. Stagflation is a situation where there is stagnation (*i.e.*, a let down in the rate of growth, though not an absolute depression like the old days) on the one hand, and inflationary problems on the other hand, at the same time. This is the problem faced by almost all industrial countries. Even communist countries are not immune. When, for example, planners in Hungary or Poland or Yugoslavia began to depend more upon decentralized mechanism, some of the same difficulties found in non-communist economies reasserted themselves—in the form of a mismatch between the total of jobs and total number of job-seekers, or a mismatch between the amount of money which the consumer brings to the market to spend and the amount of goods which are available in the market.

We shall now have some idea about his views on population problem, international monetary reforms and the future role of the United States in the world economy.

Population Problem

He believes that population growth without limit is a problem. It will result in exhaustion of irreplaceable natural resources, in more pollution, and in a lower standard of life. According to him, the trend towards zero population growth is a very important one and he believes that in the United States, it actually arrived in mid-1973. But he is no Malthusian.

International Monetary Reform

According to Samuelson, the Bretton Woods Agreement, which set up the post–World War II international system, was a great agreement". The world has benefited from it. The quantum of international trade has grown at 8 and 10 per cent a year. But one fatal flaw in the system was the pegging of exchange rates. We have learned that cannot be done. We are on the threshold of a new, gradual breakthrough to a more rational system in which there is flexibility. There is already a measure of floating of most of the major exchange rates in the world. That is an advance. And he approves of the new kind of international currency reserves, the SDRs—the Special Drawing Rights at the International Monetary fund.

The Future Role of the United States in the World Economy

The United States will have a big role to play in future. But it has to face a fact. At the end of World War II, United States with six per cent of the population had about 50 per cent of World's' GNP. Then, because of the Marshall Plan, because of the recovery of Japan, because of improvement all over the world, the U.S. share is now below 30 per cent. It may even go down to 25 per cent. So the United States does not enjoy the same unilateral power and that is a good thing. It will continue to be one of the important countries and it can afford to be more generous.

Conclusion

In economics, talk is cheap, it is performance that is hard. Samuelson is a great performer. The brief outline of his contribution clearly brings out how he has raised the level of scientific analysis in economic theory.

SIMON KUZNETS

Simon Kuznets was awarded the Nobel Prize in Economics in 1971 for his contributions to national income accounting that made possible quantitative studies of the comparative growth of nations. The prize was awarded "for his empirically founded interpretations of economic growth". The Royal Caroline Institute emphasized that "more than any other scientist, he has illuminated with facts and explained through analysis the economic growth from the middle of the last century." The Institute noted that Professor Kuznets has shown "little sympathy" for abstract theories that could not be tested.

Kuznets was born in Kharkov in what is now the Soviet Union in 1901. Professor Kuznets earned his bachelor of science and his doctorate from Columbia. He taught at the Universities of Pennsylvania and John Hopkins before joining Harvard in 1960. He retired from Harvard University on July 1, 1971.

Kuznets had shown that income derived from labour was more important than capital income and that qualified labour was an essential need of economies, especially in developing countries.

In explaining the award, the Royal Institute said that Dr. Kuznets had upset the belief that economic progress "could be measured in dollars and cents and that capital movements were of major importance to national income." Instead, Kuznets had shown that the well-being of a nation is not dependent on its gross national product but on its structural rationalization, technical development and the quality of its labour.

In more than 30 books and articles, the 1971 Nobel Laureate has, developed theories for calculation of the national income and the growth of a nation's economy. Professor Kuznets is one of the recognized authorities on national income estimates. In 1941, he published in two volumes *National Income and its Composition*, 1919-38. It describes, in detail, the methods used in the computation of national income. He cautions against double counting in the measurement of national income. For instance, he tells us "we assume that the final goal of economic activity is provision of goods to consumers, the final products are those turned during the year to flow either to consumers or to capital stock, and that everything else, by the nature of the cases, is intermediate product whose inclusion in the total output would constitute duplication."

Kuznet's study on *Commodity Flow and Capital Formation* is a document on the methodology of estimating capital formation. This volume may even be termed as a treatise on commodity-flow approach.

Kuznets has made both theoretical and empirical contributions in the field of economic growth. *Economic Growth of Nations* and *Modern Economic Growth* are among his best known books. According to him, "the enormous increase in per capita product is largely the result of a rise in efficiency, *i.e.*, output per unit of input."

Kuznets has produced some hard information—even statistical data—to show that the rate of modem economic growth is much greater than the rate of growth throughout history upto the 19th century. Knowledge has accumulated at a rapid rate in modern times and it has been applied with an increasing efficiency. The main problem in the developing countries is the dual character of their economies. We have two sectors in these countries, existing side by side: a very small modern sector, which tends to be isolated and a much larger traditional sector. And there is not sufficient interaction between the very different technologies found in these two sectors. To rectify these imbalances, generally speaking, developing countries can choose from the stock of the modem technology that exists in the world. Often the technology used in the more advanced countries is too capital-intensive to be efficient in the developing countries. For example, let us take agriculture. The U.S.A. has developed labour saving machinery for farms because it has plenty of land and a relatively limited and a fairly expensive labour. But this labour saving machinery is less useful in developing countries that have abundant suply of relatively inexpensive labour. So Kuznets thinks that one of the most important steps a developing country can take toward modernization is to develop technological and inventive talent among its own people. Japan, for example, began to develop its economy late in the 19th century. It did not blindly imitate modern technology. The Japanese began to develop certain types of machinery that were particularly appropriate for the kinds of simple production they needed. For example, they found that spinning mills were more efficient in Japan. Again, when the Japanese began to set up heavy industry, they economized on capital by importing second-hand machinery.

Still later, when they began to supply their people with more and better goods, they retained traditional types of housing, clothing and other items, utilizing a unique technology that took special advantage of the resources available then to Japan.

Kuznets assigns key role to agriculture in the economic development of a developing nation. He points out that underdeveloped countries are further behind the developed countries in product per worker in agriculture than they are in product per worker in the non-agricultural sectors. But agricultural revolution—a marked rise in productivity per worker—is a pre-condition for industrial revolution for any sizeable region in the world. If agriculture itself grows, it makes a product contribution; if it trades with others, it renders a market contribution; if it transfers resources to other sectors, these resources being productive factors, it makes a factor contribution.

During the process of development, a country may have to give up some of its cultural heritage because some of its institutions may be incompatible with a high level or production. It should consider which elements of its cultural heritage it wishes to retain and which it is willing to give up. Japan, for example, chose not to give up its basic style of housing and other characteristic aspects of the historical Japanese experience. And India almost certainly would not abandon its religious legacy. This bias toward tradition is a source of strength because it preserves a kind of community unity.

Kuznets agrees that a developing country should give priority to the industries in the export sector which enjoy comparative advantage. But he warns that the country should realize that its comparative advantage at any given time will not last forever. Sweden is a small country, whose comparative advantage has changed almost continuously over years. First it had comparative advantage in iron ore, then in raw lumber and later on in paper. So a country should not get caught in a situation that might be called "export obsolescence".

Economic development is a complicated business and it involves many inter-related elements. No country will achieve economic growth with complete efficiency. There are always errors; there will always be some waste. But by studying the established record of modern economic growth, developing countries can learn to reduce the costs and hasten the process of economic development.

Conclusion

The foregoing analysis describes in outline the contributions made by Kuznets mainly in the field of national income analysis and economic growth. His work has made possible, quantitative studies of the comparative growth of nations.

KENNETH J. ARROW

Kenneth J. Arrow of United States was awarded the Nobel Prize in economics in 1972 along with John R. Hicks of Britain. They were awarded the prize for their pioneering work in the highly abstract field of equilibrium theory, which holds that a state of balance results when economic forces cancel each other out. They have done pioneering work in the field of welfare theory also. The general equilibrium theory explains the determination of prices and the allocation of resources in the economy. According to Professor Bertil Ohlin, a member of the Prize Committee, "the general equilibrium theory is the basis for most of the direct application of economic theory such as localisation of industrial plant, resource allocation, financial and employment theory and foreign trade, all these being used to increase the welfare of the people." The welfare theory tries to analyse how you reach au optimum economy by changes, in the institutional situation of a nation's economy.

Kenneth J. Arrow was born in 1921. He took his Master's Degree in 1941 and obtained his Doctorate in 1951. He has served in many American Universities such as Chicago, Stanford, Cambridge. He became the President of the Econometric Society in 1965.

Some of the important works of Arrow are: *Social choice and Individual values* (1951), *Studies in Linear and Non-linear programming* (1958), *Essays in the theory of Risk–Bearing* (1971), *Readings in Welfare Economics* (edited by Arrow and Scitovsky) (1969), *Mathematical Methods in Social*

Sciences (1959) and *Studies in Applied Probability and Management Science* (1962).

Arrow has made many important contributions to economic theory. However, mention may be made of his development of the theory of uncertainty and its incorporation within the framework of general equilibrium and further more, his analysis of the possibilities for decentralised decisions in a society where price system is fixed by the central authority. He made this analysis in collaboration with Leonid Hurwicz.

From general equilibrium theory to welfare theory is but a short step and both Hicks and Arrow have, on several points, developed the welfare economic consequences of their achievements.

"Perhaps the most important of Arrow's many contributions to welfare theory is the possibility theorem, according to which it is impossible to construct a social welfare function out of individual preference functions".

The possibility theorem may be described as follows: "If we exclude the possibility of interpersonal comparisons of utility, then the only method of passing from individual tastes to social preferences which will be satisfactory and which will be defined for a wide range of sets of individual orderings are either imposed or dictatorial".

In an article "on the stability of the competitive equilibrium", which Arrow wrote jointly with some other economists, he has proved that "competitive equilibrium is stable in a class of cases where the demand for each particular commodity is more sensitive to change in the price of that commodity itself than it is to be a price change in any other commodity".

Conclusion

The above brief description gives in outline the pioneering contributions of Arrow to the general economic equilibrium theory and welfare economics. Arrow has added many tools to the kit of economics.

SIR JOHN HICKS

Sir John Hicks of Oxford University was awarded the Nobel Prize in Economics in 1972 along with Kenneth J. Arrow of the United States: Hicks was the first British economist to receive the Nobel Prize. They were awarded the prize for their pioneering contributions to the general equilibrium theory and welfare theory. As Bertil Ohlin put it, "the general equilibrium theory is the basis for most of the direct application of economic theory such as the localisation of industrial plant, resource allocation, financial and employment theory and foreign trade, all this being used to increase the welfare of the people".

Hicks was born in Warwick in 1904. He taught at London School of Economics, Cambridge and at Oxford. He retired from Oxford University in 1965. He was knighted in 1964.

Some of the important works of Hicks are: *Theory of Wages* (1932), *Value and Capital* (1932), *The Social Framework: An Introduction to Economics* (1942), *A Contribution to the Theory of the Trade Cycle* (1950), *A Revision of Demand Theory* (1956), *Capital and Growth* (1965), and *Critical Essays in Monetary Theory* (1967).

Value and Capital is one of the monumental works of Hicks. It became the starting point of most of the subsequent microeconomic theories in Britain and United States. The chief characteristic of Hicks's work was that he moved away from the partial equilibrium approach of Alfred Marshall back towards the older "general equilibrium" approach of Walras.

Everything Hicks writes bears the hallmark of quality. *The Social Framework* and *A Revision of Demand Theory* are his other pioneering works.

The former is a beautiful introduction to economics. The beginner coming to this book will find concepts with which he has long been familiar in a vague way clarified and given a more significant meaning and he will also acquire a good deal of actual knowledge. Hicks's style is easy and popular, the presentation is straightforward and dignified.

Hick's book *A Revision of Demand Theory* has been acclaimed as "a superb exercise of exposition" and "probably the last word there is to be said on this aspect of demand theory." He has shown that the law of demand can be extended to study the behaviour of groups from that of individuals. The theory of demand for a single commodity is only the beginning of a demand theory. The general theory of demand is a theory of the relation between the set of prices, at which purchases are made, and the set of quantities which are purchased.

Hicks has made notable contribution to the study of consumer equilibrium by making use of indifference curve approach. The ordinalist approach of Hicks is considered superior to the Marshallian utility approach or cardinalist approach. In his *A Revision of the Demand Theory*, Hicks has taken note of some of the recent developments in demand theory and incorporated them. Samuelson's "revealed preference theory" is one such thing. According to Hicks, one major advantage of revealed preference theory is that it is explicitly designed to allow econometricians to make use of it.

Hicks's study of change of price on demand in terms of income effect and substitution effect has had great import in the study of consumer equilibrium by means of indifference curve analysis.

Consumer's surplus, as developed by Marshall, is based on the assumption that the marginal utility of money is constant. This assumption is considered wrong. If we relax the assumption, the size of the consumer's surplus is smaller than the Marshallian theory of cardinal utility implies. Indifference curve analysis has been used to demonstrate this.

Hicks has developed beautiful theory of the business cycle by making use of the accelerator-multiplier interaction principle and Harrod-Domar theory of growth. There are many brilliant and original pieces of analysis in Hicks's theory. Duesenberry describes it as an "ingenious piece of work" and "the first coherent theory of the cycle to appear in some years." Despite the fact that the model has been with us for more than sixty years and despite the other work that has been done in business-cycle theory during this period, Hicks's model remains, in a sense, the last word in business-cycle theory.

Hicks has pointed out three main weaknesses in Pigou's approach to welfare economics. First of all, Pigou had correlated economic and general welfare. Second, he has made interpersonal comparisons of utility. Third, he has identified the sum of consumer surpluses with the real value of the national dividend. To remedy the defects in the analysis of Pigou and Pareto, Hicks along with Kaldor and Scitovysky and some other modern economists have introduced the concept of compensation principle and reorganization principle. The compensation principle is generally known as new welfare economics. "Reorganisation" refers to alterations in economic circumstances. For instance, there may be change of tax structure, tariff policy and so on. A change in tax structure which helped someone without affecting someone else improved welfare. Theoretically, it was an ideal reorganisation. But it was difficult to come across such actual situations. So Hicks has introduced the compensation principle. According to the compensation principle, a society's economic welfare would increase if it were possible for those gained from a reorganization to compensate those who lost and still retain some net advantage. Hicks has given the compensation principle as follows: "If A is made so much better off by change that he could compensate B for his loss and still have something left for, then the reorganization is unequivocal improvement".

Conclusion

From general equilibrium theory to welfare theory is but a short step and both Hicks and Arrow have, on several points, developed the welfare economic consequences of their achievements.

WASSILY LEONTIEF

Wassily Leontief of the United States of America was awarded the Nobel Prize in Economics for the year 1973 for his "input-output" technique for quantifying and studying specific inter-dependencies in an economy and using it to predict major trends. The Royal Swedish Academy in its citation said that "Prof. Leontief is the sole and unchallenged creator of the input-output technique. This important innovation has given to economic science an empirically useful method to highlight the general interdependence in the production system of a society." It further said that "one of the advantages of input-output analysis is its use in different types of economic systems, decentralised market economies with mainly private enterprise as well as centrally planned economies dominated by public ownership. In particular, it provides tools for a systematic analysis of the complicated inter-industry transactions in the economy.

Born in St. Petersburg (Leningrad) in 1906, Leontief studied at the University of Leningrad and obtained his master's degree in 1925. Then his family migrated from Russia. He earned a doctorate in economics at the University of Berlin and in 1931 he joined the faculty of Harvard. Samuelson, who won the second Nobel Prize in Economics in 1970 was a student of Leontief in 1935. In 1954, Leontief became the President of the Econometric Society.

The main contributions of Leontief are in the fields of general economic theory, economic and social accounting, economic planning–theory and policy. His main areas of research relate to input-output system and multi-sectoral analysis of international trade. Some of his important books are *Input-output Economics* (1966) and *Studies in the Structure of the American Economy* (1953).

The input-output analysis of Leontief is an improvement over the general equilibrium analysis of Walras. In the words of Leontief, the input-output analysis is "an attempt to apply economic theory of general equilibrium. . . . . . . to an empirical study of inter-relations among the different parts of a national economy."

The input-analysis deals exclusively with production and it is devoted to empirical investigation. A great advantage of input-output analysis is that it is applicable to capitalism as well as socialism or a mixed economy.

Leontief himself has explained his theory by a simple example "when you make bread you need eggs, flour and milk. And if you want more bread, first you must get more eggs. There are similar cooking recipes for all the industries in the economy." In the words of Simon Kuznets, "In essence, it (input-output analysis) is an attempt to study the structure of the economy." Leontief breaks the economy down industry-by-industry.

For a long time, the popular view was that American exports were capital-intensive. By making use of the input-output analysis, to the astonishment of many people, Leontief was able to demonstrate that the commodities which the United States exports, strangely enough, contain a lot of labour and relatively little capital, while the imports were vice-versa." This is the well-known *Leontief Paradox*. He has explained it as follows: "When you compare workers in different countries, you compare incomparable things. Using machines, a US worker can produce more than an average worker almost anywhere else. So you should make an analysis not in terms of how many heads you can count, but in the amount of efficiency. Suppose the United States has 70 million workers. France has 20 million and India 150 million. We might have a few workers but a lot of labour".

Leontief has become the pathfinder for the planners. The measurement of inter-dependent quantities was an almost impossible task before Leontief came on the scene. Modern economic planning involving fixation of targets and the search for resources would have been impossible but for Leontief's many discoveries, notable among them being the input-output method. The input-output method is a new tool for the analysis of the structure of an economic system or unit. It enables the planner to know how much output can be obtained with a given unit of resources. In Leontief's own words, "The input-output method is an empirical study of the quantitative inter-dependence between inter-related economic activities. It can be applied to small or bigger units—even to the analysis of international economic relationships. It describes the flow of goods and services between all the individual sectors of a national economy over a stated period of time, say a year".

The usefulness of the method is such that by 1963 some 40 countries had constructed such tables, despite the enormous quantities of statistical data and computational labour it called for.

The main economic applications of Leontief's method are in working out projections of demand, output, employment, and investment for individual sectors of entire countries and of smaller economic regions; for analysis of the effects of wage, profit and tax changes of prices and for development planning.

Conclusion

Leontief and input-output analysis go together. When the French economist Quesnay developed *Tableau Economique*, it was considered a great discovery. Although, Leontief based his work on the foundations laid by Quesnay and the later neo-classical economists (Walras, in particular), he is the first to illuminate the path. The discovery of the input-output analysis, has been compared to Harvey's discovery of blood circulation in the human system.

FRIEDRICH A. VON HAYEK

The Nobel Prize in Economics for the year 1974 was shared by Friedrich A. Von Hayek of Britain along with Gunnar Myrdal of Sweden. They were awarded the prize for their influence on two poles of economic thought. Myrdal argued for government intervention in the business cycle, while Von Hayek argued that a laissez-faire approach is the best. They have done pioneering work in the theory of money and economic fluctuations. Their penetrating analysis of the inter-dependence of economic, social and institutional phenomena was taken into account by the Royal Swedish Academy of Sciences while considering them for the award. As both of them have carried out important inter-disciplinary research so successfully, it was decided that their combined contribution should be awarded the prize for economic science.

Hayek belonged to the younger generation of Austrian school. Ludwig Von Mises and Joseph A. Schumpeter were other prominent economists of this school. Hayek was born in Vienna in 1899. He received the degree of Doctor of Jurisprudence from Vienna University in 1921. And he received the degree of political science in 1923. He was in Austrian civil service for a number of years. He joined the London School of Economics in 1931. He stayed there as Professor of Economics and Statistics until 1949. Then he was in United States at Chicago University for some years.

The early contributions of Hayek were in the field of business cycles and capital theories. Later on, he turned his attention to the broader questions of economic organization and economic philosophy. He has explained business cycle in terms of (monetary) over-investment. Hayek is well-known for his "neutral money policy." He is a great critic of price stabilisation policy.

Hayek has written many books. Some of his important books are: *Prices and Production* (1931), *Monetary Theory and Trade Cycle* (1933), *Collectivist Economic Planning* (1935), *The Road to Serfdom* (1944), *The Great Depression* (1934), *The Constitution of Liberty* (1960) and *Individualism and Economic Order* (1967).

Some of the important points made by Hayek in his works are: (*i*) the market is never in equilibrium; (*ii*) competition is more efficient than totalitarian planning; (*iii*) post-war inflation is largely wage inflation. There has been a tremendous growth in the power of trade unions to demand autonomous increases in real wages. This implies in its turn, a process of accelerated monetary expansions, to avoid unemployment; (*iv*) Society, consumption, investment, capital etc. are aggregates. These are aggregates of heterogeneous components. So, Hayek argues that there is no logical basis, for macro-economic concepts; and (*v*) we cannot have an optimum mix of planning and of private enterprise. Economic systems fundamentally do not tend to converge.

We may describe Hayek as a leading spokesman of the 19th century liberal political, economic, and legal philosophy. His influence has grown as people have become disillusioned with big government.

The Road to Serfdom was written in England by Hayek during the years of World War II. It was designed as a warning to the socialist intelligentsia of England about the real nature of the totalitarian movement in Germany, Italy and Russia. Hayek's position in *The Road to Serfdom* was that centralized economic planning—which, along with government's ownership of at least some major means of production, makes up the method of socialism—would not achieve its aims of social justice, greater equality and security. In a detailed and logical analysis, he has illustrated from Germany's experience, that planning would lead in successive stages to dictatorship, loss of liberty and increasing repression.

What was original and important in Hayek's analysis was the patient and detailed examination of why planning would produce such unlooked-for results.

The 20th century move toward socialism, Hayek argued, affected personal freedom slowly but steadily. So, he suggested that to protect people's private spheres of action, government should function through the Rule of Law. This form of society is not opposed to change, far from it. It is not laissez-faire. Government has a positive role to play in the fullest development of human personality through protection of private spheres of action. It will be instrumental in promoting education and culture. But wholesale income redistribution, monopoly labour unions, price controls, subsidies to any special groups or protection of domestic manufactures from competition of imports are all inconsistent with the Rule of Law.

Central planning aims at substituting the so-called "*social good*" or the "general welfare" for the happiness and welfare of millions. But what really happens is that expert planners impose their own views on the community. As control begets control, collectivism becomes total; that is, it becomes totalitarianism. In Leon Trotsky's words: "who does not obey shall not eat." Soon, thought, like industry, becomes nationalized. Slavery returns.

It would be wrong to brand Hayek as a laissez-faire economist. For in his scheme of things, government has a positive role to play in promoting the competitive system. His liberalism provides for "an extensive system of social services." In fact, he supports the idea of minimum income in rich societies as a right. In the words of J.W.N. Watkins, Hayek has developed a "coherent and comprehensive, distinctive and uncompromising political philosophy."

Freedom of individual, within the law, is one of Hayek's leading ideas. He no longer believes in terms such as "social justice". "What is social justice?" he asks, "I have spent a long time trying to find out and have come to conclusion the term has precisely no meaning whatever."

Conclusion

The foregoing analysis clearly tells that Hayek had the ability to find new and original ways of posing questions. And he had put forward many new ideas. There are some who think that it was a joke that he shared the Nobel Prize with Gunnar Myrdal, an advocate of state intervention to set right many economic and social ills and a great believer in social justice.

GUNNAR MYRDAL

The Nobel prize in Economics for the year 1974 was shared by Gunnar Myrdal of Sweden along with Friedrich A. Von Hayek of Britain. They were awarded the prize for their influence on two poles of thought. Myrdal argued for government intervention in the business cycle while Von Hayek argued that laissez-faire is the best. As both of them carried out important inter-disciplinary research successfully, it was decided that their combined contribution should be awarded the prize for economic science. These two great economists had, in common, ability to find new and original ways of posing questions and put forward many new ideas which often made them controversial figures.

Myrdal was born in Sweden in 1898. He is one of Sweden's best known economists. His book *An American Dilemma* (1944) deals with the problems of the American Blacks. It is a much quoted study. In the thirties, Myrdal along with Mrs. Myrdal brought out a pioneering work, *The Population Issue : a Crisis*. It is a profound study of the problems of under-population faced by Sweden. In it, they have also suggested the remedial policies that could be followed without diluting the concept of Welfare State.

For nearly two decades, Myrdal was active in domestic policies as a social democrat but after World War II, he associated himself with different agencies of the U.N. in the field of economics. Mr. Myrdal was Sweden's Commerce Minister during 1945-47, before he moved to the world body. After retirement, he continued to be active as a visiting professor and research fellow at several universities.

Myrdal's methodology is characterised by an interdisciplinary approach to social problems. As a young economist, Myrdal took a lot of interest in the debate on saving-investment relationship. His studies are wide in their scope. They range from technical economics to broad questions of scientific method, economic policy, international trade, economic development, the American race problem and the development problems of the Third World. Myrdal's *Price and change* was an exercise in dynamic analysis. His *Monetary Equilibrium* is a critique of Wicksell's theory of interest. Myrdal is one of the distinguished members of the Swedish School of Economics. *The Political Element in the Development of Economic Theory* (1953), *Rich Lands and Poor* (1954), *Economic Theory and Underdeveloped Regions* (1957). *Beyond the Welfare State* (1950). *Asian Drama: An Inquiry into the Poverty of Nations* (1968) and *The Challenge of World Poverty : A World Antipoverty Program in Outline* (1970) are some of his notable works besides *An American Dilemma* (1944).

"Economic Theory and Under-developed Regions" is considered one of the most brilliant essays ever written on the economic problems of the world. The thinking of this outstanding social scientist had an impressive range and he possessed one of the rarest qualities—a truly international outlook.

Myrdal's *Assian Drama* is a moumnental work. It is a collection of descriptive and analytical studies with emphasis on the analytical side of change in social, economic and political conditions in South Asian countries, in the post-war world. The main point he makes in it is that the theories of growth based on the experience of the developed countries of the West are inappropriate for the developing countries of South Asia like India, Pakistan, Ceylon, Burma. His thesis is that as there are sociological and institutional obstacles to growth, in any plan of development, priority should be given for removing these obstacles. Myrdal is one of those who believed that the Green Revolution had created more problems than it had solved. For instance, in his address to the third International Congress of Food, Science and Technology, he painted a grim picture of mass poverty in the developing countries resulting partly from a misplaced faith in the Green Revolution as a cure all. He said, "The green revolution is killing the interest in land reform which is essential to solve the basic social ills of many developing nations." He stated that an agricultural middle class was developing with a vested interest in applying labour saving .machinery to agriculture. But much of the technology would have the effect of making the underemployed agricultural workers even less necessary and of driving them to the already teeming city slums. Without land reform, Myrdal said institutional reforms such as credit co-operation and agricultural extension services would only benefit those who were already better off.

The basic concept he uses is that of "social system." It consists of a number of inter-related conditions. They have been grouped under six broad categories: (*i*) output and incomes, (*ii*) conditions of production, (*iii*) levels of living, (*iv*) attitude towards life and work, (*v*) institutions and (*vi*) policies. According to him, a change in the upward direction of any of the above conditions will have both an independent and an instrumental value for development.

Myrdal has a good word to say about Indian technical planning. He thinks that it is marked by a high level of competence. But the social technology is rather backward. He tells that "India is ruled by a selected group of upper class citizens who use their political power to secure their privileged position." Again, whereas the expansion of education in developed countries was marked by emphasis on science and technology, there has been quantitative expansion in education in developing countries but the progress in science and research has not been much. Myrdal does not think that there is any conflict between the goals of growth and social justice. The "*Asian Drama*" thus has served as an eye-opener to many on the problems of developing countries, most of them with their economies wrecked by the withdrawing colonial powers. Myrdal has made a cause for equitable distribution of wealth at the global level. He is against the protectionist policies followed by the developed countries. And he wants the developed countries to give aid for moral reasons rather than for military or political strategy reasons.

conclusion

Myrdal has been rightly hailed as the *Adam Smith of Poverty*. His intellectual integrity, deep humanism, and inter-disciplinary research have influenced economic thought and policy for over half a century since the thirties.

TJALLING KOOPMANS

The Nobel Prize in Economics for the year 1975 was shared by Tjalling Koopmans of United States along with Leonid Kantorovich of Soviet Union. They were awarded the prize for their work—aimed at diametrically opposed systems—on economic planning and the technical problems involved in deciding upon an optimum allocation of resources. The Royal Swedish Academy of Sciences, in its citation, said that both these men, working largely independent of each other, had "renewed, generalized and developed methods for the analysis of the classical problem of economics as regards the optimum allocation of scarce resources." It further said that "both of them had studied the problem of how the available productive resources can be used to the greatest advantage in the production of goods and services."

Koopmans is Dutch by birth. He is one of the economists who contributed to the early growth of econometrics. He has taught at different universities in U.S.—New York, Princeton, and Chicago.

Koopmans has demonstrated that on the basis of certain criteria of efficiency, it is possible directly to make important deductions concerning optimum price systems. He has developed the activity analysis. It deals with the relationship between inputs and outputs of production processes and the calculation of prices. One of his important books is *Three Essays on the State of Economic Science*. He has also edited *Activity Analysis of Production and Allocation*.

Koopmans has done a lot of work on linear programming. Activity analysis makes use of it. Besides, he has made significant contributions to comparative statics, dynamics, and structure of minimum equilibrium system. His work on minimization of costs and optimization of resources are of special significance to the developing countries.

In one of his *Three Essays*, Koopmans considers the relation between tools of analysis and choice of problems. He has always emphasized on the tools of economics.

The input-output analysis concentrates only on quantitative description of technological possibilities and it gives little attention to the effect of economic behaviour on the utilisation of these possibilities.

Conclusion

The foregoing description tells us in outline Koopmans has developed methods with regard to the optimum allocation of scarce resources.

LEONID KANTOROVICH

The Nobel Prize in Economics for the year 1975 was shared by Kantorovich of Soviet Union along with Tjalling Koopmans of United States. They were awarded the prize for their work—aimed at diametrically opposed systems—on economic planning and the technical problems involved in deciding upon an optimum allocation of resources. The Royal Swedish Academy of Sciences in its citation said that both these men, working largely independent of each other had, "renewed, generalised, and developed methods for the analysis of the classical problem of economics as regards the optimum allocation of scarce resources." It further said that "both of them had studied the problem of how the available productive resources can be used to the greatest advantage in the production of goods and services."

Professor Kantorovich is a leading mathematical economist of Soviet Russia. He has applied linear programming to demonstrate how Soviet planning can be improved. In his book, *the Best use of Economic Resources* he has analysed the conditions of efficiency in an economy and demonstrated the connection between allocation of resources and price growth. He is a strong advocate of the decentralisation of the rigidly centralised Soviet planned economy. He is of the view that the Soviet investment policy, because of its deficiencies, has failed to achieve optimum economic growth.

Kantorovich was born in 1912. He studied mathematics at the Leningrad University. Even as a young man, he made a mark on his work in linear programming techniques.

Kantorovich is of the view that the mathematical methods of planning can be applied effectively to Soviet economy. Mathematical programming enables one to balance the system with precise statement of aims. While the non-mathematical planning is essentially qualitative, programming approach and technique can make it quantitative as well. Linear programming methods are very effective in determining the feasibility conditions to make the plan viable and in determining environmental and policy constraints within the framework of a set of prices.

Kantorovich introduced the systems of optimally functioning economic system to ensure efficient allocation of resources. Social ownership of the means of production is only a necessary but not a sufficient condition for efficient allocation of resources. The sufficient condition exists only when the views of the specialists on the functioning of the economy and on economic calculations are accepted and implemented by the policy-makers.

Conclusion

Kantorovich has done pioneering work in theory and application of linear programming techniques to Soviet planning. He has been described as "the greatest living economic mathematician". He is "one of the fathers of the Soviet school of application of mathematics to economy" and "the Soviet inventor of linear programming" (Yuri Rubinski). Kantorovich himself has said that his work has provided a basis for "studies destined to change planning methods in the Soviet Union and socialist countries."

MILTON FRIEDMAN

Milton Friedman of United States was awarded the Nobel Prize in Economics for the year 1976 for his "achievements in the fields of consumption analysis, monetary history and theory, and for his demonstration of the complexity of stabilisation policy." Friedman had a far-reaching influence as the foremost American exponent of monetarism, the school of economics that stresses the control of the supply of money.

Milton Friedman was born in 1912 in New York State. He took his Ph.D. in 1946 from Columbia University. He served in many American universities and on many governmental bodies. But his name is popularly associated with the Chicago university. He was the President of the American Economic Association in 1967.

Milton Friedman is a prolific writer. Some of his important works are: *Essays in Positive Economics* (1953), *Studies in the Quantity Theory of Money* (1956), *A Theory of Consumption Function* (1957), *Capitalism and Freedom* (1962), *Price Theory* (1962), *A Monetary History of the United States* (Co-author Anna Schwartz) (1963).

Consumption Function : Permanent Income Hypothesis

The ideas of Keynes have helped a great deal for the development of macro-economics. Consumption function is one of the corner-stones of Keynesian system. Keynes made consumption solely a function of current income.

In recent times, Milton Friedman has given another theory of consumption function. It is known as Permanent Income Hypothesis. He has divided a consumer's income into "permanent income" and "transitory income". He has argued that consumption is mainly a function of "permanent income". Changes in "transitory income" such as windfall gains or loss will lead only to changes in accumulated balances or holding of durable goods. Changes in "transitory incomes" will not generally affect ordinary consumption.

The basic arguments of the permanent income theory have raised a lot of controversy and generated sizable literature. Empirical evidence has been presented on both sides but the debate is not yet resolved.

The Utility Analysis of Choices Involving Risk : Milton Friedman and Savage Hypothesis

Marshall explained consumer demand in terms of cardinal utility. Hicks has criticized it and popularized the Indifference curve analysis (ordinal approach) to explain consumer's equilibrium. But indifference curve analysis deals with situations involving riskless choices.

Milton Friedman and Savage have suggested that an important class of reactions of individuals to risk can be rationalized by a rather simple extension of orthodox utility analysis.

Friendman-Savage hypothesis is based on Neumann-Morgenstern hypothesis which tells us that "under the conditions of which the indifference curve analysis is based, very little extra effort is needed to reach a numerical utility," the expected value of which is maximized in choosing among alternatives involving risk.

Neumann and Morgenstern seek to measure the expected utility from the monetary gain rather than the expected value of monetary gain itself.

While the original properties of utility functions can be used to rationalize riskless choices, the numerical properties can be used to rationalize choices involving risk.

A criticism against Friedman-Savage hypothesis is that it is based on the assumption that marginal utility of money depends on the absolute level of income. It is argued that marginal utility of money income relates only to the changes in the level of money income rather than the absolute level of income.

Modern Quantity Theory of Money

The modern statement of the quantity theory is associated primilarily with Milton Friedman of chicago School. This is different from Fisher's quantity theory. The modern statement no longer assumes that full employment is the normal state of the economy or that the velocity of money is as stable as is required to yield the conclusions of the quantity theory in its extreme form.

Modern quantity theory is similar to Keynesian theory in that it refers to income level rather than to price level. However, modem quantity theory continues to assign a very important role to money, whereas Keynesian theory, at least in its extreme form argues that "money does not matter." Keynesian theory allots only a passive role to money. Even if it is active, its role is limited to its effect on interest rates, and through interest rates, on investment. But investment depends more importantly on factors other than the rates of interest, the quantity of money becomes a minor factor in explaining investment and so in explaining income.

Modern quantity theory argues that changes in income can be more accurately predicted from changes in the money supply than from changes in investment. The advocates of modern quantity theory have produced empirical evidence to suggest that the velocity of money exhibits a greater regularity of behaviour than does the investment multiplier.

The modern quantity theory emphasizes that inflation is the result of excessive expansion of the money supply. But velocity of money and output are both recognized as variables. So the relationship between prices and the quantity of money is not as simple as assumed by the earlier quantity theory.

The modern quantity theory has attracted a large number of supporters in recent years. But most economists still regard the approach of Keynesian theory as more fruitful in explaining income changes.

Business Cycles

Friedman is one of the main advocates of the monetary theory of business cycles. The theory attributes the cycle to the expansion and contraction of bank money and credit. Friedman has attributed cyclical instability to the sporadic changes in the rate of growth of the money supply. In fact, he has identified the shortage in the supply of money caused by the tight money policy of the Federal Reserve Board of America from 1929 to 1932 as the main cause of the Great Depression. He calls Great Depression the *Great Contraction*. He further asserts that the overly loose money policy in 1967 was responsible for the post-Vietnam inflation in United States.

State and Education

Milton Friedman is a strong advocate of capitalism and freedom. In the matter of State and education, he belongs to the school of thought which suggests that financial assistance from government should go in the form of subsidies to individuals and not to institutions. The individuals might be granted the right to spend the amount at the institutions of their own choice. Friedman's argument is that "the subsidization of institutions rather than of people has led to indiscriminate subsidization of all activities appropriate for such institutions, rather than of activities approporiate for the state to subsidize." Besides Friedman, the ease for state assistance to parents, instead of direct provision of education by the state, finds support in the writings of Peacock, Wiseman and E. G. West and they all suggest the voucher scheme (the distribution to parents of coupons with a prescribed purchasing power over educational services, which they may supplement out of their own resources if they wish) in some form or other. The Friedman type voucher scheme has also been recommended on the ground that it would increase educational investment and range of consumer choice.

Conclusion

Though Milton Friedman's name is popularly associated with monetary theories, the Nobel Committee was more admiring of his contributions to our understanding of a market system's workings and merits. They went out of the way to stress the later contributions. Even Friedman considers that the final pages of his *Price Theory* dealing with capital theory are important and deserve most to be remembered. Friedman may be compared to Hayek ,in his devotion to capitalism (market economy) and individual freedom.

BERTIL OHLIN

The Nobel Prize in Economics for the year 1977 was awarded to Bertil Ohlin of the Stockholm School of Economics (Sweden) along with James E. Meade of Cambridge University (Britain) for their contributions to international trade. Their contributions have been appreciated only recently as the world economy has moved toward greater internationalization. This is the first recognition of the specialization of international economics. International trade used to be the central focus of classical economics in the tradition of David Hume, Adam Smith, David Ricardo and John Stuart Mill.

Ohlin's award was given for his pioneering work *Inter-regional and International Trade*, published in 1933. The award was based on his contribution to the theory of comparative advantage, originally propounded by Ricardo on the basis of the labour theory of value. The labour theory of value survives today only in Marxian economics. Opposed to the labour theory is the law of variable proportions that asserts that factors of production—labour, land, capital and sometimes business enterprises, are combined in the production of given goods in varying mixes depending on the relative prices of such factors. The prices of factors determine their incomes, in the first instance, at least.

Eli. F. Heckscher, the Swedish economic historian of mercantilism, in a pioneering article in 1919, observed that international trade altered factor prices and, therefore, redistributed income within a country. But he failed to break out of labour theory mould.

Ohlin, who was a student of Heckscher, developed his theory in his 1924 thesis. The labour theory of value had difficulty in explaining why costs of production for given goods were different in different countries. Ohlin stated different commodities were typically produced with disproportionate inputs of particular factors—wheat especially with land, for example, and machinery especially with labour. A country's comparative advantage lay in the production of those goods produced with the intensive use of factors which that country had in particular abundance. Following Heckscher, he found that trade tended to raise the price of the abundant factor as exports increased the demand for it, and that imports tended to lower the relative price and incomes of the scarce factor. On this basis, he found that trade had a tendency to equalize incomes of factors between countries. The relation between factor endowments explaining trade, and trade, in turn, altering factor incomes gave rise to a number of applications.

Paul Samuelson has developed and made rigorous and extended the Heckscher-Ohlin Theorem so much that it is now called as Heckscher-Ohlin-Samuelson (HOS) theorem. Samuelson has detailed the conditions under which international trade can bring about full equalization of factor prices and thus, if the necessary assumptions are met, eliminate the need for migration from over-populated to underpopulated countries.

Practical Impact of HOS Theory

Does the HOS theory work in the real world? The answer is yes and no. Kindleberger is of the view that in the European Economic Community (Common Market), trade does go a long way to equalize wages and rates of interest, though aided by some migration and capital flows. Between the developed and developing countries economists like Gunnar Myrdal felt that international trade tends to widen the gap because of 'backwash effects' that draw off the most productive factors from poor countries and condemn them to specialize in lines of production limited in growth potential. In 1953, Leontief has brought out some proof to disturb the acceptance of HOS.

After his breakaway from the labour theory of value, Ohlin has insisted on the parallels between "interregional" and "international trade" and he has introduced into both strong doses of location theory.

The League of Nations connection

In September 1932, Ohlin wrote a report for the League of Nations Assembly, entitled *"The course and phases of the world economic depression"*. Twenty-five years later, he headed a group of experts writing *"Social aspects of European economic co-operation"* for the International Labour Office.

JAMES E. MEADE

The Nobel Prize in Economics for the year 1977 was awarded to James E. Meade of Cambridge University (Britain) along with Bertil Ohlin of the Stockholm School of Economics (Sweden) for their contributions to international trade.

Meade was educated at Oxford. He visited Cambridge under Keynes before going to Geneva and the League of Nations. During the war he worked in the British government, writing, among other things, a pioneer book on British National Income with Richard Stone. Thereafter, he went to teach at the London School of Economics. There he wrote the classic two-volume work on *The theory of International Economic Policy* which won him the Nobel Prize. In 1957, he was appointed Professor at Cambridge University. Though he has retired now, he remains a research fellow. He has written a number of books on economic priniciples. His important works are: *The Stationary Economy* (1965), *The Growing Economy* (1971), *The Intelligent Radical, Guide to Economic Policy: The Mixed Economy* (1975), *and The just Economy* (1976). Besides, for several years Meade edited the League's annual *World Economic Surveys*, which remain today indispensable to understanding the 1930s.

Volume I of *The Theory of International Economic Policy was entitled The Balance of Payments*. It appeared in 1951 Volume II on *Trade and Welfare* appeared in 1955. A by-product of the over-all work was *A Geometry of International Trade*, with 50 diagrams. It has solved a number of problems in the theory of international trade.

Meade's approach was slow to win recognition. But by the time of Volume II, it was already clear that Meade had made an enormous breakthrough. It was a landmark of creative codification, "gathering up most of the content of the best known articles on the gains from trade, the terms of trade, and the effects of trade on factory earnings......." (T.C. Schelling).

Other contributions of Meade

Jan Tinbergen had devised the Theory of Policy. In simple terms, it means this : one needs as many instrumental variables-policies as one has targets or objectives. In other words, you can't hit two birds with one stone. In the language of mathematics, one needs as many equations as one has unknowns. Meade studied the implications of these statements and raised in addition the problem of over-determination. For example, if all countries try to manage their floating exchange rates, the system is over-determined. Either one major currency must respond passively letting other countries choose whatever exchange rate they want and accepting the consequences for its balance of payments or policy actions must be co-ordinated.

In trade and welfare by making use of the device of cardinal utility analysis, Meade works through the theory of economic welfare and explores at length "the theory of the second best."

Conclusion

While Ohlin and Meade shared the Nobel award for 1977 and wrote on the same subject, they are entirely different sorts of persons. Ohlin is a public man, Meade a private man. They barely knew one another. But the economic profession and the world is in their debt.

HERBERT A. SIMON

Herbert A. Simon of the United States was awarded the Nobel Prize in Economics for the year 1978 for "his pioneering research into the decision making process within economic organizations". The Nobel Committee acknowledged that "modern business economics and administrative research are largely based on Simon's ideas."

The neo-classical theory of the firm is based on the basic assumption that the sole aim of a firm is maximization of profits. Simon contends that in a complex world, businessmen lack enough information to make decisions that maximize profits; they, therefore, merely seek to reach satisfactory targets. Simon's interest in decision-making has also led him into the fields of political science, psychology and computer science. The Swedish Academy of Sciences has described Simon as "one of the greatest of inter-disciplinary researchers."

After submitting a dissertation on decision-making in organizations, Simion obtained his Ph.D. degree in political science from the University of Chicago in 1943, That dissertation, with modifications and additions was published in 1947 under the title of *Administrative Behaviour; a study of Decision-*

making process in Administrative Organization. In that study, Simon attacked the uselessness of the existing administrative theory in public administration and other organizations—commercial, industrial, military and private non-profit organizations. Simon's object was to construct a set of tools, a set of concepts and vocabulary—suitable for describing an organization and the way an administrative organization works. Simon himself has pointed that, "if any 'theory' is involved, it is that decision-making is the heart of administration, and that the vocabulary of administrative theory must be derived from the logic and psychology of human choice."

By the mid-1950s, Simon had come to the conclusion that in the complex economic organizations of today, individuals cannot possibly process or even obtain all of the information relating to the decisions they must make. He, therefore, maintained that instead of getting the target of maximization of projects, companies merely try to set goals that represent reasonable achievement levels or minimally acceptable targets, a course of action that he called "satisfying behaviour." Simon has rejected the classical notion of "economic man" as unrealistic, and offered in its place what he referred to as "administrative man," who, "satisfies—looks for a course of action that is satisfactory or good enough". Simon's ideas have greatly influenced teaching methods in business schools.

During the mid-1950s Simon's work took a crucial turn. After deciding that the understanding of administrative decisions required a more adequate theory of problem-solving, around 1954. Simon, along with Allen Newell of the Rand Corporation, decided that the right way to study problem-solving was to simulate it with computer programmes. Simon has developed computer programmes that could solve problems in a humanoid fashion. These experiments are called "artificial intelligence." As a result of his investigation in artificial simulation of human thought processes, his work fell primarily within the academic disciplines of psychology and computer science, although his fundamental intellectual concern remained the area of decision-making. Because of his experiences with artificial intelligence, Simon is called a "technological radical" in the computer science field.

Simon tells that "in our time, a computer will do anything a man can do. They can already read, think, learn and create." He and his associates have programmed computers to play chess and proved thirty-eight out of the fifty-two theorems from Bertrand Russel's *Principia Mathematica*. Simon is of the view that most of the occupations including the higher status occupations, and those requiring the most education will be automated in due course. In his own words, "there are perhaps as good prospects technically and economically for automating the job of a physician (but not a surgeon), a corporate vice-president or a college teacher as for automating the job of the person who operates a piece of earth moving equipment."

Conclusion

The foregoing description proves that Simon has been rightly described as "one of the greatest of interdisciplinary researchers."

ARTHUR LEWIS

The Nobel Prize in Economics for 1979 was shared by Arthur Lewis of Britain and Theodore W. Schultz of the United States for their work on the problems of development in the Third World. They have focussed on the same two dimensions of a complicated problem : the importance of the quality of a system's agricultural sector and the importance of its human resources.

The full significance of the work of Lewis and Schultz can be seen only in historical context. During the 1950's and early 1960's both were successful in helping to transform the conventional wisdom on the central issues of development economics. What both men were saying in the 1950s and early 1960s has now become a part of conventional wisdom. According to them, successful development is likely to depend more heavily on the quality of human resources available than on the simple accumulation of the more traditional inputs; and that a lack of understanding of the role of agricultural sector (Schultz) or of the non-capitalist sector (Lewis) is likely to adversely affect the success of development efforts.

Lewis has always emphasized the importance of education in his writings. He has written more than 10 books and more than 100 articles. *"Development with Unlimited Supplies of Labour"* (1954) is one of the best known works of Lewis. It emphasizes the organizational differences between the major sectors of a developing economy with labour surplus. In this fundamental contribution, he presented a simple two-sector model in which a large non-capitalist sector gradually gives way to a growing capitalist sector. The non-capitalist sector contains a reservoir of underemployed labour that could be mobilized for the expansion of the capitalist sector. In this early work, Lewis was concerned with the "hidden rural savings" that could be mobilized when low productivity workers in the non capitalist sector are reallocated to higher productivity jobs in the capitalist sector. Thus he emphasizes on the initial "organizational dualism." Lewis, however, did not focus on product dualism – for example, on the peculiar characteristics of food, which is produced mainly in the non-capitalist (agricultural) sector. Others have since pointed to the importance of this special product dualism superimposed on organizational dualism. It may be important to note that Lewis and Schultz differed rather sharply on the question of the existence of surplus labour. Schultz does not accept Lewis's notion of organizational dualism with its income-sharing arrangements in the subsistence or non-capitalist sector.

More recently, Lewis explained the terms of trade between countries of the North and the South in his 1963 lecture on *Aspects of Tropical Trade*. It is a subject of considerable interest in the context of the New International Economic Order. In that lecture. Lewis has extended his domestic two-sector model to the international scene. This model has attracted much attention, both for its simplicity and its efforts to elucidate many aspects of development and of trade.

In recent years, Lewis has been paying increasing attention to the international aspects of development. He has emphasized that maximum growth in the North is likely to be in the South's best interests in future. As a native West Indian, he has been particularly sensitive to the cause of the South, and hard on the North for its protectionism, its unwillingness to maintain even meagre foreign aid levels, and its often automatic support of multinational corporations abroad.

Lewis has served for years as Vice-Chancellor of the University of the West Indies, for which he was knighted by Queen Elizabeth. He was the first President of the Caribbean Development Bank.

Conclusion

Lewis is not an ivory tower economist. He has spent much of his adult energies in public service, giving policy advice to governments or sitting on international commissions. He is motivated by the desire to throw light on the questions such as the elusive relationship between growth and distribution in human affairs, within as well as between nations. Lewis saw the problems of the under-privileged as the world's most important economic and political problems. He is basically sentimental about the culture of poverty he is trying to affect. Lewis insists on emphasizing the realism of given political or institutional pitfalls along the road of beautiful models and perfect policies. Both Schultz and Lewis realize that careful, dispassionate analysis is the best way to be of help.

THEODORE W. SCHULTZ

The Nobel Prize in Economics for 1979 was shared by Theodore W. Schultz of the United States and Arthur Lewis of Britain for their work on the problems of development in the Third World. *Shultz* is of the firm belief that successful development is likely to depend more heavily on the quality of human resources available than on the simple accumulation of the more traditional input; and that a lack of understanding of the role of agricultural sector is likely to adversely affect the success of development efforts.

Long before world food shortages drew attention to the neglect of agricultural production in most developing countries, Schultz had contributed a book on *Transforming Traditional Agriculture* (1964). In it, he laid out in detail both the costs of neglecting the agricultural sector and what it would take to set things right. Schultz has emphasized the large potential role of agriculture and offered specific advice on how to harness its contribution to the total development effort. At a time when agriculture was thought to be an inherently unproductive activity characterized by unresponsive peasants, Schultz's work pointed out to the bargains to be had by introducing modern inputs and offering higher returns to farm families. His basic twin propositions were: (*i*) that the policies generally followed were heavily biased in favour of industry and against food producing agriculture (this is done both via a neglect of resource allocation to rural areas and via market interventions to maintain artificially cheaper prices for the wage goods facing urban consumers), and (*ii*) that farmers, given proper price signals and access to modern inputs, including the technology of the then new Green Revolution, could be expected to respond in their self-interest and, in so doing permit the sector to make a major contribution to the prospects for overall development.

Schultz fervently believes in the responsiveness of farmers to economic opportunity; thus, ending the agricultural neglect and urban bias of development policy is the common message of both Schultz and Lewis and this message is increasingly being listened to in the Third World.

Schultz analysed the negative impact of food imports on agricultural productivity and became an early enemy of P.L. 480 food aid programes by which United States still try to augment its foreign assistance budgets. His view on P.L. 480 imports was largely ignored then, but now it is generally accepted that aside from relief shipments in case of natural disaster, tying aid to a particular commodity may well turn out to be counter-productive. The transfer of resources in the form of surplus food is almost bound to depress agriculture's terms of trade and serve as a disincentive to farmers in the recipient underdeveloped country.

In an earlier work *Redirecting Farm Policy* (1943), Schultz saw the market as the most effective way of mobilizing the talents of the agricultural population in a relatively rich country facing cyclical problems.

Economics of education is a new branch of economics. It has been with us only since the last five decades. According to Mark Blaug, its birth was announced in 1960 by Schultz. *Shultz* would be remembered also for his analysis of the importance of investment in human beings, whether in agriculture or elsewhere, as a generator of technology change and as a major factor in determining growth. His message is simple : education and research represent important types of investments and that their rates of return must be estimated and compared with the more conventional type of investment as a basis for rational overall resource allocation. It follows from this that the convenient, simplifying notion that labour represents a more or less homogeneous entity entering our production function must be abandoned.

In education, as in research, especially agricultural research, Schultz recognized the importance of government in improving the environment for individual private actions. Schultz's faith in the ability of the individual to make the appropriate rational choice, given the information and opportunity, really represents the cornerstone of his emphasis on human capital and of his early support of the "new household economics."

Conclusion

Schultz is no ivory-tower economist. He has spent much of his life in public service, giving policy advice to governments, sitting on international commissions. Like Lewis, he is motivated by a desire to throw light on the question of relationship between growth and distribution in human affairs, within as well as between nations. Schultz, in his own words, was always "trying to provide a small room for poverty in the house that economists have built." It may be interesting to note that both Schultz and Lewis specialize in ideas rather than in mathematical niceties; both tend to rely on old-fashioned empirical proofs rather than modern econometric methods.

LAWRENCE R. KLEIN

The Nobel Prize in Economics for the year 1980 was awarded to Lawrence R. Klein of the United States for creation of econometric models and their applications to the analysis of economic fluctuations and economic policies. His econometric models are now widely used in charting the future course of the economy and predicting its response to perturbations such as increased oil costs, inflation, high interest rates, and the like. Almost all economic forecasters today use some variant of models developed originally by Klein.

Klein is commonly known as the "father of econometrics." The field of econometrics was actually begun in the 1930s by Dutch economist Jan Tinbergen, who shared the first economic Nobel Prize in 1969 with Ragnar Frisch of Norway. Tinbergen aimed primarily at the analysis of business conditions and price movements and his models had only a limited success. When Klein began working with econometrics in 1940s, he wanted to make an instrument for forecasting the development of business fluctuations and for studying the effects of economic-political measures. To do so, he compressed the then revolutionary theories of John Maynard Keynes into a system of equations and turned to a different statistical technique for solving the equations. As Jerry Adams of the University of Pennsylvania puts it, "while he was not the first to build the models, he was the first to take them and turn them into useful tools."

Lawrence Robert Klein was born in 1920 in the United States. The Great Depression had an important influence on his youth. He was for a brief while a member of the communist party of the United States of America. He graduated from the University of California at Berkeley in 1942 and just two years later received the first economics Ph.D. awarded by M.I.T. His doctoral thesis, *The Keynesian Revolution* later became a successful book. Klein did post-doctoral research at the University of Chicago, then joined the University of Michigan. But his membership of the communist party during his Chicago years cost him his job at Michigan. His infatuation with communism ended in 1947 when he "got bored with it," as he himself says. Because of the bitter episode at Michigan, Klein spent several years at Oxford University before returning to the United States in 1958 to join Penn. Ever since, he has remained there.

In 1975, Klein was recruited as an economic adviser to Jimmy Carter. Carter was relatively unknown then. He assembled a task force of economists to help. After the election, Klein rejected an official role in the Carter administration saying that he was not a politician but a teacher.

A simple econometric model of a developing country might have as few as 30 equations to represent its economy. Klein's quarterly Wharton model of the United States has more than 1,000 such equations. The annual Wharton model, which forecasts conditions to the year 2,000, has more than 2,000 equations that must be solved simultaneously. Other models are of comparable size. The Wharton models have a very good reputation for their analysis of business conditions.

The equations and thus, the models, may not be 100 per cent accurate "but they are better than chance, and they, are better than naive models, which use momentum and extrapolation to, say, guess tomorrow's value from what today's is (Samuelson). Judgement is put in the model at the last stage. Samuelson thinks that part of the success of the Wharton model is due to Klein's judgement.

Klein constructed a model in 1946. That was rather a crude model. But, it contradicted widespread predictions that the postwar economy would fall into another depression. The standard view at the time was that there would be as many as 6 million unemployed people in the United States. Klein's model, however, indicated that there was a large pent-up demand for consumer goods among the civilian population and a large amount of cash available to returning soldiers, suggesting that the economy would thrive. That proved to be the case. A slightly more developed model later correctly predicted that there would be only a modest recession following the Korean War while many other economists were again predicting depression.

While he was at the University of Michigan in the mid-1950's, Klein and his student Arthur J. Goldberger, who is now at the University of Wisconsin, developed the first of what proved to be the current generation of econometric models. Most of the Michigan models were much larger and more complex than those developed by Tinbergen. The Michigan model is considered the first to be used on a regular basis for business forecasting. Klein subsequently collaborated in the construction of similar models for other countries, including Canada and the United Kingdom.

Since 1969, Klein has been an initiator and active research leader in *Project Link*, an effort to co-ordinate the econometric models of several countries. It is an ambitious effort to build mathematical "models" of the world economy, and is yielding new insights into how and why nations are becoming increasingly interdependent. Economic development in areas of the world that were relatively isolated are now becoming increasingly interdependent with development in other areas. In Klein's words,

"we can see this pretty clearly in the Link simulations. We can see bilateral trade-flows building up where they hardly existed before. And we can see how countries become dependent on imports of essential materials." Thus Project Link seeks to show how the changing conditions in individual economies interact worldwide.

The Wharton group has been working on the application of econometric techniques and model building to the problems of developing countries for several years. They have built Indian models, Korean models, Ghanaian models and so on. The Wharton group has given special attention to the commodity markets. The Royal Swedish Society in its Nobel citation said that 'Project Link' has opened up completely new line of development of great theoretical and practical value. It has also had a great influence in promoting the building of econometric models in those countries taking part in the project. This includes not only most of the OECD (Organization for Economic Co-operation and Development) countries, but also the socialist nations and some less developed countries.

Conclusion

The techniques used in the econometric models are relatively young. During the 1920s and 1930s they were considered very much ivory tower and mainly of academic interest. But now, in the words of Klein, they are "a bread-and-butter proposition. Daily decision-making in many of the major governments, international bodies, and large corporations relies heavily on econometrics." Econometric methods are just catching on in the countries with centrally planned economies. Klein believes that the level of work in the field of econometrics being done in those countries today is similar to what Klein and other econometricians were doing in the United States in 1950s and 1960s.

With his econometric models, Klein could have made tons of money. But as Samuelson puts it "Klein is rather worldly and he resisted for a long time becoming an instant millionaire. . . . " It is a tribute to him that he resisted the temptations of power and money. Klein was really interested in using that organization (Wharton Economic Forecasting Association) to advance the state of art and not to make money. Klein has put a very powerful tool in the hands of political leaders and civil servants of the United States and other countries. By making use of the models, we understand the economy better and we have a more consistent picture of what is going on in the world.

JAMES TOBIN

James Tobin of Yale University of the United States was awarded the Nobel Prize in Economics for the year 1981 for providing "a basis for understanding how subjects actually behave when they acquire different assets and incur debts." This was a reference to Mr. Tobin's creation of "Portfolio Theory", which, in his own shorthand, tells investors not to put all their eggs in one basket. The Nobel committee declared that Mr. Tobin's work had "unquestionably inspired substantial research during the 1970's on the effect of monetary policy, the implications of government budget deficits and stabilisation policy in general."

Professor Tobin was born in Champaign, Illinois on March 5, 1918. He graduated from Harvard in 1939, received his master's degree there in 1940, and went to Washington for his first experience as a government economist. During the war, Tobin joined the Navy and picked up the customary gold watch for best officer in his training class.

In 1946, he returned to Harvard and in 1947 he was awarded a Ph.D. degree. He worked as a junior fellow there until 1950, when he left to become an Associate Professor of Economics at Yale. Tobin was a member of the Council of Economic Advisers at the time of President Kennedy. He received many awards including the American Economic Association's prestigious bronze medal given to an economist under 40.

Portfolio Theory

Portfolio theory is one of the basic scientific contributions of Tobin in economics.

Keynes's *General Theory of Employment, Interest and Money* had a profound influence on Tobin while at the University as a freshman. Keynes, faced with the Great Depression, had to explain why people held so much idle cash relative to their annual dollar incomes. Irving Fisher, America's greatest economist of pre-1930 era, believed that the velocity of circulation of money, V, was a fundamental constant (rather like the speed of light). To understand the Depression drop in V, Keynes developed a theory of 'liquidity preference' along the following lines.

Although you can buy long-term bonds that pay an annual coupon yield, you will still keep some of your wealth in the form of zero-interest cash because you fear that interest rates will soon rise back to their prosperous times level, thereby causing bond prices to fall by even more than the bonds' interest returns.

This is perhaps not a bad theory for the depression years. But young Tobin came up with better theory to fit the 1950 facts, which were that investors could rationally expect that bond prices might go up or go down depending on the uncertainties of future interest rates.

The portfolio theory says that investors do not, and should not seek only the highest average rate of return they can get from an investment portfolio. Rather, in order to avoid taking undue risks, investors both do and should pay attention to the "variance"—the instability—of stocks and bonds or other assets they hold. They thus should balance their cash holding and their investments to achieve some combination of rate of return and security that meets their own objectives.

The 'Q-Ratio' Theory

The 'Q-Ratio' theory is one of Tobin's most important theories. It is important to the investment community as well as to the government policy-makers and theorists. This ratio, which is derived empirically, measures the relationship of the market value of physical capital—such as existing plants or other corporate assets—to its replacement cost. When the Q-ratio is low, corporations tend to acquire existing assets rather than build new plants or equipment. The present sluggishness, of capital spending by business looks like a consequence of a low Q-ratio, resulting from high interest rates that make existing assets look cheap—and make them expensive to replace.

Similarly in housing, the current steep mortgage rates greatly dampen new investment housing.

By such discoveries as the portfolio theory and 'Q-Ratio' theory, Tobin has long been working to bring about a grand union of the financial and 'real' aspects of the national economy.

Tobin has worked in the tradition of John Maynard Keynes, who in the 1930s laid the basis for the efforts of government in America and in many other countries to use fiscal policy to stabilize national economies. But he did not blindly follow Keynes. In fact, he described some of his research as an effort to "fix up some of the implausibilities in Keynesian economics and to make more sense of it." He said, "there has been justified criticism of the Keynesian model, that it was too depression-oriented." Tobin calls himself a "post-Keynesian" and is a great critic of those supply-side economists who say that "Keynes is dead."

Many economists believe that Tobin did add to Keynesian Theory. According to Robert Solow, an economics professor at M.I.T., "one of his (Tobin's) important contributions is the idea that what we think of money is just one of a whole spectrum of assets that people may choose to hold," He added, "An important consequence of that is that squeezing one end of the spectrum, such as the Federal Reserve's concentration on controlling M-1, is unlikely to work, since the whole spectrum will react."

Tobin has challenged Milton Friedmam on his monetarist theories. He has argued that a monetary policy that pays attention only to money supply and not to interest rates as well, as Friedman and his followers recommend, is likely to damage the economy.

Tobin has long advocated efforts to achieve the right mix of fiscal and monetary policy to achieve a strong rate of economic growth. He tends to favour a tax and budget policy that would yield substantial Federal surpluses at full employment, in order to generate higher national savings, and that would, at the same time make possible an easier monetary policy and lower, interest rates, thereby encouraging productive investment in plant, equipment and new knowledge.

Conclusion

Tobin richly deserves the Nobel Prize for the breadth of his work in 'empirical macro-economics and the depth of his many analytical innovations. He is the 19th Nobel Laureate—the 10th American Laureate—in Economics.

GEORGE J. STIGLER

The 1982 Nobel Prize in Economics was awarded to George J. Stigler of the Chicago School of America for his research on the working of industry and the role of Government regulation in the economy. Stigler is esteemed by his colleagues as "the first deregulator." He began challenging "the pretended competence of the state in economic affairs" nearly half a century ago. Stigler has made pioneering studies in industrial organization, price theory, the functioning of markets, and the causes and effects of public regulation. Those microeconomic studies made clear, among other things, that massive governmental programmes regulating the stock market and utility rates had no clear beneficial effects and that regulation routinely resulted in inefficiency without consumer protection.

Stigler is to microeconomics and regulation what Milton Friedman, a previous Nobel Laureate is to macroeconomics and monetarism. Both men contributed to the popularity of Reagonomics. But Stigler remains adamantly his own man. "I am not a Reagonomics man," he told the press on the occasion of his winning the Nobel Prize. "I am not a supply-sider. But reducing unnecessary government burdens on production is a wonderful thing." In differentiating himself from Friedman, he has explained that he is less the preacher. "Milton's out to save the world, and I'm out to understand it."

The important works of Stigler include *Roofs or Ceilings* (1946) (co-authored with Friedman), *The Theory of Price* (1946), *The Intellectual and the Market Place* (1963), *The Citizen and the State* (1975), *The Economist as Preacher* (1982). *Capital and Rates of Return in Manufacturing Industries* (1963) and *The Behaviour of Industrial Peace* (1968), (Co-authored with J. K. Kindahl).

In *Roofs or Ceilings*, Stigler along with Friedman argued that rent controls were counterproductive, leading to decreased construction and housing shortages. In *The Theory of Price*, Stigler covered not only perfect competition but imperfect competition, multiple products and capital theory, thus offering a comprehensive textbook on the mechanisms of a stationary enterprise economy.

The essays by Stigler published in pamphlet form by the National Bureau of Economic Research are considered classics in their field. In the late 1940s and the 1950s those essays included studies of employment in science, the service industries, and other sectors of the economy and the relationship of that employment to other factors, including federal minimum-wage legislation. Later, during President Lyndon B. Johnson's push for the massive federal social legislation known overall as the Great Society Programme, Stigler related the minimum wage to civil rights. His argument runs as follows:

"The present method of widening employment opportunities (for unskilled youths, especially black youths) is by direct legislation, laws which say that no one can discriminate against an applicant for a job. This all sounds fine; nevertheless discrimination continues to exist. The best way we can reinforce the anti-discrimination trend is by increasing the financial incentives to employers to hire Negroes. We do this not by increasing their wage rates—the market place will do this—but by increasing their skills. He recommended a two-pronged movement to train the unemployed for employment: a comprehensive programme of tuition and support grants for teen-agers of any race who wish to obtain vocational training in an accredited school and the removal of barriers to the employment of unskilled young workers at low wages while they are acquiring training on the job." Those barriers include minimum wage rates and apprenticeship restrictions.

In much of his writing and speaking in the 1950s Stigler proposed "the survivor method" of determining the efficient sizes of enterprises. He was much concerned with the evil effects of monopolies and he argued that giant companies like steel firms should be broken up to restore competition to the industry.

"The Economics of Information" is another significant contribution of Stigler to economic theory. Even before Stigler came to Chicago, he got interested in the existence of dispersion of prices under conditions which economic theory said would yield a single price. That interest culminated in the 'Economics of Information' and later work. Before the publication of Stigler's landmark essay "The Economies of Information" (Journal of Political Economy, of June 1961), the amount of information possessed by individuals in any market was arbitrarily postulated rather than derived from economic principles. As Stigler pointed out in his Nobel lecture, "The consensus was that consumers knew little, traders in any market a great deal : investors were either gullible or omniscient......
I proposed (in the Economics of Information) the use of the standard economic theory of utility—maximizing behaviour to determine how much information people would acquire, with special attention to the prices at which they would buy and sell, and a year later made an application of the analysis to labour markets (in "Information in the Labour Market," supplement to the Journal of Political Economy, October 1962)." In other words, while most economic studies had assumed that all actors in the market place possessed "perfect information," Stigler argued that information like other commodities has its cost, and different parties will be led to acquire different amounts of it when "shopping" thus accounting for divergent prices to different buyers. His proposal to study the economics of information was promptly and widely accepted without any controversy. And to-day, economics of information has become one of the popular branches of economics, and more than a hundred articles a year are now devoted to the subject.

Stigler's studies of public regulation are even more influential than his economics of information. His views on regulation were presented in such papers as "Administered prices and oligopolistic Inflation" (1962), and "Public Regulation of Securities Markets" (April 1964). In "What can Regulators Regulate? The case of Electricity Rates" (1962), he and Clare Friedland showed that unregulated utility companies charged no more for electricity than regulated ones. He later refined his theory on the costs and benefits of regulation in such essays as "The Theory of Economic Regulation" (1971), and "The Process of Economic Regulation" (1972). In his essays, Stigler turned around previous assumptions regarding regulation. Those assumptions had been that consumers welcome the "protection" of government regulation while business and industry see it as an enemy. Not so, Stigler said. He maintained that regulation is the enemy of consumers, who instinctively want the most efficient economy possible, whereas businessmen, labour unions and professionals often approve of the regulations because it tends to work in favour of those who are established and against would be new entrants to the market. Most regulatory agencies are "taken over" by the businesses and industries they are supposed to control and government officials and employees favour regulations not because they benefit consumers but because they enhance the power of the bureaucracy. Walter Heller, the Chairman of the Council of Economic Advisers in the Administration of John F. Kennedy said that using "Stiglerian theory" helped him to obtain Kennedy's approval to reduce transportation regulations despite the desire of the Department of Commerce to increase them. As the 1970s progressed, Stigler's ideas on regulation became more and more popular. Under the presidency of Jimmy Carter, major steps were taken to deregulate the oil industry, the airlines, and the trucking industry. And in the 1980 presidential campaign, one of the insistent themes of Ronald Reagon was lifting the burden of regulation from business. No wonder that on October 20, 1982. The Royal Swedish Academy of Sciences, while naming Stigler the recipient of the Nobel Prize in economic Science cited his seminal studies of industry, the market and government regulation that produced evidence that "legislation is no longer an exogenous force which affects the economy from outside, but is an endogenous part of the economic system itself."

GERARD DEBREU

Gerard Debreu, the French-born mathematician and economist (at present, American citizen) who is Professor at the Berkeley Campus of the University of California won the 1983 Nobel Prize in Economics. The Royal Swedish Academy of Sciences announced that it was awarding the Nobel Prize to him for three decades of distinguished service. Debreu made his mark on the profession more than 25 years ago in a 114 page book filled mostly with elaborate mathematical formulae. The title of the book was *Theory of Value : on axiomatic analysis of economic equilibrium* (1959). That book turned out to be one of the few classics of our period.

Debreu is a pure theorist. While commenting on the selection of Debreu, Asar Lindbeck, the Chairman of five member Nobel Committee said, "we have never before awarded the prize for contributions of such pure basic research." According to Bent Hanson, Chairman of the Berkeley Economics Department, "Gerard Debreu is an economist's economist. His work is very abstract, very fundamental. But everyone in the profession quotes him and must demonstrate that they know his work."

The *"Theory of Value"* has been described as "beautiful and austere." But it is not easily accessible to the layman. Yet in his elegant and mathematical equations, Debreu has created a model of a theoretical market place and has provided an analytical framework for some of the most fundamental tenets of classical economics.

Since 1776, when Adam Smith published his "Wealth of Nations, " economists believed that the conflicting desires of producers and consumers can be reconciled through the pricing mechanism, thereby creating an "equilibrium" of supply and demand. The best explanation that Smith could offer was that individual economic agents were guided to the common good "as if by an invisible hand." Debreu's chief contribution was to make that invisible hand somewhat more discernible. His 1959 classic showed that a freely competitive economy can, in theory, reach a state in which supply balances demand in every market and there are neither shortages nor surpluses of any product. Such a condition is called "General equilibrium." In collaboration with then Harvard Prof. Kenneth Arrow who himself won the Nobel Prize in 1972—Debreu developed a model in which producers, distributors and consumers each attempt to maximize their own economic welfare by manipulating prices and other factors such as land, labour and capital. Debreu found that—at least in his theoretical world— equilibrium could, in fact, be attained. The Royal Swedish Academy of Sciences, in its citation said that Debreu "confirmed the internal logical consistency" of the classical view of markets.

To obtain that result, Debreu had to assume an ideal world of flexible prices and unfettered competition. But these conditions simply do not exist in today's mixed economy. In developing his model, Debreu also created new mathematical tools that enable economists to better analyze conditions as they do actually exist. If, for example, bad weather causes a drop in a country's agricultural output, Debreu's model suggests how reduced farm incomes might affect sales of automobiles or how rising food prices might influence workers' wage demands. According to Karl-Goran Maler, a member of the Royal Academy, both the World Bank and International Monetary Fund use models that are based on Debreu's work, and "the economic political planning in many nations is also, to a great extent, built directly on Debreu's efforts." The models have also influenced the work of fellow Nobel Laureates, James Tobin of Yale and George Stigler of the University of Chicago.

Professor Kenneth J. Arrow, a Stanford University Professor in Economics and Operations Research said that Professor Debreu has made great strides in recent years in developing mathematical tools for discovering the prices at which supply meets demand in several complex economies. Arrow said that "his work includes a number of major innovations with practical applications."

Professor Debreu is greatly concerned with how economic models are framed. This, as Professor Debreu himself has pointed out makes him a heir to the pioneering theories of the late John Von Neumann, the originator of the Game Theory. He said, "I have been greatly influenced by Von Neumann."

In his first interview, following the announcement of the award. Debreu was asked whether he would grade the economic policies of Ronald Reagon. In reply, Debreu said that he won't and that he would try to be scientific and objective and not comment on the day-to-day developments in the economy. His theoretical bent leads him to shun disputes such as those waged by liberal Keynesians and conservative monetarists. "I do not consider myself involved in economic policy in any way," he says. Nevertheless, his work does have some practical applications in the hands of other economists. His equilibrium theory is used by private forecasters and government planners to predict such things as the impact of a tax change on various industries.

Debreu has strong feelings on the need for commitment to basic science. He is concerned that "very eager young mathematicians" are dropping out of the profession because of funding shortages or insufficient time for research...... The impact will show up in all scientific fields, including technology, usually with a great lag." According to Arrow, the most striking qualities of Debreu are "the quickness of his mind and the elegance of his thought."

SIR RICHARD STONE

Sir Richard Stone of Cambridge University was awarded the 1984 Nobel Prize in Economics. The Royal Swedish Academy of Sciences chose to stress the importance of Stone's work in formulating the system of integrated national-income accounts that have proved so useful in the post–World War II era. He was awarded the prize for "fundamental research on national accountancy systems that had radically improved the basis for empirical economic analysis."

Stone has two other important achievements to his credit : innovations in econometric measurement of demands for groups of goods and services; and in linear matrix models permitting extrapolation and testing of growth relations. The important works of Stone include "*Definition and Measurement of the national income and related totals,*" (Appendix to *Measurement of National Income and Construction of Social Accounts* (United Nations, Geneva, 1947); *A Programme for Growth* (ed.) (1962-1971) Vols. 1-11, *Mathematics in the Social Sciences and other Essays* (1966), pp. 20-21.

The Anatomy of Social Accounts

J. R. N. Stone first gained world fame for almost a half century for measurement of families' budget patterns with respect to spending and saving. Anyone who doubts that there is such a thing as economic law need only look at these well documented ancient regularities. Stone's statistical investigations of the propensities to consume and save assumed an especial importance in the revolutionary new work of Keynes's *General Theory of Employment, Interest and Money* (1936).

During World War II itself, Stone worked closely on setting up national-income accounts with James Meade (himself to share the 1977 Nobel Prize for innovation in international trade analysis). It was during World War II period that Stone and Meade made their first estimates, and forged the tools of interlocking accounts appropriate to a nation, and by extension, to a region or the whole world.

Cambridge University was not a friendly environment in the postwar years for a Department of Applied Economics. Still, a chair designated for finance and accounting went to a don (Stone himself) who had never met a payroll and whose double-entry items referred to societies and sectors and not to corporations and wholly owned subsidiaries.

Stone's work became popular soon. What was good for the United Kingdom was found to be good for the United States and became the pattern for the United Nations community generally as the Stone square matrices of interlocking fund flows became the *lingua franca* of world statisticians: involved was a *production* account, and one each for *consumption, accumulation* and *foreign finance.*

Physiology of the Circular Flow

Parallel with these accounts at the national level, Wassily Leontief developed at Harvard a similar system of input-output relations, in which a vector of industries is seen to be connected by a vast matrix of transaction flows—the dollars received by industry i from the total expenditure flow of industry j. The general notion of such a *Tableau Economique* goes back a long way, to Francois Quesnay, Physician at the court of Louis XV and founder of the Physiocratic school of economics. Quesnay's disciples called the Tableau, the greatest invention since fire and writing. That might be an exaggerated claim. We may note that both Karl Marx and Schumpeter admired this first attempt to grapple with an economy's general equilibrium.

Simon Kuznets in America had pioneered in defining and measuring national income and received the 1971 Nobel Prize for this work. Stone followed in his tradition, and in the tradition of such other laureates as Jan Tinbergan, Leontief and Lawrence Klein. Going beyond the formal anatomy and taxonomy of social accounts, Stone set up behaviour-equation hypotheses to rationalize and project future saving and income growths. A large team at Cambridge has produced volumes dealing with linear growth models.

Measurement in Terms of Theory

While announcing the 1984 Nobel award, the Royal Swedish Academy of Sciences stated : "*Economic Theory* is at the back of Stone's system for national accounts, and these therefore provide a systematic base for economic analysis, forecasts and ,economic policy." Thus, behind the dollar or pound numbers of the gross national product (GNP), an economic theorist tries to discern some real scale of output of goods and services.

What is needed is some proper index number of prices that can be used to deflate the dollar totals. When making calculations for all the countries in the Organization for Economic Co-operation and Development (OECD), Professor Stone proposed reasonable use of conventional price index numbers as deflators. The same general philosophy has been common among experts. Correct theoretical methods matter a lot. Thus, it was recently thought that half-a-dozen countries had surpassed the U.S. real per capita level of income: West Germany, Sweden, Switzerland and so forth. And that is what the World Bank Atlas used to show even though the experts there knew better.

When the United Nations and World Bank commissioned a team at the University of Pennsylvania to do the research correctly, the team used the same general methodology that Stone followed. They did not use merely exchange rates as deflators, knowing that short-term depreciations of the dollar would excessively lower the U.S. estimates. Instead they gathered prices actually paid in each country and constructed from them the proper index numbers needed as deflators. The result : America is still more than 10 per cent above the European nations named.

There is one further theoretical innovation of Stone's that is closely related : the Stone-Geary or Klain-Ruling system of demand functions. Rich people are known to spend a smaller fraction of their income on food than poor people do. So instead of assuming fixed fractions—the so-called Cobb-Douglas model—Stone gets a better fit by assuming people spend on each good a fixed fraction of the income they have left after they have bought a fixed market basket of the goods. This is also an oversimplification. But it is one in the good cause of arriving at tolerable econometric fits to whole systems of observations. Fairly recently the Kravis-summers-Hesten team (Pennsylvania team) has verified that such a model does approximately fit their data on more than a score of countries, ranging from poor Kenya and India to Hungary, Britain, Japan, and the United States. We may conclude by saying that Richard Stone has done fruitful interdisciplinary work in the realms where demographic and economic analysis overlap.

FRANCO MODIGLIANI

Franco Modigliani of the Massachusetts Institute of Technology (U.S.A.) was awarded the seventeenth Nobel Prize in Economics in 1985. Modigliani has made great contribution to modern economics for more than four decades. He is recognized as an outstanding economic theorist.

The Swedish Royal Academy of Sciences has said in its citation that Modigliani has been awarded the Nobel prize in recognition of "his development of a life cycle hypothesis of household savings and the formulation of theories on the valuation of firms and capital costs." The chairman of the Prize committee has further stated that "Modigliani's contribution lay in developing a model of how people save for their old age, integrating it into economic theory and drawing and testing implications from his model."

The Life-Cycle Saving Model

Modigliani has many brain children to his credit. According to professor Samuelson, "The jewel in the Modigliani crown is his life cycle hypothesis of saving, developed in collaboration with Richard Brumberg. It is one of the best explanations of saving and investment behaviour and their responsiveness to policy programmes. In the words of John Muelbaur, "The Life Cycle Hypothesis has been the dominant theoretical basis for empirical work on the aggregate consumption function for above a quarter of a century."

Modigliani is a versatile scholar and prolific writer. Some of his important contributions are found in (i) The collected papers of Franco Modigliani: *Essays in Macro Economics*, volume I (edited by Andrew Abel, 1980); (ii) The collected papers of Franco Modigliani: *The Life Cycle Hypothesis of Saving*, volume II (edited by Andrew Abel 1980); (iii) The collected papers of Franco Modigliani: *The Theory of Finance and other Essays*, volume III (edited by Andrew Abel 1980) and (iv) *The Determinants of Saving and Wealth* (edited with Richard Hemming, 1983).

Most of us will live beyond our prime earning years. So we must save during our working and earning years to accumulate the assets on which we will live in retirement. Though this theory appears simple, it is a fundamental one.

We gain many insights about consumption, saving and investment. Suppose there is no growth of population (as in Denmark). Suppose there are no improvements in productivity which raise real incomes (It happened from 1973 to 1980 in many countries of the world). A life cycle system without growth involves zero net saving and investment because the saving of the young will be cancelled by the dissaving of the old. In other words, growing nations will save much and stagnating nations will save little.

During the empirical investigation of his hypothesis, Modigliani found that the early Americans, though poor, saved much. The modern affluent Americans save little. The fast growing Japanese and

Germans save much. The French and the Italians, though they are generally considered romantic and carefree, have high saving rates between those of Japan and the United States.

The basic idea underlying the life cycle hypothesis is that the consumer plans his expenditure not on the basis of the income received during the current period but rather on the basis of his long-run or lifetime income expectations.

In the theory of consumption function, the life cycle hypothesis is similar to that of the permanent income hypothesis developed by Milton Friedman. Both theories divide income into permanent income (Y_p) and transitory income (Y_t) and consumption into permanent consumption (C_p) and transitory consumption (C_t).

The basic argument of both the theories is that permanent consumption depends on permanent income. Friedman tells that permanent consumption is constant proportion of permanent income in which the proportion depends only on the interest rate, on the ratio of non-human wealth to total (human plus non-human) wealth and on tastes. Tastes are affected by factors such as age and family composition. We may note that permanent consumption of different families will vary with their tastes and other specified characteristics. Modigliani accepts the same determining variables but gives importance to time and emphasizes the age of the consumer unit.

In both models, an increase in real income may raise the saving ratio. In the life cycle hypothesis, the effect varies with the age of the household. It will be positive for younger households and negative for older, and retired households.

We may note that Modigliani-Brumberg life cycle hypothesis of consumption function is different from the absolute income hypothesis of Keynes and relative income hypothesis of Duesenberry.

The life cycle hypothesis thus is based on the general idea, subject to resource constraint, households distribute their consumption over the life time to maximize their utility. The theory is made more specific by adding two assumptions. First, there is the absence of an estate motive, that is households save only for the sake of consuming later in their life span, but not for the sake of passing wealth to their heirs. And second assumption is proportionality hypothesis. It tells that contrary to the measured income theories, the allocation of consumption over time is independent of the level of income.

According to Stephen Marglin "the life cycle and permanent income approaches gained favour more because they provided a link between (Keynesian) macro economics and (Neo-classical) micro economics than because of their success in explaining the empirical evidence on consumption and savings."

The practical significance of the life cycle hypothesis lies in the fact that it has formed the basis for the study of pension and retirement schemes. In the words of the Royal Swedish Academy, "In particular, it has proved an ideal tool for analyses of the effects of different pension systems. Most of those analyses have indicated that the introduction of a general pension system leads to a declining saving."

Neutrality of Leveraging

Modigliani has made significant contributions both to macro economics of business cycles and inflation and to the micro economics of relative prices and rational decision-making. He has made important contributions in financial markets and investment decisions.

The Nobel Award cited his work dealing with "efficient market" analysis and leading to the 1958 Modigliani-Miller theorem concerning the neutrality of corporate leveraging.

Corporate finance deals with all operations of business firms aimed at the procurement of capital funds and their investment in various types of assets. Firms make decisions to invest in plant and equipment and inventories, pay dividends and borrow through the bond and stock markets at the same time. The debt/asset ratio, the interest rate and the depreciation will have an effect on investment to the extent that they influence the external borrowing. If a firm can obtain funds at an interest rate which is lower than its internal rate of return, this will increase the rate of return on its equity capital. This is known as the principle of "Financial leverage" or "Trading on Equity".

Modigliani and Miller in their analysis of the cost of capital, corporation finance and the theory of investment have argued that under certain assumptions (*e.g.*, absence of taxation and of any difference in the availability and cost of credit for individuals and corporations), the market value of shares of all firms belonging to the same risk class and having the same profit before interest would be equal irrespective of their capital structure (debt-to-equity ratio).

Generally companies float bonds as well as stocks. Some abstain from debt and any such "leveraging". The conventional wisdom before 1958 was that business corporations should borrow a certain optimal fraction of its total capital needs. The company that achieves this golden leveraging ratio lifts the total market value of its owners share. The management which either stays zero leveraged or over-leveraged, loses prospective wealth, and may in the long will be forced out of business.

Modigliani and Miller argued otherwise. "Chicken legs and breasts can be separately packaged at the super market: the values of each package must add up closely to the value of whole chickens. Otherwise, consumers can do their own packaging." Similarly, Modigliani and Brumberg showed that firm A with much debt and firm B with no debt cannot command a premium. Their point is that total value to the owners of a company is invariant, independent of the degree of leverage. Empirical testing also has not factually established the advantages of optimal leveraging.

It has also been found that the percentage payment of earnings as dividends will not affect a stock's valuation.

We live in an age of corporate borrowings. This only shows that leveraging in neutral. The 1950-86 trend toward debt confirms the Modigliani-Miller analysis.

Preferred Habitat Theory

Modigliani and Sutch (1966) have given the preferred habitat theory to explain the relationship between the yields on various securities and their terms (shorter/longer) to maturity. The theory is based on the assumption that different investors have different preferred habitats according to the pattern of their liabilities. An implication of the preferred habitat model is that a spread between the long rate and the short rate will depend primarily on the expected change in the long rate. Modigliani and Sutch have pointed out that all the factors expectations, liquidity or risk premium and market segmentation—may play a part in determining the term structure.

By making use of the Habitat model, Modigliani and Sutch (1966) have examined the behaviour of the divergence between long term and short term interest rates in the context of an attempt made by the U.S. Monetory authorities in the early 1960s to alter this gap, which has come to be known as "Operation Twist". It refers to the attempt to lower the long run interest rates in order to boost investment, and to reduce unemployment level, and to raise the short-run rate in order to attract foreign funds and to improve the balance of payments. The empirical results have suggested that the link between the expected short term rates and long term rates is fairly strong. This has indicated the expectations theory. But the operation twist had only a mild effect on the yield gap. It shows that traders are reluctant to move from their preferred habitat.

JAMES BUCHANAN

James Buchanan of George Mason University, Virginia, U.S.A. was awarded the Nobel prize in Economics for the year 1986.

Buchanan was awarded the prize for his public choice theory. The theory essentially predicts that democratically elected governments are more likely to serve their own interests than those of the people who elected them.

Buchanan has applied market place analysis to government decision making and brought more reality to political science.

The traditional idea of government is that it is a beneficent one. But Buchanan argues that as politicians are motivated more by self-interest than by an altruistic commitment to ideals such as statesmanship and national interest, the traditional idea of beneficent government fails. According to Buchanan, this should be no surprise because governments are made up of individuals and individuals operate from self-interest when they are engaged in a system of exchange, whether this is in the market economy or in politics.

Public choice theory is nothing more than the application of economic theory to political choice. Self-interest dominates the analytical formulation, whereas altruism, which was assumed to be of considerable importance is excluded. According to the supporters of public choice theory, the assumption of self-interest adds more reality to political science models.

Buchanan argues that, "taken directly, there is no ideological aspect to the logic of public choice theory." It is a straightforward analysis. "But if the analysis leads you to conclude that there are limits to what governments can do, then that will create a negative reaction in those who want government to do more and more."

The notion of self-interest as an important component of decision-making has a long tradition. For example, Adam Smith, the Father of Economics, explained how enlightened self-interest operated in the market place in his famous book "Wealth of Nations" (1776). Contrary to expectations, he showed that the exchange system of the market produced mutual advantage to buyers and sellers by the operation of the "invisible hand."

Another basic assumption of the main stream economics is that government would act in public interest to correct the so-called market failures. These government actions would include the application of mechanical methods and policies to achieve the macroeconomic and socioeconomic goals relating to employment, inflation or growth rates. The Royal Swedish Academy of Sciences in its award initiation said that "Buchanan and others in the public choice school have not accepted this simplified view of political life. Instead, they have sought explanations for political behaviour that resemble those used to analyse behaviour on markets."

In other words, as Michael Weinstein of Haverford College, Pennsylvania put it "Buchanan changed the question that people were asking. Instead of asking, "What is the ideal solution to market failure?" or "What should government do?" Buchanan asks "What do governments do?" It was a simple but revolutionary change.

Buchanan acknowledges the contribution made by the eminent Swedish economist Knut Wicksell in laying some of the intellectual foundations upon which the public choice theory is built. In the U.S.A., the first major work on the subject was a book "An Economic Theory of Democracy" by Anthony Downs in 1957. But it was Buchanan, who took this simple idea and pushed it hard.

We may also note that public choice theory was maturing side by side with social choice theory, which was developed by Kenneth Arrow, the 1972 Nobel Prize winner. Both the public choice theory and the social choice theory emphasize rational choice, the former at the institutional level and the latter more at the individual level. According to William Riker of the University of Rochester, "rational choice had not been a component of political science models until recently. But it is now a key phrase in our field."

Public choice theory can be applied to almost every level of government where agreements are made between two parties. Borcherding says that "It is directly analogous to market theory, where you have firms on one side and individual consumers on the other. In public choice, the firms are the political parties and the bureaucracies, while consumers are sometimes individual voters, sometimes, coalition of voters, such as trade unions. . . . . and so on."

One of the main pillars of Buchanan's public choice theory is that, given the propensity for self-interest in both politicians and voters, the existence of certain rules is of utmost importance in determining what will actually happen in government. It is the rules which keep self-interest in check. For example, before the advent of the Keynesian economic theory in the 1930s, there was an unwritten but powerful rule that governments did not spend more than they collected in taxes. In other words, budgets were usually kept in check.

The Keynesian theory gave approval for deficit budgets during the special circumstances of an economic recession. But in due course, deficit budgets became the order of the day. Buchanan argued that under such circumstances, financial disaster was inevitable. He wrote recently, "The fiscal outcome of ordinary politics now resembles the behaviour of the compulsive gambler who finds himself in Lasvegas or Atlantic city. "Who can expect, the gambler to refrain from irresponsible behaviour, given the temptations he faces? Because of electoral politics in modern democracy politicians make tall promises in return for votes to ensure reelection and they tend to give more largesse than might be appropriate for the overall good. The result is "pork barrel politics and budget deficits."

In the pre-Keynesian days, most of the economists believed in balanced budgets. But today there is a natural tendency among politicians to inflate the budget while keeping down taxes. According to the public choice theory, there is need for a balanced budget amendment. Buchanan says that this is a clear example of the importance of fundamental rules "and you need rules that are relatively stable so that people can make predictions and operate within those rules."

If we look at the public choice theory as a whole, we can see that it attempts to describe the behaviour of self-interested groups as they interact in systems of exchange. It applies to the highest level of government or the lowest level of local politics, and even of the church and the family. At the most fundamental level, it seeks to explain why self-interested individuals agree to operate within a majority-vote system in which inevitably, any particular individual or group will sometime lose. It is therefore all pervasive.

The public choice theory is not without its critics. For example, Colman McCarthy, a political commentator for the Washington Post, wrote that Buchanan's conclusions are "ordinary and obvious". To that Buchanan's answer is that such critics are ignorant of just how pervasive the body of theory is. In his own words "It is very difficult to explain a whole complex body of thought that has built up over a period of 40 years." He says, "So, to try to explain it, you search around for simple examples and the one I have focused on is the proclivity to have deficits. And of course, this looks like commonsense. It is very simplistic. But some parts of public choice theory are as esoteric mathematically as anything you can imagine in economic theory. You can model voting rules of parties and platforms, and that can get into many dimensions of policy. But you can't explain that to the lay public."

Weinstein is not ideologically sympathetic with the predictions of public choice theory. But he defends its power. "Yes, it is all commonsense, but no one said it before, no one explored it systematically like Buchanan did."

Another criticism of public choice theory relates to its fundamental notion that there is no altruism in the system. Critics say that the notion is wrong. In addition, it is pointed out that budget deficits are a relatively recent phenomenon. Public choice theory has to explain why they did not happen before.

According to Theodre Lowi, a political scientist, the main weakness of the public choice theory is that it does not take note of the cultural factors that influence the way governments work. In his own words, "it is true that public choice theory has enabled political scientists to formalize questions about government in a way that was not previously possible. But it leaves out tradition and institutional patterns of commitment that shape the behaviour of governments. Of course, he acknowledges that "institutions develop a life of their own, and this is not necessarily described by the rational analysis of maximising political profit."

We may conclude by saying that with regard to the impact of public choice theory, in the general sense and in the context of the growth of social choice theory, the notion of rational choice and utility maximization has been extremely important.

ROBERT M. SOLOW

The Nobel prize in Economics was awarded to Robert M. Solow of the MIT (U.S.A.) for the year 1987. The Nobel Committee cited the papers which Solow published in 1956 and 1957 in which he proved that technology, not capital, is the key factor in making economies grow. The first paper proposed the novel theory to explain how national economics grow. The second paper offered a means of testing the theory, laying out a system by which the inputs to growth could be broken down into pieces and the pieces measured. This work established some new economic truths and proved them by vigorous methods. Those two papers were "A contribution to the Theory of Economic Growth" (1956) in Quarterly Journal of Economics, February 1956 and "Technical Change and Production Function" which was published in the review of Economics and Statistics in August 1957.

Fifty years ago, Solow asserted that technology plays the key role in economic growth. Since then, his idea has been examined in hundreds of journal articles and dozens of books, leading to a cottage industry in the profession known as "growth accounting". As Solow puts it, "The idea has matured. I know of no case where it has been disconfirmed in modern industrial economies."

Solow's idea seems obvious now, but was not obvious when first described. Solow was drawn to this topic after World War II by the economic drama of the newly decolonized nations. Everyone expected them to follow the path of the industrial nations. But how? What would make their economies grow? These were the questions.

Economists at that time were preoccupied with the fluctuations of business cycles, the periods of growth and recession in the long-term trends of growth in the gross national product. But relatively, very little attention had been given to the question of why one country has a growth trend of 3%, a second 4% and a third 2%. Most of the economists focused their attention on the behaviour of the economies in 10-year periods. But solow wanted to look at longer periods.

The conventional wisdom at that time was that investment of savings was the key to growth. The more a nation saved, the faster it could grow. What distinguished poor countries from rich countries was that poor countries were able to save very little because they were poor. The economists believed that the rich ones would grow faster because they started out rich. It was this idea that Solow rejected.

Another popular notion at the time was an industrial economy-once launched on a path of high growth-would have no choice but to continue along a very narrowly prescribed growth trend line. "If it ever drifted off in one direction or the other, those movements would be magnified" leading to crisis.

Solow came forward with a new theory that put an end to "razor's edge" description of growth allowing for greater flexibility in planning. He found that the existing theories omitted forces that tend to balance one another and keep the economy in good health. In his attempts at a deep study of economic growth, Solow came up with a startling conclusion: Capital investment is not the key factor in economic growth. Neither the increase in workers. Solow proved with statistics on wage and property income between 1909 and 1957 that neither of these two was the most significant factor. Instead, it was a residual factor. It was an undefined, broad category and it has come to be known as innovations or technology. Solow has thus proved that technological change, rather than the capital stock or the labour force emerges as the most important factor in the actual rate of growth of an economy.

Solow won the Nobel prize for his study demonstrating that the rate of technological progress does more to determine an industrialized country's growth than the size of its labour force or its investment in new factories or equipment.

When we speak of technological progress, we may note that it is embodied technological progress that is important. Embodied technological progress must be physically incorporated in newly produced capital goods or newly trained or educated workers before it can contribute to the rate of growth of economy's output. Capital can no longer be assumed to be homogeneous. The capital stock becomes a mixed stock of different "vintages" (*i.e.*, period of manufacture). As the new machines embody more technological progress, they are more productive than older ones. Like units of the capital stock, different persons in the labour force are of different vintages distinguished by age, education or training. Persons who belong to the current vintage will be more productive than the persons of earlier vintages.

The award cited that "Solow's theoretical model had an enormous impact on economic analysis."

The publication of Solow's finding in 1957 had a tremendous impact on the thinking of fellow economists and administrators on economic growth. It coincided with the Soviet launch of Sputnik. Solow provided the intellectual basis and the society provided the political stimulus for an intense national drive to promote science and technology. Since then, the governments started investing sizeable funds in basic research. The American President Reagan in his 1987 budget priorities statement justified a 76% increase in research funding between 1982 and 1988 as follows: "Support for basic research, particularly at Universities, is a key factor in generating sufficient new knowledge to ensure continued technological innovation........". It went on to describe the "critical importance" of research for the economy.

In the decades since Solow published his papers, many other economists have tried to break down the residual "technology" factor into smaller pieces to get a clearer picture of the processes that work to promote economic growth.

Recently, Denison, who surveyed 500 articles on technology and growth, warns that it is rather difficult to pin down the elements of this vague factor known as innovation. He has concluded from his own work that government funded research and development are not probably the most important parts for the economy. He thinks that an unstructured kind of innovation may be more important. "You know, when people are working, they notice things" and make numerous small improvements. Others such as Griliches stress the importance of education as a promoter of knowledge and invention. Ideas like these have led to further debates on American education.

Solow and Samuelson are leaders in Keynesian school. The Keynesian school has come under attack from the monetarists in the 1970s, led by Milton Friedman of the University of Chicago. Friedman pointed to the Keynesian policies of the 1960s as a cause for the prolonged inflation of the 1970s. Under the slogan "money matters", the monetarists argued that through inattention to financial effects, the government has created a dangerous condition in which productivity was sinking, unemployment was high, and inflation was rising. Solow agrees that money matters but not as much as Friedman says.

Solow is a leading advocate of government intervention to the natural imbalances of the market place. As senior economist on the staff of Economic Advisers in the early 1960s, Solow helped shape the interventionist policies that dominated the Kennedy and Johnson administrations. And he is opposed to Reaganomics. In his own words, "The best thing you can say about reaganomics is that it probably happened in a fit of inattention."

MAURICE ALLAIS

Maurice Allais, the eminent French economist, won the 1988 Nobel prize in Economics at the age of 77. He has won the prize for his pioneering contribution to the theory of markets and efficient utilisation of resources.

The Nobel Committee cited Professor Allais mainly for basic research in the theory of markets, but also stressed that his work had important implications for making decisions on investment and pricing especially in the state-run monopolies.

The Nobel Committee further said that Allais had been instrumental in the investment and pricing decisions made by younger economists working for state owned monopolies in Western Europe after World War II. France, in particular, was engaged in a programme of nationalisation in the post-war years, resulting in state-owned enterprises in industries including railways, electric utilities and coal mining.

During the 1980s there was a worldwide trend toward privatising formerly state-owned business. But many of the enterprises sold off to the private sector continued to remain as monopolies. At the same time, public service projects such as road systems and the tunnel under the English Channel linking Britain and France continued to be started. All these require investment and pricing decisions aimed at providing a service that is socially efficient as well as economically viable. The work of Allais is of immense help in taking investment and pricing decisions in such cases.

Dr. Allais was the first French citizen to win the Nobel Prize in Economics. He has developed the theoretical foundation that showed that even in monopolies, which have no competition, there is a means for determining an optimum price that is socially efficient in the sense that no one can be better off without making someone else worse off, if there is a price change.

The principle developed by Allais proved important for guiding the planning of state enterprises by means of prices, instead of direct regulation by the State. In short, his work supplied the basis for applying some of the efficiency—increasing principles of market economics to large state monopolies.

The Nobel Committee noted that international recognition had been delayed to Dr. Allais partly because of the length and complexity of some of his most important works and partly because he wrote in French.

Allais' two pioneering works are "*Trait d' Economic Pure*" (1943) and "*Economic Interest*" (1947). The first book contains a general and rigorous formulation of the two basic propositions of welfare theory. Through his analysis of market equilibrium and social efficiency, Allais laid the foundation for the school of post-war French economists who not only analysed the conditions for efficient use of resources in state-owned monopolies but also applied the theory to business management.

In his works, Allais made use of new mathematical methods to analyse the stability of equilibrium, that is the condition, under which an economy—after disturbance—will return to equilibrium, through price formation. Allais anticipated many important results in research which led to the modem theory of economic growth in the late 50s and early 60s.

The Nobel committee described Allais' contribution to the field of economics, especially his two major books which he published in 1943 and 1947 as parallel to research published around the same time by two well-known economists Sir John Hicks of Britain and Paul A. Samuelson of the U.S.A. Both of them were awarded Nobel prizes more than a decade back. Samuelson won the prize in 1970 and Sir John Hicks in 1972.

The Nobel Committee further said that the work of Allais served as "a basis" for the mathematical analysis of markets and social efficiency carried out by one of his former pupils Dr. Gerard Debreu and Dr. Kenneth J. Arrow. Debreu a Frenchman won the Nobel prize in 1983 after he became an American citizen and Arrow won the Nobel prize in 1972.

Allais has also made contributions in theoretical and empirical studies on the significance and determinants of the volume of money. In the last two decades, he has tried to generalise the market theory by emphasizing its dynamic aspects.

Allais has developed theories on many economic relationships, including those between interest rates, growth and investment. Some of the important formulae given by him demonstrate how a monopoly can set prices for products such as coal or electricity at a level that would be best for society.

Allais is a great supporter of privatisation of industries. He has always argued that even state-run monopolies are most efficient when they set prices and allocate resources according to market prices.

TRYGVE HAAVELMO

Professor Trygve Haavelmo of Norway was awarded the Nobel prize in Economics for the year 1989. When the prize was announced, Haavelmo was completely unknown to the general public in his own country. Although, he was keenly interested in policy questions, he has never entered public debate and has always avoided publicity. But Haavelmo had enormous influence on the economists of his country. Schumpeter has paid a rich tribute to Haavelmo in his *"History of Economic Analysis"* as follows: "Haavelmo, during his brief sojourn in the United States, without holding a teaching position, exerted an influence that would do credit to the lifetime work of a professor."

Haavelmo was honoured for his pioneer work in the early 1940s that laid the foundation for econometrics, which uses mathematical models to study the behaviour of an economy. Assar Lindbeck, the chairman of the Nobel Selection Committee said that "Every time you open a newspaper and see an analysis of economic trends, it is based on Haavelmo's econometric theories."

Haavelmo's key contribution was to show that the relationship between such factors as income and spending was far more complex than had been thought, since those factors affect one another and the rest of the economy. For instance, he demonstrated that an economist could not gauge the impact of a change in tax rates on consumer spending without using sophisticated statistical methods.

Lawrence Klein, who won the 1980 Nobel prize in economics, said that Haavelmo had a tremendous influence on him and on many other young econometricians in the 1940s. Robert Solow, another Nobel Laureate who won the 1987 prize said that 'it is like giving the Nobel prize for Physics to Thomas Edison .....''

Haavelmo was in the United States from 1939 to 1947, and during this period he published most of his pathbreaking contributions to Econometrics for which the Nobel Committee awarded him the prize. The bulk of Haavelmo's teaching has been embodied in a number of papers published in *Econometrica*. But his work "The Probability approach in Econometrics", *Econometrica Supplement*, July 1944, 12,1-115 is of special importance. Some of his other important works are "The Statistical Implications of a System of Simultaneous Equations" (*Econometrica*, 1943), "Statistical Testing of Business cycle Theories". (*Review of Economic Statistics*, 1943), "On the Notion of Industry Economic Decisions (*Econometrica*, January, 1950) and "The Role of the Econometrician in the Advancement of Economic Theory" (*Econometrica*, July 1958).

A wide range of subjects are covered in Haavelmo's writings. But he seemed to have been more occupied with the followings themes, the relationship between population, natural resources and growth; investment and capital theory; the notion of equilibrium and disequilibrium; the nature and stability of preference; the nature of problems of democracy.

Background

Economists from the university of Oslo played a key role in the transformation of economics from an armchair activity to an empirical science expressed in mathematical language between 1930 and 1960. In 1931, when Haavelmo was a first-year undergraduate student, Ragnar Frisch (1895-1975) became professor in the Economics Department in Oslo. As Haaveltno later put it, "........ as seen by the students, the economics curriculum shook in its foundations". Haavelmo became Frisch's assistant in 1933. During 1938-39, Haavelmo worked as lecturer at the University of Aarhus, Denmark. He went to the United States as a Fulbright Scholar in 1939. He was in the United States from 1939 to 1947. He completed his doctoral thesis "The Probability Approach in Econometrics" at Harvard in 1941 and submitted to the University of Oslo after World War II. Haavelmo was appointed full-time Professor at the University of Oslo in 1948. He held that position until he became emeritus in 1979.

The Probability Approach in Econometrics

Haavelmo is best known for his work on identification, estimation and testing in models where the variables are determined to a system of simultaneous equations. The Swedish Academy of Sciences cited his contributions in this area and in introducing probability theory to econometrics in his dissertation and in his articles in Econometrics through the 1940s as the main reason for awarding him the prize.

Today almost every econometrician makes use of probability models as a matter of course. But it was almost a revolution when this tool was first taken into use. As Haavelmo put it "........ the adoption of definite probability models has been deemed a crime in economic research, a violation of the very nature of economic data. It may be noted that Keynes was one of the outspoken critics of the use of probability approach in economics. But economists like Aldrich consider Haavelmo's 'Probability Approach' as one of the masterpieces of twentieth century methodological writing in economics". Again, Morgan (1990) who has written the most comprehensive history of early econometrics has said that "Haavelmo's 1944 paper marks the end of the formative years in econometrics and the beginning of its mature period."

Although Haavelmo's main contributions were in econometric theory, we may note that he also contributed to the field of applied econometrics and studied problems such as the demand for milk in Norway, the market for pork in Denmark, share prices in Norway and the United States and the U.S. demand for food.

Rich and Poor Nations

Haavelmo's 1954 book is remarkable in many respects. It gives insights into some of the recent advances in economics such as the integration of accumulated human skills in growth models, the analysis of strategic behaviour in international affairs, and the economics of rent-seeking behaviour.

The book focuses on the problem why some countries are 'backward' while others are 'advanced'. He discussed this question in a purely theoretical way with a focus on macro dynamic methods and on the merits of different types of explanations from a methodological point of view. But he has not offered any final conclusions to the question why some countries are rich and why some countries are poor.

While discussing the relationship between living standards, population growth and incomes, he has observed that the living conditions of workers may rise or stagnate depending on how strongly population growth reacts to improving living standards. If population growth reacts strongly to higher incomes, the working class will remain on the subsistence level. However, if population growth reacts less, the model predicts an increasing real wage. In his later works and lectures, Haavelmo has shown keen interest in the study of the race between population growth and economic progress.

Haavelmo's book also offers an interesting discussion of conflict and co-operation between countries. His model may also provide micro foundations for the political economy of unequal exchange in international trade, which is often emphasized by radical economists.

Haavelmo's book is also related to the recent literature on rent-seeking on the basis of the contribution of Ann Krueger in 1974. The basic principle is that improving one's position to capture rents will often involve a waste of resources. But in Haavelmo's book, the same is between countries rather than between interest groups and government.

The book, further deals with certain aspects of the theory of migration, environmental problems and the long run consequences of pollution. During the process of development, each consumer faces a trade off between immediate pleasure related to higher consumption and the endless pain from the extra pollution it generates. It is obvious that free-rider problems exist, since consumption is a private good and pollution is a public bad. Hence unguarded development may become very harmful.

The Theory of Investment

Haavelmo was interested in the theory of investment since 1940s. The main purpose of Haavelmo's book "*A Study in the Theory of Investment*" (1960) was to destroy the standard Keynesian demand function for investment, where net investment is a simple function of the rate of interest, and to offer an alternative explanation. The other major questions discussed in the book relate the to why net investments are so volatile, and why they are almost always positive.

Haavelmo's main contribution to the macro theory of investment is a two-sector model, where at any point in time, the stock of real capital is given from the past. According to him, the level of real investment is determined by the relationship between the price of the existing capital goods and the factor costs and technological efficiency involved in producing new capital. In this, "one may notice the similarity to Tobin's theory of investment. "The rate of investment .... should be related .... to q, the value of capital relative to its replacement costs". The difference is that Tobin seems to have had a one-sector model in mind.

Haavelmo has also dealt with the problems of equilibrium and disequilibrium, preferences, democracy and welfare.

We may conclude by saying that Haavelmo is one of the founders of modern econometrics.

HARRY M. MARKOWITZ, F. SHARPE AND MERTON MILLER

The Nobel prize in Economics for the year 1990 was jointly awarded to Harry M. Markowitz of the City University of New York, William F. Sharpe of Stanford University and Merton Miller of the University of Chicago. They were awarded the prize for their pioneering work which helped explain how prices for corporate securities are established in financial markets. All the three have done pioneering work in the field of financial economics.

The theories developed by these three economists collectively explain how risks and rewards can be balanced in a given investment portfolio, how their weighing of risks and rewards helps determine securities prices, and how factors like tax changes or bankruptcy affect the price of a company's securities.

These theories have wide application today. For instance, they are made use of by investment firms to predict stock prices and to pick securities for a customer's portfolio. They are also used by financial experts to make decisions on dividends and financings.

Government use these theories to assess the potential impact of a tax change on a given sector of the economy. And public utility commission might use them to fix prices that would enable an electricity undertaking to realize fair return on its investment so that it can afford to build the power plants that a community needs.

According to James Tobin, who won the Nobel prize in 1981, "in many ways, the School that believes that financial markets are rational or efficient—or always accurately reflect the value of a company by the way it prices its securities-rests on their work". He further said that "They are all pioneers in finance theory, which has been flourishing in recent years. But these guys were way ahead of the fashion."

Professor Assar Lindbeck, the chairman of the prize committee at Royal Swedish Academy of Sciences observed that while the three did not collaborate, there work was a continuum. In his own words, "Each one of them gave one building block for a unified theory of financial economics. This theory would have been incomplete if one of these pieces were missing."

Markowitz was cited by the Academy for developing the theory of portfolio choice. This is a theory of how households and companies allocate their financial assets under certain conditions. The theory analyses how wealth or saving can be optimally invested in assets that differ in terms of their expected return and risk. Investors might use his formula to choose a portfolio of stocks that yielded the highest possible return with the lowest possible risk. They might also use it to take higher risks in return for a higher profit. He provided an analytical support to the insight that a diversified portfolio would reduce an investor's risk and maximize return.

Markowitz's theory offered investors the concept of a menu of portfolios with different blends of assets that seek to generate the best tradeoff between returns and risks. His theory encouraged the growth of mutual funds which rely on the portfolios of different stocks geared to the desires of different investors for safety and growth.

Markowitz first published his theory in 1952 in an essay entitled "Portfolio Selection: Efficient Diversification."

Economists and investment managers had long been aware of the necessity of taking potential returns as well as risks into account in making investment decisions and of the value of diversifying investment risks. But Markowitz provided a formula for doing so.

Sharpe took Markowitz's theory to develop a model for explaining how securities prices are established in the market to reflect risks and potential returns. He was cited for his formulation of the Capital Asset Pricing Model which enables an investor to choose exposure to risk through a combination of lending and borrowing and a suitably composed portfolio of securities. He argued that by refusing to diversify, the investor ran the risk without raising the prospects for reward. The theory is now used by investment firms to predict how a given stock, for example, will perform in relation to the stock market.

Miller is widely recognized as a dominant force in theoretical and empirical analysis in corporate finance. He was awarded the economics prize for his theory of corporate finance and the evaluation of companies on markets.

Miller's theory explained the relation, via the capital markets, between the capital asset structure and dividend policy of manufacturing companies on the one hand and their market value and cost of capital on the other.

Miller, initially collaborated with professor Modigliani on what is now known as Miller-Modigliani theorem. Modigliani won the Nobel prize for Economics in 1985. Their work demonstrated that the value of a business corporation was determined more by the skill of its managers and the expected future cash flow from its operations rather than by the debt level and dividend payment policies of the firm.

Miller often emphasizes the need for liquidity in futures markets and the avoidance of heavy regulatory burdens or investment transaction taxes on futures or other financial markets.

In a recent article, Miller distinguished between the "Casino view" and "information view" of markets. Those who hold the "Casino view" of markets think that markets provide no benefits to the larger economy. But the "information view" to which he subscribes, argues that "the prospect of speculative profits is the 'bribe' so to speak that society offers investors to speed the incorporation of dispersed bits of information into prices."

RONALD COASE

Ronald Coase was awarded the 1991 Nobel prize in Economics for his pioneering work in the ways in which transaction costs and property rights affect business and society. He was the ninth professor from the University of Chicago to win the prize and the first member of the faculty of Law to do so. Coase is an important figure in the field of law and economics. The Royal Swedish Academy of Sciences while announcing the prize said that Coase's theories "are among the most dynamic forces behind research in economic science and jurisprudence today."

Coase was born in England in 1910 and graduated from the London School of Economics in 1932. He taught at the London School of Economics from 1935 to 1951, when he moved to the United States. First, he joined the faculty at the University of Buffalo, New York, and then at the University of Virginia. He moved to the University of Chicago in 1964.

Ronald Coase has written two great theoretical articles, one in 1937 and the other in 1960 dealing with more or less the same theme. His first article was entitled "The Nature of the Firm" (1937) and the second article was "The Problem of Social Cost" (1960).

While working for his degree, Coase toured U.S. factories, during which time he developed theories for his paper "The Nature of the Firm". In his paper, Coase asked why firms exist, and suggested in reply that in many cases, organizations can minimize transaction costs incurred in a market economy by facilitating stable contractual relationships.

Coase always attacked "high theory" in economics. He tells that for the first 40 years or so of his professional life, micro economists were preoccupied with "The problem of Monopoly". They saw monopoly everywhere. "Monopolistic Competition" and "oligopolistic interdependence" were the theoretical models that extend the monopoly concept beyond classic single-firm monopolies and cartels. And they recommended government intervention by means of anti-trust laws and/or other forms of regulation. For example, they regarded vertical integration as a monopolizing device, one that employed "leverage" or created "barriers to entry" to extend or protect monopoly power.

Coase, in his article "The Nature of the Firm" had offered an alternative nonmonopolistic explanation of vertical integration. He termed it "the firm". His argument runs more or less as follows. Businessmen bring a part of the process of production within the firm, rather than arranging for it by contract with other producers, when the costs of coordinating the inputs of the firm by market transactions exceed the costs of coordinating them hierarchically. The hierarchy is itself a contractual one. But employment contracts that entitle the employers to direct the employee's work are different from contracts with outside suppliers who are independent contractors for outputs. The outputs are specified with regard to price, quality, quantity, date of delivery, and so on. Thus Coase did not like the monopoly explanations of the firm. He has praised Stigler's paper on the economics of information because it offers a nonmonopolistic explanation for a variety of business arrangements, such as advertising and department stores.

The second paper, "The Problem of Social Cost" (1960) formed the other half of the core of his work. This paper challenged the logic of prohibiting behaviour that damages others. Coase felt that it was much more important to focus on solutions that would benefit the most people rather than to focus on who is to blame. His work was a call to legal scholars to pay attention to the importance of an efficient market and to negotiate rather than litigation. Coase's theories on resolving disputes in the most cost effective manner greatly influenced a generation of both lawyers and economists and redirected thinking in critical areas of economic thought.

The Nobel Prize Committee also cited Coase for "Pioneering the study of how property rights are distributed among individuals by law, contract and regulations, showing that this determines, how economic decisions are made and whether they will succeed."

Coase's paper "The Problem of Social Cost" introduced the Coase Theorem (a term coined later, by Stigler). The Theorem states: If transaction costs are zero, the initial assignment of a property right-for example whether to the polluter or to the victim of pollution-will not affect the efficiency with which resources are allocated. The major significance of the theorem is that it has focused economists' attention on a neglected but very important aspect of the economic system, the costs of market transactions. We may restate the theorem as a hypothesis: If transacting costs are low, the law's assignment of rights and liabilities is unlikely to affect the allocation of resources much. The Coase theorem has guided important empirical research. The main point of both the articles of Coase is the importance of transaction costs in the operation of markets. And Coase emphasizes the need for studying contracts empirically because they are methods by which business firms can minimize, overcome or adjust to transaction costs.

In his Nobel lecture, Coase, remarked modestly that he has "made no innovations in high theory" but added quickly that he believed that the ideas in these articles, once they were absorbed into mainstream economic analysis, would bring about a complete change in the structure of economic theory, at least in what is called price theory or micro economics."

Coase has expressed his "dissatisfaction with what economists have been doing .... This dissatisfaction is not with the basic economic theory itself but with how it is used. The objection essentially is that the theory floats in the air. It is as if one studied the circulation of the blood without having a body."

Coase is a great admirer of Adam Smith. In an article on the "Wealth of Nations" he asks, "what have we been doing in the last 200 years. Our analysis has certainly become more sophisticated but we display no greater insight into the working of the economic system and, in some ways our approach is inferior to that of Adam Smith" (*Economic Inquiry*, July 1977, 15 P. 325).

In addition to his major articles on transaction costs, Coase has also written very fine articles on public utility pricing, monopolization of durable goods. He has done good work on the case studies of public institutions such as the British Post Office, the British Broadcasting Company, and the Federal Communications Commission. He has also published articles dealing with the methodology of economics.

Coase is opposed to public intervention because government is not omniscient. He insists that in evaluating the case for public intervention, one must compare real markets with real government, rather than real markets with ideal government assumed to work not only flawlessly but costlessly.

Coase is opposed to public intervention beyond what is defensible in strict wealth-maximization terms. Modem economists have used terms such as "externality", "public good", "social welfare function" and "market failure" that seem like invitation to state intervention. They think that the government is robust and the market is fragile. But Coase believes the other way. He believes in the roubustness of markets and the fragility of government.

Coase's article "The Problem of Social Cost" has had a great influence on American legal scholarship in the last twenty-five years. Many doctrines, procedures and institutions of law can be viewed as response to the problem of transaction costs. They are designed either to reduce those transaction costs or, if they are highly prohibitive, to bring about the allocation of resources that would exist if they were zero. The influence of this article is so great on legal scholarship, there are some who believe that Coase looms large in Law than in Economics.

The significance of the Coase theorem is that it is a "stepping stone on the way to an analysis of an economy with positive transaction costs". He feels that there is no need for fancy theoretical or empirical tools to conduct the study. Basic economic theory is enough. Even the concepts like maximization" and "equilibrium" may not be necessary.

Coase is regarded as a guru of "new institutional economics". Modern institutional economics studies man as he is, acting within the constraints imposed by real institutions. Coase has criticized the original institutionalists like John R. Commons for their hostility to classical economic theory, because "without a theory they had nothing to pass on except a mass of descriptive material waiting for a theory, or a fire". By "theory", Coase means Adam Smith's view of economics. Douglass North is another eminent modem institutional economist, who was jointly awarded the Nobel prize in Economics for the year 1993 along with Robert W. Fogel.

There are some economists who believe that Coase's influence in economics would have been more if he had spoken the language of modem economics which is mathematics in his articles. (Coase does not make use of geometry and mathematics. He uses instead arithmetic examples to explain his theories). To that, Coase's answer is, "In my youth, it was said that what was too silly to be said may be sung. In modem economics, it may be put into mathematics."

Coase does not like the effort of economists such as Stigler and Gary Becker to push economic theory into other disciplines such as law, sociology, biology, education, health, demography. As he put it humorously, "The reason for this movement of economists into neighbouring fields is certainly not that we have solved the problems of the economic system; it would perhaps be more plausible to argue that economists are looking for fields in which they can have some success."

Coase's view is not accepted by some economists because in the last 30 years, a good deal of work has been done in fields such as economics of education, the family, the political process, health and law which belong to the economics of non-market behaviour.

Coase agrees that economics is the most advanced social science but that is not because of any theoretical sophistication. It is because economics makes use of money as a convenient measuring rod. That measuring rod is more or less absent when economists move into disciplines that do not study explicit markets.

Richard A. Posner calls Coase "perhaps the finest English economist of the 20th century after Keynes."

GARY S. BECKER

The 1992 Nobel prize in Economics was awarded to professor Gary S. Becker of the University of Chicago. The Royal Swedish Academy of Sciences said that the work of Gary S. Backer had encouraged social scientists to apply economic theory to areas not previously associated with market forces: sociology, demography and criminology. As Becker himself put it: "What I try to do is to take economic-type thinking and apply it with social type problems."

Becker is an economist and sociologist by training. George Bernard Shaw said that "Economy is the art of making the most of life". Becker's philosophy is also the same.

In awarding the prize, the Royal Swedish Academy of Sciences said that Becker "has applied the principle of rational, optimizing behaviour to areas where researchers formerly assumed that behaviour is habitual and often downright irrational."

Becker's major works include "*The Economics of Discrimination*" (1957), "*Human Capital*" (1964) and "*A Treatise on the Family*" (1981).

The Economic Approach

Becker uses the economic approach to analyse social issues that range beyond those usually considered by economists. He extends the traditional theory of individual rational choice to analyze social choice by incorporating into the theory a much wider class of attitudes, preferences and calculations. Though Becker's approach to behaviour is based on the theory of individual choice, it is not mainly concerned with individuals. It uses theory at the micro level as a powerful tool to derive implications at the group or macro level.

Becker does not believe that individuals are motivated solely by selfishness or material gain. Human behaviour is based on a large number of values and preferences.

Becker's analysis assumes that individuals maximize welfare as they conceive it, whether they be selfish, altruistic or loyal. He further assumes that their behaviour is forward looking and it is also assumed to be consistent over time. Of course, Becker agrees that forward looking behaviour may still be rooted in the past, for the past can have influence on attitudes and values.

Our actions are constrained by income, time, imperfect memory and calculating capacities and other limited resources and also by the opportunities available in the economy and elsewhere. But the most fundamental constraint is the limited time. There are only 24 hours in a day. While the goods and services have increased enormously in rich countries, the total time available to consume them has not increased. So time allocation assumes importance in taking economic decisions.

We shall study briefly Becker's contribution to the economics of discrimination, economics of crime, human capital and the economics of the family.

In his Nobel lecture, Becker said that "To understand discrimination against minorities, it is necessary to widen preferences to accommodate prejudice and hatred of particular groups. The economic analysis of crime incorporates into rational behaviour illegal and other anti-social actions. The human capital perspective considers how the productivity of people in market and non-market situations is changed by investments in education, skills and knowledge. The economic approach to the family interprets marriage, divorce, fertility, and relations among family members through the lens of utility-maximizing, forward-looking behaviour".

Economics of Discrimination

As a young man, Becker began to worry about racial, religious and gender discrimination and he used the concept of discrimination coefficients to study the problem of prejudice, hostility and discrimination against minorities such as the Blacks and women. In fact, Becker's dissertation (1955) is about the economics of discrimination. It analyses how racial and ethnic discrimination affects labour markets. Employers, sometimes develop a taste for discrimination. For example, white employers may refuse to employ black workers. Even employees may refuse to work under a woman or a black even when they are well paid to do so. Becker argued that discrimination costs not only the victims but also those who practise discrimination. For instance, employers who refuse to employ black workers may have to pay higher wages to white workers.

In the words of Becker, "the economic theory of discrimination based on prejudice implies that actual discrimination by firms or workers is measured by how much profits or wages they forfeit to avoid hiring or working with members of a group that is disliked."

Becker's approach to discrimination is different from Arrow's statistical theory of discrimination. The latter theory is based on the beliefs of employers, teachers and other influential groups that minority members (e.g., blacks) are less productive. These beliefs may cause minorities to underinvest in education, training, and work skills, such as punctuality. The underinvestment does make them less productive.

Crime and Punishment

In the 1950s and 1960s, discussions of crime were dominated by the opinion that criminal behaviour was caused by mental illness and social oppression, and that criminals were helpless "victims". This opinion began to exert a major influence on social policy.

Becker, however, has assumed that criminal behaviour is rational. His theories on decision-making by criminals assume that most offenders are sane. His studies show that when criminals are deciding whether to commit a crime, the probability of getting caught weighs more heavily than the type of punishment they might face. Such an analysis would indicate that stronger law enforcement would be more effective than severe punishments.

In the early stages of his work, it was a puzzle to Becker why theft was considered socially harmful. It appeared to him that theft merely redistributed resources usually from wealthier to poorer individuals. He resolved the puzzle by pointing out that criminals spend on weapons and on the value of time in planning and carrying out their crimes. He thought that such spending is socially unproductive. Nowadays, it is called "rent seeking" because it does not create wealth, only forcibly redistributes it.

Becker's economic approach to crime has become influential because the same analytic apparatus can be used to study the enforcement of all laws, including minimum wage legislation, clean air Acts and income tax evasions. Becker observes that "The U.S. Sentencing Commission (1992) has explicitly used the economic analysis of crime to develop rules to be followed by judges in punishing violators of federal statutes".

Human Capital

Schultz (1963) emphasized that investments in human capital are a major contribution to economic growth. In 1964, Becker in his book "*Human Capital*" made the case as an economic decision. This, in turn, led to new theories regarding labour economics, and how capitalist economies determine wages and incomes.

Human capital analysis is based on the assumption that individuals decide on their education, training, medical care, other additions to knowledge and health by calculating the benefits and costs. Benefits include cultural and other nonmonetary gains along with improvement in earnings and occupations. And costs usually depend upon the foregone value of the time spent on these investments.

Nowadays, everyone speaks of human capital. But when the concept was introduced in the 1950s and 1960s, there was lot of opposition to the concept itself because, some economists argued that it treated people as machines. Even the approach to schooling as an investment rather than as a cultural experience was criticized. But gradually, economists have accepted the concept of human capital as a valuable tool in the analysis of various economic and social issues.

Becker's work on human capital began with an attempt to estimate both private and social rates of return to men, women, blacks and other groups from investments in different levels of education. Later on, he developed a more general theory of human capital that includes firms as well as individuals.

Economics of the Family

Becker's economic analysis of the family is based on maximizing behaviour, investments in human capital, the allocation of time and discrimination against women.

Becker wrote *A Treatise on the Family* in 1981. Though economists have dealt with the analysis of fertility, until recent years, issues such as marriage and divorce, and the relations between husbands, wives, parents and children had been largely neglected by economists. Becker's work on the family is based on the assumption that when men and women decide to marry, or have children or divorce, they attempt to raise their welfare by comparing benefits and costs. So they marry when they expect to be better off than if they remained single, and they divorce if that is expected to increase their welfare.

In the economics of the family, Becker saw the household as a productive unit (a firm) whose decisions could be analyzed in the same way as those of a business. According to Becker, economic incentives determine how much and what kind of work is undertaken by partners in a marriage as well as how many children they have. As one of the colleagues of Becker noted, "Economists have a tendency to steer away from the real world. Becker brings them back". Becker's analysis of the family has influenced family planning policy, employee training and welfare programmes. The theories of Becker in the field of family economics have today become the core of "The New Household Economics."

Becker is known today throughout the world for integrating economics with the other social sciences. Because of his influence, many economists want to work on social issues.

ROBERT W. FOGEL AND DOUGLASS C. NORTH

Two economic historians Robert W. Fogel and Douglass C. North of the United States have won the 1993 Nobel prize in Economics for using modern statistical methods to explain events and for questioning long held theories about growth and development.

Fogel is with the University of Chicago and North is with the Washington University in St. Louis. The Royal Swedish Academy of Sciences cited the two for providing a better understanding of why economic change occurs. The Swedish Academy described Fogel and North as leading figures within the field of "new economic history" whose works challenged widely held ideas.

Since the Nobel prize in Economics was established in 1968, Americans have won 21 out of the 34 prizes. Fogel is the seventh winner from the University of Chicago. Lindbeck, chairman of the

Nobel Prize Selection Committee said that the string of American winners illustrated that the United States was leading Europe in economic research, both history and analysis.

The Royal Swedish Academy said that modern economic historians contribute to the development of economic sciences in at least two ways: "by combining theory with quantitative methods and by constructing and reconstructing databases or creating new ones. This has made it possible to question and reassess earlier results, which has not only increased our knowledge of the past but has also contributed to the elimination of irrelevant theories."

The Nobel Prize Selection Committee cited a book written by Fogel in 1964 which argued that U.S. economic development was the result of many factors and did not depend solely on the building of the railroads, as others had claimed. The committee also referred to a controversial 1974 book by Fogel that argued that pre-civil war slavery in the United States, despite its inhumanity, was economically efficient. It may be noted that Fogel was not defending slavery as an institution. He was of the view that the collapse of slavery was due more to political decisions rather than economic weaknesses.

Much of Fogel's research has focused on the retrieval of data that clarified the relationship between the current and past behaviour of households.

According to "who is who in Economics" Fogel has constructed data sets upto ten generations "to analyse the interaction of economic and cultural factors on such variables as the savings rate, the female participation rate, fertility and mortality rates, economic and social mobility and migration rates".

The Royal Swedish Academy of Sciences called Douglass North "an inspirer, a producer of ideas who identifies, new problems and shows how economists can solve the old ones more effectively".

North in a paper for the American Historical Review wrote in 1991, "Understanding how an economy works (price or micro economic theory) is a necessary condition to writing economic history, but economic theory is static in its implications, and the key to good economic history in explaining change-over time—something missing in economic theory. It is precisely that missing ingredient that should be the contribution that economic history could make to improving economic theory. Economic theory has become more and more mathematical, formal and precise about less and less".

North has developed a model of growth in the American economy during the period 1790 to 1860. The Swedish Academy cited that his analysis of one sector—cotton plantations that stimulated development in other sections and led to specialization and interregional trade.

In an article for the Journal of Economic Perspectives in 1991, North wrote: "Institutions provide the incentive structure of an economy; as that structure evolves, it shapes the direction of economic change towards growth, stagnation, or decline".

The Swedish Academy said that North maintains that new institutions arise when groups in society see a possibility of availing themselves of profits that are impossible to realize under prevailing institutional conditions".

The Swedish Academy further said that North in his book published in 1990 examines why some countries are rich and others poor and concludes that "the lack of opportunity of entering binding contracts and other institutional arrangements is a cause of economic stagnation, both in today's developing countries and the former socialistic states".

While explaining his work, North cited the experiences of some countries such as Czechoslovakia. He said "we try to explain how institutional structures work". "The political system ultimately shapes the economic institutions. For instance, we have helped in Czechoslovakia where they have attempted to shift ownership from public hands to private hands through a voucher system". He further said, "My theory says that if economics work well and perform well, it is because you have a set of institutions that provide incentive for people to be productive".

Professor Lindbeck, the chairman of the prize committee said "that the Soviet-block countries fell apart because they did not have institutions that functioned".

JOHN C. HARSANYI, JOHN F. NASH AND REINHARD SELTEN

The Nobel Prize in Economics for the year 1994 was awarded to John C. Harsanyi, a retired professor from the University of California at Berkely, John F. Nash, a mathematician at Princeton University and Reinhard Selten of the University of Bonn for their groundbreaking work in integrating "game theory" into the study of economic behaviour. All the three have helped discover that economic performance has as much to do with moves and countermoves by business rivals as with traditional notions of supply and demand.

They refined the foundations of the game theory- discovered 70 years ago - to be able to make predictions by devising strategies based,on unknown factors.

Game theory emanates from studies of games such as chess or poker. Everyone knows that in these games, players have to think ahead and devise a strategy based on expected countermoves from the other player. Such strategic interaction also characterizes many economic situations, and game theory has therefore proved to be very useful in economic analysis.

The researchers focused on a fonnula in which players in games—or executives in corporations—received information about each other's position to form strategies. Their research has been used in everything from the study of environment to analysis of foreign trade and information.

Classical economic theory is based on the assumption of perfect competition among hundreds of buyers and sellers, with no party strong enough to challenge the "invisible hand" in setting prices. But, in modem times, oligopoly is the dominant form of market where a handful of players engage in a constant game to outwit one another with new products, marketing schemes and pricing strategies in ways that affect prices and economic performance.

Nash, Harsanyi and Selten gave economists some of the theoretical foundations and mathematical tools to incorporate such observations and intuitions into economic models.

In his doctoral thesis, in mathematics at Princeton in 1955, Nash showed that in economic interactions between any number of parties, the process of move and countermove often led to a stalemate. He called it an equilibrium, a point at which each player cannot improve his or her position by changing strategy because it would only be met by offsetting countermoves. This has come to be known as "Nash equilibrium".

The Royal Swedish Academy of Sciences said that "Nash equilibrium has become a standard tool in almost all areas of economic theory in order to improve our understanding of complex strategic interaction".

Harsanyi was lauded by the Academy both for showing how games of incomplete information can be analyzed and for "significant contributions to the foundations of welfare economics".

Selten co-authored a book with Harsanyi on equilibrium selection in games and he was the first to refine the Nash equilibrium concept and apply it to analysis of competition with only a few sellers. Harsanyi and Selten by expanding on Nash's work, have made it more applicable to real-life situations. They hybridized game theory to take account of the less-than-perfect knowledge of participants in many everyday transactions, and they found ways to begin exploring the complexities of multiple-move games.

The Swedish Academy said that the theory of equilibrium analysis–the theory that enables people to make skilled predictions–had become widely accepted in economic analysis and is even used when financial markets are seeking to determine how a central bank will behave. Thus, "Nash equilibrium" has become a standard tool in almost all areas of economic theory", the Academy said. Though Von Neumann and Oskar Morgenstern adapted game theory for economics in 1939, Nash, Selten and Harsanyi added invaluable refinements so that game theory could be applied to almost any strategic decision.

ROBERT E. LUCAS JR.

Robert E. Lucas Jr. of Chicago University, whose work challenged many assumptions of Keynesian economists won the Nobel Prize in Economics for the year 1995.

Lucas received the Nobel Prize for his groundbreaking work on "rational expectations". He was awarded the prize for "having developed and applied the hypothesis of rational expectations and, thereby, having transformed macroeconomic analysis and deepened our understanding of economic policy".

The Royal Academy said that "Mr. Lucas' work had become part of high-level decision making". The great thing about. Lucas is that his theories have really meant a lot for economic policy as well as for economic theory. His work has to do with peoples' expectations, and expectations are what people get from information.

Lucas has shown how important the rational expectations idea is. Government's models of the economy are, of necessity, based on the past behaviour of consumers and firms. Lucas said that unless they incorporate rational expectations, they are useless for assessing changes in economic policy. That is because economic behaviour in the past will have depended on the economic policies of the time. When governments change their policies, expectations will change too; so the economy's response to a new policy may be different from what governments expect.

The rational expectations hypothesis, thus, tells that the economy is influenced not only by actual events and past performance, but also by expectations of future events. Lucas contends that shifts in economic policy may produce a completely different result if people adapt their behaviour to the expected policy.

The bulk of Lucas' work came in the 1970s when he wrote the "Lucas Critique". It took aim at Keynesain economic policy that used economic models of past economic behaviour to predict what the economy will do in the future.

Under Keynesian thinking, prevalent through the 1960s, government was expected to increase spending when the economy was slowing and to boost taxes when the economy began to overheat. But in 70s, that is, about 40 years ago, Lucas shattered the widely held belief that government could fine-tune the performance of the economy.

The Royal Swedish Academy of Sciences, in its citation said that he was "the economist who has had the greatest influence on "macroeconomic research since 1970". Lucas is an economist's economist. While others have gained fame and influence by translating their economic insights into policy prescriptions, Lucas has focused on theoretical issues.

In its citation, the Royal Swedish Academy said that Lucas "had made the most important contribution to the field of macroeconomics since the 1970s, when he pioneered what is now called the "rational expectations" school.

During the post-war period, economists were mainly interested in constructing precise mathematical models of components of the economy which interact with one another. On the basis of their elaborate models, these economists offered government officials the ability to predict how changes in interest rates or spending or tax policy would affect things like inflation and high unemployment.

Until the mid-1960s, it worked like a charm. When the economy showed signs of slowing, a tax increase or interest rate cut seemed to get it back on track, just as the great British economist John Maynard Keynes had predicted. The government's job was to fine-tune the line between too much growth, as measured by inflation, and too little, as measured by unemployment rates.

But within a decade, the policies suddenly were not working so well and the American economy was affected by "stagflation", a phenomenon where there was stagnation on one hand and inflation on the other at the same time. In other words, there was the unholy combination of high inflation and high unemployment. During the period, workers acted to protect the value of their income by demanding higher wages when the U. S. Central Bank lowered interest rates and boosted the money supply.

Lucas contends that if consumers and investors anticipated government actions, it makes it nearly impossible for a government to systematically manipulate the economy. Therefore, Lucas says, the past is a poor predictor of the future.

In the early 1970s, Lucas said that the Keynesian view failed to consider the economic actors-business owners, investors and consumers - would soon learn to anticipate the government's actions and build those rational expectations into their own behaviour. These individual decisions would collectively magnify the impact of government policies or nullify them even before they were implemented.

In the words of the Royal Academy, "rational expectations have become a standard part of the economic tool box". Many forecasting models now include at least some element of rational expectations.

The rational expectations approach holds that the economy will eventually sort itself out and the government is largely powerless to improve it. This conclusion has found favour with conservatives that have long argued for less government intervention in the market place. In Lucas's own words, "the practical implication of my work has been, along with others, to make us a lot more sceptical about our ability to use monetary policy to fine-tune the economy".

Critics of the rational expectations approach argue that it offers no alternative in providing policy advice. As a result, there remains a conviction that while the government cannot directly manage the economy, policies can have modest, short-term impact in smoothing out the business cycle. In fact, after the Nobel award was announced, Lucas himself conceded that "the Keynesian orthodox hasn't been replaced by anything yet".

JAMES A. MIRRLEES AND WILLIAM VICKREY

James A. Mirrlees of Cambridge University in Britain and William Vickrey, Professor emeritus at Columbia University won the 1996 Nobel Prize in Economics for their fundamental contribution to the economic theory of incentives in an area of microeconomics dealing with situations where decision makers have different information. They were awarded the prize for their work in "asymmetric information" which assumes that in every business transaction, buyers and sellers don't have the same information. They have studied separately how people and institutions make choices when they do not share the same information. Their work in "asymmetric information" has helped in the design of more efficient auctions and tax systems.

Their work focused on situations in which one party has the advantage of more information than the other. For example, a seller knows more about the problems with a used car than the buyer.

The Royal Academy said that their work has generated better understanding of insurance markets, credit market, auctions, the internal organization of firms, wages forms, tax systems, social insurance, competitive conditions and political institutions.

Prior to Vickrey's work, most of the economic theory assumed that economic "agents" whether individuals, firms or governments, had the same information. If they nevertheless behaved differently, it was put down as difference in "preferences". We all know that not everyone shares the same information, but that fact had not been incorporated into theoretical models of how the economy works.

The Royal Academy said in its citation that an essential part of William Vickrey's research was concerned with the nature of "different kinds of auctions, and how they can best be designed so as to generate economic efficiency".

Vickrey's auction theory has shaped the behaviour of the government in the area of auctions. The U.S. Treasury sells its two - and five - year notes every month using what some call a "Vickrey auction" because the structure is based on his work in the 1960s. In Vickrey auction, would be buyers still make a single sealed bid and the highest bidder still wins. But there is a twist. The winner only pays the second highest bid. Each bidder thus knows in advance that he will not have to pay as much as he bid.

In the sale based on Vickrey auction, all successful bidders are guaranteed that they will pay the same price - or in the case of the Treasury notes, get the same rate of return on their investment. Knowing that will be the case, bidders are less worried about what is known as "winner's curse" of bidding more than is really necessary to win. With less fear of bidding too much, winners are actually apt to bid more than they otherwise might. This means a lower cost to the Treasury for financing the public debt. But should a person fail to bid the most he is willing to pay, he faces a greater prospect of losing to a bid that is far below what he views as the item's true value.

Vickrey is probably best known for his research in "congestion pricing". Many public services like roads, public transit and energy utilities, require enormous initial investments. Charging the same fee to every user to recover these costs can head to heavy congestion in period of peak demand (e.g., think of the subway at the rush hour and the sparse use the rest of the time). In the 1960s, Vickrey devised the pricing structure for smoothing the peaks and troughs by linking prices to demand.

Time-of-day pricing is now widely used by electric utilities to limit their need to build expensive new generating capacity. Singapore has long employed roadway user fees to thin traffic during business hours and increase the capacity of the road system by charging fees reflecting the cost of the congestion that vehicles actually create.

Mirrlees, who has taught in Africa, Pakistan and the U.S. devised an income-tax system that was intended to provide the maximum amount of revenue. And to the surprise of this former adviser to Britain's Labour Party, his own theory led to the conclusion that a progressive tax is not necessarily the best. We may also add that Mirrlees provided the first mathematically rigorous treatment of efficiency and equity that is central to modem economic policy debate.

Mirrlees's work on the optimal income tax was a starting point for a vast-amount of research. His work was used by Bengt Holmstrom of M.I.T. in his widely cited analysis of "moral hazard". The problem of moral hazard arises in many practical situations, such as generous insurance coverage that might encourage a policy holder to take extra risks or not to do as much as he could to prevent a loss.

ROBERT C. MERTON AND MYRON S. SCHOLES

The Nobel Prize in Economics for the year 1997 was awarded to two American economists Robert C. Merton and Myron S. Scholes for developing "a pioneering formula for the valuation of stock options", which laid the foundation for the rapid growth of markets for stock options and other so-called "derivates" during the past decade. "A new method to determine the value of derivatives stands out among the foremost contributions to economic science over the last 25 years", the Academy said.

Stock options and derivatives are financial instruments, tied to stocks, that allow investors to purchase or sell a fixed number of shares at a specified future date at a predetermined price. In other words, the value of derivatives was linked to fluctuations in the price of other assets such as bonds, stocks currencies and commodities.

In purchasing derivatives, investors are not buying a stock but a financial instrument to a stock. For instance, purchasing a so-called call option gives the purchaser the right to purchase a stock at a certain price. Derivatives are used by investors to insulate themselves from losses because of sudden market shifts.

The uncertain value of these instruments makes them particularly risky to investors. But the formula developed by the economists allows thousands of traders each day to place a value on options based on such factors as interest rates, changes in stock price, and the probability that the auctions will be exercised.

The two economists developed their method for assessing value in collaboration with Fischer Black, a mathematician who died in 1965. Nobel Prizes are not awarded posthumously. Otherwise, he too would have shared the prize along with Merton and Scholes.

The Academy said that "their methodology has paved the way for economic valuations in many areas. It has also generated new types of financial instruments and facilitated more efficient risk management in society".

According to the Royal Swedish Academy of Sciences, the idea was born in 1973 when Black and Scholes published what has come to be known as the "Black-Scholes formula" to make valuations of options.

According to the formula, the value of the call option is given by the difference between the expected share value and the expected cost, if the option right is exercised at maturity.

Dr. Merton later generalized the formula and "devised another method to derive the formula that turned out to have very wide applicability".

Other Research Contributions

In addition to their valuation method, Merton and Scholes have made many significant contributions to financial economics. Merton has developed a new and powerful method for analysing consumption and investment decisions over time, and generalized the so-called CAPM from a static to a dynamic setting. We may note that William Sharpe was awarded the Prize in 1990 for developing the so-called CAPM valuation mode. Scholes has clarified the impact of dividends on stock market values together with Black and Miller. Merton Miller was awarded the Prize in 1990 for his contributions to corporate finance. Scholes also made empirical contributions. For example, he made a significant contribution concerning estimation of the so-called beta value (a risk measure in the CAPM).

AMARTYA SEN

The Nobel Prize in Economics for the year 1998 was awarded to Professor Amartya Sen, an Indian citizen, for his contributions to welfare economics.

Sen was born at Santiniketan (West Bengal) in 1933. He graduated from Presidency College (Calcutta) in 1953. And he became Professor of Economics at a young age of 23 at Jadavpur University. He became Fellow at Trinity college (England) during 1957-63. He was Professor at Delhi School of Economics during 1963-71. Later on, he became Professor at many prestigious institutions in England and America. When he was awarded the Nobel Prize, he was master of Trinity college.

Sen's important works include *Collective Choice and Social Welfare* (1970), *On Economic Inequality* (1973), *Poverty and Famines : An Essay on Entitlement and Deprivation* (1981), *India : Economic Development and Social Opportunity* (1995). The last book, he co-authored with Jean Dreze, a Belgian economist:

The award of Nobel Prize to Amartya Sen was a matter of joy not only in India but all over the world. Kenneth Arrow, who won the Nobel Prize for Economics in 1972 said "I have learnt much from him (Sen)." Robert Solow, another Nobel laureate in Economics described Sen as " the conscience of economics."

Amartya Sen has made many key contributions to research on fundamental problems in welfare economics. His contributions range from "the axiomatic theory of social choice, over definitions of welfare and poverty indexes, to empirical studies of famine." Sen has tied together these concepts and theories to study the distributional issues, especially the problems relating to most impoverished members of the society. In other words, Sen is interested in the problems of the poor. In empirical studies, Sen's application of theoretical approach has helped us gain insight into the economic mechanisms underlying famines.

Individual Values and Collective Decisions

Some of the important questions in the field of the social welfare in a democracy are: Can the values which the individual member of society attach to different alternatives be aggregated into values for society as a whole, in a way that it is both fair and theoretically sound? Can we use the majority principle as a workable decision rule?

When there is general agreement, the choices made by society are uncontroversial. When options differ, the problem is to find methods for bringing together different opinions in decisions which concern everyone. The theory of social choice is concerned mainly with the link between individual values and collective choice.

The fundamental questions are whether and if so, in what way, preferences for society as a whole can be consistently derived from the preferences of its members.

In the early 1950s, Professor Kenneth Arrow, on the basis of certain assumptions, arrived at the conclusion that by applying the majority rule, we cannot aggregate individual preferences (values, votes) that would promote social welfare. This is, roughly, the so-called *impossibility theorem*. Sen's book Collective Choice and Social Welfare pointed out that even in a democracy, by applying majority rule, and by relaxing some assumptions which Arrow made, we can promote social welfare. Sen firmly believed in individual rights. According to him, a prerequisite for collective decision-making rule is that it should be non-dictatorial.

Indexes of Welfare and Poverty

We need some kind of indexes to measure differences in welfare or income of people living within a country or in different countries. The construction of such indexes is an important application in the theory of social choice . Inequality indexes are closely linked to welfare functions. Sen has made valuable contributions by defining poverty indexes and other welfare indicators.

Poverty indexes

A common measure of poverty in a society is the share of population below a tolerable standard of living. But the poverty line ignored the degree of poverty among the poor. Sen developed a new index, to measure the inequality of people below the poverty line: Sen's Index, is now a standard tool for calculating the Human Development Index (HDI).

Welfare Indicators

According to Sen, what creates welfare is not goods as such, but the activity for which they are acquired. He believes that income is significant because of the opportunities it creates. But the actual opportunities (Sen calls them capabilities) also depend upon a number of factors such as basic education and health. These factors also should be taken into account while measuring welfare. We may note that United Nations Human Development Index is constructed in this spirit.

Welfare of the Poorest

Sen, in his very first article, analysed the choice of techniques to be followed in production in developing countries. His works deal mostly with development economics, as they are often devoted to the poorest people in the society.

Analysis of Famines

Sen analyses famines in his well-known work *Poverty and Famines: An Essay on Entitlement and Deprivation* (1981). In that book, Sen challenges the common view that a shortage of food is the most important (sometimes the only) explanation of famine. On the basis of a careful study of famines in India, Bangladesh and Saharan countries from 1940s onwards, he found that other factors were responsible for famines. In the Bengal famine (1943) nearly five million people died. Shortage of food alone cannot explain famines. For example, famines have occurred even when the supply of food was not significantly lower than during previous years (without famines). And, sometimes areas affected by famines have exported food.

To understand famines, we must make a thorough analysis of how various social and economic factors influence different groups in society and determine their actual opportunities. For example, he has explained the Bangladesh famine of 1974 this way : the flooding throughout the country that year significantly raised food prices and work opportunities for workers declined drastically as one of the crops could not be harvested. Because of these reasons, the real incomes of agricultural workers declined so much that they were badly hit by the famine.

ROBERT A. MUNDELL

Robert Mundell was awarded the 1999 Nobel Prize in Economics for the work he did nearly six decades back, that was in 1960s at the University of Chicago. Mundell worked for a short while at the Research Department of the I.M.F. during 1961-63.

Mundell's work on monetary dynamics and optimum currency areas remain outstanding and constitute the core of teaching in international macroeconomics.

What is great about Mundell's analysis is that he made accurate prediction about the future development of international monetary arrangements and capital markets.

Robert Mundell has reshaped the macroeconomic theory by posing and answering questions such as

- How are the effects of monetary and fiscal policy related to the integration of international capital markets?
- How do these effects depend on whether a country fixes the value of its currency or allows it to float freely?
- Should a country even have a currency of its own?

Mundell's scientific contributions are original and they have transformed the research in international macroeconomics and attracted increasing attention in the application oriented discussion on stabilization policy and exchange rate system.

Effects of Stabilization Policy

In many papers published in 1960s, Robert Mundell developed his analysis of monetary and fiscal policy, so-called stabilization policy in open economies. As Marcus Fleming of I.M.F. (who died in 1976) presented similar research on stabilization policy in open economies, at approximately the same time as Mundell, the model is sometimes referred to as Mundell-Fleming model.

In a pioneering article in 1963, Mundell dealt with the short-run effects of monetary and fiscal policy in an open economy. Through a simple analysis, he has arrived at clear and robust conclusions. He has introduced foreign trade and capital movements into the IS-LM model of a closed economy, which was initially developed by Hicks. This allowed him to show that the effects of stabilization policy hinge on the degree of international capital mobility. In particular, he demonstrated the far reaching importance of exchange rates: *Under a floating exchange rate, monetary policy becomes powerful and fiscal policy powerless, whereas the opposite is true under a fixed exchange rate.*

Under floating exchange rates, monetary policy becomes a powerful tool for influencing economic activity. Expansion of the money supply tends to promote lower interest rates, resulting in capital outflows and a weaker exchange rate, which in turn expand the economy through increased net exports.

Floating exchange rates and high capital mobility accurately describe the present monetary regime in many countries. But in the early 1960s, an analysis of their consequences must have seemed like an academic curiosity. Almost all countries were linked together by fixed exchange rates within the so-called Brettenwoods system. International capital movements were highly curtailed, in particular, by capital and exchange rate controls. However, during 1950s, Mundell's own country, Canada had allowed its currency to float against the US dollar and had begun to ease restrictions. His far-sighted analysis became increasingly relevant over the next ten years, as the international capital markets opened up and Brettenwoods system broke down.

A Critique of original Mundell-Fleming Model

The original Mundell-Fleming model had certain limitations. For instance, as in all macroeconomic analysis at the time, it makes highly simplified assumptions about expectations in financial markets and assumes price rigidity in the short-run. These shortcomings have been remedied by later researchers, who have shown that gradual price adjustment and rational expectations can be incorporated into the analysis without significantly changing the results.

Monetary Dynamics

Mundell's research did not stop at short-run analysis. Monetary dynamics is the key theme in many of his articles. He emphasized differences in the speed of adjustment on goods and assets markets (called the principle of effective market classification). These differences can explain how the exchange rate can temporarily 'oversoot' in the wake of certain disturbances. Mundell formulated dynamic models to describe how prolonged imbalances in the balance of payments could arise and be eliminated. This approach is known as monetary approach to the balance of payments. For a long time, it was regarded as a kind of benchmark for analyzing stabilization policy in open economies. And insights from this analysis have been often applied in practical economic policy making - particularly by IMF economists.

Mundell has also made another important contribution to stabilization policy. In the past, the stabilization policy had not only been static, it had also assumed that all economic policy in a country is coordinated in a single hand. By contrast, Mundell used a simple dynamic model to examine how each of the two instruments, monetary and fiscal policy, should be directed towards either of two objects, external and internal balance, in order to bring the economy closer to these objectives over time. This implies that each of the two authorities – the Government and the Central Bank – is given responsibility for its own stabilization policy instrument. And he has arrived at a straightforward conclusion: To prevent the economy from becoming unstable, the linkage has to accord with the relative efficiency of the instruments.

In this model, monetary policy is linked to external balance and fiscal policy to internal balance (Internal balance refers to domestic full employment with price stability. External balance refers to equilibrium in the balance of payments).

We may note that Mundell's primary concern was not decentralization itself. But by explaining the conditions for decentralization, he has anticipated the idea that the central bank should be given independent responsibility for price stability.

The short-run and the long-run analysis carried out by Mundell arrive at the same fundamental conclusion regarding the conditions for monetary policy. With (*i*) free capital mobility, monetary policy can be oriented towards either, (*ii*) an external objective – such as the exchange rate – or, (*iii*) an internal (domestic) objective – such as the price level – but not both at the same time.

When fixed exchange rates predominated in the 1960s, almost everyone thought that a national currency was must. But Mundell posed a seemingly radical question in his article on Optimum Currency Areas (1961):

When is it advantageous for a number of regions to relinquish their monetary sovereignty in favour of a common currency?

It is true that the pioneering work in the area was done by Meade and Scitovysky in 1957-58. According to Meade, a common currency area offered the best long-term solution for the balance of payments problems of countries. Meade studied the problems of common currency area with reference to the European Economic Community (EEC). In 1969, the EEC decided to create a common currency area - in the form of a Monetary Union - by 1980. However, the first theoretical contribution to the theory of Optimum Currency Area was made by Mundell in 1961.

Changes in technology, market structure, and politics will confront policy makers with a choice between floating exchange rates and monetary unification.

The literature on optimum currency areas points to economic characteristics that shape countries' choices between managed floating and monetary union. Small, open, specialized economies are most likely to opt for monetary union. The same will be true of countries with flexible labour markets and institutional means of relaxing fiscal constraints.

Countries immune to inflationary pressures but vulnerable to asymmetric macroeconomic disturbances, in contrast, may prefer to float.

We may also note that the choice between floating and monetary union is not based on economic considerations alone. Political rather than economic factors, in fact, often seem to dictate the decision. That is, political objectives that can be attained through the maintenance of a separate currency or by the establishment of a monetarty union may dominate any strictly economic calculus of costs and benefits.

The literature on optimum currency area suggests that regions within which fiscal federalism is well developed are ideal candidates for monetary union. But political rather than economic factors may pose the principal obstacle to the development of such arrangements.

The government's power to tax and spend (in addition to the power to issue currency) is the essence of sovereignty. Governments, therefore, are reluctant to compromise their fiscal prerogatives.

In conclusion, we may say that the countries' choice between managed floating and monetary unification will be guided by economic as well as political factors. The implication is that international monetary options in the present century will be shaped as much by political as by economic factors.

The Euro

The *Euro* is the European common currency since January 1, 1999. Long back, Mundell posed a question, "Should a country even have a currency of its own?" The Euro tells that it is not necessary. Eleven out of fifteen European countries have adopted *Euro* as their future national currency. In 2002, the *Euro* started replacing local currencies in the Euro-zone area and Euro bank notes and coins were put into circulation. The main international trading currencies in the Euro-zone region are the German deutsche mark and French franc. When the Euro was launched, its exchange rate was fixed at $1.17 to Euro.

JAMES J. HECKMAN AND DANIEL L. McFADDEN

The Nobel prize in Economics for the year 2000 was awarded to two American economists James J. Heckman and Daniel L. McFadden. It was awarded to James Heckman for his development of theory and methods for analyzing selective samples and to Daniel McFadden for his development of theory and methods for analyzing discrete choice.

In the field of microeconometrics, each of them has developed theory and methods that are widely used in the statistical analysis of individual and household behaviour, within economics as well as other social sciences.

Microeconometrics is an interface between economics and statistics. It encompasses economic theory and statistical methods used to analyse micro data – economic information about individuals, households and firms.

Greater availability of microdata and increasingly powerful computers have opened up entirely new possibilities of empirically testing microeconomic theory. Researchers have been able to examine many new issues at the individual level. For instance, what factors determine whether an individual decides to work and, if so, how many hours? How do economic incentives affect individual choices regarding education, occupation or place of residence? What are the effects of different labour-markets and educational programmes on individual's income and employment?

The use of microdata has also given rise to new statistical problems, owing primarily to the limitations inherent in such (non-experimental) data. As the researcher can only observe certain variables for particular individuals or households, a sample might not be random and thereby not representative. Even when samples are representative, some characteristics which affect the behaviour of individuals remain unobservable, which makes it difficult, or impossible, to explain some of the variations among individuals.

Dr. James Heckman and Dr. Daniel McFadden have each shown how one can resolve some fundamental statistical problems associated with the analysis of microdata. Their methodological contributions share a solid foundation in economic theory. They emerged in close interaction with applied empirical studies. The microeconometric methods developed by them are now a part of the standard tool kit, not only of economists, but also of other social scientists.

Heckman's Contributions

Heckman has made many significant contributions to microeconometric theory and methodology, with different kinds of selection problems as a common denomination. His publications include (*i*) *Longitudinal Analysis of Labour Market Data*, (*ii*) *Performance Standards in a Government Bureaucracy* (edited collection) and (*iii*) *Lecture Notes on Longitudinal Data Analysis* (with W. Singer, and G. Tsiang).

Heckman developed his methodological contributions in conjunction with applied empirical research, particularly in labour economics. His analysis of selection problems in microeconometric research has had profound implications for applied research in economics as well as in other social sciences.

Selection Bias and Self-Selection

There are a number of selection problems in microeconometric studies. They can arise when a sample available to researchers does not randomly represent the underlying population. Selective samples may be the results of rules governing collection of data or the outcome of economic agents' own behaviour. The latter situation is known as *self-selection*. For example, wages and working hours can only be observed in the case of individuals who have chosen to work and the earnings of university graduates can only be observed for those who have completed their University education. The absence of information regarding the wage an individual would earn, had he or she chosen otherwise, creates problems in many empirical studies.

Dr. Heckman's methodological breakthrough regarding self-selection took place in the mid 1970s and is closely related to his studies of individuals' decision about their labour force participation and hours worked. As we observe variations in hours of work solely among those who have chosen to work, we could again encounter samples tainted by self-selection. In an article on the labour supply of married women, published in 1974, he devised an econometric method to handle such self-selection problems. This study is an excellent illustration of how microeconomic theory can be combined with microeconometric methods to clarify an important research topic. Dr. Heckman's achievements have generated a large number of empirical applications in economics as well as in other social sciences.

Dr. Heckman is the world's leading researcher on microeconometric evaluation of labour-market programmes. He has proposed tools for solving closely related problems with individual differences unobserved by the researcher; such problems are common, for example, when evaluating social programs or estimating how the duration of unemployment affects chances of getting a job. In collaboration with many colleagues, he has extensively analysed the many properties of alternative non-experimental evaluation methods and has explored their relation to experiment methods.

McFadden's Contributions

Dr. McFadden's most significant contribution is his development of the economic theory and econometric methodology for analysis of *discrete choice*, that is, choice among a definite set of decision alternatives. In economic theory, traditional analysis presupposes that individual choice be represented by a continuous variable, thereby rendering it inappropriate for studying discrete choice behaviour. Prior to Dr. McFadden's contributions, empirical studies of such choices lacked a foundation in economic theory. Evolving from a new theory of discrete choice, the statistical methods developed by Dr. McFadden have transformed empirical research. His theory of discrete choice emanates from microeconomic theory, according to which each individual chooses a specific alternative that maximises his utility. However, as the researcher cannot observe all the factors affecting individual choices, he perceives a random variation across individuals with the same observed characteristics. Dr. McFadden developed microeconometric models that can be used, for example, to predict the share of a population that will choose different alternatives. His seminal contribution is his development of so-called conditional logit analysis in 1974. Even though logit models had been around for sometime, McFadden's derivation of the model was entirely new, and was immediately recognized as a fundamental breakthrough.

Dr. McFadden's methods are readily applicable. His models are highly useful and are applied in studies of urban travel demand. They can thus be used in traffic planning to examine the effects of policy measures as well as other social and/or environmental changes. For example, these models can explain how changes in price, improved accessibility or shifts in the demographic composition of the population affect the shares of travel using alternative means of transportation. The models are also useful in other areas, such as in studies of the choice of dwelling, place of residence and education. McFadden has applied his own methods to analyse a number of social issues, such as the demand for residential energy, telephone services and housing for the elderly. In his own words, "what I did in working with that theory was to develop models to figure out a way to study what one might call 'life's big choice'. Like the choice of occupation, when to get married, and how many children to have".

GEORGE A. AKERLOF, A. MICHAEL SPENCE AND JOSEPH E. STIGLITZ

The Nobel Prize in Economics for 2001 was jointly awarded to George A. Akerlof, A. Michael Spence and Joseph E. Stiglitz (all from the U.S.) "for their analyses of markets with asymmetric information".

Many markets are characterised by asymmetric information: actors on one side of the market have much better information than those on the other. Borrowers know more than lenders about their repayment prospects, managers and boards know more than shareholders about the firm's profitability, and prospective clients know more than insurance companies about their accident risk. During the 1970s, these Nobel Laureates laid the foundation for a general theory of markets with asymmetric information. Applications have been abundant ranging from traditional agricultural markets to modern financial markets. The laureates' contributions form the core of modern information economics.

The economics of information has developed in parallel with the new economics of Industrial Organization.

When the information is asymmetrically distributed among agents, these decisions involve the designing of contracts intended to provide incentives and/or to induce the revelation of private information.

We say asymmetric information exists in a contract when one participant knows something that another doesn't. The important themes relating to asymmetric information are moral hazard, adverse selection and signalling. The models in which the themes are studied can be used to explain a large number of economic situations in the areas of finance, insurance, technology transfer, firm regulation and public subsidies. The problems that arise in this context may be described as the problems of constrained maximisation and solutions are found by making use of the theory of maximisation.

Different types of models appear when there is asymmetric information. We have a moral hazard problem when the informational asymmetry arises after the contract has been signed. There is an adverse selection problem when the agent has relevant private information before the contract is signed. Finally, a signalling situation occurs when the informed party is able to reveal private information via individual behaviour before the agreement is formalised.

We are interested in the theory of contracts under asymmetric information. This theory analyses the characteristics of optimal contracts and the variables that influence these characteristics, according to the behaviour and information of the parties to the contract. This will allow us to tackle questions such as: Should the employees of an office be paid a fixed amount, or should they receive some part of the profits of the firm? Or why does an insurance company offer several types of policy, one of which has an excess voluntary clause? Or what is the sense of a situations vacant advertisement in which the only relevant characteristic is being a graduate, without any reference to a specific subject? Our Objective must be to identify the characteristics of the relationship especially those relevant to the distribution of information that may be important in answering these questions.

Contributions of George Akerlof, Michael Spence and Joseph Stiglitz.

GEORGE AKERLOF

George Akerlof is generally regarded as the founder of the field of economics of asymmetric information. The Swedish Academy has rightly described Akerlof's 1970 essay "The Market for "Lemons" : Quality Uncertainty and Market Mechanism" as "the single most important study in the economics of information. In it, he has offered the revolutionary idea that when one side of the market has better information than the other, some markets may entirely fail to emerge.

Akerlof's paper relates quality and uncertainty. The paper attempts to give structure to the statement : "Business in underdeveloped countries is difficult". In particular, a structure is given for determining the economic costs of dishonesty.

To illustrate and develop his thought, Akerlof has made use of the example of used cars in the automobile market. Among the used cars, there may be good cars and bad cars (Bad cars are known as "lemons" in America). The owner of the car, that is the seller, has more information about the car than the buyer. So an asymmetry in available information has developed. But good cars and bad cars must still sell at the same price- since it is impossible for the buyer to tell the difference between a good car and a bad car. So Akerlof tells that "Gresham's law has made a modified appearance. For most cars traded will be "lemons" and good cars may not be traded at all. The "bad" cars tend to drive out the good (in much the same way that bad money drives out the good)".

If there are different grades of goods, Akerlof tells that "it is quite possible to have the bad driving out the not-so-bad driving out the medium driving out the not-so-good driving out the good in such a sequence of events that no market exists at all".

One can assume that the demand for used cars depends most strongly upon two variables-the price of the car and the average quality of used cars traded. Both the supply of used cars and the average quality will depend upon the price. And in equilibrium, the supply must equal the demand for the given average quality. As the price falls, normally the quality will also fall. And it is quite possible that no goods will be traded at any price level. Akerlof has derived such an example from the utility theory.

Akerlof's theory can be applied to (*i*) insurance, (*ii*) the employment of minorities, (*iii*) to study the costs of dishonesty, and (*iv*) credit markets.

In the economic models discussed by Akerlof, "trust" is important. Informal unwritten guarantees are preconditions for trade and production. Where these guarantees are indefinite, business will suffer as indicated by generalised Gresham's law. But the difficulty of distinguishing good quality from bad is inherent in the business world; this may indeed explain many economic institutions and may in fact be one of the more important aspects of uncertainty".

MICHAEL SPENCE

Spence is the author of the concept of "market signalling". If you take the job market, the problem of the job seeker is signalling one, and that of the employer who is faced with an investment decision uncertainty, is that of interpreting signals. Though Spence discusses the concept of signalling with reference to job market, he is of the view that a considerable variety of market and quasi-market phenomena like admission procedures, promotion in organizations, loans and consumer credit can be usefully viewed through the conceptual lens applied to the job market. Spence looks at hiring as investment under uncertainty. In most job markets, the employer is not sure of the productive capabilities of an individual at the time he hires him. This information will not necessarily become available to the employer immediately. The job may take time to learn. The fact that it takes time to learn an individual's productive capabilities means that hiring is an investment decision. The fact that these capabilities are not known beforehand makes the decision one under uncertainty. As Spence put it; "To hire someone, then, is frequently to purchase a lottery (The term "lottery" is used in the technical sense, imparted to it by decision theory). Spence's essay 'Job Market Signalling' is basically about the endogenous market process whereby the employer requires (and the individual transmits) information about the potential employee, which ultimately determines the implicit lottery involved in hiring, the offered wages, and in the end the allocation of jobs to people and people to jobs in the market.

Among the observable personal attributes that collectively constitute the image the job applicant presents, some are immutably fixed, while others are alterable. For example, education is something that the individual can invest in at some cost in terms of time and money. On the other hand, race and sex are not generally thought to be alterable. Spence refers to the unalterable attributes as indices and reserves the term signals for those observable characteristics attached to the individual that are subject to manipulation by him. Some attributes like age, do change, but not at the discretion of the individual. These are indices.

A potential employee faces an offered wage schedule whose arguments are signals and costs. The applicant cannot do much about indices but he can alter the signals by manipulation. But there are costs of making these adjustments. For example, education is costly. These costs are known as singalling costs. An individual will invest in education if there is sufficient return as defined by the offered wage schedule. Individuals select signals so as "to maximise the difference between offered wages and signalling costs. So signalling costs play a key role in this type of signalling situation.

Broadly, signalling costs include psychic and other costs, as well as the direct monetary ones. For example, one element of cost, is time.

During the course of his discussion on market signalling, Spence has made a provocative observation that "Looked at from outside, education might appear to be productive. It is productive for the individual, but, in this example, it does not increase his real marginal product at all".

Spence's assertion that education does not contribute to productivity has generated a controversy: "An important issue in the controversy about human capital model is whether or not human capital investments, particularly in education or in training actually increase productivity. An alternative explanation is that the attainment of such education is merely a means by which a capable individual signals his or her capabilities to potential employers".

Apart from his work on signalling, Spence has made distinguished contributions to the field of industrial organization. During the period 1975-1985, he was one of the pioneers in the wave of game-theory inspired work within the new industrial organization theory. His most important studies in this area deal with monopolistic competition and market entry. Spence's models of market equilibrium under monopolistic competition have also been influential in other fields, such as growth theory and international trade.

While Spence's research emphasised education as a productivity signal, in job markets, subsequent research has suggested many other applications, *e.g.*, how firms may use dividends to signal their profitability to agents in the stock market.

JOSEPH E. STIGLITZ

Stiglitz is one of the pioneers in field of the "Economics of Information". Basic concepts such as theories of adverse selection and moral hazard, which have now become standard tools in economic theory and policy were developed by him and Akerlof almost about the same time.

While awarding the Nobel Prize, the Swedish Academy said that in the mid-1970s, Stiglitz "showed that poorly informed agents can indirectly extract information from those who are better informed, by offering a menu of alternative contracts for a specific transaction-so called screening through self-selection". One example is the insurance market, in which companies are able to gather information about the risk associated with various clients by offering policies with different deductibles.

Generally, we consider the type of insurance which provides full coverage of the cost of medical care. However, various devices are written into insurance, in part to reduce the moral hazard, of which the most important are deductibles and coinsurance.

A deductible is the exclusion of a certain amount of expenses from coverage; coinsurance requires the individual to pay some fraction of each rupee of cost.

Coinsurance is a scheme in which the individual is, in effect, charged a positive price for medical care, but a price less than the market price. The higher the price paid by the individual, the more his usage will be curtailed.

MORAL HAZARD

It has been recognized in the insurance literature that medical insurance, by lowering the marginal cost of care to the individual, may increase usage; this characteristic has been termed "moral hazard". We may note that while the insurance companies want to follow the strategy of "restrain use", those who have insured want to "use excess care".

The Swedish Academy further said: "Stiglitz has made many other contributions regarding markets with asymmetric information.... He is probably the most cited researcher within the information economics literature-perhaps also within a wider domain of microeconomics".

Stiglitz's classic article with Rothchild on adverse selection, "Equilibrium in Competitive Insurance Markets: *An Essay on the Economics of Imperfect Information*" (1976) is a natural complement to the analyses in Akerlof (1070) and Spence (1973, 1074).

Rothchild and Stiglitz establish that equilibria may be divided into two main types: pooling and separating. In a pooling equilibrium, all individuals buy the same insurance, while in a separating equilibrium, they purchase different contracts. Rothchild and Stiglitz show that their model has no pooling equilibruim....In Akerlof's model, the price became too low for high quality sellers, whereas here the premium would be too high for low-risk individuals. The only possible equilibrium is a unique separating equilibrium, where two distinct insurance contracts are sold in the market.

The uniqueness of equilibrium is typical of screening models, as is the correspondence between the screening models and the socially most efficient signalling equilibrium. Rothchild and Stiglitz's classification of equilibrium has now become a paradigm; pooling and separating equilibrium are now standard concepts in microeconomic theory in general and in information economics in particular.

Stiglitz has made many other contributions regarding markets with asymmetric information. He has time and again pointed out that economic models may be quite misleading, if they disregard asymmetric information.

Stiglitz and Weiss (1981, 1983) have analysed credit markets with asymmetric information. They show that to reduce losses from bad loans, it may be optimal for banks to ration the volume of loans instead of raising the lending rate. These insights were an important step towards a more realistic theory of credit markets. They have had a substantial impact in the fields of corporate finance, monetary theory and macroeconomics.

Stiglitz is one of the founders of modem development economics. He has shown that economic incentives under asymmetric information are highly concrete phenomena with far-reaching explanatory value in the analysis of institutions and market conditions in developing economies. One of his first studies of informational asymmetries deals with sharecropping, an ancient but still common form of contracting. As the term implies, the contract regulates how the harvest should be divided between a landowner and his tenants. The size of a harvest generally depends on external circumstances such as weather and on the tenant's work effort. Generally, the harvest is divided between parties according to fixed shares, usually half each. Both Stiglitz and Akerlof attempted to explain this relation, in terms of asymmetric information between the two parties. Since the landowner usually cannot observe the tenant's work effort, an optimal contract strikes a balance between risk sharing and incentives, letting the tenants assume some share of the risk.

In addition to his work on the economics of information, Stiglitz has made significant contributions to public economics, especially the theory of optimal taxation, industrial organization and the economics of natural resources.

The analyses of markets with asymmetric information by Akerlof, Spence and Stiglitz are fundamental to modern economic theory. Their research has increased our understanding of phenomena in real markets which could not be fully captured by traditional neoclassical theory.

DANIEL KAHNEMAN AND VERNON L. SMITH

Two American economists Daniel Kahneman and Vermon. L. Smith have won the Nobel Prize in Economics for the year 2002 for laying the foundations of Behavioural and Experimental Economics. Their work has helped to explain decision-making and behaviour on markets, especially financial markets.

Some of the important works of Kahneman and Smith include Kahneman D and A.. Twersky (1079), *Prospect theory: An analysis of decision under risk",* Econometrica, 47, 263-291 ; Kahneman D and A..Twersky (red), *"Choices, Volues and Frames",* Cambridge University Press, 2000; Smith V. L. (1962). *"An Experimental study of competitive market behaviour",* Journal of Political Economy 70, 111-137 : Smith V.I., *"Bargaining and Market Behaviour: Essays in experimental Economics",* Cambridge University Press, 2000.

In the traditional economic theory, decision-making is based on self-interest and rationality. And Economics has been regarded as a non-laboratory science where the researchers have had to rely exclusively on field data based on the direct observation of the real world. That is why Alfred Marshall stated; "the laws of economics are to be compared with the laws of tides rather than with the simple and exact laws of gravitation". Things changed during the last two decades. Controlled laboratory experiments have become an essential part of economic research and the results have pointed out the need for modifying some of the assumptions of economic theory. This has been made possible by the pioneering work done in the field of cognitive psychology and experimental economics by Daniel Kahneman and Smith.

VERNON L. SMITH

Foundations of Experimental Economics

Vernon Smith's most significant work relates to market mechanisms. He did a lot of innovative experiments with competitive markets. He tested different auction forms and designed the so-called *induced value method*.

Smith laid the foundations of experimental economics. The Royal Swedish Academy cited that he "established laboratory experiments as a tool in empirical economic analysis, especially in the study of alternative market mechanisms". Though there are some early predecessors in experimental research (*e.g.*, Samuelson, Reinhard Selton, John Nash), the main researcher in experimental research is Prof. Vernon Smith. In a way, we may look at the Nobel Prize awarded to him as a reward for his lifetime achievement in the field of experimental economics in a subject which is traditionally considered as non-experimental science.

The early controlled experiments of Smith dealt with determination of equilibrium under perfect competition. He divided his subjects randomly into buyers and sellers with different valuations of a good. The valuations were expressed as a lowest acceptable selling price and a highest acceptable buying price. Based on such "reservation prices", Smith determined the equilibrium price. To his surprise, he found that the prices he obtained in the laboratory experiments were close to their theoretical values, in spite of the fact that the subjects lacked the information necessary to calculate the equilibrium price.

Auctions are generally used to organize markets for raw materials and shares. In recent times, auctions have also been designed for deregulation and privatisation of public monopoly. The four auction forms used in the sale of a single good are (*i*) The English auction (Buyers announce their bids in an increasing order until no higher bid is submitted); (*ii*) The Dutch auction (A high initial bid is lowered until a buyer declares his acceptance) ; (*iii*) The first-price auction (Sealed bids where the highest bidder pays his own bid to the seller); and (*iv*) The sealed-bid second-price auction (the highest bidder pays the second highest bid).

Smith along with his colleagues conducted a number of experiments in the auction method in the theory of price formation. For example, he found that a seller can get the same revenue in English and second-price auctions.

Smith and Plott made use of laboratory experiments as a "wind tunnel" (a laboratory setup used to test prototypes for aircraft) to study the performance of the proposed auction mechanisms for deregulation, privatisation and provision of public goods. These experiments are found to be useful because it is rather difficult to assess their performance solely on the basis of economic theory. By making use of computer assisted markets, Smith developed mechanisms to allocate airport time slots. He has also done experiments on organizing energy markets in Australia and New Zealand. These results have influenced actual market design in those countries.

In a seminal article in American Economic Review (1978) titled "Experimental economics: Induced-value theory", Smith provided a practical guide to the design of economic experiments in the laboratory and a motivation for these guidelines. This method emphasises the importance of providing subjects with sufficient monetary incentives. A major problem in conducting experiments is that own (unobservable) preferences of the subjects can affect their behaviour in an experiment. As a result, he who is given the role of a buyer, with a given demand function for a good, will not simply behave in accordance with this demand curve. So Smith introduced a technique, known as the induced-value method, which solves the problem. For, it provides the subject with incentives to behave as intended by the experimenter.

Thus, Smith has made significant contribution in the study of markets and auctions and also on methodology.

DANIEL KAHNEMAN

Foundations of Behavioural Economics

Daniel Khaneman laid the foundation of Behavioural Economics by applying the methods of cognitive psychology to decision-making in Economics. Thereby, he built a bridge between research in economics and psychology.

In traditional economics, economic decisions are governed mainly by self-interest and rationality. In psychology in general and cognitive psychology in particular, human being is regarded as a system that codes and interprets available information in a conscious and rational manner. But other, less conscious factors also govern human behaviour in a systematic manner. Those factors include perception, mental models for interpreting specific situations, emotions, attitudes and memories of earlier decisions and their consequences.

After an extensive research on human behaviour based on surveys and experiments, Daniel Kahneman, in collaboration with Amos Tversky, has questioned the assumption of economic rationality in decision-making. He is of the view that decision-making in the real world often does not evaluate uncertain events according to the laws of probability. People do not also make decisions according to the theory of expected-utility maximisation. Under such complex and uncertain situations, they make decisions based on the rule of the thumb. Based on their own experimental data, Kahneman and Tversky have shown that there is fundamental bias in the way in which individuals judge random events. Most people assign the same probabilities in small and large samples, without taking into account that uncertainty about (the variance of) the mean that declines drastically with sample size. People thus seem to follow the law of small numbers, without due consideration of the law of large numbers in probability theory. In a well-known experiment, subjects believed that on a given day, more than 60 per cent of the births would be boys in a small hospital (with few births) as well as in a large hospital (where many children were born).

Another rule of the thumb is *representativeness*. Kahneman and Tversky carried out an experiment in which subjects were asked on the basis of given descriptions to categorize individuals as a "salesman" or a "Member of Parliament". When a randomly chosen person was portrayed as interested in politics and participating in debates, most subjects though he was a Member of Parliament, regardless of the fact that the relatively higher share of salespersons in population increases the likelihood that he was a salesperson. Even after the subjects were informed that the proportions of Members of Parliament and salespersons in the population had been altered substantially, the results were not affected by this and remained more or less the same.

Kahneman's most influential contribution relates to decision-making under uncertainty. An important finding is that individuals are much more sensitive to the way an outcome deviates from a reference level (often the status quo) than to the absolute income. When individuals are faced with a series of decisions under risk and uncertainty, they appear to base each decision on its gains and losses in isolation than on the consequences of a decision for their wealth as a whole. Moreover, most individuals seem to be more averse to losses, relative to a reference level, than partial to gains of the same size. Results like these contradict predictions from the traditional theory of expected utility maximisation.

Kahneman and Tversky have not stopped with criticizing standard theories of decision-making under uncertainty. They have developed an alternative theory known as *prospect theory* to provide explanation for empirical observations. Prospect theory explains many types of behaviour which may appear to be anomalies according to the traditional theory. The propensity of people to sign up for costly small-scale insurance for appliances; willingness of people to drive many miles for a small discount on a minor purchase, but reluctance to do so in order to save the same amount on a more expensive good; and resistance to reducing consumption in response to bad news about lifetime income are some of the examples.

Insights from psychology have had a strong impact on contemporary developments in financial economics. Behavioural finance today has become a lively research area. Kahneman's experiments in probability theory showed a shortsightedness in interpreting data that could explain large fluctuations on financial markets that cannot be explained by existing models. There is no doubt that Vernon Smith and Kahneman have been key figures in the traditions of experimental economics and economic psychology.

ROBERT F. ENGLE III AND CLIVE W. J. GRANGER

The Nobel Prize in Economic for the year 2003 was jointly awarded to Robert F. Engle and Clive W. J. Granger. While Engle was awarded the prize "for methods of analysis of economic time series with time varying volatility (ARCE), Granger was awarded the prize" for methods of analysis of economic time series with common trends (cointegration).

Empirical research in macroeconomics as well as financial economics is largely based on time series. Both Granger and Clive have deepened our understanding of two central properties of many economic time series—nonstationarity and time-varying volatility—which have led to a large number of applications.

Nonstationarity is a property common to many macroeconomic and financial time series. It means that a variable has no clear tendency to return to a constant value or a linear trend. Price series, exchange rate series, and other aggregate variables such as gross national product, consumption, employment and asset prices share the property.

"An important objective of empirical research in macroeconomics is to test hypotheses and estimate relationships, derived from economic theory, among such aggregate variables. The statistical theory that was applied till 1980s in building and testing large simultaneous–equation models was based on the assumption that the variables in these models are stationary. The problem was that statistical inference associated with stationary processes is no longer valid if the time series are indeed realizations of nonstationary processes". This difficulty was not understood well by model builders three decades ago. This is no longer the case.

Clive Granger has shown that macroeconomic models containing nonstationary stochastic variables can be constructed in such a way that the results are both statistically sound and economically meaningful. His work has also provided the basis of modelling with rich dynamics among interrelated economic variables. Granger has achieved the breakthough by introducing the concept of cointegrated variables. This has radically changed the way empirical models of macroeconomic relationships are formulated today.

The second central property of economic time series which is common to many financial time series, is that their volatility varies over time.

Volatility is a key issue for researchers in financial economics and analysis in financial markets. The prices of stocks and other assets depend on the expected volatility of returns. Banks and other financial institutions make assessment of volatility as a part of monitoring their risk exposure. Till 1980s, the models used in the financial market were based on the assumption that volatility was constant over time. But volatility may considerably vary over time. Large (small) changes in return are followed by large (small) changes. The forecasting of volatility is very important in financial markets.

Robert Engle did a lot of research in volatility models in the early 1980s and made many outstanding contributions. He developed a new concept called auto regressive conditional heteroskadasticity (ARCH). Since then, models built around ARCH concept have become an indispensable tool for bankers, financial and fund managers throughout the world.

Cointegrated economic variables

Time-series models are used by macroeconomics for testing economic theories, for forecasting and for policy analysis. For a long time, economists estimated equations involving nonstationary variables in macroeconomic models by straightforward linear regression. This, sometimes, led to spurious results.

The importance of cointegration in the modelling of nonstationary economic series becomes clear in the Granger representation theorem.

For the concept of cointegration to be useful, there is need for statistical theory for testing for cointegration and for estimating parameters of linear systems with cointegration. Engle and Granger (1987) jointly developed the necessary techniques in their paper on cointegrated variables. The paper gives the proof for Granger representation theorem.

Often, deviations from equilibrium are explained by transaction and information costs. Granger and Swanson (1996) have demonstrated how such costs may be incorporated into models with cointegrated variables and how this may give rise to non-linear error correction model.

Cointegration has become a common econometric tool for empirical analysis in a number of areas, where long-run relationships affect currently observed values. For example, current consumption is restricted by expected future income, and current long-term interest rates are determined by expected short-term rates.

Some of the cointegration studies based on economic theory have been used for studying bubbles in asset prices, predictability of stock prices; and for testing the hypothesis that consumption is determined by permanent income.

Modelling Volatility

Many financial economists are concerned with modelling volatility in asset returns. Engle's modelling of time-varying volatility by way of auto regressive conditional heteroskedasticity (ARCH) signified a genuine breakthrough. ARCH plays an important role in value-at-risk analysis.

In 1982, Engle applied his ARCH model to macroeconomic series such as the inflation rate. Soon, he realized that the ARCH model was useful in financial economics as well. In fact, in 1963, Mandelbrot had already observed that ".... large changes tend to be followed by small changes...." But he did not go further and model the returns, as time dependent.

Engle's ARCH model is an efficient tool for estimating second moments of statistical distributions–*i.e., variances* and covariances. Financial theory deals mainly with the connection between the second moments of asset returns and the first moments (expected asset returns).

Based on the ARCH models, Engle recently developed new models for the empirical analysis of market microstructure. This literature helps to clarify the behaviour of individual agents in stock markets.

In addition to its use in asset pricing, ARCH models have also been applied in other areas of financial economics like the pricing of options and other derivatives (where the variance of the underlying assets is a key parameter).

ARCH (and GRCH) models have become popular and indispensable tools in modern risk management situations. Banks, other financial institutions and many large companies use value-at-risk analysis. The advantage of the analysis is that it reduces the market risk associated with a portfolio of assets.

Conclusion

Both Engle and Granger have made valuable contributions in many areas of time-series econometrics. Granger developed a testable definition of causality. He has also contributed to the theory of long-memory models that have become popular in econometric literature. Besides, Granger was the first to make use of special analysis as well as nonlinear models in research on economic time series. He has also made a noteworthy contribution to the theory and practice of economic forecasting.

Since its inception, cointegration has become a vast area of research in theory and practice. It has become a standard topic in econometric textbooks. Similary, auto–regressive conditional heteroskedasticity has generated extensive literature in time series.

The work of Granger on nonstationary time series and that of Clive on time-varying volatility have exercised a great influence on applied economic and financial research. Thus the two concepts of cointegration and ARCH and the methods these two economists have developed around these concepts have changed the way modelling is done in econometrics.

FINN E. KYDLAND AND EDWARD C. PRESCOTT

The Nobel Prize in Economics for the year 2004 was jointly awarded to Finn E. Kydland and Edward C. Prescott (both teaching in the Universities of U.S.A.) "for their contribution to dynamic macroeconomics: the time consistency of economic policy and the driving forces behind business cycles" (The Royal Swedish Academy of Sciences).

New Theory on Business Cycles and Economic Policy

The driving forces behind business cycle fluctuations and the design of economic policy are key areas in macroeconomic research. Finn Kydland and Edward Prescott have made fundamental contributions to these areas of great significance, not only for macroeconomic analysis, but also for the practice of monetary and fiscal policy in many countries. These major contributions are found in the following original papers which they have jointly contributed: (i) Rules rather than discretion: The inconsistency of optimal Plans (1977); and (ii) Time to build and aggregate fluctuations (1982).

The time consistency problem and their analysis of business cycles are by now well established elements in macroeconomic analysis.

The fundamental contributions of Finn Kydland and Edward Prescott are in two closely related areas of macroeconomic research. The first one is related to the design of macroeconomic policy. These two economists have brought to light inherent imperfections-credibility problem—in the ability of governments to implement desirable economic policies. The second area concerns business cycle fluctuations. Kydland and Prescott demonstrated how variations in technological development which are the main source of long-run economic growth can lead to short-run fluctuations. In doing so, they offered a new and operational framework for macroeconomic analysis based on microeconomic foundation. Their work has resulted in a major change in the theory and practice of macroeconomic analysis and policy making.

General Background

During the early post-war period, macroeconomic analysis was dominated by Keynesian theory. According to it, short-run fluctuations in output and employment are mainly due to variations in aggregate demand (i.e., investors' willingness to invest and consumers' willingness to consume). To avoid recurring fluctuations in output, macroeconomic policy should systematically control aggregate demand. These ideas were born out of the experience of the Great Depression of 1930s. As the market system failed to coordinate aggregate demand and aggregate supply, it provided a motive for government intervention.

Until the mid-1970s, Keynesian policy was found to be successful in explaining macroeconomic fluctuations. But real-world developments in the late 1970s revealed serious shortcomings in Keynesian policy. It could not explain the new phenomenon of stagflation - simultaneous inflation and unemployment. Stagflation seemed closely related to the shocks on the supply side of the economy: increase in the price of oil and worlwide slowdown of productivity growth. Monetary and fiscal policies based on conventional macroeconomic policy appeared to make matters worse in many countries.

Robert Lucas in the 1970s demonstrated that the effects of macroeconomic policy could not be properly analyzed without explicit microeconomic foundations. Only by carefully building models of the behaviour of individual economic agents, such as consumers and firms, we can derive reliable conclusions regarding private sector responses to economic policy. Consumers' preferences, technologies of firms and market structures are the building-blocks of such an analysis. They are likely to be robust to changes in economic policy.

Lucas critique based on rational expectations and microfoundations of macroeconomics gained wide acceptance. It called for an alternative and operational macroeconomic framework based on solid microeconomic foundations. The award-winning contributions of Kydland and Prescott provided just this alternative framework.

Main contributions of Kydland and Prescott

Time Consistence of Economic Policy

The paper, "Rules rather than Discretion: The Inconsistency of Optimal Plans" (1977) studies the sequential choice of policies, such as tax rates or monetary policy instruments. The key insight of the analysis of Kydland and Prescott is that many policy decisions are subject to a fundamental time consistency problem.

If households expect higher taxation of capital in the future, they will save less; if the government follows an expansionary monetary policy and if firms expect higher inflation, they will set higher prices and wages. Kydland and Prescott showed how such effects of expectations about future economic policy can give rise to a time consistency problem. If economic policy makers lack the ability to commit in advance to specific decision rule, they will often not implement the most desirable policy later on. The inability of the government to make binding commitments regarding future policies will result in a credibility problem. Especially the public will realize that future government policy will not necessarily coincide with the announced policy unless the plan already has the incentives for future policy change. In other words, sequential policy making faces a credibility constraint. By making use of the game theory and rational expectations hypothesis, Kydland and Prescott showed that the outcome in a rational expectations equilibrium where the government cannot commit to policy in advance—discriminatory policymaking—results in lower welfare than the outcome in an equilibrium where the government can commit.

Kydland and prescott's 1977 article had a great impact not only on theoretical policy analysis, but also provided a new perspective on actual policy experience, such as the stagflation problem. The analysis showed that a sustained high inflation may not be the consequence of irrational policy decisions. On the other hand, it might be a reflection on the inability of policymakers to commit to monetary policy. This insight shifted the focus of policy analysis from the study of individual policy decisions to the design of institutions that make the time consistency problem less severe. The reforms undertaken by central banks in many countries since 1990s are based on the research findings of Kydland and Prescott. These reforms are an important factor underlying the recent period of low and stable inflation in several countries.

Driving Forces Behind Business Cycles

The article" Time to Build and Aggregate Fluctuations (1982) by Kydland and Prescott gave a theory of business cycle fluctuations far from the Keynesian tradition. In this article, they transformed the theory of business cycles by integrating it with the theory of economic growth. In this article, both economists integrated the analysis of long-run economic growth and short-run macroeconomic fluctuations, by maintaining the that growth in technology can also generate short-run cycles. The earlier research on business cycles has emphasized macroeconomic shocks on the demand side of the economy, whereas Kydland and Prescott demonstrated that shocks on the supply side may have far-reaching effects. Their work showed that technology shocks should be taken seriously as a cause of business cycles.

In Kydland and Prescott's business cycle model, realistic fluctuations in the rate of technological development brought about covariation between GDP, consumption, investment and worked hours close to that observed in actual data. The earlier business cycle models were typically based on historical relations between key macroeconomic variables. But models that functioned well before 1960s began to breakdown during the 1970s, when there was stagflation marked by oil-price shocks and inflation and unemployment at the same time. The work of these two economists laid the foundation for robust business cycle models by regarding them as the collective outcome of several forward-looking decisions made by households, and firms regarding consumption, investment, labour supply and so on. Kydland and Prescott's research methods have been widely adopted in modern macroeconomics.

ROBERT J. AUMANN AND THOMAS C. SCHELLING

The Nobel Prize in Economics for the year 2005 was jointly awarded to Robert J. Aumann (Israel and U.S.A.) and Thomas C. Schelling (U.S.A.) "for having enhanced our understanding of conflict and cooperation through game-theory analysis." The essence of game theory is the analysis of strategic interaction of all kinds. The most important applications of game theory are found in such vital issues as security and disarmament policies, price formation of markets, as well as economic and political negotiations.

War and other conflicts have tormented mankind since time immemorial. They have caused great suffering and extensive material losses. Yet many societies live in prosperity based on cooperation and peaceful competition. Why do some groups, organizations and countries succeed in promoting cooperation while others suffer from conflict? Auman and Schelling approached this age-old question against the backdrop of cold war. While the former approached the problem from mathematical angle, the latter approached it from the angle of economics. Both of them shared a vision that game theory had the potential to reshape the analysis of human interaction.

Thomas Schelling

In the mid-1950s, Thomas Schelling applied the game-theory methods to the issue of global security and arms race.

The negotiating strength of parties in a conflict could be affected by a number of factors such as the initial alternatives at their disposal and their potential to influence their own and each other's alternatives during the process. He clarified why it could be advantageous to limit one's own alternatives or worsen one's own options to get concessions from the opponent. It can be wise for a general to burn bridges behind his troops as a credible commitment to the enemy not to retreat. And a politician may gain from making promises that would be embarrassing to break. Such tactics work if the commitment is irreversible or can only be undone at a great cost. Schelling was interested in building a climate of confidence, whereby long-term cooperation could be built up over a period of time, and in the long-run gains a party could achieve by making short-run concessions. His analysis is found in his book "The Strategy of Conflict" (1960), which became a classic. It has influenced generations of strategic thinkers.

Schelling was also concerned with the ability of individuals to coordinate their behaviour in situations without any strong conflict of interest, but where unsuccessful coordination would give rise to high costs for all parties. He found that coordinative solutions—which he called focal points—could be arrived at more often than predicted by theory. The ability of the parties to coordinate appears to be related to their common frames of reference. Social conventions and norms are intergral parts of this common ground. Under the influence of Schelling, philosopher David Lewis declared that language originated as a means of coordination.

Why does Segregation Arise?

Schelling was concerned with the question: What happens when individual's plans and patterns of behaviour are confronted in the social arena. His book "Micromotives and Macrobehaviour"

(1978) deals with the analysis of the above problem. It includes an analysis of racial and sexual discrimination.

Segregation is usually associated with oppression. In fact, this has been an important historical explanation. But segregation is also a stable phenomenon in developed countries. Schelling formulated a simple model where he assumed that all individuals are tolerant. That is, they are willing to live in a neighourhood with people belonging to different cultures, religion or skin colour, but they want to have at least a few neighbours that share their own characteristics. If not, they will move to a neighbourhood where they can find more people like themselves. Schelling showed that even rather weak preferences regarding the share of like persons in a neighbourhood can result in strongly segregated living patterns. In other words, for a social problem to arise, no extreme preferences on the part of the individuals are required.

ROBERT AUMANN
Long-run Coperation

Robert Aumann's primary contributions consist of using the tools of mathematical analysis to develop concepts and hypotheses, provide them with concise formulations and draw precise conclusions. The strength of Thomas Schelling, on the other hand, lies largely in his ability to introduce original ideas and concepts with a minimum of mathematical technique.

Aumann shared Schelling's early interest in "repeated games". Repeated games deal with interaction where the parties interact many times over a long period. He showed that peaceful cooperation is often an equilibrium solution in a repeated game; even between parties with strong short-run conflicts of interest. Aumann and other researchers have extended and generalized Schelling's results in different directions, for example, regarding credibility in "threats of punishment" for deviating from cooperation. Aumann along with another researcher Michael Maschler, also established the theory of repeated games with asymmetric (or incomplete information) i.e., situations where one party knows more than another about certain aspects of the repeated game (For example, information regarding the real costs of a competitor or the military strength of another country).

The theory of repeated games is now the common framework for analysis of long-run cooperation among parties with conflicting interests in the social sciences. It has helped to explain economic conflicts such as price wars and trade wars. The theory is applied to study many situations such as the competing firms which collude to maintain a high price level, and farmers who share pastures or irrigation systems, to countries which enter into environmental agreements or are involved in territorial disputes.

Common Knowledge and Correlated Equilibria

Another fundamental contribution of Aumann concerns the known foundations of the game theory, i.e., the implications of the parties' knowledge about various aspects of the game, including "knowledge about each others' knowledge".

Aumann also introduced a new equilibrium concept called correlated equilibrium. This is weaker than Nash equilibrium. Correlated equilibrium can explain why it may be advantageous for negotiating parties to allow an impartial mediator to speak to the parties either jointly or separately, and in some instances give them different information.

Conclusion

Aumann and Schelling have shared a common trait : an interest in considering aspects neglected by established theory and in developing new concepts and analytical tools, thereby extending the scope of analysis. As a consequence of their efforts, the concept of rationality has a wider interpretation. Behaviour which was considered irrational then has become rational. Their work has bridged the gap between economics and other behavioural and social sciences.

EDMUND PHELPS

The Nobel Prize in Economics for the year 2006 was awarded to the American economist Edmund Phelps for helping us understand the tradeoff between inflation and unemployment and the tradeoff between the consumption of current and future generations.

Some of Phelps' important and popular books and articles are *Inflation policy and unemployment theory,* (1972) (a book), *The Origin and further development of the natural rate of unemployment* (1995) (a paper), *"A Life in Economics"* (1995) (an essay). *The golden rule of accumulation*: *A fable for growthmen,* (1961) (an article) and Phelps Volume, the anthology that Phelps published under the title *Microeconomic Foundations of Employment and Inflation Theory* (1970).

Inflation and Unemployment

In the early postwar period, macroeconomics was dominated by Keynesian views on how the economy operates. According to Keynesian theory, there was no conflict between full employment and price stability. As long as the economy was below full employment, an increase in aggregate demand which could be achieved through fiscal or monetary measures, would not result in inflation. From the Keynesian point of view, stabilization policy appeared to be simple. But Phillips curve changed all this.

According to Phillips curve, there was a stable negative relationship between inflation and unemployment. This led to a revision of the standard Keynesian model of the economy. The Phillips curve implied a tradeoff between inflation and unemployment. That means, though employment could be increased using aggregate demand policy, this would occur at the cost of higher inflation. There would be one-time increase in the rate of inflation. The Phillips curve implies that policymakers could choose between inflation and unemployment according to their preferences.

The Phillips curve had some limitations. It was a purely statistical relationship. There was no clear link to microeconomic theories about the behaviour of individual firms and households. Not only that, there was also no theory about the minimum possible unemployment.

In the late 1960s, Edmund Phelps challenged the earlier view on the relationship between inflation and unemployment. He recognised that inflation does not only depend on unemployment but also on the expectations of firms and employees about price and wage increases. Thus he brought agents' expectations to the forefront of the analysis, and made the crucial distinction between expected and unexpected inflation, and examined the macroeconomic implications of this distinction. He formulated the first model of what has come to be known as *expectations – augmented Phillips curve.* Phelps emphasized that it was the difference between actual and expected inflation, and not inflation, per se, that is related to unemployment. The expectations augmented Phillips curve says that, for a given unemployment rate, a one percentage point increase in expected inflation leads to a one percentage point increase in actual inflation. Thus in setting prices and negotiating wages and salaries, firms and employees base their decisions on their beliefs about the development of prices and wages in general. This hypothesis has received a lot of support in subsequent empirical research.

By making use of his analysis, Phelps arrived at the conclusion that there is no long-run tradeoff between inflation and unemployment, since inflationary expectations will adapt to the actual inflation. According to him, in the long run, the economy is bound to approach the *equilibrium unemployment rate* at which actual and expected inflation coincide. *Equilibrium unemployment* is only determined by the functioning of the labour market. Any attempt to permanently reduce unemployment below the *equilibrium* rate will only result in continuously increasing inflation. Stabilization policy still has an important role to play in dampening the short-run fluctuations in unemployment around its equilibrium level.

Phelps' contributions highlight the importance of analyzing how future possibilities of reaching the goals of stabilization policy are affected by today's policy: high inflation today means higher inflation expectations in the future. This renders future policy choices more difficult. A policy of maintaining low inflation can therefore be regarded as an investment in low inflation expectations, enabling more favourable conditions of inflation and unemployment in the future.

Phelps also developed the first model of the determinants of equilibrium unemployment. His contribution was also the first to integrate the hypothesis of the efficiency of high wages into macroeconomic theory. This hypothesis states that it may be in the best interest of a firm to set high wages in order to improve workers' morale, reduce labour turnover and attract better qualified employees.

Phelps' work has fundamentally altered our views on how the macroeconomy operates. The theoretical framework he developed in the late 1960s soon proved fruitful in understanding the causes of increases in both inflation and unemployment that took place during the 1970s. He also clarified the limitations of macroeconomic policy. This has brought about a radical change in macroeconomic policy. For example, central banks now base their decisions regarding interest rate on assessment of equilibrium unemployment rate and tradeoffs between effects of policy at different horizons.

Capital Formation

Phelps made significant contribution to the research on intergenerational welfare through his earlier work on capital formation (physical capital as well as human capital i.e. education as well as research and development). Phelps has tried to find out the answer to the question: What fraction of national income should be consumed now and how much should be invested in order to increase the capital stock, thereby boosting future production and consumption? This question is crucial for the distribution of consumption and welfare across generations. In this area as well, Phelps' contribution had a profound impact on the debate over economic policy.

In one of his articles (1961), Phelps derived the concept of *golden rule* of capital formation. By taking an intergenerational perspective, he posited that the goal is to attain the maximum consumption per capita that is sustainable in the long run. The term "golden rule" refers to the ethic: "Do unto others as you would have them do unto you". Hence the interpretation is that the consumption level should be the same for all generations. According to this rule, the savings rate should be high enough to maintain a capital stock that yields a return (a real rate of interest) that is equal to the rate of growth in the economy.

Phelps' original analysis was restricted to long-run situations. But the process of *changing* the savings ratio from one level to another may create distributional conflicts. If an increase in savings rate is required in order to attain the golden rule, the welfare of future generations will increase but the current generation will lose. The reason is that the current generation has to reduce its consumption in order to save more, whereas later generations will benefit from a larger capital stock allowing them to increase both consumption and saving. However, later by making use of the concept of *dynamic inefficiency*, Phelps demonstrated that there may be situations, where the capital stock is so large that it is possible to increase the welfare of all generations by reducing the savings rate. By reducing the savings rate, consumption can be increased immediately. If the original savings rate is above the golden-rule level, this reduction also implies a long-run gain in consumption.

Phelps also analysed the role of investment in education (human capital) and research and development (R&D) in the growth process. In order to achieve maximum long-run consumption, R&D investments (which raise the technology level) should also be adjusted to the level where their return is equal to the growth rate in the economy. From 1966, in joint work with Richard Nelson, Phelps emphasized how a better educated work force facilitates the dissemination of new technology, thereby making easier for poor countries to "catch up" with richer countries. This, in a way, explains the findings of the recent empirical research that GDP growth appears to depend on existing stock of human capital, not just its growth rate. The analysis of Nelson-Phelps offered a possible explanation of why the returns to education is often high in periods of rapid technological change. During such periods, a well educated workforce is particularly important for increased productivity. Arguments of this kind have been put forward to explain why the salaries of highly educated employees have increased in many countries in recent decades with the advent of I.T revolution which has initiated a rapid diffusion of new technology.

Summary

Edmund Phelps' contributions have had a profound influence on macroeconomic theory and policy. The focus on the intertemporal nature of macroeconomic policy tradeoffs provides a unifying theme for his work on inflation and unemployment as well as on capital formation.

Phelps developed the first models of the expectations augmented Phillips curve and equilibrium unemployment. They provided a completely new setting for the analysis of monetary (and fiscal) demand management of policy.

Phelps' contributions to the analysis of optimal capital accumulation demonstrated conditions under which all generations would benefit from changes in aggregate savings rate. He also pioneered research on the role of human capital for technology and output growth.

LEONID HURWICZ, ERIC S. MASKIN AND ROGER B.MYERSON

The Nobel prize in Economics for the year 2007 was awarded to three American economists Leonid Hurwicz, Eric S. Maskin and Roger M.Myerson for *laying the foundations of mechanism design theory,* which plays a central role in contemporary economics and political science. The theory explains situations in which markets work and others in which they do not work. It helps explain how incentives and private information affect the functioning of markets. For example, it explains what insurance polices will provide the best coverage without inviting misuse. It also explains how sellers and buyers can maximize their gain from a transaction.

Mechanism design theory was initiated in 1960 by Hurwicz and further developed by Maskin and Myerson in the 1970s and 1980s. Essentially, the three economists studied how the game theory could help determine the best, most efficient method for allocating resources given the available information, including the incentives of those involved.

The original scientific articles of the economists are : Hurwicz: *"Optimality and information efficiency in resource allocation processes"* (1960), *"On informationally decentralized systems"* (1972), Maskin, E. *Nash equilibrium and welfare optimality* (1977); and Myerson R. *Optimal auction design* (1981).

Asymmetric information and economic institutions

An important goal of economic theory is to understand what institutions, or *allocation mechanisms,* are best suited to minimize the economic losses generated by private information. What trading mechanisms will realize the larger gains from trade and what mechanisms will maximize the sellers' expected revenue? What collective decision – making procedures will succeed in implementing desirable joint projects while denying funds for undesirable projects? What insurance schemes will provide the best coverage without inviting misuse?

Mechanism design theory provides tools for analyzing and answering all these questions and many others like them. For example, it shows why an auction is typically the most efficient institution for the allocation of private goods among a given set of potential buyers, and it also specifies often what auction format will give the largest expected revenue for the seller. Likewise, mechanism design theory explains why there is often no good market solution to the problem of providing public goods.

Before the advent of the mechanism design theory, microeconomic analysis of resource allocation mechanisms was very largely a theory of markets. A central question was: When will a market mechanism suffice to allocate resources efficiently? We know that the market implements fully efficient outcomes under very stringent and unrealistic conditions such as perfect competition, freely available information, private goods, and the absence of any environmental effects of production and consumption. Mechanism design theory asks a much more general question. What resource allocation mechanism produces the best attainable outcome under more general conditions? One part of the answer is that markets, even if they do not attain full efficiency, perform at least as well as any other mechanism under conditions that are considerably less stringent than the conditions for full efficiency. For example, *double auctions,* where buyers as well as sellers submit bids, are quite often unbeaten mechanisms for trading private goods. Another part of the answer is that markets can be ill suited for providing public goods. The funding of such joint projects may require another institutional framework. For example, taxation of potential users.

Mechanism design theory provides a tool for characterizing the optimal institution for any given set of conditions. By that way, it provides a much deeper scientific analysis of the merits of alternative institutions. Mechanism design theory has been applied in many areas of economics, including regulation theory, corporate finance, the theory of taxation and voting procedures.

Key concepts and results

In his mechanism design theory, Hurwicz defined a mechanism as a game in which the participants send messages to each other and / or a "message centre", and where a pre-specified rule assigns an outcome (such as an allocation of goods and services) to every collection of received messages. For given assumptions about participants' preferences and beliefs, each rule induces one or more predicted outcomes or equilibria. Within this framework, the predicted outcomes associated with markets and market-like institutions can be compared with the predicted outcomes of a vast array of alternative trading institutions. Hurwicz introduced the key notion of *incentive – compatibility* in his analysis. It allows the analysis to incorporate the incentives of self – interested participants. In particular, it enables a rigorous analysis of economies where agents are self-interested and have relevant private information.

In the 1970s, the formulation of the *revelation principle* and the development of *implementation theory* led to great advances in the *theory of mechanism* design. The revelation principle states that any equilibrium outcome of an arbitrary mechanism can be replicated by an incentive capable direct mechanism. The revelation principle is an insight that greatly simplifies the analysis of mechanism design problems. It states that the researcher, when searching for the best possible mechanism to solve a given problem, can restrict attention to a small subclass of mechanisms called *direct mechanisms* that satisfy Hurwicz's condition of incentive compatibility. The first version of the revelation principle was formulated by Gibbard in 1973. Several researchers including Maskin and Myerson independently extended it to the standard notion of Bayesian Nash equilibrium. In 1979, 1982 and 1986 Myerson developed the principle in its greatest generality and pioneered its application to specific economic problems such as auctions and regulation.

The revelation principle has transformed the analysis of economic mechanisms. There is, however, one problem. In many cases, one mechanism admits several different equilibria (Equilibrium is attained when all participants in the mechanism send a message that is in their own best interest). Even if the best outcome is achieved in one equilibrium, other inferior equilibria may also exist. For example, conventional double auctions tend to have many equilibria, some of which are associated with very low volumes of trade. So a question arose. Can a mechanism be designed such that *all* its *equilibria* are optimal. The first general solution to this problem was given by Eric Maskin in 1977. The resulting theory, known as *implementation theory* is a key part of modern mechanism design.

Multiple - equilibrium problems are endemic in social – choice theory. Voters who are to select one out of many candidates face, in effect, a coordination problem. To vote for a candidate who has little chance of winning means "wasting one's vote." Accordingly, if there is a commonly held belief in the electorate that a certain candidate has no chance of winning, then this expectation can be self-fulfilling. Such phenomena easily generate multiple equilibria some of which lead to suboptimal outcomes.

In view of these difficulties, it is desirable to design mechanisms in which all equilibrium outcomes are optimal for the given goal function. The quest for this property is known as the *implementation problem*. Implementation theory has played, and continues to play an important role in several areas of economic theory, such as social choice theory and the theory of incomplete contracts.

Mechanism design theory allows a characterisation of the best mechanism of all conceivable mechanisms. Myerson and Satterthwaite (1983) established a precise upper limit for the expected gains from trade that are realizable in *any* trading mechanism in bilateral situations. Moreover, they showed that this upper limit can be realized by way of double auction.

Conclusion

The foregoing analysis shows that market, is general, and auctions in particular, can be efficient institutions for the allocation of private goods. Though the study of optimal trading institutions is one important application, mechanism design theory has a much broader scope. It has been used to sharpen the analysis of many other issues in economics and political science. For example, the theory has been used to analyse the institutions for the provision of public goods, of optimal forms of regulation, and of voting schemes. Finally, we may note that the mechanism design theory defines institutions as non-cooperative games and compares different institutions in terms of equilibrium outcome of these games. It allows economists and other social scientists to analyze the performance of institutions relative to the theoretical optimum.

PAUL KRUGMAN

The Nobel Prize in Economics, for the year 2008 was awarded to Paul Krugman, an American economist "for his analysis of trade patterns and location of economic activity". Some of the important articles and books by Paul Krugman include" Krugman, P (1979). Increasing Returns, Monopolistic Competition and International Trade", *Journal of International Economics;* "Krugman, P (1980), Scale Economics, Product Differentiation, and the Pattern of Trade, *American Economic Review;* Krugman, P (1991). Increasing Returns and Economic Geography, *Journal of Political Economy;* Krugman, P (2000) *Geography and Trade.,* M.I.T. Press, Cambridge, MA and Krugman P and Obstfeld (2009) *International Economics, Theory and Policy,* 8th edition, Pearson.

International Trade and Economic Geography

How are we affected by globalization? What are the effects of free trade? Why do increasing number of people migrate to large cities while rural areas become depopulated?

We cannot answer these questions without a theoretical foundation.

Over the centuries, international trade and the location of economic activity have been some of the central themes in economic thought. Traditionally, trade theory and economic geography have been treated as separate subfields of economics. The theoretical insights by Paul Krugman emphasize that the same basic forces simultaneously determine specialization across countries for a given international distribution of factors of production (trade theory) and the long-run location of those factors across countries (economic geography).

Until the mid – 1970s, trade theory was explained in terms of comparative advantage. It was assumed that trade took place between countries because of differences in some respect—either in terms of technology, as assumed by David Ricardo in the early 19th century, or in terms of factor endowments, according to the Heckscher-Ohlin theory developed in the 1920s. It may be noted that Ohlin was awarded the 1977 Nobel Prize in Economics for his contributions to trade theory.

The above theories provided good explanations of the trade patterns in the first half of the 20th century. But in recent times, many researchers have found that comparative advantage seemed less relevant in the modern world. Today, most trade takes place between countries with similar technologies and similar factor endowments. Quite similar goods are often both exported and imported by the same country. For example, Sweden exports and imports cars. This is known as intra-industry trade, and it has expanded between rich countries. (If a country exports agricultural commodities and imports industrial products, it is a case of inter-industry trade). The comparative advantage theories cannot provide a satisfactory explanation of intra-industry trade.

More than 30 years ago. Krugman introduced a new theory of international trade to explain the occurrence of intra-industry trade. It is based on the assumption of economies of scale which help in reducing cost per unit produced.

Consumers appreciate Diversity

Besides the economies of scale in production, Krugman's new theory was based on the assumption that consumers appreciate diversity in their consumption. One of the salient features of monopolistic competition is product differentiation. That is, the same product (*e.g.,* toothpaste) is produced as a different product with a different brand by firms. After basic wants such as food, clothing and housing have been satisfied, people opt for diversity and variation in their consumption. In 1977, Avinash Dixit and Joseph Stiglitz introduced a model for analyzing consumers' preferences for product diversity. According to this model, each producer, working under increasing returns to scale, is a partial monopolist as far as his brand is concerned, even though he has to face stiff competition from other brands.

We can use such a model to show that foreign trade will arise not only between countries which are *different* (as in the traditional theory), but also between countries which are identical in terms of access to technology and factor endowments. Moreover, the model can be used to demonstrate that extensive intra-industry trade will occur. In fact, it becomes advantageous for a country to specialize in manufacturing a specific car, and to produce for the world market, while another country specializes in a different brand of car. By that way, each country can take effective advantage of economies of scale. It also implies that consumers all over the world will benefit from greater welfare due to lower prices and greater product diversity, as compared to a situation where each country produces solely for its domestic market, without international trade.

Krugman's simple, straightforward and realistic analysis of the vital mechanisms in the economy has become popular among the economists. We may note that Krugman's theory does not supplant the earlier theories, rather, it is a complement to traditional Heckscher-Ohlin theory. The new international trade theory of Krugman has inspired a lot of research in the particular field. That speaks of its theoretical quality.

Economic Geography

Economic geography deals not only with what goods are produced where, but also with the distribution of capital and labour over countries and regions. Krugman has demonstrated that the assumptions which he has made in his approach to new international trade theory, namely the assumption of economies of scale in production and consumers' preference for diversity in production were found appropriate for analyzing geographical issues. This allowed Krugman to integrate two *disparate* fields in a cohesive model. This theory has come to be known as *new economic geography*. The embryo of this theory is found in Krugman's 1979 article itself. In it, he asks a simple question: what would happen if foreign trade became impossible, for example, due to very high transport costs or other obstacles? He answers the question in the following way. If two countries are identical, that is, they are exactly alike, then welfare will be the same in both the countries. But if the countries are alike in all respects except that one of them has a slightly larger population than the other, then the real income of labour will be somewhat higher in the country with larger population. The reason, he gives is that firms in the more highly populated country can make better use of economies of scale. That implies, lower prices for consumers and/or greater diversity in the supply of goods. This, in turn, will increase the welfare of the consumers. As a result, labour, *i.e.*, consumers, will tend to migrate to the country with more inhabitants, thereby increasing its population. Real wages and the supply of goods will then continue to increase even more in that country, and that will further increase the migration and so on.

It was only in 1991 that Krugman developed these ideas into a comprehensive *theory of location of labour and firms*. Here, he makes the assumption that although trade is possible, high transport costs stand as an obstacle. Otherwise, labour is free to move to the country or region which can offer the highest welfare, in terms of real wages and diversity of goods. The location decisions of firms imply a trade–off between utilizing economies of scale and saving on transport costs.

Concentration or Decentralization?

The above considerations have given rise to a *core-periphery model*. It shows that the relation between economies of scale and transport costs can result in either concentration or decentralization of population. Sometimes, the forces which contribute to concentration will be at work. It will result in regional imbalances and most of the population will be concentrated in a high technology core, whereas a small minority will inhabit the periphery with agriculture, as its livelihood. This mechanism can be used to explain the explosive urbanization witnessed today throughout the world, with rapidly growing megacities surrounded by increasingly depopulated rural areas. However, this is not necessarily the only possibility. Under different conditions, the forces which give rise to decentralization will dominate. This promotes more balanced development. Krugman's model explains the mechanisms at work in both the directions. For example, his model explains that declining transport costs result in concentration and urbanization. And it may be noted that throughout the 20th century, transport costs witnessed a declining trend.

ELINOR OSTROM AND OLIVER E. WILLIAMSON

Introduction

The Nobel Prize in Economics for the year 2009 was awarded to two American Scholars Elinor Ostrom and Oliver E. Williamson for their contribution to the field of economic governance. The former has been awarded the prize "for her analysis of economic governance, especially the commons" and the latter "for his analysis of economic governance, especially the boundaries of the firm". Both the Laureates explain how non-market institutions like natural resources managed by common property and firms, exist and work.

According to the Commission on Global Governance "governance is the sum of many ways individuals and institutions, public and private, manage their common affairs. It is a continuous process through which conflicting or diverse interests may be accommodated and cooperative action be taken. It includes formal institutions and regimes empowered to enforce compliance, as well as informal arrangements that people and institutions will either have agreed to or perceive to be in their interests".

Williamson defines economics of governance as "an effort to implement the study of good order and workable arrangements". Good order includes both spontaneous order in the market and intentional order of a "conscious, deliberate, purposeful kind". Workable arrangements are feasible modes of organization, all of which are flawed in comparison with a hypothetical model.

Elinor Ostrom

Elinor Ostrom is the first woman to get a Nobel Prize in Economics in the last forty five years. She is basically a political scientist. But she considers her work to be political economy or the study of social dilemmas. Rather her work is Interdisciplinary Covering Law, History, Economics, Political Science and Sociology. Her analysis is based on rich empirical evidence and laboratory experiments based on game theory and it provides practical guidance for policy.

Ostrom's important works include: (1) Ostrom E (1965). Public Entrepreneurship: *A Case Study in Ground Water Management,* Ph.D. Dissertation, University of California at Los Angeles; (2) Ostrom, E. (1990) *Governing the Commons: The Evolution of Institutions for Collective Actions,* Cambridge, Cambridge University Press; (3) Ostrom, E. (1999). *Coping with the tragedies of the Commons,* Annual Review of Political Science 2:493-535, (4) Ostrom, E. *Collective action and the evolution of social norms,* Journal of Economic Perspectives, 14:137-158. Summer; 5) Ostrom, E. (2005) *Understanding Institutional Diversity,* Princeton N.J., Princeton University Press; (6) Ostrom, E., R. Gardner and T. Walker (1994). *Rules, Games and Common Pool Resources.* Ann Arbor MI University of Michigan Press; (7) *Covenants with and without a Sword: Self – governance is possible,* American Political Science Review 86:404-417; and 8) Ostrom, E et al. (1999). *Revisiting the Commons: Local lessons, global challenges,* Science, 284:278-282.

Ostrom's work relates mainly to the management of common property by common ownership. And she has found that common ownership can be more effective than other forms of governance of commons. She does not say that it is a panacea, her findings reveal that it is much more effective than our common understanding.

"The word *Commons* originally denoted pastureland treated as a common resource, where individual herders were free to graze their sheep or cattle. The land can support a limited number of grazing animals. The temptation to graze more than one's share is a rational strategy for an individual herder. But if all succumb to the same temptation, the grass ceases to grow and the value of the pasture to everybody disappears".

Nowadays, the "commons" is used as a general term for shared resources in which each shareholder has an equal interest. In the information commons, we study issues relating to public knowledge, the public domain, open science and the free exchange of ideas. All these issues are at the core of a direct democracy.

Common-pool resources (CPRs) are natural or human-made resources where one person's use subtracts from another person's use, but difficult and costly, to exclude other users outside the group from using the resource. In the CPRs, a lot of research has been done in the areas of fisheries, forests, grazing systems, wild life, water resources, irrigation systems, agriculture, land tenure and use, social organization, theory (social dilemmas, game theory, experimental economics etc.) and global commons (climate change, air pollution, transboundary disputes, etc.) but CPRs can also include the broadcast spectrum.

We begin to study the Game Theory with the example of Prisoner's Dilemma. People are trapped by the Prisoner's Dilemma only if they treat themselves as prisoners by passively accepting the suboptimum strategy that locks them into. But if they try to work out a contract with the other players, or find the ones most likely to cooperate, or agree on punishing cheaters, or artificially change the incentive ratios, *they can create an institution* for collective action that benefits them all. This is one of the strategies (changing the rules of the game) for dealing with social dilemmas. Ostrom looks at some of the observed institutions as equilibrium outcomes of repeated games.

Social dilemmas act as obstacles on the path to creating institutions for collective action. These dilemmas must be overcome if institutions are to succeed or exist at all. *Lack of information* about the system can be an obstacle to agreement among individuals who make up the system. Another obstacle, *free-riding,* creates the second order social dilemma concerning who will bear the cost of policing the rules once they are agreed upon. Social dilemmas can be solved through institutions for collective action that are built by overcoming known obstacles.

Ostrom tells that the arc of civilization for the past 8000 years evolved by changing the rules of the game to turn zero-sum games into non-zero sum games. By examining legal records and public documents, she found that in many different cultures all over the world, some groups would find ways to overcome the obstacles that defeated others—by creating contracts, agreements, incentives, constitutions, signals, media to enable cooperation for mutual benefit.

The main issues in common pool resources are: whenever a group of people depend on resource that everybody uses but nobody owns, and where one person's use affects another person's ability to use the resource, either the population fails to provide the resource, overcomes and/ or fails to replenish it, or they construct an institution for undertaking and managing collective action. As already mentioned, the common pool resources can be a fishery, a grazing ground, the Internet, the electromagnetic spectrum, a park, the air, and scientific knowledge. The institution can be a body of informal norms which are passed from one generation to another or a body of formal written laws that are enforced by state agencies, or a market place that treats the resource as a private property or a mixture of these forms. In the real world of fishing grounds and wireless competition, CPR institutions that succeed are those that survive, and that fail sometimes cause the resource to disappear (e.g., salmon in the Pacific Northwest).

Elinor Ostrom challenged the accepted wisdom about institutions for collective action by her careful inductive examination of empirical studies of common pool resource management, and her insistence on interdisciplinary analysis.

She studied a number of small to medium groups that have taken on the responsibility for organizing resource governance. For example, she studied several hundred irrigation systems in Nepal. Her finding is that farmer-managed irrigation systems are more effective in terms of getting water to the tail end, higher productivity, lower cost, than the fancy irrigation systems built with the help of the Asian Development Bank, World Bank, USAID, etc. The locally managed irrigation systems with small and primitive dams built from stone, mud and trees have successfully allocated water between users for a long time whereas many of the modern dams of concrete and steel built with foreign aid, despite a flawless engineering have ended in failure. The reason is that the presence of durable dams has severed the ties between head-end and tail-end users. Since the dams are durable, there is little need for cooperation among users in maintaining the dams. Therefore, head-end users can extract a disproportionate share of the water without fearing the loss of tail-end maintenance labour. Ultimately, the total crop yield is higher around the primitive dams than around the modern dams. This is a classic case of failed modernization.

There is another example relating to failed collectivization and privatization. It refers to the management of grasslands in the interior of Asia. Scientists have studied satellite images of Mongolia and neighbouring areas in China and Russia, where livestock has been feeding on large grassland areas for centuries. Historically, the region was dominated by nomads, who moved their herds on a seasonal basis. In Mongolia, the traditions were largely intact in the mid-1990s, while neighbouring areas in China and Russia—with closely similar initial conditions—had been exposed to radically different governance regimes. There, central government imposed state-owned agricultural collectives, where most users settled permanently. As a result, the land was heavily degraded in China and Russia.

In the early 1980s, in an attempt to reverse the degradation, China dissolved the people's communes and privatized much of the grassland of Inner Mongolia. Individual households gained ownership of specific plots of land. Again, as in the case of the collectives, this policy encouraged permanent settlement rather than pastoral wandering, with further land degradation as a result. As satellite images clearly reveal, both socialism and privatization are associated with worse long-term outcomes than those observed in traditional group-based governance.

The above mentioned failures refer to economically poor regions of the world. But the lessons are much more far-reaching. Ostrom's first study concerned the management of ground water in parts of California and highlighted the role of users in creating workable institutions.

One thing, we must note here. She doesn't simply say "Oh, well, just leave it to the people, they will always organize". There are many settings that discourage self-organization.

The lesson is not that user management is always preferable to all other solutions. There are many cases in which privatization or public regulation yield better outcomes than user management. For example, in the 1930s, failure to privatize oil pools in **Texas** caused massive waste. Rather, the main lesson is that common property is often managed on the basis of rules and procedures that have evolved over long periods of time. As a result, they are more adequate and subtle than outsiders have tended to realize. Things like village sabhas during the Chola period and *Oor kattupadu (village discipline)* can also be cited as examples.

Besides demonstrating that self-governance can be feasible and successful, Ostrom has elucidated the key features of successful governance. Active participation of users in creating and enforcing rules is the key to successful governance. Rules that are imposed from the outside or unilaterally dictated by powerful insiders are more likely to be violated. Similarly, monitoring and enforcement work better when conducted by insiders than by outsiders. These principles radically differ from the common view that monitoring and sanctioning are the responsibility of the state and should be conducted by public employees.

Ostrom extracted from the cases of successful CPR management the following *design principles:*

1. Group boundaries are clearly defined.
2. Rules governing the use of collective goods are well matched to local needs and conditions.
3. Most individuals affected by these rules can participate in modifying the rules.
4. The rights of community members to devise their own rules are respected by external authorities.
5. A system for monitoring member's behaviour exists; the community members themselves undertake this monitoring.
6. A graduated system of sanction is used.
7. Community members have access to low-cost conflict resolution mechanisms; and
8. For CPRs that are parts of larger system: appropriation, provision, monitoring, enforcement, conflict resolution, and governance activities are organized in multiple layers of nested enterprises.

Conclusion

Ostrom argued forcefully that neither direct intervention by the state nor total privatization is necessary for people to evolve successful institutions. Of course, she agrees that state-provided courts lower the costs of creating the institutions and the market value of well-managed CPRs provides strong incentive to create, agree and maintain such arrangements.

Oliver E Williamson

Oliver Williamson has been awarded the Nobel Prize "for his analysis of economic governance, especially the boundaries of the firm".

Williamson's works include: 1) Williamson, O.E. (1968) *Economies as an antitrust defence: The Welfare tradeoffs*, American Economic Review 58:18-36; 2) Williamson O.E. (1971). *Vertical integration of production: Market failure considerations.* American Economic Review, Papers and Proceedings 61:112-123; (3) Williamson O.E. (1975). *Markets and Hierarchies*, New York, Free Press; 4) Williamson O.E. (1985). *The Economic Institutions of Capitalism*, New York, *Free Press;* 5) Williamson O.E. (1988). *Corporate Finance and Corporate Governance, Journal of Finance 43:567-591;* and 6) Williamson, O.E. (2000). *The New Institutional Economics: Taking Stock, Looking Ahead,* Journal of Economic Literature 38:595-613.

His work is an interdisciplinary effort to draw economics and organization theory together, to try to understand the boundaries of the firm and a whole set of practices that firms engage in, and more generally to understand complex economic organizations, of both private and public sector kinds. It analyses why firms can accomplish some transactions better than the markets can accomplish them. It also appeals to aspects of the law, mainly contract law. It has a lot of public *policy ramifications for antitrust and regulations.* A plus point about his work is that it provides for empirical testing of his theories. Economics of governance is influential in significant measure, because it does speak to the real world phenomena and invites empirical testing and much of it has been corroborated. One of the recommendations that flows from his work for public policy is that "all feasible forms of organization are flawed in comparison with a hypothetical ideal and that we need to understand the trade - offs that are going on, the factors that are responsible using one form of the governance rather than another, the strengths and weaknesses that are associated with each of them, and to fashion policy, with respect to anti-trust. It relates to corporate governance, as well. It adopts a different orientation than a standard one which looks at the firm and market organization in significant measure from a technological point of view. But Williamson looks at firm and market organization from a contractual point of view. That is, he looks at the theory of firm as governance structure through the lens of contract.

9. In contrast with the orthodox lens of choice (prices and output, supply and demand) the economics of governance is a lens of contract construction, broadly in the spirit of Buchanan's observation- that "mutuality of advantage from voluntary exchange ... is the most fundamental of all understandings in economics".

The economics of governance is basically an exercise in *bilateral private ordering*. It means that immediate parties to an exchange are actively involved in the provision of good order and workable arrangements. As against simple market exchange, governance is predominantly concerned with *ongoing contractual relations for which continuity of the relationship is a source of value*.

The four conceptual cornerstones out of which the economics of governance works are governance, transaction costs, adaptation and interdisciplinary social science.

J.R. Commons, one of the leaders of the institutional school was interested in "going concerns". The orthodox (classical) economics was preoccupied with simple market exchange and resource allocation paradigm. But Commons observed that the *continuity* of exchange relationship was important and reformulated the problem of economic organization as follows: *"the ultimate unit of activity ... must contain in itself the three principles of conflict, mutuality, and order. This unit is a transaction* (Commons, 1932, p4). And governance is the means by which to infuse order, thereby to mitigate conflict and realize mutual gains.

Ronald Coase (1937) in his article on "The Nature of the Firm" noted that the standard assumption that the transaction costs were zero presented neoclassical economics with a logical lapse. Sometimes, we glibly talk of market failure. Market failure is not absolute. Transaction cost can impede and sometimes and in particular cases completely block the formation of markets (Arrow, 1969). Arrow's remarks about vertical integration are especially pertinent: "An incentive for vertical integration is replacement of the costs of buying and selling on the market by the costs of intrafirm transfers; *the existence of vertical integration may suggest that the costs of operating competitive markets are not zero, as is usually assumed by theoretical analysis* (1969, p48).

Adaptation is the central problem of economic organization. While Hayek considered the price system as a mechanism for communicating information, Chester Barnard thought that consciously coordinated adaptations were accomplished through the use of management administration within the firm. So, to Hayek's "marvel of the market", Barnard added the "marvel of hierarchy".

Interdisciplinary social science is the last of the four cornerstones associated with economics of governance. As noted already, organization theory and aspects of the law (especially contract law) bear importantly on economics of governance.

It is a mistake to confuse the neoclassical theory of the firm with its real-world namesake. The chief mission of neoclassical economics is to understand how the price system coordinates the use of the resources, not the inner workings of real firms (Harold Demsetz, 1983, p 37).

There is a lot of confusion in the regulatory area. The main reason is regulatory issues are treated in a one-sided way. There is an extensive literature on market failure but there is no mention of, much less a corresponding literature on regulatory failure (Coase, 1964). Taken together, antitrust and regulatory policies toward business were careening out of control.

By way of digression, we may say that the recent global financial crisis, in a way is a case of regulatory failure.

Oscar Lange (1938, p. 109) described bureaucratization as "the real danger of socialism".

In economics of governance, we are not interested in one all-purpose law of contract that can be enforced in a legalistic way. Rather, we are interested in the idea of "contract as a framework" (Karl Llewellyn). The object of contract, so construed, was not to be legalistic, but *to get the job done*. The key idea is this: the legalistic view of contract that applies to simple transactions needs to make way for a more flexible and managerial conception of contract as the preservation of ongoing relations takes on economic importance. The convenient notion of one all purpose law of contract gives way to contract laws (plural) in the process.

Within a firm, transactions are organized by hierarchy. But what then is the contract law of internal organization? Williamson tells that "the implicit contract law of internal organization is that of forbearance" (Williamson, 1991b): the courts will hear cases relating to contracts between firms when there are disputes over prices, the damages to be ascribed to delays, failures of qualities and the like. But they will refuse to hear disputes between one internal division and another over identical technical issues. As access to courts is denied, the parties must resolve their differences internally. In other words, the firm becomes its own court of ultimate appeal. In effect, forbearance law authenticates hierarchy.

The strength of economics of governance lies in the fact that it has derived refutable implications and invited empirical testing.

Conclusions

The conclusions that we can drive from the economics of governance are:

1. Institutions matter and are susceptible to analysis;
2. Adaptation to disturbances is a key purpose of economic organization;
3. The action is in the microanalytics.
4. Positive transaction costs can be addressed in a comparative way;
5. Public policy toward business needs to be informed by a broad (organizational) understanding of the efficiency purposes served by complex contract and economic organization.
6. In short, economics of governance treats simple market exchange, as a special case and features *ongoing* transactions for which adaptations are needed. The firm exists because of its ability to economize on transaction cost.
7. Although Williamson's main contribution was to formulate a theory of vertical combination, the broader message is that different kinds of transactions call for different governance structures. Today, the general idea of economic governance has been extended to theories of marriage (Pollak, 1985), to theories of regulation (Goldberg, 1976) and to theories of corporate finance. Finally, both through his writings and founding editorship of the *Journal of Law, Economics and Organization*, Oliver Williamson has contributed to eliminating many of the barriers to intellectual exchange among different disciplines of the social sciences.

PETER A. DIAMOND, DALE T. MORTENSEN AND CHRISTOPHER A. PISSARIDES

The Nobel Prize in Economics for the year 2010 was awarded to Peter A.Diamond and Dale T. Mortensen of United States and Christopher A. Pissarides of Cyprus "for their analysis of markets with search frictions".

In most of the real world transactions, there are many impediments to trade. We can call these impediments "frictions". Buyers may have trouble finding the goods they are looking for and sellers may not be able to find buyers for the goods which they want to sell. These frictions can take many forms and may have many sources. They include worker and firm heterogeneity, imperfect information, and costs of transportation. An important question in this context is "how are market outcomes influenced by such frictions?" That is, how should we expect prices to form and how are quantities determined? Do these frictions warrant government intervention? These questions are pertinent in the labour market where unemployment is a major problem: Some workers will not find job openings or their applications will be turned down in favour of other workers.

As already noted, the 2010 Economics Nobel Prize was awarded for fundamental contributions to *search and matching theory*. This theory offers a framework for studying frictions in real-world transactions and has led to new insights into the workings of markets. The prize was granted for the closely related contributions made by Peter Diamond, Dale Mortensen, and Christopher Pissarides. Their contributions include the analysis of price dispersion and efficiency in economies with search and matching frictions as well as the development of what has come to be known as the *modern search and matching theory of unemployment*.

The major contributions of the three Nobel Laureates are found in the following works: (1) Diamond, P (1971), A Model of Price Adjustment, *Journal of Economic Theory, 3,* 156-168; (2) Diamond, P (1982a), Wage Determination and efficiency in Search Equilibrium, *Review of Economic Studies* 49, 217-227; (3) Diamond, P (1982b), Aggregate Demand Management in Search Equilibrium, *Journal of Political Economy* 90, 881-894; (4) Diamond, P (1984), *A Search Equilibrium Approach to the Micro Foundations of Macroeconomics* MIT Press; Mortensen, D (1970b) Job Search, the Duration of unemployment and the Phillips Curve, *American Economic Review* 60, 847-862; (6) Mortensen, P (1977), unemployment Insurance and Job search Decisions, *Industrial and Labour Relations Review 30,* 505-517; (7) Mortensen, D (1982a), The Matching Process as a Noncooperative Bargaining Game, in J McCall (ed.), *The Economics of Information and Uncertainty,* University of Chicago Press; (8) Mortensen, D (1988), Matching: Finding a Partner for Life or Otherwise, *American Journal of Sociology 94* (Supplement), 5215-5240; (9) Mortensen, D (2005), Wage Dispersion: *Why Are Similar Workers Paid Differently,* M.I.T. Press; (10) Mortensen, D and C. Pissarides (1994), Job Creation and Job Destruction in the Theory of Unemployment, *Review of Economic Studies* 61, 397-415; (11) Mortensen, D and C. Pissarides (1998), Technological Progress, Job Creation and Job Destruction, *Review of Economic Dynamics,* 733-753; (12) Mortenson, D and C. Pissarides (1999b) New Developments in Models of Search in the Labour Market, in O. Ashenfelter and D. Card (eds.) Handbook of Macroeconomics, Vol I, Part 2, Elseevier; (13) Pissarides, C (1984a), Search Intensity, Job Advertising and Efficiency, *Journal of Labour Economics* 2, 120-143; (14) Pissarides, C (1984b), Efficient Job Rejection, Economic Journal 94 (Supplement), 97-108; (15) Pissarides, C (1985), Short-Run Equilibrium Dynamics of Unemployment, Vacancies and Real Wages, *American Economic Review* 75, 676-690; (16) Pissarides, C (1990/2000), *Equilibrium Unemployment Theory* Basil Blackwell, Second Edition, MIT Press; (17) Pissarides C (1992), Loss of Skill during unemployment and the Persistence of Employment Shocks, *Quarterly Journal of Economics* 107, 1371-392; and (8) Pissarides, C (2009), The unemployment volatility Puzzle; Is Wage Stickiness the Answer? *Econometrica* 77, 1339-1369.

The research of Diamond, Mortensen and Pissarides focuses on specific frictions due to costly search and pairwise matching, i.e., the explicit difficulties buyers and sellers have in locating each other, thereby resulting in failure of markets to clear at all points, in time. Buyers and sellers face costs in their attempts to locate each other ("search") and meet pairwise when they come into contact ("matching"). This is in contrast to the standard market description of large number of buyers and sellers who trade at the same time. It is also assumed in the standard description that market information is easily available without any cost. And that there would be only one price in the market at which the sellers sell their good. But in the new theory, one of the main issues is, how price formation works in a market with search frictions. The theory considers in particular, how much price dispersion will be observed, and how large are the deviations from competitive pricing?

Peter Diamond's research shows that the mere presence of costly search and matching frictions is not sufficient to generate equilibrium price dispersion. Diamond also found that even a minute search cost moves the equilibrium price very far from the competitive price. He has shown that the only equilibrium price is the monopoly price. This surprising finding is called "Diamond Paradox".

Another important question in search markets is whether there is too much or too little search, that is, whether or not the markets deliver efficient outcomes. Since there will be unexecuted trade and unemployed resources—buyers who have not managed to locate sellers, and vice versa—the outcome might be regarded as necessarily inefficient. On the basis of the assumption that the friction is a fundamental problem that the economy cannot avoid, the relevant issue is whether the economy is *constrained efficient*, i.e., delivers the best outcome, given this restriction. It may also be, noted that aggregate welfare is not necessarily higher with more search since search is costly. All the three economists contributed important insights into the efficiency question. Their finding is that efficiency cannot be expected and policy intervention may therefore become desirable.

Peter Diamond argued that a search and matching environment can lead to macroeconomic unemployment problems as a result of the difficulties in coordinating trade. A model he developed provides a rationale for "aggregate demand management" so as to steer the economy towards the best equilibrium.

The research on search and matching theory has a deep impact within labour economics. One of the most central issues in economics is why unemployment exists and what can and should be done about it? Labour markets do not appear to "clear": there are jobless workers who search for work (unemployment) and firms that look for workers (vacancies). It is a difficult challenge to formulate a fully specified equilibrium model that generates both unemployment and vacancies. The research by Diamond, Mortensen and Pissarides has fundamentally influenced our views on the determinants of unemployment, and more generally on the working of labour markets. Their major contribution is the development of a new framework for analyzing labour markets, for both positive and normative purposes in a dynamic general equilibrium setting. The resulting class of models has become known as the *Diamond – Mortensen – Pissarides model* (DMP model). The DMP model helps us to consider simultaneously (1) how workers and firms jointly decide whether to match or to keep searching. (ii) in case of a continued match, how the benefits from the match are split into a wage for the worker and a profit for the firm; (iii) firm entry, i.e., firms' decisions to "create jobs"; and (iv) how the match of a worker and a firm might develop over time, possibly leading to agreed upon separation.

Conclusion

The search and matching theory developed by Diamond, Mortensen and Pissarides has evolved from microeconomic decision theory to the leading paradigm in macroeconomic analyses of the labour market. The theory has also proved to be fruitful in many other areas. It has been used to study issues in consumer theory, monetary theory, industrial organization, public economics, financial economics, housing economics, urban economics and family economics.

THOMAS SARGENT AND CHRISTOPHER SIMS

Introduction

The Nobel Prize in Economics for the year 2011 was awarded to two American economists Thomas Sargent and Christopher Sims "for their empirical research on cause and effect in the macroeconomy". The whole idea behind their work is that individuals are rational and capable of making informed choices.

"One of the main tasks of macroeconomic research is to comprehend how both shocks and systematic policy shifts affect macroeconomic variables in the short and long run", the Royal Swedish Academy said in a statement. It further stated that "Sargent and Sim's awarded research contributions have been indispensable to this work".

Sargent has specialized in the field of macroeconomics, monetary economics and time series econometrics. He is known as "one of the leaders of the rational expectations revolution" and the author of a number of path – breaking papers.

In a series of articles written during the 1970s, Sargent showed how structural macroeconomic models could be constructed, solved and estimated. His approach is very useful in the analysis of economic policy, but is also used in other areas of macro-econometric and economic research.

Sargent has shown how structural macroeconometrics can be used to analyse permanent changes in economic policy. This method can be applied to study macroeconomic relationships when households and firms adjust their expectations concurrently with economic developments.

Christopher Sims introduced a new way of analyzing macroeconomic data. He also concurred with Sargent in emphasizing the importance of expectations.

Sims proposed a new method of identifying and interpreting economic shocks in historical data and of analyzing how such shocks are gradually transmitted to different macroeconomic variables.

Sims has developed a method based on vector autoregression to analyse how the economy is affected by temporary changes in economic policy and other factors.

The major works of Sargent and Sims include (1) Sargent Thomas J., (1973) "Rational Expectations, the Real Rate of Interest, and the Natural Rate of Unemployment", *Brookings Papers on Economic Activity* 2, pp. 429-72; (2) Sargent, Thomas J. (1977), "The Demand for Money: Hyperinflations under Rational Expectations: I", *International Economic Review 18, pp 59-82;* (3) *Sargent, Thomas J. and Christopher Sims (1977),* Business Cycle Modelling without pretending to Have Too Much A Priori Economic Theory", Federal Reserve Bank of Minneapolis, Working Paper 55, (4) Sargent, Thomas J. (1979, 1987). *Macroeconomic Theory.* New York: Academic Press; (5) Sargent, Thomas J. and Lars P. Hansen (1980) "Formulating and Estimating Dynamic Linear Rational Expectations Models". *Journal of Economic Dynamics and Control 2(1) 7-46;* (6) Sargent Thomas J. and Neil Wallace (1981). "Some unpleasant Monetarist Arithmetic". Federal Reserve Bank of Minneapolis Quarterly Review 5(3)1-17; (7) Sargent Thomas J. (1987). Dynamic Macroeconomic Theory. Harvard University Press, and Sims Christopher (January 1980). "Macroeconomics and Reality" (PDF) Econometrica 48(1)1-48.

One of the main tasks for macroeconomists is to explain how macroeconomic aggregates—such as GDP, investment, unemployment and inflation—behave over time. How are these variables affected by economic policy? A primary aspect in this analysis is the role of the central bank and its ability to influence the economy. How effective can monetary policy be in stabilizing unwanted fluctuations in macroeconomic aggregates? We can raise similar questions about fiscal policy. Sargent and Sims have developed empirical methods that can answer these kinds of questions.

In any empirical analysis based on observational data, it is rather difficult to disentangle cause and effect. This becomes especially cumbersome in macroeconomic policy analysis because of an important stumbling block: the key role of *expectations*. Economic decision-makers form expectations about policy, thereby linking economic activity to future policy. The methods developed by Sargent and Sims tackle these difficulties and they have become standard tools among the researchers and are commonly used to inform policymaking.

Both the economists have made seminal contributions that allow researchers to specify, empirically implement and evaluate dynamic models of the macroeconomy with a central role for expectations. The Keynesian macroeconomic model that was in vogue till 1970s was found unsuitable to explain the *stagflation*—high rates of inflation combined with slow output growth and high unemployment—which most western countries experienced since 1970s.

Sargent: Structural Econometrics

During the 1970s, Sargent developed an alternative theoretical macroeconomic framework with emphasis on rational expectations to interpret stagflation of the 1970s. Sargents' contributions to rational-expectations econometrics were purely methodological. His methods for characterizing and structurally estimating macroeconomic models with microeconomic foundations broke new ground in economic research. Sargent also raised important points of immediate policy relevance. For instance, his early studies of linkages between fiscal and monetary policy guides policymakers even today.

Sims: Vector Autoregression (VAR)

Sims launched a forceful critique of the macroeconometric paradigm of the 1970s by focusing on *identification*, which is a central element in making causal inferences from observed data. He argued that existing models relied on "incredible" identification assumptions and the interpretations of "what causes what" based on these assumptions in macroeconomic time series were flawed. He thought the models based on wrong estimates would not serve as useful tools for monetary policy analysis and for forecasting.

Sims proposed as an alternative that the empirical study of macroeconomic variables could be built around a statistical tool, the vector autoregression (VAR). He believed that properly structured and interpreted VARs might overcome many identification problems. Not only that, they were of great potential value not only for forecasting but also for interpreting macroeconomic time series and conducting monetary policy experiments. Today, VARs have become a major research tool in many areas outside of monetary economics.

Conclusion

Sargent and Sims have developed methods which have become predominant in empirical studies of the two-way relations between monetary policy and broader macroeconomy.

Sargent is the father of modern structural macroeconometrics. He has shown how to characterize and estimate modern macroeconomic models relying on full microeconomic foundations. He has also pioneered the empirical study of expectations formation.

Sims is the father of vector autoregressions (VARs) as an empirical tool in macroeconomics. This has become an indispensable tool in applied research and in structural econometrics. The tools of VARs is used today for studying macroeconomic aggregates for interpreting time series, for forecasting and for policy analysis.

LLOYD SHAPLEY AND ALVIN ROTH

Introduction

The 2012 Nobel Prize in Economics was awarded to two American economists Lloyd Shapley and Alvin Roth for providing a theoretical framework for analyzing resource allocation, as well as empirical studies and actual redesign of real-world institutions such as labour market clearing houses and school admissions procedures.

Generally, resources are allocated through the price system. For example, high wages attract workers into a particular occupation. But in many cases, price system cannot solve allocation problems because it would encounter legal and ethical objections. Let us consider, for example, the allocation of public – (government) school places to children, or the allocation of human organs to patients who need transplants. It is true that there are many markets where the price system operates. But in a majority of cases, we do not have perfect competition. The market for some goods is very thin. The allocation of resources in these thin markets depends on the institutions that govern transactions.

The major works of the two Nobel Laureates include: (1) Gale D. and L.S. Shapley (1962) College admissions and stability of marriage, *American Mathematical Monthly,* 69, 9-15; (2) Roth A.E. (2008). What have we learned from market design? *Economic Journal, 118;285-310;* (3) Roth, A.E. (1984). The evolution of the labour market for medical interns and residents: A case study in game theory *Journal of Political* Economy 92:991-1016. (4) Roth A.E. and Gotomayor M. (1990)

Two-sided Matching: a Study in *Game-theoretic Modeling and Analysis,* Econometric Society Monograph Series, Cambridge University Press. Two important lectures by Roth are: 1. Roth A.E. (2007) *What Have We Learned from Market Design?* Rosenthal Memorial Lecture, Boston University; and 2) Roth, A.E. (2007) *Market Failure and Market Design, Google Tech Talks.*

Lloyd Shapley: Stable Allocations

The foundations for theoretical framework for analyzing allocation of resources were laid in 1962, when David Gale and Lloyd Shapley published a mathematical inquiry into a certain class of allocation problems. They considered a model with two sets of agents (*e.g.*, workers and firms) that must be paired with each other. Let us suppose that a particular worker is hired by employer A. But this worker would have preferred employer B, who would have also liked to hire this worker (but did not), then there are unexploited gains from trade. If employer B had hired this worker, both of them would have been better off. Gale and Shapley defined that for a pairing to be *stable,* unexploited gains from trade should not exist. In an ideal market, where workers and firms have unlimited time and ability to make deals, the outcome would always be stable. But, real-world markets differ from this ideal in important ways. However, Gale and Shapley discovered a "deferred – acceptance" procedure which is easy to understand and always leads to a stable outcome. The procedure specifies how agents on one side of the market (*e.g.*, the employers) make offers to those on the other side, who accept or reject these offers according to certain rules.

The notion of stability is a central concept in cooperative game theory, which seeks to determine how a group of rational individuals might cooperatively choose an allocation. The primary architect of this game theory was Lloyd Shapley, who developed its main concepts in the 1950s and 1960s.

In 1962, Shapley applied the idea of matching to a special case. In a joint paper with David Gale, he examined the case of *pairwise matching:* how individuals can be paired up when they all have different views regarding who would be the best match.

Matching Partners

Gale and Shapley analysed matching at an abstract level. They used marriage as an example. They posed the question: How should ten women and ten men be matched, while respecting their individual preferences? The main challenge was to design a simple mechanism that would lead to a simple matching, where no couples would break up and form new matches which would make them better off. Gale and Shapley provided the solution—"deferred acceptance" algorithm—which was a set of simple rules that always led straight to a stable matching.

The Gale-Shapely algorithm can be set up in two different ways: either men propose to women or women propose to men. In the latter case, the process begins like this: each woman proposes to the man she likes the best. Each man then looks at the different proposals he has received (if any), retains what he regards as the most attractive proposal (but defers from accepting it) and rejects the others. The women, who were rejected in the first round then propose to their second-best choices, while the men again keep their best offer, and reject the rest. This continues until no woman wants to make further proposals. As each of the men accepts the proposal he holds, the process comes to an end. Gale and Shapley proved mathematically that this algorithm always leads to a stable matching.

The real-world significance of Gale and Shapley's work was recognized in the early 1980s when Alvin Roth set out to study a very practical problem: the market for newly examined doctors.

Alvin Roth and Market Design

Alvin Roth and his colleagues used Gale – Shapley theoretical framework, in combination with empirical studies, controlled laboratory experiments and computer simulations, to examine the functioning of other markets. This has led to the emergence of a new branch of economics known as *market design.* We may note in this context that the term "market" does not presuppose the existence of a price system. Monetary transfers are ruled out in many important applications.

Two properties of key importance for market design are *stability*, which encourages groups to voluntarily participate in the market and *incentive compatibility*, which discourages strategic manipulation of the market. While the notion of stability is derived from cooperative game theory, the concept of incentive compatibility comes from the theory of mechanism design, a branch of non-cooperative game theory.

Controlled laboratory experiments are often used in the field of market design. Vernon Smith shared the 2002 Nobel Prize in Economics for his work in experimental economics. Alvin Roth is another major contributor in this area.

The combination of game theory, empirical observations and controlled experiments has led to the development of an empirical science with many important practical applications. For example, Roth made use of the Gale-Shapley algorithm to study the market for new doctors who are employed as residents (interns) in U.S.A. The Gale-Shapley algorithm proved to be useful in other applications such as high school choice and matching kidneys and patients.

Conclusion

A striking feature of the above examples is that prices are not part of the process. But it has not limited the applicability of Gale-Shapley algorithm. The work by Alvin Roth has enhanced our understanding of how markets work. The contribution of both the economists have led directly to the successful redesign of a number of important real-world markets.

EUGENE FAMA, ROBERT SHILLER AND LARS PETER HANSEN

Introduction

The Nobel Prize in Economics for the year 2013 was awarded to three American economists Eugene Fama, Robert Shiller and Lars Peter Hansen for their empirical work aimed at understanding how asset prices are determined.

The behaviour of asset prices are of crucial importance for the investors and for the macroeconomy. Mispricing of assets may contribute to financial crises. As the recent recession illustrates such crises can damage the overall economy.

The Nobel Laureates and their contribution

What are the determinants of asset prices? Whether asset prices are predictable? These are all central questions. The methods developed by the three Nobel Laureates have greatly improved our understanding of asset prices and revealed a number of important empirical regularities as well as plausible factors behind these regularities.

The important works of the three Laureates include: (1) Fama, E.F. (1965) "The behavior of stockmarket prices", Journal of Business 38, 34-105; (2) Fama E.F., L. Fisher, M.Jensen and R. Roll (1969). "The adjustment of stock prices to new information". *International Economic Review* 10, 1-21; (3) Fama E.F. and K.R. French (1988a). "Dividend yields and expected stock returns". *Journal of Financial Economics* 22, 3-26; (4) Fama E.F. and K.R. French (1988b). "Permanent and temporary components of stock prices". *Journal of Political Economy* 96.246-273; (5) Fama E.F. and K.R. French (1996). "Multifactor explanations for asset pricing anomalies", *Journal of Finance 53(6),* 1975-1999; (6) Hansen, L.P. (1982). Large sample properties of generalized method of moments estimators, *"Econometrica,* 50 1029-1054; (7) Hansen L.P., J.C. Heaton and A. Yaron (1996), "Finite-Sample properties of some alternative GMM estimators", *Journal of Business & Economic Statistics* 14; (8) Hansen L.P. and R. Jagannathan (1991), "Implications of Security market data for models of dynamic economics", *Journal of Political Economy* 99, 225-252; (9) Hansen L.P. and S.F. Richard (1987), "The role of conditioning information in deducing testable restrictions implied by dynamic asset pricing models," *Econometrica*, 55, 587-613; (10) Shiller R.J. (1981a), "Do Stock prices move too much to be justified by subsequent changes in dividends". *American Economic Review* 71, 421-436; (11) Shiller R.J. (1981b), "The use of volatility measures in assessing market efficiency", *Journal of Finance* 36 (2) 291-304; (12) Shiller R.J. (1984), "Stock prices and social dynamics", *Carnegie Rochester Conference Series on Public Policy, 457-510;* (13) Shiller R.T. *(2000), Irrational Exuberance,* Princeton University Press; (14) Shiller R.J. and P. Perron (1985), "Testing the random walk hypothesis: Power Vs. frequency of observation" Economics Letters 18. 381-386; and (5) Shiller R.J. (2008) *The Subprime Solution: How today's global financial crisis happened and what to do about it,* Princeton University Press.

In a seminal *event study* from 1969, and in many other studies, Fama and his colleagues studied short-term predictability from different angles. They found that the amount of short-run predictability in stock market is very limited. The empirical result has had a profound impact on academic literature as well as on market practices.

If we cannot predict stock prices in the short-run, many economists believed that we cannot predict in the long-run. Shiller's empirical research proved that the belief was incorrect. Shiller's 1981 paper on stock-price volatility and his later studies on long-run predictability provided the key insights: stock prices are excessively volatile in the short-run, and at a horizon of a few years, the overall market is quite predictable.

In the long-run, compensation for risk should play a more important role for returns, and predictability might reflect attitudes towards risk and variation in market risk over time. And interpretations of findings of predictability need to be based on the theories of the relationship between risk and asset prices. Here Hansen made fundamental contributions first by developing an econometric method—the Generalized Method of Moments (GMM) presented in a paper in 1982 – designed to make it possible to deal with the particular features of asset-price data and then by applying it in a sequence of studies. Hansen's findings broadly supported Shiller's preliminary findings: asset prices fluctuate too much to be reconciled with standard theory, as represented by the Consumption Capital Asset Pricing Model (CCAPM).

Influences on Market Practice

Asset pricing is one of the fields in economics where academic research has had profound impact on market practice. The research initiated by Fama, Shiller and Hansen has produced a body of robust empirical findings, which have important practical implications.

1. In the short term, predictability in stock returns is limited.
2. In the long term, there is economically significant predictability in stock returns.
3. In the cross-section of stocks, a number of factors such as book – to – market predict differences in expected returns. Higher returns come with higher risk.

The work of Fama, Jensen and others inspired the emergence of *index funds* and Exchange Traded Funds (ETFs) and in 2012, they accounted for 41% of the worldwide flows into mutual funds.

The research on market predictability and on cross-sectional return differences across financial assets has also had considerable practical impact and has contributed to the growth of "quantitative investment management", where investors use quantitative factors and statistical modelling to make investment decisions. The academic work on the determinants of cross-sectional returns has also had a large impact on the practice of portfolio performance measurement.

Research findings from empirical asset pricing have also had practical impact outside the investment management industry. The event study methodology of Fama, Fisher, Jensen and Roll (1969) has become an important tool in legal practice for assessing damages in law suits, for example, in securities fraud cases.

Another area of practical impact is the measurement of asset returns and price indexes.

Beyond stock prices, Case and Shiller (1987) constructed the first systematic high quality index of U.S. house prices. It is now the standard real estate price index in the U.S. In his 1991 book *Macro Markets,* Shiller highlighted the fact that major risks in society, like house-price risks are uninsurable despite their importance.

Conclusion

Fama, Shiller and Hansen have developed empirical methods and used them to gain important insights about the determination of asset prices. Their findings have become highly influential both academically and practically.

We now know that it is very difficult to predict asset prices in the short-run, but their movements can be predicted in the long-run. We also know more about the determinants of the cross-section of returns on different assets. Subsequent research has further investigated how asset prices are fundamentally determined by risk and attitudes towards risk, as well as behavioural factors.

JEAN TIROLE

Introduction

The Nobel Prize in Economics for the year 2014 was awarded to Jean Tirole, a French economist 'for his analysis of market power and regulation'.

After taking a degree in Engineering and another degree in Mathematics in Paris, Tirole went to USA to study Economics and he was awarded Ph.D. in economics in 1981 by the Massachusetts Institute of Technology in Cambridge, USA. He is now Scientific Director at Toulouse School of Economics, Toulouse, Capitole University, France. The new tools of economic theory and deep insights into the production conditions of a number of regulated industries gave Tirole a very good foundation to review and deepen the analysis of market power and regulation.

Tirole did considerable amount of research work along with Laffont J.J. Some of the important books which he wrote jointly are: Laffont J.J. and Tirole: *Competition in Telecommunications* (1999), Laffont J.J. and Tirole: *A Theory of Incentives in Procurement and Regulation (1993)* and Dewatripont, M., Rochet, J. Tirole, J: *Balancing the Banks : Global Lessons from the Financial Crisis (2010) Tirole, J.: The Theory of Industrial Organization (1988).* Besides, he published innumerable number of papers related to regulation and market power.

In the market, many industries are dominated by a few large firms or a single monopoly. Without regulation, such markets often produce undesirable results. They will charge prices much higher than costs or some unproductive firms survive by preventing the entry of new and more productive firms.

Before Tirole, economists and policymakers followed some general principles for all industries. They advocated simple policy rules. For example, capping prices for monopolists and prohibiting cooperation between competitors. Tirole theoretically showed that such policies worked well only in certain conditions. They had good and bad effects. For example, price caps can provide dominant firms motives to reduce costs. It is a good thing for the society. But, it may also permit excessive profits, which is a bad thing for society. The merger of a firm and its supplier may encourage innovation but may distort competition

There is not much of competition in many industries. A few firms controls the market and they enjoy a lot of market power. Such a situation warrants intervention by the government. Theories of regulation and competition policy aim to provide useful scientific guidance for such intervention. And there is no perfect competition. Imperfect competition is more or less the rule. When a firm has market power, how will it behave? How does its behavior affect the firm's suppliers, customers, and competitors? All these questions are studied within the field of Industrial Organization. George Stigler was awarded the Nobel Prize in Economics in 1982 "for his seminal studies of industrial structure, functioning of market and causes and effects of public regulation". Since then, Industrial Organization field has undergone rapid development. This enhanced our understanding of imperfectly competitive markets. And this in turn has laid the foundation for better informed competition policy. Good progress has been made in the theory of optimal regulation of firms with market power.

Tirole's Contributions

Jean Tirole is one of the most influential economists of our time. He has made important theoretical research contributions in a number of areas. His most significant contribution is he has clarified how to understand and regulate industries with a few powerful firms.

The developments in the study of industrial structure, markets and regulation witnessed two methodological breakthroughs, namely game theory and the theory of mechanism design. By 1970s, economists started applying these tools to the major issues of imperfect competition, regulation and competition policy. Over the next decade, many economists took part in this analytical revolution. It was to a large extent a collective effort. But, among the many contributors, Jean Tirole stands out. No other scholar has done more to enhance our understanding of Industrial Organization in general and of optimal policy interventions in particular.

At a time when theoretical advancements took place, public-policy also got interested in these issues. Regulatory reforms and pro-competitive liberalization in conjunction with privatization were followed in many countries. The European Union became a single market. Many issues arose and they could not be solved with the existing theory. The analysis of the new issues required a combination of oligopoly theory and contract (principal – agent) theory and an integration of industrial economics with public economics. And Tirole became an ideal candidate to make lasting contribution.

It may be noted that Tirole's overall contribution is greater than the sum of individual contributions. He has created a unified framework for Industrial organization theory and regulation, founded on a rigorous analysis of strategic behaviour and information economics.

Tirole's research is marked by the following salient features: First, he derived his results from fundamental assumptions about preferences, technologies (including contracting technologies) and asymmetric information. He had the technical expertise to deal with the issues in game theory and contract theory. Economics is sometimes described as 'a box of tools'. Tirole made significant contributions to the tool box itself. Second, his research facilitated realism. He has carefully designed his models to capture essential features of economic environments so that his theories could be immediately applicable to policy. Third, by creating a consistent conceptual framework, he became a leader in the formulation of coherent theory of Industrial organization. Fourth, Tirole's models have sharpened policy analysis. For example, economists before him thought that monopoly power in one market cannot be profitably leveraged into another market by vertical integration. But Tirole challenged that view. This made the competition authorities to become more alert to the potential dangers posed by vertical integration.

Tirole made very important contribution to the theory of Industrial Organization and the regulation of dominant firms. His insights apply to more regulatory settings as well as to the related topic of government procurement. Some of his most significant contributions are the *modelling of regulatory capture* (collusion between regulatory agencies and regulated firms) and *dynamic contracting*. These advances were inspired by fundamental contributions to contract theory.

It is true that general theories of regulation are of great value. But in the end, all regulation must be industry-specific. For example, Laffont and–Tirole in their book *Competition in Telecommunications* (2000) consider the issues related to the regulation of telecommunications industry. Tirole has also studied the regulation issues of other industries ranging from banking to electricity. Tirole has an exceptional ability to grasp the central features of an economic environment, to formulate these features mathematically and to analyse the resulting model. Thereby, he arrives at normative conclusions of great practical importance.

Tirole was awarded the prize mainly for his focus on normative theories of optimal regulation and competition policy. But any normative theory must rest on positive analysis of how firms interact. For competition and regulation policy, it is important to understand interaction among firms working under imperfect competition. So, *oligopoly theory* becomes the most central theory in Industrial organization. Tirole played a major role in the transformation of oligopoly theory during the 1980s.

Tirole's contribution to theoretical advances changed the way economists think about competition policy. He analyzed public policies regarding vertical contractual relationships in a convincing manner. He expressed the view that vertical relations require regulation only if they impose costs on outsiders that are greater than the benefits to insiders. His analysis helped to have a clear understanding of mutually beneficial contracts between sellers and buyers in a vertical chain . This problem closely resembles that of optimal regulation of monopolies. Another important thing to understand is the nature of strategic behaviour towards competitors. Tirole's analysis of vertical contractual relationships contributed to a significant revision of competition policy in the U.S.

As already mentioned, Tirole has not only developed general theoretical frameworks of analysis but also adapted them to the circumstances of specific and quite different industries (e.g. telecommunications and financial intermediaries).

Tirole has made many contributions to other fields as well: general economic theory, financial markets, asset-market bubbles, organization economics, corporate finance and behavioural economics.

Conclusion

Jean Tirole's research is marked by respect for the particulars of different markets and skillful use of new analytical methods in economics. He has provided deep insights about essential nature of imperfect competition and contracting under asymmetric information. His contributions provide a fine example of how economic theory can be of great practical significance.

ANGUS DEATON

Introduction

The Nobel Prize for Economics in 2015 was awarded to Angus Deaton of Princeton University, U.S.A. 'for his analysis of consumption, poverty and welfare'

The Royal Swedish Academy, while announcing the prize, in its press release stated: "To design economic policy that promotes welfare and reduces poverty, we must first understand individual consumption choices. More than anyone else, Angus Deaton has enhanced this understanding. By linking detailed individual choices and aggregate incomes, his research has helped transform the fields of microeconomics, macroeconomics and development economics.

The work for which Deaton has been honoured revolves around three questions:

(1) How do consumers distribute their spending among different goods?

(2) How much of society's income is spent and how much is saved?

(3) How do we best measure and analyze welfare and poverty?

Angus Deaton is a UK and US citizen. He was born in 1945 in Edinburgh, U.K. He took his Ph.D. degree in 1974 from the university of Cambridge, UK. He has been Professor of Economics and International Affairs at Princeton University, USA, since 1983.

His Works

Deaton published some important books and a large number of papers in the field of consumption, poverty and welfare. They include, Deaton, A: *Measurement of Welfare: Theory and Practical guidelines* (1980), LSMS, Working Paper No.7, The World Bank, Washington, D.C., Deaton, A: *Understanding Consumption* (1992); Deaton, A: *The Analysis of Household Surveys: A Microeconomic Approach to Development Policy* (1997), Deaton, A: *Looking for Boy – Girl Discrimination in Household Expenditure Data* (1989), World Bank Economic Review 3(1) 1-15; Deaton, A : *Prices and Poverty in India,* 1987-2000, Economic and Political Weekly 38(4) 362-368 (2003c); Deaton, A. and J. Dreze: *Food and Nutrition in India: Facts and Interpretations,* Economic and Political Weekly 44(7), 42-65 (2009); Deaton, A. and J. Muellbauer: *An Almost Ideal Demand System* American Economic Review 70(3), 312-326 (1980a); Deaton, A. and T.Muellbauer: *On Measuring Child costs: with Applications to Poor Countries, Journal of* Political Economy 94(4) 720-744 (1986) and Deaton, A. and A. Tarozzi: *Prices and Poverty in India,* Princeton Working Paper (2000).

Deaton's Contributions

There has been enormous progress in the study of consumption over the last three to four decades. Though many economists have contributed to this progress, Angus Deaton stands out. He has made many fundamental and interconnected contributions to the measurement, theory and empirical analysis of consumption. His main achievements are three.

First, his research enabled the estimation of demand systems, that is, the quantitative study of consumption choices across different commodities to a new level of sophistication and generality. The Almost Ideal *Demand System* which Deaton and John Muellbauer introduced more than three decades ago is widely used even today in academic circles, as well as in practical policy evaluation.

Second, Deaton's research on aggregate consumption was the first step in microeconometric revolution in the study of consumption and saving over time. He is a pioneer in the analysis of dynamic consumption behaviour under uncertainty and liquidity constraints. He devised methods for designing panels from repeated cross-section data. This has made it possible to study individual behavior over time. He explained why researchers must take aggregation issues seriously to understand total consumption and saving. His later research has mostly addressed macroeconomic issues through microeconomic data.

Third, Deaton popularized the use of household survey data in developing countries, especially data on consumption, to measure living standards and poverty. By doing that, Deaton helped transform development economics from a largely theoretical field based on crude macro data, to a field dominated by empirical research based on reliable micro data. He showed the value of using consumption and expenditure data to analyse the welfare of the poor. He identified shortcomings when comparing living standards across time and place.

Demand Analysis

While studying consumption, demand analysis is of paramount importance. Deaton has brought about a major transformation in the research on demand systems. He has identified important limitations in earlier systems. In his paper "An Almost Ideal Demand System" which he published jointly with Muellbaur in 1980 he has developed a model that overcomes some of the limitations. This model forms the basis of modern demand analysis. Deaton has also pointed out many limitations in the Almost Ideal Demand System. By doing that, he has provided the agenda for further research on consumer demand.

Consumption Over Time

In the earlier demand study system, we study consumption by following two-stage procedure. First, the consumer decides how much to spend on consumption at each point in time. Then she decides how much to spend on different commodities or commodity groups. While the latter decision can be captured by the demand system, the determination of total expenditure on consumption is taken as given.

In a series of contributions during the 1980s, Deaton studied how much of an individual's income is spent on consumption (or, equivalently, how much is saved) at each point in time.

Changing the Focus on Individual Data

Deaton rejected the earlier aggregation data for three reasons. First, the theoretical model could be wrong because consumers may not be rational second, while working with aggregate data, the notion of representative consumer is problematic. Even if the individuals are rational, the conditions for aggregation are not satisfied in reality. Third, many constraints faced by individuals as consumers may not be accounted for in the models. For example, borrowing constraints, which have implications for consumer behaviour and aggregation. So Deaton in his book *understanding consumption* argued : "Progress is most likely to come when aggregation is taken seriously and when macroeconomic questions are addressed in a way that uses the increasingly plentiful and informative microeconomic data".

Thus he argued that one should study individual consumption, where observed behaviour may reflect a degree of consistent rational choice, and to explicitly address the aggregation problem.

As a result of Deaton's insights, macroeconomists nowadays devote a lot of time to the analysis of income dynamics. Macro-economics today is not only about studying the dynamics of aggregate variables, it is about studying the dynamics of the entire equilibrium distribution of allocations across individual economic actors. Deaton played a major role in starting this transition.

"..The hallmark of Deaton's research on consumer behaviour over time is the interplay between theory and data; and the interplay between individual behaviour and aggregate outcomes. His work on consumption and saving showed that aggregate data could only be reconciled with theory if one took individual consumption behaviour based on individual income processes seriously. In this way, he played a fundamental role in shifting the macroeconomic literature on consumption and savings towards micro-based empirical models" (The Royal Swedish Academy of Sciences Scientific Background on 2015 Economics Nobel Prize, P. 21).

Welfare in Developing Countries

In the 1980s, development economists faced problems in answering with credibility, the basic questions on the extent of poverty, and how poor households respond to their economic and physical environments due to lack of data and appropriate analytical methods.

All that has changed now. Today, development economics is dominated by microeconometric research, high-quality microdata, especially household data. The last two decades of research has improved our understanding of the essential mechanisms at play in developing counties. It has provided a large number of insights that are highly relevant for policy making.

Angus Deaton has played a fundamental role in this transformation, similar to the role played by him in the study of demand analysis, aggregation consumption and savings. He has made a number of methodological and substantial contributions to the measurement of poverty by his pioneering analysis of microdata from household surveys.

Household Survey Data Analysis

During 1980s, Deaton made use of household surveys as a means of measuring poverty and living standards, and to find out their determinants. He played an important role in a major study ("Living Standards Measurement Study") commissioned by the World Bank in 1980s. He ensured that expenditure data were collected as the basis for welfare measurement. Consumption – as opposed to income – remain the core variable in poverty measurement in low income countries. That is because it is easier to measure and provide an accurate measure of material welfare when income varies seasonally throughout the year.

Income and Nutritional Status

Deaton jointly with Subramanian investigated the relationship between income and nutritional status, as measured by calories consumed in poor countries. The investigation is important for three reasons:

First, poverty is closely related to whether people get enough to eat. When we document the living standard of the poor, through household surveys, it helps us to know whether they get adequate nutrition. Second, knowledge about the relationship between nutrition and income will help the government to design policies to reduce poverty. Third, it helps us study the relationship between nutritional status, productivity and income. The theory of nutritionally based efficiency wages tells that productivity depends on nutrition. That means, those who do not get enough food (calories) may not be productive enough to be employed even below the current market wage. As a result, they will be stuck in unemployment trap and find themselves in the vicious circle of low productivity, low income and poverty.

Discrimination within Family

Deaton's study, "Looking for Boy-Girl discrimination in Household Expenditure Data" (1989) deals with discrimination within the household. There is strong evidence that sons are favoured over daughters in many developing countries. One possible mechanism is that girls are systematically provided with fewer resources than boys. Testing this is rather difficult because household data do not contain each individual member's consumption. Deaton, in a skillful way, used household consumption data to indirectly estimate whether girls are given less resources than boys. In a poor country, when a child is born, the household becomes poorer because there is then one more mouth to feed. There will be drop in the consumption of "adult goods" such as adult clothing, alcohol and tobacco. This provides an indirect estimate of the "cost of a child". If the household cuts its expenditure on adult goods by less when the child is a girl, that provides evidence that there is discrimination against girls.

Poverty Measurement

Consumption data is normally collected at the household level but poverty is measured naturally at the individual level. As consumption data are aggregated at the household level, there is a problem in comparing individuals in households of different sizes and compositions. In a household, there will be adults and children. Normally, individual welfare is measured as per capita total expenditure of the household. But children consume less of most things than do adults. The extent of poverty among children or among households with children is overstated by per capita estimates. Deaton made important contributions to this study. While discussing child costs, on the basis of Sri Lankan and Indonesian data collected and analyzed jointly with Muellbauer. (A Deaton and J. Muellbauer: "On Measuring Child Costs: with Applications to Poor Countries" Journal of Political Economy, (1986)), Deaton concluded that child costs are about 30-40 percent of per capita adult expenditures.

There is another issue in welfare measurement. That is, how to treat goods with different prices and qualities, On the basis of a theoretical model of quantity and quality choice, Deaton suggested an important methodology to deal with the problem.

Measurement of Poverty in India

Deaton has made significant contribution to measurement of poverty in India. In 2010, one-third of the world's extreme poor lived in India (Chen, S. and M. Ravallion (2010), "The Developing World is Poorer Than We Thought, but No Less Successful in the Fight Against Poverty", Quarterly Journal of Economics, 125 (4), 1577-1625). But Deaton questioned their methodology and the authors adopted new methodology partly in response to Deaton's Critique. As a result of the new methodology, they found that rural poverty was significantly higher than in previous estimates. Thus, Deaton actively participated in the debate about the method of measurement of poverty and the relationship between poverty and growth.

Deaton took a lot of interest in comparing welfare, across time and across countries. Today, this issue is at the heart of many practical policy debates. He has also made important contribution to the study of the relationship between health and income. He has also analysed the connection between inequality and health.

Conclusion

Deaton championed the use of household survey data in developing countries, especially data on consumption, to measure poverty and living standards. We can study important development issues by making use of such data. Deaton's contribution has made careful microeconometric analysis a corner stone of modern development economics.

Deaton has made major contributions in three fields: consumption demand systems, the fluctuations of consumption over time, and the measurement of consumption and poverty in the developing world. He has consistently tried to bring theory and data closer together through his mastery of measurement and statistical methods. He has brought the analysis of individual and aggregate incomes closer together by attending to issues of aggregation. And he helped us in understanding in a better way the determinants of consumption and thereby human welfare.

OLIVER HART AND BENGT HOLMSTROM

Introduction

The Nobel prize in Economics for the year 2016 was jointly awarded to Oliver Hart of Harvard University, Cambridge USA and Bengt Holmstrom, Massachusetts Institute of Technology, Cambridge, USA for their contributions to Contract Theory.

Oliver Hart was born in 1948 in London, UK. He took his Ph.D. from Princeton University, N.J., USA. He is Professor of Economics at Harvard University, Cambridge, USA.

Bengt Holmstrom was born in 1949 in Helsinki, Finland. He took his Ph.D. in1978 from Stanford University, US. He is Paul A. Samuelson Professor of Economics, and Professor of Economics and Management at Massachusetts Institute of Technology, Cambridge, USA.

A main obstacle to human cooperation is that people have different interests. In modern societies, conflicts of interests are mitigated by contracts. A contract that is designed well provides incentives for the contracting parties to exploit prospective gains from cooperation. For example, we have labour contracts, insurance contracts and credit contracts. Labour contracts include pay and promotion conditions that are designed to retain and motivate employees; insurance contracts combine the sharing of risks with deductibles, and co-payments to encourage clients to exercise caution; credit contracts specify payments and decision rights aimed at protecting the lender, while encouraging sound decisions by borrowers.

In the 1770s, Adam Smith argued that sharecropping agreements did not give tenants sufficient incentives to improve the land.

Their Works

Some of their important works include Hart, O. (1975): "On the Optimality of Equilibrium when the Market Structure is Incomplete"; Hart, O. (1983): "The Market Mechanism as an Incentive Scheme"; *Hart, O. (1995): Firms, Contracts and Financial Structure,* Hart, O (2003): "Incomplete Contracts and Public Ownership Remarks and Application to Public-Private Partnerships"; Hart, O. and B. Holmstrom (1987): The Theory of Contracts; Hart, O. and J. Moore (1988): "Incomplete Contracts and Renegotiation", Hart, O and J. Moore (1990): "Property Rights and the Nature of the Problem"; Hart, O. and J. Moore (1999): "Foundations of Incomplete Markets"; Hart, O. and J. Tirole (1988): "Contract Renegotian and Coasean Dynamics" Holmstrom, B (1979): "Moral Hazard and Observability"; Holmstrom, B. (1982) "Managerial Incentive Problems: A Dynamic Perspective"; Holmstrom, B and P. Milgrom (1991): "Multi-Task Principal Agent Analysis"; Holmstrom, B and P. Milgrom (1994): "The Firm as an Incentive Scheme; and Holmstrom, B. and J. Tirole (2001): "A Liquidity – Based Asset Pricing Model".

Hart and Holmstrom's Contributions

HOLMSTROM

Hart and Holmstrom created important new theoretical tools which are valuable in understanding real-life contracts and institutions, as well as potential pitfalls in contract designs. They have given us new insights into the nature of optimal contracts. As a result, contract theory has made great progress during the last few decades. Incentive problems are studied today through the lens of contract theory. It has had major impact on Organizational Economics and Corporate Finance. It has profound influence on other fields such as Industrial Organization, Labour Economics, Public Economics, Political Science and Law.

A contract has the following structure. There will be an agent and a principal. The Principal cannot directly observe the agent's actions, and this creates a problem of *moral hazard*. The agent may take actions that promote his own interest. For example, suppose the principal is the main shareholder of a company and the agent is the manager of the company. Long back, Adam Smith noted that the separation of ownership and control in a company might cause the manager to make decisions contrary to the interest of shareholders.

Paying for Performance

To get over the moral hazard problem, the principal may offer a compensation package which ties the manager's income to some performance measure that is observable and measurable. This is known as *paying for performance*. The company's profit or stock-market value are commonly used performance measures. But these measures have some drawbacks. They may depend largely on factors beyond manager's control. That means, the manage may be rewarded for luck. So it may be necessary to measure the firm's performance relative to other firms in the same industry. But we do not have a precise performance measure. So in any optimal compensation schedule, there will be a trade-off between incentive-provision and risk-taking.

The Informativeness Principle

Besides characterising the optimal trade-off between incentives and risk-sharing, Holmstrom's work contained a fundamental result on optimal performance measures, namely the *informativeness principle*. In the 1980s, Holmstrom developed moral hazard models with concepts such as dynamic moral hazard and multi-tasking. These concepts are largely being used in Organizational Economics.

Holmstrom has made many significant contributions to contract theory. A simple contract model captures many real-life settings. In any contract, there will be a principal and an agent. For example, the agent could be a worker, a CEO, a lawyer, a firm, or a supplier of public services. The corresponding principal could be an employer, a board of directors, a client, a regulator or a public authority. In many cases, the outcome is random. Risk-sharing is a crucial aspect of the contracting problem.

The agent's compensation should depend on variables (signals) that provide information about his work. This intuition is captured well in *the informativeness principle*. For example, a manager's pay should depend not only on accounting measures and the firm's own stock price, but also on signals that are correlated with the stock price, such as observable cost and demand conditions or the stock prices of other firms in the same industry. By linking the manager's pay to these signals, we can filter, out the effect of the manager's performance from general industry and macroeconomic fluctuations that are beyond the manager's control.

We may note that the informativeness principle is based on statistical considerations only, with no reference to preference parameters.

Using the insights from the informativeness principle, Holmstrom and Tirole in their paper Market Liquidity and Performance Monitoring (1993) investigated the role of stock market liquidity in determining optimal managerial compensation and incentives.

The Holmstrom – Milgrom model (1987) "Aggregation and Linearity in the Provision of Intertemporal Incentives" explains common sharecropping contracts, as well as the use of shares to motivate managers. However, the model does not explain why contracts have a pay floor, e.g., in the form of a sizable salary which is independent of performance.

The Multi-Tasking Model

Holmstrom extended the basic moral hazard model by analyzing cases with several tasks as well as several agents. In the basic moral hazard model, the agent performs a single task. But, in many cases, the agent performs many tasks. They are complex and multi-dimensional. Those tasks can only be imperfectly observed and measured. If only measurable activities are rewarded, it may lead to dysfunctional behaviour because agents will then concentrate too much attention on the activities that are more likely to be rewarded. For instance, if a manager's bonus is tied to short-term earnings, he might sacrifice long-term investments, since these investments involve lower current earnings. And the benefits will arise only after a long time. Holmstrom provided a multi-tasking model, to cover actions and outcomes that are multi-dimensional. For example, a school teacher is expected to stimulate curiosity, responsibility and ability to think independently. But, a teacher may be "teaching to the test". Let us suppose there are two teachers A and B. If A focuses on the first aim, he would bear too much risk, if his salary is tied to such a measure. If B is provided incentives by tying his salary to the students' grades on standardized tests, he will neglect teaching broader set of skills. So, an optimal contract for the teacher may specify a fixed salary with no explicit (incentive) pay at all. This illustrates an important point about the informative principle. That is, its recommendation to link the agent pay to any informative measure of effort applies only to the simplest cases, where the effort is one-dimensional.

The basic idea behind the multi-tasking model is that agents will reallocate their effort away from uncompensated activities and toward compensated activities that provide incentives. For example, in a field experiment in Chinese factories, Hong et al. (2013) in their paper "Testing the Theory of Multitasking: Evidence from a Natural Experiment in Chinese Factories: found that output increases but quality falls when a piece-rate bonus scheme is introduced.

We may note that agents who are concerned about their future careers may have an incentive to work hard even under simple fixed-wage contracts. Fama, the 2013 Economics Nobel Laureate, argued that career, concerns might solve moral hazard problems, without any need for explicit performance-based contract. The idea of career concerns was formalized by Holmstrom.

The career-concerns model has been extensively used in political economy and political science to develop a model of the behaviour of career-motivation politicians, who care about re-election rather than future wages. We find that some politicians are more productive than others. They do good work and produce good result in their constituencies. Voters appreciate this and are more likely to re-elect him. This provides incentives for the incumbent politicians. And they generate a "political business cycle".

Oliver Hart

Oliver Hart has done pioneering work on *the theory of incomplete contracts.*

In order to alleviate the moral hazard problem, contracting parties enter into performance – based contracts *ex ante* and enforce the suitable rewards *ex ante*. Such a contract has drawbacks. For example, it may be difficult to enforce the contract because a third party (e.g. a judge) may not be able to verify the performance *ex post*. Many of the contracts we actually observe are found to be incomplete. This is the basic idea behind the *incomplete contract* approach to contracting (Oliver Hart).

Decision Rights and Property Rights

A central point in the incomplete – contract literature is that carefully allocated decisions or control rights can substitute for rewards specified through contracts. As decision rights are allocated through ownership, incomplete-contract theory generates a rich theory of property rights. As Hart puts it: "ownership of an asset goes together with the possession of residual rights of control over the asset; the owner has the right to use the asset in any way not inconsistent with a prior contract, custom or any law.

Incomplete contracts and the Theory of the Firm

Property rights play an important role in incomplete contracts. The 1991 Economics Nobel Laureate Ronald coase argued in his paper "The Nature of the Firm" (1937) that firms may organize certain transactions more efficiently than markets can. Unlike market transactions most of the economic activity inside firms is not regulated by explicit contracts. Based on these ideas, 2009 Economics Laureate Oliver Williamson developed a theory of firm based on incomplete contracts, known as transaction – cost economics.

The Grossman – Hart property rights theory is the first theory that explains in a straightforward manner why markets are so critical in the context of organizational choice. Though transaction cost economics investigated the boundaries of the firm, Grossman and Hart model not only predicts where the boundaries of the firm should lie; it makes specific predictions about who should own a particular asset. Ownership should be given to the party that makes the most important investment outside the contract. When both parties, separately own their assets, that is, when there is no integration, it is optimal when the investments of the parties are equally important.

Hart and Moore in their 1990 paper "Property Rights and the Nature of the Firm" arrived at the conclusion that joint ownership is inefficient. The reason they gave was, if each party can hold up other party by denying her him the use of the asset after separation, incentives could be weakened for both parties. And outside ownership would be inefficient because the outsider could deny both parties the use of the asset.

The real world contracts are, more often than not, highly incomplete and allocation of control and property rights play a central role.

Privatization and Pubic versus Private Ownership

The property rights framework helps us understand the costs and benefits of privatization and public versus private ownership.

Hart et al. in a 1997 paper studied privatization by combining the incomplete contract approach with the multi-tasking model.

A government owned service provider will have little incentive to invest in cost innovation or quality innovation. Private contractor will have incentive to improve quality and reduce cost but he will have stronger incentive to reduce cost. If the cost-cutting has adverse impact on quality, then there is a strong case for government ownership. Privatization and outsourcing will be harmful in such a context.

Conclusion

Contract theory identifies a variety of obstacles to cooperation and suggests which contracts are appropriate to overcome them. It provides a number of testable hypotheses that can be tested with empirical data. It has provided a strong foundation for the design of various policies and institutions, from bankruptcy legislation to political institutions. Thus, Hart and Holmstrom, through their key concepts of 'incomplete contracts' and "informativeness principle" have played a major role in the development of the contract theory.